create™

Course	Dunn: REA Accounting Systems
Course Number	**Resources-Events-Agents:**
	An ontology for designing, controlling, and using integrated enterprise systems

http://create.mheducation.com

ISBN-10: 1121555853   ISBN-13: 9781121555853

Contents

Credits

REA Accounting Systems: Resources-Events-Agents: An ontology for designing, controlling, and using integrated enterprise systems

1

REA Accounting Systems

Resources-Events-Agents: An ontology for designing, controlling, and using integrated enterprise systems

CHERYL L. DUNN
Grand Valley State University

for Jimmy D, Jimmy, Sarah, Theresa, Bob, Issie, James, and Janet

with special thanks to Eric Denna, Anita Hollander, and Owen Cherrington, and especially to Bill McCarthy, without whom this text would not exist.

REA Accounting Systems: Resources-Events-Agents: An ontology for designing, controlling, and using integrated enterprise systems

3

Letter to the Instructor

Dear Colleague,

I am pleased to offer *REA Accounting Systems,* fourth edition, as a revision of *Enterprise Information Systems: A Pattern-Based Approach*, third edition. I realize this edition has been too long in coming, and I appreciate your patience. The delay is entirely my fault.

You probably wonder why the title is changed and how major a change in the content that signifies. Although I have restructured and updated the content to reflect advances in REA theory, conceptual modeling tools (UML), and software (Microsoft Access), the primary reason for the title change is that the latter title failed to communicate the importance of the accounting foundation for enterprise systems. Many enterprise systems exist that have not taken advantage of innovations to re-invent the integration of accounting into the systems. This edition continues to develop the design, control, and use of systems for all business uses. Most of the examples focus on accounting uses to help illustrate the difference in how the accounting is done in systems built with the REA ontology compared to more traditional systems.

As many of you know, J. Owen Cherrington passed away since publication of the previous edition of this text. Anita Sawyer Hollander has withdrawn from authoring due to serious health issues that I pray will be resolved. My sincere hope is that I continue to capture their innovative and pioneering spirits in this and future editions of this book.

Sincerely,
Cheryl Dunn

About the Author

Cheryl L. Dunn   *Grand Valley State University*
Cheryl L. Dunn (PhD, Michigan State University) is Associate
Professor of Accounting at Grand Valley State University. Cheryl also
served as associate professor at Florida State University and has
held visiting positions at University of Notre Dame and Michigan State
University. She has also served as an instructor at the American
Accounting Association's Workshop on Teaching AIS.

   Cheryl has written many articles for scholarly journals, including
Journal of the Association for Information Systems, *Decision
Sciences*, *Journal of Information Systems*, *International Journal of
Accounting Information Systems*, and *Issues in Accounting
Education*, as well as a chapter in the American Accounting
Association research monograph *Researching Accounting as an
Information Systems Discipline*. She has also served as book review
editor for *Journal of Information Systems* and on the editorial boards
of *Issues in Accounting Education*, *Journal of Database Management*,
and *International Journal of Accounting Information Systems*. Cheryl
has taught undergraduate and graduate courses in accounting
information systems, graduate accounting theory, and undergraduate
principles of financial and managerial accounting. Her primary
research interests are in conceptual modeling, enterprise system
design, and corporate financial reporting.

REA Accounting Systems: Resources-Events-Agents: An ontology for designing, controlling, and using integrated enterprise systems

5

WHAT'S INSIDE?

Theory-Driven REA Focus

This text follows the REA model, an innovative approach to teaching accounting and enterprise systems, developed by William McCarthy of Michigan State University. REA is an ontology that defines an enterprise's **R**esources, **E**vents, and **A**gents, and various associations among them. The new text title emphasizes the fact that while REA is an enterprise-wide ontology, accounting is its foundation. Some accounting systems academicians lament that their field does not have an underlying theory. This text reflects the belief that REA *is* the theory underlying accounting and enterprise systems.

A Pattern-Based Approach to Understanding

This book focuses on the use of ontology and patterns to understand enterprises and enterprise activities and to consider how details of the activities should be represented in accounting and enterprise systems. System designers should certainly be interested in this book; however, the intended audience is much broader. Business students and practitioners who currently use, manage, design, or evaluate accounting and enterprise systems need to understand how business phenomena may be represented in enterprise information systems. This text provides a foundation for such an understanding, with a focus on the necessary components of information systems versus artifacts that are often maintained in information systems.

Objectives and Content: Chapter by Chapter

In this book you will see an integration of concepts from business and computer science to create a framework for developing a theoretical understanding of integrated enterprise information systems. You will also be provided with practical details for designing systems for small enterprises; these serve as a proof of concept. Additional complexities arise when extrapolating the concepts to very large systems that are beyond the scope of this text.

The book begins with a review of some of the history of enterprises and information systems to reveal the need for changes in the integration of accounting and enterprise systems today. Some methods are discussed by which current enterprise information systems achieve integration and the importance of including only necessary components in the core architecture of an enterprise information system. Chapter 2 provides an overview of pattern and representation use for learning and understanding, along with an introduction to the four levels of the REA enterprise ontology. The value system and value chain levels of the REA ontology are described in detail using an example enterprise to help illustrate application of the concepts.

Task level modeling is introduced in chapter 3 in the form of system flowcharting. The workflow and documents commonly used in enterprise revenue and acquisition cycles are introduced, giving readers some domain knowledge to which to apply the documentation technique. Whereas many texts don't introduce revenue and acquisition cycle workflow until halfway or three quarters of the way through, this text advocates thorough understanding of those two cycles early in the course to enable application of concepts to those cycles throughout the entire course.

Chapter 4 introduces the concepts of enterprise risk and controls to mitigate that risk. Students are introduced to legislation and authoritative guidance surrounding risk and control (Sarbanes Oxley, PCAOB Auditing Standard #5, ISA 315 and 330, ISACA's COBIT framework and COSO's Integrated Internal Control Framework. Next the REA pattern is used as a template for considering risk. Controls are suggested to mitigate the various types of risks and students are encouraged to use creativity in thinking of additional controls that could be implemented.

Chapter 5 introduces conceptual modeling with UML class diagrams and illustrates how to convert conceptual models into relational database tables. The conceptual modeling in this edition has been updated from the older Chen notation to the more current Universal Modeling Language (UML). Instructors who have used the Chen notation in the past should not find the transition to be difficult, and the resulting models are less cluttered and easier to create.

Chapter 6 details the REA core business process pattern and provides step-by-step instructions for creating a core business process conceptual model. The example enterprise used in chapter 2 is again used to illustrate application of the concepts for the acquisition cycle. The revenue cycle is then described without an example enterprise to enable instructor guided insight generation by students. Chapter 7 goes beyond the REA core business process to illustrate modeling of the expanded acquisition and revenue cycles. Example database tables are provided encompassing data describing each of the events and related classes.

Implementation of the relational tables into Microsoft Access is provided in Chapter 8 with screen shots to help guide students' understanding of concepts. Students are encouraged to work through the illustrated examples in the chapter on a computer with Microsoft Access. Chapter 9 presents an introduction to querying that starts with the conceptual foundation of relational algebra, then describes the move to structured query language and query by example. Once again, Microsoft Access screen shots are provided and the chapter database is available upon request so that students may work through the examples themselves.

Chapters 10 and 11 provide detailed descriptions of the querying needed to meet enterprise information needs. Stored information has little value if it cannot be obtained when needed in an appropriate format to support decisions. Generation of various financial statement line items is emphasized in these chapters; however, ways to meet additional types of enterprise information needs are suggested in these and later chapters.

Chapter 12 introduces advanced REA modeling constructs such as abstraction mechanisms that are needed to capture enterprise policies and contract or product specifications. Enterprises are described as having policy and accountability infrastructures, within which we can capture (and compare) what could be or should be, what is planned or scheduled, and what has already happened. Students will begin to see how concepts such as variance analysis are facilitated with data captured with these advanced modeling constructs. The need for enterprises to sometimes make compromises from the pure theory is acknowledged and suggestions are provided for how to make such compromises.

Chapters 13 through 15 discuss application of the REA ontology's business process level pattern to the conversion, human resources, and financing transaction cycles. We refrain from focusing student attention on memorizing a series of process sequences, tasks, or a series of control procedures. Instead we focus their attention on the pattern and on matching the reality of enterprises against the pattern to determine which pieces of the pattern are relevant and necessary. Each transaction cycle is described as to the activities, the participants in those activities, and the data items that are commonly captured in the form of documents or computer entry screens. Information needs are suggested with descriptions of how those needs can be met with queries.

REA Accounting Systems: Resources-Events-Agents: An ontology for designing, controlling, and using integrated enterprise systems

7

The text wraps up with a summary in Chapter 16 of the organizing principles of current accounting and enterprise systems with speculation as to what future development of such systems may look like as enterprises evolve and take on new business models.

End of Chapter Learning Opportunities
To help students apply their knowledge, each chapter includes an ample number of review and discussion questions, multiple choice questions, and applied learning problems.

CONTENTS

REA Accounting Systems: Resources-Events-Agents: An ontology for designing, controlling, and using integrated enterprise systems

9

REA Accounting Systems: Resources-Events-Agents: An ontology for designing, controlling, and using integrated enterprise systems

11

BRIEF CONTENTS

CHAPTER 1

Why REA? Accounting and Enterprise Systems for Economic Storytelling

LEARNING OBJECTIVES

The objectives of this chapter are to explain the primary purpose of accounting and enterprise systems as telling the economic story of the enterprise, to discuss the degrees to which systems are commonly integrated, to advocate for complete integration across enterprise systems, deriving traditional accounting data from that captured for other purposes, and to describe the REA approach to re-inventing accounting/enterprise systems. After studying this chapter, you should be able to

1.   Describe the purpose of accounting and enterprise systems
2.   Identify the extent to which a described system is integrated
3.   Identify impediments to integrating components of enterprise systems
4.   Explain the need to eliminate silos in operations and in enterprise systems
5.   Explain the difference between paving cowpaths and reengineering
6.   Describe in general terms the REA approach to reinventing accounting/enterprise systems

ECONOMIC STORYTELLING: THE PURPOSE OF ENTERPRISE SYSTEMS

An **enterprise** is an organization established to achieve specific undertakings involving industrious, systematic activities. Enterprises existed long before computers, calculators, formal corporations, and the double-entry bookkeeping system. Among the earliest enterprises were families who labored together in fields tending to crops, trees, or animals, and families who fished, hunted, or trapped in order to have enough food to eat. These families traded goods with other families who grew different crops, herded or successfully hunted different types of animals, or who created other products from their land's resources (furniture from trees, for examples).

Historians have described many attempts by ancient agrarian enterprises to account for their activities. As far back as 5000 B.C. in Babylonia, Egypt, China, and Greece, concepts of economic value and profit existed, as did attempts to record information regarding enterprise activities or business transactions[1]. Accounting was accomplished by methods such as making notches in sticks to indicate quantities of goods for which one was responsible, or having scribes write business transactions onto moist lumps of clay using wooden rods with blunt triangular ends. Such records noted the names of the parties involved in the transactions, the items paid or received, promises made, and any other pertinent details. The clay tablets were then dried and kept as accounting records.   Ancient records also include periodically prepared inventory lists of assets on hand and evidence of audit examinations.

---

[1] Chatfield, M. 1977. *A History of Accounting Thought*. Huntington, New York: Robert E. Krieger Publishing.

REA Accounting Systems: Resources-Events-Agents: An ontology for designing, controlling, and using integrated enterprise systems

13

The Sumerians in 3250 B.C. used sealed clay receptacles containing tokens that represented the portion of one person's wealth that had been loaned to another[2]. Imprints on the seals indicated the contents.

An **information system** is a network of communication channels used within an enterprise. The purpose of the information system is to store the story of the enterprise – to be able to describe who, what, where, when, why, and how with respect to the enterprise's activities. The ancient agrarian systems described in the previous paragraphs were not just accounting systems; they were enterprise systems. The same systems were used for accounting, management, and any other decision making needs. Of course such enterprises were much smaller than modern enterprises and their information needs were easily met with just a few descriptive records for each business transaction or audit activity. Much information needed was simply retained in the memory of the sole proprietor until such time as that information was no longer needed. Success of such enterprises was measured in terms of asset increases; income was not isolated. Accountability was the focus – keeping track of the assets and measuring the give and the take of economic transactions. Only limited details could be captured with notches in sticks, tokens in clay pots, or the laborious carvings on clay tablets. Additional details of the economic stories of enterprises were typically stored only in the proprietor's memories and passed verbally to other interested parties.

As society progressed to the mercantile and industrial age, new forms of business organizations and new technologies emerged. Merchant traders, also called adventurers, journeyed to distant places to trade their goods. Some traveled by land, others by sea. Records recovered by archaeologists indicate the primary information they kept track of was the value of the cargo with which they returned home. That was what mattered most: if they returned home with a valuable shipment, the voyage was said to be profitable. Because a merchant trading voyage was expensive and labor-intensive, the joint venture form of business was created. The owner of the ship or caravan was typically not the owner of the merchandise to be traded. The merchant entrusted his goods to the adventurer who, if all went well, returned many months later with the merchandise for which the original goods had been traded. The merchant and adventurer divided the return cargo according to their joint venture agreement and the venture was over. Such enterprises needed more than the lists, clay tablets, and notched sticks of earlier times. The double-entry bookkeeping system formally described by Pacioli in 1494 met most of the enterprise information needs, at least in terms of written records kept. However, no financial statements were prepared, probably because each joint venture was considered a separate business. There was no concept of the business as an ongoing entity[34].

As the Industrial Revolution spread throughout the world, manufacturing enterprises emerged that required substantial purchases of fixed assets that were beyond the financial means of most sole proprietors or even joint ventures. The corporation as a business entity thus evolved, allowing for many investors each contributing relatively small amounts of capital.[5]

---

[2] Mattesich, R. 1989. Accounting and the input-output principle in the prehistoric and ancient world. *ABACUS*. September. 74-84.

[3] Irish, R.A. 1968. The evolution of corporate accounting. *Contemporary Studies in the Evolution of Accounting Thought*. Dickenson Publishing. 57-85.

[4] Littleton, A.C. 1968. Ancient and modern bookkeeping compared. (ed. Chatfield) *Contemporary Studies in the Evolution of Accounting Thought*. Dickenson Publishing. 48-56.

[5] ten Have, O. 1976. *The History of Accountancy*. Bay Books. Palo Alto, California.

These investors were called shareholders. Merchants began to form corporations for their trading voyages, whereby the profits from one voyage were reinvested in the next voyage. Administration of enterprises in many sectors was taken over by salaried managers. Because the shareholders of corporations did not have ready access to the bookkeeping records, periodic financial statements were created to summarize the profit and loss activities and to list the assets and equities. This enabled the shareholders to see how their money was being used. The underlying information system for accounting remained the double-entry bookkeeping system. Late in the Industrial Age the emergence of cost accounting revealed one of the weaknesses of Pacioli's system. The original data needed for cost accounting purposes had been summarized from the underlying transactions before being entered into journals and posted to the accounts; accrual accounting entries were also posted into the accounts, thereby becoming part of the account balances. To obtain the detail needed for cost accounting would require reverting to the original source documents and re-summarizing according to the cost accounting decision needs. Cost accountants developed estimation techniques based on the financial accounting journal entries and other readily available data to circumvent the need for the original source transaction data.

As enterprises became more complex, with numerous employees working in various departments, and multiple layers of management, the demand grew for all types of information needed to run the enterprises. Before 1865, the information sector – that is, the portion of the workforce who handled data – was negligible. In 1920 that sector had grown to 17.7% of the overall workforce.[6] Information handling was a labor intensive process in those years. Large enterprises had dozens of calculators. Not electronic calculators like the ones we use today, but people hired full-time to make and double-check calculations. Machines such as typewriters, telephones, cash registers, and tabulating equipment were designed to assist with information gathering, processing, and communicating. Sales of such machines grew rapidly as enterprise information needs increased. Enterprises had many distinct operating units, each of which had its own administrative offices and managers and each of which kept its own set of books and accounts. Today's enterprises are more complicated than ever – many are global conglomerates, many achieved their growth through numerous mergers and acquisitions, and many are involved in multiple alliances and cooperatives with other enterprises.

The more an enterprise grows, the more impossible it becomes for any one person to see and know everything that happens – that is, to see and be able to tell the complete economic story of the enterprise. When the sole proprietors of the agrarian and mercantile ages were not directly involved in their enterprises' activities, they were in frequent direct communications with those who were directly involved (who were usually family members). The explosive growth of the industrial and information ages made such comprehensive first-hand and second-hand involvement in enterprise activities impossible in all but the smallest enterprises. Renowned economist Alfred Chandler proposed that enterprises become large multi-unit entities once administrative coordination (i.e. use of salaried managers) of flow through the production and distribution processes is more profitable than market coordination of that flow[7]. What could make such flow more profitable with administrative coordination? Lowered transaction costs have been suggested by some[8]. Increased ability to manage the activities and the information

---

[6] Cortada, J.W. 1993. *Before the Computer*. Princeton University Press, Princeton, New Jersey.

[7] Chandler, A.D. 1977. The Visible Hand: The Managerial Revolution in American Business. Belknap Press of Harvard University Press, Cambridge, Massachusetts.

[8] Bucheli, M., Mahoney, J. and Vaaler, P. 2010. Chandler's living history: *The Visible Hand* of vertical integration in nineteenth century America viewed under a twenty-first century transaction costs economic lens. *Journal of Management Studies*. 47:5, July 2010.

describing those activities is undoubtedly part of the explanation. As the activities of the enterprise become too cumbersome for the sole proprietor to manage, he must hire additional labor and eventually additional managers.

A natural way of dividing workload is by area of expertise. As the enterprise grows, producing more workload and necessitating more managers and more specialized areas of responsibility, the information across all the areas is more difficult for the owner(s) to assimilate. That was especially true when enterprises expanded their reach to national and even global levels even before computers and the Internet facilitated wide-scale sharing and processing of information. Silo operations and silo systems resulted. **Silo operations** are the division of enterprises into functional areas such that different activities occur in different parts of the enterprise. **Silo systems** are separate information systems for each of the different functional areas of an enterprise. Envision a farm, on which each silo is used for a different type of grain to keep each type of grain separate from each other. For grain on farms, separation is a good thing unless a specific recipe calls for a mixture of grains. For a business, separation of the activities and information of different functional areas may actually be dysfunctional. Some use the term stovepipes to describe this phenomenon whereby the walls of each functional area go straight up, with no pathways of communication between them. Using stovepipes as the analogy may help you to see that the only openings through which communication can flow are at the top. Smoke rises from the stove where a fire is burning through the stovepipe until it escapes out the top of the pipe. Only when it has escaped the walls of the pipe can it mix with smoke that has arisen from other stovepipes.

Typical departments in enterprises include accounting/finance, advertising, customer service, human resources, information systems, logistics, manufacturing, marketing, procurement, research and development, sales, and others. Employees in each of these areas are typically focused on what they as individuals need to do for their jobs. In today's economic environment, employees are trained to specialize in something. Assembly line workers specialize in a few specific tasks, which they repeat over and over each day. Credit managers specialize in making a few specific decisions, which they make over and over each day. Accountants specialize in journalizing a limited number of types of transactions, and they make those entries over and over. These departments consisting of people similarly trained in specialized activities serve as silos or stovepipes. Other authors have described these functional areas as islands. The common theme of these descriptors is that each functional area is relatively isolated from the other functional areas and decisions may be made without a realization of how they may affect the other functional areas. The isolation of functional areas need not be physical; two departments that are physically located on the same floor of the same building may not fully understand each other's operations and objectives, nor how they fit together within the broad scope of the enterprise.

Even the members of top management in organizations tend to be specialists – the CFO (chief financial officer) focuses on financial decisions, the COO (chief operations officer) focuses on daily operations, the CIO (chief information officer) focuses on information systems issues, etc. Yet these top-level executives provide the primary pathways of communication by which the functional areas of many enterprises pass information back and forth. Is it any wonder, then, that in most enterprises, separate information systems were created to support the separate, specialized functions? Thus enterprises have accounting information systems, marketing information systems, personnel information systems, etc. Because accountants were technologically able to tell only limited details of the economic story of enterprises, and then they were separated into a single functional area, it is not surprising that they have continued telling only limited details of the economic story even as technology is available to facilitate telling more. This has resulted in a crisis in accounting with numerous business failures and audit failures in the past two decades. Lack of transparency of financial statements and the failure of financial statements to include important business details is often cited as contributing to such failures. If more details are needed for the economic story of the enterprise to be clear and complete, then change is overdue. Either the non-accounting areas' information systems need to capture the remaining details, in such a way as to be easily combined with the accounting details into the complete story, or the individual area systems (including accounting) must be replaced with one system that can capture, store, and report the full story. Whether that is done by accountants or by some other area is not as important as that it is done.

EXHIBIT 1-1 Silo or Stovepiped Operations

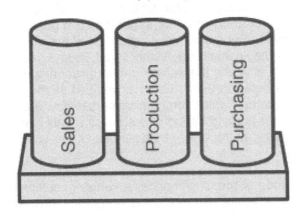

If it isn't enough of a problem that silo operations generate silo systems, next consider how silo systems perpetuate silo operations. When decision-making is based on information obtained from within one functional area, those decisions are likely to be made from a narrow perspective. If systems are not integrated, it is unlikely that decision-makers will obtain information from multiple areas, because that would require obtaining information from multiple systems. If decisions are not based on integrated information, then enterprises may not realize the advantages that such information may provide.

INTEGRATION OF ENTERPRISE SYSTEMS

Integration is defined in most dictionaries as the combination of parts into a whole. This definition may bring to your mind the disassembled pieces of a jigsaw puzzle, and their assembly into one completed picture, as in Exhibit 1-2. To achieve the integration of these pieces into the finished whole, each piece must be connected to another piece that fits and which in turn fits with another piece. The integration of pieces in most jigsaw puzzles is a relatively simple task that has a single correct solution. A picture on the box in which the puzzle pieces are stored illustrates how the assembled end product should look. The puzzle solver uses that illustration to help determine how to integrate the pieces.

For this book, the puzzle pieces we are interested in combining together into a whole are the building blocks of an enterprise information system, and there is not a sole predefined solution. Although the pieces of the story must be coherent once assembled, a story can be told in various sequences and still make sense. The pieces we need to integrate are less similar to jigsaw puzzle pieces and are more similar to various types of children's building blocks, such as Legos, K'nex, Tinkertoys, and so on. To build something from such building blocks, a person may start with a predefined solution (e.g., a picture of an end product to build) and follow a set of directions to arrive at that solution. However, a person may instead visualize something to build, and then start integrating the pieces, gradually shaping the desired end product. The builder's visualization may change as the product takes shape and additional possibilities are identified. As with jigsaw puzzles, these specialized building pieces must fit together in a certain way. Unlike jigsaw puzzles, these pieces may be correctly assembled in many different ways.

EXHIBIT 1-2 Integration of Jigsaw Puzzle Pieces

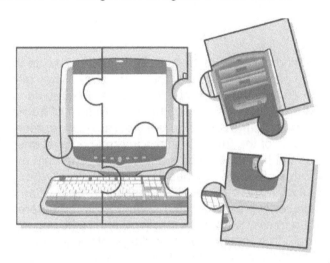

Integration can be achieved to various degrees. Today many enterprises have what they consider to be integrated information systems. However what you might picture in your mind as an integrated information system might not be consistent with the systems they actually have in place.   Consider the following example as a rough analogy of the extent to which information systems may be integrated. Two children decide to build toy trains using popular building blocks. One child builds a train using Legos; the other builds a train using K'nex Lincoln Logs. (See Exhibit 1-3.)

EXHIBIT 1-3 Lego and K'nex Lincoln Log Trains

Say each train car contains a different kind of candy as freight. The children decide they want to connect their tracks together so as to expand the territory they can cover. They also want to be able to unhook a train car from one engine and connect it to the other train so as to send the freight to a different destination. The first question is whether the two sets of tracks are compatible such that both trains can run on both tracks. Picture the tracks as representing the hardware platforms and operating systems of the functional area information systems. If the tracks for which the trains were built do not have the same specifications, one train may not be able to operate on the other's track. Once one train reaches the end of its track, the freight from the train car that needs to be hauled by the other engine to reach its destination must be unloaded and then reloaded into a train car compatible with that engine. In an enterprise system this is similar to printing the data from one software package and re-keying it into the other or, better yet, downloading the data from one software package into a generic format such as ascii or .csv and uploading it into the other system. Depending on the extent of interaction between the integrated pieces of our system, such an integration solution may be adequate although not ideal. Such a system is filled with redundancy (duplication of data), which leads to data inconsistencies. For example, an enterprise's marketing department software and its credit department software may each capture data about customers. When a customer calls to change his address and telephone number, if those data are stored separately in each software application, they must be changed in both places or data inconsistency will result.

If the two trains can operate on the same track, the next decision is how to connect the different trains' freight cars to the opposite engines. Because Legos and K'nex have different types of connectors, this will not be straightforward. One approach to connect the freight car to the engine is to tie them together with string. Such a connection may work, but is not ideal because it is likely to be loose and to result in the freight car swaying to and fro when the train is in motion. Other possible integration solutions for the train car example require intervention from either the Legos and K'nex manufacturers or from a third party manufacturer. One such solution is to have these manufacturers collaborate to build a special combination building block that has a Lego compatible connector on one end and a K'nex compatible connector on the other end. Another similar solution is for the Lego manufacturer to build a special building block that has a Lego compatible connector on one end and a generic type of connector on the other end, and for the K'nex manufacturer to build another special building block that has a K'nex compatible connector on one end and a generic type of connector on the other end.

Then, of course, the Lego end can be connected to the Lego train car and the K'nex end can be connected to the K'nex train car and their two generic ends can be attached together. Of course the manufacturers would first need to develop standards for the specifications of the generic connectors. As long as the integration needed is exclusively between cars (i.e. the only connections needed are at the edges) these solutions are likely to be effective.

Nearly all large companies and many small to medium sized enterprises have implemented enterprise resource planning (ERP) system software such as SAP or Oracle Applications in an effort to get all of their corporate data into a common database. **ERP software** is a group of commercial software applications integrated to form an enterprise-wide information system solution. Others have developed internal enterprise system software applications instead of purchasing packaged enterprise software solutions. Although a goal of enterprise software is to provide one integrated enterprise-wide system with a common database, in reality most implementations of these software packages do not end up with seamless integration.

Most enterprise software that purports to be integrated actually combines separate applications for manufacturing, MRP (materials resource planning), general ledger, human resources, procurement, order entry, and SCM (supply chain management). Programming code forms connections between the modules of these applications in much the same way that the combination Lego/K'nex pieces that could be manufactured for the purpose of connecting the train cars in our toy example. Within a specific enterprise software package, implemented uniformly throughout an enterprise, the connections are likely to be solid, so if a sale order is entered into the order entry module, information will flow through to the warehouse, manufacturing, and accounting modules.

However, many enterprises do not implement the same ERP software package uniformly throughout their organizations. Instead they take a **best-of-breed** approach, an approach to ERP software implementation in which an enterprise chooses different software packages for different areas of its business such that each package best suits the business area for which it is chosen. For example, an enterprise may choose one package for manufacturing process, another for human resources, and another for financials. While best-of-breed may result in the best overall solution for meeting an enterprise's needs, and despite the fact that ERP software packages are often themselves glued together applications, the uniform ERP software implementation is usually more fully integrated than the best-of-breed.

A more radical approach than any yet mentioned is for one of the children to start over and build a new train out of the same type of blocks as the other child's train. That would result in the best fit for connecting a train car from one to the engine of the other. Of course, that approach would involve an incredible amount of cooperation on the part of one child, each of which is likely to want the other child to rebuild. Unless one child recognizes the other child's building blocks as somehow superior for building trains, or one child bribes the other child to rebuild, or unless one child would rather build trains than use them, it is conceivable that a mediator (such as a parent) will need to step in and declare which train should be rebuilt. Otherwise the two children will likely decide not to connect their trains after all. Similarly, the managers of some functional areas could opt to give up their existing systems and change to the one that is deemed best for the overall enterprise. However, that would involve an incredible amount of cooperation on the part of each changing functional area and unless each of them recognize the system to which they are changing as somehow superior, or unless they enjoy the upheaval of system change, most likely a mediator such as the enterprise president or CEO will need to step in and declare which system should be used.

RE-INVENTING ENTERPRISE SYSTEMS WITH REA

Many top-level corporate executives have recognized the problem of silo operations. Some have tried to break down the silos by encouraging interdepartmental interactions. Some enterprises assign building space so people from different departments are next to each other, with the thought that those employees will develop friendships with each other and perhaps engage in cross-departmental topic discussions. For some enterprises such physical integration of employees from different departments may not be possible or practical. For example, it wouldn't make sense to physically locate a member of an assembly line in an office with a credit manager.

Many years ago, renowned management consultant Michael Hammer recommended that enterprises get rid of traditional departments and focus instead on workflow processes. Known as a champion of **reengineering** (the redesign of business processes or systems to achieve a dramatic improvement in enterprise performance), Hammer recognizes that most enterprise workflow processes are cross-functional and that passing information from one department to another in a nonintegrated enterprise system environment takes unnecessary time. He also recognizes that to take full advantage of their information systems' capabilities, enterprises must do more than just automate their existing processes. In a 1990 article he wrote

> It is time to stop paving the cowpaths. Instead of embedding outdated processes in silicon and software, we should obliterate them and start over.....use the power of modern information technology to radically redesign our business processes in order to achieve dramatic improvements in their performance. (p. 104) [9]

What does **paving the cowpaths** mean? It means automating existing processes as is, without considering whether they are the most efficient and effective means of achieving the goal. That analogy comes from a time when the technology for building paved roads was new and leaders were deciding how to design the road systems. Many road systems were designed by simply paving the paths that were already trodden by cattle or other livestock when being herded from one place to another. Such an approach has the advantage that the paths are well known and will not cause a high degree of resistance to change. The disadvantage is that the cowpaths do not always represent the best way to get from one location to another. Those paths may have been the best way for livestock to get from one place to another, based on the speed at which they could travel, the features of the surrounding land, the difficulty of controlling the cattle's behaviors, and the physical needs of the cattle to be able to stop periodically where there were sources of food and water. If the shortest route went through too many trees or over too many hills to easily herd cattle, or if the route went too close to the edge of a cliff, or contained no convenient food or water sources, or offered no adequate overnight resting area, the herders would choose a more circuitous route. So while the cowpaths may have been brilliantly designed for their intended purpose, they may not be wise at all to use for human vehicle traffic. Analysis of some cowpaths may reveal they are also the best route for vehicles. Analysis of others may reveal much more efficient and effective routes.

Despite this article's age, Hammer's principles are still valid today. Examination of many computerized software packages reveals that few have attempted to take advantage of the new available power of the computer and have simply automated the legacy manual

---

[9] Hammer, M. "Business Process Reengineering: Don't Automate, Obliterate." *Harvard Business Review*, July-August 1990, pp. 104-12.

procedures, even taking care to make the screen interfaces look like the manual tools such as ledger paper with red pencil markings.

What is a business process? Business process is a term widely used in business to indicate anything from a single activity such as printing a report to a set of activities such as an entire transaction cycle. In this text, a **business process** is a set of activities that comprise a transaction cycle such as the procure-to-pay (acquisition) process or the order-to-cash (revenue) process. We will discuss transaction cycles more completely in later chapters. For now, simply be aware that Hammer encouraged enterprises to carefully examine every step in their business processes and question the necessity of each and every step. Is this step designed this way because it is the best way to accomplish the goal with current technology, or is it designed this way because it is the way we have done it for the last 45 years even though our current tools are completely different? Many reengineering efforts that have been publicized have focused on streamlining workflow and reducing headcount. Other reengineering efforts have focused on consolidating disparate information systems to eliminate duplication of effort in collecting, maintaining, and reporting information.

An example of a reengineering effort made to streamline workflow and reduce headcount was undertaken by Ford and is described in Hammer's article. Economic times were tough and the entire automotive industry was in cost-cutting mode. Management believed Ford would realize significant cost savings by reengineering its accounts payable (A/P) department. Initially managers hoped to cut Ford's accounts payable headcount (redirecting the displaced workers to more challenging, meaningful, and revenue-generating positions) by 20 percent. Upon comparing itself to Mazda, a much smaller automotive manufacturer, Ford realized that even accounting for the size difference, Ford should be able to cut its A/P staff by 80 percent. The reengineers started by taking a close look at the existing A/P processing function, which began when the purchasing department wrote a purchase order (PO) and sent a copy of the PO to the A/P department and sent the original PO to the vendor. The vendor sent the goods to Ford's material control department and an invoice to Ford's A/P department (not necessarily at the same time). Upon receipt of the goods, material control staff prepared a receiving report and sent a copy to A/P. An A/P clerk compared the three documents received (PO, vendor invoice, and receiving report) matching them on 14 data items. If the 14 fields all matched, the clerk issued payment to the vendor. Most of the time and effort in accounts payable was devoted to reconciling the mismatches.

Ford could have chosen to pave the cowpaths by simply automating the existing process. Instead of the purchasing department, the vendor, and the material control department sending paper documents to A/P, they could have each entered the data into an information system that would automatically compare the 14 fields on the three documents and issue an electronic payment to the vendors for whom there were no mismatches. The mismatches would still need to be flagged for human intervention. This would have sped up the process by eliminating the lead time associated with transferring paper documents to A/P, by eliminating the manual matching process and by eliminating the issuance of manual checks for those transactions with no mismatches. The faster lead time would undoubtedly have enabled some reduction of headcount and also would have enabled Ford to take advantage of more early payment discounts. However, Ford did even better.

The reengineers questioned the purpose of the three-way match, and whether mismatches could be prevented from the start rather than being detected after they had already entered the system. The three-way match is an age-old internal control that serves the purpose of ensuring that companies don't pay for something they didn't order and/or that they didn't receive. Notice two risks the three-way match mitigates: (1) they might receive (and pay for) goods they didn't order, and (2) they might pay for goods they didn't receive. Ford's more effective procedure had its purchasing department enter POs into an integrated information system. Upon receipt of goods, material control clerks immediately entered the receipt information into the system and have the computer check to see if the item numbers and the quantities agreed (within pre-determined acceptable ranges). If they agreed, the shipment was accepted; if they disagreed, the shipment was rejected. Vendors quickly learned not to deliver a shipment that didn't match the order! This control mitigates the risk of receiving goods that were not ordered. Ford mitigated the second risk of paying for goods not received by issuing payment based on goods receipts rather than basing payments on invoices. In fact, Ford asked its vendors to not send invoices and even threw away the invoices that were received! Upon the acceptance of a shipment of goods, the computer automatically flagged the record for payment and the check was issued within the early payment discount period.

We began this discussion saying that Ford reengineered its accounts payable function. But is that really true? Actually, Ford reengineered its acquisition/payment business process. That process (as we will describe further in later chapters) is sometimes called the expenditures cycle or the procure-to-pay process. The reengineering project involved three of the major events found in this business process: the ordering of goods, the receipt of goods, and the payment for goods, and cut across three different departments (Purchasing, Material Control, and Accounts Payable. That meant many people had to change their job functions. This radical change approach paid off for Ford, which achieved a 75 percent reduction in head count, and improved accuracy of inventory information with fewer discrepancies between the physical inventory records and the financial inventory records. Vendors enjoyed on-time payments, although they had to get used to not sending invoices. One vendor complained that their own system didn't allow them not to print an invoice; Ford countered that the vendor could print the invoice as its system required, but then just throw it away rather than wasting postage to mail it to Ford.

Ford's re-engineers are not the only ones to question an age-old accounting practice such as the three-way match internal control. William McCarthy, a professor at Michigan State University, questions the need for debits and credits to accomplish accounting[10]. He proposed an alternative accounting model that he labeled as the REA (*Resources-Events-Agents*) accounting model. In a series of papers since his original proposal in 1982, he and a colleague Guido Geerts have expanded the REA accounting model into an enterprise domain ontology that can be used as a foundation for building enterprise systems to provide information not just for accounting purposes, but for most decision-making needs[11].

The premise is that the **base objects**, the foundational building blocks, in an enterprise information system should not reflect only one **view** (decision-making need) within the

---

[10] McCarthy, W.E. "The REA Accounting Model: A Generalized Framework for Accounting Systems in a Shared Data Environment." *The Accounting Review*, July 1982, pp. 554-77.

[11] Geerts, G.L. and McCarthy, W.E. "Modeling Business Enterprises as Value-Added Process Hierarchies with Resource-Event-Agent Object Templates" in *Business Object Design and Implementation*, edited by J. Sutherland, D. Patel, C. Casanave, G. Hollowell, and J. Miller (London: Springer-Verlag, 1997) pp. 94-113. Also see "An Accounting Object Infrastructure for Knowledge-Based Enterprise Models." *IEEE Intelligent Systems and Their Application*. 14, no. 4(1999), pp. 89-94; "The Ontological Foundation of REA Enterprise Information Systems" presented to the American Accounting Association annual meeting, Philadelphia, Pennsylvania, 2000; and "An Ontological Analysis of the Economic Primitives of the Extended-REA Enterprise Information Architecture." *International Journal of Accounting Information Systems* 3, no. 1 (March 2002), pp. 1-16.

REA Accounting Systems: Resources-Events-Agents: An ontology for designing, controlling, and using integrated enterprise systems

23

enterprise, but that they should reflect the real underlying activities in which the enterprise engages. System in which foundational building blocks are artificial constructs that represent a perspective needed for a particular decision-making need (e.g. debits, credits, journals, and ledgers) are **view-driven systems**. Systems whose foundational building blocks are representations of the actual underlying activities are **event-driven systems**. **Ontology** is the study of what things exist. Domain ontologies attempt to define things that are relevant to specific application domains. The **REA ontology** is a domain ontology with the purpose of defining constructs common to all enterprises and demonstrating how those constructs may be represented in an integrated enterprise information system. Effective REA modeling requires and enables thorough understanding of an enterprise's environment, business processes, risks, and information needs.

The term *enterprise system* for many people brings to mind ERP software. Such software has the same objective as the REA ontology – to store enterprise information one time, in a disaggregated format from which it can be retrieved by many different users to assist in making many different types of decisions. O'Leary compared the REA ontology with SAP, the market leader in enterprise resource planning software[12]. He concluded that many similarities exist between the underlying SAP models and the REA pattern, but that the SAP models contain many view-driven constructs as base objects, which is something REA discourages[13]. In other words, while some parts of the SAP software use representations of underlying business activities as the foundational building blocks, they also use many view-driven base objects. His analysis confirms that REA provides a good theoretical foundation for studying enterprise system design.

Like REA models, ERP software packages are representations of business processes. If the software is not an adequate representation of an enterprise's existing business processes, either the business process must be changed or the software must be changed. Either type of change is problematic. When an enterprise customizes ERP software to fit its business processes, considerable care must be taken to avoid creating bugs in the software. The software changes take extra time, and every time the vendor upgrades the software the customizations need to be redone. On the other hand, when an enterprise changes its business processes, people must change. People don't like to change. If change management in such cases is not handled well, the software implementation is doomed to fail. Most failed ERP software implementations have been blamed on people issues rather than on technological software issues. Some practitioners have pinpointed one of the biggest problems as lack of education about the underlying business processes for system users.

In the chapters that follow, we introduce you to a set of building blocks that are the best blocks for interoperability because they focus on the common elements of the reality of enterprises. They focus on real things, not on artificial constructs. An **artificial construct** is a concept that represents a man-made rule or concept rather than something with physical substance. The best news is that even if you do not agree that these are the best building blocks for designing integrated enterprise information systems, the discussions in this book will lead you to thoroughly analyze the major business processes that are common across enterprises. By developing a strong understanding of business processes, you will gain the business-and-people processes education so many ERP software users lack. The REA ontology approach

---

[12] O'Leary, D.E. On the Relationship Between REA and SAP. *International Journal of Accounting Information Systems*, 5, no. 1 (2004), pp. 65-81.
[13] Dunn, C.L. and McCarthy, W.E. The REA Accounting Model: Intellectual Heritage and Prospects for Progress. *Journal of Information Systems*. 11, no. 1 (1997), pp. 31- 51.

attempts to eliminate silos and is based on a set of building blocks that could be used by all enterprises, and by all functional areas within an enterprise. Wherever two areas of an enterprise (or two different enterprises) use these same building blocks as the foundation of their database design, their systems may be effectively integrated.

Key Terms and Concepts

Artificial construct	Integration
Base object	Ontology
Best-of-breed	Paving the cowpaths
Business process	REA ontology
Enterprise	Reengineering
ERP software	Silo operations
Event-driven systems	Silo systems
Information system	View-driven system

Review Questions

LO1   R1. Describe the purpose of accounting and enterprise systems.

LO2   R2. What are three common types of information system integration attempts currently used by enterprises?

LO3   R3. What are some impediments enterprises may encounter in their efforts to integrate their information systems? Describe at least three.

LO4   R4. What does it mean to have silo operations?

LO4   R5. What does it mean to have silo systems?

LO4   R6. Explain the need to eliminate silos in operations and in systems.

LO5   R7. What does the phrase paving the cowpaths mean with respect to reengineering?

LO6   R8. What do the letters in the acronym *REA* stand for?

LO6   R9. Who invented the REA ontology and for what purpose?

LO6   R10. Why does REA not include debits and credits?

Multiple Choice Questions

LO2
1. Which of the following statements about ERP systems is true?
   A) Most ERP software implementations fully achieve seamless integration.
   B) Some ERP software packages are themselves combinations of separate applications for manufacturing, materials resource planning, general ledger, human resources, procurement, and order entry.
   C) A specific enterprise software package implemented uniformly throughout an enterprise is likely to contain very flexible connections to allow changes and software variations.
   D) ERP systems are designed primarily for small businesses.
   E) Integration of ERP systems can be achieved in only one way.

LO1, LO2, LO4

2. Which of the following is <u>FALSE</u> with regard to an integrated enterprise information system?
   A) An integrated enterprise information system is a set of communication channels in a business organization.
   B) The goal of an integrated enterprise information system is to form one network by which information is gathered and disseminated.
   C) Redundancy in an integrated information system can lead to data inconsistency.
   D) Integration can be achieved in only one way.
   E) Some ERP software packages are themselves combinations of separate applications for manufacturing, materials resource planning, general ledger, human resources, procurement, and order entry.

LO4

3. Which of the following is used to solve the problem of silo departments?
   A) Encouragement of interdepartmental interactions.
   B) Reengineering of traditional departments and focus on workflow processes.
   C) Assign building space such that people in the same department are all in the same physical location.
   D) Both A and B
   E) Both B and C

LO5

4. Which of the following often result from reengineering?
   A) Streamlined workflow
   B) Reduced head count
   C) Consolidation of disparate information systems to eliminate duplication of efforts in various activities
   D) All of the above
   E) None of the above

LO6

5. Geerts and McCarthy's proposed expansion of the REA accounting model presumes that base objects in an enterprise information system should...
   A) Reflect the underlying activities in which an enterprise engages.
   B) Reflect aggregations of numbers needed for decision-making needs within the enterprise.
   C) Reflect artifacts needed to support specific decision-making views within the enterprise.
   D) Include debits, credits, and accounts.
   E) All of the above

LO6

6. Which of the following is false about the REA ontology?
   A) It attempts to eliminate silos.
   B) It is based on a set of building blocks.
   C) It can be used by all enterprises and by all functional areas within an enterprise.
   D) Wherever two areas of an enterprise use the same building blocks as the foundation of their database design, their systems may be effectively integrated.
   E) None of the above is false (i.e., all of the above are true).

LO3, LO5
7. Most failed ERP software implementations have been blamed on...
    A) People Issues
    B) Technological software issues
    C) Hardware issues
    D) Both A and B
    E) None of the above

LO5
8. The redesign of business processes or systems to achieve a dramatic improvement in enterprise performance is called
    A) Reengineering
    B) Interruption
    C) Siloing
    D) Intra-enterprise integration
    E) Inter-enterprise integration

LO6
9. Which of the following about the REA ontology is false?
    A) The REA ontology began as a generalized accounting model but has since developed into an enterprise ontology.
    B) The REA ontology encourages the use of artificial constructs, such as the many artificial constructs included in SAP systems.
    C) REA ontology has the same objective as enterprise systems.
    D) The purpose of the REA enterprise ontology is to define constructs common to all enterprises and to demonstrate how those constructs may be represented in an integrated enterprise information system.
    E) Effective REA modeling requires and enables thorough understanding of an enterprise's environment, business processes, risks, and information needs.

LO6
10. REA stands for...
    A) Reality Exchange for Activities
    B) Reapplication of Enterprising Accounting
    C) Resources, Events, and Agents
    D) Resources, Events, and Applications
    E) Revenues, Exchanges, and Acquisitions

Discussion Questions

LO1   D1. What pieces of the enterprise's economic story are captured and told by traditional accounting systems, and to what audience are those pieces of the story told? What pieces of the story are captured and told by the non-accounting parts of traditional enterprise systems and to what audience are those pieces of the story told? Is the complete story being told to those who need it?

LO2   D2. What are the different degrees to which an information system may be integrated and what are the pros and cons of each approach?

REA Accounting Systems: Resources-Events-Agents: An ontology for designing, controlling, and using integrated enterprise systems

27

LO3   D3.   Suppose you wanted to implement REA enterprise ontology concepts in an enterprise system once you enter the workplace. What obstacles and challenges are you likely to face, and how might you deal with them?

LO4   D4.   Explain the statement "Silo operations lead to silo systems; silo systems perpetuate silo operations." Do you agree or disagree, and why?

LO5   D5.   Read Michael Hammer's article on reengineering. How is reengineering different from automating or computerizing the traditional methods of conducting business? Explain.

LO5   D6.   Use your library to research whether Michael Hammer's concept of business process reengineering has been widely referred to in the past four years. How many journal articles appeared in your search results? Do you think the topic is still as important today as it was in 1990? Explain your position.

LO6   D7.   Would you describe the REA enterprise ontology as paving the cowpaths of accounting or as reengineering of accounting? Explain.

LO6   D8.   If REA were adopted, what additional details of the economic story of enterprises would be told that are currently not told by accounting systems? Discuss the pros and cons of telling those additional details.

Applied Learning

LO1-6   A1.   Reengineering the Business School. This chapter discussed functional silos in enterprises and the need to reengineer business processes and enterprise systems to better share information across functions. Consider your university's college of business (or the equivalent area of business study at your institution)

Required:
a. Describe the structure of your college of business. What departments or other subdivisions exist within the business area? Who is in charge of each department? Where are faculty offices located for each department? To what extent do faculty members from different departments co-author research? To what extent are business courses team-taught by faculty from multiple departments? Does anything about the structure of your college of business seem remarkable?
b. Based on your description in part (a), to what extent do you think functional silos are present in your university's college of business?
c.   How does the presence (or absence) of silos in your college of business affect your curriculum?
d. What recommendations do you have for reengineering your college of business? Explain.

LO1-6   A2.   Many people, business students and practitioners alike, believe that managers and accountants do not need to understand how an enterprise system is designed, only how to use it. Russell Ackoff in 1967 contended that to be effective, managers must understand how systems are designed. His reasoning is summarized below.

Required: Read Professor Ackoff's reasoning. Write a one-page report discussing your reaction to this assumption and Professor Ackoff's contention. Before reading this did you believe it was unimportant for accountants to understand how to design an accounting information system? What do you think now? What was the most important point Professor Ackoff made in favor of managers understanding their information systems? What is the strongest argument you can think of in favor of managers merely needing to know how to use the system?

Professor Ackoff[14]: Most MIS designers seek to make their systems as innocuous and unobtrusive as possible to managers lest they become frightened. The designers try to provide managers with very easy access to the system and assure them that they need to know nothing more about it. The designers usually succeed in keeping managers ignorant in this regard. This leaves managers unable to evaluate the MIS as a whole. It often makes them afraid to even try to do so lest they display their ignorance publicly. In failing to evaluate their MIS, managers delegate much of the control of the organization to the system's designers and operators who may have many virtues, but managerial competence is seldom among them.

Let me cite a case in point. A Chairman of the Board of a medium-size company asked for help on the following problem. One of his larger (decentralized) divisions had installed a computerized production -- inventory control and manufacturing -- manager information systems about a year earlier. It had acquired about $2,000,000 worth of equipment to do so. The Board Chairman had just received a request from the Division for permission to replace the original equipment with newly announced equipment which would cost several times the original amount. An extensive "justification" for so doing was provided with the request. The Chairman wanted to know whether the request was really justified. He admitted to complete incompetence in this connection.

A meeting was arranged at the Division at which I was subjected to an extended and detailed briefing. The system was large but relatively simple. At the heart of it was a reorder point for each item and a maximum allowable stock level. Reorder quantities took lead-time as well as the allowable maximum into account. The computer kept track of stock, ordered items when required and generated numerous reports on both the state of the system it controlled and its own "actions."

When the briefing was over I was asked if I had any questions. I did. First I asked if, when the system had been installed, there had been many parts whose stock level exceeded the maximum amount possible under the new system. I was told there were many. I asked for a list of about thirty and for some graph paper. Both were provided. With the help of the system designer and volumes of old daily reports I began to plot the stock level of the first listed item over time. When this item reached the maximum "allowable" stock level it had been reordered. The system designer was surprised and said that by sheer "luck" I had found one of the few errors made by the system. Continued plotting showed that because of repeated premature reordering the item had never gone much below the

---

[14] Ackoff, R.L. "Management Misinformation Systems," Management Science 14, no. 4 (December 1967), pp. B-147—B-156

maximum stock level. Clearly the program was confusing the maximum allowable stock level and the reorder point. This turned out to be the case in more than half of the items on the list.

Next I asked if they had many paired parts, ones that were only used with each other; for example, matched nuts and bolts. They had many. A list was produced and we began checking the previous day's withdrawals. For more than half of the pairs the differences in the numbers recorded as withdrawn were very large. No explanation was provided.

Before the day was out it was possible to show by some quick and dirty calculations that the new computerized system was costing the company almost $150,000 per month more than the hand system which it had replaced, most of this in excess inventories.

The recommendation was that the system be redesigned as quickly as possible and that the new equipment not be authorized for the time being.

The questions asked of the system had been obvious and simple ones. Managers should have been able to ask them but—and this is the point—they felt themselves incompetent to do so. They would not have allowed a hand-operated system to get so far out of their control.

No MIS should ever be installed unless the managers for whom it is intended are trained to evaluate and hence control it rather than be controlled by it.

CHAPTER 2

Representation and Patterns: An Introduction to the REA Enterprise Ontology

LEARNING OBJECTIVES

The objective of this chapter is to help you understand how to analyze and create enterprise representations that serve as the core foundation for their information systems. After studying this chapter, you should be able to

1. Explain the importance of representation and modeling in enterprise system design and use
2. Identify various types of patterns and recognize patterns in the world around you
3. Describe the purpose and the components of the four levels of the REA ontology
4. Describe the usefulness of the REA pattern as a framework for database design
5. Identify an enterprise's external business partners
6. Identify the resources that are exchanged between an enterprise and its business partners
7. Develop a value system level REA model for an enterprise
8. Identify an enterprise's business processes (transaction cycles)
9. Identify the resource flows between an enterprise's internal business processes and the economic events that cause those resource flows
10. Develop a value chain level REA model for an enterprise

REPRESENTATION AND MODELING

You may wonder why **representation** and modeling are important for understanding accounting and enterprise systems[1]. The general answer to this question is that we can't understand accounting and enterprise systems without **models** that serve as representations of the systems and their underlying **reality**. The systems are too large and complex for most people to comprehend in their entirety. The creation and use of models to help build and understand complex things in life is common. Engineers who build automobiles create models before they create the real cars. Automotive repairpersons use models to help them understand the cars on which they work. Architects create models of the buildings they design; once the building is built, other users often refer to the model to understand some aspect of the building (such as where the support beams are located).

To design and understand accounting and enterprise systems, we must be able to develop and understand representations of the enterprise's reality. Representations are surrogates for the real constructs; in other words, they are **symbols** of those constructs. To design an information system that closely resembles the underlying reality of the enterprise about which the information is stored, we must build a set of symbols that represents that reality. Some models are better than others. Consider model cars as an example. First, envision a molded plastic toy car that was created for use by a baby or toddler. For safety reasons, such a toy may be created with no removable parts that could choke a baby – the wheels

---

[1]Much of the material on representation and patterns is based on materials prepared by Professor William E. McCarthy at Michigan State University. The script material is also based on books written by Roger Schank, including *Tell Me A Story*, Northwestern University Press 1990; *The Connoisseur's Guide to the Mind*, Summit Books 1991; and *Dynamic Memory Revisited*, Cambridge University Press 1999.

REA Accounting Systems: Resources-Events-Agents: An ontology for designing, controlling, and using integrated enterprise systems

31

wouldn't turn, and the doors wouldn't open. Contrast that mental image with that of a model car intended for an adult (one, for example, that a teenager or an adult builds from a kit). Such a model car may have doors and a trunk that open, headlights that light up, perhaps a battery operated convertible top or even a power source that propels it across the floor. Which is the better representation, and why? Most would consider the adult model car the better representation because it more closely resembles a real automobile than does the baby's toy car.

In modeling enterprise systems, our symbol representations must not only map as directly as possible to the underlying reality, but they must also be convertible into a computerized format. In the case of designing enterprise databases, that means we must be able to create paper-based representations of the enterprise reality and then convert the paper models into a format compatible with a database software package.

Representations may be created at different levels of abstraction. More specifically, a representation may symbolize individual **objects** or categories of objects. In database design, individual objects are sometimes referred to as tokens, and categories of objects are known as types. For example, see Exhibit 2-1

EXHIBIT 2–1
Representation at Token and Type Levels of Abstraction

Adapted from: G. L. Geerts and W. E. McCarthy, "An Ontological Analysis of the Economic Primitives of the Extended-REA Enterprise Information Architecture," *International Journal of Accounting Information Systems* 3, no. 1 (March 2002), pp. 1–16.

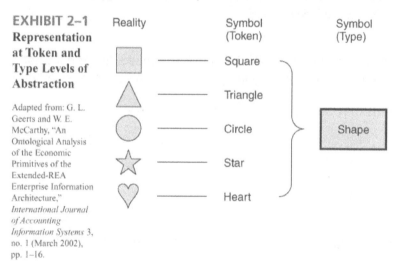

Exhibit 2-1 demonstrates that the reality of shapes can be represented in different formats and at various levels of abstraction. Each shape is represented at the token level by a word that once upon a time was created as a representation for that shape. The string of characters s-q-u-a-r-e is a representation of the square shape. A **token** is an individual instance of something. For example *Fred's little red corvette* is a token. Please understand that it is not the fact that the shapes are represented by words that makes the middle column of Exhibit 2-1 a token-level representation, it is the fact that each individual instance in the reality is represented as a separate token.   For the corvette example, the tokens in the middle column could include *Fred's little red corvette*, *Samantha's hot pink corvette*, *Samantha's little red corvette*, and *Andrew's royal blue corvette*. In other words, token level representation is a one-for-one correspondence of symbols to actual instances in reality.

The shapes (reality) in the first column of Exhibit 2-1 may also be represented at the type level. A **type** is a category of instances that have something in common with each other. The box with the word *shape* inside it in the third column of Exhibit 2-1 is a type-level representation of the individual shape instances. Each separate shape fits into the *shape* category. *Corvette* is a type, of which *Fred's little red corvette* and *Samantha's hot pink corvette* are tokens[2]. In other words, type level representation yields a one-to-many correspondence of symbols to actual instances in reality. This reality-to-category mapping is a very important concept in building enterprise system models, because often we need to represent categories of things as well as the individual things themselves. Imagine an enterprise that has 4,000 different types of inventory items, 895 employees, 25 different cash accounts, 12 branch locations, and engages in thousands of transactions each day. A system must be built to store data about all those individual things, but the conceptual model of the system must represent those things at the type level to make the complexity manageable.

PATTERNS

A **pattern** is an arrangement of repeated or recognizably consistent objects or actions. People use patterns of various kinds every day in understanding the environment around them. Patterns allow us to make predictions about future events and to make sense of the present based on our past experiences. Patterns are used in learning from the time that we are very young children throughout the rest of our lives. Preschoolers and early elementary school students are given a row of symbols such as

♥ ♦ ♥ ♦ ♥ ___

and are asked to fill in the blank with the appropriate symbol. Go ahead, figure out what goes in the blank! It probably didn't take you very long to identify the correct answer as ♦!

As students progress, patterns may be more complicated, for example,
♣ ♦ ♥ ♠ ♣ ♦ ♥ ♠ ___

Of course the correct answer is ♣.

Try this one, which is a little more complex:
⊕ ⊠ ⊖ ⊞ ⊗ ⊟ ⊕ ⊠ ⊖ ⊞ ___

The answer is ⊗ and requires recognition that the + × − pattern is embedded inside the pattern.
○ □ ○ □

Object Patterns

An **object pattern** is a commonly observed constellation of things and relationships between those things. Such a pattern serves the purpose of associating like objects with each other. For example, an early learning pattern was (and perhaps still is) popular on the children's television show "Sesame Street". A group of four objects was shown on the screen and a song said something like "One of these things just doesn't belong here; one of these things just isn't the same." The children were asked to identify which thing was different. Simple patterns of this type might include three things that are identical (e.g. three copies of the same picture of a cow) and one unique thing (e.g. a picture of an airplane). A slightly more difficult pattern of this type could include three things that could be combined

---

[2] Types also exist at different levels of detail; we have sub-types and super-types (corvette is a sub-type of car, which is a sub-type of vehicle). We will save this level of complexity for later chapters.

REA Accounting Systems: Resources-Events-Agents: An ontology for designing, controlling, and using integrated enterprise systems

33

into a category contrasted with another thing that doesn't fit the category. For example, a group could include a cow, a dog, a monkey, and an airplane; of course it is the airplane that is not like the others. Even more advanced patterns of this type might include three things that are related to each other by some kind of domain (e.g. a cow, a barn, and a tractor are related to each other as part of the farm domain) and one thing that is unrelated to that domain (e.g. a monkey). Note that it is especially complicated if the object that is unrelated to the domain common to the other three is part of a different domain with at least one of the other objects; in this example cow and monkey are part of the animal domain, but barn and tractor don't fit that domain.

In conceptual modeling, object patterns consist of expected groupings of things and the relationships between them. Let's use the farm example. What things and activities would you expect to find on a farm? A partial list would include

> Animals
> Crops
> Barn
> Silo
> Farmer
> Tractor

> Harvesting Equipment
> Field
> Harvesting of Crops
> Feeding of Animals
> Caring for Animals

What relationships between these objects would you expect to find on the farm? A partial list would include

> Animals take shelter in the barn
> Crops (unharvested) grow in the field
> Crops (harvested) are stored in the silo
> Farmer participates in harvesting of crops
> Crops participate in harvesting of crops
> Farmer responsible for caring for animals
> Animals benefit from caring for animals
> Farmer drives the tractor
> Harvesting equipment is used in harvesting of crops

You can probably think of additional objects, activities, and relationships between them that you could expect to find on a farm – these lists are intended just to get you thinking. How do you know what things are likely to be part of the farm's reality? You probably know from past experience. That experience could have been personal (from visiting or growing up on a farm) or second-hand (from seeing a farm on television or hearing stories about a farm on which your grandfather was raised, for example).

You may not have realized you have a farm object pattern stored in your memory! In fact, you have many object patterns stored in your long-term memory. Whether the information is actually stored as patterns or whether you simply have an indexing scheme that triggers recall of those objects from various parts of your memory is a matter of debate among academic researchers, but that distinction is unimportant for purposes of this book. My goal is to lead you along a lifelong path of using pattern matching to solve problems. When you are faced with what looks like a new problem, this approach requires you to find some similarity to old problems for which you have already developed a solution. You may then apply the old solution to the new problem, adapting the solution for anything that is different in the new situation. For enterprise system modeling, you will need to think about the objects you expect to find in an enterprise, match the reality to your expectations, and adapt as necessary. Such an approach enables you to avoid having to reinvent the wheel every time you design or evaluate a new enterprise system.

Script Patterns

Whereas object patterns focus on objects and the relationships between them, a **script pattern** is a sequence of events that typically occur in combination with each other. Imagine you are in a friend's house and he came in from his car and said he had just come from the grocery store. If you are a polite person, you will likely ask if he would like you to help him carry in the groceries. How do you know he has groceries to carry? Based on past experience, you have stored in your memory a script pattern for a sequence of events that frequently occur when someone goes to the grocery store. That script leads you to infer he drove to the grocery store (not necessarily from home), took groceries off the store shelves, transported the groceries to the checkout lane, placed the groceries on the checkout counter so the prices could be summed and the groceries could be bagged, paid for the groceries, and drove home. The script that is evoked in your mind is not necessarily accurate for the particular situation. Perhaps the friend was only looking for one thing and was unable to find it so he came home empty-handed, or perhaps he went to the grocery store because it contained a postal station and he needed to mail a letter. In spite of exceptions, the script patterns you have developed based on your past experiences will help you more often than not in understanding your present and future experiences.

Context is important in determining which script is invoked, and part of what determines someone's knowledge is that person's ability to invoke the most appropriate script for a situation. For example, imagine that someone starts to tell you a story that begins with the following sentences. "Once upon a time a boy named Jimmy met a girl named Theresa. They fell in love." You likely have at least two scripts to invoke based on those sentences, and you need to know more about the context in order to guess the ending. If you are told that the story is a traditional romance, you are likely to guess the ending reads something like this: "They lived happily ever after." If you are told the story is a romantic tragedy, you are likely to guess the ending reads more like this: "One of them died and the other was very sad."

You may be surprised to learn that many of the critical steps of building an information system have little to do with programming a computer. The process begins with identifying the need for a business solution and acquiring a better understanding of the environment you plan to support and/or improve. You must examine that environment from different perspectives and at different levels of detail. To thoroughly understand the enterprise domain and to completely represent the activities of the enterprise in its information system we must identify object patterns that communicate things in the enterprise that are usually associated with each other, and we must also identify script patterns that communicate typical sequences of events. A combination of such patterns for a particular domain is known as a domain ontology.

THE REA ENTERPRISE ONTOLOGY

McCarthy proposed a generalized model for accounting systems after analyzing many accounting transactions and identifying the common features of the transactions[3]. McCarthy and Geerts have further developed the constructs of the original model to form an enterprise domain ontology. This ontology is called the REA Enterprise Ontology because three of the principle constructs are <u>R</u>esources, <u>E</u>vents, and <u>A</u>gents. **Resources** are things of economic value (with or without physical substance) that are provided or consumed by an enterprise's activities and operations. Resources found in many enterprises include cash, raw materials, finished goods inventory, equipment, employee labor, and land. (Note: this is not a comprehensive list!) **Events** are activities within an enterprise that need to be planned, controlled, executed, and evaluated. A carefully designed REA model will include only those events that are necessary and in a sense natural, as opposed to those that could be eliminated without changing the substance of the enterprise and thus are in a sense artificial. We return to this distinction later. For this chapter we focus only on **economic events**, which are those events that increase or decrease one or more resources in the enterprise. Later in the book other types of events are introduced. **Agents** are individuals, departments, divisions, or organizations that participate in the control and execution of events.

The REA ontology views enterprises at four levels of detail[4]. The first level of detail is called the value system level. A **value system level REA model** focuses on the resources that are exchanged between the enterprise and its various external business partners. **External business partners** are people or organizations with which an enterprise trades resources, such as suppliers, customers, creditors, investors, and employees. External business partners are sometimes called external agents. A supply chain is made up of the value system level models of interconnected business partners. The second level of detail is called the value chain level. A **value chain level REA model** focuses on the resource flows between interconnected business processes and on the economic events that accomplish the resource flows. Resource flows are the increases or decreases of things of economic value as a result of those things being provided or used up by economic events. In a value chain, the resource flows indicate transfer of availability of or responsibility for the resource from one business process to another. Once a resource is made available to a different business process, that process needs to do something with it and will therefore

---

[3] The REA Ontology material included in this chapter is based on the McCarthy 1982 paper (see footnote 1) and on the following papers:

Geerts, G. and McCarthy, W.E. "Modeling Business Enterprises as Value-Added Process Hierarchies with Resource-Event-Agent Object Templates" in J. Sutherland and D. Patel, eds., *Business Object Design and Implementation*, London: Springer-Verlag, 1997, pp. 94-113.

Geerts, G. and McCarthy, W.E. "Using Object Templates from the REA Accounting Model to Engineer Business Processes and tasks." *The Review of Business Information Systems*, Fall 2001, vol. 5, no. 4, pp.89-108.

Geerts, G. and McCarthy, W.E. "An Accounting Object Infrastructure for Knowledge-Based Enterprise Models." *IEEE Intelligent Systems and Their Application*. Vol. 14, Issue 4, 1999, pp. 89-94.

Geerts, G. and McCarthy, W.E. "The Ontological Foundation of REA Enterprise Information Systems." Presented to the American Accounting Association annual meeting, Philadelphia, Pennsylvania, 2000.

Geerts, G. and McCarthy, W.E. "An Ontological Analysis of the Economic Primitives of the Extended-REA Enterprise Information Architecture." *International Journal of Accounting Information Systems* 3, no. 1 (2002), pp. 1-16.

[4] In the Geerts and McCarthy papers, they describe the REA ontology as a three-level architecture consisting of the value chain, business process, and task levels; however, many professors also find it helpful to discuss the value system level.

include an economic decrement event to use up the resource. That in turn is linked to an economic increment event that acquires or produces a different resource which must then be made available to another business process. The term *business process* is a term widely used in practice to mean anything from a single activity of producing a report to an entire transaction cycle. For this textbook, business process is the term used to describe an entire transaction cycle.

The commonly interconnected business processes included in a value chain level REA model are the **financing process**, the **acquisition/payment process**, the **human resources process**, the **conversion process**, and the **sales/collection process**. Each of these processes is discussed in more detail in this chapter and in later chapters. The third level of detail is the business process level. A **business process level REA model** focuses on one or more transaction cycles in an enterprise's value chain, expanding the representation to include various types of resources, events, agents, and relationships among them. The fourth level of detail is the task level. A **task level REA model** focuses on workflow – the individual steps involved in accomplishing events in an enterprise. Tasks include activities that may be changed or eliminated and therefore should not serve as foundational elements in an enterprise system.

Where are the Patterns in REA?
The value system level is an object pattern that depicts a macro level view of the firm, with the objects being the enterprise itself, its external business partners, and the resources that are exchanged between them. An **exchange** is a trade or swap of one resource for a different resource between business partners.

The value chain level is based on a script pattern. McCarthy proposes that there is a **business-entrepreneur script** (with several possible variations) that serves as a starting point for modeling enterprises. The script says (from the enterprise's point of view)

The enterprise gets some money
- ❖ The enterprise engages in value-added exchanges, such as (but not limited to)
  - ➢ Purchase equipment and raw materials
  - ➢ Purchase labor
  - ➢ Manufacture finished goods
  - ➢ Sell finished goods
- ❖ The enterprise pays back the money and lives off the profit

Variations on this script include value-added exchanges that involve performing services rather than manufacturing and selling finished goods, and any of a number of other revenue-generating and resource-expending activities that are not covered in this version of the script. The value chain level models should be created with this overall script in mind, but adjusted and embellished as appropriate for the specific enterprise being modeled.

Scripts consist of scenes and involve actors, roles, and props. You have probably experienced a dramatic production (e.g. a play, musical, or opera) either as an actor or as an audience member. Members of the audience are typically given a program that outlines the scenes that will take place in the drama. Each scene involves actors and actresses playing roles according to a written script. Sometimes props (physical items used to help communicate the message of the scene) are used. The value chain level is somewhat analogous to the program given to the audience – it provides an outline of the scenes (internal business processes) that will take place for the enterprise.

REA Accounting Systems: Resources-Events-Agents: An ontology for designing, controlling, and using integrated enterprise systems

37

Each scene in the value chain then needs to be portrayed as a business process level REA object pattern model. The REA object pattern identifies the roles and props involved in the scene's events and also relates the events within the scene to each other.

No pattern has yet been identified at the task level. Although best practices in workflow have been recommended in many industries, much variation exists among companies. Still it is important to consider and document workflow when designing, using, or auditing an enterprise system.

Exhibit 2-2 illustrates the relationships between the four levels of the REA ontology

Exhibit 2-2 Four Levels of the REA Enterprise Ontology

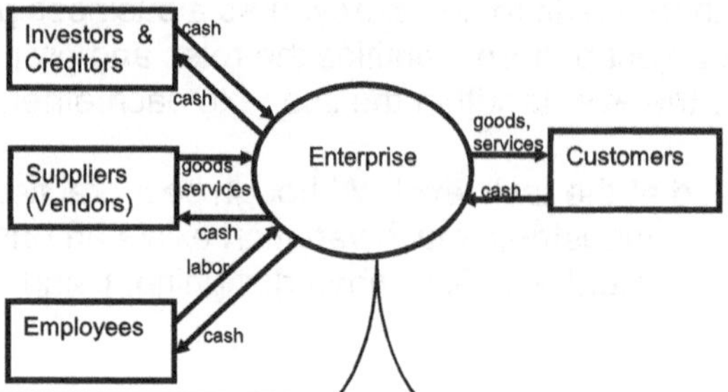

Value System Level
External connections between enterprise and its business partners as indicated by resource flows

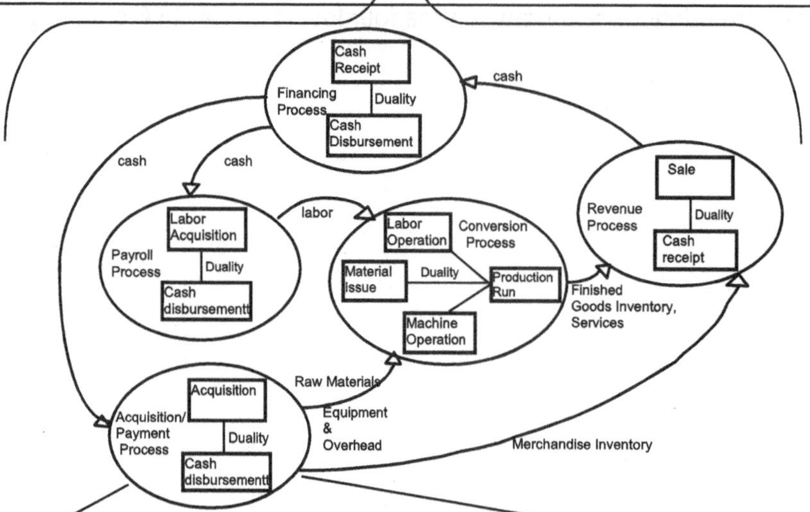

Value Chain Level
Internal resource flows <u>within</u> an enterprise, between its various business processes. Notice NO external business partners are included on this level. The value chain level describes what occurs inside the bubble labeled Enterprise at the value system level.

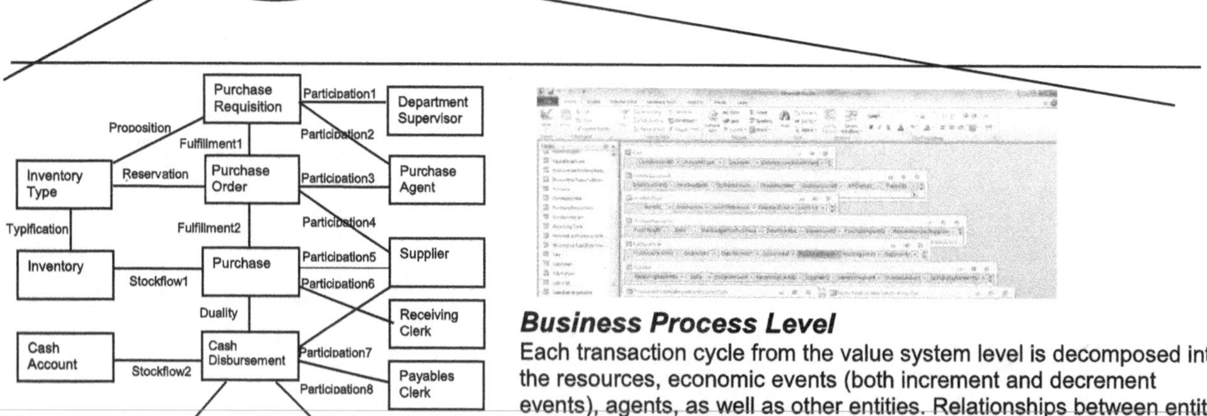

Business Process Level
Each transaction cycle from the value system level is decomposed into the resources, economic events (both increment and decrement events), agents, as well as other entities. Relationships between entities include duality, stockflow, participation, and many others. Business process level models from each of the transaction cycles are integrated into one overall conceptual model for the company, merged on common entities and relationships. Once merged, the conceptual model is converted into relational database tables or some other type of physical storage.

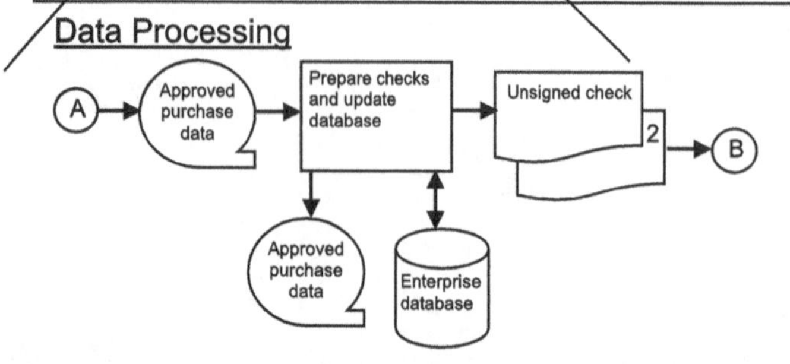

Task Level
Each event from the Business Process Level is decomposed into the workflow by which the event is accomplished, including the inputs, processes, and outputs as well as identifying areas of responsibility. Task Level models may be represented in many different formats including document flowcharts, process maps, data flow diagrams, and others. The flowchart shown at left is only a small piece of a flowchart to represent purchase and payment activities for an enterprise.

VALUE SYSTEMS

The first level of detail in the REA ontology is the least detailed – the big picture view that is called the value system level. You may have heard the saying "they couldn't see the forest for the trees" used to describe someone who is so mired in detail that they forget the big picture of what they are trying to accomplish. Examining the forest level of an enterprise first and trying to develop a plan for analyzing the enterprise a section at a time will help you keep your perspective and avoid getting mired in the detail. Obviously there is plenty of detail in which to get mired, so try to constantly envision the end goal and the plan for getting there to keep you on the path.

Examining the value system level of a firm includes thinking about the enterprise's mission and **strategy**, that is, an enterprise's planned course of action for achieving its objectives. Understanding this level is crucial because later you must ensure that activities within the enterprise's business processes are consistent with its overall mission and strategy. The REA ontology is about much more than developing information systems; it is about understanding enterprises.

To really understand and analyze an organization, you must understand more than internal operations and functions. You must look outside the organization at the industry, the enterprise's **suppliers** (people or organizations from which the enterprise purchases goods or services), its **customers** (people or organizations to whom the enterprise sells goods or services) and all the other parties that affect organization performance. In other words, you must examine the enterprise at its value system level, and also consider how the enterprise's value system interacts with the value systems of the other enterprises in its supply chain. An enterprise **supply chain** encompasses all of the enterprises involved in providing a product or service to an end customer. For example, a manufacturer may purchase materials and equipment from suppliers, then the manufacturer may sell its finished products to wholesalers which then sell the products to retail stores which then sell the products to the end customers.

Eventually managers must look at the entire supply chain to streamline inter-enterprise activities and gain efficiencies in operations. However, the best first step is to focus on the enterprise in the context of its immediate business partners, then to focus on the enterprise value chain and the business processes that comprise that chain. An enterprise **value chain** is the interconnection of business processes via resources that flow between them, with value being added to the resources as they flow from one process to the next. Once an understanding of the enterprise in the context of its immediate business partners and its internal processes is achieved, then examination of the more distant links on its supply chain will be helpful.

VALUE CHAINS

Everything an enterprise does should create value for its customers according to Michael Porter in *Competitive Advantage*[5]. Creating value has a cost. For example, an enterprise that assembles automobiles creates something of value but also must pay for various inputs (e.g., materials, supplies, and time of employees). Porter computes an organization's margin as the difference between value and cost. This calculation includes all value and all

---

[5]M. Porter, *Competitive Advantage: Creating and Sustaining Superior Performance* (New York: The Free Press, 1985), p. 12.

cost, much of which is difficult to measure financially, but which the REA value chain model can capture if measurements are available.

The concept of creating value applies to both for-profit and not-for-profit organizations. For-profit organizations try to maximize their margins. Not-for-profit organizations, such as charitable or governmental entities, seek to maximize the goods and services they provide with the resources (funds) they receive. Over the long run, charitable and governmental organizations seek to optimize their services while matching outflows to inflows. Whether for-profit or not-for-profit, viable organizations provide goods and services that customers value in a cost-effective way. The main difference between for-profit and not-for-profit enterprises is that at the value system level, the input resources and output resources are paired with different external business partners. That is, some of the partners who give resources to the not-for-profit enterprises do not receive resources directly from the not-for-profit enterprises and some of the partners who receive resources from the not-for-profit enterprises do not give resources to the not-for-profit enterprises. The overall notion of input resources being transformed into output resources is still valid, however, because one would expect that if the not-for-profit organization failed to provide the expected goods and services, its contributing external business partners would discontinue their contributions.

Every organization seeks to create value by providing goods and services customers want. For example:
♦ A grocery store creates value by providing food in a clean and convenient location for customers to purchase.
♦ An airline company creates value by safely transporting passengers and cargo in a timely manner.
♦ An automobile manufacturer creates value by manufacturing safe, reliable vehicles to transport people and cargo.
♦ A municipality creates value by providing essential community services (e.g., police protection, fire protection, emergency services, and utilities) to its citizens.

Enterprises that provide goods and services of value to their customers will survive and grow while those that do not will shrink and die. Due to competition for scarce resources, each enterprise must provide value in a cost-effective manner. Although some organizations manage to defer their demise through deceit, disguise, or political influence, ultimately every organization must answer to the final arbiter of value – the customer.

BUSINESS PROCESSES
Developing a value chain level model provides a great deal of insight about the enterprise and is useful for understanding the enterprise's mission, strategy, and overall operations. Facilitating high-level strategic analysis is certainly a goal of the REA enterprise ontology. The primary goal, though, is to provide a structure for the creation of an enterprise-wide database in which to store disaggregated transaction data. The physical implementation of the shared data storage may vary; the relational database is the most widely used format as of this book's publication and is the format demonstrated herein.

Once an enterprise's business processes have been identified along with the specification of the resource flows and the events that caused the resource flows, a pattern has been established from which an enterprise-wide database may be designed. To develop the business process level model, each bubble in the value chain level model is further

REA Accounting Systems: Resources-Events-Agents: An ontology for designing, controlling, and using integrated enterprise systems

41

specified as to the resources, events, agents, and the various types of associations between them. At this level, the external business partners are once again included – you may think of the business process level as a combination of value system and value chain components but at a more detailed level. The specific components of the business process level REA model are discussed in more detail in chapter 5; however, an illustration of the basic business process model for the acquisition of materials is included within Exhibit 2-2, together with some example corresponding relational table structures.

Exhibit 2-2 is over-simplified in order to provide a manageable example; additional complexities that provide more realism are introduced and discussed in later chapters. In chapter 5 we will describe how business process level models like the one in Exhibit 2-2 are derived and further explain what the symbols and the names of the constructs shown mean. For now, you need to understand that each rectangle represents a resource, an event, or an agent. You also need to understand that each of these rectangular constructs corresponds to a table in the enterprise-wide database and that the notations on the relationships between the rectangles determine how the database tables are linked to each other. The procedures for converting the business process level conceptual model (the diagram with the boxes and lines between them) to relational database tables will be detailed in chapter 5 of this book, so don't be concerned that you don't know how that works yet. For now the purpose of Exhibit 2-2 is to show you a small piece of a deliverable obtained from the REA ontology: an operational enterprise-wide transaction database.

One goal of this book is to teach you the basics involved in designing such a deliverable as the partial relational database illustrated in Exhibit 2-2. There are complexities involved in scaling up such a design, optimizing its performance, and designing effective user interfaces that are beyond the scope of this book. Thus once you master the material covered in this book you will have only a partial toolset to use in designing a working database for a real-world enterprise. However, the toolset you acquire by mastering the material in this book can help you to use and evaluate relational database tables in actual enterprises.

TASKS
The final level of detail in the REA ontology is the task level. Recall that any activities that are not essential parts of an enterprise's operations – in other words those activities that can be reengineered away – should not serve as foundational building blocks for an integrated enterprise information system and thus should not become base objects in the enterprise-wide database. However, enterprises need to document all activities and to include information about them in their enterprise systems. A variety of workflow activities are possible and no pattern has yet been identified to represent the task level. Further, a variety of representation techniques for documenting workflow activities are used in practice, including narrative descriptions, system flowcharts, data flow diagrams, process models, fishbone diagrams, and others. Although a specific pattern has not yet been discovered for tasks, in chapter 3 of this book we introduce system flowcharting as a commonly used workflow representation technique. The ability to document tasks and to interpret task documentation is important for designing, using, and evaluating enterprise information systems. The task level of Exhibit 2-2 shows a tiny portion of a system flowchart representing part of a company's workflow needed to accomplish a cash disbursement event. The portion of the system flowchart included in this exhibit does not represent the entire workflow needed by a typical company; the complete flowchart would

not fit in the space available within the exhibit. Chapter 3 provides more guidance on how to prepare complete system flowcharts.

AN EXAMPLE ENTERPRISE

Many abstract concepts have been introduced in this chapter. Robert Scott Woodwind Shop (RSWS) is a fictitious enterprise (based on a real enterprise) we use to illustrate some of these concepts and make the abstract more concrete. To help separate fact from fiction, Robert Scott is a real person and truly is an accomplished woodwind instrument repairman, player, and teacher.   See Exhibit 2-3 for a photo of the real Robert Scott.

Exhibit 2-3 Robert Scott, of Robert Scott Woodwinds

RSWS' primary line of business has been woodwind instrument repair, and many concert musicians claim Mr. Scott is the best in the world because he has near perfect pitch and can detect subtle tone and pitch changes that other repairmen can't hear. Mr. Scott provides repair services and he manufactures clarinet mouthpieces, clarinet barrels, oboe reeds, and bassoon reeds. In years past he sold a few instruments and taught some lessons to a few lucky students. He never took on more work than he could perform by himself, with a little help now and then from whichever one of his children showed an interest in learning how to perform some of the simpler repair or manufacturing activities. To keep his workload manageable, he never advertised; word of mouth proved sufficient to generate enough business to support his family while doing something he loved with a minimal amount of administrative work. He is currently in semi-retirement and has only limited need for an information system to maintain complete control of his tiny sole proprietorship. To make this an appropriate enterprise for which to discuss the need for an integrated enterprise information system, we have scaled up this example to include a high volume of transactions and multiple locations, thus necessitating the use of multiple employees, division of labor, and other complicating factors that evolve small sole proprietorships into large corporations that need integrated enterprise information systems.

RSWS as a whole has two types of financing: debt and equity. The debt financing reflects occasional loans RSWS obtains from banks to help with short-term cash flow needs. As RSWS expanded in volume and needed additional cash infusions to purchase new equipment, rent new store buildings, and pay employees, Robert Scott decided to change from a sole proprietorship to a corporation, completed all the necessary legal paperwork, and sold shares of stock representing ownership interest to a dozen of his concert musician friends.

RSWS generates revenues in four ways. First, RSWS purchases woodwind instruments from its suppliers at wholesale prices and sells them to its customers at retail prices.

REA Accounting Systems: Resources-Events-Agents: An ontology for designing, controlling, and using integrated enterprise systems

43

Second, RSWS purchases woodwind instruments from its suppliers at wholesale prices and rents them to customers who are not yet sure they want to buy an instrument. Most often these rentals are made to the parents of schoolchildren who are just beginning to play an instrument and the parents want some evidence that their child's interest in the instrument is more than just a passing fancy. Third, RSWS manufactures various instrument parts and accessories and sells them to customers. For example, RSWS manufactures clarinet barrels, clarinet mouthpieces, oboe reeds, and bassoon reeds. This involves purchasing the equipment and raw materials and performing the labor and machining operations needed to transform the raw materials into the finished goods. Fourth, RSWS performs repair services for customers. This involves evaluating the customer's woodwind instrument to diagnose the problem, purchasing any repair parts that are needed (or taking them from stock), and performing the labor and machining operations needed to repair the instrument.

Value System Level REA Modeling

One question to answer in order to develop a value system level REA model is "Who are the enterprise's external business partners?" To answer this question, it is helpful to focus on resource flows and ask the question this way, "To whom does the enterprise give resources and from whom does the enterprise receive resources?" Recall that resources are defined as things that have economic value to the enterprise. Recall also that we are taking a pattern-based approach to developing enterprise information systems. Thus we want to consider what is true for most enterprises and then make adjustments as necessary for our particular enterprise. Most enterprise resources fit into one of the following categories:

- Cash
- Inventory (raw materials, finished goods, merchandise, parts, and supplies)
- Labor
- Property, plant and equipment
- Insurance
- Services (such as advertising, cleaning, or government services)
- Utilities (water and energy)

To determine an enterprise's external business partners, a helpful step is to examine which of these resources the enterprise provides or uses and then determine to whom they provide the resources and from whom they acquire the resources. To make matters even simpler, in the current economic environment cash is the universal resource for which most other resources are exchanged. Very seldom do companies engage in **barter transactions** (exchanges of a non-cash resource for a different non-cash resource). Therefore if you concentrate on identifying the various partners to whom the enterprise pays cash and from whom the enterprise receives cash, you will very likely have identified all the appropriate external business partners. Typically the external business partners fit into the following categories:

- Vendors or suppliers (of inventory, equipment, utilities, insurance, and services)
- Employees
- Investors and creditors
- Customers

Sometimes examining the cash outflows of an enterprise does not reveal a resource received in exchange. For example, when an enterprise pays cash to government agencies (such as the Internal Revenue Service) what resource does the enterprise receive in exchange? Some resources the government provides are easy to identify, such as a license to do business, or police and fire protection services. However, the amounts paid in taxes and fees to the government often exceed an identifiable resource received in exchange and we must simply label the resource as government services. Payments to charitable organizations pose a similar dilemma. If an enterprise donates money to a university, what resource does it receive in exchange? The enterprise must believe it receives a resource, because enterprises are assumed to make economically rational decisions. The enterprise may expect goodwill, an increased reputation in the community (in effect, advertising), or an advantage in recruiting the university's students. Based on the assumption that the enterprise does in fact receive resources in exchange for these payments, hopefully you have figured out that government agencies and charitable organizations would be included in the external business partner category of vendors or suppliers.

Once the resources an enterprise uses are identified and the external business partners with whom these resources are exchanged are determined, the information is portrayed in a diagram. The enterprise being modeled is represented as a circle or oval in the center of the diagram. Each external business partner is represented as a square or rectangle; these are placed around the outside of the circle that represents the enterprise. Arrows are drawn between the circle and the squares as appropriate to indicate the resource exchanges between the enterprise and its business partners.

RSWS Value System

From the narrative summary of RSWS's operations earlier in this chapter, we can identify RSWS's external business partners and the resources that are exchanged among them. Exhibit 2-4 illustrates RSWS's value system level REA model. The external business partners for RSWS include investors, creditors, suppliers, customers, and employees. At first glance, you may wonder why employees are considered to be external business partners. After all, they perform services on behalf of RSWS. Although they perform services on behalf of RSWS, they are being paid by RSWS to perform those services and as such are external business partners. We return to the distinction of employees' functioning as internal agents and external business partners later.

Exhibit 2-4
RSWS Value System Level REA Model

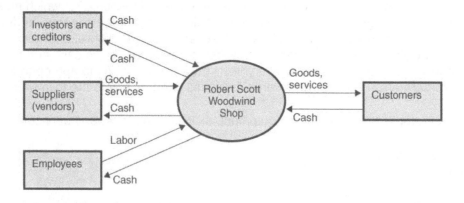

The first step in constructing this model is to examine the various resources RSWS uses in its operations. Cash is certainly used by RSWS. Let's consider the sources from which cash is received, and then the parties to whom RSWS pays cash, and also consider how the cash is used. We identify that cash is received from investors (for equity financing), from creditors (for debt financing), and from customers. Thus we draw a rectangle to represent the set of investors and creditors and another rectangle to represent the set of customers.

Investors and creditors are willing to give cash to RSWS because they expect to receive an amount of cash that is worth more to them than the cash they initially gave up (with the excess being interest, dividends, and/or capital appreciation). Therefore we draw one arrow from investors and creditors to RSWS and label it *cash* to represent cash inflows from investors and creditors and we draw another arrow labeled *cash* from RSWS to investors and creditors to represent cash outflows to investors and creditors (e.g. for interest payments, dividends, principal repayments, and treasury stock purchases).

Customers are willing to give RSWS cash because they expect RSWS to provide goods (e.g. instruments, accessories), repair services, or the use of goods (i.e. rental of instruments). Therefore we draw an arrow labeled *cash* from customers to RSWS to represent the cash inflows from customers and we draw an arrow labeled *goods and services* from RSWS to customers to indicate that RSWS provides those resources to its customers.

We then inspect the narrative to determine what types of cash payments are made by RSWS and to whom. We identify cash payments made to employees and realize that those payments are made in exchange for labor provided by the employees (which for now we will say also includes skills and knowledge). Therefore we draw a rectangle to represent the set of employees. We draw an arrow labeled *cash* from RSWS to employees to represent the cash outflows to employees and we draw an arrow labeled *labor* from employees to RSWS to represent the labor inflow from employees. You might notice that there is no arrow to represent benefits such as health insurance paid to employees. Is it because RSWS doesn't offer any such benefits or is it because they have forgotten to represent them? The answer is neither. Payments made for health insurance for employees is a cash outflow to suppliers made by RSWS on behalf of the employees. The actual insurance benefit is an outflow from the health insurance supplier to the employees and is outside the scope of RSWS's value system model, which only examines the direct resource flows between RSWS and its external business partners.

This leads us to the other external business partner for RSWS – the suppliers (some enterprises may call these vendors). Suppliers are all non-employee individuals or organizations from which an enterprise acquires goods and services. We draw a rectangle to represent the set of suppliers, an arrow labeled *cash* from RSWS to suppliers to indicate the cash outflow, and an arrow labeled *goods and services* from suppliers to RSWS to indicate the inflow of goods and services.

Note that the value system level REA model is based on expectations rather than actuality (as are all levels of the REA model). Some customers may not fulfill their end of the exchange bargain and RSWS will have given up goods and services without receiving the expected cash. Likewise RSWS may not succeed in its endeavors, in which case its investors will not receive cash in excess of their initial investment. Regardless of what actually occurs, the model must allow for the expected exchanges.

You may have some questions about how to create the value system level model from the narrative. For example, how do you choose how many different external partner categories to represent? Notice that we could have made separate boxes for investors and creditors. Similarly we could have made separate boxes for suppliers of goods and suppliers of services. In fact, we did make a separate box for employees, who are essentially suppliers of one type of service. As guidance for your decision about what to combine and what to separate, consider both the types of resources being exchanged and the types of information you will want to capture about the external partners. If the same types of resources are exchanged with two different types of external parties, and the same types of information need to be captured about those external parties, then it makes sense to combine them to simplify the picture. If different types of resources are exchanged and/or different types of information need to be captured about the external parties, then it makes sense to separate them. For example, the exchange between RSWS and its employees is cash for services that is similar to the exchange between RSWS and some types of suppliers (advertising agencies, accountants, and lawyers). However, RSWS needs to capture much more information about its employees than about its suppliers. To process payroll and comply with government reporting requirements, RSWS must store employees' social security numbers, number of dependents, tax filing status, bank account numbers for direct deposit, and so forth. RSWS would not capture and store such details about its non-employee suppliers.

Value Chain Level REA Modeling

Once the value system level analysis is complete, much of the initial value chain analysis has also been completed. This level of analysis focuses on the resource flows between the enterprise's internal business processes. Because you have already identified the resources flowing into and out of the enterprise, what remains at this level is to examine what the company does with its input resources and how it generates its output resources. As business processes use up resources, they should be producing resources worth more to the enterprise than those used up. As noted earlier, enterprises create value by developing and providing the goods and services customers desire. Goods and services are provided through a series of business processes. Regardless of the type of goods or services provided, each organization has at least three business processes.

1. *Acquisition/payment process*: The objective of the acquisition/payment process is to acquire, maintain, and pay for the resources needed by the organization. This process is sometimes called the expenditures cycle, purchasing cycle, or procurement process. Enterprises need many resources, including financial resources, human resources, raw materials, supplies property, plant, and equipment. Resources are acquired from external entities like suppliers or vendors. These are the inputs required by the organization to provide goods and services to its customers. Because the acquisition of financial resources and the acquisition of human resources have complexities not found in the acquisition of other goods and services, many enterprises separate these activities into additional business processes, called the *financing process* and the *human resources process*. We cover these separately in later chapters.

2. *Conversion process*: Sometimes called the manufacturing cycle, the objective of the conversion process is to convert the acquired resources into goods and services for customers. The raw inputs are transformed into finished goods and services by this process.

REA Accounting Systems: Resources-Events-Agents: An ontology for designing, controlling, and using integrated enterprise systems

47

3. *Sales/collection process*: The objective of the sales/collection process is to sell and deliver goods and services to customers and to collect payment. The finished goods and services from the conversion process are sold to customers (external entities) in exchange for their payment, usually in the form of cash (for simplification in this book checks and credit card payments are treated as cash payments).

Creating a value chain model that illustrates the linkages between these processes requires understanding of two very important concepts in the REA ontology: *duality* and *stockflow*. These concepts characterize a core economic phenomena – that of an exchange. As noted earlier, enterprises are assumed to make rational economic decisions. Rational economic theory precludes decision-makers from giving up something with no expectation of anything in exchange. For every event in which an enterprise gives something up we expect a related event in which the enterprise receives something. The causal relationship between a give event and a take event is a **duality** relationship. **Stockflow** is defined as the inflow or outflow of a resource. Stockflow relationships exist between give events and resources (these stockflows are outflows) and between take events and resources (these stockflows are inflows). The value chain level of the REA ontology is constructed based on these two concepts. Geerts and McCarthy say "Duality relationships are the glue that binds a firm's separate economic events together into rational economic processes, while stock-flow relationships weave these processes together into an enterprise value chain. (p.98) [6]"

The first step in creating a value chain model is to write the enterprise script to identify the business processes that need to be included in the value chain. We use the value system level model along with whatever other information we have, such as a narrative description of the enterprise activities. The second step in creating a value chain model is to draw the resource flows to link the business processes together. The third step is to determine the economic exchange events and the duality relationships that make up the core of each business process in the value chain. Let's revisit our RSWS example to clarify these steps.

RSWS VALUE CHAIN
Once the external business partners and the resource exchanges between them are identified, we can proceed to develop a model of RSWS's internal business processes and the resource flows that link them together. Such a model is called a value chain level model, and an example is illustrated as Exhibit 2-5. Let's examine the steps for creating this picture.

---

[6] Geerts, G. and McCarthy, W.E. "Modeling Business Enterprises as Value-Added Process Hierarchies with Resource-Event-Agent Object Templates" in J. Sutherland and D. Patel, eds., *Business Object Design and Implementation*, London: Springer-Verlag, 1997, pp. 94-113.

Exhibit 2-5: RSWS Value Chain Level Model

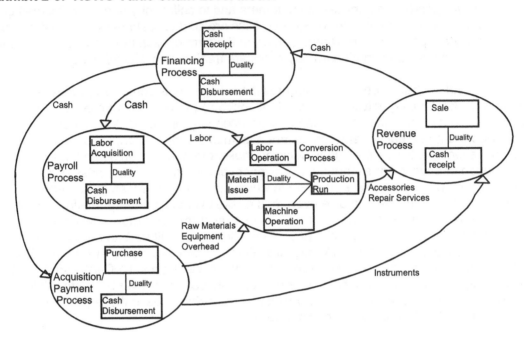

Step 1: Write the entrepreneurial script

To complete this step, we examine the typical scenes of the entrepreneurial business script to see which of the typical scenes RSWS has. Based on our value system level analysis, the typical script pattern, and the narrative description of RSWS we write RSWS's script as follows:

- RSWS gets cash from investors and creditors
- RSWS engages in value-adding activities
  - uses cash to buy instruments, raw materials, and overhead from vendors
  - uses cash to acquire labor from employees
  - uses materials, equipment, and overhead to manufacture accessories and to provide repair services
  - sells instruments, accessories, and repair services to customers for cash
- RSWS pays cash to investors and creditors

The first and last scenes together comprise the financing process; in scene 2, the sub-scenes are (in order) the acquisition/payment process; the human resources (payroll) process; the conversion process; and the sales/collection process. Keep in mind that all of these scenes and sub-scenes come directly from our value system level analysis except for the "uses materials, equipment, and overhead to manufacture accessories and to provide repair services." That sub-scene doesn't involve resource exchanges with external business partners, so is not modeled at the value system level. Thus you must be careful when developing your value chain model to include not only the scenes that you derive from the value system level but also include any business processes that add value via internal resource transformations.

To begin re-creating the model in Exhibit 2-5, draw a bubble for each scene and subscene identified in step 1. No distinction is made between scenes and subscenes from this point forward – they are all business processes and they will all be referred to as scenes. Label each bubble with the scene name. You may notice that the example diagram shown has the bubbles drawn in a somewhat counter-clockwise order. You may prefer to draw your value chain diagrams clockwise. The layout of these diagrams does not matter; however, they should be made as easy to use as possible.

Step 2: Connect the scenes with resource flows
Once all the scenes are identified they need to be combined to form a value chain. The resource flows provide the links from one scene to the next.

Look first at the financing process scene for RSWS. Once the cash is acquired in the financing process, it becomes an outflow resource that is made available to be used as an inflow resource for the acquisition/payment and human resource processes, where it is transferred out to external business partners in exchange for instruments, raw materials, overhead, and labor. Therefore draw arrows labeled *cash* from the financing process to the acquisition/payment process and from the financing process to the payroll process.

Because the value chain model only illustrates the internal processes, we don't show the cash outflows from the acquisition and payroll processes to the external partners, nor do we show the related resource inflows from those external partners. Rather we just see the flows between the business processes within the enterprise. Picture the page as a piece of cardboard and each scene's bubble as a hole in the cardboard. Picture the resource flows as yarn. A resource that is made available by one business process results in the yarn being brought up through the hole for that scene. The yarn is then brought over and down into to the hole of the business process that is expected to use up that resource. At the value chain level, we don't see what happens to that yarn when it is below the surface of the cardboard – we just see the transfers between the scenes.

For RSWS, the acquisition process uses up the cash inflow resource and obtains raw materials, equipment, overhead, and instruments as outflow resources; and the payroll process uses up the cash inflow resource and produces labor as an outflow resource. RSWS's conversion process transforms the labor, raw materials, equipment, and overhead inflow resources into the accessories and repair service outflow resources. Therefore draw an arrow labeled *labor* from the payroll process to the conversion process and draw an arrow labeled *raw materials, equipment, and overhead* from the acquisition/payment process to the conversion process. RSWS's sales/collection process uses up the instrument, accessory, and repair service inflow resources and obtains cash as an outflow resource. Therefore draw an arrow labeled *Instruments* from the acquisition/payment process to the sales/collection process and draw an arrow labeled *accessories and repair services* from the conversion process to the sales/collection process. The cash obtained within the sales/collection process is then made available to the financing process to meet the enterprise's needs. Therefore draw an arrow labeled *cash* from the sales/collection process to the financing process. The assumption is that in each of these scenes the resources produced or obtained are worth more than the resources used up, thus value is added to the enterprise in each link of the chain.

Step 3: Specify the economic exchange events within each scene
The third step in creating the value chain diagram adds more detail to the diagram that clarifies how each scene's representation in the value chain diagram provides the starting point for a business process level model. This step entails depicting the economic

exchange events inside each scene's bubble on the value chain diagram. Each scene must contain at least one economic increment (take) event and at least one economic decrement (give) event. You can use the resource flows to determine what events are needed. This analysis will also help you to determine whether a scene in your value chain should be decomposed into multiple scenes. The general rule to follow for this step is that each process must have an economic decrement event to match up with each resource inflow and an economic increment event to match up with each resource outflow. The idea is that if a resource is flowing into a process, the process must include an event that uses it up (either by transferring it to an external partner or by transforming it into a different resource). Similarly, if a resource is flowing out of a process, the process must include an event that produced the resource (either by transferring it in from an external business partner or by creating it as a transformation of some other resources.

In our RSWS example, let's add detail first to the financing process. Because cash is a resource inflow to that process, the process must include an event that uses it up (i.e. a cash disbursement event). Cash is also a resource outflow from financing, so the process must include an event that acquired it (i.e., a cash receipt event). The cash receipt and cash disbursement events are linked via a duality relationship. So we draw two event boxes inside the financing process bubble and connect them via a relationship line labeled *duality*. We label the events *cash receipt* and *cash disbursement*. Note that even though cash flows from the financing process to multiple other processes, only one cash receipt event is typically used. That is because the data attributes of all cash receipts are likely the same, so we combine all cash receipts for all purposes into one event set. The fact that cash is used for different purposes doesn't matter.

Next we examine the payroll process. Because cash is a resource inflow, the process must include an event that uses it up (i.e., a cash disbursement event). Notice that the enterprise will likely only have one cash disbursement event set that will encompass all cash disbursements made for all purposes, but we must depict the event set in each business process that uses cash. The payroll process obtains labor as its resource outflow, so there must be an event within the payroll process that obtains that labor (labor acquisition, an event that transfers the labor into the enterprise). So we draw two event boxes inside the payroll process bubble and connect them via a relationship line labeled *duality*. We label the events *cash disbursement* and *labor acquisition*.

The acquisition/payment process is similar to the payroll process. Cash is a resource inflow to acquisition/payment, so the process must have an event that uses it up (i.e., a cash disbursement event). The acquisition/payment process has instruments, materials, services, and equipment as outflows, so the process must include an event that obtains those things from external sources (i.e., an acquisition event set). Here we must determine whether the same data attributes are recorded for acquisitions of each of these types of items. For any that are different, the events should be modeled separately and the recommendation would be to make separate acquisition cycle bubbles. Let's say we determine that RSWS records all acquisitions using a common set of forms and captures the same data attributes for them. Thus we need only one acquisition event set and only one acquisition process (scene). We draw two event boxes inside the acquisition/payment process bubble and connect them via a relationship line labeled *duality*. Label the events *cash disbursement* and *acquisition*.

Next we examine the conversion process. The conversion process is typically the most complicated scene. RSWS's value chain diagram shows input resource flows as materials,

REA Accounting Systems: Resources-Events-Agents: An ontology for designing, controlling, and using integrated enterprise systems

51

equipment, labor, and overhead. That indicates the conversion process must have events that use up each of those items. We determine that raw materials are used up as they are issued into a manufacturing or repair job so draw a box labeled *material issue*. Next note that employee labor is used up through the employees' involvement in labor operations, so draw a box labeled *labor operation*. Equipment and overhead are used up in machine operations, so next draw a box labeled *machine operations*. Next we need to determine what event produces the finished accessories and/or repaired instruments. We determine that for RSWS every repair service and each job to produce a batch of parts or accessories is called a production run. Therefore draw a box labeled *production run*. We realize that the material issues, labor operations, and machine operations are economic decrement events (they use up resources) that are matched with the production run, which is an economic increment event (it produces resources). Therefore we draw relationship lines to connect material issues, labor operations, and machine operations to the production run and label them each as *duality*.

Now all our scenes are detailed except for the Sales/Collection or Revenue process. We see that the input resources are the instruments (from the acquisition process), and the manufactured accessories and repair services (from the conversion process). The instruments get changed into cash either by selling them or renting them to customers. The repair services and manufactured accessories are also changed into cash by selling them to customers. As with the acquisition process, we need to make a choice as to whether there is a common sale event set for which the same set of data attributes will be maintained, or whether the activities are dissimilar enough to warrant being maintained as separate event sets. For this example, we assume RSWS uses the same set of forms and captures the same data attributes for each of these revenue-generating activities, so we will combine them into one economic decrement event called sale. The output resource flow is cash, indicating that the process must include an event that produces or obtains the cash, in other words an economic increment event called cash receipt. We draw two boxes with a duality relationship line connecting them; we label one box *sale* and the other box *cash receipt*. Now the value chain is complete and may be used to facilitate creation of the business process level models for RSWS. We discuss that process in detail in Chapter 5.

CONCLUDING COMMENTS

In this chapter we discussed techniques for representing elements of an enterprise's reality in a conceptual model (set of symbols on paper) that serves as a basis for designing an enterprise wide database. We discussed the REA enterprise ontology and illustrated how the enterprise can be viewed from multiple perspectives to ensure the database is designed to capture information consistent with the enterprise's value-adding activities and overall strategy. The coverage of these topics in this chapter provides only a high level overview. In the remaining chapters of this book we will provide more details regarding each level of the ontology.

Value system and value chain analyses are valuable because they compel you to understand both the internal operations of a firm as well as the forces and parties outside the firm that affect its ability to create value. The direct actions of an organization are only part of its overall value chain process. It is also important to look at external linkages, such as the activities of customers and suppliers to understand the ability of an organization to create value. For example, some organizations may be more successful at creating value because they elicit quality response from their customers and use the feedback to quickly change or upgrade their products. Other organizations may achieve success because they have worked effectively with their suppliers to reduce costs and improve the ability to respond to customer desires. A thorough analysis of the value system and value chain helps your thought process by enabling you to understand all the activities that are strategically relevant to an organization, not just the portion of activities in which an organization directly participates or controls.

Key Terms and Concepts

Acquisition/Payment process
Agent
Barter transaction
Business-entrepreneur script
Business process level REA model
Context
Conversion (manufacturing) process
Customer
Duality relationship
Economic event
Event
Exchange
External business partner
Financing process
Human resources (payroll) process
Model
Object
Object pattern
Pattern

REA ontology – 4 Levels
Reality
Representation
Resource
Sales/Collection process
Script pattern
Stockflow
Strategy
Supplier
Supply chain
Symbol
Task level REA model
Token
Type
Value chain
Value chain level REA model
Value system
Value system level REA model

Review Questions

LO1   R1.   What is a model? Why do we create models of systems?

LO8   R2.   What is a business process?

LO1, LO3   R3.   Is it better to make one model of an entire enterprise, or several smaller models of individual processes? Why?

LO1   R4.   What is the difference between token level and type level representation?

LO2   R5.   What is the difference between an object pattern and a script pattern?

LO3, LO4   R6.   Describe the four levels of the REA ontology, and explain what type of pattern (object or script) exists at each level.

LO8   R7.   Describe each of the major business processes found in most enterprises.

LO5-7   R8.   To begin creating a value system level REA model, what does the chapter recommend as the first thing you should try to identify?

LO9   R9.   What do duality associations consist of?

LO9   R10.   What is the difference between a stock inflow and a stock outflow? What types of events are associated with stock inflows and with stock outflows?

LO9, LO10   R11.   When creating a value chain level REA model, if a transaction cycle has two resource inflows and one resource outflows, what do you know about the events in that transaction cycle?

LO9, LO10   R12.   When creating a value chain level REA model, if a transaction cycle has three economic decrement events and one economic increment event, what do you know about that transaction cycle's resource inflows and outflows?

REA Accounting Systems: Resources-Events-Agents: An ontology for designing, controlling, and using integrated enterprise systems

53

Multiple Choice Questions

LO2
1. Which of the following is true about script patterns?
   A) Script patterns are sequence of events that occur in combination with each other.
   B) Script patterns focus on objects and relationships between them.
   C) Script patterns are always accurate.
   D) Past script patterns rarely help you for the future
   E) None of the above.

LO9
2. Which of the following is NOT an example of a resource in the REA ontology?
   A) Employee Labor
   B) Land
   C) Finished Goods
   D) Customers
   E) Raw Materials

LO5-7
3. Which of the following models focuses primarily on the resource exchanges between the enterprise and its various external business partners such as suppliers, customers, creditors/investors, and employees?
   A) Value system level REA model
   B) Value chain level REA model
   C) Business process level REA model
   D) Task level REA model
   E) None of the above

LO3
4. Which of the following models focuses on the individual workflow steps involved in accomplishing events in an enterprise?
   A) Value system level REA model
   B) Value chain level REA model
   C) Business process level REA model
   D) Task level REA model
   E) None of the above

LO1, LO2
5. In database design, individual objects are sometimes referred to as _____, and categories of objects are known as _____.
   A) Symbols, Types
   B) Types, Tokens
   C) Tokens, Types
   D) Symbols, Tokens
   E) Tokens, Symbols

LO3
6. For which level of the REA ontology has a specific pattern not yet been discovered?
   A) Business process level
   B) Task level
   C) Value system level
   D) Value chain level
   E) None of the above; specific patterns have been discovered for all four levels

LO5-7

7. The external partners to whom cash is the primary resource typically given in a traditional manufacturer's value system level REA model include all of the following **except**...
   A) Employees
   B) Customers
   C) Suppliers
   D) Investors
   E) Creditors

LO8, LO10

8. Which of the following is NOT included in a typical Value Chain Level REA model?
   A) Financing process
   B) Human resources process
   C) Sales process
   D) Acquisition process
   E) Consumption process

LO3, LO5, LO7

9. In the REA Ontology, Agents can be
   A) Individuals
   B) Departments
   C) Organizations
   D) Divisions
   E) All of the above

LO5-7

10. Employees of Brymer Bridge Design (BBD) can elect to have $50 per month deducted from their paychecks to pay for dental insurance. BBD transmits the insurance premiums to DentaRight Dental Insurance (DDRI). When an insured BBD employee visits a participating dentist, the employee pays only half the bill. The remaining half is paid by DDRI. Which of the following statements best describes why the dental benefits paid by DDRI to the dentists should not be included on BBD's REA Value System Model?
    A) Payment of employee benefits such as dental insurance falls within the scope of BBD's conversion cycle, and conversion cycles are typically not depicted on value system models.
    B) Payment of the dental benefits relates to the resource exchanges between DDRI and its suppliers, therefore it is outside the scope of BBD's value system model.
    C) Payment of the dental benefits by DDRI to the dentists should be included on BBD's value system model.
    D) Payment of dental benefits is an event, not a resource exchange; therefore it should not appear on a value system level model.
    E) Payment of dental benefits does not involve cash flow, therefore it should not appear on a value system level model.

REA Accounting Systems: Resources-Events-Agents: An ontology for designing, controlling, and using integrated enterprise systems

55

LO8, LO10

11. Regardless of the type of goods or services provided, each organization typically includes these three business processes/transaction cycles:
   A) Inventory, Wage Payments, and Sales
   B) Payments, Collections, and Debt Financing
   C) Acquisition/Payment, Conversion, and Sales/Collection
   D) Inputs, Outputs, and Returns
   E) Financing, Wage Payments, and Inventory

LO9

12. The causal relationship between a give event and a take event is a _____, and _____ is defined as the inflow or outflow of a resource.
   A) Difference association; Process
   B) Duality association; Stockflow
   C) Conversion association; Timing
   D) Value Chain association; Resource flow
   E) Stockflow association; Duality

LO8-10

13. Which of the following are economic increment events?
   A) Production Runs
   B) Material Issues
   C) Labor Operations
   D) Machine Operations
   E) Cash Disbursements

LO8-10

14. Resource flow connections between the internal business processes (transaction cycles) of an enterprise are most commonly illustrated in:
   A) REA Value System models
   B) REA Value Chain models
   C) REA Business Process models
   D) REA Task models
   E) None of the above

LO8-10

15. What is likely the most appropriate label to put on the arrow going into the financing process for this partial value chain level model for a privately held pharmacy?

   A) Loan
   B) Common stock
   C) Cash
   D) Pharmaceuticals
   E) Derivatives

LO8-10
16. In a REA value chain level model, what event inside the financing process bubble corresponds to the arrow coming into the financing process bubble?

A) Cash disbursement
B) Cash receipt
C) Labor acquisition
D) Purchase
E) Sale

LO3
17. In order from the top down, the hierarchy levels in the REA enterprise ontology are
A) Task, business process, value system, value chain
B) Business process, task, value system, value chain
C) Value chain, value system, business process, task
D) Value system, value chain, business process, task
E) Business process, value chain, task, value system

LO3, LO7
18. Which level of the REA ontology represents the big-picture view?
A) Value system
B) Value chain
C) Business process
D) Task
E) Both C and D above

LO8-10
19. To which other internal business process are manufactured goods typically made available by the conversion business process?
A) Financing
B) Revenue
C) Payroll (Human Resources)
D) Acquisition/Payment
E) Both C and D above

LO3
20. Which REA ontology level focuses on the resource flows between interconnected business processes?
A) Task
B) Business process
C) Value system
D) Value chain
E) Both A and B above

Discussion Questions

LO4 D1. Dramatic productions follow scripts that contain scenes, actors, props, and roles. Describe how each of these components map to levels of the REA enterprise ontology. Explain why you believe or don't believe it is useful to think about enterprises from the script perspective.

LO2 D2. The chapter gave an example of a romantic script that some would say is the theme for many happy romantic movies. Write a similar script for a typical action/adventure movie. What, if anything, do romantic and action/adventure movie scripts have in common?

LO2-3 D3. Exhibit 2-2 includes an example business process level model for an acquisition/payment cycle. List at least two resources, two events, and three agents that you think Robert Scott Woodwinds would need to include in its revenue cycle business process level model.

LO4 D4. Explain why you think activities that could be re-engineered away should or should not serve as foundational building blocks in an enterprise information system.

LO4 D5. The REA ontology was originally created as an accounting model intended to replace the traditional double-entry model Assets = Liabilities + Owners' Equity. Using your knowledge of business and accounting, what do you believe are the essential parts of accounting systems that can never be re-engineered away? In other words, what makes up the essence of accounting? What parts of the traditional double-entry model are artificial constructs that could be replaced with other methods or approaches?

Applied Learning

LO2,6,7 A1. Picture in your mind a pizza delivery retailer of your choice. Using the knowledge you have based on your previous experience ordering pizza, combined with your general business understanding, try to guess what the value system level model for this enterprise includes. Draw a value system level model similar to Exhibit 2-3 using labels specific to the pizza delivery retailer.

LO2 A2. Imagine this scenario. Midsize University in Midtown, USA, has a library. You have never been to Midsize University or even to Midtown, USA. You have been asked to create an object pattern model for Midsize University's library. Such a model illustrates the set of things the library would need to keep track of and the relationships between those sets of things. You are told you will earn a large bonus if you can complete the model in a very short time frame. Your flight to Midtown, USA has been delayed by four hours, which is going to make it very difficult to finish on time. Whatever you can complete while waiting for your flight will help you to meet your bonus deadline, so you start to prepare a list of things and relationships between things that you think the library will need to track. Prepare this list in either diagram or list format.

LO 5-10 A3. China U-Town is a very successful restaurant that delivers Chinese food to customers in a medium-sized city that has a large public university. China U-Town has four locations, one on each side of town (north, south, east, and west) in order to provide delicious food and quick delivery (30 minutes or less, or the customer gets $5 off) to the majority of the city. China U-Town's operational cash flow is augmented by occasional owner contributions and a Wells-Fargo line of credit. China U-Town's owner, Hui Zhong (pronounced Hoy Zong) frequently generates and analyzes reports that give her information about her company's competitors and customers. Using these reports, Hui Zhong decides whether to change menu items, prices, delivery areas, and so forth. She is able to gauge relative performance of the four store locations. China U-Town has approximately 60 employees. Order clerks take customer orders over the telephone and instruct the cooks as to what they need prepared. Cooks prepare the requested food and give it to the order clerks who package it for delivery. Delivery people take the final packaged orders to the customers' residences using company-owned delivery vehicles. Customers pay the delivery people either by check or with cash. Delivery people return a copy of the delivery ticket along with the customer's remittance to the company's order clerk who records the cash receipt using the company's electronic cash register. Each day's receipts are totaled and Hui Zhong decides which bank account to replenish and deposits the receipts into that account. China U-Town's purchasing agent acquires the finest organically raised raw food ingredients from leading Asian markets where, because of her outstanding reputation, she is allowed to purchase all items on account. Hui Zhong approves all purchases in excess of $250. China U-Town's accounts payable clerk pays for all such ingredient purchases within 30 days. Hui Zhong also regularly updates her restaurant equipment, seating furniture, and computer systems through on-account purchases from trusted merchants. Those purchases are typically paid by the accounts payable clerk with sufficient dispatch to take advantage of the 2/10, n/30 payment terms.

Required
1) Create a value system level model for China U-Town
2) Create a value chain level model for China U-Town

LO5-10 A4. Frankie is a 10-year old entrepreneur. He is a big fan of sports trading cards and has a great idea for making money: 1) buy cards in bulk, 2) buy sleeves in bulk, 3) put cards in sleeves, and 4) sell single sleeved cards at a profit to other sports trading card fans. Frankie surveyed his friends and identified Melissa, Steven, Anthony, and Kyle as sports card fans willing to pay fairly high prices to get the cards they want, and are willing to pay cash. Besides those four, many other potential customers exist.

Frankie's dad doesn't think Frankie's brainstorm is such a great idea because (a) Frankie has no money, and (b) Frankie may not have time to sort and assemble cards because he has too much homework. Frankie's Aunt Frances has plenty of money, no kids of her own, and is happy to lend some money to her namesake Frankie. Frankie's dad says she must charge simple interest at an annual interest rate of 10% to make it a real business transaction, otherwise no deal. Frankie's little sister Sally, who is 6 years old, is in the first grade, very smart, extremely industrious, and exceptionally trustworthy. She has lots of time because first graders don't have much homework. Sally is willing to work for Frankie for 2 cents per assembled card.

Moved by his son's initiative and the support of Frankie's aunt, Frankie's father decides to allow Frankie to try out his scheme. He even agrees to be Frankie's supplier, since Frankie doesn't have a credit card. However, he makes it clear that Frankie must pay his father as soon as the sleeves and cards arrive and he must pay Sally as soon as she does her work, not after Frankie sells the cards. Their research indicates the best deal for the most desirable trading card brand is $3 for a pack of 9 cards, and the best deal for sleeves is $7.50 for a box of 250 sleeves. Those costs include shipping and any applicable tax.

Frankie borrows $180 from Aunt Frances. He buys 48 packs of cards and two boxes of sleeves from his dad. Sally takes all 432 cards (48 packs x 9 cards per pack) out of their packages and puts them into the card protector sleeves. She sorts them by type (super-rare, rare, common, and so forth). Frankie pays her the agreed upon $8.64 ($.02 x 432 cards). Slowly, but surely, over the next 3 months Frankie sells all 432 cards and generates total revenue of $400. At the end of the 3 months, Frankie pays Aunt Frances $184.50 ($180 principal + $4.50 in interest -- $180 x .10 x 3/12 = $4.50).

Required

1. Create a value system level model for Frankie's business
2. Create a value chain level model for Frankie's business – include all duality relationships
3. Create the Income Statement, Statement of Owners Equity, and Balance Sheet for Frankie's business
4. Explain how you were able to create the financial statements in (3) above without having used journals and ledgers to store the transaction data.

CHAPTER 3

Task Level Modeling

LEARNING OBJECTIVES

The objective of this chapter is to introduce document flowcharts as a tool for representing the task level detail of business processes. The task level in REA modeling is the level at which workflow is documented. Details of common activities in the revenue and acquisition cycles are introduced to provide context and to demonstrate application of the flowcharting constructs to enterprise activities. After studying this chapter you should be able to:

1. Explain the difference between task level and business process level representations of an enterprise
2. Identify the various symbols used on document flowcharts
3. Describe various kinds of physical media, file types, and processing methods used in enterprise systems
4. Identify the typical tasks, instigation events, commitment events, economic events, economic reversal events, and documents used in the revenue and acquisition cycles of many enterprises
5. Create a system/document flowchart from a narrative description of an enterprise business or information process
6. Create a narrative description of an enterprise business process from a system/document flowchart

INTRODUCTION

In Chapter 2 we defined tasks as the individual steps involved in accomplishing events in an enterprise. The events themselves are in fact tasks; however, many tasks should not be represented as events. Tasks for which measurements are either not feasible or not cost effective should not be represented as events. Tasks that are activities that may be changed or eliminated should not serve as foundational elements in an enterprise system database. The purpose of task level modeling is <u>not</u> to design a database; instead it is to document the flow of data through an enterprise. Tasks may be included in the workflow for an enterprise even though they are not represented as base objects in the enterprise database. Data captured as a result of tasks may be included in the tables as attributes, and data needed to accomplish tasks can be retrieved from the database via queries.

Pattern discovery at the task level is not as straightforward as at the value system, value chain, and business process levels. Although there are best practices for how certain activities can be accomplished in enterprises, workflow may include steps or activities that could be re-engineered away without substantively changing the nature of the enterprise. Tasks may also occur in various sequences for different enterprises (or for different areas within an enterprise) and the sequencing must be represented in task level models. For the other levels of the REA ontology, the models do not represent a sequencing of events, but merely associations between them. A sale may come before a cash receipt, or vice versa; the order does not matter for establishing the architecture of the enterprise system's core database as long as one can be traced to the other. For the task level, sequencing is important, as enterprises need to document details about the procedural aspects of the business activities and corresponding data entry into and information retrieval from the enterprise system.

COMPARISON OF REA's BUSINESS PROCESS AND TASK LEVELS

The purpose of creating a business process level REA model is to design the enterprise database. Any events, or activities that make up those events, that could be reengineered away without changing the overall nature of the enterprise should not be included as core elements of the enterprise database. This avoids the need to substantially alter the enterprise database every time workflow is changed. However, firms must document those events and activities as part of the enterprise's system documentation. Such documentation is especially useful for identifying enterprise risks and internal control strengths and weaknesses, which will be discussed further in Chapter 4. An example of business process level modeling as compared to task level modeling may help you to understand the difference.

Jayvision, Inc. is an enterprise that creates video games for children. In its acquisition/payment process, Jayvision once had the following procedures:

- A department supervisor identified or confirmed the need to acquire a particular product or service, and submitted a requisition form to the purchasing department through the company mail.
- The purchasing department opened the mail, approved (or disapproved) the requisitions and sorted the approved requisitions into piles according to the type of products and services needed. Disapproved requisitions were returned to the department supervisor with explanations as to why the requisitions were denied.
- The purchasing department identified appropriate vendors for the requested products and services. Often this entailed searching the catalogs of established vendors to determine pricing and availability; sometimes the purchasing agent contacted the vendor's sales representative to obtain details about the products and services; sometimes the purchasing agent needed to prepare a request for quote or to issue requests for competitive bids from potential suppliers.
- Once appropriate vendors were selected, the purchasing department prepared purchase orders (based on one or more purchase requisitions) and mailed or faxed them to the vendors. A copy of the purchase order was sent to the accounts payable department, where it was filed in a temporary file in vendor number order awaiting further processing.
- The receiving department for Jayvision received products. Upon receipt a clerk manually counted the products and filled out a receiving report listing the product identification number, quantity received, and a note describing the condition of the items. A copy of the receiving report was sent to the accounts payable department where it was filed in a temporary file in vendor number order awaiting further processing.
- Services were received by various departments; upon receipt of a service, the appropriate department supervisor filled out a "receiving report" for services, including a description of the services received and the dates on which they were received. A copy of the report was sent to the accounts payable department where it was filed in a temporary file in vendor number order to await further processing.
- The accounts payable department for Jayvision received vendor invoices in the mail. For each vendor invoice received, an accounts payable clerk retrieved the purchase order and receiving report copies for that vendor. The clerk verified that each line item amount on the vendor invoice represented the correct amount for a product or service that had been both ordered and received. The

clerk also double-checked the invoice for mathematical accuracy. If everything was deemed okay, the accounts payable clerk wrote a check to the vendor for the amount of the invoice and forwarded the check with its underlying documentation to the controller. The controller signed the check and gave it to an accounting clerk to copy and send to the vendor. The copy was filed along with the supporting documentation in a permanent file in the accounting department.

Jayvision recently re-engineered its acquisition/payment workflow. The new procedures are described as follows:

- A department supervisor identifies or confirms the need to acquire a particular product or service, and enters requisition data into the enterprise database. This entry triggers an electronic notification that is sent to the purchasing department.
- Upon receipt of the electronic notification, the purchasing department examines and approves (or disapproves) the requisitions. Notices regarding disapproved requisitions are electronically sent to the department supervisor with explanations as to why the requisitions were denied.
- The purchasing department identifies appropriate vendors for the requested products and services. Often this entails searching the catalogs of established vendors to determine pricing and availability; sometimes the purchasing agent contacts the vendor's sales representative to obtain details about the products and services; sometimes the purchasing agent needs to prepare a request for quote or to issue requests for competitive bids from potential suppliers.
- Once appropriate vendors are selected, purchase order data is entered into the enterprise database and purchase order forms are electronically generated and are either e-mailed or printed and faxed to the vendors.
- The receiving department for Jayvision receives products. Upon receipt a clerk checks the enterprise database to verify an order had been placed for the vendor from whom the goods were received. The clerk manually counts the products and enters the appropriate receipt data into the enterprise database.
- Services are received by various departments; upon receipt of a service, the appropriate department supervisor enters receiving report data into the enterprise database.
- Each day the enterprise database's interface displays a list (based on the purchase order and purchase data in the database) of the unpaid purchases (receipts of products and services) that are due within three business days. The accounts payable clerk reviews for accuracy each electronic payment suggested by the enterprise database interface. The electronic payments approved by the clerk are submitted to the vendors' bank accounts and recorded in the enterprise database.

The REA business process level pattern in the old and reengineered acquisition/payment cycles are identical; however the steps to accomplish the workflow associated with the events in the pattern changed significantly. Both the old and the new cycles included need identification (purchase requisition) as an instigation event, ordering of goods or services (purchase order) as a commitment event, receipt of goods (purchase) as an economic increment event, and payment of cash (cash disbursement) as an economic decrement event. Thus the business process level model and resulting database design are the same under both workflow scenarios. However, representation of the document processing and data flows is

REA Accounting Systems: Resources-Events-Agents: An ontology for designing, controlling, and using integrated enterprise systems

63

quite different for the two scenarios. You will learn how to create this documentation later in this chapter.

Many different types of documentation may be used to represent tasks, including flowcharts, data flow diagrams, process models, and narrative descriptions. This chapter presents the tool most commonly used in accounting and auditing practice: document flowcharts, also known as system flowcharts. **System flowcharts** are graphical representations of the inputs, processes, and outputs of an enterprise information system; they include details about the physical as well as the logical aspects of the system components

SYSTEM FLOWCHARTING

Enterprises need to document details about workflow – what happens, in what order, and what details are captured, maintained, and reported by the information system. These details may be documented using a variety of different methods. One obviously possible method to use is a narrative description of all the steps in the workflow. Indeed, many companies do create such narratives. However, such narratives are typically voluminous and can be time-consuming to use to find information about a process. **Flowchart symbols** are specific shapes used to communicate constructs on a system flowchart; numerous different symbols are used to represent different constructs. **Flow lines** indicate the movement of documents, physical objects, or data to the next point in a system. System flowcharts graphically document information systems. Pages of narrative describing system processes and data/document flows can be succinctly summarized using flowcharts. System flowcharts focus on the physical aspects of information flows and processes. This chapter presents the rudiments of this tool to help you develop the skills needed to prepare new flowcharts and to interpret existing flowcharts.

Flowcharts are used to describe an entire information system, or some portion thereof. The system flowcharts discussed in this chapter are sometimes called **document or procedure flowcharts** because they illustrate the data flows of the enterprise and how the data flows are processed. Since many of the data flows are contained on documents, document processing typically makes up a large portion of the flowcharts. The entire information system is made up of a series of input, process, and output activities. The inputs and outputs may be paper documents or electronic data and the processes may be manual or computerized. The outputs from the various processes may be used for decision-making purposes or they may serve as inputs to other processes. System flowcharts may be created manually, either freehand or with the help of a plastic flowchart template – a stencil that allows users to trace the outline of the various symbols that are used in flowcharts. System flowcharts may also be prepared using one of several software packages designed for that purpose, such as iGrafx, Microsoft Visio, or SmartDraw. Even word processing, spreadsheet, and presentation software packages often include flowchart symbols among their drawing tools.

The Basic Elements of System Flowcharts

System flowcharts consist of three simple graphical elements combined to represent various types of physical information flows and processes:

1. Symbols
2. Flow lines
3. Areas of responsibility

Exhibit 3-1   Example System Flowchart

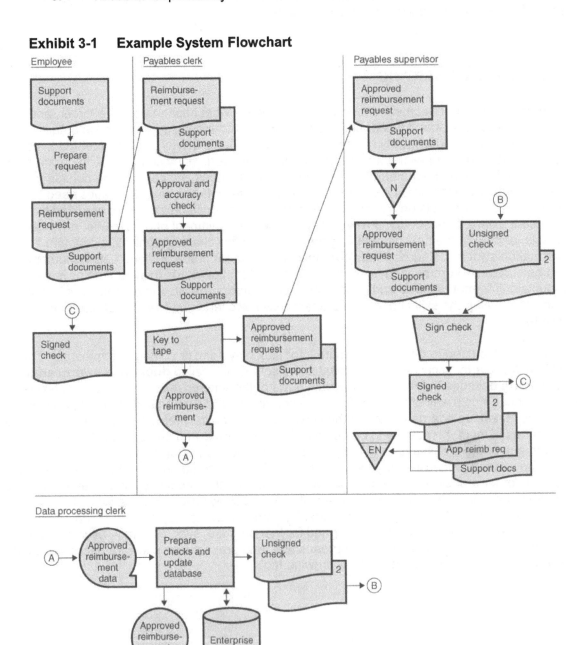

The documents and processes of information systems can be illustrated by linking various symbols together as shown in Exhibit 3-1. Compare the following explanation of the process with its flowchart before we discuss the detailed conventions for preparing flowcharts.

Exhibit 3-1 illustrates possible document flows for processing employee expense reimbursements for an enterprise. Employees in various departments throughout the enterprise spend their own money for expenses such as business-related travel, supplies, etc. They then request reimbursement for those expenditures. Employees prepare requests for reimbursement, which they submit along with supporting receipts and documentation justifying the necessity of their expenditure to the Payables department. Payables clerks check the request for accuracy and agreement with the support documents. They also verify whether the support documents are approved by the employee's supervisor and adequately justify the need for the expenditure. The payables clerks then key the approved reimbursement request data to magnetic tape using a key-to-tape encoding machine. The approved reimbursement requests are sent to the payables supervisor who puts them into a temporary file in numeric order. The magnetic tape is sent to the data processing department where it is used as input to a computerized process that generates the reimbursement checks and updates the enterprise database for the expenses and cash disbursement data. The enterprise database is stored on disk. The checks are prepared in duplicate (the copy does not look like a real check; it contains only the check stub information). The check and copy are sent to the payables supervisor. The supervisor pulls the appropriate reimbursement request and support documentation for each check from the temporary file, double-checks everything for accuracy, and signs the check. The check is sent to the employee; the check copy is attached to the request and support documents and is filed in a permanent file in employee number order.

Flowcharting symbols and methods can vary widely across professionals and organizations. There is no one set of generally accepted flowcharting principles and symbols. The flowcharting conventions and symbols we present in this chapter are representative of those commonly used in accounting and auditing.

Flowcharting Element 1: Symbols.
A variety of symbols are used to represent the physical aspects of the document/data flows and processes of an information system. Since flowcharts illustrate the physical features of a system, there are various symbols in each category. For example, there are at least four storage symbols, and the one chosen depends on the physical characteristics of the storage medium (e.g. whether it is a paper file, a disk file, or a tape file). The following describes some of the more frequently used symbols in flowcharting.

Input-Process-Output
Properly constructed system flowcharts are simply related input-process-output clusters strung together, with defined starting and stopping points. In system flowcharts, a process is defined as an activity that uses or alters an input to produce an output. An output from one process may be used as input to the next process. Exhibit 3-2 illustrates the typical input, output, and process symbols. Most of the symbols used to illustrate inputs are also used to represent outputs. For example, a document (symbol B) may be the output of one process and the input for another process. Similarly, a magnetic tape file (symbol J) or a disk file (symbol I) may serve as either input or output or both.

Exhibit 3-2   Flowchart Symbols

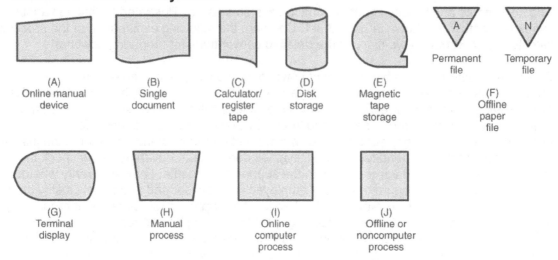

On-line Manual Input Device (Keyboard or Touch-Terminal)
Symbol A on Exhibit 3-2 is used to illustrate an online manual device, and is used to describe the entry of data into a computer through an on-line keyboard or touch-terminal. When this symbol and the computerized process symbol are used together, they are considered to comprise a single process for the purpose of *input-process-output* logic. That is, there must be some input (such as a document) to the keying/computer process and there must be an output from the keying/computer process (such as a report or an updated masterfile).

Input/Output Symbols: Paper Documents
Paper documents (symbol B in exhibit 3-2) are used as inputs and as outputs of processes in system flowcharts. The document symbol is one of the most commonly used symbols in system flowcharts, and it has variations that are not illustrated in Exhibit 3-2. Exhibit 3-3 depicts the different symbols commonly used to represent documents (e.g. checks, invoices, and reports). The name of the document is entered on the symbol's face (see symbol *A* in Exhibit 3-3). A single document symbol is used to represent one or more documents of the same type; i.e., a batch of 100 remittance advices is represented with the single document symbol, provided there is only one copy of each remittance advice. Multiple copies of a document are typically illustrated as staggered symbols for each copy of the document (see symbol *B* in Exhibit 3-3). Each copy is numbered in the top right hand corner. The numbers may be arranged in whatever sequence best suits the flow of documents from that point in the flowchart. This method easily allows the flowchart designer to communicate the separate flows of the different copies of the document, for example, one copy of a sale invoice may be sent to the customer, another copy sent to the accounts receivable department, and a third copy filed away. If copies of two (or more) different documents move together in a flowchart, they are illustrated as staggered symbols for each different document with the appropriate copy of the document noted (see symbol *C* in Exhibit 3-3). A document used to store reference information, such as a price list or tax table, as opposed to a document that is processed, such as a check or invoice, is often distinguished by darkening the left-hand edge of the symbol (see symbol *D* in Exhibit 3-3).

Exhibit 3-3 Flowchart Symbols: Documents

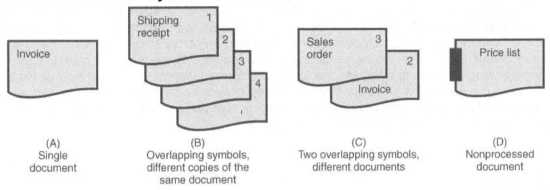

(A)
Single
document

(B)
Overlapping symbols,
different copies of the
same document

(C)
Two overlapping symbols,
different documents

(D)
Nonprocessed
document

Input/Output Symbols: Calculator/Register Tapes

Symbol *C* in Exhibit 3-2 is used to represent printouts of calculations made on a calculator, adding machine, or cash register. These are most often outputs of a manual process, but once they are processed they can also be used as inputs to other processes, such as reconciliations between the manual calculations and the computations of a computer process.

Input/Output Symbols: Files Containing Stored Data

Files of stored data may be used as input to processes or as output from processes. Computerized processes typically use and produce data stored on disk (Symbol *D* in Exhibit 3-2) or on magnetic tape (Symbol *E* in Exhibit 3-2). A description of the file contents is entered on the face of the symbol (e.g. Customer Master File or Cash Disbursements Transaction File). Examples of disk storage with which you are probably familiar include hard disks, floppy disks, CDs, and DVDs. Examples of magnetic tape storage with which you are probably familiar are audiocassette tapes and VHS videotapes. Some computer systems, especially older mainframe systems, have tape drives instead of disk drives and while you may not have seen or used such hardware, the tape media has many of the same characteristics as the audiocassette tapes and VHS videotapes you have seen and used.

Computerized processes sometimes use and produce data stored in paper files, and of course manual processes can only use and produce manual off-line stored data. Symbol F in Exhibit 3-2 represents any storage of paper documents (e.g., file cabinet, safe, cardboard box, or shelves). Two types of off-line storage files exist - temporary and permanent. A temporary file is a store of documents that will be involved in subsequent processing. A horizontal line across the top of the file symbol is often used to indicate a permanent file. The method of document order or organization is denoted using an abbreviation such as A (alphanumeric), N (numeric), or C (chronological). Whenever abbreviations or codes are used, you should place a legend on your flowchart to assist readers.

Input/Output Symbols: Terminal Display

The terminal display symbol (Symbol G on Exhibit 3-2) illustrates a computer monitor or terminal display. It is often used in conjunction with the on-line computer-device symbol to show data being entered into a computer process using an on-line terminal. Alternatively it may be used to illustrate output from a computer process that is only seen on a computer screen, such as an error message.

Process Symbols

Different symbols represent processes according to the level of automation included in the processes. The manual-process symbol (Symbol *H* in Exhibit 3-2) indicates an operation that is primarily manual (such as completing forms, verifying amounts, or making calculations with a manual calculator). Manual operations most often are used to process documents. There are two machine-processing symbols: one for on-line computer processing (see symbol *I* in Exhibit 3-2) and one for off-line processing or processing performed by a machine other than a computer, such as an optical character reader (see symbol *J* in Exhibit 3-2). A description of the operation is entered on the face of the symbol.

The input-process-output symbols on a system flowchart are supplemented with other symbols that depict the flow of data throughout the system. These other symbols are illustrated in Exhibit 3-4.

Exhibit 3-4 Additional Flowchart Symbols

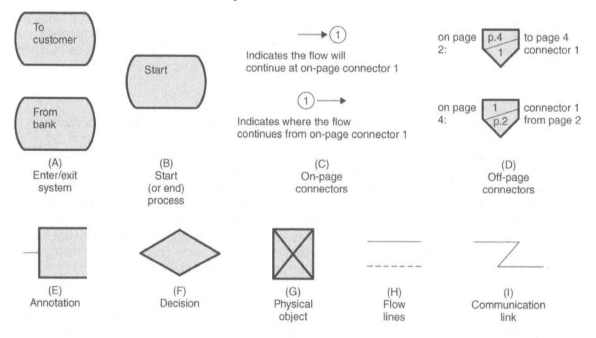

Terminal or System Exit/Entry

The terminal symbol indicates the beginning or ending point of the process represented on a flowchart, and also displays system entry or exit of data (see symbols *A* and *B* on Exhibit 3-4). If the flowchart begins at the top left corner of a page, there is no need to include a start symbol, because the default starting point for a flowchart is the top left corner.

On-Page Connector

On-page connectors allow document flows to be bridged within a single page of the flowchart. The use of on-page connectors allow a document to be shown flowing from one position on a page to a distant location on the page without drawing a line across the entire page. Each connector is numbered within a page to enable the reader to know exactly where to continue

REA Accounting Systems: Resources-Events-Agents: An ontology for designing, controlling, and using integrated enterprise systems

69

reading. An arrow pointing to a connector identifies the other connector on the same page where the document flow continues. An arrow pointing away from the connector identifies the connector from which the flow is continuing (see the symbols labeled *C* in Exhibit 3-4).

Off-Page Connector

Rarely do entire system flowcharts fit on a single page. Off-page connectors are used to connect multiple pages of a document flowchart. The use of off-page connectors is similar to on-page connectors, except they illustrate the continuance of the data flow on another page of the flowchart. Shown within the off-page connector symbol is the page number to which the flow continues (or from which the flow came) and a connector number (see the symbols labeled D on Exhibit 3-4).

Annotation

The annotation symbol includes important supplementary information or explanations that are difficult to describe graphically within the flowchart itself (see symbol E on Exhibit 3-4). Use annotations sparingly.

Decision

Sometimes in a system, the course of action depends on making a decision or choice. For example, if a clerk's task is to review a document for completeness, the clerk must make a decision. If the document is complete, the clerk files the document. On the other hand, if the document is incomplete, the clerk sends the document back to the user department. A decision symbol (see symbol *F* in Exhibit 3-4) displays the decision, and a description of the decision is included in the symbol (e.g. "Is document complete?"). Two labeled flow lines exit from the decision symbol to illustrate the indicated course of action. In this case, a line labeled with *yes* (yes the document is complete) would lead to a paper off-line file, while a line labeled *no* (no the document is not complete) would show the document flowing back to the user department.

Physical (Nondocument) Objects

Symbol *G* in Exhibit 3-4 is used to denote any physical object that may accompany a document flow (e.g., merchandise, supplies, and fixed assets).

Flowcharting Element 2: Flow Lines

Flow lines connect the symbols on the document flowchart. A solid line indicates actual physical flow of a document or object. A dotted or dashed line indicates flow of information rather than a physical document (see symbol *H* in Exhibit 3-4). For example, if information is verbally obtained, either in person or on the telephone, the data flow is represented with a dotted or dashed line.

Arrows are used when the document or information flow is not left to right or top to bottom. The assumed flow of documents and information is from top to bottom and from left to right. As long as this flow is followed, arrows are not required. Arrows must be used when there is a counter flow. However, there is nothing wrong with using arrows on all flow lines, and such use eliminates any potential confusion.

Some flowcharts also display communication link symbols (see symbol *I* in Exhibit 3-4). This symbol is used when telephone lines, microwave towers, or satellite transmitters are used to transfer data, particularly when the transfer is from one computer directly to another computer.

Flowcharting Element 3: Area of Responsibility

Areas of responsibility are displayed to enable the flowchart reader to clearly identify changes in responsibility as the documents flow through the system. They are represented on flowcharts by segmenting and labeling columns (see Exhibit 3-1).

An **area of responsibility** is a department, a section within a department, or an individual employee that is held accountable for flow of information or physical objects through a system. Areas of responsibility may be represented as columns on a page, or as separate pages, or even as groups of pages, depending on how much information flows through that area. Judgment must be used in choosing the level of subdivision that is most appropriate to designate as an area of responsibility.

FLOWCHART PREPARATION CONVENTIONS

Several techniques have been developed to guide the preparation of a flowchart. The main objective of these techniques is to enhance the readability, and thereby enable the validation, of the flowchart.

Left to Right, Top to Bottom

A page in a book is read from top to bottom and from left to right. A flowchart is most easily understood if the same convention is followed. Therefore, when preparing a document flowchart, begin in the upper left-hand corner and work from left to right and from top to bottom.

All Documents Must Have an Origin and Termination

A flowchart must clearly indicate where a document is introduced into a system and where it is permanently filed or leaves a system. Each copy of a document must flow to:

1. A permanent file symbol,

2. A symbol denoting an exit from the system, or

3. An off-page connector.

Following this convention ensures that the progress of every document has been observed and documented from cradle to grave. Whenever the final destination of a document is unknown, use an annotation symbol to indicate that additional investigation is required.

Keep Flowcharts Uncluttered

A flowchart is an important analytical and design tool; however, great amounts of detail reduce a flowchart's ability to communicate. For this reason, to the extent possible, observe the following rules:

1. Place areas of responsibility with the most frequent interchange adjacent to each other to avoid long arrows,

2. Enter narrative on charts only within symbols.

3. Avoid explaining with narrative what is already adequately described by the flowchart itself.

Make Sure Document Progress is Clear

Diagram a document before and after a process is performed, when entering or leaving a file, and on entering or leaving a page. Also, if a document is altered (e.g., updated, signed, or approved), change the name of the document to indicate its current status. For example, notice

REA Accounting Systems: Resources-Events-Agents: An ontology for designing, controlling, and using integrated enterprise systems

71

in Exhibit 3-1 the flow of the reimbursement request. The manual process "Prepare reimbursement request" creates it. It is sent to the payables clerk where it is approved. The name is changed accordingly to *approved reimbursement request*. After further processing, it is eventually filed in a permanent file. Similarly, notice the flow of the check. The computerized process in the data processing department generates the check, which at that point is unsigned. Copies 1 and 2 are sent to the payables supervisor, who performs a manual double-check and signing process. The signed check is sent to the employee and the copy along with the underlying request and support documents are filed in a permanent file.

Make Complete Flowchart: Represent Each Input, Process, Output, and Storage Step
Be sure to include all major steps in the transaction cycle or information process you are modeling. It is often helpful to remember that systems are simply a combination of inputs, processing, outputs, and storage of data.

SYSTEM FLOWCHART SUMMARY
Following the preceding instructions can guide the development of an effective flowchart for analyzing an information process or system. The flowchart is one of the easier types of documentation for information customers and management to understand. Often, auditors use system and document flowcharts to understand business and systems controls.

To test whether you are beginning to understand how to read and prepare flowcharts, go back to Exhibit 3-1, and write a short narrative of the process. Compare your narrative to the narrative provided earlier in this chapter to see how accurately you read the flowchart.

Although many individuals and organizations still use flowcharts, their usefulness is limited to decisions or information needs that require knowledge of the physical information flows and system characteristics. Often the conceptual essence of the system is somewhat obscured by the physical artifacts; other documentation techniques may be useful for information needs that focus on the concepts. Because many accounting and auditing analyses (such as risk assessment and control evaluation) require consideration of the physical tasks, system flowcharts are still widely used.

FILE TYPES, MEDIA AND PROCESSING METHODS
Because system flowcharts reflect the physical media on which data are stored and the automation level of each process, they are difficult to prepare or to interpret without adequate understanding of some features of the common physical media, file types, and tools involved in the information processes. Therefore this section provides a description of some common file types, media on which files are stored, and some common processing methods.

File Types
Files store data and processing instructions. Each file is named and saved on a storage medium like a hard disk or magnetic tape. An example of a file is a document created using Microsoft Word. The two types of files used most often by computer users are executable files and data files. *Executable files* are also called program or application files, and they usually have an .exe extension. *Data files* are used to store anything from transaction data to business reference data to a word processing or graphics document. Often files are referred to by their type or content. Types of data files used in most enterprise systems include master files, transaction files, history files, reference files, and suspense files.

Master files contain balance data or the status of an entity at a point in time. Examples of master files in enterprise systems are customer, employee, inventory, fixed asset, and supplier master files (to name a few). Master files do not contain event or activity data, but they typically contain balances that are updated by such data. For example, a customer master file may contain a field "accounts receivable balance" that is updated by sales and cash receipt activity data. **Transaction files** contain activity data that is used to update the balances on master files. Examples of transaction files in enterprise systems are cash disbursement, cash receipt, payroll, purchase, and sales transaction files (to name a few). When a transaction file is used to update a master file, it is often said the transaction file is "run against" the master file.

History files or *archive files*, as the names suggest, contain inactive past or historical data. Examples of history files include data files from years past that are no longer subject to updates. History files are distinguished from *backup files*, which are copies of files created in case the files are destroyed. At least one backup file should be stored at a location other than the location at which the original files are stored in case of a disaster such as a fire or flood that could potentially damage or destroy both the original and the backup files. *Reference files* contain referential data such as tax rate schedules or customer price lists. *Suspense files* are files of data that are awaiting some action to complete their processing. Examples include records identified as incomplete or erroneous that need correction and reentry for processing (e.g. a payment by a customer who is not listed in the customer master file or a journal entry that doesn't balance).

Media

Data for most enterprises are stored on media that fall into three categories: paper, magnetic tape, and disk. Each of these media types was discussed earlier in this chapter; however, most of you probably need a more detailed discussion of them in order to understand some of the processing issues associated with them. Paper is the most common form of media used in enterprises. Source documents (documents that contain details about transactions) are used as inputs for many information processes, and paper reports are produced as outputs for many information processes. Paper is the media type most people prefer to use. Although increasingly people are asked to read output screens, reports, and even textbooks on computer monitors, most people still prefer to have the files printed out and to read them on hardcopy. Although paper has many advantages, including ease of use and lack of dependence on electricity, it also has many disadvantages such as bulk (for storage), lack of search and automated processing capability, and susceptibility to destruction (although all media types may be easily destroyed, backup copies to mitigate inadvertent destruction are more easily made with non-paper media).

Magnetic tape stores data from source documents and reports in a format that is computer readable. As noted earlier, if you who have used audiocassette tape recordings of music, or videocassette tape recordings of movies, then you have used magnetic tape media. One important feature of magnetic tape media is the fact that data on it are stored sequentially and may only be accessed sequentially. **Sequential storage** implies that records are stored one after another in some order (chronologically, by account number, alphabetically, etc.). **Sequential access** requires that all data be read in sequential order to find a particular record. For example, suppose you purchase a cassette tape containing songs performed by your favorite recording artist. The songs are stored sequentially (one after another) on the tape. To listen to your favorite song, you must fast forward or rewind (searching the songs one after another) to sequentially access the desired song – there is no faster access option. Enterprises use magnetic tape cartridges and open reel tapes to store transaction and report data and those files require sequential storage and access of data.

Disk technology is increasingly replacing magnetic tape as the preferred media type, both for personal audio-visual needs and for enterprise processing applications. Examples of disk technology include internal and external hard disks, thumb drives, and sd cards on computers, and CDs and DVDs for computers and personal audio/visual needs. From an information processing standpoint, the primary advantage of disk-based storage over magnetic tape storage is the random storage and direct access capability of disk technology. **Random storage** allows information to be stored in any order on the disk device; in fact a file need not be stored in its entirety in a single location on a disk – part of it may be stored in one location and part of it in another location, although processing is more efficient if files are not "fragmented" in that manner. **Direct access** allows each record to be retrieved without reading all the records that precede it in the file. The computer maintains an index to keep track of the location of each record, thus allowing the computer to retrieve any record requested by the user regardless of its physical position in a file. There is no need to sequentially search part or all of the other records stored on the storage device. Suppose instead of purchasing a cassette tape of songs performed by your favorite recording artist you instead purchased a CD containing those songs. With the CD player you can choose your favorite song from the index and listen to it without having to listen to or fast-forward through the other songs on the CD.

The most obvious distinction between these media types for system flowcharting is that different symbols are used to represent them. However, there are other distinctions. One distinction that must be made is whether updates are made to the same physical file or whether a new file must be created that merges the original data with the updates. If a master file is stored on magnetic tape, updates may not be made to the same physical medium but rather a new magnetic tape must be used and data read from the old master file and the transaction file containing the updates and the updated records re-written onto the new master file. The reason the updates may not be written directly to the old master file is that they may take up a different amount of space, and could potentially destroy existing data. For example, if you taped four 30-minute television shows on a VCR tape and you want to replace one of those shows with a 60-minute television show, you couldn't do that without destroying one of the other 30-minute television shows. To clarify this even further, suppose the four shows (in order) on your tape were episodes of *Gilligan's Island*, *Seinfeld*, *I Love Lucy*, and *Cheers*. Further supposed you only wanted to keep the episodes of *Gilligan's Island* and *I Love Lucy*, and you wanted to record a one-hour episode of *Matlock*. So you have a 2-hour tape and you want to end up with 2 hours worth of shows, deleting two 30-minute episodes and replacing them with one 60-minute episode. If you position the tape so that it begins recording where *Seinfeld starts*, you will end up replacing *I Love Lucy* instead of replacing *Cheers*. There is no way to tell the tape to skip over the *I Love Lucy* episode when it comes to it and then start recording again.

Contrast that with the updating of a master file stored on disk. Updates may be written directly to the disk, because it doesn't matter where physically the data is located on the disk. As long as there is space available for all the needed data, if you update a customer street address that was 123 Pine St. to 12345 Appleyard Ave. (notice the new address is longer) it will realize the allotted space is not big enough and will add a pointer to a new location on the disk that has adequate space. The logical view (what the user sees when the computer displays this data) does not show the fact that the data is stored in fragments, but physically it is stored in that manner. If the data becomes stored in too many fragments, processing efficiency may decrease; that is why occasionally on your personal computer you may get an error message suggesting that you "de-frag" your hard disk drive. The defrag process rearranges the physical locations of data on the drive to make processing more efficient.

Processing Methods

The timing of processing reveals the point at which activity data are posted to update the master files. Therefore the processing method determines the timeliness of the data stored in master files. Processing is often identified by type: batch, online, real-time, or report-time processing.

Batch processing accumulates transaction data for a period of time to collect a *batch*, or group, of transaction data. Then all of the transactions in the transaction file are posted to the master file in one processing run. Therefore, processing (i.e. updating of the master file) occurs after a group of transaction data is collected. Processing involves merging the data in the transaction file with the current master data to create a *new, updated* master file. Thus, with batch processing, transaction data may not be entered in the computer system until some time after a business activity occurs, and master files may be updated even later. The only time the master file is accurate and up-to-date is immediately after a batch of transaction data has been processed.

Online processing means the computer-input device is connected to the CPU so that master files are updated as transaction data are entered. *Real-time* denotes immediate response to an information user; transaction data are entered and processed to update the relevant master files and a response is provided to the person conducting the business event fast enough to affect the outcome of the event. Although they sound similar, online and real-time processing can differ. **Real-time processing** updates master files as a business activity occurs, while online processing updates master files whenever transaction data is entered (which may *not* be when a business activity occurs). Real time processing generally requires an online input device.

Report-time processing means the data used to generate the requested report is processed as the report is created. Report-time processing is a term used primarily in event-driven systems and it is similar to real-time updating. Most event data are stored in a detailed or disaggregated form and the relevant data are selected, processed, and any master files are updated as the information customer's report is generated.

Due to the sequential access limitations of tape, tape storage mediums always use batch processing. Disk storage mediums can handle batch, online, or real-time processing.

ACQUISITION CYCLE: WORKFLOW AND DOCUMENTS

The **acquisition cycle** includes the activities associated with buying, maintaining, and paying for goods and services needed by enterprises. This includes acquiring raw materials, component parts, and other resources contained in finished products or services. It also includes acquiring, and paying for, a variety of other goods and services (e.g., utilities, supplies, insurance, repairs, maintenance, research, development, professional and legal services, and property, plant, and equipment). Processes that are special cases of the acquisition cycle, but that are typically considered separate business processes include the payroll cycle (also called the human resources business process, which involves the acquisition of and payment for employee labor) and the financing cycle (acquisition and repayment of financial capital). We discuss these processes separately in later chapters. The acquisition cycle is sometimes alternatively called the acquisition/payment business process, the expenditures cycle, or the procure-to-pay process.

No pattern exists for the specific procedures and information/document flows that are used by specific enterprises in their acquisition cycles. However, it may be helpful for you to learn about the general categories of activities and some of the documents that are commonly (but not always) used to record data regarding those activities. For each workflow stage, we indicate in parentheses the type of REA event the workflow comprises, if any.

Need Identification (Instigation Event)

The acquisition cycle begins with someone within an enterprise communicating a need to acquire a good or service, either to satisfy a new requirement or to replenish an existing supply that is either low in quantity (as with a supply or inventory item or an advertising services contract) or useful life (as with property, plant, and equipment items). The identification of need for additional goods and services may be triggered externally, such as by a supplier's presentation of a new product and its capabilities. Alternatively the need identification may be triggered internally. Various supervisors identify the need for goods and services by monitoring enterprise activities such as production levels, sales levels, capital improvement plans, capital budgets, sales forecasts, trends and projections. Once supervisors or other authorized individuals identify a need for goods, they communicate that need to an authorized buyer (internal purchasing agent) via a **purchase requisition** form such as that shown in Exhibit 3-5. This form may be either a paper document or it may be part of a software application interface. In either case, similar data are captured and transmitted from user departments to authorized purchase agents (usually the purchasing department).

Vendor Selection

Once the need for additional goods or services has been identified, the enterprise must determine the most appropriate source from which to purchase those goods or services. Most enterprises have procedures in place to evaluate vendors before placing orders for goods and services that are of a significant dollar value. Such procedures may include discussing with the vendor's existing customers the vendor's performance for on-time deliveries, quality of the vendor's goods or services, and post-purchase service for warranty work or product returns. Such procedures may also include evaluating the vendor's financial condition to determine the probability that the vendor will have the wherewithal to actually deliver the promised goods and services and to provide post-purchase services.

Once vendors are approved as satisfactory potential sources, many enterprises have additional procedures to inform the decision of with which vendor to place an order. Often the decision involves price and delivery time considerations. The enterprise's purchase agents may look up prices, availability, and expected delivery times by perusing vendor catalogs or websites or by calling a vendor sales representative. **Requests for quote** (also called RFQs) may be sent to potential vendors either to formalize the vendor selection process or because the enterprise believes it qualifies for special pricing not available for lookup in the vendor's catalog or website. A RFQ is typically several pages long so we do not attempt to reproduce an example in this chapter. Information on a RFQ typically includes a confidentiality statement that specifies the vendor may not share the information in the RFQ with anyone else, details of how and where to submit their quotation, submission deadline, information about the enterprise and the intended use for the product or service, detailed specifications , assumptions and constraints, terms and conditions, and criteria by which the vendor will be selected.

Exhibit 3-5 Purchase Requisition

YOUR SOURCE COMPANY **PURCHASE REQUISITION**			No. R17	
Date Prepared: 4/20/2014	Prepared by: E12		Suggested Vendor: V7	
Deliver To: Product Warehouse	Attention: Patrick Wellesley		Date Needed: 5/2/2014	
Item Number	Quantity	Description	Price/Unit	
BIS1	100	Big Stuff	$20.00	
LIS1	200	Little Stuff	$36.00	
HUS1	100	Huge Stuff	$30.00	
TIS1	300	Tiny Stuff	$48.00	
Reason Needed: To meet customer demand for these products.				
Approved by: E5	Department: Sales	Date Approved: 4/22/2014		

Interested vendors respond with a **quote**, an offer to sell an item at a stated price. The quote may be submitted electronically or on paper; it may be a multiple-page detailed document similar to the RFQ with responses to each section, or it may be a simple form such as that shown in Exhibit 3-6. Once the deadline for submitting quotes is reached, the enterprise will evaluate the quotes it received and select the most appropriate vendor.

Agreements/Contracts (Mutual Commitment Events)

Once a vendor is selected, the enterprise makes a commitment to the vendor to receive and pay the quoted price for the goods or services according to the quoted terms. This is accomplished by the purchase agent placing an order with the vendor on behalf of the enterprise. A **mutual commitment** exists when the enterprise and an external business partner have each agreed to exchange resources at one or more defined future times. A **purchase order** is a mutual commitment event in which a supplier agrees to transfer title of goods to an enterprise at an agreed upon future time and price and the enterprise agrees to pay for those goods. If the agreement involves temporary use of an asset to which title is not transferred, the mutual commitment is typically called a **rental agreement**. If the commitment involves the vendor performing a service rather than providing goods, the event is typically called a **service agreement**. In most states these agreements are enforceable as contracts.

Details of commitments to purchase products or services that typically should be captured include the date, time, a list of products or services, the quantities needed and unit prices of each, the total dollar amount of the order or agreement, the date by which the enterprise needs the goods or services delivered, the delivery method to be used (e.g., Federal Express, UPS, or customer pick-up), the desired location of the delivery, and the payment terms. Data regarding purchase order commitment events are often captured on a purchase order form such as that shown in Exhibit 3-7. This form may be either a paper document or part of a software application interface used to update the enterprise database. Similar types of data would be captured on similar types of documents regarding service and rental agreements as

REA Accounting Systems: Resources-Events-Agents: An ontology for designing, controlling, and using integrated enterprise systems

77

are captured for the purchase order events. Until the vendor delivers the products or services specified, the purchase order is considered unfilled or open. The phrase **open purchase order** simply means a purchase order for which the products or services have not yet been received.

Exhibit 3-6: Example Quote

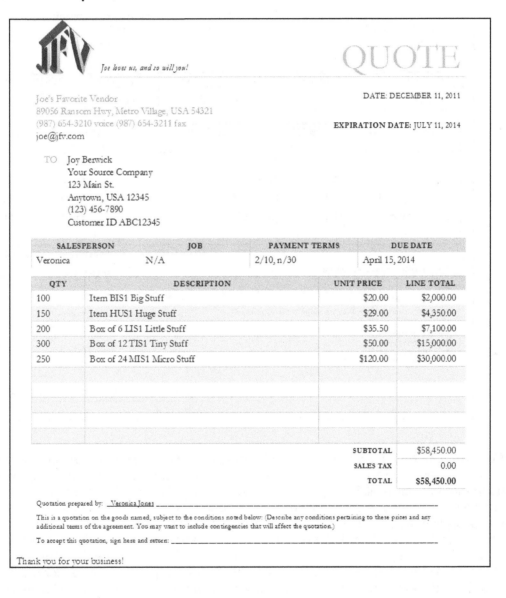

QUOTE

Joe loves us, and so will you!

Joe's Favorite Vendor
89056 Ransom Hwy, Metro Village, USA 54321
(987) 654-3210 voice (987) 654-3211 fax
joe@jfv.com

DATE: DECEMBER 11, 2011

EXPIRATION DATE: JULY 11, 2014

TO   Joy Berwick
Your Source Company
123 Main St.
Anytown, USA 12345
(123) 456-7890
Customer ID ABC12345

SALESPERSON	JOB	PAYMENT TERMS	DUE DATE
Veronica	N/A	2/10, n/30	April 15, 2014

QTY	DESCRIPTION	UNIT PRICE	LINE TOTAL
100	Item BIS1 Big Stuff	$20.00	$2,000.00
150	Item HUS1 Huge Stuff	$29.00	$4,350.00
200	Box of 6 LIS1 Little Stuff	$35.50	$7,100.00
300	Box of 12 TIS1 Tiny Stuff	$50.00	$15,000.00
250	Box of 24 MIS1 Micro Stuff	$120.00	$30,000.00
		SUBTOTAL	$58,450.00
		SALES TAX	0.00
		TOTAL	$58,450.00

Quotation prepared by: _Veronica Jones_ _____

This is a quotation on the goods named, subject to the conditions noted below: (Describe any conditions pertaining to these prices and any additional terms of the agreement. You may want to include contingencies that will affect the quotation.)

To accept this quotation, sign here and return: _____

Thank you for your business!

Exhibit 3-7 Purchase Order

Your Source Company	**Purchase Order**
Your Source for Everything You Need	NO. ____16____
123 Main St.	
Anytown, USA 12345	This number must appear on all related correspondence, shipping papers, and invoices

To: Joe's Favorite Vendor
89056 Ransom Hwy.
Metro Village, USA 54321

Ship To: Your Source Company
123 Main St.
Anytown, USA 12345

P.O. DATE	REQUISITION#	REQUISITIONER	SHIP VIA	F.O.B. POINT	TERMS
4/24/2014	R17	E5	UPS	Shipping	N/30

QTY	UNIT	ITEM NO.	DESCRIPTION	UNIT PRICE	TOTAL
100	Each	BIS1	Big Stuff	$20.00	$2,000.00
150	Each	HUS1	Huge Stuff	$29.00	$4,350.00
200	Box/ 6	LIS1	Little Stuff	$35.50	$7,100.00
300	Box/12	TIS1	Tiny Stuff	$50.00	$15,000.00

SUBTOTAL	$28,450.00
SALES TAX	$0.00
SHIPPING & HANDLING	$0.00
OTHER	$0.00
TOTAL	**$28,450.00**

1. Please send two copies of your invoice.

2. Enter this order in accordance with the prices, terms, delivery method, and specifications listed above.

3. Please notify us immediately if you are unable to ship as specified.

4. Send all correspondence to:
   Purchasing Manager
   Your Source Company
   123 Main St., Anytown, USA 12345

Joy Berwick	E12	4/24/2014
Authorized by		Date

Performance by Vendor – Delivery of Goods or Services (Economic Increment Event)
In contract law, **performance** is the fulfillment of an obligation in a manner that releases the performer from all liabilities. The vendor's performance is typically the delivery of the products or services specified in a commitment. If the vendor delivered products, this activity is called an acquisition, a **purchase**, or a receipt of goods. If the vendor provided a temporary right to use goods, the event is called a rental; the rental begins when the right to temporary possession of the goods transfers from the vendor to the enterprise and ends when possession of the goods transfers back from the enterprise to the supplier. If the vendor provided services or utilities, the event is usually called a service acquisition or a general and administrative service acquisition. Whatever label is used, the important consideration is that performance represents the enterprise receiving a resource or a benefit that it didn't previously possess. Therefore, an economic increase has occurred and this is called an economic increment event. At this point, unless the enterprise pre-paid for the product or service, a liability is incurred. While many companies do not record the liability until the vendor sends an invoice to document its performance, in theory, the performance is what causes the liability. Therefore systems in which the liability is not recorded until the vendor invoice is received are technically inaccurate.

REA Accounting Systems: Resources-Events-Agents: An ontology for designing, controlling, and using integrated enterprise systems

79

Receiving reports are documents indicating the quantities and condition of goods received by an enterprise from an external business partner. These reports are typically completed by inventory or receiving clerks when goods or services are received from suppliers (or from customers in the case of sale returns, to be discussed later in this chapter). Similar to Exhibit 3-8, such reports list the items and the quantities and condition of each item received. In general, we believe it is unwise for the enterprise to use an externally prepared document as a base object in its system when an internally prepared alternative is available. Because receiving reports are typically prepared as the vendor's performance occurs and the liability is thereby incurred, most enterprises should consider using the receiving report together with the underlying commitment document to record the liability rather than waiting for the **vendor invoice** – a document sent by a supplier to the enterprise to communicate the fact that the supplier has fulfilled its commitment to transfer title of goods to the enterprise. While data captured on vendor invoices may provide additional details of the acquisition; such data could be used to update the data captured via the receiving report and underlying agreement. Meanwhile the system would be more accurate than when nothing is recorded until the invoice arrives. Exhibit 3-9 illustrates an example vendor invoice.

Exhibit 3-8 Receiving Report

RECEIVING REPORT			NO. 18	

Your Source Company
Your Source for Everything You Need
123 Main St.
Anytown, USA 12345

DATE **4/30/2014**	PURCH ORD NO./ SALE RETURN AUTH NO.	**PO16**	
RECEIVED FROM	Joe's Favorite Vendor		PREPAID XX
ADDRESS	89056 Ransom Hwy. Metro Village, USA 54321		COLLECT
FREIGHT CARRIER **UPS**		FREIGHT BILL NO. **XYAT31253**	

	QUANTITY	ITEM NO	DESCRIPTION
1.	100	BIS1	Big Stuff
2.	200	LIS1	Little Stuff
3.	150	HIS1	Huge Stuff
4.	300	TIS1	Tiny Stuff
5.			
6.			
7.			
8.			
9.			

REMARKS: CONDITIONS, ETC.
  Perfect condition

RECEIVED BY E111	DELIVERED TO E5

BE SURE TO
MAKE THIS RECORD
ACCURATE AND COMPLETE

Exhibit 3-9 Vendor Invoice

Invoice

NO: <u>4167</u>
DATE: <u>5/3/2014</u>

Joe's Favorite Vendor
Let us be your favorite too!
89056 Ransom Hwy.
Metro Village, USA 54321

Sold To:

Your Source Company
123 Main St.
Anytown, USA 12345

Ship To:

Same

P.O. NUMBER	SALESPERSON	PACKING LIST#	DATE SHIPPED	SHIPPED VIA	TERMS
16	Veronica	4199	4/27/2014	UPS	N/30

QUANTITY	STOCK #	DESCRIPTION	UNIT PRICE	AMOUNT
100	BIS1	Big Stuff	$20.00	$2,000.00
200	LIS1	Little Stuff	$35.50	$7,100.00
150	HUS1	Huge Stuff	$29.00	$4,350.00
300	TIS1	Tiny Stuff	$50.00	$15,000.00
		SUBTOTAL		$28,450.00
		SALES TAX		0
		SHIPPING & HANDLING		0
		TOTAL DUE		$28,450.00

Make all checks payable to: Joe's Favorite Vendor
Please make sure your account number is on all correspondence and checks.

THANK YOU!

Performance by Enterprise - Payments (Economic Decrement Events)

The commitment made by the enterprise was to pay for the goods or services detailed in the purchase order, rental agreement, or service agreement. Contracts may require the enterprise to pay for the goods or services in advance, at the time of vendor performance, or within a specified time period after the vendor performance. The payment made by the enterprise is also sometimes called a **cash disbursement**. Payments may be made via **check** (a document used to authorize the transfer of cash from one entity to another), debit card, electronic funds transfer, or with currency and coins. If the enterprise uses a credit card to pay a vendor, the enterprise has not yet disbursed cash. Such a payment does decrease the balance of the accounts payable balance with the vendor to whom the payment was rendered; however, it creates a new payable balance with the credit card company. Therefore, the cash disbursement does not occur until the enterprise pays the credit card company.

Several documents may be involved in task activities that comprise the cash disbursement event: disbursement vouchers, vendor invoices, purchase orders, and receiving reports. A **disbursement voucher** is a document that indicates underlying documents have been examined to confirm goods or services were received and thus payment should be made. Two main concerns in the acquisition/payment process are for enterprises to ensure they do not receive goods or services they did not order, and more importantly to ensure they do not disburse cash for goods or services that they did not receive. To address these concerns, many enterprises prepare disbursement vouchers to authorize cash disbursements, using the purchase orders, receiving reports, and vendor invoices as support documentation. Exhibit 3-10 illustrates a disbursement voucher. The comparison of the vendor invoice with the purchase orders and receiving reports to ensure the enterprise is paying only for goods and services ordered and received is commonly known as the three-way match.

Some enterprises have reengineered the workflow in the acquisition/payment process in a manner similar to Ford Motor Company as described in Chapter 1. Ford implemented an integrated automated system that completely eliminated the vendor invoices and disbursement vouchers. Rather than having an individual employee perform the three-way match after the events had occurred, Ford's information system matched the purchase to the purchase order as the receipt of goods occurred. Payment was then automatically generated based on the quantities received and the contractual costs per the purchase order.

Exhibit 3-10 Disbursement Voucher

Disbursement Voucher
Number: __40__

Your Source Company
Your Source for Everything You Need
123 Main St.
Anytown, USA 12345_____

Date Prepared: 5/25/2014
Authorized By: E36

Vendor Number: V7
Remit Payment To:
Joe's Favorite Vendor
89056 Ransom Hwy.
Metro Village, USA 54321

VENDOR INVOICE NUMBER	DATE	INVOICE AMOUNT	RETURNS & ALLOWANCES	DISCOUNT	NET PAYMENT AMOUNT	SUPPORT DOCUMENTS EXAMINED BY
4167	5/2/2014	$28,450.00	$0.00	$0.00	$28,450.00	*DJB*
PAYMENT TOTALS:		$28,450.00	$0.00	$0.00	$28,450.00	

CHECK NUMBER:	41235
CASH ACCOUNT#:	Ca123501

Post-Purchase Activities: Returns & Allowances (Economic Increment Reversal Events)
If goods and services received do not meet the identified needs, the enterprise may decide to return the goods or request an allowance for the unsatisfactory services. A **purchase return** is the transfer of title (usually concurrent with transfer of physical custody) of goods from the enterprise back to the vendor.   Several documents may be used in workflow tasks that make up the purchase return event: requests to return goods, packing slips, bills of lading, and debit memos. A **request to return** is a notification to a supplier of the enterprise's dissatisfaction with goods that seeks permission to return those goods instead of paying for them (or in exchange for a refund). In response, the enterprise receives return authorization information

from the supplier via a paper document, an e-mail, or a phone call. Inventory or shipping clerks complete **packing slips** which detail the contents of each package shipped to an external business partner. If the goods are returned via common carriers, bills of lading usually are also prepared. A **bill of lading** is a document that indicates transfer of custody of goods from the enterprise to a common carrier, including details about how many packages comprise the shipment and the dimensions and/or weight of those packages. Packing slips list the items and quantities of each item returned; bills of lading list the number and dimensions of boxes in which the returned goods are packed. **Debit memorandums**, also called debit memos, are internal documents used to communicate the need for a journal entry to debit (decrease) the enterprise's accounts payable balance for that supplier. In Exhibits 3-11 through 3-13 we illustrate a sample request to return, packing slip, and debit memorandum. Sometimes a vendor will negotiate with the enterprise such that the enterprise will keep the unsatisfactory product and the vendor will refund part of the enterprise's purchase price. That refund is called a purchase allowance. Because purchase allowances do not involve the return of the product, no packing slip or bill of lading need be created; however, a debit memo will still be used to communicate to the accounts payable department the need to debit accounts payable.

Exhibit 3-11: Example Request to Return Goods Document

REQUEST TO RETURN FROM →	**Your Source Company**

Your Source for Everything You Need
123 Main St.
Anytown, USA

Ret. Request No. __3__
Date of Request _____

VENDOR:

All returns will be clean, in saleable condition, and shipped prepaid. A prompt reply will be greatly appreciated. Thank you for your cooperation.

RETURN CODES:

A Overstock
B DAMAGED
C DEFECTIVE
D WRONG PRODUCT BILLED & SHIPPED
E CORRECT PRODUCT BILLED BUT
    WRONG PRODUCT SHIPPED
F OTHER

☐ Cash Refund - Please

☒ Credit to Account - Please

Account No. _____

Request by _____

FOR CLARIFICATION CONTACT

Name Patrick Wellesley _____

Phone 555-3333 _____

DEPT.	QUAN. REQ.	PRODUCT NUMBER	DESCRIPTION		RETURN CODE	INVOICE NO.	QUAN. RET.	LIST PRICE	COST OR DISC.	EXTENSION
Sales	48	TTP12	Tiara		C	48592	48		$10.00	$480.00

Patrick Wellesley, E5
Return Authorized by

TOTAL	$480.00

REA Accounting Systems: Resources-Events-Agents: An ontology for designing, controlling, and using integrated enterprise systems

83

Exhibit 3-12: Packing List

Your Source Company	**RETURNS PACKING LIST __22__**
Your Source for Everything You Need	Clerk ID _137_
123 Main St.	
Anytown, USA 12345	If there are any questions about this shipment, contact our sales department (999) 555-3333

Trina's Trinkets	**RETURN AUTHORIZATION NUMBER:** 485
1612 Myway Rd.	**ORIGINAL PURCHASE NUMBER:**
Hinterland, USA 23456	
Contact: Trina Weeble	

PART NUMBER	QUANTITY RETURNED	UNIT OF MEASURE	ITEM DESCRIPTION
TTP12	48	each	Tiara, faux gold with inlaid baubles

Exhibit 3-13: Debit Memorandum

DEBIT MEMO

Your Source Company   No.___3___
Your Source for Everything You Need
123 Main St.
Anytown, USA 12345

DEBIT TO   Trina's Trinkets   DATE   5/22/2014

SUPPLIER
ACCOUNT NO.   V90

RETURN AUTH NO.	VENDOR INVOICE NO.	INVOICE DATE	PURCHASE ID	
485	48592	5/15/2010	RR25	
ITEM NUMBER	DESCRIPTION	QUANTITY	UNIT COST	AMOUNT
TTP12	Tiara	48	10. 00	480. 00
			TOTAL DEBIT	480. 00

REVENUE CYCLE: WORKFLOW AND DOCUMENTS

The **revenue cycle**, also called the **sales/collection process** or the order-to-cash process, is the transaction cycle in which goods or services are exchanged to customers for cash or some other form of compensation. The activities that comprise a typical revenue cycle are actually the same activities that comprise a typical acquisition cycle; the activities are simply viewed from the opposite party's perspective. Consider a transaction in which Bikes Unlimited sells a racing bike to customer Joe Green in exchange for $250. To Joe Green the transaction is a purchase. To Bikes Unlimited the transaction is a sale.

To exchange goods and services for cash with the customers, we must attract customers, then help those customers select goods and services, deliver the goods and services requested, and collect payments for the goods and services. Generating revenue is the key to achieving growth and profitability. Enterprises can produce an abundance of goods and create a variety of services, but the real test of value is whether someone will pay a price that covers the cost of goods and services and provide the enterprise with an acceptable return on invested funds.

No pattern exists for the specific procedures and information/document flows that are used by specific enterprises in their revenue cycles. However, it may be helpful for you to learn about the general categories of activities and some of the documents that are commonly (but not always) used to record data regarding those activities.

Marketing Events, Customer Inquiries (Instigation Events)

Instigation events may be internally instigated (i.e., by the enterprise) or externally instigated (i.e., by an external business partner of the enterprise). The sales/collection process is instigated by the attraction of a customer's decision to buy the enterprise's goods or services.

Sometimes customers know they want a particular product or service and they search for a source for that product or service. They may call an enterprise to see if the product or service they need is available, without having participated in a marketing event. Such customer inquiries are externally generated instigation events. Quotes or bids may be provided to the customer as part of instigation events. Quotes in the revenue cycle are the same as that illustrated in Exhibit 3-6 in our discussion of the acquisition cycle

In an effort to influence customer decision making, an enterprise plans, executes, and evaluates a variety of marketing events (e.g., sales calls, advertising campaigns, or promotions) intended to inform customers about products and/or services and hopefully influence them to trigger the sales/collection process. Therefore marketing efforts are typically considered to be internally generated instigation events.

A **sales call** is an event in which an enterprise representative describes features of products or services to potential customers in an attempt to generate sales to those customers. Usually sales calls are pre-arranged and face-to-face and may involve product demonstrations. Data regarding sales calls are often captured on a sales call form such as that in Exhibit 3-14. This form may either be a paper document or it may be part of a software application interface. In either case, similar data are captured and stored.

REA Accounting Systems: Resources-Events-Agents: An ontology for designing, controlling, and using integrated enterprise systems

85

Exhibit 3-14: Sample Sales Call Report

Your Source Company	**Sales Call Report**
Your Source for Everything You Need 123 Main St. Anytown, USA 12345	No. _42_

Salesperson Name	Jimmy Vitale	**Salesperson #**	E23
Customer Name	Needmore Stuff	**Customer #**	C2323

Sales Call Location	Needmore Stuff warehouse

Date	5/4/2014	**Start Time**	9:12 a.m.	**End Time**	10:00 a.m.

Customer Representative Called on	Sarah Gibson
What is this person's position?	Procurement supervisor

What products/services were presented at this sales call?

Big stuff (Item BIS1)
Little stuff (Item LIS1)
Huge stuff (Item HUS1)
Tiny stuff (Item TIS1)

Did a sale order result from this sales call? Yes ☒ Order Number__14____ No ☐

If yes, what products/services were ordered by the customer?

TIS1
LIS1

Follow-up comments (e.g. customer reaction to products, other notes):

Customer likes small things! Had no interest at all in big or huge stuff, don't bother presenting again.
The smaller the better!

Agreements/Contracts (Commitment Events)

In the sales/collection process the most common commitments/contracts are sale orders, rental agreements, and service agreements. They are the same activities as we discussed for the acquisition cycle but viewed from the seller's perspective. A commitment event doesn't always happen at a discrete point in time; often it involves a series of activities. Typically a customer places an order with the enterprise for goods or services. A **customer order** is information in the customer's own format regarding what goods and services the customer is committing to purchase from an enterprise. Sales or customer service representatives and/or order entry clerks may assist the customer and collect the order data. The enterprise determines whether to commit by checking the availability of requested goods or services, verifying all price and date information, and contacting the customer if necessary to adjust pricing or dates promised. The enterprise also determines whether to extend credit to the customer, therefore the credit department will also play a role in the activities associated with the commitment event.

These determinations are important because the enterprise shouldn't commit unless it is confident both parties can fulfill their parts of the sales transaction (i.e., the enterprise must be able to fill the order and the enterprise must be confident that the customer has the ability to pay). An approved customer order becomes a **sale order** – a mutual commitment event in which the enterprise agrees to transfer title of goods to a customer at an agreed upon future time and price and the customer agrees to pay for those goods. Ideally an enterprise wants to be able to trace each commitment to a sales call or other instigation event. Sometimes it is impossible to determine which marketing effort led to a commitment. Other times, for example in vacation ownership (time share) sales, a commitment typically occurs only as part of a marketing event. In those rare cases, it is very clear whether the instigation activities were successful in generating the commitments and eventual sales. Linking marketing efforts to commitment events provides valuable information with which to evaluate marketing effectiveness, so enterprises should consider the feasibility and cost of materializing this link.

Data regarding sale order events are often captured on sale order forms such as that shown in Exhibit 3-15. This form may either be a paper document or part of a software application interface that is used to update the enterprise database. Notice the similarity between the sale order in Exhibit 3-15 and the purchase order in Exhibit 3-7. For many enterprises, the data for sale orders are obtained from a customer purchase order form, commonly referred to as a customer order. The primary difference between a customer order and a sale order is that the customer order is in the customer's format, whereas the sale order is in the seller's format.

Similar types of data are captured on similar forms (again, either in electronic interfaces or on paper documents) for other mutual commitment events such as service agreements and rental contracts. Exhibit 3-16 shows a service agreement; note the similarities in the types of data captured regarding the service agreement and the sale order events. Similar data would also be captured for rental agreements.

Exhibit 3-15 Sale Order

Your Source Company   **Sale Order**
Your Source for Everything You Need
123 Main St.   ORDER NO: ___14___
Anytown, USA 12345

DATE: ___5/4/2014___

Ordered By:	Ship To:
Sarah Gibson	Needmore Stuff
	86906 Enterprise Dr.
	Anytown, USA 12345

SALESPERSON	P.O. NUMBER	EST. SHIP DATE	TO SHIP VIA	TERMS
E23	Verbal	5/5/2014	FedEx	N/30

QUANTITY	STOCK #	DESCRIPTION	UNIT PRICE	AMOUNT
2	LIS1	Little Stuff, box of 6	$70.00	$ 140.00
10	TIS1	Tiny Stuff, box of 12	$96.00	$ 960.00
			SUBTOTAL	$1,100.00
			SALES TAX	0
			SHIPPING & HANDLING	0
			ORDER TOTAL	$1,100.00

REA Accounting Systems: Resources-Events-Agents: An ontology for designing, controlling, and using integrated enterprise systems

87

Exhibit 3-16: Sample Service Agreement

Your Source Company	**Repair Service Order**
Your Source for Everything You Need	
123 Main St.	**ORDER NO:** _____
Anytown, USA 12345	**DATE:** _____

Ordered By: Deliver To:

SALESPERSON	P.O. NUMBER	ESTIMATED COMPLETION DATE	TO SHIP VIA	TERMS

Parts and Supplies

QUANTITY	STOCK NO.	DESCRIPTION	UNIT PRICE	AMOUNT
			SUBTOTAL	

Labor Charges

HOURS	SERVICE TYPE	DESCRIPTION	REPAIR PERSON	HOURLY RATE	AMOUNT
				SUBTOTAL	
				SALES TAX	
				SHIPPING & HANDLING	
				TOTAL DUE	

THANK YOU FOR YOUR BUSINESS!

Performance by Enterprise - Sale, Delivery, Shipment, Rental, or Service Engagement (Economic Decrement Event)

The enterprise's delivery of the products or services specified in the commitment represents the revenue-generating activity of the enterprise and may also be called the enterprise's performance. If the revenue generating activity involves the sale of merchandise, the event may be called *Sale*, *Delivery*, or *Shipment* depending in part on whether the customer is on-site to accept possession of the goods or whether the enterprise must deliver or ship the goods to the customer. The important consideration is that the **sale** occurs when title to the merchandise transfers from the seller to the buyer. If title has not transferred, then revenue has not been earned.

If the enterprise sells services rather than goods, then the resource given up to the customers is a set of employee services, making those services unavailable to provide to someone else.

Such an event is usually called **Service Engagement** or something that more specifically describes the kinds of services performed by the enterprise (such as *Repair Service*, *Audit Engagement*, or *Consultation*) In the case of enterprises that rent merchandise to customers, the revenue generating activity is usually called Rental. A **rental** is an event that does not involve the transfer of title of goods, but instead involves a transfer of the right to use goods for an agreed upon length of time. The rental event begins when the right to temporary possession of the goods transfers from the lessor to the lessee and ends when possession of the goods transfers back from the lessee to the lessor.

Notice the similarity between this description and that of the performance by vendor in the acquisition cycle discussion. The activities are identical if viewed from an independent perspective. They are part of the acquisition cycle if viewed from the customer's perspective and they are part of the revenue cycle if viewed from the vendor's perspective.

Whether the revenue-generating activity is a sale, delivery, shipment, rental, or service, these economic decrement events in the revenue cycle do not always happen at discrete points in time. Rather they are often made up of a series of workflow activities. The fulfillment of an enterprise's commitment is accomplished by the tasks that make up the economic decrement event. For enterprises that sell or rent merchandise that must be shipped to the customer location, these tasks include picking the inventory from the warehouse, packing the inventory into boxes, and shipping the boxes to the customer via a common carrier. The rental event also includes receiving the returned merchandise, inspecting it, and returning it to the warehouse. Economic decrement events for service enterprises generally require active involvement of trained employees who perform the services. The enterprise must identify the requirements of the services to be rendered and select an individual or group of individuals to perform the services. Services may be provided over an extended period of time by a variety of people.

An enterprise may have multiple revenue generating activities. For example, some enterprises ship finished products to customers and also provide services. Some enterprises provide various combinations of products/services for different customers. For example, a computer manufacturer may serve one customer by shipping a new computer and letting the customer install it and handle all conversion. For another customer, the enterprise may deliver the computer, assist with installation, and convert existing applications for processing on the new computer. Yet another customer may request the enterprise to repair a computer that the enterprise had previously sold to the customer.

Several documents often are prepared in conjunction with the activities that comprise the revenue-generating activities: picking slips, packing slips, bills of lading, and sale invoices. A **picking slip** is a document that identifies the goods taken out of the warehouse and made available to be shipped (see Exhibit 3-17). Other names for this document include pick ticket, picking ticket, pick list, and picking list.

REA Accounting Systems: Resources-Events-Agents: An ontology for designing, controlling, and using integrated enterprise systems

89

Exhibit 3-17: Picking List

Your Source Company			**PICKING TICKET** __15__	
Your Source for Everything You Need			Clerk ID __137__	
123 Main St.				
Anytown, USA 12345				

Order Number: 14   **Order Date:** 5/4/2014   **Warehouse:** WH1

Sold To: Needmore Stuff	**Ship To:** Needmore Stuff
86906 Enterprise Dr.	86906 Enterprise Dr.
Anytown, USA 12345	Anytown, USA 12345

CUST NUMBER	**P.O. NUMBER**	**TERMS**	**REP NUMBER**
E2323	Verbal	n/30	E23

SHIP VIA	**DATE-TO-SHIP**		
FedEx	5/5/2014		

ITEM ID	**DESCRIPTION**	**QTY ORDERED**	**QTY PICKED**
LIS1	Little Stuff, box of 6	2	2
TIS1	Tiny Stuff, box of 12	10	10

LINE ITEMS	**TOTAL QUANTITY**
2	12

Often a picking slip is initially prepared by the sale order clerk and sent to the warehouse to authorize an inventory clerk to "pick" the goods out of the warehouse; the inventory clerk then completes the picking slip. Sometimes the pick ticket is actually a copy of the sale order with the cost column replaced by a "quantity picked" column (picking list copies may be designed to accomplish this without having to fill out separate documents). The inventory clerk notes the quantities of each item picked, notes any stockout problems, and signs the form to indicate the transfer of custody of those goods to the shipping area.

A **packing slip** (sometimes called a packing list) is a document that identifies the goods that have been shipped to an external business partner (see Exhibit 3-18). Often the packing slip is a copy of the picking slip on which a shipping clerk fills in the quantities of each item packed, notes any discrepancies from the picking slip, and signs to indicate transfer of custody of the goods to a common carrier.

Exhibit 3-18: Packing List

Your Source Company	PACKING LIST __15__
Your Source for Everything You Need	Clerk ID _137_
123 Main St.	
Anytown, USA 12345	If there are any questions about this shipment, contact our sales department (999) 555-3333

Needmore Stuff	YOUR PURCHASE ORDER NUMBER
86906 Enterprise Dr.	Verbal
Anytown, USA 12345	
Contact: Sarah Gibson	**# Items Ordered:** 2

WAREHOUSE LOCATION	YOUR SOURCE PART #	FILL QUANTITY	ITEM DESCRIPTION	YOUR LINE	YOU ORDERED	WE SHIPPED
WH1	LIS1	2	Little Stuff	1	2	2
WH1	TIS1	10	Tiny Stuff	2	10	10

The bill of lading also indicates transfer of custody of goods from the enterprise to a common carrier; however, it contains different data from the packing slip. Rather than documenting details about each type of item shipped and the quantities of those items, the bill of lading documents details about how many boxes made up the shipment and the dimensions and/or weight of those boxes. See the bill of lading in Exhibit 3-19.

Sale invoices (electronic or paper) communicate to customers that the enterprise has fulfilled its commitment and request the customer to remit payment to fulfill its commitment. If the customer already paid for the merchandise, the invoice indicates that no balance is due. Exhibit 3-20 shows a sales invoice. A sale invoice represents an information event; that is, it does not communicate anything new but rather confirms details that were previously known and agreed upon. As noted when discussing the acquisition cycle, invoices may be reengineered out of a system as long as some mechanism is in place to ensure payment results directly from the non-cash economic event. Elimination of vendor invoices is much less scary to consider then is elimination of sale invoices, but keep in mind they both represent the same phenomena – simply from two different perspectives.

Creating separate documents for the picking, packing, and shipment of inventory and for customer billing is not a requirement of any enterprise information system, nor is it required that those activities be separated into four tasks. An interface to an enterprise-wide information system may make approved sale order data available on the company intranet and the shipping function may be integrated with the warehousing function. Thus an inventory clerk may view the approved order details, pick, pack, and ship the goods and transmit an electronic invoice to the customer's information system all in one task, with no need to document transfers of custody (i.e. the picking and packing) because custody did not change until the goods were shipped to the customer.

REA Accounting Systems: Resources-Events-Agents: An ontology for designing, controlling, and using integrated enterprise systems

91

Exhibit 3-19 Bill of Lading

UNIFORM STRAIGHT BILL OF LADING – Domestic				Document No. __15__

Your Source Company
Your Source for Everything You Need
123 Main St.
Anytown, USA 12345

Shipper's No. ___14789B___
Carrier's No. ___8796801___
Date ___5/5/2014___

___Federal Express___
(Name of Carrier)

Route: _____ Vehicle Number: _____

No. shipping units	Kind of Packaging, Description of Articles, Special Marks and Exceptions	Weight (Subject to Correction)	Rate	Charges (for Carrier use only)
1	Box, stuff	15 lbs.	1.14	

REMIT
C.O.D. TO: N/A
ADDRESS

COD
Amt:$ 0.00

C.O.D. FEE: $ N/A
PREPAID ☐
COLLECT ☐

Note – Where the rate is dependent on value, shippers are required to state specifically in writing the agreed or declared value of the property.
    The agreed or declared value of the property is hereby specifically stated by the shipper to be not exceeding.

$ __1,200.00__   per __box__

Subject to Section 7 of the conditions, if this shipment is to be delivered to the consignee without recourse on the consignor, the consignor shall sign the following statement:
    The carrier shall not make delivery of this shipment without payment of freight and all other lawful charges.

_____
(Signature of Consignor)

Total Charges $ 17.10

FREIGHT CHARGES
Check Appropriate Box:
☐ Freight prepaid
☒ Bill to shipper
☐ Collect

Received subject to the classifications and tariffs in effect on the date of the issue of this Bill of Lading, the property described above in apparent good order, except as noted (contents and condition of contents)

Shipping Clerk ID: 137

Performance by the Customer – Payments to Enterprise (Economic Increment Event)

Payments made by the customer to the enterprise are often referred to as **cash receipts**. The enterprise receives cash from the customer. These cash receipts are economic increment events that increase the enterprise's cash balance. Cash receipts may take the form of checks, currency, or coins – anything that can be deposited into a cash account held either in a bank or on hand in petty cash. Notice that if a customer pays with a credit card, the enterprise has not yet received cash; the cash receipt does not occur until the credit card company pays the enterprise. In the latter case, the cash receipt must be connected to two external agents – the customer, whose accounts receivable balance will be decreased as a result of the cash receipt, and the credit card company, from whom the cash was literally received.

Exhibit 3-20: Sale Invoice

Your Source Company
Your Source for Everything You Need
123 Main St.
Anytown, USA

Sale Invoice

INVOICE NO: ___12___
DATE: __5/5/2014__

Sold To:

Needmore Stuff
86906 Enterprise Dr.
Anytown, USA 12345

Ship To:

Needmore Stuff
86906 Enterprise Dr.
Anytown, USA 12345

SALESPERSON	P.O. NUMBER	S.O. NUMBER	DATE SHIPPED	SHIPPED VIA	TERMS
E23	verbal	14	5/5/2014	FedEx	N/30

QUANTITY	STOCK NO.	DESCRIPTION	UNIT PRICE	AMOUNT
2	LIS1	Little Stuff, box of 6	$70.00	$ 140.00
10	TIS1	Tiny Stuff, box of 12	$96.00	$ 960.00

SUBTOTAL	$1,100.00
SALES TAX	0
SHIPPING & HANDLING	0
TOTAL DUE	$1,100.00

Make all checks payable to: Your Source Company

THANK YOU FOR YOUR BUSINESS!

Cash receipts occur at various times in the revenue cycle. Some cash receipts may occur as orders are placed (i.e., a prepayment); other cash receipts may occur at the point of sale or upon delivery of goods or services; still other cash receipts may occur days or weeks after sales take place. The receipt of cash is a custodial function. Two documents are typically involved in task activities that comprise the cash receipt event: remittance advices and deposit slips. When payment is received, cashiers, accounts receivable clerks, or other company employees verify the payment information is correctly recorded on a remittance advice. A **remittance advice** is a document (usually the portion of a customer invoice or customer statement that says "return this stub with payment") that advises the enterprise the customer is remitting payment. A **customer statement** is a document that summarizes the economic transactions for a customer and reflects the customer's account balance status. Exhibit 3-21 shows a customer statement with a detachable remittance advice.

A **deposit slip** is promptly prepared summarizing all payments for a prescribed time period (usually a day). The deposit slip and payments are deposited into one of the enterprise's bank accounts. Due to the risk of loss, cash should be deposited at least daily, all employers who have access to cash should be bonded, and two employees should verify cash transactions. In addition to having customers mail or bring payments directly to the business, an enterprise can use the *lockbox method* or electronic funds transfers to collect customer payments. When the lockbox method is used, customers mail their checks to a post office address, and for a fee, a bank will pick up, total, and directly deposit the funds into the company's account. In such situations the post office serves as an external agent. The bank then sends a copy of the deposit information and the remittance advices to the company. Electronic funds transfers reduce human involvement with cash by having customers electronically transfer funds from their bank accounts directly to the company's bank account. The form of payment is incidental to the occurrence of the event.

Enterprise systems should include the ability to record a cash receipt without linking it to a specific customer. For example, suppose someone sends a check but neglects to send the remittance advice and the name on the check does not correspond to the name of any existing customer account. The enterprise should be able to deposit the funds and tag the transaction as "unapplied cash" (a cash payment that was received but was not posted to a customer's receivable balance). If this occurs, the system should generate a listing of "unapplied cash" transactions and, as with all errors, they should be investigated and corrected as soon as possible. The enterprise system should also allow enterprises to choose how they want to link customer payments to customer accounts. Two methods include specific invoice and balance forward. As the name implies, the specific invoice method involves matching payments to specific sales invoices. When enterprises use a balance forward approach, they apply payments to a customer's total account balance, rather than any specific invoice.

Exhibit 3-21 Customer Statement with Remittance Advice

Your Source Company *Your Source for Everything You Need* 123 Main St. Anytown, USA 12345			PAGE 1 **STATEMENT**				PAGE 1 REMITTANCE ADVICE # __20__	

	DATE	CUSTOMER NUMBER		DATE	CUSTOMER NUMBER
Needmore Stuff 86906 Enterprise Court Anytown, USA 12345	5/19/2014	C2323			C2323

TERMS: N/30

← PLEASE DETATCH HERE AND RETURN THIS STUB WITH YOUR REMITTANCE
TO: Your Source Company
123 Main St.
Anytown, USA 12345

INVOICE NUMBER	DATE	CURRENT	PAST 1-30	PAST 31-60	PAST 61-90	PAST 91-120	INVOICE NUMBER	AMOUNT APPLIED
12	5/5/2014	1,100.00					12	$ 960.00
TOTAL DUE		**TOTAL CURRENT**	**TOTAL PAST 1-30**	**TOTAL PAST 31-60**	**TOTAL PAST 61-90**	**TOTAL PAST 91-120**	**TOTAL DUE**	**TOTAL REMITTED**
$1,100.00		**$1,100.00**	**$0**	**$0**	**$0**	**$0**	**$1,100.00**	**$ 960.00**

REVIEWED BY _____

Post-Sale Activities: Sales Returns & Allowances (Economic Decrement Reversal Events)

The same activities we discussed for the acquisition cycle also occur in the revenue cycle. Just as the purchase/sale activities are identical when viewed from an independent perspective, the purchase return and allowance/sale return and allowance activities are also identical when viewed from an independent perspective. If products do not meet quality standards represented in the sale agreement or the product specifications of the customer; or if the customer's needs changed while the goods were in transit, the customer will not want to keep the goods. Three options are available to handle disagreements like these: The enterprise may allow the customer to keep the product and receive an adjustment or allowance in the price, or the enterprise may allow the customer to return the product and decrease the customer's account receivable or issue a cash refund. Alternatively the enterprise may take a no returns – all sales final approach.

A **sale return** is the transfer of title (usually concurrent with transfer of physical custody) of goods from a customer back to the seller. Several documents may be used in workflow tasks that make up a sales return event, including return authorizations, receiving reports, and credit memos. A **return authorization** is a document that gives permission for the customer to return merchandise and is typically prepared in response to a customer's request to return goods through the mail or via a common carrier. In retail stores a modified document is used that combines the customer request, and store authorization; it indicates what inventory items were returned. Receiving reports are completed by inventory or receiving clerks when returned goods are received from customers. The receiving report lists the items and the quantities and condition of each item received. If the customer already paid for the merchandise, the enterprise issues a cash refund (either in currency/coin or via check). If the customer did not already pay for the merchandise, or if the enterprise policy only allows returns for credit toward future customer purchases, then the enterprise will credit the customer's account receivable balance. A **credit memorandum** (also called credit memo) is an internal document used to communicate to the accounting department that a journal entry needs to be made with a credit to the customer's account receivable. A copy may also be sent to the customer to confirm to them that they were given credit. Exhibits 3-22 through 3-24 illustrate a sample sales return authorization, receiving report, and credit memorandum. Because the receiving report indicates the actual return of physical custody of the goods back to the selling enterprise, the receiving report is the most appropriate document to represent the sale return.

Exhibit 3-22: Sales Return Authorization

RETURN AUTHORIZATION __1__

Your Source Company
Your Source for Everything You Need
123 Main St.
Anytown, USA

Date __5/12/2014__

Customer No. __C2323__
Address: 86069 Enterprise Dr.
Anytown, USA 12345
For clarification contact
Name __Sarah Gibson__
Phone __555-8989__

All returns must be clean, in saleable condition, and shipped prepaid. Thank you for your cooperation.

Customer Return Request No. __3__
Date of Request __5/9/2014__

RETURN CODES:

A OVERSTOCK   D WRONG PRODUCT
                 BILLED & SHIPPED
B DAMAGED
              E CORRECT PRODUCT
C DEFECTIVE   BILLED BUT WRONG
                 PRODUCT SHIPPED

F OTHER

☐ Cash Refund - Please

☒ Credit to Account - Please

ITEM ID	DESCRIPTION	RETURN CODE	INVOICE NO.	QTY. RETURNED	UNIT PRICE	EXTENSION
LIS1	Little Stuff	F – too big	12	2	70.00	$140.00
					TOTAL	

Exhibit 3-23: Receiving Report

RECEIVING REPORT   NO. __25__

Your Source Company
Your Source for Everything You Need
123 Main St.
Anytown, USA 12345

DATE	5/12/2014	PURCH ORD NO./ SALE RETURN AUTH NO.	SR1	
RECEIVED FROM	Needmore Stuff			PREPAID 10
ADDRESS	86906 Enterprise Dr. Anytown, USA 12345			COLLECT
FREIGHT CARRIER **Federal Express**		FREIGHT BILL NO. **FE78901256**		

	QUANTITY	ITEM NO	DESCRIPTION
1.	2	LIS1	Little Stuff
2.			
3.			
4.			
5.			
6.			
7.			
8.			
9.			

REMARKS: CONDITIONS, ETC.
Perfect condition

RECEIVED BY	DELIVERED TO
E111	E23

BE SURE TO
MAKE THIS RECORD
ACCURATE AND COMPLETE

Exhibit 3-24: Credit Memorandum

CREDIT MEMO

Your Source Company   No.   **1**

Your Source for Everything You Need
123 Main St.
Anytown, USA 12345

CREDIT TO   Needmore Stuff   DATE   5/19/2014

CUSTOMER
ACCOUNT NO.   C2323

RETURN AUTH NO.	INVOICE NO.		INVOICE DATE	RECEIVING REPORT NO.	
SR1	12		5/5/2014	25	
ITEM NUMBER	DESCRIPTION		QUANTITY	PRICE EACH	AMOUNT
LIS1	Little Stuff		2	70. 00	140. 00
				TOTAL CREDIT	140. 00

You must present this copy when applying to future orders.	APPLY ON FUTURE ORDER ONLY ☐ REFUND BY CHECK ☐ CREDIT ACCOUNT ☒	Prepared by *Elmore Kirk* Credit Manager Emp#_16_

CONCLUDING COMMENTS

This chapter presented an overview of document flowcharting and introduced some of the associated information processing considerations. Some organizations and consultants have developed their own diagramming techniques. Whether you use flowcharting or some other diagramming tool is really a matter of choice and what you are trying to analyze or design. Diagramming tools combine the efficiency of graphics and the rigor of rules to communicate the nature of the process being modeled. It is important for analysts to develop the skills to both read and create documentation of information and business processes using tools such as document flowcharts. This chapter also described common workflow activities and documents often used in the acquisition and revenue cycles. Document flowcharting and other task level representation tools work very well for summarizing the specific workflow for an enterprise in such a way that inefficient processes or weak internal controls may be revealed.

Key Terms and Concepts

Acquisition cycle
Area of responsibility
Batch processing
Bill of lading
Cash disbursement
Cash receipt
Check
Contract
Credit memorandum
Customer order
Customer statement
Debit memorandum
Deposit slip
Direct access
Disbursement voucher
Document/procedure flowchart
Flow lines
Flowchart symbols
Magnetic tape
Master file
Mutual commitment
Online processing
Open purchase order
Packing slip
Performance
Picking slip
Purchase
Purchase order

Purchase requisition
Purchase return
Quote
Random storage
Real-time processing
Receiving report
Remittance advice
Rental
Rental agreement
Report-time processing
Request for quote (RFQ)
Request to return
Return authorization
Revenue cycle
Sale
Sales call
Sales/collection business process
Sale invoice
Sale order
Sale return
Sequential access
Sequential storage
Service agreement
Service engagement
System flowchart
Transaction file
Vendor invoice

Review Questions

LO1   R1.   Explain the difference between the REA ontology's task level modeling and business process level modeling.

LO2   R2.   Draw the flowcharting symbols and describe the use of each.

LO2, LO5   R3.   List the important conventions you should follow when preparing a flowchart to make the flowchart easier to understand.

LO2   R4.   When should you use an overlapping document symbol instead of a single document symbol in a system flowchart?

LO3   R5.   What is the difference between online processing and real-time processing? Can processing be both online and real-time? Can processing be online without being real-time? Explain your responses.

LO4   R6.   Explain the difference between a customer order and a sale order.

LO4   R7.   Explain the difference between a sale order and a sale invoice.

LO4   R8.   Which document best represents the economic increment event in the acquisition/payment cycle: a purchase order, a receiving report, a vendor invoice, or a check ? Explain your response.

LO4   R9.   Explain what it means for a transaction or document to be *open*, e.g., an open sale order, open sale invoice, open purchase order, or an open vendor invoice.

LO4   R10.   During which event should an enterprise recognize revenue for a FOB shipping point sale transaction: Sale Order, Shipment, or Cash Receipt? Explain.

Multiple Choice Questions

LO2, LO6

1. In the following flowchart segment, the most likely action to take with the customer remittance advices once they've been keyed into the system, AND the corresponding symbol to replace circle B is

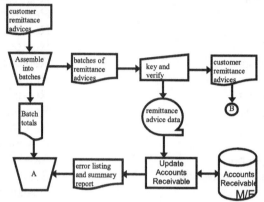

A) Discard them immediately; manual process symbol
B) Forward them to the internal audit department for review; dashed line
C) Forward them to the treasurer to compare with the monthly bank statement; dashed line
D) File them by customer number; file symbol
E) Compare them to the customer check amounts, manual process symbol

LO2, LO5

2. In a system flowchart, which symbol should be used to represent a backup of the general ledger master file that can only be accessed sequentially?
    A) ▱
    B) ▭
    C) ◒
    D) ◗
    E) ▱

LO3

3. The primary purpose of executable files is to store which of the following?
    A) Business reference data
    B) Transaction data
    C) Word processing documents
    D) Graphics documents
    E) Application programs

LO3

4. Which of the following can best be described as a master file?
    A) A file of event data
    B) An income statement
    C) A trial balance
    D) An accounts payable subsidiary ledger
    E) A journal voucher file

LO1
5. The purpose of task level modeling in the REA ontology is
   A) To design a database
   B) To represent the specific workflow activities that combine to form events in a business process, and to document the flow of data through an enterprise
   C) To represent the enterprise in the context of its external business partners
   D) To represent the resource interconnections among the enterprise transaction cycles
   E) To represent resource flows among external partners that do not directly involve the enterprise (e.g. a customer payment to a credit card company for the amount of the credit sale a store made to the customer)

LO2, LO5, LO6
6. System flowcharts consist of these three simple graphical elements combined to represent various types of physical information flows and processes:
   A) Charts, lines, and documents
   B) Charts, symbols, and annotations
   C) Symbols, lines, and documents
   D) Symbols, flow lines, and areas of responsibility
   E) Circles, squares, and flow lines

LO5
7. Which rules should be followed to keep flowcharts uncluttered?
   A) Enter narrative on charts only within symbols
   B) Avoid explaining with narrative what is already adequately described by the flowchart itself
   C) Place areas of responsibility with the most frequent interchange adjacent to each other to avoid long arrows
   D) All of the above
   E) None of the above

LO3
8. Media that can be used to store data include
   A) Paper
   B) Magnetic tape
   C) Flash drives
   D) Hard disks
   E) All of the above

LO3
9. Which type of processing occurs during the course of a business event and provides immediate response to an information user's request
   A) Online processing
   B) Batch processing
   C) Report-time processing
   D) Real-time processing
   E) Suspense processing

LO 4

10. Which of the following is a document that identifies goods taken out of the warehouse and made available to be packed?
    A) Picking slip
    B) Packing slip
    C) Bill of Lading
    D) Sale invoice
    E) Customer statement

LO 4

11. Which document indicates transfer of custody of goods from the enterprise to a common carrier?
    A) Picking slip
    B) Sale return authorization
    C) Sale invoice
    D) Customer statement
    E) Bill of lading

LO4

12. Which of the following documents is usually the portion of the customer statement that says "return this stub with payment"?
    A) Picking list
    B) Customer invoice
    C) Bill of Lading
    D) Remittance advice
    E) Receiving report

LO4

13. What is the primary document prepared by the enterprise in conjunction with the economic increment event in the acquisition/payment process?
    A) Vendor invoice
    B) Receiving report
    C) Purchase order
    D) Debit memorandum
    E) Disbursement voucher

LO4

14. Which of the following internal documents is used to communicate the need for a journal entry to decrease the enterprise's accounts payable balance for that supplier?
    A) Credit memorandum
    B) Debit memorandum
    C) Return voucher
    D) Request to return goods
    E) Receiving report

LO4

15. Which of the following represents an unfulfilled request by a department supervisor for the purchasing department to acquire a good or service?
    A) Open purchase order file
    B) Closed purchase order file
    C) Open purchase requisition
    D) Closed purchase requisition
    E) Acquisition voucher

LO4

16. Match the flowcharting segments with the descriptions to which they correspond by writing the number of the segment on the blank next to the description. Leave one of the descriptions blank (i.e., none of the segments apply).

_____ a. A payroll clerk reconciles a timesheet with an unsigned paycheck and approves (or rejects) the check for signature.

_____ b. A report is printed from a computer.

_____ c. A payroll supervisor signs a paycheck.

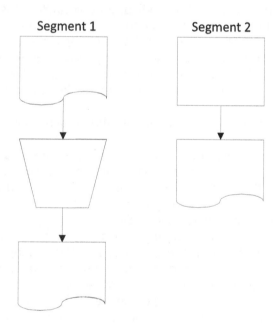

Applied Learning

LO2   A1. Create a system flowchart to represent the acquisition/payment tasks for Jayvision, Inc., as described in the first scenario in this chapter. Next create a system flowchart to represent the acquisition/payment tasks for Jayvision as described in the second scenario in this chapter. How are they similar? How are they different? How much would the business process level models differ for the two scenarios?

LO5, LO6 A2. Working as a team, visit a local enterprise and interview a manager or owner to get information needed to flowchart a source document (e.g. a customer order, sale invoice, or purchase order) from origination to its final destination. Also flowchart at least one task performed by one of the organization's clerical staff. In class, exchange your team's flowcharts with those of another team and write narratives that describe the activities illustrated on their flowcharts. Finally, prepare a written critique of how well the other team interpreted the flowchart your team prepared.

LO5 A3. The following describes the process to execute a credit sale at Willie's Furniture Store. Sales clerks assist customers in locating and pricing merchandise. A sales clerk prepares a sales invoice with an original and three copies. If the merchandise on an invoice is priced differently than the list price, the price change must be approved with a signature by the sales manager. Copy #3 of the sales invoice is filed by the salesperson in a salesperson file.

The salesperson walks the customer and the remaining copies of the invoice to the credit approval department where the invoice is checked for mathematical errors by a clerk. The credit manager evaluates the credit standing of the customer, approves or rejects the application based on standard company policy, and marks "credit sale" on the invoice along with the results of the credit evaluation. Invoice copy 2 of credit approved sales is given to the customer. The credit approval department keeps the original copy of the invoice in their files (filed numerically) and sends the other copy to shipping.

The shipping department uses its copy as a guide to pull and deliver merchandise to the customer. The customer is asked to sign the invoice copy as evidence of delivery. The delivery person files the invoice copy by date.

Required

Prepare a document/procedure flowchart for the process just described.

LO5 A4. Motor Building Industry (MBI) Incorporated develops and manufactures natural-gas powered motors. Capital tools are the larger, more-prominent assets of the organization. Because of their long life and significant value, considerable attention is devoted to their acquisition and use. The following procedures are used in acquiring capital tools for MBI Inc.

A capital tool is defined as any individual item that costs over $10,000. Capital tools must be requested by a department manager and reviewed and approved by the capital tool planning committee. The department manager prepares a purchase request and a copy (which is filed numerically) and sends the original copy to the planning committee. The planning committee reviews all purchase requests and decides whether to approve the tool request. The committee remits disapproved purchase requests to the requesting manager and forwards approved purchase requests to MBI's purchasing department.

Approved capital tools are purchased by the purchasing department manager. Using the approved purchase request, a purchasing agent prepares a purchase order and a copy for each order. The original is filed numerically and the copy is sent to MBI's receiving department. Each tool is assigned to only one purchasing agent, and the assignment is made according to the vendor from whom the tool is intended to be purchased. Several vendors are assigned to each purchasing agent to establish a personal relationship with the vendor and secure a more favorable price because of their knowledge of the vendor.

Receiving clerks at the dock receive the tools, inspect them, match the tool to a purchase order, complete a receiving report, and route the tool to the department that originally requested it. Receiving clerks send the receiving report to the treasury department and file a copy alphabetically. Purchase orders are filed numerically. Occasionally, tools are received that were never ordered. Even though the number of these items is relatively small, sorting them out and returning them occupies a major portion of the receiving clerk's time.

The treasury department is informed of capital tools received by the receiving report. They pay vendors monthly for the items invoiced by the vendor during the month. An elaborate matching process is required to verify that the price paid is the same as the price negotiated by the purchasing agent.

Required

Prepare a flowchart of MBI's tool acquisition process (excluding the payment process) as described

LO5   A6.   The Warehouse Club is a small merchandise discount store that sells everything from grocery items to automotive parts. The Warehouse Club is able to secure low prices by buying in bulk and by operating out of a leased warehouse. In addition, only paid members are allowed to shop at a Warehouse Club location. The following is a description of the yearly member renewal process.

At or near the first day of each month, an accounts receivable clerk queries the membership database to identify those whose membership expires during the following month. For example, on January 1st a query is executed to identify memberships that expire during February. A membership renewal list is printed for use in preparing individual invoices and for documentation. Using the computer and the membership renewal list, an accounts receivable clerk prepares each individual invoice for members. This process automatically updates accounts receivable records. The computer prints two copies of the invoice. The original invoice is sent to the customer and the invoice copy is stored numerically in a filing cabinet. The membership list is also stored in a filing cabinet, but is filed according to the date. When payment checks are received they are immediately processed. First, a copy is made and stored alphabetically in customer files. Next, account receivable records are updated and customers are given another year of shopping privileges. Finally at the end of the day, checks are endorsed and deposited in the bank.

Required

Prepare a flowchart of this process.

LO5   A7.   Convenient Computing Associates (CCA) operates a mailing-order operation and sells a vast array of computer products and accessories. The following is a description of Convenient Computing's collection process:

The policy of CCA is to collect all accounts receivable as quickly as possible. CCA encourages prompt payment by sending reminder statements at the end of each month and calling customers whose balance is more than 30 days past due. On the last working day of the month, the accounts receivable clerk prints a statement for each customer showing a balance due on their account. Statements are automatically generated by a computer which maintains the accounts receivable files and records. The original statement is mailed to the customer and a copy of the statement is filed alphabetically according to customer last name. On the 15th and the last day of the month, the accounts receivable clerk prints an open accounts receivable aging report by customer.

The clerk calls the customer on all invoices more than 30 days past due. The purpose of the call is to verify the accuracy of the invoice data. If the information is correct, a polite reminder is given to encourage prompt payment. The open receivable report is marked with the clerk's initials and the date the call was made, and filed by date when all calls are complete.

Required

Prepare a flowchart of this process.

LO5   A8.   Wiltex Research is a company that performs energy research on a contract basis for major oil and chemical companies. The following narrative describes the process to acquire materials for research projects.

A project manager determines the materials needed for a project and purchases them from a vendor. The project manager completes a purchase order for each piece of materials. A catalogue price is used, or the vendor is contacted by telephone to determine the price. The purchase order has an original and two copies (Copy #1 and Copy #2). The project manager sends the purchase order to the project supervisor for approval/disapproval. The project manager writes "approved" or "disapproved" on the purchase order, signs it, and returns it to the project manager. The project manager sends the original copy of approved purchase orders to the vendor; sends Copy #1 to the accounting clerk; and files Copy #2 in a permanent project file (ordered numerically by project number). Disapproved purchase orders are thrown in the garbage can by the project manager. The accounting clerk files Copy #1 in a temporary file (numeric by PO#).   The project manager receives and inspects materials sent from the vendor and compares them to the packing slip. The packing slip is sent to the accounting clerk as evidence that the materials have been received. The accounting clerk matches the packing slip with the Copy #1 of the purchase order and prepares a check (which has an original and one copy). The check is attached to the packing slip and Copy #1 of the purchase order is sent to the project supervisor for a signature. Once signed, the entire set of documents is returned to the accounting clerk who sends the original copy of the check to the vendor, and files the copy of the check with the supporting documentation attached to it in a permanent file (ordered numerically by check number).

Required

Prepare a flowchart of this process.

CHAPTER 4

Enterprise System Risks and Controls

LEARNING OBJECTIVES

Before we discuss REA modeling at the business process level, we need to consider risks and controls. This area is a consideration of utmost importance for enterprise system designers, managers, and auditors. Because the task level system documentation techniques discussed in chapter 3 represent the physical activities associated with capturing, storing, maintaining, and reporting data for enterprises, managers and auditors often use them to help assess enterprise risk and evaluate control. Managers and auditors also consider other sources of information regarding risks and controls.

In this chapter we discuss some types of enterprise risk and means by which enterprise system controls may mitigate such risks. We introduce selected regulations and authoritative guidance including Sarbanes Oxley, PCAOB Auditing Standard #5, the International Federation of Accountants International Standards on Auditing (ISA) 315 and 330, the ISACA's COBIT framework and the Committee of Sponsoring Organizations' (COSO) Internal Control – Integrated Framework. We also demonstrate how the REA ontology may be used as a framework for business process risk identification. After studying this chapter you should be able to:

1. Describe the relationship between enterprise risks, opportunities, and controls
2. Describe the various legislations and authoritative guidance related to enterprise risk and control
3. Explain the levels at which enterprise risks occur
4. Use the REA ontology to identify some common sources of enterprise risk
5. Identify the three primary types of control objectives and five components of internal control recommended by COSO
6. Identify specific controls commonly used in enterprises to prevent, detect, and recover from enterprise risks

THE RELATIONSHIPS BETWEEN RISKS, OPPORTUNITIES, AND CONTROLS

Risk
A **risk** is any chance of injury or loss. **Exposure** is uncontrolled risk, i.e., the potential impact of a threat of loss on an enterprise. Every enterprise faces a multitude of risks. If a risk materializes it threatens some aspect of the entities' operations and more serious risks threaten the ongoing existence of the entity. Every day the news is filled with examples of risks that have developed into major losses, scandals, or total collapses of enterprises. **Threat** is another word some people use to describe these situations because they represent a possible or probable loss to the entity.

The following are just a few examples of risks or threats that have plagued many companies:

- Bad decisions by management to discontinue popular product lines
- Faulty product design that causes costly recalls
- Fabrication of product quality tests to enhance the value of the company's stock
- Invasion of a company's network by hackers through the Internet
- Recognition of revenues a company has not actually earned
- Overstatement of inventory or operating assets on a company's balance sheet
- Understatement or misclassification of debt on a company's balance sheet

Every time one of these risks materializes, critics ask, "Why?" They criticize management for lack of due care. They criticize the auditors for not detecting the problem. Questions are always asked about how such a thing could happen within the enterprise and not be noticed by other people. Risks need to be identified and controlled, but they must be balanced with opportunities, objectives, and the cost of controls. Enterprises must balance operational efficiency with operational effectiveness. Enterprise information systems may sometimes facilitate efficient and effective controls.

Opportunity

Why do individuals and enterprises take risks? Why expose themselves to threats of loss? **Opportunity** (the potential for reward) and risk go hand in hand. You can't have an opportunity without some risk and with most risks there is potential opportunity. Typically greater opportunities are accompanied by higher risks, and vice versa. For example, investments in stock are generally riskier than investments in government bonds; those stock investments also provide the potential for greater returns than do the bonds. Individual and enterprise objectives determine the extent to which risks will be sought or avoided. Conservative objectives that can be easily achieved require less risk. More aggressive objectives create greater risk as more difficult and complex activities are pursued to achieve them. As an example, say you have $10,000 available to invest, and you do not need this money back until after you retire 40 years from now. If over the course of those 40 years your goal is to simply double your money for a total of $20,000 then there is no need to invest in risky investments, as investments that are considered "risk-free" are likely to double your money in 40 years. If your objectives are more aggressive; for example, to increase your $10,000 by 500%, then you will need to consider more risky investments that have a higher potential return. With every opportunity there is some element of risk. We seek to manage these risks by a system of controls.

Control

To mitigate the risk of loss while gaining the advantages afforded by risky activity, most enterprises implement a system of **internal controls**: activities performed to minimize or eliminate risks. For example, a control to mitigate the risk of stock market investments is to maintain a diversified portfolio rather than holding only one company's stock. Similarly, an enterprise that sells goods on credit rather than requiring immediate cash payment for sales creates an opportunity for additional sales, but also incurs a risk of bad debts. An internal control that may be adopted to mitigate this risk is to check customers' credit ratings before approving sales to the customers.

Cost/Benefit of Controls

Two major concerns regarding controls are the time they consume and the cost. Often multiple controls could each mitigate a particular risk; sometimes the controls differ in terms of cost and effectiveness. So many potential risks exist that it may seem overwhelming to try to control all of them. It may also be cost prohibitive to control every potential risk. Only significant risks for which controls are cost effective should be controlled. The significance of a risk is determined by (a) its impact on the enterprise, and (b) the likelihood of it occurring. *Exposure* is a word some people use to describe the potential impact on the entity, i.e. uncontrolled risk. Some people also use the term risk in a more narrow sense to describe the probability of a loss occurring. Risks that prevent an enterprise from achieving its objectives are very costly and may have a catastrophic impact on the on-going viability of the entity. **Materiality of risk** (i.e. how significantly will risk affect the firm's financial statements) illustrated in Exhibit 4-1, is a function of:

1.   The size of the potential loss and its impact on achieving the enterprise's objectives
2.   The likelihood of the loss

Exhibit 4-1 Materiality of Risk

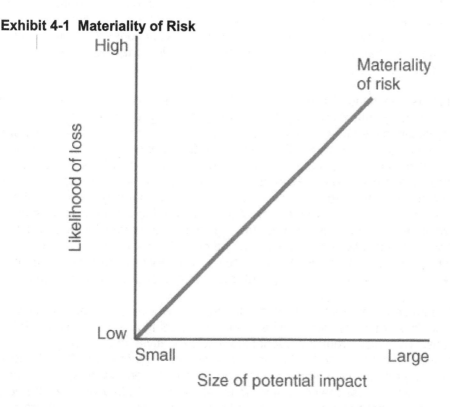

As either the likelihood or size of the loss increases, the materiality of the risk also increases. With higher materiality comes a greater need to manage risk. In many situations these evaluations can only be measured in rough, order-of-magnitude amounts.

Management may choose to ignore risks that have a low impact and a low likelihood of occurrence except those for which controls are costless. Controlling all risks to the point of eliminating all potential losses is quite unrealistic and unnecessary. In fact, a commitment to "zero risk" could leave an enterprise totally ineffective since many controls add inconvenience to business processes. Enterprises typically concentrate their control design efforts on risks that have a high impact and a high likelihood of occurrence. Many enterprises choose to purchase insurance to mitigate risks that have a high impact and a low likelihood of occurrence. For risks that have a low impact and a high likelihood of occurrence, management will design controls only if the cumulative costs of the controls are less than the cumulative probable losses based on the risk. The key is identifying and controlling risks in a manner such that the benefits of controlling the risks exceed the costs of the controls, while balancing enterprise efficiency and effectiveness.

REGULATIONS AND AUTHORITATIVE GUIDANCE FOR INTERNAL CONTROL SYSTEMS

Internal controls within enterprise systems are increasingly important in today's economy. In 2002 as a response to several corporate collapses and scandals involving nontransparent and fraudulent financial statements, Congress passed the Sarbanes-Oxley Act, commonly referred to as SOX. SOX is a U.S. federal law intended to reinstate the trust of investors and the general public. SOX holds all executives of publicly traded companies accountable for the accuracy and completeness of all financial information released by those companies. SOX is a lengthy law; it consists of eleven titles, each of which contains sections. We won't discuss every section in this book; rather, we will focus on those most important for enterprise accounting systems.

Title I of SOX includes Sections 101 through 108. The most notable component of this title is the establishment of the **Public Company Accounting Oversight Board (PCAOB)**. PCAOB is a nonprofit organization intended to monitor public accounting firms to be sure they are conducting high quality audits. Section 103 gives PCAOB authority to set standards for auditing, quality control, and ethics relating to audit reports. Sections 104 and 105 give the SEC limited jurisdiction to oversee the PCAOB; however, the SEC is prohibited from controlling the PCAOB's inspections and special investigations of public accounting firms. Title II of SOX has nine sections (201-209) that detail the regulation of auditor independence. Title III of SOX contains eight sections (301-308) and lays out the regulations for corporate responsibility – especially holding chief executive officers (CEOs) and chief financial officers (CFOs) accountable by requiring them to certify the accuracy of all financial reports filed with the SEC and to verify the effectiveness of a company's internal controls and to report any changes.

Title IV of SOX regulates enhanced financial disclosures. These nine sections (401-409) require all material financial transactions to be reported, including adjustments and off-balance sheet transactions. They also prohibit personal loans to executives and require disclosure of insider stock trades and outline a code of ethics for senior financial officers. **SOX Section 404** is perhaps of most importance with respect to enterprise information systems, as that section requires management to assess the company's internal controls. Title V of SOX attempts to eliminate conflicts of interest between analysts and companies and between analysts and investment bankers. The goal is to ensure analyst reports are unbiased, therefore protection is provided for analysts who issue negative reports. Title VI expands the SEC's power and enables it to obtain the resources it needs to effectively oversee auditors and audit firms. Title VII authorizes the creation of studies and reports to improve SOX compliance. Title VIII imposes criminal penalties and extends the statute of limitations for **fraud** (intentional efforts to cause harm to an enterprise), including falsification or destruction of financial records and auditors' failure to maintain records for the five-year minimum. Title VIII also facilitates reports of whistle-blowers and protects them from retaliation. Title IX increases criminal penalties for mail and wire fraud and other white-collar crimes and establishes penalties for executives who

REA Accounting Systems: Resources-Events-Agents: An ontology for designing, controlling, and using integrated enterprise systems

109

do not certify the accuracy of the company's financial reports. Title X requires CEOs to sign corporate tax returns. Title XI expands the SEC's powers to combat and investigate fraud by enabling the SEC to freeze payments. This title also prohibits people who have been convicted of fraud-related activities from being executives.

The **PCAOB's Auditing Standard #5** (AS5) provides a comprehensive and rigorous expectation of the responsibilities of auditors involved in an engagement that includes both audits of a company's financial statements and of the company's management's assessment of the effectiveness of internal control over financial reporting. In such engagements, auditors' focus on internal control is doubly important as observed weaknesses in the company's internal control over financial reporting not only inform the auditors' evaluation of managements' assessments about that system but also affect the extent of detailed testing the auditors will need to formulate an opinion to issue on the conformance of the company's financial reports with generally accepted accounting principles. AS5 takes a top-down, risk-based approach and provides a framework for best practices such as automating internal controls, training, and using internal resources to apply audit work. Other standards and regulations such as the AICPA's AT501 and IFAC's ISA315 and ISA 330 have recognized the value of and have attempted to maintain consistency with AS5. Similarly, the Auditing Standards Board issued Statement on Auditing Standards (SAS) 115: *Communicating Internal Control Related Matters Identified in an Audit* (which replaces SAS 112), recommending a more risk-based approach that is intended to be more effective and less expensive to implement. **SAS 94**: *The Effect of Information Technology on the Auditor's Consideration of Internal Control in a Financial Statement Audit* and **SAS 109**: *Understanding the Entity and its Environment and Assessing the Risks of Material Misstatements,* also provide guidance for auditors with respect to internal controls, information technology, and risk.

While this flurry of regulatory activity occurred in the 2000s, it is noteworthy that these standards and regulations primarily direct company managers and auditors to follow the *Internal Control - Integrated Framework* that was issued by COSO[1] in 1992. The **Committee Of Sponsoring Organizations (COSO)** is a joint initiative of the American Accounting Association, the American Institute of CPAs, Financial Executives International, the IMA (Association of Accountants and Financial Professionals in Business) and the Institute of Internal Auditors. COSO formed the 1985 Treadway Commission in response to the 1977 Foreign Corrupt Practices Act that required all companies whose securities were listed in the United States to maintain adequate internal control systems. The Treadway Commission's meetings resulted in a recommendation for the development of a common definition for internal control, ways to improve internal control, and guidance for evaluating internal controls' effectiveness. The next seven years were spent drafting a report that included those definitions and guidance; the result was COSO's 1992 *Internal Control – Integrated Framework*. COSO has continued to provide guidance over the past two decades; COSO states its goal as "to provide thought leadership dealing with three interrelated subjects: enterprise risk management (ERM), internal control, and fraud deterrence." Consistent with that goal, COSO published *Enterprise Risk Management – Integrated Framework* in 2004, *Internal Control over Financial Reporting – Guidance for Smaller Public Companies* in 2006, *Guidance on Monitoring Internal Control Systems* in 2009, *Fraudulent Financial Reporting 1987-1997* and *Fraudulent Financial Reporting 1998-2007*. COSO has also issued several thought papers regarding these publications.

---

[1]Internal Control – Integrated Framework (New York: Committee of Sponsoring Organizations of the Treadway Commission, 1992.)

Whereas COSO began as a framework for financial controls and has gradually added emphases on information technology, security, and risk management, **Control Objectives for Business and Information Technology (COBIT)** began as a framework for IT controls and has gradually added emphases on enterprise governance and risk. The first version of COBIT was issued in 1996; that has undergone several revisions and the most recent version COBIT 5 (currently in exposure draft status with expected publication in 2012) integrates concepts from COBIT 4.1 with its former Val IT governance, Risk IT, and IT Audit frameworks and also with its Business Model for Information Security. If you are reading this textbook prior to 2012, the exposure drafts for *COBIT 5 The Framework* and *COBIT 5 Process Reference Guide* may be downloaded at www.isaca.org. Both COBIT 5 and COSO are valuable and complementary frameworks.

Although more than two decades have passed since COSO's *Internal Control – Integrated Framework* was published, the three types of objectives and five control components outlined therein remain relevant and intact. The more recent documents listed in the previous paragraph provide additional guidance but do not change the underlying framework. COSO is currently updating the Internal Control – Integrated Framework; expected completion date is mid-2012. COSO has indicated most of the changes involve guidance for the rapidly changing technologies in business and remain resolute that the three objectives and five control components are timeless. If you are reading this book after mid-2012, see www.coso.org for updates. COSO makes executive summaries of its frameworks available to read at no charge and has the full frameworks available for purchase.

COSO OBJECTIVES AND COMPONENTS OF INTERNAL CONTROL SYSTEMS

The COSO report lists three primary objectives of internal control system: to ensure (1) efficient and effective operations, (2) reliable financial reporting, and (3) compliance with laws and regulations. With those three objectives in mind, COSO's recommended framework consists of five essential components: (1) the control environment, (2) risk assessment, (3) control activities, (4) information and communications, and (5) monitoring. As noted earlier, these objectives and components are likely timeless; what will change is their application to ever-changing advances in business and technology. We discuss each component in turn.

The COSO ICIF is often presented as a cube that depicts the five components across each of the three objectives and within all organizational units and activities. See Exhibit 4-2.

Exhibit 4-2 The COSO Internal Control Integrated Framework, aka the COSO Cube

Control Environment

A company's **control environment** sets the tone of the enterprise, which influences the control consciousness of its people. Some people refer to the control environment as "the tone at the top"; however, notice it forms the bottom layer of the COSO Cube. That is because the control environment is the foundation that provides discipline and structure upon which all other components of internal control are built. The control environment includes the following areas[2]:

a. Integrity, ethical values and competence of the enterprise's people
b. Management philosophy and operating style
c. The way in which management assigns authority and responsibility and in which it organizes and develops its people
d. The attention and direction provided by the board of directors

The attitudes and actions of top management largely determine the climate of an enterprise. Consider the environment of one enterprise with a top management who has very high standards of moral and ethical conduct, who is committed to hiring competent people and properly training them for their work, who develops an organizational structure where the work of one person is checked by the work of another person, and who is conservative in their management style and financial reporting. Contrast this with the climate of a second enterprise in which top management constantly tries to take unfair advantage of their employees, in which its people are poorly trained, in which employees' work is poorly defined, and in which management constantly tries to overstate their achievements and minimize their problems. Since the attitudes and actions of lower level employees typically mirror the attitudes and actions they see in top management, we would expect to find a strong control environment in the first enterprise but a rather weak control environment in the second enterprise.

Within the control environment, management should assess threats to the achievement of its desired objectives and should take reasonable actions to minimize those threats. Management must establish and enforce appropriate policies and procedures that foster shared values and teamwork. These policies and procedures should specifically include effectively communicated anti-fraud expectations. An especially eloquent phrase by COSO says "The effectiveness of internal controls cannot rise above the integrity and ethical values of the people who create, administer and monitor them.[3]"

Risk Assessment

Risk assessment is an element of an internal control system that involves the identification and analysis of relevant risks associated with the enterprise achieving its objectives. Risk assessment forms the basis for determining what risks need to be controlled and the controls required to manage them.

Risk assessment should include consideration of previous company losses and the reasons for those losses, consideration of similar companies' losses and reasons for those losses, and communication with employees as to where errors and irregularities are most likely to occur. An historical analysis of past errors and irregularities identifies potential future losses and provides information by which both the probability and the magnitude of the loss may be estimated. Much can also be learned by analyzing other companies' mistakes by examining

---

[2] Guidance on Monitoring Internal Control Systems Volume II: Application (New York: Committee of Sponsoring Organizations of the Treadway Commission, 2009.)

[3] Guidance on Monitoring Internal Control Systems Volume II: Application, page B-2 (New York: Committee of Sponsoring Organizations of the Treadway Commission, 2009.)

information available directly from the company or through published literature. Most employees are honest and want to do a good job. They know where errors and irregularities have occurred and have not been reported, and they know where irregularities could occur and not easily be detected. Effective communication with employees may reveal critical information needed for risk assessment.

Risk assessment should include consideration of potential fraud schemes as well as financial reporting risks, selection of appropriate accounting principles, IT issues, and business process risks.

Control Activities

Control activities are policies and procedures enterprises use to ensure necessary actions are taken to minimize risks associated with achieving enterprise objectives. Controls have various objectives and may be applied at various organizational and functional levels.

Control activities may be classified as to whether they are used to prevent, detect, or recover from errors or irregularities. The purpose of each control is evident by its name.
- **Preventive controls** focus on preventing errors or irregularities.
- **Detective controls** focus on identifying that errors or irregularities have occurred.
- **Corrective controls** focus on recovering from, repairing the damage from, or minimizing the cost of errors or irregularities.

An **error** is an unintended mistake on the part of an employee while an **irregularity** is an intentional effort to do something that is undesirable to the enterprise. Often our attention is focused too much on irregularities; but more money is lost as a result of errors than is lost as a result of irregularities.

It is better to prevent an error or irregularity rather than detect it and then have to incur the cost of recovering from the consequences. However, preventive controls are not always possible or cost-effective and it is important to have a means for determining if the prevention has been effective; therefore detective and corrective controls are also needed. As an example, a control to prevent theft of cash by a sales clerk is to have a second clerk assist with each cash sale. Collusion, two or more people acting together or conspiring to commit fraud, may cause this preventive control to fail. Another preventive control that lessens the possibility of collusion is to eliminate the use of cash entirely, instead requiring all payments to be made with a credit card or through an electronic fund transfer. The latter preventive control may not be cost effective. The costs include the transaction costs associated with using credit cards and electronic funds transfers (sellers who accept credit cards pay fees to the credit card companies) and the opportunity costs associated with lost revenues from customers who do not want to pay with credit cards or electronic fund transfers. If the enterprise weighs these costs against the benefit of preventing employee theft, the enterprise may conclude it is an undesirable control. Therefore the enterprise may implement one or more detective and corrective controls to back up the preventive control and ensure its effectiveness. For example, as the sales clerk(s) Scanning items sold and pricing them automatically by the cash register, along with a rule that requires a comparison of the cash in the cash drawer with total sales accumulated by the cash register during an employee's shift, is an example of a detective control. If the cash in the cash drawer does not equal total sales, we know the employee either pocketed some of the money, or made an error in giving change to a customer. An example of a corrective control is a policy of deducting the amount of a cash shortage from the employee's pay.

REA Accounting Systems: Resources-Events-Agents: An ontology for designing, controlling, and using integrated enterprise systems

113

Information and Communication

The **information and communication** element of the COSO framework provides guidance as to enterprise information systems and the distribution of information from the systems to the people who need it. The information system consists of the methods and records used to record, maintain, and report the events of an entity, as well as to maintain accountability for the related assets, liabilities, and equity. The quality of system-generated information affects management's ability to make appropriate decisions in managing and controlling the entity's activities and to prepare reliable financial reports.

The information system should do each of the following to provide accurate and complete information in the accounting system and correctly report the results of operations.

1. Identify and record all business events on a timely basis.

2. Describe each event in sufficient detail.

3. Measure the proper monetary value of each event.

4. Determine the time period in which events occurred.

5. Present properly the events and related disclosures in the financial statements.

The communication aspect of this component deals with providing an understanding of individual roles and responsibilities pertaining to internal controls. People should understand how their activities relate to the work of others and how exceptions should be reported to higher levels of management. Open channels for communication help ensure that exceptions are reported and acted upon, and ensure support of the company's anti-fraud expectations. Communication also includes the policy manuals, accounting manuals, and financial reporting manuals. Both internal and external communications of the company are important, especially as communications about companies are becoming increasingly public as a result of technologies such as Twitter, Facebook, and Google-Plus. Company management should take special care to train all personnel as to what types of external communications are appropriate.

Monitoring

Monitoring is the process of assessing the quality of internal control performance over time. This is extremely important as most enterprises are constantly changing their operations to meet new demands in the market place and capitalize on new opportunities. Monitoring involves assessing the design and operation of controls on a timely basis and taking corrective actions as needed. This process is accomplished by ongoing monitoring activities by management as they question reports that differ significantly from their knowledge of operations. Internal auditors or system evaluators also accomplish it through periodic evaluations to review internal controls, evaluate their effectiveness, report their results, and provide recommendations for improvement. Information from external entities is also valuable in monitoring internal controls. Complaints by customers or suppliers about billings or payments, reviews by various governmental agencies, and reports by external auditors all provide information on the adequacy of internal controls and how to improve them. A company's monitoring process should include an evaluation and report of any deficiencies in the company's anti-fraud program and should provide details of any fraud occurrences.

Performance reviews are any assessments of an enterprise's performance that provide a means for monitoring. Some of the more common reviews compare actual data to budgeted or prior period data, operating data to financial data, and data within and across various units, subdivisions, or functional areas of the enterprise. An example of a performance review is a comparison of actual production costs of the current period to last period's production costs to identify any significant deviation. Any cost category that deviates significantly from last year should be investigated so the cause may be identified. Another example is a comparison of the dollar value for sales within each region of an enterprise to the quantity of inventory shipped to each region to determine whether the ratio of sales to quantity shipped is similar for each region. If a region's ratio is lower than others, the cause should be investigated – it could be due to theft, damaged inventory, or some other explanation.

EVALUATION OF INTERNAL CONTROL SYSTEMS
The COSO report recommends that evaluation of internal control systems focus first on risk identification, next on identification of mitigating controls, and finally on tests to determine whether the controls are operating effectively. The increased monitoring and attestation regarding internal control systems recommended by COSO and demanded by the Sarbanes-Oxley Act is facilitated by business process and information system designers similarly focusing on risk identification, development of cost-beneficial mitigating controls that can be designed into the business process and/or into the supporting information systems, and then implementation of those controls.

RISK IDENTIFICATION
Enterprise risks occur at several levels: economy, industry, enterprise, business process, and information process. Table 4-1 illustrates these levels and lists some types of risk at each level. Keep in mind that the risks identified in Table 4-1 are not a comprehensive list. In fact, a comprehensive list is impossible because the environment, technology, and people are constantly changing and new risks continually arise. Also please realize that the categorization of risks is not an exact science. Overlaps may sometimes make it difficult to distinguish an economy risk from an industry risk, an industry risk from an enterprise risk, etc. The most important objective is for you to recognize the risks as potential threats of loss, whether they are economy wide, industry, enterprise, business process, or information process risks. You must apply critical thinking for risk identification; however, this framework will provide guidance for your thinking.

Economy and Industry Risks
Enterprises do not operate in a vacuum; they operate in an industry that is part of a local economy and also part of the overall global economy. Failure to consider local and global economy risks and industry risks and to adequately address those risks may prove disastrous for enterprises. **Economy risks** are threats to an entire economy; examples include those resulting from war, epidemics, financial market changes, terrorist attacks, and natural disasters such as floods, hurricanes, and drought. Many of these factors can lead to global economic downturn. Sometimes economy risks particularly devastate selected industries and thereby become industry risks. **Industry risks** are those that affect an entire industry. For example, the terrorist attacks of September 11, 2001 contributed to global economic downturn, but were especially damaging to certain industries such as travel and tourism. Another type of industry risk is widespread cost increases that particularly affect a specific industry. For example, if the cost of raw materials that are used intensively in an industry increases significantly, the entire industry is negatively affected. A sudden increase in a product's price may lead to a sudden decrease in demand for that product. Decreased product demand is an industry risk that is sometimes independent of price increases. Such decreases may result from simple trend shifts (e.g. the popularity of fad products is ever-changing) or from the development of superior replacement products developed in another industry (e.g. many years ago the invention of the

telephone replaced much of the demand for telegraph and personal messenger services. More recently, cell phones replaced the need for most – but not all – pagers and two-way radios, aka walkie talkies).

Table 4-1: Risk Identification Levels

Economy risks	Risks associated with factors that affect the entire economy e.g. Global economic downturns Wars Epidemics Terrorist attacks Environmental disasters (floods, hurricanes, etc.)
Industry risks	Risks associated with factors that affect the enterprise's industry e.g. Industry-wide cost increases Industry-wide decrease in demand for products economy risk especially bad for a specific industry unexpected competition from another industry
Enterprise risks	External factors e.g. Increased competition from other enterprises Reduction of perceived brand quality and/or firm reputation Crises involving business partners (value system relationships) Catastrophe that causes an interruption of operations Merger or acquisition involving another enterprise Internal factors e.g. Lack of ethics Low employee morale Employee incompetence
Business process risks	Risks associated with actual business process objects Resources (R's) Events (E's) Agents (A's) Resource-Event relationships Event-Event relationships Event-Agent relationships Resource-Agent relationships
Information process risks	Risks associated with Recording information about R's, E's and A's Maintaining information about R's, E's and A's Reporting information about R's, E's and A's

Enterprise Risks

Enterprise risks reflect potential threats of loss to the enterprise as a result of internal and external factors that result from the actions or circumstances of the enterprise itself or of one of its external business partners. Internal risk factors include such threats as low employee morale, lack of ethics in the enterprise, and employee incompetence. These internal risk factors are largely determined by management's philosophy and operating style, therefore interviews with management may identify the extent to which these risk factors represent a concern. If management's philosophy and operating style encourage a high-risk environment, greater risk also exists at the business process and information process levels. Questions that may help to identify a high-risk environment include:

- Is the enterprise committed to hiring competent people who possess the knowledge and skills needed to perform their assigned jobs?

- Does management have a conservative or reasonable approach in accepting business risks and in reporting the financial results of operations?
- If there is a board of directors, are there outside representatives on the board?
- If the entity undergoes an annual audit of their financial statements, does it have an audit committee to oversee the audit?
- Does the company have a well defined organizational structure with appropriate division of duties and responsibilities and identified reporting relationships so that important activities are planned, executed, controlled, and monitored on a timely basis?
- Do employees understand the company's policies and practices, what they are individually responsible for, and to whom they report?
- Has management developed a culture that emphasizes integrity and ethical behavior?
- Does the enterprise have a "whistleblower" policy that encourages employees to inform management or the board of directors of fraudulent activities observed in the firm's operations?

Enterprises that can answer these questions in the affirmative likely have favorable control environments. Enterprises that have not taken these and similar steps to encourage integrity and competence face a high degree of internal enterprise risk.

Enterprise risk also results from external factors such as increased competition from other enterprises within the industry, loss of perceived brand quality or firm reputation, catastrophes that cause business interruptions, crises involving one or more of the enterprise's external business partners, and risks resulting from mergers or acquisitions. Increased competition may lower the enterprise's market share. Events that cause a perceived loss of brand quality or firm reputation (e.g. if quality control fails to prevent a defective batch of products from being sold and the market generalizes the problem to all of the firms' products) may result in long-term negative consequences for the enterprise. All enterprises face some risk of business interruption due to catastrophes such as fire, flood, tornado, power outages, or technology failures. All enterprises also face risks that one or more of its external business partners may experience a business interruption catastrophe that will in turn cause a threat to the enterprise. For example, a warehouse fire that destroys a key supplier's entire inventory and interrupts the supplier's business for several months may cause the enterprise to be unable to fulfill customer orders until an alternative source is found. Another external enterprise risk enterprises sometimes face is involvement in a business combination such as a merger or acquisition. While a voluntary business combination may appear to be an attractive option during negotiations, sometimes plans fail to consider all circumstances and unexpected negative consequences result. The risk of such a consequence is an enterprise risk.

Business Process Risks
Because the REA pattern represents the reality of an enterprise's business processes, it provides a useful framework to help system designers, managers, and auditors identify business process risks. In this section we provide some examples of risks specific to resource, events, agents, and various relationships in the REA pattern for business processes. The examples in this section do not provide a comprehensive list of business process risks; indeed a comprehensive list cannot exist because as controls for known risks are developed, additional means for misappropriating enterprise assets and misstating results of operations for enterprises are also being created that existing controls may not sufficiently mitigate. Thus, although the REA pattern provides a useful framework, we discourage students from adopting a checklist mentality when considering risks (and controls).

REA Accounting Systems: Resources-Events-Agents: An ontology for designing, controlling, and using integrated enterprise systems

117

Business process risks are defined for this textbook as risks associated with actual business process objects, including resources, events, agents, and relationships among resources, events, and agents. Some of the resources most commonly found in enterprises are inventory, supplies, operating assets, and cash. Risks associated with resources include threats associated with theft or loss, obsolescence, waste, and damage (either intentional or unintentional). Risks associated with events include failure to execute an event that should occur, execution of an event that should not occur, or executing an event at the wrong time (too soon or too late).

Most risks do not involve resources or events in isolation, but rather involve some combination of resources, events, and/or agents. Risks associated with resource-to-event relationships include execution of an event involving an incorrect resource, an incorrect quantity of a resource, or an incorrect cost or price for a resource. Risks associated with resource-to-resource relationships include an incorrectly specified correspondence of one resource to another resource. An example is a bill of materials for a finished good inventory type that specifies an incorrect raw material or an incorrect quantity of a raw material. The primary risk associated with event-to-event relationships is incorrect sequencing of corresponding events. For example, if a company has a policy requiring all sales to be accompanied by cash receipts (down payments) equal to at least 50% of the selling prices, a risk is that a sale will be accepted without receiving the required cash receipt. Similarly, a risk exists that a cash disbursement may be made without confirmation that goods were actually received for which the cash is disbursed.

Event-to-agent relationships in the REA enterprise ontology represent participation relationships linking internal and external agents to events. Risks include execution of events involving unauthorized external agents (e.g. sales made to non-existent customers) or unauthorized internal agents, (e.g. cash disbursements made by inventory clerks). Resource-to-agent relationships reflect custody arrangements (i.e. internal agents responsible for physical custody of a resource type); risks include unauthorized agents having custody of resources. Examination of single relationships is useful for risk identification; however, full risk analysis also requires simultaneous examination of multiple relationships. For example, queries may be formulated to evaluate whether linked purchase orders, purchases, and cash disbursements are all related to the same vendor. If not, there may be a data entry error or an irregularity that warrants investigation.

Information Process Risks
Information process risks are threats of loss associated with recording, maintaining, and reporting information about resources, events, agents, and relationships among them. On the surface, these risks may seem very similar to business process risks. The difference is that business process risks have to do with the actual execution of the events and the actual physical resources and agents. Information processing risks have to do with the information that gets recorded, maintained, and reported about those objects. For example, if a sale is made to a non-existent customer, it is a business process error. If a sale is actually made to an approved customer, but a data entry error is made such that it appears the sale is made to a non-existent customer, it is an information processing error. Information process risks include recording, maintaining, or reporting information that is incomplete, inaccurate, or invalid. Incomplete information reflects failure to record, maintain, or report information about resources, events, agents, or relationships. Inaccurate information reflects the recording, maintaining, and reporting of data that is incorrect as to the reality it represents. Invalid information reflects the recording, maintaining, and reporting of information about non-existent

resources, events, agents, or relationships. All of these types of information processing risks need to be controlled.

IDENTIFICATION OF MITIGATING CONTROLS

Once risks have been identified at the various levels of detail outlined in Table 3-1 for an enterprise, its management must identify and implement controls to mitigate those risks.

Controls for Economy and Industry Risks

You may be wondering what an enterprise could possibly do to shield itself from economy and industry risks. These risks can be very difficult, if not impossible, to control. One control that is likely to be cost effective is the gathering and monitoring of enough information to be able to predict trends and product replacements. Enterprises that focus inwardly and tend to ignore the environment in which they operate are likely to be caught unaware by economy and industry risks. Enterprises that focus outwardly and pay attention to industry and economy trends and market demands are likely to be prepared for most shifts in prices and quantities at the economy and industry levels.

Controls for Enterprise Risks

Like economy and industry risks, external enterprise risks are often difficult to predict and identify and are therefore difficult to control. Constant analysis and awareness of the external environment may help enterprises anticipate and prepare for increased competition. Strong commitment to quality and extra quality control procedures may help to prevent loss of perceived brand quality or firm reputation; effective responsiveness to the market in case of a quality problem may help to correct any loss of perceived brand quality or firm reputation (possibly at the expense of a short-term financial loss). For example, it may cost a manufacturer a significant dollar amount to recall a production run of a defective product and replace the products at no cost to the customers; however, the cost of not recalling and replacing the products would likely result in a much more costly loss of perceived brand quality and firm reputation. Enterprises may purchase insurance to mitigate some external risks such as business interruptions caused by natural disasters or computer disruptions such as hard disk crashes or attacks by hackers, viruses, or worms. Companies may also create contingency plans such that in case of business interruptions operations may be transferred to a backup location. A **contingency plan** is a set of procedures to enact if a disaster occurs. Business interruptions of external business partners are more difficult to insure. A supplier whose warehouse burned down may have insurance to replace lost inventory, but usually that insurance does not compensate the supplier's customer who lost money because the inventory was not available when it needed to be issued to the production floor. To help mitigate such risks, enterprises should consider identifying multiple sources for each type of raw material or merchandise inventory they use in their conversion and revenue processes.

Many of the controls for enterprise risks form management's philosophy and operating style. Some high level policies that contribute to a well-controlled enterprise include sound human resource policies and practices. Human capital is often considered to be the most important resource of many enterprises. However, employees who are mismatched with their job responsibilities or who are not managed properly may become more of a liability than a resource. Human resource policies and practices relate to hiring, orienting, training, evaluating, counseling, promoting, compensating, and terminating employees.

Sound personnel practices are essential in controlling both operating activities and information processes. This is becoming increasingly important as enterprises empower employees in an attempt to streamline operations and cut costs. The quality of an enterprise's employees directly influences the quality of the goods and services provided to the customers. Generally speaking, competent, trustworthy employees are more likely to help the enterprise create value. Controls that help ensure success in hiring and retaining quality employees include completion of background checks, full explanation of enterprise policies and procedures, clear definition of promotion and personal growth opportunities as well as termination policies, and clear definition of work schedules. Many enterprises have suffered significant losses at the hands of individuals who had histories of incompetence, fraud, or other dishonest acts. Simple background checks could have prevented these losses. The other controls mentioned are summarized in a phrase: effective communication with employees. Employees must understand what is expected of them and they must be equipped with the training and tools they need to meet those expectations. They also need to be very aware of the consequences of not meeting expectations.

Controls for Business Process Risks

Resource Controls
Some of the resources most commonly found in enterprises are inventory, supplies, operating assets, and cash. Risks associated with resources include threats associated with theft or loss, obsolescence, waste, and damage (either intentional or unintentional).

Separation of Duties
An important control principle for all types of resources is separation (or segregation) of duties. Effective **separation of duties** prohibits one employee from performing two or more of the following functions: authorization of transactions involving assets, custody of assets, record keeping, and reconciliation. Separating those functions reduces the opportunity for one employee to steal enterprise assets and to conceal the theft in the normal course of his or her work. Of course, **collusion** (two or more employees in different positions working together to perpetrate fraud) is still a risk even with separation of duties.

Resource Theft and Loss: Cash
Theft of resources is a rampant problem for many enterprises, costing billions of dollars worldwide every year. Because cash is the most liquid of all resources and is universally desirable, it is particularly susceptible to theft and enterprises need strict controls over those who have access to cash. Cash is most often stolen by employees, but could potentially be stolen by customers. **Physical access controls**, which are features, barriers, or procedures designed to prohibit unauthorized people from touching a resource, are especially important when the resource is cash. Currency should obviously be kept locked in a container to which only authorized employees have access. In the sales/collection process most enterprises keep cash in cash registers that may only be opened under certain circumstances. Control over the enterprise checkbook is especially important in the acquisition/payment, payroll, and financing processes, as access to the checkbook provides access to the cash in the checking account. **Bonding** of employees who handle cash is a form of insurance whereby if an employee with an adequate rating from the bonding (insurance) company is proven to have stolen cash from the enterprise, the bonding company recompenses the enterprise. Bonding is considered a corrective control. Just as the purchase of automobile insurance does not prevent a driver from being involved in a car accident, bonding does not prevent a seemingly trustworthy employee from deciding to steal cash from the company. The purpose for buying automobile insurance is so that if an accident occurs, the owner may be recompensed for the loss incurred. Similarly the purpose for bonding employees is so that if a theft occurs, the enterprise may be recompensed for the loss incurred.

Enterprises may take advantage of electronic funds transfers for cash transactions as a means of reducing theft. In electronic funds transfers-in, customers send cash receipts directly to the bank; the bank deposits the cash directly into the enterprise cash account. In electronic funds transfers-out, the enterprise authorizes the bank to directly transfer funds from the enterprise cash account to a designated vendor. Such transfers also ensure accuracy of record keeping because the transaction data is usually made available to be automatically input into the enterprise information system.

Case in Point

Most gas stations now allow customers to pay for gas at the pump. These pay-at-the-pump stations automatically bill the customer's credit card and eliminate the need for customers to pay a cashier. All the data about the gasoline sale event (e.g., customer's credit card information, type of gas, quantity, pump location, and station location) are recorded as the customer is pumping gas. Benefits include decreased time customers spend at the station, decreased number of employees needed to run the station, decreased data entry errors, and virtual elimination of nonpaying customers.

Lapping is a method of stealing cash that enterprises need to control. To accomplish lapping an employee steals cash from a customer payment and delays posting a payment to the customer's account. The employee uses funds from a subsequent customer payment to post to the first customer's account. This process continues with the employee continually stealing from subsequent customer payments to post as prior customer payments. Employees who engage in lapping often attempt to conceal the fraud by writing off as uncollectible customer accounts that have actually been paid. Eventually, lapping becomes so difficult to hide that the perpetrator leaves the company or the lapping is detected.

One of the most important detective controls with respect to cash and other assets are periodic **reconciliations of physical to recorded quantities**. Such reconciliations compare a physical count of the on-hand dollar values of the assets to the dollar values the information system reports as being on-hand. An example with which you are probably familiar is the monthly reconciliation of a bank statement. Bank statement reconciliation compares details of the inflows and outflows depicted on the bank statement with the details of the inflows and outflows for the same account as recorded in the enterprise information system. Discrepancies in the bank statement versus the records in the enterprise system may reveal fraudulent cash-related activities as well as bank or enterprise errors. An employee with no other cash responsibilities should perform the monthly reconciliation.

Case in Point

The bookkeeper for White Electric Company had sole responsibility for the company's checkbook and accounting records. Because of lax controls throughout the company, she felt justified in stealing cash from the company. Her method was quite simple and is illustrated with the following example. She received a vendor invoice for $10,000. She wrote check 5421 for the actual invoice amount of $10,000. However, in the check register she recorded check 5421 as $15,000. She then wrote check 5422 to herself for $5,000 but recorded it in the register as "Void". Because she herself performed the monthly bank reconciliation, no one realized what she was doing. Because inventory controls were also lax, apparently no one questioned why the recorded inventory costs were overstated. After guilt feelings overwhelmed her, the bookkeeper hired an attorney and confessed her crime to her employer. She had stolen approximately $150,000 and was sentenced to time in prison. Notice that the risk of her stealing from the company could have been prevented by adequate separation of duties, and could have been detected by requiring an alternative employee or manager perform the monthly bank reconciliation (because they would have noticed the mismatched check amounts on the bank statement as compared to the check register. Most current automated enterprise information systems also provide protection against this particular fraud scheme, because each check stub and entry into the check register are automatically generated to match the actual dollar amount of the check.

-Source: *Red Flags: What Every Manager Should Know about Internal Fraud*, video, Association of Certified Fraud Examiners, 1991.

Periodic counts of actual cash and reconciliation to account balances in the information system records (similar to bank statement reconciliation) help to detect theft or loss due to errors in petty and on-hand cash accounts such as those stored in cash registers.

Case in point

Fast food restaurant managers typically count each cash register drawer's contents before and after each cashier's shift. They compare the difference in cash to the sales rung up on the cash register to see if the amounts agree or if the cashier ended up with and overage (too much) or a shortage or (too little) cash in the drawer. Overages indicate errors by the cashier that cost the customers; shortages result either from theft or from errors by the cashier. Tracking discrepancies over time for each cashier reveals whether a cashier needs additional training or whether the enterprise should conduct additional surveillance to uncover theft by the cashier.

Resource Theft and Loss: Inventory, Supplies, and Operating Assets
Restriction of access to non-cash resources is the most common preventive control to reduce theft of those resources. In enterprises for which inventory, supplies, and operating assets are delivered to the enterprise via common carriers or suppliers, the receiving dock should be secured and the goods immediately transferred from the receiving dock to a locked storeroom or warehouse to which only authorized employees are allowed access. They may then be transferred to less secure environments as needed. In enterprises for which merchandise is sold via shipments (e.g. mail order catalog companies or internet stores), inventory is typically kept locked in the storeroom or warehouse with access limited to authorized employees. In other enterprises customers need to be able to physically examine inventory, so the inventory must be transferred to a less secure sales floor. For high value items, access is still often limited. For example, in retail stores, high priced items that are small enough to be easily stolen are typically kept in locked display cases and can only be examined by customers under the direct supervision of a sales representative. When supplies and operating assets are made

available to the business processes in which they are to be used up, their access should still be restricted when practical. For example, employee offices containing furniture, computer equipment, and other operating assets should be locked when not in use. Buildings in which offices are located should be locked during non-working hours. Precautions such as tagging each operating asset with a permanent id tag help to deter theft and to facilitate periodic counts of operating assets and reconciliation of the counts with the recorded assets on hand. As with cash, all enterprise resources should periodically be counted and the balances compared to the recorded balances in the enterprise information system. Discrepancies should be brought to management's attention.

Case in Point
Cook & Campbell, a construction firm for residential homes, was surprised to find they had one more vacant lot on their financial records than they actually owned at the end of their first year of operations. Upon closer examination they found they had constructed a home on one of the vacant lots and sold it without recording the sale of the lot on the financial records. The lot had actually been sold with the home, but the value of the lot was not included as they priced the home and it was not shown as part of cost of goods sold on the income statement. The anticipated $15,000 profit on the speculative home actually turned into a $20,000 loss as they corrected their mistake.

Supplies are the resources employees are most likely to steal from enterprises. Most supplies are small, relatively inexpensive, and easily mixed in with employees' personal supplies. Many employees don't consider personal use of enterprise supplies as theft; and some firms may view personal use of supplies by employees as acceptable. Enterprises that want to monitor supply use typically keep supplies locked in a cabinet, closet, or room that can only be opened under the watchful eye of an employee who is assigned custody of those assets. The enterprise may require documentation of what supplies were removed and by whom to help detect excessive or unnecessary use of supplies. Such procedures have become more important in recent years, as employees have developed personal needs for more expensive supplies such as printer toner, computer storage media, etc.

When people are made aware of detective controls, those detective controls may also serve as deterrents. They don't prevent all people from stealing; however, they may deter many people due to their fear of getting caught. One such primarily detective control that may also have secondary deterrent benefits to reduce resource theft is the use of surveillance equipment such as security cameras to identify theft or damage as or after they occur and to identify those responsible for theft or damage. Surveillance equipment is frequently used in the less secure environments such as the sales floor, and employee offices, but may also be used even in the more secure storerooms and warehouses.

Case in Point
Security control equipment is being used in retail stores at cash registers to prevent fraud and promote efficiency. Cash registers and video cameras are connected to, and controlled by, a computer. The computer maintains a record of each transaction and the amount of time the clerk takes to execute it. All clerk activities are videotaped. The computer provides summary statistics at the end of each shift with unusual transactions highlighted based on type or amount of time to execute. Security personnel review the videotape of selected transactions to determine if fraud was present or if a clerk needs additional training.

REA Accounting Systems: Resources-Events-Agents: An ontology for designing, controlling, and using integrated enterprise systems

123

Tracking the chain of custody of resources is a preventive and detective control for loss. Several technologies exist to assist with tracking the chain of custody of inventory. One is the application of barcodes to inventory and/or inventory containers and the subsequent scanning of the barcode labels as the inventory and/or inventory containers move throughout the enterprise's acquisition and sales processes. An example of the use of barcodes to track the location and chain of custody of assets with which you may be familiar is that offered by enterprises such as Federal Express and UPS. When you ship a package with one of these enterprises, a barcode is applied to the package. At each location, and when custody of the package changes hands, the barcode is scanned to update the database with the current status of the package in the chain of custody. To enhance customer service, these companies provide customers with tracking numbers that correspond to the barcodes applied to their packages. Customers may enter the tracking numbers on the company websites or via telephone to determine the location and status of the packages.

Radio frequency identification (RFID) tags are another type of technology available to track the chain of custody of resources. These tags communicate electronically with a reader via radio waves, thus eliminating the need to scan the tags with barcode readers. The readers are connected to a networked information system. Items or containers of items are automatically tracked as they move from location to location. Some envision these tags playing a role in future grocery shopping, allowing shoppers to simply associate their shopping cart with a debit or credit card; put desired items into bags in their carts and then leave the store with the merchandise. The readers would transmit details to the networked information system and the customer's debit or credit card vendor would be billed for the transaction total.

Resource Obsolescence and Waste

The risk of obsolescence is the likelihood of a resource becoming outdated or superseded by new products. This risk is particularly great for inventory, but is also a concern for some operating assets and supplies. Some types of resources are more susceptible to decreased value due to obsolescence than are other types of resources. To control the risk of obsolescence, enterprises need to avoid purchasing or producing more inventories, supplies, and operating assets than they expect to sell or use up in a reasonable timeframe. An integrated enterprise system can help to mitigate the risk of obsolescence by shortening the entire cycle from estimating demand for a product to acquiring the raw materials, manufacturing the product, selling the product, and collecting the cash.

Resource Damage: Inventory and Supplies

Another risk associated with resources is the risk of damage while in storage or while in transit. Damage could result from various causes, including a lack of climate control, inadequate packaging, careless handling, haphazard placement of inventory on storage shelves, etc. Well-communicated inventory storage and handling procedures and employee training of those procedures are one form of preventive control for such damage. Insurance is a corrective control; it will not necessarily prevent the damage from occurring but the firm will be compensated for the loss.

Event and Relationship Controls

Business and information process risks associated with events and the relationships in which they participate generally include

- failure to execute an event that should occur
- failure to record an event that did occur
- execution of an event that should not occur
- recording of an event that did not occur
- execution of an event at an incorrect time or location, or involving the incorrect resources and/or agents
- incorrect recording of event details (such as time, location, affected resources, and agents involved)

We next examine specific risks that fit into these general categories for each type of event in various business and information processes.

Instigation Event Risks and Controls

Some risks reduce the likelihood of the enterprise fulfilling its strategic and operational objectives with respect to its instigation events. Instigation events are those events that initiate the chain of events within each transaction cycle. For the revenue cycle, instigation events include marketing efforts, sales calls, and customer inquiries. Some examples of risk associated with such instigation events include:

- ☐ Failure to make potential customers aware of product features that would entice them to buy the product.
- ☐ Mistakes made in the advertising or promotions regarding the products or services available for sale.
- ☐ A sales call presentation to a customer including products the customer has no reason to be interested in, or for which they have previously declared no interest.
- ☐ Inability of customer making an inquiry to find the information they need about desired products or services.
- ☐ Inability to track which customer orders result from each separate marketing effort (tracking is desired in order to know which marketing efforts to continue, which to discontinue, which to further develop, etc.).
- ☐ Salespeople spending too much time with non-target customers, i.e. people who never buy anything or who don't buy enough to justify the time commitment of marketing personnel.
- ☐ Salespeople spending time doing unproductive things that do not influence potential customers.

In the acquisition cycle the most common instigation event is a purchase requisition. When a department supervisor identifies a need for a good or service and communicates that need to the Purchasing department, that communication is a purchase requisition. Some examples of risk associated with purchase requisition instigation events include:

- ☐ Failure to identify needs for resources in a timely manner.
- ☐ Requisitioning resources that are not actually needed by the enterprise or that do not have the features the enterprise needs.
- ☐ Inability to locate a reliable source from which to obtain needed items.
- ☐ Failure to approve a requisition for items for which need was appropriately identified.
- ☐ Requisitioning items for which they do not have available funding in their budgets.

This list is only a beginning; many risks exist that may inhibit an enterprise achieving its strategic and operational objectives for instigation events. The list of possible controls to mitigate risks associated with instigation events is even longer, thus we do not attempt to provide an exhaustive list. However, one major control is an effective enterprise information system. The more complete the design of the enterprise-wide database, the more information-related risks are mitigated. For example, if the database is designed in conformance with the REA pattern (and if data is entered correctly and completely) the enterprise will be able to track which instigation events lead to customer orders. Sales and marketing personnel should be able to run queries to effectively identify desirable customers and to help schedule their activities to minimize wasted time. The information system can also accurately report salespeople's activities. Merely recording and reporting the activities performed and the amount of time spent on each activity encourages effective use of time. Similarly, if production schedule data from the conversion cycle is integrated with the acquisition cycle, need for the raw materials involved in upcoming production runs can be communicated automatically. Such an information system can also integrate information linking departmental budgets to requisitions to determine whether funding is available or whether the proposed purchase will cause budget overruns.

Mutual Commitment Event Risks and Controls

Mutual commitment events in the REA ontology are those events that obligate the enterprise to participate in a future exchange with an external business partner that will result in one or more economic events that increase a resource and will also result in one or more economic events that decrease a resource. In the revenue and acquisition cycles, sale orders and purchase orders are the most common mutual commitment events. Risks associated with these events include:

- ☐ Failure to accept an order that both the enterprise and the potential customer would have been willing and able to fulfill.
- ☐ Acceptance of an order from an undesirable or unauthorized customer (e.g., a bad credit risk, thus increasing bad debt losses).
- ☐ Acceptance of an order for a product or service that is not currently sold by the company and can't be made available.
- ☐ Acceptance of an order by an unauthorized internal agent.
- ☐ Commitment to provide products or services with an unrealistic delivery date.
- ☐ Commitment to provide products or services at an unprofitable price.
- ☐ Failure to place a purchase order for items the enterprise needs and can pay for, and which a reliable vendor could fill.
- ☐ Placement of a purchase order from an undesirable or unauthorized vendor.
- ☐ Placement of a purchase order for items the company no longer needs, or for too many items as compared to the quantity needed by the enterprise.
- ☐ Placement of a purchase order by an unauthorized employee.
- ☐ A purchasing agent placing an order for a dollar amount that is higher than his or her authorized limit.
- ☐ Failure to provide adequate lead-time to vendors when placing orders, leading to impossible situations or leading to exorbitant shipping and handling costs.
- ☐ Failure to obtain the lowest possible cost for the highest possible quality items.

Some of these risks can be controlled declaratively within an integrated enterprise information system. For example, the interface can be programmed to prevent placement of a purchase order with an unauthorized vendor, and to prevent acceptance of a sale order from a customer who is not in the system as an approved customer. The interface can also be programmed to allow only items on the "approved list of goods and services" to be purchased or sold, to allow them to be purchased and sold only by selected internal agents (identified by passwords and access codes), to automatically insert the quoted costs and selling prices from the master cost sheet and price list (and possibly to allow adjustments within a specified range), and to automatically calculate line item extensions and total order amounts. Such automation not only improves the efficiency of the business processes, it also improves the control over business and information process risks.

Economic Decrement Event Risks and Controls

Because economic decrement events involve an outflow of economic resources such as inventory or cash, this type of event is particularly susceptible to risks associated with theft of those resources (see *Resource Risks* earlier in this chapter). Risks associated with sales, shipments, or service engagements in the revenue cycle include:

- ☐ Failure to ship goods in response to a sale order commitment.
- ☐ Shipment of goods that were not ordered by a customer.
- ☐ Shipment of goods by an unauthorized internal agent.
- ☐ Shipment of goods to the wrong customer or to an unauthorized location.
- ☐ Shipping the wrong product or the incorrect amount of product.
- ☐ Shipping poorly packaged products.
- ☐ Selecting a poor carrier or route.
- ☐ Losing sales due to untimely shipments.

An effective integrated enterprise information system can help control several of these risks. The system itself can verify who ships products and to whom they are shipped. Passwords can prevent an unauthorized internal agent from gaining access to the system to ship products. Computer generated address labels can prevent shipping products to the wrong customers and product bar codes can help prevent shipping the wrong products.

Risks associated with cash disbursements include:

- ☐ Failure to pay for goods that were received, or making late payments, thus earning a bad credit rating.
- ☐ Recording a cash disbursement that did not in fact occur.
- ☐ Making duplicate cash disbursements for the same purchase.
- ☐ Recording incorrect details about cash disbursements
- ☐ Failure to take advantage of early payment discounts.

Independent checks on performance (i.e., someone else checks what you do) are crucial to mitigate risks in the cash disbursement event activities. Employees other than those who make the cash disbursements can do these independent checks, or the checks may be done by the enterprise system interface. For example, one employee may write checks based on the supporting documentation, and another employee may verify the accuracy of the checks and the entries to record them. Alternatively as the underlying acquisitions are made, the system may generate and record the checks and an employee may verify their accuracy and sign them.

Case in Point
Marty's Distributing Company is a distributor of alcoholic beverages and soft drinks. Under the pre-computerized system, a delivery clerk took a load of beer to a retail outlet and manually prepared a sales slip. There was no independent check on the accuracy of the amount of beer recorded, the extension of quantity multiplied by price, or the summation of the total charge. At the time the computer was installed, the old system and the new system were operated in parallel for two months to verify the accuracy of the new systems. During this time many errors were identified, and further investigation revealed the delivery clerk made all the errors in manually preparing the sales tickets. The savings the computer system generated by catching and preventing these errors more than paid for the computer system in less than one year.

Economic Increment Event Risks and Controls

Because economic increment events involve resource inflows, these events are also particularly susceptible to risks associated with theft (see *Resource Risks* earlier in this chapter). In the revenue and financing transaction cycles, the most common economic increment event is the receipt of cash. Risks associated with cash receipts include:

- ☐ Failure to receive cash as a result of a sale, or failure to record cash that was received.
- ☐ Recording a cash receipt that did not in fact occur.
- ☐ Accepting duplicate cash receipts for the same sale.
- ☐ Recording incorrect details about cash receipts
- ☐ Failure to deposit cash into the bank in a timely manner, or depositing cash into the wrong cash account.

When cash is received in the mail, two employees should open the mail together. One employee should take the money and prepare the deposit and the other person should send a receipt to the customer and record the receipt in the company's information system. The system should compare the deposit total with the total of the receipts to verify their equality. A control to reduce the risk of data entry errors is the use of computer-readable remittance advices. If a customer pays the exact amount of an invoice and returns the remittance advice with the payment, the computer can read the information on the remittance advice and know the amount of the payment and the customer information needed to correctly process the payment.

In the acquisition cycle, the most common economic increment is the receipt of inventory, supplies, services, or operating assets. Risks associated with such acquisition events include:

- ☐ Failure to receive goods or services in response to a purchase order commitment.
- ☐ Receipt of goods or services that the enterprise did not order.
- ☐ Receipt of the wrong goods or services or an incorrect quantity of goods or services.
- ☐ Damaging goods during unpacking on the receiving dock.
- ☐ Failure to receive goods or services in a timely manner.
- ☐ Failure to record acquisitions quickly enough to take advantage of early payment discounts.

Access restriction controls for resource-related theft risks as described earlier in this chapter should also be enforced for acquisition events. An effective integrated enterprise information system can help control several of the other risks identified. The system can be used during the acquisition event to verify the goods received were in fact ordered. In an automated integrated enterprise system, acquisitions are recorded in a timely manner (as the goods are received) such that early payment discounts may be taken. The system may also be queried on a regular basis to identify to follow up with vendors regarding unfilled purchase orders (i.e., orders for which goods have not yet been received).

Economic Decrement Reversal Risks and Controls
Economic decrement reversal events in the sales/collection process should be subject to close scrutiny because they are the alternative to the expected economic increment event and because they involve custody of inventory. Sales returns are sometimes used as a means to cover up theft of cash (for example without proper controls, a clerk may steal a customer payment for an invoice and then process a sales return for the invoice amount. Other risks associated with sales returns include:

- ☐ Failure to accept a sale return for which a customer has a legitimate reason.
- ☐ Acceptance of returned goods that were not originally sold by the enterprise.
- ☐ Approval of a sale return by an unauthorized employee.
- ☐ Recording a sale return that did not in fact occur.

These risks may be controlled with the aid of an integrated enterprise information system. No person without a proper password or access code should be able to authorize a sales return event. Access restriction controls and chain of custody tracking should be enforced for the receipt of the returned merchandise into the warehouse.

Economic Increment Reversal Risks and Controls
Similarly, economic increment reversal events in the acquisition/payment process are the alternative to the expected economic decrement event and they involve custody of inventory. Purchase returns are sometimes used as a means to cover up theft of inventory, supplies, or operating assets (for example without proper controls, a clerk may steal goods and then process a fictitious purchase return for the purchase amount. Other risks associated with purchase returns may include:

- ☐ Failure to return goods that did not satisfy the enterprise's needs.
- ☐ Return of goods that the enterprise does in fact need.
- ☐ Approval of a purchase return by an unauthorized employee.
- ☐ Recording a purchase return that did not in fact occur.

These risks may be controlled with the aid of an integrated enterprise information system. No person without a proper password or access code should be able to authorize a purchase return event. Restriction of access controls should be employed in the activities of packaging and shipping the goods back to the appropriate vendor. The integrated enterprise information system may be used to verify who ships goods and to whom they are shipped to help resolve any dispute with a vendor as to whether goods were actually returned. Passwords can prevent unauthorized employees from gaining access to the system to ship products. Computer generated address labels can prevent shipping products to the wrong vendors and product bar codes can help prevent returns of the wrong products.

Controls for Information Process Risks
Many of the controls for business process risks involved information system controls that overlap with controls for information process risks. Indeed, it is often difficult to distinguish between controls over actual business process objects and the recording, maintenance, and

REA Accounting Systems: Resources-Events-Agents: An ontology for designing, controlling, and using integrated enterprise systems

129

reporting of information about those objects. This section focuses on information processing risks and controls that are reasonably separable from the business process objects themselves.

Although all information processing errors and irregularities are undesirable, those that occur during the recording and maintenance processes are particularly harmful. Why? The old adage, "Garbage in, Garbage out!" If inaccurate, invalid, or incomplete data are either recorded or maintained, the result is erroneous reporting. Since important decisions regarding the enterprise's strategy and direction are based on reports produced by the system, the errors may prove disastrous.

System Resource Risks and Controls

The enterprise information system is an important resource of the enterprise and as such should be protected. Several types of protection should be implemented, including protection against system failure, protection from unauthorized physical access, and protection from unauthorized logical access.

Protection Against System Failure

Until we have a fail-safe technology, we must guard against possible failures in the computer hardware and its power source, as well as protect system hardware from the environment. Such failures can result in the interruption of business operations and the loss of data. As a preventive measure, enterprises should properly maintain computer equipment and facilities, and operate equipment in an appropriate physical environment (environmental controls). For larger systems, specially prepared rooms are sometimes necessary to house computer equipment. Some enterprises have backup system components (e.g., extra disk storage devices, extra printers, and extra communication channels) so that if a component fails, processing can quickly be transferred to another component without interrupting the flow of processing for an extended period of time.

Not only can computer components fail, but the power source for the components can also fail or provide an irregular power supply. The loss of power shuts down the entire operation and any data in temporary storage will be lost. Protection from the loss of power is usually provided through the use of special battery units called uninterruptable power supplies (UPS). These devices provide battery support and sound an alarm when power is interrupted. This allows needed time to stop computer processes and back up data and instructions (programs). An irregular power supply can damage or destroy the computer hardware. Sudden and dramatic increases in power are called power surges or spikes. Protecting against surges or spikes involves the use of a surge protector or line conditioning. Conditioning power lines is sometimes provided by utility companies, but can also be provided by a simple and relatively low cost, device called a surge protector.

Protection from Unauthorized Physical Access

In the business process risk section we discussed the need to restrict access to enterprise resources. The enterprise information system is one of the resources to which access should be restricted. Critical system hardware such as file servers should be locked in restricted areas; however other components of networked information systems usually need to be accessible to authorized users to complete business and information processes. Unauthorized access to systems represents a tremendous risk to enterprises, so prevention of unauthorized system access is important. Controlling access is critical when systems have online, real-time transaction processing capabilities. Any computer that is connected to the Internet is vulnerable to attempted break-ins by unauthorized users. Unauthorized users are sometimes referred to as hackers. Hackers may seek personal gain from intruding into an enterprise's information system, or they may seek only to cause destruction to the enterprise such as has been accomplished by denial of service attacks in recent years. In a denial of service attack, an intruder typically logs into the system and launches an application that inundates the server with logins such that it gets overloaded and has insufficient resources to serve legitimate user's needs. The most likely way to ensure the secrecy of data that is stored on a computer is to keep the computer as a standalone (i.e., never connect it to the Internet) and keep that computer locked in a secure place. Most enterprises can't operate effectively in standalone environments; therefore logical access controls for each layer are needed.

Protection from Unauthorized Logical Access

Logical access controls restrict unauthorized access to the programs and data in systems. Networked information systems have several layers of potential access points, each of which must be secured. Besides controlling access to the enterprise's application software packages, it is also necessary to control access to the underlying database, and to the overall network operating system. If adequate controls are not built into the system at each layer, unauthorized users may gain access to the application software through a back door in the network operating system or in the underlying database. System access controls involve the use of passwords and an access control matrix.

A **password** is a unique identifier that only the user should know and is required to enter each time he/she logs onto the system. Passwords are a weak form of protection. Unless passwords are formally assigned, routinely changed, and protected from use by other people, they will quickly get into the wrong hands and provide unauthorized access to the system. An **access control matrix** identifies the functions each user is allowed to perform and what data and programs the user can access once he or she gains access to the system. For example, only a limited number of individuals are allowed access to payroll data. Some users are only allowed to read data, while other users are given the right to read and update the data. Access controls require users to authenticate themselves (i.e. give evidence that they are who they say they are) by providing something they know, something they possess, or something they physically are. Examples of access controls that represent things users know are passwords and personal identification numbers (PINs). Examples of access controls that represent things users possess are identification cards or tokens (see cases in point below). Examples of access controls that require physical characteristics as input include voice recognition, fingerprint identification, retinal scanners, and digital signature recognition technology. Enterprises can also use terminal identification codes to prevent access by unauthorized terminals over communication lines. A host computer can require a terminal to electronically transmit its identification code that identifies it as an authorized terminal and defines (and limits) the type of transaction a terminal user can perform. The host computer compares the identification code it receives from the terminal with a list of approved terminal identification codes to verify that it is an approved terminal.

A strong form of protection against unauthorized access to a network is the **token system**, which authenticates a user through a hardware device combined with a log-in password process. A **smart card** is a device that generates a random code in sync with the host system that changes at predetermined intervals and must be matched against the host system to authorize access. Such devices make the network tougher to hack because of the randomly generated, one-time-only password codes. Like a bankcard, the smart card works in sync with the host system to authenticate access. But instead of a single code or PIN, the card generates a random code, which can change every 60 seconds, and is read into the system. If the code matches the software on the host, access is granted. Some cards can be configured to provide

REA Accounting Systems: Resources-Events-Agents: An ontology for designing, controlling, and using integrated enterprise systems

131

access to selected network components. Elaborate ones may include electronic eyes on the card that capture the resemblances of the users, read them into the system, and allows them to be viewed by the network managers.[4]

Encryption is used to protect highly sensitive and confidential data. **Encryption** is a process of encoding data entered into the system, storing or transmitting the data in coded form, and then decoding the data upon its use or arrival at its destination. This prevents unauthorized access to the data while it is stored or as it is transmitted. Unauthorized users can easily intercept information broadcast over networks by applications that do not use encryption.

Information Processing Controls

Information processing controls check the accuracy, completeness, and authorization of information to be recorded, maintained, and reported. Two broad categories of information processing controls are general controls and application controls.

General Controls

General controls include all controls over data center operations, access security, systems software acquisition and maintenance, and application system development and maintenance. A high level executive who reports to the president of the enterprise (e.g. a Chief Information Officer or CIO) should administer the information systems functions of an enterprise. An IS Steering Committee, composed of several other key officers of the enterprise, should work with the CIO to develop a plan that identifies the strategic use of information technology within the enterprise and prioritizes the development of individual components.

The responsibility for all aspects of the information systems functions of the enterprise falls under the CIO. This individual has the responsibility to see that there is adequate separation of duties and responsibilities, adequate access security, and that the operations of the data center are properly controlled as we have discussed above. The other general controls of acquisition, development, and maintenance of both systems and application software are discussed in the next sections.

Development and Maintenance of Systems and Application Software

Systems software consists of the computer programs that make the computer hardware run. They include the operating system, networking and communication software, and various utilities programs to back up and maintain files. Application software consists of the programs that process the business events of the enterprise such as the acquisition of goods and services and the production of finished products. Because of the high cost to develop custom software, there is a growing trend to purchase both systems and application software and modify them as necessary to meet the needs of the enterprise. Care must be taken in specifying the requirements of the software, analyzing available software to see which package best meets the requirements, modifying the software as necessary, and testing individual applications and the entire system to make sure it processes the data accurately.

User departments are generally responsible for developing the list of software requirements. People from the user departments, the systems analysts, and the programmers work together to identify potential software packages in the market and compare their features with those

---

[4]D. KcKay, "Network Managers Face Formidable Challenge," *Computer Dealer News*, July 13, 1994, p. 29.

desired by the enterprise. When modifications are required, the systems analysts design the changes and the computer programmers write the code to make the changes. *Test data* are generally used to verify that the programs and the entire system work correctly. Test data is a set of business events to test every logic path within the programs. The correct results from running the test data are developed independently from the system being tested and are compared with the results obtained when processed by the new system. If the new system correctly processes the test data we assume it has been modified correctly. The data control group is responsible for reviewing the testing and the test results to verifying that they are adequate and that the systems is ready for use.

This same process must be followed every time a modification is required in a program. The request comes from the user department. Systems analysts design the change, programmers write the code, test data are used to verify that the program functions properly, and the data control group verifies the program is ready for use. Once the modification is complete, it is turned over to the operating people and controlled by the systems librarian. Controls over developing and maintaining a system are very important. The way a system is developed is as important as how it is operated in preventing errors and irregularities.

Financial losses because of software defects are an international problem. As institutions become dependent on electronic funds transfers, the software itself becomes more complex. Individual programmers have taken advantage of this complexity by concealing code in programs that transfer minute amounts from individual transactions to their own accounts. What's the true magnitude of the financial shrinkage due to faulty software? No one knows.

Application Controls
Application controls are controls that apply to the processing within individual software programs. These controls help ensure that transactions are valid, properly authorized, and completely and accurately processed. Our discussion of application controls will be divided into data input controls, processing controls, and file controls.

Data Input Controls
Some of the most important controls are those dealing with the accuracy and completeness of data as the data are entered into the computer. Accuracy of input data is checked by event processing rules, data entry verification, and several edit checks.

Event processing rules should be built into the system to verify that prescribed business rules are followed when executing an event. Some examples of potential business rules include:

A customer may exist in our database before participating in a related sale event, but it is not permissible to record a sale event without identifying the related customer.

Products can be shipped (Sale event) only after a valid customer order has been taken (Sale Order event).

Each customer order can have one or more types of inventory associated with it; each inventory type can be involved in many customer orders; and information about inventory types may be entered into the system before any orders are taken.

As we discuss in chapters 5 and 8, business rules such as these can be designed into the relational database table definitions. Alternatively such rules or business logic can be programmed into the user interface software. In some cases these event processing rules and programmed business logic can help enterprises detect errors or irregularities; in other cases it will help prevent errors.

If data is entered after the events actually occurred, the control is detective rather than preventive. The data entry clerk will not be able to enter the data into the system and will need to bring it to a manager's attention, thereby identifying the error or irregularity. For example, consider a mail order company that does not normally have prepaid sales and very rarely generates cash sales. Because the company also receives cash from non-sale sources (such as bank loans), the information system must allow cash receipts to be entered without having previously processed a corresponding sale. A risk exists that a cash receipt that actually resulted from a sale was not matched to any corresponding sale in the system. To detect such a case, a query may be developed to identify any unmatched cash receipts in the system so that someone can verify whether they match loans or whether they should have been matched to a sale. That investigation could reveal that the sale was inadvertently not recorded in the system (the enterprise's error). Alternatively a query could identify "overmatched" cash receipts in the system – those for which the cash receipt amount exceeded the related sale amount(s); such a query could reveal that a customer paid for the same sale twice (the customer's error, but the enterprise should return the overpayment).

Event processing rules can also help prevent errors or fraud, if the data input functions are embedded in the business process procedures. That is, if the data is entered on a real-time basis as the events occur, enforcement of business rules by the database or user interface software will prevent the noncompliant events from being recorded which will then result in non-execution of the events. In other words, the system can note activities that represent exceptions to the prescribed rules and send exception messages to a responsible person for review. Based on the authorized person's response, the system can allow or prevent execution of the activity. For example, is a shipment normally necessary to record an order? No; instead, an order event should precede the shipping event. Is an order necessary to execute a shipment? For many enterprises the answer is yes! The authorization for a shipment is the existence of a valid order. Without a valid order, the shipping event should not be executed. An IT application could deny the execution and recording of a shipment that is not supported by a valid order. If shipping personnel can only generate shipping labels through the system, the likelihood of shipping merchandise without an order is reduced significantly. Notice that if an enterprise does not embed the data entry function into the business process procedures, but instead inputs data after the events have occurred; then the system's ability to prevent errors and irregularities is substantially reduced; it can only detect rather than prevent.

Data Entry Verification. As event data are entered into systems they must be checked to verify the accuracy of the record being updated and the accuracy of the data itself. Two controls often applied in this area are closed loop verification and key verification.

> **Closed-loop verification** uses one input data item to locate the record to be updated and displays other data from the record so the data entry person can verify it as the correct record to be processed. For example, if a sales order clerk enters a customer number for a customer buying merchandise on account, the computer uses the number to locate the customer record, then display additional customer data (such as name and address) on the computer screen. This way the user can verify that the correct customer record is being updated.

Key verification (also called **rekeying**) requires one data enterer to key input data twice, or requires two different data people to enter the same data. The computer compares the data entered on the second keying operation with the original data and highlights any differences. The clerk verifies and corrects any differences.

Edit checks are incorporated into computer instructions to verify and validate the completeness, reasonableness, and/or accuracy of data. Edit checks can help reduce both operating risk and information processing risk. Their use is not limited to one type of risk or circumstance. The following is an overview of some of the edit check logic used in information systems. Edit checks may be applied to individual fields or to records or batches of records.

Several edit checks can be used to check the accuracy, reasonableness, and completeness of individual data input fields.

Check digit. A formula can be applied to an account number, part number, or similar standard number to calculate a check digit. The check digit is appended to and maintained as part of the number (usually as the last digit). For example, suppose we want a five-digit account number (including the check digit) and the first four digits of the account number (based on style, division, color, and product type) are 1534. A check digit formula is used to add the fifth digit. There are several check digit formulas, and one rather simple, but less than adequate, formula adds the account number digits and extracts the second digit of the sum. The resulting account number using this formula is 15343 (the 3 is the second digit of $1 + 5 + 3 + 4 = 13$).

Completeness check. A completeness check verifies that all critical field data are entered. It checks for missing data or blanks.

Default value. Default values set the field contents to a pre-specified (default) value. In some cases the default values may be overridden, while in other cases they may not.

Field or mode check. A field or mode check verifies that the entered data type is the appropriate mode for a field. For example, if a field is declared as a text or an alphanumeric field, the data input should be alphanumeric (letters and numbers). Other field modes include numeric, date, logical, counters, memo, and embedded objects (such as video, audio, or graphics).

Range check. A range check compares entered data to a predetermined acceptable upper and/or lower limit. Data is not accepted without special authorization if the data fall outside the specified limits.

Validity check. A validity check compares entered data against pre-specified data stored within the computer to determine its validity. For example, to determine the validity of a user identification number, the computer would compare the entered primary key of the user to a stored list of valid user numbers.

The next level of edit checks examines an entire record, generally a record in the file being updated by business event data. Some of the more common record edit checks are:

Master reference check. A master reference check verifies that an event/transaction record has a corresponding master record to be updated. An error occurs when there is no corresponding master record for the transaction record. For example, there is an error if you input a sale for a customer not currently included in your customer data files.

Reasonableness check. Reasonableness checks verify whether the amount of an event/transaction record appears reasonable when compared to other elements associated with each item being processed. For example, if an employee is coded as a clerk, it is probably unreasonable that her pay per week is $5,000. Note that a reasonableness check is not the same as a limit check. It might be reasonable for the president to have a weekly check of $5,000. The reasonableness of the pay is based on the relationship between position (clerk versus president) and the amount of the pay, not a fixed dollar amount.

Referential integrity. Referential integrity is a safeguard to ensure that every posted foreign key attribute relates to a primary key attribute. For example, suppose you have two tables: a Salesperson table and a Sales event table. Since the two tables have a relationship (a salesperson participates in each sale), you must include the primary key attribute of the Salesperson table (e.g., salesperson number) in the Sale event table; salesperson number is a foreign key attribute in the Sales event table. You want to invoke referential integrity to ensure a link between the two tables. Referential integrity prevents writing a sale in the Sale event table without a valid salesperson number from the Salesperson table. It also prevents deleting a sales person from the Salesperson table as long as the salesperson has sales in the Sale event table.

Valid sign check. The valid sign check is used to highlight illogical balances in a master file record. For example, a negative balance for the quantity on hand for a particular item in inventory is a likely error.

The third level of edit checks is for an entire batch of events or transactions. Sometimes business events can be grouped into batches for a period of time, such as one day, and processed together. Controls are needed to make sure none of the events are lost, no unauthorized events are added, and that all events are in the proper sequence and correctly processed.

Sequence check. A sequence check verifies the records in a batch are sorted in the correct sequence. For sequential processing (often used in batch processing), the transaction records must be sorted in the same order as the master file's primary key. A sequence check can be used to highlight missing batch items (e.g. a missing check).

Transaction type check. A transaction type check verifies that all transactions included within the batch are of the same category or type. For example, we would not want to confuse the addition of a new customer with the addition of a new employee.

Batch control totals. When transactions are processed in batches, each batch should be dated and assigned a unique batch number. Batch control totals are used to verify that all transactions within a batch are present and have been processed. They verify that no transactions were added or deleted during processing. There are several types of batch control totals. Let's use a record that includes a customer number field and an invoice amount field to illustrate three types of control totals: hash, financial/numeric, and record count control totals.

Hash control total. A hash control total is the sum of an attribute in a file that has no real meaning or use. For example, the sum of the customer number field of all the records in a batch is a meaningless number for purposes other than as a control total. But, if it is calculated when the batch is first assembled, the computer can recalculate it after the records have been entered for processing. If the computer-generated sum is the same as the original amount, we have some assurance that all records were accurately processed. If they are not the same, one or more transactions may have been either added or deleted from the batch.

Financial/numeric control total. A financial control total is the sum of a financial field, such as the invoice amount, of all records in a batch. Usually, this is a meaningful numeric or financial field. For example, the total of the invoice amounts is meaningful because it represents the increase in account receivable and it is useful to evaluate the effectiveness of those taking orders for the day.

Record count control total. A record count control total is a total of the number of records in a batch. So if a batch contains 46 records, the record count is 46.

All the control totals can be used to verify batch input, processing, and output. For example, suppose a clerk enters 46 customer invoices totaling $14,678.93 in charge sales into a computer file. Also assume that the sum of the customer account numbers on the invoices is 738476846. Once these records are entered into a batch transaction file, the file should include 46 records (the *record count*), the customer number field should total 738476846 (a *hash total*), and the sum of the invoice amount field should total $14,678.93 (a *financial total*). When the records are processed to update the customer receivable master file, the update run should show that 46 records were affected, and the accounts receivable total should increase by $14,678.93.

Batch control totals may be generated by one computerized process compared with another computerized process that uses the same batch as input; in those cases, a hash total is as easy as a record count or financial/numeric control total. Often, however, the initial batch control total is generated manually with a ten-key adding machine as the batch is created. The batch control total (usually a financial total, but sometimes a record count) is written on the batch header along with the batch number and date. Once a manual batch control total is computed and the batch is processed in a computerized process, the computer process should generate a control total of the same type (financial, numeric, record count, or hash) and the manual total should be compared to the computerized total. If they match, the enterprise has a reasonable confidence that all items in that batch were in fact processed in the computer system processes.

Notice that batch totals do not identify errors in individual records. Batch totals only highlight errors in the group as a whole. Batch totals do not ensure that individual records are updated correct. For example, if the total of an accounts receivable subsidiary ledger equals the total in a general ledger accounts receivable control account, this does not signify that the posting to the individual customer accounts are correct. It only indicates that the same total amount was posted; some individual items could have been posted to the wrong customer's account!

REA Accounting Systems: Resources-Events-Agents: An ontology for designing, controlling, and using integrated enterprise systems

137

Information Processing Controls

Information processing controls are designed to verify that event, resource, agent, and location information are recorded and maintained accurately, completely, and in a timely manner. They also help ensure the information on reports is complete, properly summarized, and reported to the appropriate people.

Process controls verify that the input data are properly recorded in the database and any balances maintained within the system are properly updated. Many of the program development and maintenance controls, data input controls, and edit check controls identified above are also used as process controls. The following examples illustrate the application of these controls to verify process accuracy.

Test data to verify that computer programs function properly are an important element in verifying the accuracy of information processing. Once a program is correctly written and tested it is very reliable in performing the same operations again and again.

Closed-loop verification is used when the input data are being processed in an online, real-time mode. For example, closed-loop verification is used to make sure the customer account being updated is accurate. Because of the mode of processing, this serves as an input and a process control.

Edit checks on the record and batch levels are also used as process controls. For example, a reasonableness check when used in a sequential batch process is a process control. As a transaction is being processed, the computer can compare one element of input with the master record to see if it appears reasonable. If it does not, an error is recorded on the error log. An example of this is a sales order process. Selling ten computers to a customer with an occupation listed as "housewife" would not seem reasonable and the transaction would be printed on an error report. If however, the sales clerk was entering the transaction by an online, real-time process and the sales clerk attempted to execute such a transaction, the computer could perform the reasonableness check as the data are entered and highlight the unreasonableness. In this case it is an input control.

As you can see, many online, real-time controls become process controls when the mode of processing is shifted to batch processing. This explains why real-time processing helps enterprises prevent errors more easily than enterprises that perform batch processing after a transaction has already occurred. With batch processing, error detection is more common than error prevention.

One of the benefits of an architecture based on the REA pattern is the simplicity of data storage and processing. Most event data are stored in a raw, unprocessed form. Processing consists of recording the individual characteristics and attributes about each business event. Most classifications, summarizations, and balances are developed as part of the reporting process. This is much more streamlined and less complex than a traditional processing environment where you have to control not only the input but also a complex posting process to perform classifications, summarizations, and balance calculations. Processing in a REA-based architecture is very simple; it is a direct recording of the event attributes. This allows for straightforward controls. The key to control is making sure the event record is being recorded in the correct file in a timely, complete, and accurate manner. Then we accurately report this data per the request parameters of the information customer.

File Security Controls

Devices or techniques are available to verify that the correct file is being updated and to prevent inadvertent destruction or inappropriate use of files. Some of these controls include the following:

External file labels (as simple as stick-on labels) identify a storage media's contents. They also help prevent someone from inadvertently writing over the contents of the disk or tape.

Internal file labels record the name of a file, the date it was created, and other identifying data on the file medium to be read and verified by the computer. Internal labels include *header labels* and *trailer labels*. Header labels are a file description recorded at the beginning of a file. Trailer labels mark the end of a file and contain control or summary data about the contents of the file.

Lockout procedures are used by database management systems to prevent two applications or users from updating the same record or data item at the same time.

The read-only file designation is used to mark data available for reading only. The data cannot be altered by instructions from users, nor can new data be stored on the device.

Data Loss and File Reconstruction Capability

Regardless of the controls taken to secure the computer and prevent problems, files are occasionally lost and programs are occasionally destroyed. Therefore, it is necessary to maintain backup or duplicate copies of current data files, programs, and documentation. At least one set of backup copies of all these items should be stored at a location that is physically removed from the computer facilities. Enterprises should develop a policy concerning how long to retain backup copies. The length of time will depend on the managerial and regulatory requirements of the enterprise. The purpose of backup copies is to allow an enterprise to reconstruct its data should a disaster strike and cause a loss or corruption of data. The basic task is to retain copies of reference (resource and agent) data and event data for use in reconstructing any lost data.

CONCLUDING COMMENTS

This chapter introduced you to the importance of understanding enterprise risks and provided some examples of controls that are available to reduce enterprise risks. Some of the control examples cited are useful for preventing errors and irregularities, while others are helpful in detecting and correcting errors and irregularities. Just as change has become a constant feature of enterprises and information technology, the need for creativity and innovation in identifying risks and in developing control procedures to reduce risks is becoming consistent across enterprises. The tools provided in this chapter are only a beginning; as new risks arise, new controls must also be developed. The key is to adequately assess risks, determine which of the risks need to be controlled, and design cost-effective controls to mitigate those risks. When measuring the cost of controls, any decreases in operational efficiency and effectiveness must be considered.

Key Terms and Concepts

Access control matrix
Application controls
Batch control total
Bonding
Business process risks
Check digit
Closed loop verification
Collusion
Committee of Sponsoring Organizations
  (COSO)
Completeness check
Contingency plan
Control activity
Control environment
Control Objectives for Business and
  Information Technology (COBIT)
Corrective controls
Default value
Detective controls
Economy risks
Edit check
Encryption
Enterprise risks
Error
Exposure
Field (mode) check
Financial/numeric control total
Fraud
General controls
Hash control total
Independent checks on performance
Industry risks
Information and communication
Information process risks
Internal control
Irregularity

Key verification (rekeying)
Lapping
Logical access controls
Master reference check
Materiality of risk
Monitoring
Opportunity
Passwords
PCAOB Auditing Standard 5 (AS5)
Performance reviews
Physical access controls
Preventive controls
Public Company Accounting Oversight
  Board (PCAOB)
Range check
Reasonableness check
Reconciliation of physical to recorded
  quantities
Record count control total
Referential integrity
RFID (radio frequency identification) tags
Risk
Risk assessment
Sarbanes Oxley Act (SOX) – section 404
Separation/segregation of duties
Sequence check
Smart card or token
Statement of Auditing Standards (SAS) 94
Statement of Auditing Standards (SAS) 115
Threat
Token system
Transaction type check
Valid sign check
Validity check

Review Questions

LO1	R1.	What is a system of internal controls?
LO1	R2.	Distinguish between risk, exposure, and threat.
LO1	R3.	Describe the relationship between risk, opportunity, and objectives.
LO1	R4.	How do you determine the materiality of risk?
LO1	R5.	Should enterprises attempt to control all risks? Explain.
LO6	R6.	Describe separation of duties and responsibilities.
LO1, LO2	R7.	Who is ultimately responsible for internal controls within an enterprise?
LO5	R8.	List and describe the five interrelated components of an internal control system per the COSO Integrated Control Framework.

LO5   R9.   List and describe the three objectives of internal control systems per the COSO Integrated Internal Control Framework.

LO6   R10.   Which type of control is needed more in today's risk environment: prevention, detection, or correction? Explain.

LO1   R11. If an enterprise changes from a manual information system to a computerized information system, does its internal control objectives change? Explain.

LO1   R12. Is it better to build controls into an information system or add them to the system after it is built? Why?

LO3, LO4   R13. What risks do enterprises face with respect to resources?

LO3, LO4   R14. What risks do enterprises face with respect to agents?

LO3, LO4   R15. What risks do enterprises face with respect to events?

LO3, LO4   R16. What is the difference between business process risks and information process risks?

LO6   R17. What are three means by which system users can prove their identity to the system? Which of these means is least vulnerable to falsification?

LO6   R18. Explain the purpose of encryption techniques.

LO6   R19. Describe a website or an application you have used that incorporated some form of closed-loop verification.

LO6   R20. How do check digits help ensure that field contents are valid?

LO6   R21. Give an example of a completeness check.

LO6   R22. A clerk at Wilfred Hanks Inc. has just keypunched a week's worth of sales records. When the items were given to her for data entry, the clerk was told that there were 1,800 records, totaling $4,000,000, and that the sum of the customer identification numbers was 211,825,814. When she finished the data entry, the keypunch machine verified that she had put in 1,800 records, totaling $4,000,000, and that the sum of the last four digits of the customer identification numbers was 211,825,814.
a. What type of batch total is the sum of the customer numbers? _____
b. What type of batch total is the number of records she keypunched? _____
c. What type of batch total is the $4,000,000 sum of sale amounts? _____

LO6   R23. List three physical assets that should be counted regularly and compared with the asset value reported on the financial records.

LO6   R24. How are master reference checks and referential integrity similar?

Multiple Choice Questions

LO3, LO6
1.   An example of an internal control designed to mitigate the risk of stock market investments is
A) An enterprise sells goods on credit rather than requiring immediate cash payment for sales.
B) An enterprise checks customers' credit ratings before approving sales to customers.
C) An enterprise maintains a diversified portfolio rather than holding only one company's stock.
D) An enterprise never pays dividends but rather reinvests all earnings.
E) An enterprise invests only in penny stocks because they are low cost.

LO1
2.   Which goal should enterprises have for internal controls?
A) Enterprises will typically live with high materiality risks because the cost of controlling all risk far exceeds the potential benefit.
B) Enterprises should control all risks to the point of eliminating all potential losses.
C) Risks that have a low impact and a low likelihood of occurrence must always be controlled.
D) The key in establishing internal controls is to identify and control risks in a manner such that the benefits of controlling the risks exceed the costs of the controls.
E) Management should usually ignore risks that have a high impact and a high likelihood of occurrence.

LO3, LO6
3.   What is collusion?
A) Collusion is an internal control designed to prevent fraud.
B) Collusion is the act of two or more employees acting together to conspire in a fraud.
C) Collusion is the act of two internal controls contradicting each other and negating the intended benefit.
D) Collusion is a clash or disagreement between two middle-tier managers.
E) Collusion occurs as a result of the elimination of cash through the use of electronic payments.

LO3
4.   Which is an example of an enterprise risk?
A) A global epidemic
B) Unexpected competition from another industry
C) An industry-wide cost increase
D) A merger or acquisition of another enterprise
E) Failure to record information about an economic resource acquisition

LO6
5.   Use of one customer's payment to pay off another customer's account receivable is part of a fraud scheme known as
A) Checking
B) Lapping
C) Crediting
D) Kilting
E) Funding

LO1
6.   Which of the following is FALSE regarding risks?
A) Opportunities often cannot exist without risks.
B) When a risk materializes, it threatens some aspects of the entity's operations and more serious risks threaten the ongoing existence of the entity.
C) Internal controls are implemented to mitigate risks.
D) Risks need to be identified and controlled, but they must be balanced with objectives, opportunities, and the cost of controls.
E) All of the above are true statements.

LO1
7. The materiality of risk is a function of:
    A) The size of the potential loss
    B) The impact of a loss on achieving the enterprise's objectives.
    C) The possibility of a loss
    D) Two of the above
    E) All of the above

LO6
8. Which type of control focuses primarily on ensuring that errors or irregularities cannot happen?
    A) Preventive
    B) Detective
    C) Corrective
    D) All of the above
    E) None of the above

LO3
9. Which of the following is an example of an economy risk?
    A) Loss of brand quality
    B) The increasing cost of computer memory chips
    C) Sales made to non-existent customers
    D) A change in the financial market
    E) A new competitor entering the enterprise's market

LO3, LO4
10. Which risks are associated primarily with recording, maintaining, and reporting information about resources, events, agents, and relationships among them?
    A) Business process risks
    B) Information process risks
    C) Industry risks
    D) Enterprise risks
    E) Economy risks

LO6
11. What kind of control is bonding?
    A) Primarily preventive
    B) Primarily detective
    C) Primarily corrective
    D) Primarily substitutive
    E) Primarily premeditative

LO6
12. What identifies the functions each user is allowed to perform and specifies which data and programs the user can access after gaining access to the system?
    A) Passwords
    B) Logical access controls
    C) Access control matrix
    D) Application controls
    E) Operating system controls

LO6
13. A formula applied to an account number, part number, or similar standard number is used to calculate what?
    A) Key verification
    B) Edit checks
    C) Referential integrity
    D) Check digit
    E) Closed loop verification

LO6
14. Which edit check compares entered data to a predetermined acceptable upper and lower limit?
    A) Predetermined check
    B) Range check
    C) Validity check
    D) Field check
    E) Sequence check

LO3
15. Which guideline helps to distinguish industry level risks from economy level risks?
    A) An industry risk primarily affects the industry in which the enterprise operates, whereas an economy risk affects all industries within the enterprise's local or global economy.
    B) An industry risk affects all industries within the enterprise's local or global economy, whereas an economy risk is a result of the enterprise not taking advantage of production economies of scale.
    C) an industry risk is associated with a specific business object such as a resource-event association; whereas an economy risk affects all industries within the enterprise's local or global economy.
    D) An industry risk primarily affects the industry in which the enterprise operates, whereas an economy risk is a result of the enterprise not taking advantage of production economies of scale.
    E) None of the above is a valid guideline to differentiate industry from economy risks

Discussion Questions

LO1   D1. Why is it important to consider both the costs and benefits of internal controls?
LO1   D2. Is risk 100% controllable? Explain your response.
LO4   D3. On January 1, CBU installed a new computer system for tracking and calculating inventory costs. On December 31, at closing, CBU's system reported inventory at $4.5 million for financial statement purposes. At midnight, the auditors performed a physical inventory count and found the inventory total to be $3.5 million. To correct the discrepancy, CBU's accounting staff processed an adjusting entry to reduce inventory by $1.0 million. The next day, two accountants were discussing the events of the previous night. Accountant A was proud of the audit and said it illustrated a benefit of having a good system of internal control. CBU had followed good internal control procedures by having a regular physical inventory count to safeguard a valuable enterprise resource. Accountant A was relieved that the problem was resolved: the financial numbers were corrected before they were reported. In short, he felt successful and thought CBU should feel fortunate to have his accounting staff as control advisors. Accountant B felt differently. She was concerned about the bad

decisions that were made throughout the year based on the incorrect inventory numbers. She felt that she and the other accountants should have helped develop more timely and effective system controls. With which accountant's philosophy do you agree? How can you explain the diverse opinions? What policies or procedures, if any, should CBU develop to avoid such problems in the future?

LO1   **D4.** Some people believe that information technology has made enterprise internal control systems more difficult to design and use. Others believe that information technology has made it easier to control enterprise risks. Which do you believe is true, and why?

Applied Learning

LO4, LO6 **A1.** A customer calls a mail order catalog to order merchandise. The order clerk takes the customer's name, mailing address, credit card number, and the merchandise numbers, sizes, colors, and quantities. After the order clerk hangs up, he or she verifies the merchandise numbers given by the client are valid (that the company does indeed sell an item with that number) and checks with the Shipping Department on availability of the merchandise item.

Required
a. What business process and information process risks exist in this scenario?
b. What control(s) may be implemented to mitigate the risks identified in part (a).

LO4, LO6 **A2.** ABC recently decided to analyze its expenditures. During the analysis, ABC discovered that all orders for repair services always go to a company owned by the vice president's sister. The repair company has a reputation for high prices and poor service. During the analysis, ABC also discovered that many of its purchases for supplies were delivered to the vice president's home address.

Required
a. What business process and information process risks exist in this scenario?
b. What control(s) may be implemented to mitigate the risks identified in part (a).

LO4, LO6 **A3.** A truck driver for a food distributor loads his truck early in the morning according to the invoice purchase orders. He is responsible for picking up COD delivery payments and, on his return trip, for picking up the inventory from major distributors. Currently the POs are hand written by the floor manager the day before the delivery.

Required
a. What business process and information process risks exist in this scenario?
b. What control(s) may be implemented to mitigate the risks identified in part (a).

LO4, LO6 **A4.** Bob owns a small recreational trailer business in a suburban community located close to the mountains. The community is relatively small but growing rapidly. Bob's business is growing, not because of his effective sales style and personality, but because of the growth of the community. Currently, Bob's competition has been nearly nonexistent, but as the area grows he expects to encounter increasing competition. Bob sells mostly trailers for vacationing and camping. When customers arrive on Bob's lot, they are greeted by a salesperson. The salesperson may show the customers the trailers on the lot, but the salesperson need not be present during the entire showing. Depending on customer preference, the salesperson will either take the customer on a tour or the customer may roam the lot freely, inspecting trailers at their leisure. Since recreational trailers are fairly large-ticket items, customers often leave the lot without making a purchase, only to return another day to purchase a trailer. When the customer decided to make a purchase, the salesperson initiates a series of procedures to properly document the order and sale transaction. First, the salesperson determines the model of the selected trailer and offers the customer a list of options that correspond to the particular model. The customer may (1) purchase a trailer off the lot with no added features, (2) purchase a trailer off the lot with additional features, or (3) special order a trailer that is not currently on the lot. In most cases, customers do not pay cash for their trailers. If, however, the customer pays cash, a simple sales contract is prepared and the customer drives off with the trailer. The majority of the customers use an installment method of purchase. Before an installment purchase is authorized, the customer's credit must be verified to determine credit worthiness. With an installment purchase, an installment agreement is prepared in addition to the sales contract. Bob has arranged financing through a local bank for all installment sales. When an installment sale is made, the bank sends Bob a lump-sum payment equal to the price of the trailer. Instead of making payment to Bob, customers pay the bank plus interest. In either case, Bob receives a lump-sum payment for each trailer sold, whether that lump sum comes from the customer or from the bank. Once the credit is approved, the customer can take delivery of the trailer. This involves a delivery person who checks the trailer before delivering it to the customer. The customer picks up the trailer or has it delivered by Bob.

Required

What are Bob's Trailer Sales' instigation, mutual commitment, economic decrement, and economic increment events, and what risks are associated with those events? What are Bob's Trailer Sales' resources, and what risks are associated with those resources? Who are the agents for Bob's Trailer Sales' and what risks are associated with those agents? What controls could be implemented to address all of these risks?

LO1, LO6 **A5.** A computer operator at the local data processing center decides to visit work on a Monday evening. She has a key to the outside door, and since there is no key required for the computer room, she simply walks into the computer room. The operator, who is really one of the nation's most notorious computer programmer/hackers (having been convicted five time for manipulating various firms' data files), opens the documentation bookcase, located in the corner of the computer room. In the bookcase she finds the procedural documentation, the systems documentation, user manuals, application documentation, and operator manuals. She examines the documentation to understand the payroll program and to find the location of the payroll files. She accesses the information systems library, which is available to all computer operators at all times, accesses the payroll program, reprograms it, and runs a payroll job that creates one electronic funds transfer (to a new account opened by the operator under an assumed name). On Tuesday, the operator transfers the funds to a Swiss bank account and does not show up for work.

Required

Prepare a summary that details any internal controls violated in this situation.

CHAPTER 5

Conceptual and Logical Relational Database Models

LEARNING OBJECTIVES
Before we delve into explanations of how to create business process level REA models, you must first learn some useful tools for creating them. These tools are not specific to REA; they were created in the computer science field and have been used by many computer scientists and by many information systems professionals in a variety of contexts. The objective of this chapter is to provide details of conceptual modeling with UML class diagrams and also to provide details of converting conceptual models into logical relational database models.

1. Explain the difference between conceptual, logical, and physical database models
2. Describe constructs that comprise UML class diagrams
3. Describe constructs that comprise relational databases
4. Prepare and interpret UML class diagrams
5. Convert conceptual models into logical models in relational database format
6. Interpret logical relational models to determine what the underlying conceptual models must have been
7. Create data consistent with multiplicities

INTRODUCTION
A **conceptual model** is a representation that depicts the important objects and relationships between the objects that must be captured in a database. It is independent of any hardware, software, or any type of software. The purpose of the conceptual model diagrams created in this chapter is very different than the system flowchart diagrams created in chapter 3. Whereas system flowcharts represent the physical flow of documents and other information throughout a system, showing the areas of responsibility for the information and documents, as well as data's sources, destinations, and formats, conceptual models design a structure for the data an enterprise needs to store to meet its information needs. The conceptual model may be converted into a set of database tables therefore you may think of it as a blueprint with the specifications for the resulting database table structures.

Several different conceptual modeling languages exist. The REA pattern is independent of any specific modeling language and can be implemented using many different types of software. REA can be communicated using (1) narrative descriptions, (2) diagrams of various types with different notations (3) structured grammar, (4) predicate logic notation, (5) tags such as are used in XML and XBRL, and (6) programming language notation. It is very difficult for some people to separate the pattern that is REA from the notation that is used to communicate the pattern. Many of the published REA materials have used entity-relationship (ER) diagrams to demonstrate REA concepts.

Unified Modeling Language (UML) is a widely accepted notation for system analysis and design that includes several types of diagrams for different levels of analysis; its class diagrams are appropriate for conceptual modeling of REA concepts. Later in this textbook we illustrate the REA pattern using class diagrams.

In database design, a conceptual model is converted into a **logical model** once the type of database to be used has been determined. Logical models are independent of any specific software package, but may only be implemented using a software package of a certain category. Examples of logical database models include relational, object-oriented, hierarchical, network, and others.

Once a conceptual model is converted to a relational logical format, it can no longer be implemented in object-oriented, hierarchical, or network database software (unless you go back to the original conceptual model and re-convert it to the corresponding format). Instead the relational logical model must be implemented in one of many relational database software packages. Similarly, if a conceptual model is converted into an object-oriented format, it can no longer be implemented in non-object-oriented software but may be implemented in a variety of object-oriented software packages.

The third type of model used in database design is the **physical database** model. Such a model is created based on the specific database software package in which the database is implemented and is therefore dependent on the software choice.

Because most enterprises use relational database software of some kind, and because most universities make relational database software available to students, we have chosen in this book to focus only on the relational database logical model.

CONCEPTUAL MODELING with UML CLASS DIAGRAMS

Conceptual modeling has historically been the most commonly used tool for presenting REA business process level patterns. Before we discuss the details of the REA business process level pattern, we need to introduce the constructs of conceptual modeling using UML class diagrams. You've actually already seen some of these constructs represented in the examples we used in chapters 1 and 2. The four constructs we discuss are classes, associations, attributes, and multiplicities.

An **entity** is a real world object that has a separate existence (either physical or conceptual). Entities that share the same characteristics (but may each have different values for those characteristics) form an entity set, which may also be called a **class**. The individual members of that set are called instances. For example, each individual customer of an enterprise is an instance of the customer class. The customers share a set of characteristics (e.g. CustomerID, name, address, telephone number, credit limit, account balance due, etc.) Each customer in the set may have different values for these characteristics, but they are expected to possess these characteristics. The specific customer whose ID is C1234, named Brenda Brenton, who lives at 236 Bonair St., Lansing, MI 48917, whose telephone number is (517) 555-2236, whose credit limit is $4,000, whose account balance due is $100 is an instance of the Customer class.

An **association** is a relationship between classes. Notice that because classes are set level constructs, associations represent sets of relationships between entities. Consider a Student class and a Course class. The association between them may be called Enrollment, and that association represents the set of all associations between individual students and the individual courses in which they are or have been enrolled. Exhibit 5-1 illustrates an association between the student class and the course class.

Exhibit 5-1
Students, Courses, and the Enrollment Association

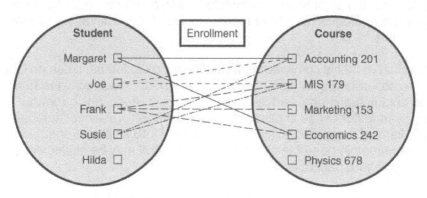

Notice that to describe instances of the association, we need to use characteristics of both of the related classes. Instances of the enrollment set in Exhibit 5-1 are

- Margaret enrolled in Accounting 201
- Margaret enrolled in Economics 242
- Joe enrolled in Accounting 201
- Joe enrolled in MIS 179
- Frank enrolled in MIS 179
- Frank enrolled in Marketing 153
- Frank enrolled in Economics 242
- Susie enrolled in Accounting 201
- Susie enrolled in MIS 179

Associations may also possess characteristics of their own; associations that have such characteristics are described as either an association class or a reified association. For example, the enrollment association may possess a characteristic "grade earned" to reflect the result of a student's enrollment in a course. An **association class** represents a relationship in which there can be only one link between the related entities. For example, if each student can enroll in each course only one time, the relationship is an association class. Each student may enroll in multiple classes, and each class may have multiple students enrolled, but there can be only one grade earned for each combination of student and course. A **reified association** represents a relationship in which there can be multiple links between the related entities. For example, if each student can enroll in the same course multiple times, the relationship is a reified association and there can be multiple values of grade earned for each combination of student and course.

An **attribute** is a characteristic possessed by a class or an association. Several different kinds of attributes are distinguished in conceptual modeling. A **primary key attribute** is used to uniquely and universally describe each instance of a class or association class. For a primary key to be unique, each instance must have a different data value for that attribute. For a primary key to be universal, each instance must possess a data value for that attribute. Consider the Student class and some possible attributes we could use to uniquely and identify each instance in the set of students. Could we use Last Name? No; it is likely that more than one student will share the same last name so it would not be unique. Could we use Drivers' License Number? No; it is likely that some students will not possess a drivers' license so it would not be universal.

If the school in question is in the United States, it may be reasonable to use social security number, substituting an equivalent government-assigned identification number for non-US citizens.

In cases where there is not a naturally occurring attribute that uniquely and universally describes each instance (or if there is one but for some reason the enterprise doesn't want to use it), a primary key may be arbitrarily assigned. Because privacy issues associated with social security numbers make its widespread availability undesirable, the university may choose to assign student ID numbers.

In some cases it may be possible to uniquely and universally identify an instance of a class or association using a combination of two (or more) attributes. For example, to identify instances of the Enrollment association class between Student and Course, we can't use student ID (not unique, since the same student may enroll in multiple courses) or course ID (not unique, since the same course may have multiple students enrolled). However, a combination of the student ID attribute with the course ID attribute would suffice as a primary key. Such a key is called a **concatenated primary key**.

A **simple attribute** is an attribute that cannot be further decomposed; whereas a **composite attribute** may be decomposed into other attributes. An example of a commonly used composite attribute is "address", which may be decomposed into street address, city, state or province, country, and postal code. In general, it is best to store only simple attributes to facilitate querying and maintenance of the data once it is entered. For example, to query all customers who live in a particular city, it will be most efficient if city is stored as a separate attribute rather than as part of "address".

A **derivable attribute** is an attribute that can be derived (computed) from the values of other attributes in the database. For example, a student's overall grade point average is an attribute that is computed based on all of the instances of "grade earned" in the enrollment association for that student. There are two types of derivable attributes: those for which the derived value will not change if new data is entered into the database (i.e., a **static derivable attribute**), and those for which the derived value will change if new data is entered into the database (i.e., a **volatile derivable attribute**). Student's overall grade point average is an example of a volatile derivable attribute. Each time a student completes another course, the value for overall gpa must be re-calculated. "Total sale amount" as an attribute of a Sale class is an example of a static derivable attribute. This attribute may be calculated as the sum of the quantity x selling price of each item sold.

For example, we may compute the total sale amount for Sale #1 as $100. As we enter data for Sales #2 through #50 into the database, that new data does not change the value we computed as the total amount for Sale #1. In general, derivable attributes should not be stored in a relational database, because they take up valuable storage space. Ignoring the cost of storage space, from a theoretical perspective we recommend storing static derivable attributes if they are likely to be needed as base element in queries, because those queries will be much less complex and more efficient. For example, "total sale amount" is likely to be needed as a base element in other queries such as "accounts receivable as of the balance sheet date" or "total sales for region Y during the marketing campaign". We do not recommend storing volatile derivable attributes unless the database software is capable of storing them as triggers (in essence storing the formula by which the data value is computed instead of storing an actual data value).

However, keep in mind that the conceptual model is independent of any specific logical model or physical implementation. Therefore the conceptual model <u>should</u> include derivable attributes attached to the class or association they describe. In fact, the decision to exclude derivable attributes from the company database tables should not be made until the physical implementation level, at which point the specific software has been chosen and its capability of storing triggers is known.

Multiplicities are assigned to represent business rules for how many times an instance of a class is allowed to participate in an association. **Minimum multiplicities** represent the minimum number of times each instance of a class must participate in an association with another class. The most common possible values for minimum participation are zero and one. This indicates whether the participation of each instance of the class in an association with another class is considered optional or mandatory. **Optional participation** means that any specific instance of the class can exist in the database without a corresponding instance of the associated class; optional participation is represented with a zero minimum multiplicity. **Mandatory participation** means that each instance of the class must be related to at least one instance of the associated class in order to be included in the database; mandatory participation is represented with a one minimum multiplicity.

Maximum multiplicities represent the maximum number of times each instance of a class may participate in an association with another class. The most common possible values for a maximum multiplicity are one and many. The term *many* for multiplicities is somewhat misleading because it actually means *more than one*. So if the maximum participation of a class is two or three, it could be depicted as many. Multiplicities may be set to a specific number when appropriate. For example, if a store says each customer may redeem a special offer coupon a maximum of 2 times; the maximum could be specified as 2 rather than * to constrain the data entry to comply with the specific policy.

Exhibit 5-2 displays a UML class diagram using as examples the Purchase and Cash Disbursements events and the Duality association between them.

Exhibit 5-2 UML Class Diagram

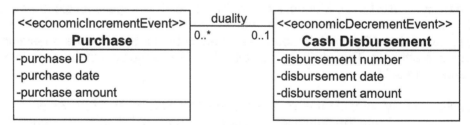

UML Class diagrams represent classes as boxes split into three compartments. We use a simplified version of classes in this textbook because we use relational databases rather than object oriented technology to implement the conceptual models. The first compartment of the box is the name compartment; that section shows the name of the class and may or may not preface the name with a stereotype for the class. In Exhibit 5.2, <<economicIncrementEvent>> and <<economicDecrementEvent>> are stereotypes. The second compartment of the box is the attribute compartment. For simplicity sake, we list only the attribute names in this compartment; more complicated UML class diagrams may also list data types, visibility (whether an attribute is public or private), and other aspects of the attributes. The third compartment of

REA Accounting Systems: Resources-Events-Agents: An ontology for designing, controlling, and using integrated enterprise systems

151

the box is the operation compartment. An operation is a method or function that can be performed by instances of the class. We will leave that compartment blank for this chapter.

Associations between classes are represented in UML class diagrams as lines drawn between the related classes; the lines are labeled with the association names. The minimum and maximum multiplicity representing participation of a class instance in an association is noted on the association line next to the related class's box. The 0..1 next to the Cash Disbursement class in Exhibit 5-2 indicates an instance of purchase may be entered into the system without relating it to an instance of cash disbursement, and each instance of purchase may be related to a maximum of one instance of cash disbursement. The 0..* next to the Purchase class in Exhibit 5-2 indicates an instance of cash disbursement may be entered into the system without relating it to an instance of purchase and each instance of cash disbursement may relate to multiple instances of purchase.

With that explanation in mind, look back at Exhibit 5-1. The lines drawn between the instances of the Student and Course classes indicate which instances of Student are related to which instances of Course. See if you can fill in the multiplicities on the association between Student and Course for Exhibit 5-3. That is, determine what values should replace the A, B, C, and D along the enrollment association line in Exhibit 5-3.

Exhibit 5-3 Student Enrollment in Course in UML Class Diagram format

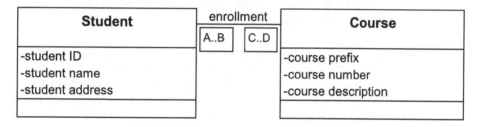

The A represents the minimum participation of Course in its association with related Students. Physics 678 is an example of a course for which no students have yet enrolled, therefore the participation of course in that association is optional and the appropriate value for A is 0. The B represents the maximum participation of Course in its association with related Students and at least one course (Accounting 201) has multiple students enrolled and therefore the appropriate value for B is *. Notice that MIS 179 and Economics 242 also have multiple students; however, once you identify any one instance of course that has multiple related students you don't have to look any further.

The C represents the minimum participation of Student in its association with related Courses. Hilda is an example of a student who has not yet enrolled in any courses, therefore the participation of student in that association is optional and the appropriate value for C is 0. The D represents the maximum participation of Student in its association with related Courses. At least one student (Margaret) has enrolled in multiple courses therefore the appropriate value for D is *. Although Joe, Frank, and Susie have also enrolled in multiple courses, once you notice that Margaret has, you need look no further.

Alternative Conceptual Modeling Notations

Conceptual models are usually portrayed in diagram format; however there is no requirement that diagrams be used, and several different modeling notations exist. Chen[1] introduced one of the first conceptual modeling notations; the entity-relationship model in diagram format. In Chen's notation, entities are represented as rectangles and relationships between entities are represented as diamonds. Chen's notation uses cardinalities instead of multiplicities; the concepts are very similar but the notation placement is slightly different. The previous edition of this textbook used the Chen notation. Other information systems and computer science courses use other notations such as crow's feet diagrams. The current edition of this textbook has changed to UML, as that has become the most widely accepted notation in practice.

It may seem disconcerting that there is not just one notation that everyone uses for conceptual modeling. The differences in notation are especially pronounced for multiplicities/cardinalities. You must not let these differences frustrate you any more than you can let the fact that there are thousands of different languages spoken across the globe. Be aware of the different notations and be sure you understand which "language" an enterprise has used when you try to interpret its system documentation. At least when different spoken languages are written, they look different on paper so that when you are presented with לודג, for example, you immediately recognize that you are not reading English. While you may not be able to tell exactly what language the non-familiar notation is, you will at least recognize that it is not the same as a language you know. With conceptual modeling notation (especially for multiplicities) you must be very careful because at first glance the notation may look similar but upon closer examination you may find it is backward from your approach. You must become multi-lingual with regard to conceptual modeling notations!

UML Class diagrams are similar to entity-relationship models. Classes are similar to entities and Associations are similar to relationships. Multiplicities are similar to participation cardinalities. Nearly every diagrammatic notation in practice represents entities with rectangles (or rounded rectangles). Notations vary as to whether they represent relationships using diamonds, some other symbol, or just connection lines. It is usually reasonably easy to tell at a glance what the entities and relationships are in any notation. Cardinalities are sometimes more difficult to interpret across notations. To clarify cardinalities and to illustrate the difference between the Chen notation and two other notations, examine Exhibit 5-4.

We ask (and answer) 4 questions to determine what this "picture of reality" shows:
- Q1: Must every sale relate to a customer?
    - Yes, each instance of sale involves a customer = mandatory participation minimum multiplicity = 1
- Q2: May any sale relate to multiple customers?
    - No, each instance of sale involves only one customer maximum multiplicity = 1
- Q3: Must every customer relate to a sale?
    - No, Customer 2 (Delia) is unconnected to any sale = optional participation minimum multiplicity = 0
- Q4: May any customer relate to multiple sales?
    - Yes, Customer 1 (Amy) is related to Sale 2 and to Sale 4 maximum multiplicity = *

---

[1] Chen P.P. 1976. The entity relationship model—toward a unified view of data. *ACM Transactions on Database Systems* (March) pp. 9-36.

Exhibit 5-4
Example for Comparing Multiplicity/Participation Cardinality Notations

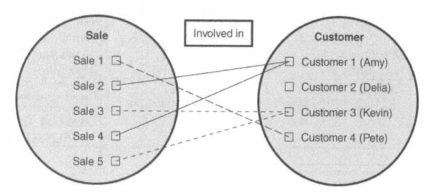

These same 4 questions are asked and answered no matter what multiplicity or participation cardinality notation is used; the difference is simply in where the answers to the questions are placed and what notation is used to communicate the answers.

UML class diagrams put the answers next to the opposite class, with the minimum participation followed by two periods and then the maximum participation. The Chen notation puts the answers next to the first entity in the question inside parentheses, with the minimum participation followed by a comma and then the maximum participation. Another cardinality notation widely used in practice, Crow's Foot, places the answers to the minimum and maximum cardinality questions are placed next to the second entity in the questions, with the minimums closest to the center of the relationship and the maximums closest to the entities.

Table 5-1 shows a side-by-side comparison of the notation used to describe the reality depicted in Exhibit 5-4 for the association/relationship and its multiplicities/cardinalities based on the answers to the four questions above.

Table 5-1 Conceptual Modeling Notation Comparison

	UML Class Diagrams	Chen (used in 3rd edition of textbook)	Crow's foot
Notation for each multiplicity/ cardinality	Min Zero = 0. Min One = 1. Max One = .1 Max Many = .*	Min Zero = (0, Min One = (1, Max One = ,1) Max Many = ,N)	Min Zero = —o— Min One = —+— Max One = ——+ Max Many = —<

Answer Placement	Sale (Q3..Q4)
	  (Q1..Q2) Customer
		Sale (Q1, Q2)
		  (Q3, Q4) Customer
			Min symbol closest to relationship center on opposite entity's side; Max symbol closest to opposite entity;
			Sale (Q4, Q2) ------
			      (Q1, Q3) Customer

Solution to Exhibit 5-4 (attributes are left off to reduce clutter)		Diagram form: 	

CONVERTING CONCEPTUAL MODELS INTO RELATIONAL LOGICAL MODELS

To understand the rules for converting a conceptual data model into a relational logical model, you must first understand the structure of the relational model. The **relational model** was developed by Codd[23] and is based on set theory and predicate logic. The primary construct in the relational model is the **relation**, which is a two-dimensional storage structure (i.e., a storage structure with rows and columns) more commonly referred to as a table. Each table in the relational model represents either a class or an association between classes. The columns in a relational database table are formally called the table **intension**, **schema**, or **fields**, and they represent the attributes of the class or association. The rows in a relational database table are formally called the table **extension**, **tuples**, or **records**, and they represent the specific instances that are members of the classes or associations. The order of columns in a table does not matter, nor does the order in which rows appear. This is because the tables are created in such a way that the rows and columns may be sorted as desired through the use of queries. For this to be possible, one requirement is that all data values in a column must conform to the same data format (e.g. date, text, currency, etc.). Another requirement is that each cell (row-column intersection) in a relational table can contain only one value. Multiple values stored in the same cell form a repeating group; a table containing a repeating group is not a relational table.

The tables in a relational database are linked to each other through primary and foreign keys. Recall that a primary key consists of one or more characteristics of a class that uniquely and universally identifies each instance of the class. A **foreign key** is the primary key of one class

---

[2] Codd, E.F. "Derivability, Redundancy, and Consistency of Relations Stored in Large Data Banks." *IBM Research Report* RJ599, August 19, 1969.

[3] Codd, E.F. "A Relational Model of Data for Large Shared Data Banks." CACM 13, No. 6, June 1970. Republished in *Milestones of Research: Selected Papers 1958-1982*. CACM 25th Anniversary Issue, CACM 26, No. 1, January 1983.

table that is "posted" (added as another column) into another class table to represent an association between those classes.

Exhibit 5-5 illustrates an example of a foreign key attribute. Salesperson ID is the primary key of the Salesperson table, and is posted into the Sale table to establish a link between the Sale and Salesperson tables. Notice that the name of the attribute in the table in which it is the primary key is not required to match the name of the attribute in the table in which it is the foreign key. There is; however, a requirement called **referential integrity** that says a value for a foreign key attribute must either be null (blank) or it must match one of the data values in the table in which the attribute is a primary key. In Exhibit 5-5, example (a) meets referential integrity because each value for salesperson in the Sale table is either blank or it matches a data value from the Salesperson table. Example (b) in Exhibit 5-5 violates referential integrity because it includes a data value for a salesperson in the Sale table for salesperson 234567, but there is no salesperson 234567 in the Salesperson table.

Exhibit 5-5
Foreign Key Examples

(a) meets referential integrity principle

Sale

SaleID	Date	Amount	Salesperson
061401A	6/14	$4,218	*123456*
061401B	6/14	$6,437	*654321*
061501A	6/15	$1,112	*654321*
061501B	6/15	$3,300	
061501C	6/15	$1,776	

Salesperson

SalespersonID	Name	Telephone
123456	Fred	555-0063
654321	Francis	555-0007

(b) violates referential integrity principle

Sale

SaleID	Date	Amount	Salesperson
061401A	6/14	$4,218	*123456*
061401B	6/14	$6,437	*654321*
061501A	6/15	$1,112	*654321*
061501B	6/15	$3,300	
061501C	6/15	$1,776	*234567*

Salesperson

SalespersonID	Name	Telephone
123456	Fred	555-0063
654321	Francis	555-0007

Referential integrity is only one principle to which relational databases must adhere. Another important principle is that of entity integrity. **Entity integrity** says that a primary key of a relational table must not contain a **null value** (which in effect would mean it did not have a value at all, as a null value is a blank value). This guarantees the uniqueness of entities and enables proper referencing of primary key values by foreign key values. As an example, consider the common practice of many enterprises of using telephone numbers as identifiers for their customers. Among the issues associated with this practice is the problem that some customers may not have telephone numbers. If a customer, Joe Smith, does not have a telephone number and telephone number is used as the primary key for the Customer table, the entity integrity principle would prohibit the enterprise from entering a row for Joe Smith in the Customer table.

A third principle to which relational databases must adhere is the **one-fact, one-place rule**[4]. To understand this rule you must understand the definition of a fact as the term is used in database design. A **fact** in database design is the pairing of a candidate key attribute value with another attribute value. A **candidate key** is an attribute value that could be used as a primary key for some class (not necessarily for the class in whose table it exists). Because the facts consist of pairs of actual data values, one must consider the likely data entry possibilities to ensure that each fact will appear only one time. In other words, facts are found in the extension (rows) of the database tables. In database design, **redundancy** is duplicate storage of the same information. One fact stored in multiple places is redundancy and should be avoided, as redundancy nearly always causes data inconsistencies.

Consider the following Sale table, and examine each of its attributes. What attributes are candidate keys? Are any other attributes paired with a candidate key for which duplicate data is expected?

Sale

SaleID	Date	Amount	CustomerID	CustomerName	CustomerAddress
8532	Oct. 2	$13	C422	Andy	456 Pine St.
9352	Oct. 14	$14	C821	Jennifer	987 Forest St.
10215	Oct. 27	$20	C363	Arlie	321 Beech St.
14332	Nov. 5	$18	C422	Andy	456 Pine St.
17421	Nov. 16	$22	C363	Arlie	321 Beech St.

The two attributes that are candidate keys are SaleID (which in fact is the primary key for this table) and CustomerID, which would be the logical primary key to use for a class of customers. Next examine the data in the table to see if there are any duplicate combinations of candidate keys and other attribute values. Each SaleID is unique, so there is no duplication of facts containing that attribute. However, values for CustomerID are not unique. To determine whether there is one fact-multiple places we must examine whether the repeated customer ids are associated with the same data values for another attribute (remember the definition of a fact is a pairing of a candidate key data value with another attribute data value!). Inspection of the data reveals that every time C422 is listed as the customer ID, Andy is listed as the customer name and 456 Pine St. is the customer address. Similarly, each time C363 is listed as the customer id, Arlie is listed as the customer name and 321 Beech St. is the customer address. Therefore the one-fact, one-place rule is violated in this table.

Another violation of the one-fact, one-place rule occurs when multiple facts are stored in one place. This phenomenon is commonly known as a **repeating group**. Consider the following table.

Employee

EmployeeID	Name	Office	Degree Earned
1	Tony	Cleveland	BS,MBA
2	Emily	New York	BA,MBA,PhD
3	Leigh	Birmingham	BA

---

[4] The one-fact, one-place rule was developed by William McCarthy in class notes as a simplified approach to normalization of relational database tables to approximately 3rd normal form.

Because employees may have earned multiple degrees, the placement of the "degree earned" attribute in the Employee table creates multiple facts in the same row. That is, there are multiple pairings of a candidate key (EmployeeID) and another attribute (Degree Earned) in at least one row. Similarly if we tried to store any other attribute (telephone number, vehicle owned, etc.) for which an employee may have multiple values, we would end up with a repeating group. To be able to retrieve and manipulate data in accordance with set theory and predicate logic, the relational model does not allow repeating groups. Therefore the Employee table above is not a relational table.

If we follow prescribed steps for converting a conceptual UML class diagram into relational tables, most violations of the one-fact, one-place rule will be avoided. We present these steps and then demonstrate their application.

Step 1: Create a separate table to represent each class in the conceptual model.

   1A: Each attribute of the class becomes a column in the relational table.

   1B: Each instance (member) of the class becomes a row in the relational table.

Step 2: Create a separate table to represent each association class (each association that has attributes of its own), and also create a separate table to represent each "many-to-many" association in the conceptual model even if it doesn't have attributes of its own. A many-to-many association is one for which the maximum multiplicities of both participating classes are many.

   2A: The primary key from each class that participates in the association is posted into the association table as a column, and the combination of those keys becomes a concatenated primary key for the association table. Any attributes of the association itself are added as columns in the association table.

Step 3: For associations that have a multiplicity pattern of 1..1-1..1 consider whether the conceptual model has correctly represented the underlying reality as two separate classes or whether the two classes should in fact be collapsed into one. If they are best represented as two separate classes, then follow steps 3A and 3B.

   3A: The primary key of one of the classes is posted into the related class table as a foreign key.

   3B: It typically does not matter which class's primary key is posted into the other class's table, but do not post both.

Step 4: For any remaining associations that have 1..1 participation by one of the classes, post the primary key of the class that the 1..1 is next to into the related class's table as a foreign key.

When Step 4 is completed, the only remaining associations should have 0..1 participation by at least one of the classes. These associations take a bit more consideration to determine the best representation in relational tables. According to pure relational theory, separate tables should be created to represent each of these associations. However, for practical purposes, posted foreign keys may be used to represent many of these associations as an implementation compromise. The decision to make the implementation compromise is based on a concept called load.

Load indicates how many data values for an attribute are expected to be non-null. A high load indicates most of the values are expected to be non-null (that is good). A low load means that most of the values are expected to be null (that is bad). A goal of efficient database design is to avoid null values as much as possible, while creating as few separate tables as possible. If posting a foreign key from a class that has a 0..1 next to it into a related class will result in a high load (i.e., most data values are non-null), then it is most efficient to post the foreign key rather than to create a separate table. If posting a foreign key from a class that has a 0..1 next to it into a related class will result in most data values being null, it is most efficient to create a separate table to represent the association and to post the primary keys of the related classes into the association table to form a concatenated primary key. Thus step 5 is stated as

Step 5: For the remaining associations that have 0..1 participation next to one of the classes, consider load.

5A: Post the class next to which the multiplicity is 0..1 into the related class's table as a foreign key for any association for which that posting results in a high load.

5B: Create a separate table for any such associations for which posting a foreign key results in low load.

These five steps are derived from three overall goals. One is to avoid repeating groups, the second is to avoid storage of null values, and the third is to create a minimal database (one that has as few separate tables as possible). Repeating group avoidance is crucial in relational database design – a table that contains repeating groups is not relational.

The most critical "rule" for avoiding repeating groups in converting an association in a conceptual model into relational format is to only allow posting of foreign keys from tables of classes that have a maximum participation of 1 in the association being converted. That is because by definition of the multiplicities, if a class has a * (many) next to it, it would potentially have multiple values to post into the foreign key field in the related class's table. Consider the conceptual model shown in Exhibit 5-6.

Exhibit 5-6: Customer-Sale Association Conceptual Model

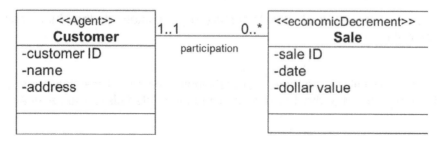

REA Accounting Systems: Resources-Events-Agents: An ontology for designing, controlling, and using integrated enterprise systems

159

Our rules require that we create tables to represent the Customer and Sale classes, as follows:

Customer

CustomerID	Name	Address

Sale

SaleID	Date	Dollar Value

Before following the remaining rules to complete this example, consider the 0..* next to the sale class, which communicates the reality that a customer may exist without participating in a sale (the 0 minimum) and that a customer may participate in many sales (the * maximum). If SaleID were posted as a foreign key in the Customer table, repeating groups would result because by definition of the * maximum multiplicity, the foreign key attribute could take on multiple values. The result would be a non-relational table. To avoid causing repeating groups via the table implementation, do not post a foreign key from a class that has a * maximum next to it into a related class's table.

Another problem would result from posting SaleID as a foreign key into the Customer table. Null values would result in the SaleID field in the Customer table, because the 0 minimum multiplicity indicates a customer can exist without a related sale. That leads us to the second goal: avoiding null values. To avoid null values in foreign key fields, only post foreign keys from class tables for which the related class has mandatory participation in the association of interest (i.e., a 1 minimum).

Examine the possibility of posting the primary key from the Customer class table into the Sale class table as a foreign key. The 1..1 next to customer reveals that a sale cannot exist in this enterprise's database without involving a customer, and that a sale involves no more than 1 customer. Therefore if CustomerID is posted into the Sale table, it will not contain any null values (because of the 1 minimum) and it will not contain multiple values (because of the 1 maximum). The general rule to follow, then, is to post foreign keys from classes that have maximum participation of 1 and mandatory minimum participation in the associations. Steps 2 through 5 are all derived from this general rule.

Once you realize that posting from a class next to a * maximum will (by definition of the multiplicity) cause a repeating group, Step 2 should be clear to you. Recall that Step 2 says to make separate tables for all many-to-many associations. The following multiplicity patterns are all many-to-many associations: 0..* - 0..*; 1..* - 0..*; 0..* - 1..*; 1..* - 1..*.

To make sure Step 2 is clear; consider the association for students' declaration of academic majors shown in Exhibit 5-7. The conceptual model for this association communicates the information that a student can exist in the database before they declare any major (minimum participation is 0) and that a student can declare multiple majors (maximum participation is *). It also communicates the information that a major can exist in the database before any students have declared it (minimum participation is 0) and that a major can be declared by multiple students (maximum participation is *).

Exhibit 5-7: Student-Major Association Conceptual Model

Student	0..* 0..*	Major
-Student ID -Name -Address	Declaration	-Major Code -Name of Major -Credit hours required

Following step 1, we create a table to represent the set of students, and another table to represent the set of majors. We have entered data into these tables to help illustrate the example. Primary keys are underlined.

Student

StudentID	Name	Address
1	Tony	Cleveland
2	Emily	New York
3	Leigh	Birmingham
4	Abe	Illinois

Major

MajorCode	Name_of_Major	Credit_Hours_Required
1110	Accounting	183
1221	MIS	180
1342	Finance	180
2104	Nuclear Physics	190

The following set of declarations is consistent with the cardinalities:
- Tony is double-majoring in accounting and finance
- Emily is double-majoring in accounting and MIS
- Leigh is majoring in finance
- Abe has not declared a major

Notice what happens if we post MajorCode into the Student table:

Student

StudentID	Name	Address	MajorCode
1	Tony	Cleveland	1110, 1342
2	Emily	New York	1110, 1221
3	Leigh	Birmingham	1342
4	Abe	Illinois	

The repeating groups in MajorCode represent multiple facts in one place and cause the table to be non-relational, so we can't do that! Similarly, if we post StudentID into the Major table:

Major

MajorCode	Name_of_Major	Credit_Hours_Required	StudentID
1110	Accounting	183	1,2
1221	MIS	180	2
1342	Finance	180	1,3
2104	Nuclear Physics	190	

The repeating groups in StudentID represent multiple facts in one place and cause the table to be non-relational, so we can't do that. Notice that it does not matter what minimum cardinalities existed for either class in the association. Even if there were mandatory participation for both student and major such that Abe had declared a major in nuclear physics, the repeating groups problem still exists. The correct table representation for this association is as follows:

Student

StudentID	Name	Address
1	Tony	Cleveland
2	Emily	New York
3	Leigh	Birmingham
4	Abe	Illinois

Major

MajorCode	Name_of_Major	Credit_Hours_Required
1110	Accounting	183
1221	MIS	180
1342	Finance	180
2104	Nuclear Physics	190

Declaration

StudentID	MajorCode
1	1110
1	1342
2	1110
2	1221
3	1342

Next, examine Step 3 more closely. Step 3 applies to associations with the multiplicity pattern 1..1--1..1. The first part of the step says to consider whether the two classes are conceptually separate or whether they should be combined. Consider an enterprise that earns its revenue by setting up hot-dog stands between the hours of 11:00 a.m. and 2:00 p.m. each day that classes are in session on college campuses. The enterprise places its stands in areas where many students are likely to be walking, and likely to be hungry because no alternative food vendors are nearby. The enterprise sells hot dogs, lemonade, chips, fruit, and cookies. All sales are made on a cash basis. The food and the cash change hands simultaneously. Therefore a sale doesn't exist without a related cash receipt, and the sale only involves one cash receipt since it must be paid in full. So the multiplicity next to cash receipt is 1..1.

Next we make a rather bold assumption that sales are the only source of cash for this enterprise (that is, they haven't borrowed money or obtained contributed cash from its owners). That is probably not realistic, but is within the realm of possibility as the owners could have contributed the equipment as capital instead of cash, and the enterprise could have purchased its initial inventory on credit, and then generated enough cash flow from sales to pay for the purchases and make new purchases. If we accept that possibility as the reality for this enterprise, the minimum multiplicity next to sale in the association with cash receipt is 1(mandatory). It also seems reasonable to assume maximum multiplicity next to sale in the association with cash receipt is also 1; that says that a cash receipt applies to only one sale. In this scenario, if we receive cash from a customer for a hot dog and lemonade, the cash receipt applies only to that sale.

You may wonder whether the maximum of 1 next to Cash Receipt is valid if a boyfriend and girlfriend approach the stand and the boyfriend pays for both their lunches. The hotdog vendor would view that as one sale and one cash receipt, with the boyfriend as the customer. Assume for example sake that this is a reasonable Sale 1..1 – 1..1 Cash Receipt association. Next it must be determined whether these two classes are conceptually separate (in the context of this enterprise) or whether they should be combined into one class. To make this determination we must consider the future of this enterprise, allowing for reasonably possible growth, as well as the present circumstances. If we determine this enterprise will never sell lunches on credit and will never obtain cash from a source other than sales, it may be reasonable to combine them into a single class.

If we determine that someday they might obtain cash from other sources, then we should maintain them as separate classes and create separate tables for them. Note that we may determine through this analysis that our chosen multiplicity pattern is not the most appropriate choice and we may decide to change the minimum multiplicity beside sale to optional, in case in the future the enterprise wants to allow cash receipts from loans and owner contributions. If we decide to keep the classes separate, and to keep the multiplicity pattern as 1..1—1..1 then we can post a key from either class into the other class's table to establish the association in the tables. Consider the tables and information about their association in Exhibit 5-8.

Exhibit 5-8: Sale and Cash Receipt Class Tables and association information

Sale

SaleID	Date	Amount
S1	6/5	$4.25
S2	6/5	$3.75

CashReceipt

ReceiptID	Date	Amount
CR1	6/5	$4.25
CR2	6/5	$3.75

Association Information:
Cash Receipt CR1 paid for Sale S1
Cash Receipt CR2 paid for Sale S2

Given the association information (notice that the association information is consistent with the multiplicities) we can see that posting ReceiptID from the Cash Receipt table as a foreign key in the Sale table creates no problems. No repeating groups result, and no facts end up stored in multiple places. Similarly we could post SaleID from the Sale table as a foreign key in the Cash Receipt table without any problem. However, we must choose one or the other.

If we post both foreign keys, we have created one fact (a pairing of a candidate key attribute SaleID with another attribute ReceiptID) in multiple places (in this case, in two different tables). Our recommendation for this particular situation is to post the ReceiptID into the Sale table because that allows the most flexibility in case of future changes in the enterprise. Thus our recommended solution is as follows.

Sale

SaleID	Date	Amount	ReceiptID
S1	6/5	$4.25	CR1
S2	6/5	$3.75	CR2

CashReceipt

ReceiptID	Date	Amount
CR1	6/5	$4.25
CR2	6/5	$3.75

From these examples, Step 4 is probably clearer to you now than when we first introduced it. This step says that any remaining associations that have 1..1 multiplicities beside one of the classes should be represented in the tables by posting that class's primary key into the related class's table as a foreign key. This step covers associations with the following multiplicity patterns: 1..1—0..*; 1..1—1..*; 1..1—0..1; 0..*--1..1; 1..*--1..1; and 0..1—1..1. There is no need to make separate tables to represent any of these associations; because posting a foreign key from a table of a class with 1..1 participation guarantees that no repeating groups or null values will result. Because fewer tables results in easier database querying, it is best to avoid making more tables than absolutely necessary.

Exhibit 5-9 revisits the example that was presented in Exhibit 5-6, with the Customer 1..1 – 0..* Sale association. Say that Frank was the customer for sale 1 and Amy was the customer for sale 2, and Frank liked what he bought in sale 1 so much that he came back the next day and bought more. That scenario fits with the given multiplicities. We have one customer (Dean) who exists without participating in a sale, and we have one customer (Frank) who participates in multiple sales. And each sale involves one and only one customer. We can't post SaleID into Customer because it will cause a repeating group, but we can post CustomerID into Sale.

Exhibit 5-9: Relational Table Implementation of a 1..1 to 0..* Association

Customer

CustomerID	Name	Address	Telephone	~~SaleID~~
C1	Frank	Dover	555-9999	~~S1, S3~~
C2	Dean	Amherst	555-8888	
C3	Amy	Chicago	555-7777	~~S2~~

Sale

SaleID	Date	Amount	CustomerID
S1	5/21	$40.00	C1
S2	5/22	$30.00	C3
S3	5/22	$80.00	C1

Once again, it doesn't matter what the multiplicities are on the class that is related to the 1..1 class; we will always have an acceptable relational table if we post a foreign key from the table of the 1..1 class into the associated class's table. By definition of the multiplicities there will be a non-null value and there will not be more than one value of that attribute to post into each row of the related table.

We have saved the most difficult associations for last. Once you learn Steps 1-4, you will be able to apply them quickly and easily, because there is very little subjectivity involved. For Step 5 you will have to be more careful. Still, once you understand the logic to use, this step will also become straightforward.

Step 5 provides guidance for establishing associations in tables to represent the following multiplicity patterns: 0..*—0..1; 1..*--0..1; 0..1—0..*; 0..1—1..*; and 0..1—0..1. For each of these multiplicity patterns the general rule for maximum multiplicities prohibits posting a foreign key from the table of the class that has multiplicities of 1..* or 0..* beside it. The general rule for maximum multiplicities cannot be broken, because it will cause a repeating group. The general rule for minimum multiplicities suggests you shouldn't post a foreign key from the table of the class that has 0..1 multiplicity because it will create null values in the database. Null values are undesirable because they waste space in the database (there is space reserved for the values even though they are not there).

To avoid creating repeating groups and to avoid creating null values, then, we would need to create separate tables to establish each of these associations. However, creating separate tables also takes up valuable space in the database, and it complicates querying. So for these multiplicity patterns we need to determine which is the least wasteful of space in the database. To make that determination we evaluate a concept called load.

Load refers to the number of non-null data values for an attribute. If most of the data values are non-null, the attribute is said to have a high load, or to be highly loaded. If most of the data values are null, the attribute is said to have a low load. This concept applies to any attribute, but for Step 5 we are only interested in load for potential foreign key attributes. The decision we need to make is whether posting from a 0..1 class table will result in more wasted space than the space creating a separate table would consume. If posting a foreign key from the 0..1 class table would result in only a few null values, less overall table space would be used than the creation of a separate association table. However, if posting a foreign key would result in mostly null values, then a separate table would take less space than the posted foreign key would waste.

Consider the following example. After an enterprise makes purchases, it either pays for the merchandise (with a separate check written for each purchase) or it returns the merchandise to the vendor. The enterprise rarely ends up returning the merchandise; most of the time the merchandise received is satisfactory and the enterprise pays for it.

On average 98 out of 100 purchases end up being paid for and 2 out of 100 purchases result in a purchase return. Sometimes the company returns two purchases made from the same vendor as a single return. Therefore, for this company, a purchase may exist without a related purchase return (minimum 0) and may result in no more than one return (maximum 1).
However a purchase return may not exist without a related purchase (minimum 1) and may result from more than one purchase (maximum *).

Also, a purchase may exist without a related cash disbursement (minimum 0) and it may result in no more than one cash disbursement (maximum 1). A cash disbursement may exist without a related purchase (in inquiring of the company you discovered that approximately 2/3 of the company's checks are written for other things like employee salaries, dividends, loan re-payments, etc.) (minimum 0) and a cash disbursement pays at most for one purchase (maximum 1). This scenario encompasses two associations of interest for discussing load: the association between Purchase and Cash Disbursement and the association between Purchase and Purchase Return. Exhibit 5-10 presents the conceptual models for this scenario.

Exhibit 5-10: Example Scenario for Evaluating "Load"

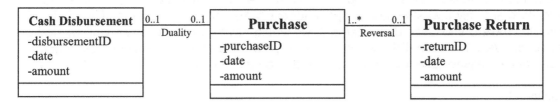

Following Step 1, we create a separate table for each of the classes as follows:

Purchase

PurchaseID	Date	Amount

Cash Disbursement

DisbursementID	Date	Amount

Purchase Return

ReturnID	Date	Amount

Next we examine the conceptual model to determine whether either of the associations have multiplicities for which guidance is provided in steps 2 through 4. They do not. Therefore we follow the guidance for Step 5 for each of the two associations. First we examine the Duality association. Because the multiplicity pattern is 0..1 – 0..1, the maximum multiplicity rule would allow us to post in either direction. That is, we could post PurchaseID into the Cash Disbursement table or we could post DisbursementID into the Purchase table. However, if neither posting results in high load, we should make a separate table to avoid wasting space. We must examine the likely load if we post in each direction and then determine the most efficient solution.

First let's examine what is likely to happen if we post PurchaseID into the Cash Disbursement table. We know from the information given to us previously that approximately 2/3 of the checks the company writes are for non-purchase transactions such as employee salaries, dividends, loan re-payments. That means if we post PurchaseID into the Cash Disbursement table, only 1/3 of the data values will be non-null whereas 2/3 will be blank. That is not a high load, so that would not be a good choice.

Consider the alternative of posting DisbursementID into the Purchase table. The information we were given revealed that the company pays for 98 out of 100 purchases. It does not matter that the payment is not made immediately; you are concerned with how many of the attribute's data values will eventually be non-null. 98% is a high load, so the best solution for this association is to post the DisbursementID into the Purchase table. The purchase table will be changed to

Purchase

PurchaseID	Date	Amount	DisbursementID

The Cash Disbursement and Purchase Return tables will remain as shown on the previous page. In the purchase table, for 2 out of every 100 records, DisbursementID will be blank (null) thus there are only 2 wasted cells of space for every 100 purchase records. If we had chosen to post PurchaseID into Cash Disbursement, we would have had approximately 66 wasted cells of space for every 100 cash disbursement records. If we had chosen to create a separate table to represent the association, we would have added a table as follows

Duality

PurchaseID	**DisbursementID**

For every 100 purchases, there will be 98 records added to this association table, as opposed to filling in 98 data values in the DisbursementID field in the Purchase table. This latter approach thus "wastes" 98 cells of space for every 100 purchase records (the purchaseID is entered 98 times more in this example than in the posted key example). This analysis leads us to conclude that the DisbursementID posted into the Purchase table is the best solution.

Next we examine the Reversal association. Because the multiplicity pattern is Purchase 1..* -- 0..1 Purchase Return, the only alternatives we need to compare are that of posting Purchase Return into Purchase versus creating a separate table. The maximum multiplicity rule prohibits the posting of PurchaseID into PurchaseReturn because by definition a purchase return may have resulted from more than one purchase and would cause a repeating group.

The information we were given revealed that 2 out of 100 purchases end up being returned. That is a very low load, so if we post ReturnID into the Purchase table nearly all the data values for that attribute will be null. That approach would "waste" 98 cells of space for every 100 purchase records. The best solution in this case is to create a separate table to represent the Reversal association. The association table will be established as follows (in addition to the original Purchase and Purchase Return tables:

Reversal

PurchaseID	**ReturnID**

For every 100 records entered in the Purchase table, 2 records will be added to this table. This approach in effect "wastes" 2 cells of space for every 100 purchase transactions (because the PurchaseID is entered 2 more times than in the posted key example). Thus for the Reversal association, the separate table is the best approach, as using 2 extra cells of space per 100 purchases is preferable to using 98 extra cells of space per 100 purchases.

ASSOCIATION ATTRIBUTE PLACEMENT

Because associations that have attributes of their own become association classes in UML class diagrams, you must create separate tables to represent those association classes. The attributes that belong to the associations must be placed in the association class table. This is especially important to prevent repeating groups for many-to-many associations. Consider the association between Student and Course shown in Exhibit 5-11.

Exhibit 5-11: Student-Course Association: Conceptual Model with Association Class

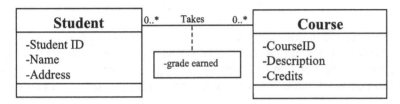

Our first rule requires that we make a separate table for the Student class and a separate table for the Course class. Our second rule requires that a separate table be created to represent the "Takes" association class, using the primary keys of each of the associated classes as a concatenated primary key and placing any attributes of the association class (in this case "grade earned") into the "Takes" table. Exhibit 5-12 displays these table structures.

Exhibit 5-12: Relational Tables for Student-Takes-Course Classes and Association Class

Student

StudentID	Name	Address
999888	Mildred	123 Almanac St.
888777	Kent	456 Market Dr.
777666	Candace	789 Harriet Ave.

Course

CourseID	Description	Credits
ACG611	Advanced AIS	3
FIN642	Financial Markets	3
MIS650	IT Management	3

Takes

StudentID	CourseID	Grade earned
999888	ACG611	B
999888	MIS650	A-
888777	MIS650	B+

If the attribute *Grade earned* (see bolded column) is placed in the Student table, what would happen when data is entered for the grades earned by Mildred in ACG 611 and in MIS 650? There would be only one cell available to hold two data values. If the attribute is placed in the Course table, what would happen when data is entered for the grades earned by Mildred and Kent in MIS 650? Again, there would be only one cell available to hold two data values. The correct placement of the attribute is in the Takes table.

SUMMARY

In this chapter we introduced the UML class diagram notation used for conceptual modeling, including the creation of classes and associations and the definition of minimum and maximum multiplicities for each association. We then introduced a set of rules that can be applied in an algorithmic manner to convert any UML class diagram into a set of relational database tables. If you apply the rules we labeled as steps 1 through 5 to a UML class diagram and then are careful when assigning attributes to ensure you don't cause one fact to be multiple places or multiple facts in one place, you will end up with a set of reasonably well normalized relational database tables.

Keep in mind, though, that we have not discussed (and will not discuss) technical issues such as optimization and database performance that would be necessary for scaling this type of database to be able to handle the volume required by most large corporations. Such a discussion is beyond the scope of this book but would need to be considered in large scale implementations.

CHECKLIST OF KEY TERMS AND CONCEPTS

Association

Association class

Attribute

Candidate key

Class

Composite attribute

Concatenated primary key

Conceptual (database) model

Derivable attribute

Entity

Entity integrity

Extension

Fact

Field

Foreign key

Intension

Load (high and low)

Logical model

Mandatory participation

Maximum multiplicity

Minimum multiplicity

Null value

One fact, one place rule

Optional participation

Physical database model

Primary key attribute

Record

Redundancy

Referential integrity

Reified association

Relation

Relational model

Repeating group

Schema

Simple attribute

Static derivable attribute

Tuple

Unified Modeling Language (UML)

Volatile derivable attribute

Review Questions

LO3   R1. What is the purpose of a foreign key?

LO3   R2. Does every table in a relational database contain a foreign key? Explain.

LO1   R3. Explain the difference between conceptual, logical, and physical database models.

LO3   R4. What is referential integrity and how can one tell if a relational database has referential integrity?

LO2   R5. How are minimum multiplicities used when designing enterprise systems?

LO2   R6. How are maximum multiplicities used when designing enterprise systems?

LO2, LO3 R7. What is the purpose of a primary key attribute?

LO2, LO4 R8.   What are the multiplicities for a class that has mandatory participation in an association and can be related to at most one instance of the associated class? Where should these multiplicities be placed on the UML class diagram?

LO5   R9.   Given the conceptual model of the association between Alpha and Omega, if 74% of alphas are related to omegas and 46% of omegas are related to alphas, what is the best relational table implementation .

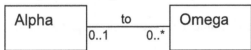

LO6, LO7 R10. Given the tables below and assuming entered data conforms to the multiplicities, what must have been the underlying conceptual model?

Course

CourseID (PK)	Days	Time	Location	Instructor(FK)
10012153102	MWF	9:00-9:50a	111D DeVos	Dunnc
10021153103	MW	3:00-4:15p	103D DeVos	Phillipss4
10021315318	TTh	8:30-9:45a	635 EC	Easlickn
10012315318	MW	3:00-4:15p	109D DeVos	Dunnc

Instructor

InstructorID (PK)	LastName	FirstName	Office	Phone
Dunnc	Dunn	Cheryl	466C	1-7379
Easlickn	Easlick	Nancy	123B	1-1112
Johnsonf3	Johnson	Frank	211A	1-2111
Phillipss4	Phillips	Steven	212A	1-2112

Multiple Choice Questions

LO2

1. Which statement accurately interprets one or more of the multiplicities that are depicted below in the Alpha to Omega relationship?

Alpha   to   Omega
0..1   0..*

A) An Alpha is related to at most one Omega
B) An Omega can be related to many Alphas
C) An Omega can happen before an Alpha
D) Omegas can be related only to Alphas
E) Alphas can be related only to Omegas

LO2, LO3

2. Primary key attributes
A) Must be unique
B) Must be universal
C) Must be used to identify the classes or associations to which they are assigned
D) Can be chosen arbitrarily
E) All of the above are true

LO2

3. Which statement accurately explains one or more of the following multiplicities between the "Customer Order" and the "Delivery" events?

Customer Order	to	Delivery
	1..* 0..1	

A) Each delivery can be associated with only one order
B) A delivery cannot be made without a valid order
C) An order cannot be accepted without a prior delivery to the customer
D) Any order can be associated with several delivery events
E) A delivery can happen before the associated order event

LO2

4. Customers that come in to Furniture Galore, Inc. may be helped by any available salesperson. If more than one salesperson helps the same customer with the same merchandise, any resulting sale to that customer will be credited to all involved salespeople, who will split the sale commission. Salespeople are added to the database as soon as they are hired. A sale cannot be made without a salesperson. The multiplicities for the association between Sale and Salesperson for Furniture Galore, Inc. are:
A) Sale 0..1 to 1..1 Salesperson
B) Sale 0..* to 1..1 Salesperson
C) Sale 1..1 to 0..* Salesperson
D) Sale 1..* to 0..* Salesperson
E) Sale 0..* to 1..* Salesperson

LO2, LO3

5. Any attribute that may be decomposed into other attributes is called a
A) Simple attribute
B) Complex attribute
C) Static derivable attribute
D) Volatile derivable attribute
E) Candidate key attribute

LO2

6. Which of the following represent invalid multiplicities for a class' participation in an association?
A) 0..1
B) *..1
C) 1..1
D) 1..*
E) 0..*

LO2

7. Which of the following minimum and maximum multiplicities represent a class that has optional participation in an association and can participate in the association multiple times?
A) 1..0
B) 1..*
C) 0..1
D) 0..*
E) 1..1

LO3
8. The intension of a relational database table is its
   A) Cells
   B) Rows
   C) Columns
   D) Relationships
   E) Referential integrity

LO3
9. In relational database design, a primary key of one table that is also included in another table
   A) Usually indicates that someone made a mistake in deriving the tables and has added undesirable data redundancy into the database.
   B) Usually results in null values being introduced into the database.
   C) Usually ensures that we can get all the information we need to make a decision by querying only one table or the other (i.e., we would not need both tables in the same query).
   D) Usually uniquely and universally identifies each instance in both tables in which it is included.
   E) Usually establishes a connection between the tables so they can be linked to generate useful information.

LO3
10. Which of the following is NOT another name for the columns in a relational database?
    A) Intension
    B) Schema
    C) Fields
    D) Records
    E) All of the above are other names for the columns in a relational database

LO3
11. Which of the following describes referential integrity?
    A) A primary key of a relational table must not contain a null value
    B) One fact must not be in multiple places
    C) The value for a foreign key attribute must either be null or match one of the data values of that attribute in the table in which the attribute is a primary key
    D) Referential integrity is a principle that prevents the use of redundancy, avoids null values, and creates a minimal database
    E) Multiple facts must not be stored in a single cell

LO3
12. Which of the following statements about is correct regarding the concept of load?
    A) High load indicates most of the values are expected to be null
    B) Low load indicates most of the values are expected to be null

LO5
13. Load indicates
    A) The capacity of the database
    B) The dollar amounts of the data
    C) Null values
    D) How many data values for an attribute are expected to be non-null
    E) None of the above

LO3

14. Which of the following is most likely a violation of the one-fact, one-place rule?
    A) Customer ID is used as the primary key of a Sale table.
    B) Cash Receipt ID is posted as a foreign key in a Sale table for a company that requires immediate cash payments in full for each sale.
    C) A separate table is created to represent a relationship between Warehouse and Inventory with cardinalities 1..* - 0..* and the attribute "Quantity On Hand" is assigned to the relationship table.
    D) Customer ID posted as a foreign key in a Sale table.
    E) A separate table is created to represent a relationship between Purchase and Cash Disbursement with cardinalities 0..1 – 0..1 and the attribute "Amount of Cash Disbursement Applied to a Purchase" is assigned to the relationship table.

LO5

15. Creating separate tables to represent associations helps to avoid
    A) Repeating groups
    B) Non-null values
    C) Null values
    D) Both A and C above
    E) Both A and B above

Discussion Questions

LO5   D1. Say you are trying to create relational database tables to implement a conceptual model that includes an association as shown.

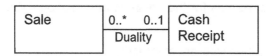

      You have created a table for Sale and a table for Cash Receipt. You are considering whether to post a foreign key from Cash Receipt into Sale. You have the following information available. Explain whether each of these statements adds to the knowledge you already had and how each affects your decision as to whether to post the foreign key. If you decide not to post a foreign key from Cash Receipt into Sale, what other choices do you have for implementing this relationship in the relational tables?

- Nearly all of this enterprise's sales are made on credit.
- The enterprise very rarely has any bad debts resulting from sales.
- Nearly all of this enterprise's cash receipts apply to sales.

LO5   D2. In creating relational tables we have three objectives. Explain what these objectives are, and how we attempt to meet them in converting a conceptual model into relational tables. Do any of these objectives contradict each other, and if so, to which do we give precedence?

LO5   D3. Explain the rule used to create relational database tables from a conceptual model association that has the multiplicity pattern 0..* – 0..*. How should the association be implemented and why does it need to be implemented that way? Does the rule differ if either or both of the minimum multiplicities are changed to 1?

LO5   D4. Explain the rule used to create relational database tables from a conceptual model association that has the multiplicity pattern 1..1 – 0..*. How should the association be implemented and why is it best implemented that way? Are there any other choices for implementing the association? What if the pattern is changed to 1..1 – 1..*; would you implement the association differently?

LO4, LO6 D5. What should be your first consideration if you encounter an association in a UML class diagram with a multiplicity pattern 1..1 – 1..1, and why? What choices do you have for implementing the association into relational tables and how will you decide which is the most appropriate implementation?

LO3   D6. When creating a physical relational database implementation, what should you do with derivable attributes? Does your answer differ for static derivable attributes compared to volatile derivable attributes? Does the specific database software to be used affect your choice? Explain.

LO6   D7. Inspect the following logical relational database tables. Construct the likely underlying conceptual model.

Library Book Loan Event

LoanID	Date	Time
L1	1/21/2015	8:32
L2	1/21/2015	8:37
L3	1/21/2015	8:48

Library Book Renewal Event

RenewID	Date	Time
R1	2/7/2015	9:10
R2	2/8/2015	8:20
R3	2/28/2015	12:40

Loan-Renewal

LoanID	RenewID
L1	R1
L1	R3
L3	R2

Applied Learning

LO5, LO7 A1. Midsize University has the following partial conceptual model to represent its system for storing information about its faculty, courses, departments, and offices. Convert the conceptual model into a logical model in relational database table format (manually, on paper, not in a database software package). Create and write data into the tables that is consistent with the multiplicities in the conceptual model. Each table should have at least 3 rows, and no more than 5 rows of data.

Additional information you may need: While at any point in time a few offices are unassigned to faculty and unallocated to any department, more than 80% are assigned and allocated. More than 90% of faculty have assigned offices.

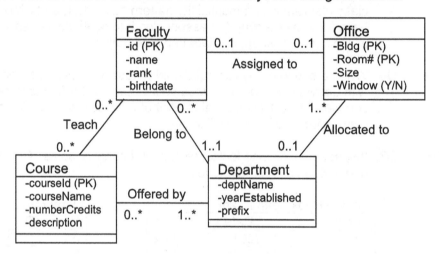

Chapter 6

REA Core Business Process Modeling

LEARNING OBJECTIVES

The objective of this chapter is to introduce constructs of the business process level of the REA ontology. We illustrate those constructs by creating conceptual models for the acquisition and revenue cycles encompassing only the core REA business process model constructs. By focusing first on the core, you can master a manageable number of constructs. Once you have the core pattern developed in your long-term memory, it will be easier to extend that pattern for the expanded business process model constructs. Similarly, by focusing first on the acquisition and revenue cycles, you can master the most common activities. Once you are comfortable applying the pattern to those cycles, it will be easier to extend that pattern-based thinking to the conversion, payroll, and financing cycles. After studying this chapter, you should be able to

1. Read, interpret, and prepare UML class diagrams that incorporate the REA pattern
2. Assign multiplicities to represent the participation of REA classes in associations
3. Identify economic exchanges that form the core of transaction cycles
4. Identify resources involved in economic events in the revenue and acquisition cycles
5. Identify agents (internal and external) involved in economic events in the revenue and acquisition cycles
6. Create a core business process level REA model for revenue or acquisition cycle

REA CORE BUSINESS PROCESS LEVEL MODELING CONSTRUCTS
While most of the business process level REA constructs were briefly mentioned throughout chapters 2, 3, and 4, we reintroduce those constructs that comprise the core REA business process level model next to make sure you have them all in one place such that you can organize them clearly in your mind.

Core REA Classes
Most of the terminology and REA constructs introduced in this chapter have been formalized into an ISO/IEC standard for business transactions[1]. ISO (the International Organization for Standardization), and IEC (the International Electro-technical Commission) form the specialized system for worldwide standardization.

The three categories of classes that comprise the core REA business process level pattern are *Resources*, *Events*, and *Agents*.

Resources are things such as goods, services, or rights that have value and are under the control of a person or enterprise. Resources are sometimes tracked at the individual instance (token) level. That occurs when each specific physical object can be differentiated from the others even though their nature and appearance may be identical. Such tracking is typically

---

[1] ISO/IEC 2007, ISO 15944-4 Information technology -- Business Operational View -- Part 4: Business transaction scenarios -- Accounting and economic ontology. http://standards.iso.org/ittf/PubliclyAvailableStandards/index.html

accomplished through some type of tags, each of which has a unique identifier such as a serial number. Resources are sometimes tracked only by the categories by which they are classified, and we thus refer to them as **resource types**. That is, one identifier will be assigned to represent the type of object and individual instances will be interchangeable and indistinguishable. Resource types may also be called bulk resources.

An example of a resource is an automobile. Each specific physical automobile is given a unique vehicle identification number (VIN) that differentiates that automobile from all others. An example of a resource type is a can of soup at the grocery store. Each specific physical can of soup has a label that identifies the type of product – brand, size, and flavor, but once all the cans that share that brand, size and flavor are put on to the shelf they are interchangeable and indistinguishable from each other.

Events are occurrences in time, i.e., something that happens of some importance. In the core REA business process level of the REA ontology, the events of interest are economic events. *Economic Increment Events* are events that increase resources, either in quantity or in value. *Economic Decrement Events* are events that decrease resources, either in quantify or in value. Purchase (receipt of goods) is an example of an economic increment event in the acquisition cycle. Cash receipt is an example of an economic increment event in the revenue cycle. Cash disbursement is an example of an economic decrement event commonly found in the acquisition cycle. Sale is an example of an economic decrement event commonly found in the revenue cycle.

Agents are individuals, enterprises, or agencies who participate in events or who control resources. Those agents acting on behalf of the enterprise whose system is being designed or operated are referred to as *Internal Agents*. Those agents operating on behalf of themselves or on behalf of other enterprises are referred to as *External Agents*.

Core REA Associations
When Bill McCarthy examined hundreds of accounting transactions in search of an underlying pattern, he noted that every accounting transaction represented part or all of an economic exchange that was made up of at least one economic increment event and at least one economic decrement event. In other words, each economic exchange involved the company giving up one resource or combination of resources to get another resource or combination of resources. *Duality* is the causal association between the economic increment and decrement events that make up an economic exchange. McCarthy also noticed that the exchange was not always immediate and that there was no rule as to whether the increment or the decrement event happened first. Sometimes there was a significant time lag between the events, for which double-entry bookkeeping entries created an account to allow its entries to balance – i.e., to keep both sides of the Assets = Liabilities + Equity equation equal with each other. McCarthy labeled these timing differences **claims** and emphasized the fact that the exchanges were not complete until the claims were satisfied by the corresponding economic events occurrence. You may recognize some of these timing differences as accounts receivable (e.g. sale happens before the related cash receipt), deferred revenue (cash receipt happens before the related sale), prepaid expenses (cash disbursement happens before the related acquisition event), accounts payable (acquisition event happens before the related cash disbursement event), and wages payable (acquisition of labor happens before the related cash disbursement event).

McCarthy also noticed that although the thing received or given up varied for different transactions, that thing always had economic value and could be thought of as a resource. He emphasized that the claims that result from timing differences between duality-related events are not resources and should not be used as foundational elements in an information system. McCarthy used the term *Stockflow* to describe the association between an economic event and the resource that event increases or decreases. Associations between economic increment events and the resources they increase may alternatively be called *Inflow* relationships. Associations between economic decrement events and the resources they decrease may be called *Outflow* relationships. Finally, McCarthy noticed that each event that made up an economic exchange involved more than just a "what" (the resource) but also a "who". In fact each event typically involved at least one person operating as an agent of the enterprise and at least one other person or company who was an external business partner. *Participation* associations relate events to the agents who participate in those events.

The core REA pattern documented by McCarthy in 1982 is shown in Exhibit 6-1.

Exhibit 6-1
Core REA Pattern

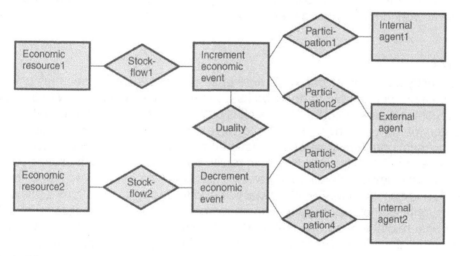

Adapted from
McCarthy, W.E. "The REA Accounting Model: A Generalized Framework for Accounting Systems in a Shared Data Environment." *The Accounting Review*, July 1982, pp. 554-77.

McCarthy realized that accounting transactions aren't recorded until part of the economic story is already over. He also understood that the full story was not being captured because the full detail was not needed for the accounting view that was driven by the content of traditional financial statements. Therefore he included some associations that were not needed for traditional accounting purposes, but in general included only economic events. In later years, he and other colleagues further developed the REA ontology to include events that happen prior to the actual economic exchange. The remaining associations McCarthy did discuss as part of the original core business process level REA ontology are as follows.

Custody is the association between an agent and a resource such that the agent either has physical control over the resource or controls access to the resource. Such a relationship is separate from any event involving the resource. In other words, if an event involves a resource and an agent, the participation of both the resource and the agent in that event does not constitute a custody association. Such information is already captured in the stockflow and participation associations. The agent who has custody of a resource may be an internal or an external agent. For example, banks have custody of an enterprise's cash held in accounts at their locations. Similarly goods may be consigned to an external agent to sell on the enterprise's behalf.

Assignment is an association between an internal agent and an external agent that is separate from any event in which they might both participate. For example, a salesperson may be assigned to a territory that includes customer number 43BYZ. That relationship exists even if 43BYZ never buys anything from the enterprise.

Responsibility is an association between two types of internal agents that is separate from any event in which they might both participate. For example a partner in a public accounting firm may be given responsibility for ten of the staff accountants in that firm. Specific responsibilities may include the partner mentoring the staff accountants, reading supervisors' reviews of the staff accountants' performance, reviewing the staff accountants' training programs and career plans, and conducting their annual evaluations. Such a relationship exists even if those staff accountants never work on a client engagement with that partner.

REA Attributes

REA does not specify attributes as part of its enterprise ontology. Enterprises may use whatever attributes are appropriate to describe its classes and associations. With that said, attribute assignment is a very important step as it is by these attributes that the system will store the economic story of the enterprise.   In order to correctly assign attributes to classes and associations, you must understand what information the attribute is supposed to communicate, and you must understand exactly what "thing" in reality each class and each association represents, and at what level of detail the data will exist. This may seem like an easy task, and for some classes it is quite simple. For other classes and for many associations it takes considerable thought. Sometimes in assigning attributes, a designer will realize he or she misunderstood what reality a class was intended to represent. Such misunderstandings are best corrected before the conceptual model is converted into a physical implementation.

Class or Association Attribute?

To determine whether an attribute describes an instance of a class or an instance of an association, you need to be able to isolate whether the attribute describes just one thing or whether it describes a combination of things. For example, consider the attribute quantity sold of an inventory item in a sale event. Assume each sale event can involve multiple inventory items and that an inventory item represents a type of inventory (i.e. a model number and description) that can be sold multiple times. Should this attribute be assigned to the inventory class, to the sale class, or to the stockflow association? To answer this question, think about what the attribute describes. Does it describe inventory separately from sale? Could you find a data value for that attribute if you knew which inventory item it was but you didn't know which sale it was related to? That is, if you knew it was Model KXPJ432, but you didn't know whether it was Sale #2, 46, or 79? No, you could not find the data value, because different quantities may have been sold on each of those sales! So quantity sold is not an attribute of inventory. Does quantity sold describe sale separately from inventory? Could you find a data value for that attribute if you knew which sale it was but you didn't know which inventory item was involved? That is, if you knew it was Sale #17 but you didn't know whether it was Model AFLQ127 or Model CLDJ1110? No! That tells you that quantity sold is not an attribute of sale. To fill in a data value for the attribute "quantity sold" you must know both the inventory item and the sale because it is really describing the relationship between them. Thus it is an association attribute, not a class attribute.

If, on the other hand, the attribute of interest was not the quantity of a specific item sold in a specific sale event, but rather the total quantity sold of an inventory item throughout the company's history (considering all sale events that have involved that inventory model) then the attribute is a class attribute assigned to inventory. Or if the attribute of interest was the total of all inventory items (of all types) included in a sale event, then it is a class attribute assigned to sale. So you must verify that you understand what data the enterprise wants for each of the attributes on your list and place the attribute accordingly.

Resource Attributes

Although REA does not prescribe a set of required attributes, there are some typical attributes we repeatedly see. Resources can be difficult classes to grasp in terms of the underlying reality and what attributes should be used to identify and describe them. Cash is a class that many people who are new to REA modeling have difficulty conceptualizing. When you pictured cash as a resource in thinking about the value system and value chain levels in chapter 2, you probably thought about physical cash – the actual coins and pieces of currency. Most of the time we do not need information about each specific coin and each piece of currency that enters and exits an enterprise, therefore we do not usually represent cash at the specific instance level. Instead, we typically represent cash at an aggregated level, representing characteristics of the accounts in which cash is stored. The instances of a cash class are usually cash accounts that have attributes such as Cash account number, cash account location (e.g. "Fourth Street Bank", "Cash register #42", or "secretary's file cabinet drawer in room 144"), cash account type (e.g. checking, savings, money market, petty cash, or cash on-hand), and account balance.

Inventory is another resource class that takes some thought, because sometimes instances of the inventory class are specifically identified physical items. Other times instances of the inventory class are categories into which the physical items are grouped – these instances typically are model or SKU numbers. What determines whether the instances are separate physical items or whether they are categories? As discussed earlier, if the enterprise does not separately identify each physical unit of inventory then the instances must be categories. For example, consider bags of potato chips at the grocery store. When a bag of potato chips is sold, the cashier scans the UPC code that tells the system what brand and what size package was just scanned. If another bag of chips (of the same brand and size) is scanned, exactly the same information is communicated to the system. There is no way for the system to distinguish between the first physical bag of chips and the second physical bag of chips. Contrast that with personal computers that have serial numbers to separately identify each physical computer. When the serial number is entered into the system, the system knows exactly which physical unit is being sold. Technically the class that represents category level inventory information should be called Inventory Type and the class that represents each physical unit of inventory should be called Inventory and they should have a typification association between them. In fact, if an enterprise wants to store data at both levels of detail, that is how the model must be constructed. If an enterprise has no need to separately identify each physical unit of inventory, then often a compromise is made and Inventory Type is substituted for Inventory and used as if it were a resource instead of a resource type.

Event Attributes

Assignment of attributes to events is usually straightforward. Consider the information that is typically needed regarding events. The five "journalism 101" questions – who, what, why, when, and where – are a good representation of what people (and enterprises) want to know about events. The "who and why" questions are answered by the participation and duality associations in which the event class participates. The "what" question actually contains two parts. One part is "what happened" and the other part is "what things were affected by the event". The "what happened" is answered by the name of the event and its identifier attribute. The "what things were affected by the event" is answered by the stockflow associations between the event and the related resources and sometimes by the inclusion of a dollar value attribute. The remaining attributes needed to fill out the whole picture, then, are those that will answer the "when" and the "where" questions, therefore date and location are often stored as attributes of events. If there is no question as to the when or where for an event set, then these attributes may be excluded. For example, if an enterprise only has one location at which it makes sales, or if the location of a sale doesn't matter for decision-making purposes, then there is no reason to record location as an attribute of sale.

Agent Attributes

To consider what attributes are likely to be assigned to agents, think about what you typically want to know about people or companies with which you do business. An identifier is needed, of course, to be able to tell one agent from another, especially if two agent instances may have the same name. Assuming you can tell them apart, what else do you need to know? You probably want to know their name and some means of contacting them, such as addresses and telephone numbers. You may also need to keep attributes that tell you something about their qualifications and their performance.

REA Multiplicities: Some Heuristics

As with attributes, REA does not specifically prescribe any multiplicities as part of its enterprise ontology. However, years of practice have produced heuristics, i.e., rules of thumb that usually apply, but don't always apply. Therefore your assignment of multiplicities is not completely ad hoc; however, you must carefully consider whether the situation you are modeling is an exception to the heuristic. We have listed some common exceptions along with the heuristics, but other exceptions certainly exist!

Resource Type-Economic Event (Stockflow) Multiplicity Heuristics

If a resource type is substituted for a resource in a stockflow association with an economic event, then the general multiplicity heuristics are as follows:

Resource Type 1..* – 0..* Economic Event

The minimum of zero for the participation of resource types in the association with economic events reflects the common business practice of entering data about resource types before any economic events involving them are recorded. Also often resource type data is entered in conjunction with instigation or commitment events that precede the economic event that causes the resource inflow or outflow.

The maximum of many for the participation of resource type in the association with economic events reflects the fact that resource type is a category level class and one would expect that if every instance of that set were only to be involved a maximum of one time with the set of economic events there would have been no need to represent the class at the category level.

The minimum of one for the participation of economic event in the association with resource type reflects the fact that an economic event must involve a resource flow – by definition an economic event either gives or takes something of economic value.

The maximum of many for the participation of economic event in the association with resource type reflects the fact that seldom does an enterprise design its business processes such that each event may involve only one instance of a resource. When an enterprise makes a sale, it would hope at least some of its sales consist of multiple items. When an enterprise purchases merchandise, it would be inefficient to create a separate purchase for each separate item it purchases, especially if multiple resources are purchased on the same day from the same vendor.

Common exception that changes the 1 minimum participation of Economic Event
If the event could involve alternative kinds of resource types that are stored in different classes, then the minimum participation for Event in its association with Resource Type would change from one to zero. For example, if a purchase could involve a fixed asset or an inventory item (assuming those are maintained as separate classes) then the participation of purchase with fixed assets would be optional, because the purchase could instead involve an inventory item. Likewise, if cash disbursements can be made to employees or to suppliers or to creditors, each of which is maintained as a separate class, then the participation of cash disbursement in its association with supplier would be optional (because it could involve an employee or creditor instead) and for the same reason, participation with creditor would also be optional and participation with employee (as payee) would also be optional. Notice also that participation with employee as processor rather than payee of the cash disbursement may still be mandatory.

Resource-Economic Event (Stockflow) Multiplicity Heuristics
If a resource class represents specifically identified resources, the expected multiplicity is

Resource 1..* – 0..1 Economic Event

The reasoning for the minimum of zero participation of Resource in its association with the related Economic Event, the minimum of one participation of Economic Event in its association with the related Resource and the maximum of many for Economic Event in its association with the related Resource is the same as in the expected multiplicity for Resource-Type – Economic Event, so we won't repeat that logic here. The only difference between the pattern for stockflow associations involving resources as opposed to resource types is the expected maximum participation of the Resource in its association with the Economic Event. Because resources are specifically identified physical units (as opposed to categories) each can typically only be involved once in an economic event. Usually the same physical unit of something can only be produced or purchased or sold one time.

Common Exceptions that changes the 1 maximum participation of Resource
One exception that changes the 1 maximum participation of Resource in its association with Economic Event to a maximum of many occurs when the economic event involves the rental of the resource rather than the permanent transfer of the resource. In this case, what is being exchanged for cash is actually the right to use a resource for a contracted period of time, rather than the resource itself. For example, a video store can rent the same specific copy of a video many times.

Another exception that changes the 1 maximum participation of Resource in its association with Economic Event to a maximum of many occurs when the same resource may be sold and reacquired multiple times. For example, a car dealership that handles both new and used vehicles may sell a car, then acquire the same car when the owner decides to trade it in for another new vehicle, then sell the car to another customer, eventually re-acquire it again, etc. In some such cases an enterprise may decide to assign a different identifier to the resource each time it is re-acquired (an argument in favor of this approach is that the condition of the resource is likely different each time) and then the maximum of one would still be appropriate. However in some cases the history of the specific physical item may be important and the enterprise may choose to keep using the same identifier and the maximum participation needs to be many.

Economic Event-Agent (Participation Association) Multiplicity Heuristics
The general participation heuristic for agent-event associations is as follows:

Economic Event 0..* - 1..1 Agent

The 1 minimum participation of the Economic Event in its association with an agent signifies that most enterprises want to record at least one internal agent for each economic event. If we don't know who represented each enterprise involved in the exchange, it will be difficult to resolve any future discrepancies about the exchange events.

The 1 maximum participation of the Economic Event in its association with an internal agent indicates that most enterprises hold one internal agent accountable for (or give them credit for) each economic event. The 1 maximum of the Economic Event in its association with an external agent indicates that most enterprises maintain information about only one external agent involved in a transaction. For example, if two college roommates decide to split the cost of a personal computer for their dorm room, the computer store records the sale as being to one of the roommates. The company can't sell half of a computer! If the two roommates purchase two computers and want the sale split between them, the computer store would typically record two sales, one to each of them. Similarly when an enterprise receives goods, each receipt of goods would come from just one vendor.

The 0 minimum participation of Agent in its association with Economic Event is typical because in most enterprises data about an agent must be entered into the system before the agent participates in any events. The * maximum participation of Agent in its association with Economic Event represents the fact that it would be very unusual to restrict the entire set of agents to participating a maximum of one time each in an event. For example, it would be completely ridiculous for a company to tell customers they can't buy anything more from the company once they have participated in one sale!

Typical exceptions to the Economic Event-Agent multiplicity heuristics are as follows:

Common exceptions that change the 1 minimum participation of Economic Event
If alternative types of internal agents can process an event, then the minimum participation of the Event in the association with Agent would change from 1 to 0. For example, if a sale could be made by either a salesperson or by a manager (and if those are maintained as two separate classes), then the participation of sale with salesperson would be optional (because it could involve a manager instead) and the participation of sale with manager would be optional (because it could involve a salesperson instead).

Similarly if alternate types of external agents could participate in an event, then the minimum participation of Event in the association with Agent would change from 1 to 0. For example, if a cash disbursement could be made to an employee or to a supplier or to a creditor (and if those are maintained as separate classes), then the participation of cash disbursement with employee would be optional (because it could involve a supplier or creditor instead) and for the same reason, participation with supplier would be optional and participation with creditor would be optional.

Common exception that changes the 1 Maximum participation of Economic Event
If multiple agents share responsibility (or credit) for an economic event then the maximum participation for the Economic Event in its association with Agent would change to *. For example, if two different salespeople assist a customer in selecting the product he or she wants to buy, and they split the commission resulting from the sale, the sale event is associated with multiple salespeople.

Economic Event – Economic Event (Duality Association) Multiplicity Heuristics
Duality associations typically allow any number of different possible multiplicities, thus no heuristic is available. The enterprise's business policies must be examined to determine the correct multiplicities.

STEP BY STEP – HOW TO CREATE A CORE REA BUSINESS PROCESS MODEL

To create a core business process level model, follow these steps.

REA Business Process Modeling Step 1: Identify Economic Exchange Events
The first step is to identify the economic exchange events that form the core of the business process. To do this, consider the resource inflows and outflows for the business process for which you are constructing a model and determine what economic exchange events provide and use up these resources. Represent the economic exchange events with a duality association between them. Note that if you already prepared a value chain level model, you have already completed this step, and the economic exchange events and duality association are inside the bubble for that business process on the value chain. So you can simply copy that to your business process level model.

REA Business Process Modeling Step 2: Attach Resources to Economic Events
The second step is to attach the resources identified in step 1 to the appropriate events via stockflow associations. If there are multiple inflow resources, determine whether the same attributes need to be stored for each inflow resource. Combine resources for which the same attributes are stored; keep separate resources for which different attributes are stored. Similarly if there are multiple outflow resources, combine resources for which the same attributes are stored and keep separate those for which different attributes are stored.

REA Business Process Modeling Step 3: Attach External Agents to Economic Events
The third step is to attach the appropriate external agents to the events via participation associations. To determine the appropriate external agents, examine the value system level and determine which external agent represents the one that gives and receives the same resource flows as are represented in your business process level model. That is the external agent for your model. If you did not prepare a value system level model, then you will need to examine any narrative description you may have for the process or ask someone knowledgeable from the enterprise who the external business partners are that participate in those economic events.

REA Business Process Modeling Step 4: Attach Internal Agents to Economic Events
The fourth step is to attach the appropriate internal agents to the events via participation associations. Internal agents are not reflected anywhere in the value system and value chain levels, so to determine the appropriate internal agents you will have to examine any narrative description you may have for the process or ask someone knowledgeable from the enterprise which type of employees are responsible for each of the economic events in the process. Keep in mind that sometimes there are multiple internal agents who participate in an event. For example, one type of employee may perform an event and another type of employee may authorize the event. Assuming the enterprise wants to track information about both roles, it will need to establish separate relationships for each role.

REA Business Process Modeling Step 5: Attribute Assignment
The fifth step is to assign attributes to each class in the model and also to assign attributes to any associations that possess their own attributes (and are thus association classes). Typically you will be provided with a list of attributes the company needs to be able to store; if not, you will need to ask someone knowledgeable in the enterprise (i.e., someone familiar with that business process and its information needs) to determine what attributes need to be assigned. Use the heuristics as well as the narrative description and common sense regarding how business works to assign the attributes to the appropriate classes and associations.

REA Business Process Modeling Step 6: Multiplicity Assignment
The sixth step is to assign multiplicities to each association in the model. Great care must be taken in assigning multiplicities, as the multiplicities form some of the business rules and will in some cases dictate what data may or may not be able to be entered into the resulting database tables. You may identify the business rules that need to be represented by the multiplicities by examining any narrative description you have and/or by asking someone knowledgeable in the enterprise. Remember to ask the questions in a "language" the business user can understand. Business rules are policies and practices the enterprise adopts in its operations. For example, an enterprise's credit policy is a business rule. If they don't offer credit, that policy will be represented one way in the multiplicities, whereas if they do offer credit sales that will be represented another way.

REA Business Process Modeling Step 7: Validate Model
The final step of constructing a REA model at the business process level is to validate the model with one (or preferably more than one) representative from the enterprise who is knowledgeable about the details and objectives of the business processes being modeled. Validation sessions should result in either confirmation of the model's accuracy or modification of the model. When validating the model with the enterprise representative(s) the REA modeler must take care to be aware of potential miscommunications due to differences in vocabulary. Unfortunately many words have multiple possible meanings, especially when used in different contexts. When one person talks about a purchase, they may in fact be referring to a purchase order. In an informal setting that might be fine; however, the REA model must be created with strict economic definitions observed, and in those definitions, a purchase does not occur until the title to goods is transferred from the seller to the buyer. At that point a sale occurs for the seller and a purchase occurs for the buyer. When asking enterprise personnel about events, then, one must be very careful to ask enough questions to ensure that the strict economic definitions are being effectively communicated.

CORE REA MODELING OF THE ACQUISITION CYCLE

The REA modeling constructs may still seem somewhat abstract to you. Let's make those more concrete by discussing them in the context of the acquisition cycle and then apply the constructs by creating a business process level REA class diagram for Robert Scott Woodwinds Shop (recall the example company we introduced in chapter 2). As introduced in chapters 2 and 3, the acquisition cycle is sometimes called the acquisition/payment business process, the expenditures cycle, or the procure-to-pay process.

The acquisition cycle includes the activities associated with buying, maintaining, and paying for goods and services needed by enterprises. This includes acquiring raw materials, component parts, and other resources contained in finished products or services. It also includes acquiring, and paying for, a variety of other goods and services (e.g., utilities, supplies, insurance, repairs, maintenance, research, development, professional and legal services, and property, plant, and equipment). Processes that are special cases of the acquisition cycle, but that are typically considered separate business processes include the payroll cycle (also called the human resources business process, which involves the acquisition of and payment for employee labor) and the financing cycle (acquisition and repayment of financial capital). We discuss these processes separately in later chapters.

Organizations can acquire a variety of goods and services. These include inventory, supplies, various services, utilities, or property, plant, and equipment. Exhibit 6-2 illustrates three typical core REA class diagrams for the acquisition cycle, first for inventory purchases, second for operating asset purchases or rentals, and third for service acquisitions. The *REA* pattern aids in analyzing business processes and events by highlighting the *what* (the resources involved in the event) and the *who* (the internal and external agents) of each event. Notice that the *where* and the *when* often are stored as attributes of each event. The events, agents, and resources involved in the acquisition/payment process vary somewhat from enterprise to enterprise. The general pattern discussed in this chapter easily can be adapted and applied to meet the exact requirements of any enterprise.

Economic Increment Event (Purchase [Receipt of Goods], Rental, or Service Acquisition)

The economic increment event in the acquisition/payment process may take on one of several labels to represent the various resources acquired. Typically if goods are being acquired, the increment event is called *Acquisition, Purchase*, or *Receipt of Goods*. If the resource acquired is a temporary right to use goods, the event is usually called *Rental.* A rental acquisition begins when the right to temporary possession of the goods transfers from the supplier to the enterprise and ends when possession of the goods transfers back from the enterprise to the supplier. When services or utilities are acquired, the label is often *Service Acquisition* or *General and Administrative Service Acquisition*. Whatever label is used, the important consideration is that an increment event must represent the point at which benefit was received by the enterprise. It is at this point that a liability is incurred (unless the acquisition was prepaid). Enterprises usually purchase several types of resources (e.g., inventory, operating assets, and general and administrative services) and therefore must decide for database design purposes whether to combine the different acquisitions into one acquisition event class (attached to multiple different resource classes) or to create separate models with different event classes and different resource classes.

Exhibit 6-2 Core REA Acquisition Cycle

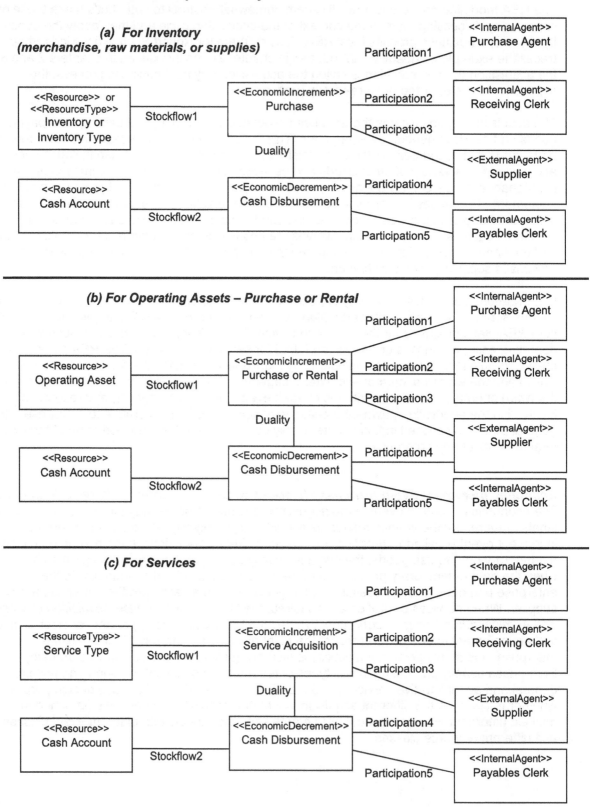

(a) For Inventory
(merchandise, raw materials, or supplies)

(b) For Operating Assets – Purchase or Rental

(c) For Services

The decision to combine or separate acquisitions of different resources usually depends on whether different attributes need to be captured for the different acquisitions. If different attributes are needed for the different increments, usually they should be represented as separate event classes, each participating in a duality association with the appropriate economic decrement event. If the same attributes are captured for acquisitions of inventory, operating assets, and service types, (and especially if the same sequentially numbered documents or interface screens are used) then they may be combined into a common acquisition event.

Internal agents typically associated with economic increment events via participation associations include purchase agents and receiving clerks. External agents typically associated with economic increment events via participation associations include suppliers, common carriers (such as UPS or Federal Express), and credit card companies. The resources typically associated with the economic increment event via stockflow associations in the acquisition cycle are usually *inventory*, *inventory type*, *service type*, *supply type*, or *operating asset*.

Most manufacturers and merchandisers do not individually identify inventory, so the resource that participates in the stockflow1 association for inventory acquisition is usually *inventory type*. For those enterprises that do specifically identify individual inventory items, the resource in the stockflow1 association is *inventory*. For general and administrative service acquisitions, the resource involved in the stockflow1 association is usually *service type*. For supply acquisitions the associated resource is usually *supply type*, and for operating asset acquisitions the associated resource is usually *operating asset* (note that typically operating assets are individually identified).

Economic Decrement Event (Cash Disbursement)
Cash disbursements are economic decrement events that decrease the enterprise's cash balance. Cash disbursements may be made via paper check, debit card, electronic funds transfer, or by cash payment. Notice that if the enterprise uses a credit card to pay a supplier, the enterprise has not yet disbursed cash; the cash disbursement does not occur until the enterprise pays the credit card company.

Attributes captured regarding cash disbursements usually include a cash disbursement identifier (such as a disbursement voucher number), date, amount paid, supplier identification, employee identification (such as employees who write the checks), the account number from which the cash is disbursed, and the check number of the payment.

ACQUISITION CYCLE CORE PATTERN EXAMPLE ENTERPRISE
Now that we have reviewed the class diagram constructs and the REA ontology constructs, and the core REA constructs of the acquisition/payment process, let's combine and apply that knowledge to the creation of a REA class diagram for Robert Scott Woodwinds Shop (RSWS), the enterprise that was introduced in chapter 2.

Recall that RSWS generates revenue through several different activities:
- selling instruments
- renting instruments
- providing repair services
- selling manufactured accessories such as clarinet barrels and mouthpieces

Recall that in order to engage in these revenue-generating activities RSWS must purchase instruments, raw materials, fixed assets, and various services from suppliers. RSWS must also purchase labor from employees, and use that labor in addition to the materials, fixed assets, and services in order to manufacture accessories and repair instruments.

We next apply the step by step procedure for creating a core business process level model to RSWS's acquisition/payment process. Because the enterprise as described doesn't exist, the model can't be validated with an enterprise representative, we complete only steps 1 through 6.

RSWS Step 1
The economic exchange events in the acquisition cycle for RSWS are Purchase and Cash Disbursement. We represent them as classes as shown in Exhibit 6-3.

Exhibit 6-3: RSWS Step 1 Result

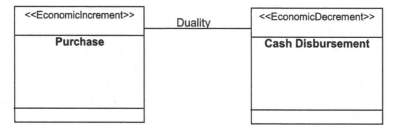

RSWS Step 2
The resource flowing into the acquisition bubble on the value chain that gets used up in a decrement event is Cash. Therefore we attach the Cash resource to the Cash Disbursement decrement event via a Stockflow association, as shown below. The resources flowing out of the acquisition bubble that were obtained by an increment event are Instruments, Raw Materials, and Overhead. At this point we must make a decision as to whether the same characteristics will be stored for the resources to know whether to show each type of resource as a separate class or whether to combine the different types of resources into a single class. In this example, let's say we determine we will track the same attributes for instrument inventory and raw materials so we combine them into one class. However, we determine the characteristics of the overhead items/services we acquire are different from the inventory attributes so we create a separate class to represent overhead. We create two resource classes; one called Inventory and the other called Overhead, and we link them to the Acquisition increment event via two Stockflow associations, as shown in Exhibit 6-4.

RSWS Steps 3 and 4
In the value system level model, the external agent with whom RSWS exchanges cash for goods and services (such as inventory and overhead) is the set of suppliers. Thus we add Suppliers as an external agent to our model and we create two participation associations; one between Supplier and Acquisition and the other between Supplier and Cash Disbursement.

Neither the value system nor the value chain level identify internal agents, therefore we must go back and look at the available narrative description for RSWS or ask someone from RSWS who

REA Accounting Systems: Resources-Events-Agents: An ontology for designing, controlling, and using integrated enterprise systems

189

has the appropriate knowledge. The narrative description provided in Chapter 2 is a very high level overview and does not contain enough detail to determine what internal agents apply.

Let's say we asked Robert Scott who processes acquisitions and cash disbursements on behalf of RSWS and we receive the following reply. "Johnny Arthur and Cheri Lynn make the acquisitions; Lorie Lisbet, Linda Kay, and Timothy Rob process the cash disbursements – those for acquisitions and all other payments we make. Oh, and Ray Edwards has to approve all checks that are written."

Exhibit 6-4: RSWS Step 2 Result

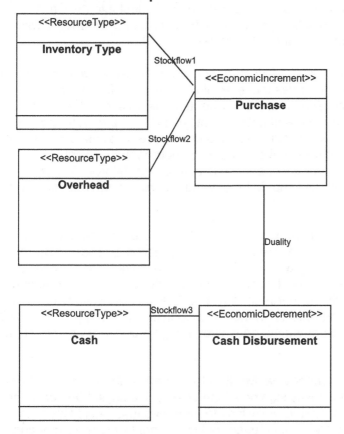

Notice that the response we received was at the token level of detail. We want our database to be able to store the token level detail, but we need to form our conceptual model at the type (set) level. We need to know what type-level names we should use to represent the set to which these individuals belong. In some companies we may not want to distinguish between different employee positions and we may choose simply to attach a class called "Employee" to events to represent internal agent participation. Whether that is a good idea depends on whether we want to store the same attributes for all categories of employee. If we need to store different attributes about different sets of employees (i.e. we need different attributes for purchasing agents than we do for accounts payable clerks or managers) then we may choose to represent each category of employee as a separate class and show associations between the event and the appropriate employee category agent.

If we represent all employees as a single class, we must take care to identify separate associations to represent different roles involving different individuals with respect to each event. For example, processing cash disbursements is a different role from authorizing them, therefore if RSWS chooses to maintain one overall class for Employee, it should create two associations between the Cash Disbursement event and the Employee agent. Let's assume that RSWS wants to keep its employees in separate classes depending on their positions.

When we interview Mr. Scott further, he tells us that Johnny and Cheri are called purchase agents; Lorie, Linda, and Timothy are called accounts payable (A/P) clerks, and Ray is a manager. Therefore we add Purchasing Agent as a class and connect it to Acquisition via a participation association. We add A/P Clerk as a class and connect it to Cash Disbursement via a participation association. And we add Manager as a class and connect it to the Cash Disbursement via an authorization association (to distinguish the role of the manager with respect to the cash disbursement from that of the A/P clerks).

We take this opportunity to ask Robert Scott a few more questions, because we know we are going to need more information about the roles these employees are playing in order to assign multiplicities. First we confirm with Mr. Scott that RSWS wants to be able to enter information about employees as soon as they are hired and not wait until after they have participated in an event. His reply: "Of course! In fact, I want your system to make sure no transaction can be entered unless a valid employee is entered as the responsible person. I also want the transaction to be rejected if an invalid product or service is entered for the transaction. Information about products we buy and sell should be entered before any information about the purchases and sales is entered."

We ask Mr. Scott whether Johnny and Cheri ever work together on a purchase and assume joint responsibility for that purchase or whether each of them processes a separate set of purchases. He replies, "Sometimes Johnny will help Cheri open the boxes and count all the different types of inventory that arrive in one of her incoming shipments, or vice versa, but Cheri signs off on and assumes responsibility for her receiving reports and Johnny signs off on and assumes responsibility for his receiving reports. In fact for all activities that happen at RSWS I want just one employee I can blame if something goes wrong or give credit when something is awesome."

We make a note of that and then remember what Mr. Scott said earlier about the A/P clerks processing cash disbursements and yet Ray signing all the checks. He says, "Oh yes, I can see why that seems contrary to what I just said. It really isn't though, because I hold Ray responsible for all payments, and in case we hire additional managers I would hold whichever manager approved a payment responsible for it. But we still need to track which A/P clerk participated in each payment so the personnel department can have that information for evaluation purposes."

Based on this interview with Mr. Scott, we attach internal and external agents to our model as shown in Exhibit 6-5.

Exhibit 6-5: RSWS Steps 3 and 4 Result

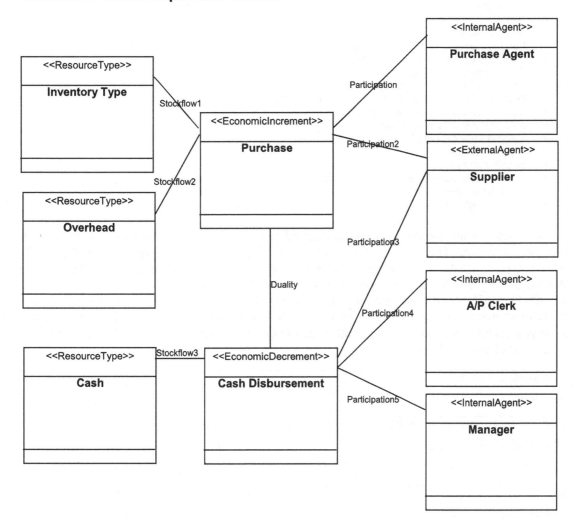

RSWS Step 5

This step is to assign attributes to the appropriate classes and associations. Assume RSWS has given you the following list of attributes.

- Acquisition ID
- Actual unit cost of an inventory item purchased on an acquisition
- A/P clerk identification number
- Bond rating for an A/P clerk
- Cash account balance
- Cash account number
- Cash disbursement identification number
- Date goods or services were acquired
- Date of cash disbursement
- Description of inventory item
- Description of overhead item
- Dollar amount of a cash disbursement applied to a specific acquisition
- ID code assigned to overhead item
- Identification number for a manager
- List selling price per unit of inventory item
- Location of a cash account
- Manager's highest degree

- Name of A/P clerk
- Name of manager
- Name of purchase agent
- Name of supplier
- Purchase agent identification number
- Purchase authorization limit for a purchase agent
- Quality rating for supplier
- Quantity of an inventory item purchased on an acquisition
- Quantity of an overhead item purchased on an acquisition
- Quantity on hand of inventory item
- SKU number of inventory item
- Standard unit cost of inventory item
- Supplier address
- Supplier number
- Total dollar amount of a cash disbursement
- Total dollar value of an acquisition
- Type of cash account

To help illustrate the thought processes needed to assign attributes, we next present a table with three columns. The first column contains the attribute description as given in the list. The second column contains an abbreviation that we can include in our model to save space and avoid crowding. A (PK) is added next to the abbreviation for any attributes we identify as primary keys. The third column contains the name of the class or association to which the attribute should be assigned. (Note: you probably won't make a table like this as a separate step once you understand the process of attribute assignment, but we hope it helps you to follow the logic of what we are doing).

Attribute description in list	Abbreviation	Assignment
Acquisition ID	Acq-id (PK)	Acquisition
Actual unit cost of an inventory item purchased on an acquisition	Item-unit-cost	Stockflow1
A/P clerk identification number	AP-id (PK)	A/P Clerk
Bond rating for an A/P clerk	AP-bond	A/P Clerk
Cash account balance	AcctBal	Cash
Cash account number	AcctNum (PK)	Cash
Cash disbursement identification number	CD-id (PK)	Cash Disbursement
Date goods or services were acquired	Acq-date	Acquisition
Date of cash disbursement	CD-date	Cash Disbursement
Description of inventory item	Item-desc	Inventory
Description of overhead item	OH-desc	Overhead
Dollar amount of a cash disbursement applied to a specific acquisition	CD-Acq-applied	Duality
ID code assigned to overhead item	OH-id (PK)	Overhead
Identification number for a manager	Mgr-id (PK)	Manager
List selling price per unit of inventory item	Item-list-price	Inventory
Location of a cash account	Acct-loc	Cash
Manager's highest degree	Mgr-degree	Manager
Name of A/P clerk	AP-name	A/P Clerk

Name of manager	Mgr-name	Manager
Name of purchase agent	PA-name	Purchase Agent
Name of supplier	Sup-name	Supplier
Purchase agent identification number	PA-id (PK)	Purchase Agent
Purchase authorization limit for a purchase agent	PA-limit	Purchase Agent
Quality rating for supplier	Sup-rating	Supplier
Quantity of an inventory item purchased on an acquisition	Item-qty-purch	Stockflow1
Quantity of an overhead item purchased on an acquisition	Oh-qty-purch	Stockflow2
Quantity on hand of inventory item	Item-qoh	Inventory
SKU number of inventory item	Item-SKU (PK)	Inventory
Standard unit cost of inventory item	Item-std-cost	Inventory
Supplier address	Sup-add	Supplier
Supplier number	SupNum (PK)	Supplier
Total dollar amount of a cash disbursement	CD-amt	Cash Disbursement
Total dollar value of an acquisition	Acq-amt	Acquisition
Type of cash account	AcctType	Cash

Next we place each of these attributes in the appropriate place on our class diagram and make sure each class has a primary key attribute and at least one descriptor attribute. See Exhibit 6-6. If no attributes describing a class are needed for decision-making purposes (and you are sure the list of attributes given to you was complete), then usually the class should not be included in your model.

Next we look at the Stockflow3 association between Cash and Cash Disbursement to see if it follows the general heuristic. We are confident that we need to establish a cash account before we can make any disbursements out of it and that from one cash account we can make many disbursements. So the 0..* Resource Type heuristic applies. When we consider the Cash Disbursement's participation in the stockflow3 association, we realize that a cash disbursement cannot exist without coming from a cash account and since all cash accounts owned by RSWS would be included in this system as members of the Cash class, participation of Cash Disbursement in the Stockflow3 association must be mandatory (minimum multiplicity = 1). We also realize that if we make disbursement of cash it can only come from one account (maximum multiplicity = 1). For example, when we write a check, the check is drawn on just one bank account. If we want to pay a supplier with money from two different checking accounts we must write two checks and that would be considered as two cash disbursements. Multiplicities for Stockflow3 are summarized as Cash 1..1 − 0..* Cash Disbursement.

**Exhibit 6-6: RSWS Step 5 Class Diagram with Attributes
(notice that associations to which attributes are assigned become association classes)**

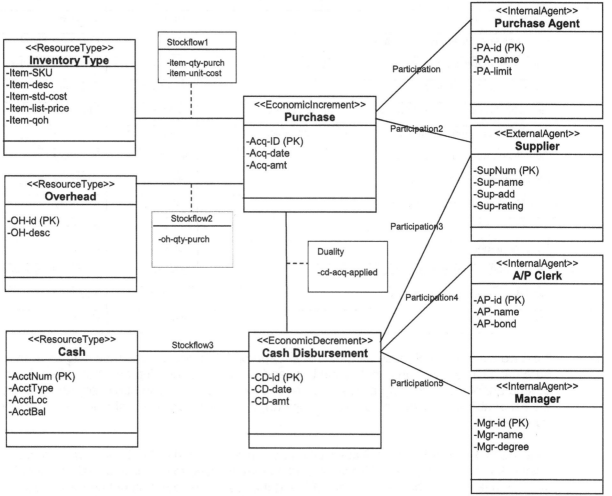

Next we evaluate the duality association and remember that there is no heuristic for duality associations. The fact that RSWS has A/P clerks indicates they make purchases on credit (otherwise they wouldn't have accounts payable) so we note the minimum participation of Acquisition is optional (zero). We are not sure whether an acquisition is ever paid in installment payments (i.e. with multiple cash disbursements) or if they are always paid in full. Similarly, while we know that some cash disbursements are made for expenditures other than acquisitions (for example, to pay employees or to repay loans), we are not sure whether a cash disbursement ever pays for multiple acquisitions.

We go to see Mr. Scott again and ask him. He tells us RSWS has never made installment payments for any acquisitions and never intends to do so, but that perhaps the system should be set up so that it would be possible. He says RSWS does make payments that combine multiple purchases. In his words, "For example, we make a folder for Emersmith and store up the bills for all the purchases we make from Emersmith in a month. At the end of the month we write one check to Emersmith that covers all of those purchases. We do the same thing for each of our other suppliers." Putting all this information together we summarize our Duality association multiplicities as Acquisition 0..* − 0..* Cash Disbursement.

Our participation associations remain to be examined. We recall our heuristic is Economic Event 0..* − 1..1 Agent and look for evidence to confirm or refute that heuristic. We recall that Mr. Scott already told us he wants no transaction to be entered without one person and one person only being identified as the responsible employee. So we know the 1..1 next to Agent is valid for all three of the participation associations that involve internal agents (Participation1, Participation4, and Participation5). When we consider Participation2, between Acquisition and Supplier, we confirm the 1..1 heuristic next to supplier (to describe the Acquisition's participation in that association) is valid because in RSWS's value system level, there is no alternative external business partner from whom we acquire goods and services. Thus an acquisition must involve a supplier (minimum = 1), and multiple receipts of goods from the same supplier would be considered as multiple acquisitions (maximum = 1).

Our examination of Participation3, between Cash Disbursement and Supplier reveals a common exception because the value system level model indicates that RSWS makes cash disbursements to external agents other than suppliers. This changes the minimum participation of Cash Disbursement in the association with Supplier to zero. The maximum of one is reasonable because it would not make sense to write one check to two different suppliers. Next we consider the 0..* heuristic for the participation of agents in the five participation associations. We know the minimum of zero holds true for the internal agent associations (Participation1, Participation4, and Participation5) because the agent data must exist in our system before any transactions are entered in order to be able to validate the responsible employee upon entry of the transactions.

We also know the maximum of many holds true for all five participation associations because it is simple common business sense. There is no business reason why an enterprise would want to limit participation in its entire set of a type of economic event to only one time per agent. That would be saying, for example, that once a purchase agent makes one purchase he or she can never make another purchase.

To evaluate the minimum multiplicities of the two external agents in their participation associations (Participation2 and Participation3) we consider whether RSWS would enter an acquisition or a cash disbursement to a supplier for which RSWS has not already entered data into the system. We recognize that good business policy would recommend RSWS should have a vendor selection policy that would result in supplier information being entered into the system before any transactions involving them may be entered. We ask Mr. Scott whether RSWS has a need to be able to enter supplier information before entering acquisitions or cash disbursements involving that supplier. He confirms that in fact, the vendor selection policy at RSWS requires approval of suppliers prior to engaging in transactions with them. We therefore assign Economic Event 0..* − 1..1 Agent to participation associations 1, 2, 4, and 5 and Economic Event 0..* − 0..1 Agent to participation3.

The results of these multiplicity assignments are reflected in our completed model as shown in Exhibit 6-7.

This acquisition cycle example only covered the core economic exchange; to complete the class diagram for the full acquisition cycle, with commitment events and instigation events and all the associations in which they participate would require additional information from Robert Scott but would use the same procedures that we demonstrated.

Exhibit 6-7: RSWS Step 6 Multiplicities in Class Diagram

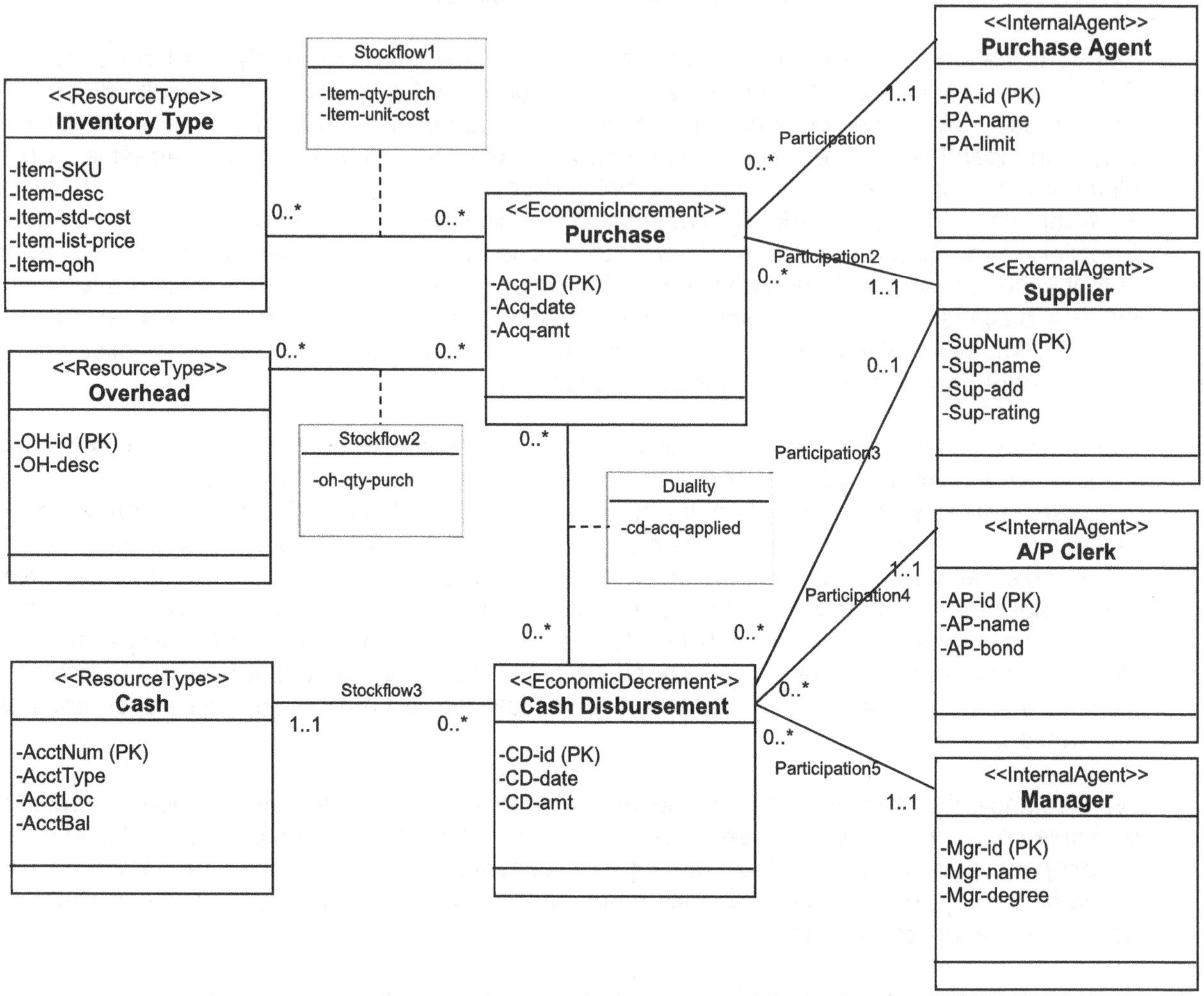

RSWS Step 6

This step is to assign multiplicities to the associations in the REA class diagram. We begin this step by filling in the multiplicities we know. We know that the instances of the inventory class and of the overhead class are types rather than tokens. We are reminded of the knowledge of multiple instances of each inventory type and of each overhead type by fact that they have a quantity purchased attribute in the stockflow associations in which they participate. That knowledge allows us to fill in the maximum multiplicity for each of those resource-types in the stockflow1 and stockflow2 associations as many. We assign zero as the minimum multiplicity for each of those because we remember from our interview with Mr. Scott that RSWS wants to enter data about resource types before they actually acquire them (following the normal heuristic for stockflow associations). For the acquisition's participation in the stockflow1 and stockflow2 associations, we realize that we have a common heuristic exception for the minimum multiplicity. Because we decided to combine acquisitions of inventory and overhead, yet to maintain them each as separate classes, we have a situation in which an acquisition can involve alternative resource types. Therefore the participation of an acquisition with either one of those classes is optional. An acquisition can either involve inventory or overhead so its participation in

REA Accounting Systems: Resources-Events-Agents: An ontology for designing, controlling, and using integrated enterprise systems

197

the association with inventory cannot be mandatory nor can its participation in the association with overhead be mandatory. When we consider the maximum multiplicity for acquisition in the two stockflow associations we realize it is common business sense that an acquisition should be capable of involving multiple types of inventory or overhead. We look back at our interview notes and confirm this with Mr. Scott's description of Johnny helping Cheri open all the boxes and counting all the types of inventory on one of her incoming shipments. Our multiplicities for the first two stockflow associations are thus summarized as Inventory 0..* - 0..* Acquisition and Overhead 0..* – 0..* Acquisition.

REA MODELING OF THE REVENUE CYCLE

Because as discussed in chapter 3, the acquisition and revenue cycles are comprised of the same overall activities viewed from different perspectives, the conceptual models for the two cycles are similar. Exhibit 6-8 illustrates a typical core REA class diagram for an enterprise revenue cycle.

Exhibit 6-8: Revenue Cycle Core REA Class Diagram

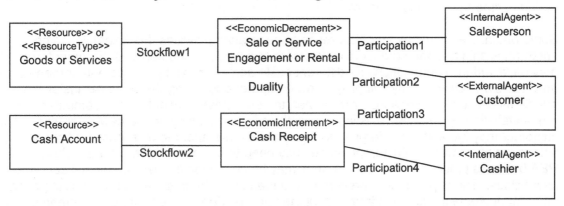

Economic Decrement Event (Sale, Delivery, Shipment, Rental, or Service Engagement)

The economic decrement event in the sales/collection process may take on one of several labels because it represents the revenue generating activity, which can take various forms. The revenue generating activity is the decrement event; resources made available to the revenue cycle by the acquisition and/or conversion cycles must be given or used up in exchange for the resource (usually cash) received from external partners. Usually the enterprise gives up goods, services, or the temporary use of goods. If the revenue generating activity involves the sale of merchandise, the event may be called *Sale*, *Delivery*, or *Shipment* depending in part on whether the customer is on-site to accept possession of the goods or whether the enterprise must deliver or ship the goods to the customer. The important consideration is that a decrement event that represents the sale of goods must represent the point at which title to the merchandise transfers from the seller to the buyer. If title has not transferred, then no decrement has occurred and the sale event cannot be materialized.

If the enterprise sells services rather than goods, then the resource given up to the customers is a set of employee services, making those services unavailable to provide to someone else. Such a decrement event is usually called Service Engagement or something that more specifically describes the kinds of services performed by the enterprise (such as *Repair Service*,

Audit Engagement, or *Consultation*) In the case of enterprises that rent merchandise to customers, the economic decrement event is usually called Rental. The rental event does not involve the transfer of title of goods, but instead involves a transfer of the right to use goods for an agreed upon length of time. The rental event begins when the right to temporary possession of the goods transfers from the lessor to the lessee and ends when possession of the goods transfers back from the lessee to the lessor.

Economic decrement events in the revenue cycle do not always happen at discrete points in time; rather they are often made up of a series of workflow activities. Once a mutual commitment is made, the enterprise's fulfillment of that commitment is accomplished by the tasks that make up the economic decrement event. For enterprises that sell or rent merchandise that must be shipped to the customer location, these tasks include picking the inventory from the warehouse, packing the inventory into boxes, and shipping the boxes to the customer via a common carrier. The rental event also includes receiving the returned merchandise, inspecting it, and returning it to the warehouse. Economic decrement events for service enterprises generally require active involvement of trained employees who perform the services. The enterprise must identify the requirements of the services to be rendered and select an individual or group of individuals to perform the services. Services may be provided over an extended period of time by a variety of people.

Some enterprises may have multiple revenue generating activities. For example, some enterprises ship finished products to customers and also provide services. Some enterprises may have various combinations for different customers. For example, a computer manufacturer may serve one customer by shipping a new computer and letting the customer install it and handle all conversion. For another customer, the enterprise may deliver the computer, assist with installation, and convert existing applications for processing on the new computer. A third customer may request the enterprise to repair a computer that the enterprise had previously sold to the customer. The different events may need to be recorded as separate classes in the REA business process level model, or they may be combined into one economic decrement event class. The appropriate representation depends on the data captured regarding each different decrement event. If different attributes are needed for the types of decrements, usually they should be represented as separate event entities, each participating in the duality association with the appropriate economic increment event.

Associations in which the economic decrement event participates typically include a fulfillment association (enabling the enterprise to trace which mutual commitment event the decrement fulfilled), a duality association (allowing the enterprise to trace a related economic increment that represents the other part of the exchange), a stockflow association (to trace the resource or resource type that was given up in the decrement event), participation associations with the internal and external agents, and occasionally a reversal association (allowing the enterprise to trace sale returns to the original sales for which they reversed the economic effect). Internal agents typically associated with economic decrement events via participation associations include salespeople, shipping clerks, delivery clerks, and engagement personnel. External agents typically associated with economic decrement events via participation associations include transportation suppliers (such as UPS or Federal Express) and customers. The resources typically associated with the economic decrement event via stockflow associations in the revenue cycle are usually *inventory*, *inventory type*, or service type. Most manufacturers and merchandisers do not specifically identify inventory, so the resource that participates in the stockflow association is usually *inventory type*. For those enterprises that do specifically identify inventory items, the resource in the stockflow association is *inventory*. For service providers, the resource involved in the stockflow association is usually *service type*.

Economic Increment Event (Cash Receipt)

Cash receipts are economic increment events that increase the enterprise's cash balance. Cash receipts may take the form of checks, currency, or coins – anything that can be deposited into a cash account held either in a bank or on hand in petty cash. Notice that if a customer pays with a credit card, the enterprise has not yet received cash; the cash receipt does not occur until the credit card company pays the enterprise. In the latter case, the cash receipt must be connected to two external agents – the customer, whose accounts receivable balance will be decreased as a result of the cash receipt, and the credit card company, from whom the cash was literally received.

Attributes captured regarding cash receipts usually include a cash receipt identifier (such as a unique remittance advice number), date, amount received, customer identification, employee identification (such as employees who count and deposit the cash), the account number where the cash is deposited, the location of payment (such as mail, or in person at the main office), and the check number of the payment.

CONCLUDING COMMENTS

The UML class diagram conceptual model and the relational database logical model are generic tools that may be used by anyone completely independent of the REA ontology. The REA ontology, with its identified patterns, is what enables the creation of integrated enterprise information systems that can be used to generate traditional financial accounting statements, calculate variances needed for cost accounting, identify situations in which the enterprise has deviated from its stated internal control policies, and much, much more (and not just accounting!).

You may be wondering why, if there is a pattern underlying all enterprises, it isn't obvious to everyone and why the patterns weren't searched for and discovered long before 1982. Even when a pattern is quite straightforward, sometimes it takes a certain perspective to be able to see it. Separating a complex reality into parts that are relevant and irrelevant for a specific context can be quite difficult. In order to see patterns, you must focus on the substance of what occurs rather than the form of the activities themselves. It is very easy to focus on the form, which has surface level similarities and differences, and miss the substance and deep level commonalities between enterprise processes.

In Chapter 2 we introduced the notion of script patterns, which have been researched extensively by Schank in his quest to figure out how to make computers that can think and learn like human beings. His most famous script example is that of restaurants. Unless you had previously read Schank's ideas in another book or heard about them in a class you took, you probably never realized that you have a restaurant script (and possible variations of the restaurant script) in your memory that you retrieve and adapt as necessary to allow you to understand your environment whenever you go to a restaurant. Close your eyes for a few moments and picture yourself going out to dinner at a fancy restaurant (but don't forget to open your eyes back up and continue reading when you are through imagining that scenario!).

What did you "see" happening? Probably you pictured some combination of the following:

- Was greeted by host or hostess upon entry into building
- Waited in lobby area until seating was available
- Was seated by host or hostess at a table in dining area
- Was provided with a menu that included descriptions and prices of available products
- Ordered beverage from waiter or waitress
- Received beverage from waiter or waitress
- Ordered food from waiter or waitress
- Stayed at table conversing with companion and sipping beverages while food was prepared by cooks in the kitchen
- Received food from waiter or waitress
- Gave waiter or waitress payment for food and beverages (and possibly tip)
- Waiter or waitress took payment to cashier
- Waiter or waitress returned any change due to you
- Left tip for waiter or waitress (if not done earlier with food payment)
- Left restaurant

The above list is not necessarily comprehensive, and may include more or less detail in each step than was included in your list, but likely there was significant overlap.   Now close your eyes again and picture yourself going out to lunch at a fast food restaurant (once again, be sure to open them back up and continue reading when you are done imagining the scenario!). The following list is likely a fairly good representation of what you imagined.

- Entered restaurant and approached the cashier's counter
- Examined menu board posted on wall while waiting in line at counter
- Ordered food and beverage from cashier
- Paid cashier for food and beverage
- Waited at cashier's counter while food was prepared by cooks in the kitchen
- Seated yourself in the dining area
- Ate food
- Threw trash away
- Left restaurant

How are the two restaurant scripts different? How are they similar?

There are many differences between them. One of the obvious differences is the order in which the different activities occur. In sit-down restaurants, we typically pay for our meal after we eat; in fast-food restaurants we pay for our meal before we eat. In sit-down restaurants, we sit down before we examine a menu, order food, or receive food. In fast-food restaurants, we examine the menu, order food, and receive food before we sit down. It is easy to focus on differences, particularly in the physical flow of what occurs. Other variations of the script are possible. For example, if the restaurant you pictured in your mind was a Japanese steakhouse you may have imagined the food being prepared at your table with the cook entertaining you in the process of preparing your food. The first time you go to such a restaurant, you immediately notice that there is something "different" about this restaurant and you create a "Japanese steakhouse" variation in your repertoire of restaurant scripts.

To find a pattern that applies to all restaurants, we need to focus on what elements of these descriptions are necessary elements for this to be considered a restaurant. The essential constructs seem to be "customer ordered food", "customer received food", "customer ate food", and "customer paid for food". If you went to a restaurant where its normal operations did not involve you ordering food, receiving food, eating food, and paying for food (not necessarily in that order), you would not know what to think! We can add to this "core restaurant pattern,"

REA Accounting Systems: Resources-Events-Agents: An ontology for designing, controlling, and using integrated enterprise systems

201

although we will not try to complete the example to its full potential; we just want to give you the idea of what kinds of thought processes are involved. We need to sift away all the details that make the scripts different from each other.

While details of the differences are important, we can't include them in a pattern unless we can discover a conceptual commonality among them. Let's look at an example of discovering a conceptual commonality. Although details such as who prepared the food, who received payment for the food and beverages, who received the order from the customer, and where the food was prepared, differed, the fact that a restaurant employee was involved in preparing the food, receiving payment, and receiving orders, and the fact that a location for food preparation was identified can become part of the pattern. Similarly in modeling enterprises to determine what data need to be stored in enterprise-wide databases, we want to store the identifiable pattern of necessary elements as base objects and ensure the other details may be stored by enterprises to which they apply, and left out by enterprises to which they do not apply.

For some management and decision-making activities, physical workflow differences are important and physical workflow and information flow certainly need to be documented, as we saw in chapter 3. Those things do not matter for the storage structure of the data. They can matter for how and when data is input and retrieved, but they do not matter for the actual storage structure, which is what the business process level of the REA ontology helps to construct with the tools introduced in this chapter. The core elements we identified in our restaurant script do not describe workflow, and indeed to form a pattern for the restaurants we do not require the activities to happen in a prescribed order. Similarly in REA conceptual models, we are less concerned about the order in which events occur and are more interested in what data attributes and relationships to other phenomena we are interested in tracking. By following the procedures outlined in this textbook for each transaction cycle in an enterprise and then integrating the views, we can create an enterprise wide database that can be used as the foundation for an integrated enterprise system. The next step in that process is to expand the pattern to include more of the economic story than the core pattern contains, and to discuss how to integrate cycles. Read Chapter 7 to learn more.

Key Terms and Concepts
Agent
Assignment
Claim
Custody
Duality
Economic decrement event
Economic increment event
Event
External agent
Inflow
Internal agent
Outflow
Participation
Resource
Resource type
Responsibility
Stockflow

Review Questions

LO3-LO6   R1. Give three examples of different types of revenue cycles.

LO3-LO6   R2. Give three examples of different types of acquisition cycles.

LO3-LO6   R3. Describe the acquisition cycle. What main activities make up this process?

LO3-LO6   R4. Describe the sales/collection process (revenue cycle). What main activities make up this process?

LO6   R5. How do you determine the scope of a business process level REA model?

LO3-LO5   R6. List the five questions typically asked in Journalism 101 and explain how they are typically answered in a business process level model.

LO6   R7. List and describe the steps in REA business process level modeling.

LO5   R8. Give some examples of nonkey attributes that would describe a customer class.

LO3   R9. What type of data does each record in an event table contain?

LO4   R10.What type of data does each record in a resource table contain?

LO5   R11.What type of data does each record in an agent table contain?

Multiple Choice Questions

LO6

MC1. The recommended Step 1 in REA business process level modeling is

     A) Attach resources to economic events.

     B) Identify the economic exchange events that form the core of the business process.

     C) Identify internal and external agents and the events in which they participate.

     D) Assign participation cardinalities to all relationships in the model.

     E) Assign attributes to all entities and relationships in the model.

LO4

MC2. Which of the following pairs of classes would typically be related to each other in a stockflow association in a REA model?

     A) Vendor and inventory

     B) Purchase and cash disbursement

     C) Purchase and purchasing agent

     D) Purchase and inventory

     E) Inventory and cash

LO2

MC3. If a resource class represents individually identified resources, the expected multiplicity pattern for its association with an economic event class is

     A) Resource 2..1 – 1..2 Economic Event

     B) Resource 0..1 – 1..* Economic Event

     C) Resource 1..* – 0..1 Economic Event

     D) Resource 1..1 – 1..0 Economic Event

     E) Resource 1..1 – 0..* Economic Event

LO4

MC4. In REA business process level modeling, resources are connected to economic events using _____ associations

     A) Participation

     B) Difference

     C) Duality

     D) Stockflow

     E) Assignment

LO1

MC5. Which example relational tables below contain data that best represents the multiplicities for the Location association Warehouse 1..* - 0..* Inventory.

Example 1:

Warehouse	
WarehouseID	Address
WH138	11 Oak
WH479	321 East
WH702	929 Paris

Location	
WarehouseID	InventoryID
WH138	BVL489
WH138	ANK18
WH702	BVL489

Inventory	
InventoryID	Description
ANK18	Rough
BVL489	Smooth

Example 2:

Warehouse	
WarehouseID	Address
WH138	11 Oak
WH479	321 East

Location	
WarehouseID	InventoryID
WH138	BVL489
WH138	ANK18

Inventory	
InventoryID	Description
ANK18	Rough
BVL489	Smooth

Example 3:

Warehouse	
WarehouseID	Address
WH138	11 Oak
WH479	321 East
WH702	929 Paris

Location	
WarehouseID	InventoryID
WH138	BVL489
WH479	ANK18
WH702	BVL489

Inventory	
InventoryID	Description
ANK18	Rough
BVL489	Smooth

Example 4:

Warehouse	
WarehouseID	Address
WH138	11 Oak
WH479	321 East
WH702	929 Paris

Location	
WarehouseID	InventoryID
WH138	BVL489
WH138	ANK18
WH702	BVL489

Inventory	
InventoryID	Description
ANK18	Rough
BVL489	Smooth
CRW177	Bumpy

A) Example 1
B) Example 2
C) Example 3
D) Example 4
E) None of the above.

LO5

MC6. Internal agents typically associated with economic increment events via participation relationships in the acquisition/payment process include:
A) Salespeople
B) Receiving clerks
C) Credit card companies
D) Suppliers
E) Accounts payable clerks

LO4

MC7. For supply acquisitions the associated resource is usually _____, and for operating asset acquisitions the associated resource is usually _____.
A) supply type, operating asset
B) service type, operating asset
C) operating asset, supply type
D) operating asset type, service type
E) supply, operation asset type

LO4

MC8. Which classes would be paired in a stockflow association in the acquisition cycle?
A) Purchase requisition and inventory type
B) Purchase and inventory type
C) Purchase order and inventory type
D) Purchase order and purchase
E) Purchase and purchase return

LO3

MC9. Which classes would be paired in a duality association in the acquisition cycle?
A) Service acquisition and cash disbursement
B) Cash disbursement and cash
C) Purchase and purchase return
D) Purchase and inventory type
E) Rental contract and cash receipt

LO5

MC10. Which classes would be paired in a participation association in the revenue cycle?
A) Customer and salesperson
B) Sale and inventory
C) Sale and sale return
D) Service engagement and employee
E) Rental contract and cash receipt

Discussion Questions

LO2, LO4 D1. What are the heuristic multiplicities for an association between cash and cash disbursement? Explain each of the four multiplicities and identify any common exceptions to the heuristic.

LO2, LO4 D2. What are the heuristic multiplicities for an association between sale and inventory, assuming the inventory is mass-produced and tracked at the type level? Explain each of the four multiplicities and identify any common exceptions to the heuristic.

LO3 D3. Explain whether the following statement is true or false. "Recording an event in a relational database simply involves adding one record to an event table."

LO1, LO2 D4. Inspect the following logical relational database tables. Construct the likely underlying conceptual model.

Inventory Type

ItemID	Description	Unit Cost
I1	Heart pin	$4.59
I2	Topaz ring	$22.35
I3	Diamond	$332.50

Stockflow InvType Sale

ItemID	SaleID	Quantity Sold
I1	S1	20
I2	S1	5
I2	S2	10

Sale

SaleID	Date	Amount
S1	1/3	$203.55
S2	1/3	$223.50

Applied Learning

LO6   **A1.** Surfer Dudes Inc. (SDI) sells handcrafted surfboards to customers through its network of company salespeople. Each surfboard is given a unique identification number and a suggested selling price when finished. Upon employment each salesperson is immediately assigned to service a separate group of customers. When customer data is initially entered into SDI's information system, the customer is immediately assigned to a salesperson. Each sale can include one or more surfboard and can be paid for in any of three ways: (1) immediately in cash, (2) on the 15th of the following month, or (3) over the course of six months. No more than one salesperson participates in making each specific sale. Sometimes surfboards are sold for a price that is lower than their suggested selling prices, especially if the customer is a high volume customer or if that surfboard is a slow seller (i.e., it has been in stock for a long time). Each cash receipt comes from either one customer or from one lender or investor. Every cash receipt is processed by exactly one of SDI's several cashiers and is deposited into one of SDI's bank accounts. Information about surfboards, employees, and customers will often need to be entered into the database before any transactions involving them have occurred. The following data items (attributes) are of interest to potential users of this model:

-surfboard-id#	-cash-account-balance
-customer-name	-number-of-surfboards-sold-on-a-specific-invoice
-salesperson-name	-cashier-name
-cash-receipt-total-amount	-description-of-surfboard
-location-of-cash-account	-customer-accounts-receivable-balance
-sale-number	-salesperson-number
-cash-receipt-amount-applied-to-a-sale	-cashier-ID-number
-cash-account-number	-cash-account-type
-customer-number	-suggested-selling-price-for-a-surfboard
-actual-selling-price-for-a-surfboard	-sale-total-amount
-salesperson-commission-rate	-remittance-advice-number

Note: Salesperson commission rate is determined per contractual arrangement with each salesperson and for a particular salesperson it is the same percentage rate no matter what items he or she sells.

Required:

Create an REA class diagram for SDI's revenue cycle. Be sure to include all relevant classes, associations, attributes, and multiplicities. Limit the scope of your model to those classes and associations covered by the above attribute list (that is, don't add any attributes and don't represent anything that can't be identified).

LO6   **A2.** FarmFresh Produce Company is a produce wholesaler that buys large quantities of produce and sells this produce to grocery stores and restaurants. Four purchasing agents arrange the acquisitions of produce; each agent is assigned to specific produce types. Only one agent is assigned to each item of produce; however, if an assigned agent is on vacation or is ill, an alternative agent may acquire the absent agent's produce types. Only one agent is involved with any acquisition. Agents can acquire several types of produce on any single purchase. A produce item may be available from more than one vendor, and FarmFresh wants to be able to track which produce types are available from which vendors.

One of FarmFresh's three disbursement clerks prepares a check drawn on one of the company's checking accounts to pay vendors for purchases. One check is prepared for all purchases made from a vendor during the previous week. Partial payments are never made. The company has checking accounts at several different banks, and the same check numbers could be used by the different checking accounts. Besides checks written to vendors (which constitute only approximately 20% of all checks written), FarmFresh's disbursement clerks also issue checks to employees, lenders, stockholders, etc. FarmFresh does not have any petty cash or on-hand cash accounts. FarmFresh does have some savings accounts and certificates of deposit, held at some of the same banks at which FarmFresh has checking accounts.

Employees, vendors, inventory items, cash accounts, and banks can be added to the database before any transactions involving them occur.

Required: Prepare a UML class diagram for FarmFresh Produce, consistent with the REA ontology. Be sure to include all classes, associations, attributes, and multiplicities. The owner of FarmFresh has identified the following attributes that she wants included in the database. Do not add or subtract any attributes. You may use the abbreviations for the attributes.

Disbursement clerk ID (DC-ID)	VendorID (VenID)
Check number (Ck#)	Cash account type (Ctype)
Check amount (Ck-amt)	Purchase date (Date-pur)
Vendor name (Vname)	Bank's phone number (B-ph)
Vendor address (Vadd)	Cash account number (Acct#)
Produce type ID (PT-ID)	Date of check (Date-ck)
Purchase number (Pur#)	Vendor's phone number (V-ph)
Purchasing agent name (PA-name)	Purchasing agent ID (PA-ID)
Bank ID (Bank-ID)	Produce type description (Desc)
Disbursement clerk name (DC-name)	Name of bank (B-name)
Cash disbursement ID (CD-ID)	
Actual unit cost of a produce type on a purchase (act-cost)	
Quantity of each produce type received on a purchase (act-qty)	

LO1, LO6   **A3.**   Use the following partial database tables to answer the required questions:

Sales Event Table

Sales Event #	Date	Terms	Salesperson ID	Customer ID
1	11/5	2 10, net 30	2	2543
2	11/5	2 10, net 30	4	635
3	11/5	COD	6	1845

Salesperson Table

Salesperson ID	Last Name	First Name
2	Cleaves	Mateen
4	Warrick	Peter
6	Peterson	Morris
8	Janakowski	Sebastian

Sale-Inventory Table

Sale Event #	Inventory Item #	Inventory Quantity	Price each
1	876	10	1.25
1	674	8	0.875
1	451	30	0.995
2	887	54	1.475
2	513	188	0.525
3	736	36	24.995
3	001	58	7.875
3	302	16	8.00
3	224	114	8.75

Cashier Table

Cashier ID	Last Name	First Name
1	Weinke	Chris
2	Outzen	Marcus

Cash Receipts Event Table

Cash Receipt #	Date	Check #	Cashier ID	Sale Event #	Customer ID	Cash Account #	Amount
1001	11/6	11097	12	2	635	110146758	$ 178.35

Customer Table

Customer ID	Last Name	First Name	Address	City	State	Zip
101	Conrad	Chris	5629 Longfellow Dr.	Paragould	AK	65323
183	Anderson	Paul	674 Sunderland Lane	Sioux City	IA	63126
635	Padgham	Donna	1264 Algonquin Road	Mason	MI	48854
1845	Oliver	Andrew	8512 Bonita Dr.	Clearwater	FL	33051
2543	Cook	Carol	536 Secondary Ave.	Fremont	CA	75518

Cash Table

Cash #	Type of account	Bank Name
110146758	Regular checking	North First
1203948102	Payroll checking account	Credit Grantors

Inventory Table

Inventory Item #	Description
001	XL T-shirt
224	XL Sweatshirt
302	XXL T-shirt
451	Felt pennant
513	Ping pong ball
674	Golf ball
736	XL Polo shirt
876	Bumper sticker
887	Foam football

Required

a. What events, resources, and agents must have been included in the underlying conceptual model from which these relational tables were designed?

b. Identify the primary key of each table.

c. Identify each foreign key in the database.

d. List the resources and agents involved in Sale event #2.

e. List the resources and agents involved in Cash Receipt #1001.

f. Suppose you wanted to generate an invoice (bill) for customer # 2543 that lists the customer name and address, the salesperson name, and all other information about the sale, including the items sold. Which tables contain the data you will need in order to generate the invoice?

g. Suppose you wanted to generate a report listing each customer name and the amount due from each customer. Which tables contain the data you will need in order to generate the report?

h. Explain why "total sales amount" did not need to be included as an attribute in the sale table. What are the pros and cons associated with leaving this attribute out of the database tables?

i. If you need to record the following sale:
    Sale event 4; on 11/10; COD terms; Salesperson 2; Customer 101; 30 units of item 887, for a total of $44.25.
    What tables would you use? How many records would you add or modify in the tables?

j. If you need to maintain your records to reflect a change in Donna Padgham's last name and address, what tables would you use? How many records would you add or modify in the tables.

k. If you need to record the following cash receipt:
    Cash receipt 1002; on 11/10; from customer 2543 to pay off sale event # 1; in the amount of $49.35 deposited into cash account # 110146758
    What tables would you use? How many records would you add or modify in the tables?

REA Accounting Systems: Resources-Events-Agents: An ontology for designing, controlling, and using integrated enterprise systems

209

CHAPTER 7

Expanded REA Business Process Modeling and View Integration

LEARNING OBJECTIVES

This chapter expands the business process level models introduced in chapter 5 to include events that occur prior to and after the economic exchange events and associations in which those events are involved. Examples are provided for both the acquisition and revenue cycles. View integration, the process by which conceptual models from multiple transaction cycles are merged together, is also introduced. After studying this chapter, you should be able to

1. Identify the various expanded business process level REA constructs for the revenue and acquisition cycles of a variety of enterprises
2. Identify instigation events that lead to mutual commitment events
3. Identify commitment events that lead to economic exchange events
4. Identify economic reversal events (both increment and decrement reversals)
5. Identify resources involved in instigation, commitment and economic reversal events
6. Identify agents (internal and external) involved in instigation, commitment and economic reversal events
7. Create expanded revenue and acquisition cycle REA models for a variety of enterprises
8. Explain the difference between view modeling and view integration
9. Explain the various types of conflict that need to be resolved in view integration
10. Identify the steps needed to integrate multiple business process level conceptual models
11. Integrate revenue and acquisition cycle REA models for an enterprise

EXPANSIONS TO THE REA CORE BUSINESS PROCESS MODEL

Chapter 6 covered the core business process level of the REA ontology which is shown as the non-bolded portion of Exhibit 7-1. The bolded portion of Exhibit 7-1 illustrates some of the expansions that were originally published in 1982 that were discussed but not illustrated in chapter 6 (custody, assignment, and responsibility) and also some of the expansions that have been made to REA in the three decades since its first publication in 1982. These expansions help make the economic story told by the accounting and enterprise system more complete by including events that occur prior to the economic exchange events and also include events that occur afterward. We next describe each of these bolded classes and associations in more detail.

The events that occur prior to economic exchanges in enterprises are instigation events and commitment events. **Instigation events** are events in which the need for future economic events are identified, thus triggering other activities and events in a transaction cycle. **Commitment events** are events in which agreements are made that will result in future economic events. In theory there is a commitment to the future economic increment event and a commitment to the future economic decrement event. If the commitments happen simultaneously, they may be bundled into a **mutual commitment event.**

One type of event that occurs after economic exchanges in many enterprises is a reversal of part or all of the economic events that make up the exchange. **Economic reversal events** are events that reverse or annul economic events that previously occurred.

As described in Chapter 6, custody is the association between an agent and a resource such that the agent either has physical control over the resource or controls access to the resource. Such a relationship is separate from any event involving the resource. In other words, if an event involves a resource and an agent, the participation of both the resource and the agent in that event does not constitute a custody association. The agent who has custody of a resource may be an internal or an external agent. For banks have custody of an enterprise's cash held in accounts at their location. Similarly goods may be consigned to an external agent to sell on the enterprise's behalf. Assignment is an association between an internal agent and an external agent that is separate from any event in which they might both participate. For example, a salesperson may be assigned to a territory that includes customer number 43BYZ. That relationship exists even if 43BYZ never buys anything from the enterprise. Responsibility is an association between two types of internal agents that is separate from any event in which they might both participate. For example a partner in a public accounting firm may be given responsibility for ten of the staff accountants in that firm. Specific responsibilities may include the partner mentoring the staff accountants, reading supervisors' reviews of the staff accountants' performance, reviewing the staff accountants' training programs and career plans, and conducting their annual evaluations. Such a relationship exists even if those staff accountants never work on a client engagement with that partner.

Fulfillment associations occur between instigation events and the commitment events to which the instigation events lead and also between commitment events and the economic events to which the commitments lead. For example, a purchase order fulfills a purchase requisition and a purchase fulfills a purchase order. **Proposition** associations occur between instigation events and the resources or resource types that the instigation events have identified a need to increase or decrease with future economic events. A proposition is essentially a proposed future stockflow. **Reservation** associations occur between commitment events and the resources or resource types that the commitment events promise to increase or decrease with the future economic events. A reservation is essentially an agreed upon future stockflow. **Reversal** associations occur between economic reversal events and the economic events that are reversed or annulled. **Typification** associations may be created between any class and its type. Exhibit 7-1 shows typification between resource and resource type, as that is a common association in many enterprise's revenue and acquisition cycles. Chapter 11 discusses typification in more depth and provides additional examples of its usefulness. Exhibit 7-1 illustrates the expanded REA ontology in diagram format. **Reciprocal** associations occur between commitment events wherein one commitment is for a future economic increment and the related commitment is for a future economic decrement. Reciprocal is essentially the commitment equivalent of duality. If the separate commitments have been replaced by a Mutual Commitment Event, then there is no reciprocal association. Reciprocal associations are discussed further in Chapter 13, as they are most common in the conversion cycle.

Exhibit 7-1: Expanded REA Ontology

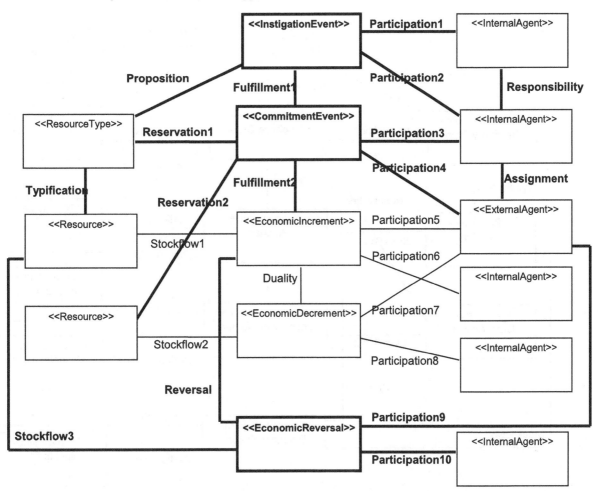

Bold classes and associations are expansions from the core business process level of the REA ontology. *Note: Internal agents on this diagram are illustrated as separate classes; however, in most enterprises the same internal agent will be connected to more than one of the events.*

EXPANDED REA ACQUISITION CYCLE MODEL

Applying the expanded REA business process level object pattern to the acquisition/payment process for an enterprise that purchases inventory that is identified at the type level for purposes of need identification and ordering but is specifically identified by a serial number upon receipt results in the class diagram shown in Exhibit 7-2.

Exhibit 7-2: Expanded REA Business Process Level Acquisition/Payment Cycle Model

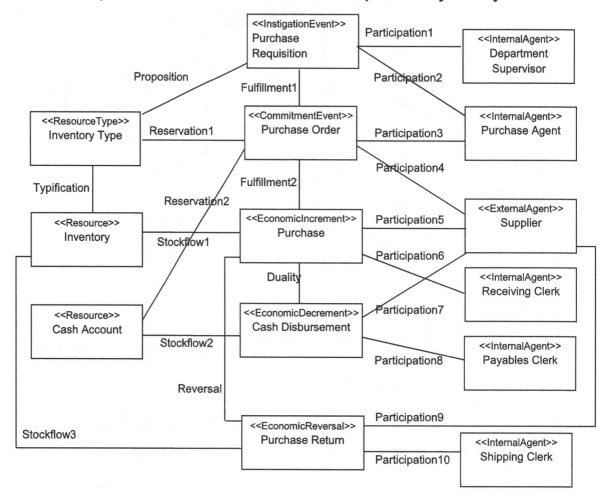

Acquisition Cycle Instigation Events
Need Identification and Request for Goods/Services

As discussed in chapter 3, in most enterprises with formal purchasing departments, once supervisors or other authorized individuals identify a need for goods, they communicate that need to an authorized buyer (internal purchasing agent) via a purchase requisition. The communication of such information is represented as an instigation event and is often labeled as *purchase requisition* as included in Exhibit 7-2. Smaller and less formal enterprises may not document the need identification event; such enterprises may therefore choose to omit this event in their acquisition cycle business process conceptual model. Others may choose to document the need identification with some other non-requisition document and label the instigation event accordingly.

Agents involved in instigation events in the acquisition/payment process usually are department supervisors (or other internal agents who initiate the requisition) and purchasing department representatives (internal agents who process or deny the requisition). Requisitions may include a recommended vendor for the requested goods or services; this data may be tracked in the database and represented by another participation association that is not currently shown in

Exhibit 7-2. Most instigation events specify the type of good or service requested and no link is needed to the exact good.   For the rare cases in which an exact good is requested, the proposition association should connect the requisition event to the specifically identified resource rather than the resource type.

Attributes of instigation events that typically should be captured include the date and time of the need identification, as well as the date by which the needed items are required. The instigation event data should also be able to be linked to data regarding the related employees, requested vendor (if one is specified), and the types of requested goods or services.

Associations in which the purchase requisition or equivalent instigation event commonly participates include *proposition*, to track the resources or resource types for which need has been identified, *fulfillment*, to track the requisition to the resulting purchase order or equivalent commitment event, and participation associations with any internal and external agents.

Exhibit 7-3 illustrates example database tables encompassing the requisition event. Data to be entered to record the purchase requisition are in bold italic font. Data that would already have been in the database are in regular font.

Exhibit 7-3   Sample Relational Tables Encompassing Purchase Requisition Event

Purchase Requisition (Instigation) Event

RequisitionID	Date	Maximum Budget for this purchase	Date Needed	SuperID[FK]	Purch AgentID[FK]	Recommended SupplierID[FK]
R17	*4/22/2015*	*$30,000.00*	*5/2/2015*	*E5*	*E12*	*V7*

Proposition Relationship

Requisition ID	Item ID	Quantity Needed	Estimated Unit Cost
R17	*BIS1*	*100*	*$20.00*
R17	*LIS1*	*200*	*$36.00*
R17	*HUS1*	*150*	*$30.00*
R17	*TIS1*	*300*	*$48.00*

Department Supervisor (Internal Agent)

Super ID	Name	Address	Telephone	DateOfBirth
E5	Patrick Wellesley	53125 Fenton Dr.	555-1112	March 4, 1958

Purchasing Agent (Internal Agent)

PurchaseAgent ID	Name	Address	Telephone	DateOfBirth
E12	Joy Berwick	1237 Kirkland Ave.	555-8914	July 14, 1960

Supplier (External Agent)

Supplier ID	Name	Address	Telephone	Performance Rating
V7	Joe's Favorite Vendor	89056 Ransom Hwy.	555-7655	Excellent

Inventory Type (Resource Type)

Item ID	Description	UnitOfMeasure	Standard Cost	List Price
BIS1	Big Stuff	Each	$20.00	$50.00
HUS1	Huge Stuff	Each	$30.00	$70.00
LIS1	Little Stuff	Box of 6	$36.00	$72.00
TIS1	Tiny Stuff	Box of 12	$48.00	$96.00

Purchase Order (Mutual Commitment) Event

Purchase Order ID	PO Date	Date Promised	Total Dollar Amt	Purchase RequisitionID^{FK}	Purchase AgentID^{FK}	SupplierID^{FK}

Note: Fulfillment1 is implemented with RequisitionID posted into Purchase Order table; Participation1 is implemented with SupervisorID posted into Requisition table; Participation2 is implemented with PurchaseAgentID posted into Requisition table; Fulfillment1 data are not yet entered, assuming a time lag between requisition and order.

Acquisition Cycle Mutual Commitment Events
Purchase Orders, Rental Agreements, Service Agreements

A mutual commitment event exists if the enterprise and an external business partner have each agreed to exchange resources at a defined future time. In the acquisition/payment process the most common mutual commitment events are purchase orders, rental agreements, and service agreements. Because Exhibit 7-2 was created for an enterprise's acquisition of inventory, the commitment event is called a *purchase order*. A mutual commitment event doesn't always happen at a discrete point in time; often it involves a series of tasks. Typically a purchase agent (the internal agent) places an order with a supplier (the external agent) for goods or services (the resource). There is usually no need to specifically identify goods or services for mutual commitment events; rather, information about the type of good or service ordered from the supplier is sufficient.

Attributes of mutual commitment events that typically should be captured include the date, time, and dollar amount of the order or agreement, the date by which the enterprise needs the goods or services delivered, the delivery method to be used (e.g., Federal Express, UPS, or customer pick-up), the desired location of the delivery, and the payment terms. Details of what resource items comprise the order are typically attributes of the reservation association that is described later in this chapter.

Associations in which purchase orders commonly participate include *reservation*, to track the resources or resource types the enterprise is agreeing to purchase, one fulfillment association to track the need identification event that led to the purchase order and two more fulfillment associations to track the order to the resulting purchase and cash disbursement events. Because the purchase order is typically considered a mutual commitment (the enterprise agrees to pay for inventory; the vendor agrees to provide the inventory), it is fulfilled both by the receipt of inventory and by the payment for the inventory.

Exhibit 7-4 illustrates example database tables encompassing the purchase order event. Data to be entered to record the purchase order are in bold italic font. Data that would already have been in the database are in regular font.

Exhibit 7-4: Sample Relational Tables Encompassing Purchase Order Event

Purchase Order (Mutual Commitment) Event

Purchase Order ID	PO Date	Date Promised	Total Dollar Amt	Purchase RequisitionID^{FK}	Purchase AgentID^{FK}	SupplierID^{FK}
PO16	*4/24/2015*	*5/2/2015*	*$28,450.00*	*R17*	*E12*	*V7*

Purchase Requisition (Instigation) Event

RequisitionID	Date	Maximum Budget for this purchase	Date Needed	SuperID^{FK}	Purch AgentID^{FK}	Recommended SupplierID^{FK}
R17	4/22/2015	$30,000.00	5/2/2015	E5	E12	V7

Reservation1 Relationship

Purchase Order ID	Item ID	Quantity Needed	Quoted Unit Cost
PO16	*BIS1*	*100*	*$20.00*
PO16	*LIS1*	*200*	*$35.50*
PO16	*HUS1*	*150*	*$29.00*
PO16	*TIS1*	*300*	*$50.00*

Purchasing Agent (Internal Agent)

Purchase Agent ID	Name	Address	Telephone	DateOfBirth
E12	Joy Berwick	1237 Kirkland Ave.	555-8914	July 14, 1960

Supplier (External Agent)

Supplier ID	Name	Address	Telephone	Performance Rating
V7	Joe's Favorite Vendor	89056 Ransom Hwy.	555-7655	Excellent

Inventory Type (Resource Type)

Item ID	Description	UnitOfMeasure	Standard Cost	List Price
BIS1	Big Stuff	Each	$20.00	$50.00
HUS1	Huge Stuff	Each	$30.00	$70.00
LIS1	Little Stuff	Box of 6	$36.00	$72.00
TIS1	Tiny Stuff	Box of 12	$48.00	$96.00

Fulfillment2 Relationship

Purchase Order ID	Receiving Report ID

Note: Participation3 is implemented with PurchAgent ID posted into Purchase Order table. Participation4 is implemented with Supplier ID posted into Purchase Order table. Fulfillment1 relationship is implemented with Requisition ID posted into Purchase Order table. Fulfillment2 data are not yet entered, assuming a time lag between order and receipt of goods.

Acquisition Cycle Economic Increment Events
Purchase [Receipt of Goods], Rental, or Service Acquisition

As described in chapter 6, the economic increment event in the acquisition cycle is that in which the enterprise receives a resource or resource type. Because the example in Exhibit 7-2 illustrates an acquisition/payment cycle in which inventory is acquired, the economic event therein is called *purchase*; however, it would be acceptable to call it *receipt of inventory* or *receipt of goods*.

Associations in which the economic increment event in Exhibit 7-2 participates include a *fulfillment* association, enabling the enterprise to trace which purchase order the purchase fulfilled, a *duality* association, allowing the enterprise to trace the purchase to related cash disbursements that represent the other part of the exchange, a *stockflow* association to track the inventory received in the purchase event, *participation* associations with the internal and external agents, and occasionally a *reversal* association, allowing the enterprise to trace purchase returns to the original acquisitions for which they reversed the economic effect.

The enterprise illustrated in Exhibit 7-2 has receiving clerks who receive the inventory as it is delivered from suppliers. This enterprise has chosen not to track directly which purchase agent authorized each purchase; however, the information is indirectly available by tracking the purchase back to the purchase order and then tracing from the purchase order to the purchase agent. Whether full traceability exists in those associations depends in part on the multiplicities, therefore if the data is needed, it makes sense to add a direct connection from the purchase event to the purchase agent.

The stockflow association for the illustrated enterprise connects inventory to the purchase event. In this enterprise each separate physical inventory item is identified with a unique number. If the inventory was not separately identified, then the stockflow would have connected to the inventory type and the inventory resource would be omitted from the model.

Exhibit 7-5 illustrates example database tables encompassing the purchase event. Data to be entered to record the purchase are in bold italic font. Data that would already have been in the database are in regular font.

REA Accounting Systems: Resources-Events-Agents: An ontology for designing, controlling, and using integrated enterprise systems

217

Exhibit 7-5: Sample Relational Tables Encompassing Purchase Event

Purchase (Economic Increment) Event

Receiving ReportID	Date	Dollar Amount	Receiving ClerkID^{FK}	SupplierID^{FK}	Vendor Invoice#	Invoice Amount	Cash DisbID^{FK}
RR18	*4/30/2015*	*$28,450.00*	*E111*	*V7*	*VI4167*	*$28,450.00*	

Purchase Order (Mutual Commitment) Event

Purchase Order ID	PO Date	Date Promised	Total Dollar Amt	Purchase RequisitionID^{FK}	Purchase AgentID^{FK}	SupplierID^{FK}
PO16	4/24/2015	5/2/2015	$28,450.00	R17	E12	V7

Stockflow1 Relationship

Receiving Report ID	Item ID	Quantity Received	Actual Unit Cost
RR18	*BIS1*	*100*	*$20.00*
RR18	*LIS1*	*200*	*$35.50*
RR18	*HUS1*	*150*	*$29.00*
RR18	*TIS1*	*300*	*$50.00*

Receiving Clerk (Internal Agent)

Receiving Clerk ID	Name	Address	Telephone	DateOfBirth
E111	Kendall Galligan	1235 Germandy Dr.	555-6812	December 12, 1970

Supplier (External Agent)

Supplier ID	Name	Address	Telephone	Performance Rating
V7	Joe's Favorite Vendor	89056 Ransom Hwy.	555-7655	Excellent

Inventory Type (Resource Type)

Item ID	Description	UnitOfMeasure	Standard Cost	List Price
BIS1	Big Stuff	Each	$20.00	$50.00
HUS1	Huge Stuff	Each	$30.00	$70.00
LIS1	Little Stuff	Box of 6	$36.00	$72.00
TIS1	Tiny Stuff	Box of 12	$48.00	$96.00

Fulfillment2 Relationship

Purchase Order ID	Receiving Report ID
PO16	*RR18*

Purchase Return (Economic Increment Reversal) Event

Purchase ReturnID	Date	Dollar Amount	Packing Slip#	Debit Memo#	Receiving ReportID^{FK}	SupplierID^{FK}	Dept SuperID^{FK}	Shipping ClerkID^{FK}

Note: Participation5 is implemented with Supplier ID posted into Purchase table. Reversal is implemented with Receiving Report ID posted into Purchase Return table. Duality and reversal data are not yet entered, assuming a time lag between Purchase and either Cash Disbursements or Purchase Returns.

Acquisition Cycle Economic Decrement Event
Cash Disbursement

Cash disbursements are economic decrement events that decrease the enterprise's cash balance. Cash disbursements may be made via paper check, debit card, electronic funds transfer, or by cash payment. Attributes captured regarding cash disbursements usually include a cash disbursement identifier (such as a disbursement voucher number), date, amount paid, supplier identification, employee identification (such as employees who write the checks), the account number from which the cash is disbursed, and the check number of the payment.

Exhibit 7-6 shows a set of relational tables that correspond to Exhibit 7-2's class diagram representation of the cash disbursement event and the acquisition cycle associations in which it participates (duality, stockflow2, participation7, and participation8). Other possible tables could be derived, depending on the multiplicities. Additional tables are likely necessary to correspond to associations in which the cash disbursement event participates in other transaction cycles such as financing and payroll. The tables shown in Exhibit 7-6 are applicable to the acquisition/payment process. New data to be added for the cash disbursement event is shown in bold italic font. Data that would already have been in the tables is shown in regular font.

Exhibit 7-6 Relational Tables Encompassing Cash Disbursement Event

Cash Disbursement (Economic Decrement) Event

Disb Voucher ID	Voucher Date	Dollar Amount	Check Number	Cash AccountID^{FK}	A/P ClerkID^{FK}	SupplierID^{FK}
40	5/25/2015	$28,450.00	41235	Ca123501	E36	V7

Cash (Resource Type)

CashAccountID	AccountType	Location
Ca123501	Checking	1st Local Bank

Purchase (Economic Increment) Event

Receiving ReportID	Date	Dollar Amount	Receiving ClerkID^{FK}	SupplierID^{FK}	Vendor Invoice#	Invoice Amount	Cash DisbID^{FK}
RR18	4/30/2015	$28,450.00	E111	V7	VI4167	$28,450.00	40

Accounts Payable Clerk (Internal Agent)

A/P Clerk ID	Name	Address	Telephone	DateOfBirth
E36	Diane Bowersox	9115 Wolfgang Court	555-7244	September 15, 1963

Supplier (External Agent)

Supplier ID	Name	Address	Telephone	Performance Rating
V7	Joe's Favorite Vendor	89056 Ransom Hwy.	555-7655	Excellent

Note: Stockflow2 is implemented with Cash AccountID posted into Cash Disbursement table. Participation7 is implemented with Supplier ID posted into Cash Disbursement table. Participation8 is implemented with A/P Clerk ID posted into Cash Disbursement table. Duality is implemented with Cash Disbursement ID posted into Purchase table.

Economic Increment Reversal Event (Purchase Returns and Allowances)

If goods and services received do not meet the identified needs, the enterprise may decide to reverse the increment event by returning the goods or requesting an allowance for the unsatisfactory services. For purchase return events, the returned products are the associated resources. Although a purchase return event decreases the inventory resource, the return is inherently different from an economic decrement event such as a sale. Because the return in effect reverses the purchase event, we call the purchase return an economic increment reversal event. If the goods were specifically identified upon acquisition, they should be specifically identified upon return; if they were measured and recorded at the type level upon acquisition, they should be measured in that same manner for the return. Typically the supplier is the external agent involved in the return event (a common carrier also may need to be linked as an external agent), a department supervisor authorizes the purchase return as an internal agent and a shipping clerk processes the purchase return as an internal agent.

Attributes typically captured regarding purchase returns include an identifier for the event, the return date, and the dollar amount of the return. Links also should be available to attributes of related agents and merchandise inventory. If a cash refund is received, it reverses the cash disbursement event, which was an economic decrement. Therefore we call the cash refund an economic decrement reversal event.

Exhibit 7-7 illustrates example database tables encompassing the purchase return event. Data to be entered to record the purchase return are in bold italic font. Data that would already have been in the database are in regular font.

Exhibit 7-7 Relational Tables Encompassing Purchase Return Event

Purchase Return (Economic Increment Reversal) Event

Purchase ReturnID	Date	Dollar Amount	Packing Slip#	Debit Memo#	Receiving ReportID^{FK}	SupplierID^{FK}	Dept SuperID^{FK}	Shipping ClerkID^{FK}
PR3	5/17/2015	$480.00	22	3	RR25	V90	E5	E41

Purchase (Economic Increment) Event

Receiving ReportID	Date	Dollar Amount	Receiving ClerkID^{FK}	SupplierID^{FK}	Vendor Invoice#	Invoice Amount	Cash DisbID^{FK}
RR18	4/30/2015	$28,450.00	E111	V7	VI4167	$28,450.00	40
RR25	5/12/2015	$480.00	E111	V90	48592	$480.00	

Stockflow3 Relationship

Purchase Return ID	Item ID	Quantity Returned	Actual Unit Cost
PR3	TTP12	48	$10.00

Shipping Clerk (Internal Agent)

Shipping Clerk ID	Name	Address	Telephone	DateOfBirth
E41	Amy Milano	8892 Eddy Ave.	555-9557	January 3, 1964

Department Supervisor (Internal Agent)

DeptSupervisorID	Name	Address	Telephone	DateOfBirth
E5	Patrick Wellesley	53125 Fenton Dr.	555-1112	March 4, 1958

Supplier (External Agent)

Supplier ID	Name	Address	Telephone	Performance Rating
V7	Joe's Favorite Vendor	89056 Ransom Hwy.	555-7655	Excellent
V90	Trina's Trinkets	1612 Myway R.	555-2424	Very Good

Inventory Type (Resource Type)

Item ID	Description	UnitOfMeasure	Standard Cost	List Price
BIS1	Big Stuff	Each	$20.00	$50.00
HUS1	Huge Stuff	Each	$30.00	$70.00
LIS1	Little Stuff	Box of 6	$36.00	$72.00
TIS1	Tiny Stuff	Box of 12	$48.00	$96.00
TTP12	Tiara	Each	$10.00	$25.00

Note: Participation9 is implemented with Supplier ID posted into Purchase Return table. Participation10 is implemented with Shipping Clerk ID posted into Purchase Return table. Reversal is implemented with Purchase ID posted into Purchase Return table.

REA Accounting Systems: Resources-Events-Agents: An ontology for designing, controlling, and using integrated enterprise systems

221

REA MODELING OF THE REVENUE CYCLE

Because as discussed in chapter 3, the acquisition and revenue cycles are comprised of the same overall activities viewed from different perspectives, the conceptual models for the two cycles are similar. Exhibit 7-8 illustrates a typical REA class diagram for an enterprise revenue cycle.

Exhibit 7-8: Revenue Cycle REA Class Diagram

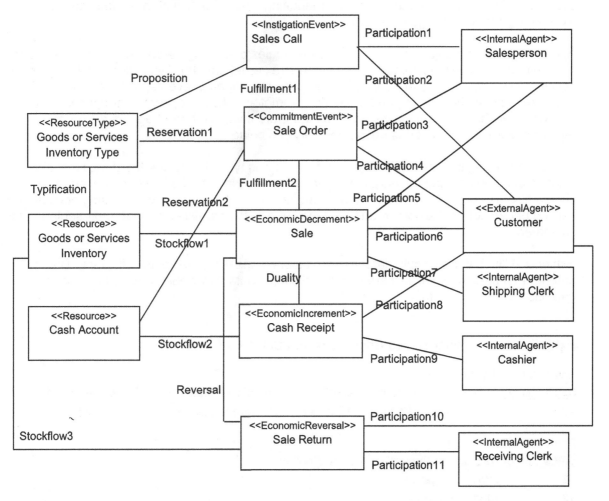

Note#1: Goods or Services Inventory may be excluded for enterprises for which it is not cost effective to use specific identification; if so, stockflow1 and stockflow3 should connect to the Goods or Services Inventory Type class. In other cases, the mutual commitment event may specify an instance of goods or services inventory; if so, reservation1 should connect to the Goods or Services Inventory class.

Instigation Events (Marketing Events, Customer Inquiries)

As described in chapter 3, in an effort to influence customer decision making, an enterprise plans, executes, and evaluates a variety of marketing events (e.g., sales calls, advertising campaigns, or promotions) intended to inform customers about products and/or services and hopefully influence them to trigger the sales/collection process. Therefore marketing efforts are typically considered to be internally generated instigation events. On the other hand, customers who know what they want may call the enterprise to see if the product or service they need is available, without having participated in a marketing event. Such customer inquiries are externally generated instigation events.

Agents involved in instigation events usually are sales/marketing personnel or customer service representatives (internal agents) and customers (external agents). Typically there is no need to specifically identify a good or service for purposes of instigation events; all that is needed is information about the type of good or service promoted. Of course, some enterprises have atypical or unusual circumstances and may therefore involve different agents and/or may require specific identification of goods and services being marketed.

Attributes of instigation events that should be captured typically include the date, time, and location of the event, and the duration of the customer contact. The instigation event data should also be able to be linked to data regarding the related sales and marketing or customer service personnel, the customer, and the types of goods or services that were presented to the customer.

Exhibit 7-9 illustrates example database tables encompassing the sales call event. Data to be entered to record the sales call are in bold italic font. Data that would already have been in the database are in regular font.

Exhibit 7-9: Relational Tables Encompassing Sales Call Event

Sales Call (Instigation) Event

Sales Call ID	Date	StartTime	EndTime	Location	SalesRepID^{FK}	CustomerID^{FK}
42	*5/4/2015*	*9:12 a.m.*	*10:00 a.m.*	*Customer*	*E23*	*C2323*

Proposition Relationship

Sales Call ID	Item ID	Customer Reaction to Product
42	*BIS1*	*Negative*
42	*LIS1*	*Positive*
42	*HUS1*	*Negative*
42	*TIS1*	*Positive*

Sales Representative (Internal Agent)

Sales Rep ID	Name	Address	Telephone	DateOfBirth
E23	Jimmy Vitale	425 ConAir Drive	555-5678	Aug 18, 1962

Customer (External Agent)

Customer ID	Name	Address	Telephone	Credit Rating
C2323	Needmore Stuff	86906 Enterprise Court	555-8989	A+

Inventory Type (Resource Type)

Item ID	Description	UnitOfMeasure	Standard Cost	List Price
BIS1	Big Stuff	Each	$20.00	$50.00
HUS1	Huge Stuff	Each	$30.00	$70.00
LIS1	Little Stuff	Box of 6	$36.00	$72.00
TIS1	Tiny Stuff	Box of 12	$48.00	$96.00

Sale Order (Mutual Commitment) Event

Sale Order ID	Order Date	Date Needed	Total Dollar Amt	Sales Tax	Shipping Charge	Sales CallID^{FK}	Sales RepID^{FK}	Customer ID^{FK}
14	5/4/2015	5/7/2015	$1,100.00	$0	$0	42	E23	C2323

Note: Fulfillment1 is implemented with Sales Call ID posted into Sale Order table; Participation1 is implemented with Sales Rep ID posted into Sales Call table; Participation2 is implemented with Customer ID posted into Sales Call table. Customer reaction to product is included as an attribute in the proposition table because it is intended to measure the reaction to the product on a specific sales call. It is assumed that the customer could react differently to the same product on a different call.

Mutual Commitment Events (Customer Orders, Rentals, Service Agreements)

A mutual commitment event exists if the enterprise and an external business partner have each agreed to exchange resources at a defined future time. In the sales/collection process the most common mutual commitment events are customer orders, rental agreements, and service agreements. A mutual commitment doesn't always happen at a discrete point in time; often it involves a series of activities. Typically a customer (the external agent) places an order with the enterprise for goods or services (the resource). Typically there is no need to specifically identify goods or services for mutual commitment events; rather information about the type of good or service promised to the customer is sufficient. Sales or customer service representatives and/or order entry clerks (internal agents) assist the customer and collect the order data. A credit manager may also serve as an internal agent as the one responsible for approving credit terms for the order.

Once the customer's order is approved, it becomes an accepted sale order and is considered a mutual commitment. Ideally an enterprise wants to be able to trace each sale order (mutual commitment event) to a sales call or other instigation event via a fulfillment association. . Sometimes it is impossible to determine which marketing efforts led to commitments for an enterprise; in such cases the fulfillment association is not materialized.

In cases in which commitments occur only as part of marketing events, the commitment and instigation events may be collapsed into a single class. If they are separate, linking marketing efforts to the commitment event provides valuable information to evaluate marketing effectiveness, so enterprises should consider the feasibility and cost of materializing this link.

Attributes of mutual commitment events that typically should be captured include the date, time, and dollar amount of the order, the date by which the customer needs the goods or services delivered, the delivery method to be used (e.g., Federal Express, UPS, or customer pick-up), the desired location of the delivery, and the payment terms. The order data should also be able to be linked to data regarding the related resources, agents, and economic decrement events, and, if possible, to the related instigation event.

Exhibit 7-10 illustrates example database tables encompassing the sale order event. Data to be entered to record the sale order are in bold italic font. Data that would already have been in the database are in regular font.

Exhibit 7-10: Sample Relational Tables Encompassing Sales Order Event

Sale Order (Mutual Commitment) Event

Sale Order ID	Order Date	Date Needed	Total Dollar Amt	Sales Tax	Shipping Charge	Sales CallID^{FK}	Sales RepID^{FK}	Customer ID^{FK}
14	*5/4/2015*	*5/7/2015*	*$1,100.00*	*$0*	*$0*	*42*	*E23*	*C2323*

Sales Call (Instigation) Event

Sales Call ID	Date	StartTime	EndTime	Location	SalesRepID^{FK}	CustomerID^{FK}
42	5/4/2015	9:12 a.m.	10:00 a.m.	Customer	E23	C2323

Reservation Relationship

Sales Order ID	Item ID	Quantity Ordered	Quoted Unit Price
14	*LIS1*	*2*	*70.00*
14	*TIS1*	*10*	*96.00*

Sales Representative (Internal Agent)

Sales Rep ID	Name	Address	Telephone	DateOfBirth
E23	Jimmy Vitale	425 ConAir Drive	555-5678	Aug 18, 1962

Customer (External Agent)

Customer ID	Name	Address	Telephone	Credit Rating
C2323	Needmore Stuff	86906 Enterprise Court	555-8989	A+

Inventory Type (Resource Type)

Item ID	Description	UnitOfMeasure	Standard Cost	List Price
BIS1	Big Stuff	Each	$20.00	$50.00
HUS1	Huge Stuff	Each	$30.00	$70.00
LIS1	Little Stuff	Box of 6	$36.00	$72.00
TIS1	Tiny Stuff	Box of 12	$48.00	$96.00

Fulfillment2 Relationship

Sales Order ID	Sale ID

Note: Participation3 is implemented with Sales Rep ID posted into Sales Order table. Participation4 is implemented with Customer ID posted into Sales Order table, Fulfillment1 is implemented with Sales Call ID posted into Sales Order table. Fulfillment2 data is not yet entered, assuming a time lag between order and shipment.

Economic Decrement Event (Sale, Delivery, Shipment, Rental, or Service Engagement)
The economic decrement event in the sales/collection process may take on one of several labels because it represents the revenue generating activity, which can take various forms. The revenue generating activity is the decrement event; resources made available to the revenue cycle by the acquisition and/or conversion cycles must be given or used up in exchange for the resource (usually cash) received from external partners. Usually the enterprise gives up goods, services, or the temporary use of goods. If the revenue generating activity involves the sale of merchandise, the event may be called *Sale*, *Delivery*, or *Shipment* depending in part on whether the customer is on-site to accept possession of the goods or whether the enterprise must deliver or ship the goods to the customer. The important consideration is that a decrement event that represents the sale of goods must represent the point at which title to the merchandise transfers from the seller to the buyer. If title has not transferred, then no decrement has occurred and the sale event cannot be materialized.

If the enterprise sells services rather than goods, then the resource given up to the customers is a set of employee services, making those services unavailable to provide to someone else. Such a decrement event is usually called Service Engagement or something that more specifically describes the kinds of services performed by the enterprise (such as *Repair Service*, *Audit Engagement*, or *Consultation*) In the case of enterprises that rent merchandise to customers, the economic decrement event is usually called Rental. The rental event does not involve the transfer of title of goods, but instead involves a transfer of the right to use goods for an agreed upon length of time. The rental event begins when the right to temporary possession of the goods transfers from the lessor to the lessee and ends when possession of the goods transfers back from the lessee to the lessor.

Economic decrement events in the revenue cycle do not always happen at discrete points in time; rather they are often made up of a series of workflow activities. Once a mutual commitment is made, the enterprise's fulfillment of that commitment is accomplished by the tasks that make up the economic decrement event. For enterprises that sell or rent merchandise that must be shipped to the customer location, these tasks include picking the inventory from the warehouse, packing the inventory into boxes, and shipping the boxes to the customer via a common carrier. The rental event also includes receiving the returned merchandise, inspecting it, and returning it to the warehouse. Economic decrement events for service enterprises generally require active involvement of trained employees who perform the services. The enterprise must identify the requirements of the services to be rendered and select an individual or group of individuals to perform the services. Services may be provided over an extended period of time by a variety of people.

Some enterprises may have multiple revenue generating activities. For example, some enterprises ship finished products to customers and also provide services. Some enterprises may have various combinations for different customers. For example, a computer manufacturer, may serve one customer by shipping a new computer and letting the customer install it and handle all conversion. For another customer, the enterprise may deliver the computer, assist with installation, and convert existing applications for processing on the new computer. Yet another customer may request that enterprise to repair a computer that the enterprise had previously sold to the customer. The different events may need to be recorded as separate classes in the REA business process level model, or they may be combined into one economic decrement event class. The appropriate representation depends on the data captured regarding each different decrement event. If different attributes are needed for the types of decrements, usually they should be represented as separate event entities, each participating in the duality association with the appropriate economic increment event.

Associations in which the economic decrement event participates typically include a fulfillment association (enabling the enterprise to trace which mutual commitment event the decrement fulfilled), a duality association (allowing the enterprise to trace a related economic increment that represents the other part of the exchange), a stockflow association (to trace the resource or resource type that was given up in the decrement event), participation associations with the internal and external agents, and occasionally a reversal association (allowing the enterprise to trace sale returns to the original sales for which they reversed the economic effect).

Internal agents typically associated with economic decrement events via participation associations include salespeople, shipping clerks, delivery clerks, and engagement personnel. External agents typically associated with economic decrement events via participation associations include transportation suppliers (such as UPS or Federal Express) and customers. The resources typically associated with the economic decrement event via stockflow associations in the revenue cycle are usually *inventory*, *inventory type*, or service type. Most manufacturers and merchandisers do not specifically identify inventory, so the resource that participates in the stockflow association is usually *inventory type*. For those enterprises that do specifically identify inventory items, the resource in the stockflow association is *inventory*. For service providers, the resource involved in the stockflow association is usually *service type*.

Exhibit 7-11 illustrates example database tables encompassing the sale event. Data to be entered to record the sale are in bold italic font. Data that would already have been in the database are in regular font.

Exhibit 7-11: Relational Tables Encompassing Sale Event

Sale Order (Mutual Commitment) Event

Sale Order ID	Order Date	Date Needed	Total Dollar Amt	Sales Tax	Shipping Charge	Sales CallID[FK]	Sales RepID[FK]	Customer ID[FK]
14	5/4/2015	5/7/2015	$1,100.00	$0	$0	42	E23	C2323

Sale (Economic Decrement) Event

Sale ID	Date	PickID	PackID	BOL#	SalesRepID[FK]	CustomerID[FK]	CashRecID[FK]	ShipClerkID[FK]
12	*5/5/2015*	*15*	*15*	*15*	*E23*	*C2323*		*E41*

Stockflow1 Relationship

Sale ID	Item ID	Quantity Sold	Actual Unit Price
12	*LIS1*	*2*	*70.00*
12	*TIS1*	*10*	*96.00*

Sales Representative (Internal Agent)

Sales Rep ID	Name	Address	Telephone	DateOfBirth
E23	Jimmy Vitale	425 ConAir Drive	555-5678	Aug 18, 1962

Shipping Clerk (Internal Agent)

Shipping Clerk ID	Name	Address	Telephone	DateOfBirth
E41	Amy Milano	8892 Eddy Ave.	555-9557	January 3, 1964

REA Accounting Systems: Resources-Events-Agents: An ontology for designing, controlling, and using integrated enterprise systems

227

Customer (External Agent)

Customer ID	Name	Address	Telephone	Credit Rating
C2323	Needmore Stuff	86906 Enterprise Court	555-8989	A+

Inventory Type (Resource Type)

Item ID	Description	UnitOfMeasure	Standard Cost	List Price
BIS1	Big Stuff	Each	$20.00	$50.00
HUS1	Huge Stuff	Each	$30.00	$70.00
LIS1	Little Stuff	Box of 6	$36.00	$72.00
TIS1	Tiny Stuff	Box of 12	$48.00	$96.00

Fulfillment2 Relationship

Sale Order ID	Sale ID
14	*12*

Cash Receipt (Economic Increment) Event

CashReceiptID	Date	DollarAmount	CashAccountID[FK]	CustomerID[FK]	CashierID[FK]
RA20	*5/19/2015*	*$1,100.00*	*Ca123501*	*C2323*	*E111*

Sale Return (Economic Decrement Reversal) Event

Sale Return ID	Date	$Amount	SalesRepID[FK]	CustomerID[FK]	SaleID[FK]

Note: Participation5 is implemented with Sales Rep ID posted into Sale table. Participation6 is implemented with Customer ID posted into Sale table. Participation7 is implemented with Shipping Clerk ID posted into Sale table. Duality is implemented with Cash Receipt ID posted into Sale table. Cash receipt data is not yet entered, assuming a time lag between shipment and cash receipt. Reversal is implemented with Sale ID posted into Sales Return table. Return data is not yet entered, assuming a time lag between shipment and sale return.

Economic Increment Event (Cash Receipt)

Cash receipts are economic increment events that increase the enterprise's cash balance. Cash receipts may take the form of checks, currency, or coins – anything that can be deposited into a cash account held either in a bank or on hand in petty cash. Notice that if a customer pays with a credit card, the enterprise has not yet received cash; the cash receipt does not occur until the credit card company pays the enterprise. In the latter case, the cash receipt must be connected to two external agents – the customer, whose accounts receivable balance will be decreased as a result of the cash receipt, and the credit card company, from whom the cash was literally received.

Attributes captured regarding cash receipts usually include a cash receipt identifier (such as a unique remittance advice number), date, amount received, customer identification, employee identification (such as employees who count and deposit the cash), the account number where the cash is deposited, the location of payment (such as mail, or in person at the main office), and the check number of the payment.

Exhibit 7-12 illustrates example database tables encompassing the cash receipt event. Data to be entered to record the cash receipt are in bold italic font. Data that would already have been in the database are in regular font.

Exhibit 7-12: Relational Tables Encompassing Cash Receipt Event

Cash Receipt (Economic Increment) Event

CashReceiptID	Date	DollarAmount	CashAccountID^{FK}	CustomerID^{FK}	CashierID^{FK}
RA20	*5/19/2015*	*$960.00*	*Ca123501*	*C2323*	*E111*

Sale (Economic Decrement) Event

Sale ID	Date	PickListID	PackListID	BOL#	SalesRepID^{FK}	CustomerID^{FK}	CashReceiptID^{FK}
12	5/5/2015	15	15	15	E23	C2323	*RA20*

Cashier (Internal Agent)

CashierID	Name	Address	Telephone	DateOfBirth
E111	Missy Witherspoon	1710 Crestwood Dr.	555-9392	May 11, 1960

Customer (External Agent)

Customer ID	Name	Address	Telephone	Credit Rating
C2323	Needmore Stuff	86906 Enterprise Court	555-8989	A+

Cash (Resource Type)

CashAccountID	AccountType	Location
Ca123501	Checking	1st Local Bank

Note: Participation8 is implemented with Customer ID posted into Cash Receipt table. Participation9 is implemented with Cashier ID posted into Cash Receipt table. Duality is implemented with Cash Receipt ID posted into Sale table. Stockflow2 is implemented with Cash Account ID posted into Cash Receipt table.

Economic Decrement Reversal Event (Sales Returns and Sales Allowances)

If sales returns are allowed, the returned products are the resources involved in the sales return event. Although the return increases the inventory resource, the return is inherently different from an economic increment event such as a purchase. In effect, the return reverses the sale event, which was an economic decrement event. Therefore we call this an economic decrement reversal event. If the goods were specifically identified upon sale, they should be specifically identified upon return; if they were measured and recorded at the type level upon sale, they should be measured in that same manner for the return. Typically the customer is the external agent involved in the return event (a common carrier may also need to be linked as an external agent) and a sales manager serves as the internal agent.

Attributes typically captured regarding sales returns include an identifier for the event, the return date, and the dollar amount of the return. Links should also be available to attributes of related agents and merchandise inventory.

Exhibit 7-13 illustrates example database tables encompassing the sale return event. Data to be entered to record the sale return are in bold italic font. Data that would already have been in the database are in regular font.

Exhibit 7-13: Relational Tables Encompassing Sales Return Event

Sales Return (Economic Decrement Reversal) Event

Sale ReturnID	Date	Dollar Amount	Receiving ReportNo.	Credit Memo#	Credit MgrID	SaleID^{FK}	CustomerID^{FK}	Receiving ClerkID^{FK}
SR1	5/12/2015	$140.00	RR25	1	E16	12	C2323	E247

Sale (Economic Decrement) Event

Sale ID	Date	PickListID	PackListID	BOL#	SalesRepID^{FK}	CustomerID^{FK}	CashReceiptID^{FK}
12	5/5/2015	15	15	15	E23	C2323	RA20

Receiving Clerk (Internal Agent)

ClerkID	Name	Address	Telephone	DateOfBirth
E247	Kenneth Barki	4312 Monticello Dr.	556-4891	April 14, 1945

Customer (External Agent)

Customer ID	Name	Address	Telephone	Credit Rating
C2323	Needmore Stuff	86906 Enterprise Court	555-8989	A+

Stockflow3 Relationship

Sale Return ID	Item ID	Quantity Returned	Actual Unit Price	Condition of Goods	Reason Returned
12	LIS1	2	70.00	Perfect	Too big

Inventory Type (Resource Type)

Item ID	Description	UnitOfMeasure	Standard Cost	List Price
BIS1	Big Stuff	Each	$20.00	$50.00
HUS1	Huge Stuff	Each	$30.00	$70.00
LIS1	Little Stuff	Box of 6	$36.00	$72.00
TIS1	Tiny Stuff	Box of 12	$48.00	$96.00

Note: Participation10 is implemented with Customer ID posted into Sales Return table. Participation11 is implemented with Clerk ID posted into Sales Return table. Reversal is implemented with Sale ID posted into Sales Return table.

VIEW INTEGRATION

We initially create business process level models separately for each transaction cycle because each cycle presents a manageable set of events and related resources and agents. The creation of separate models for different parts of a system is called **view modeling**. To create a database that can serve as the foundation for an integrated enterprise-wide information system; however, the separate views must be integrated to form a comprehensive model. Although we introduced the conversion of a conceptual model to a logical model, followed by the implementation into a physical database as if those steps would be part of each separate transaction cycle analysis, in fact the separate conceptual models for each business process view should be integrated before the conversion to the logical and physical levels occurs. This step is called **view integration**.

When you use the full REA ontology as a foundation for designing an enterprise-wide database, the first step is to consider the enterprise in the context of its external business partners and to create a value system level model. The second step is to consider the resource flows among the transaction cycles within the enterprise and to create a value chain level model. Identifying the resource flows at the value chain level model helps to identify the points of integration of the transaction cycles and therefore also helps to identify points of integration for the conceptual models of those transaction cycles.

View integration may be used in the normal course of database design for a single enterprise; alternatively it may be used to consolidate separate databases as a result of a corporate merger, acquisition, or other forms of business consolidation. Whether in the original design phase for a single enterprise or in the consolidation of separate databases, view integration involves three basic steps:
1. Identify the common classes in two views.
2. Merge the common classes, resolving any class conflicts and performing a set union of their attributes.
3. Examine each association and resolve any association conflicts.

Conceptual models are integrated based on their common classes. The resources that flow from one business process to another in a value chain are common classes to those business processes; sometimes the processes also share common agent or event classes. One potential class conflict is **class name conflict**; this occurs when the same class included in different conceptual models is not labeled identically. Often different people on the same design team separately model the different views and may use synonymous labels. Even the same individual who models different views at different times, may use **synonyms** (different words that have the same meaning) for the same class. For example, the class representing disbursements of cash may be labeled *payment* in the financing process and it may be labeled *cash disbursement* in the payroll process.

Another type of name conflict occurs when conceptually different entities are given the same label. For example, say two enterprises merged operations and need to merge their databases. One enterprise labeled its sale order class (mutual commitment event) as Sales. The other enterprise labeled its sale order class as Sale Order. That is a case of a **homonym** – the same word to represent two different things.

Attribute conflict exists if different attributes have been identified as important for describing the same class in various views. The most extreme attribute conflict exists when different attributes are assigned as primary key identifiers for the same classes. Perhaps one designer assigned a unique identifier called Employee ID as the primary key for the Employee class, and another designer used social security number for the same purpose. Other attribute conflicts include overlapping but non-identical sets of attributes assigned to the same class in different cycles. For example, a person who modeled *Inventory Type* in the acquisition/payment process may have included the attributes *item ID, description, unit of measure*, and *standard unit cost* as attributes. A different person who modeled *Inventory Type* in the sales/collection process may have included *item ID, description, unit of measure*, and *list selling price* as attributes. All necessary attributes of a class that are needed for any business processes in which that class occurs should be included in an enterprise-wide database.

To resolve class name conflicts and attribute conflicts, choose a common label for each common class, choose the most appropriate primary key, and perform a set union of the attributes needed for the different cycles. Once the classes that are shared by the views to be integrated are identified, relabeled, and assigned the complete set of attributes, the associations must be examined and relabeled if necessary to resolve any association conflicts. An **association name conflict** is a discrepancy in the labels on associations - either the same association with different names or different associations with the same name. Each association should have a unique name to avoid any possible confusion in communications about relationships in the database. Association name conflicts are resolved in the same way as class and attribute name conflicts. An **association structure conflict** is a discrepancy in the multiplicities on an association. One example is when the same association has different multiplicities in different views. Another example is when an association's multiplicities need to be changed once views are integrated.

Exhibits 7-14 through 7-18 illustrate the process of view integration. Exhibits 7-14 and 7-15 show separate view models for the revenue and acquisition cycles of a company that sells custom-made surfboards. Exhibit 7-16 reorganizes the conceptual models to align shared classes. Exhibit 7-17 illustrates the merging of the models with the set union of attributes for each shared class. This exhibit also illustrates that when a class participates in multiple associations and it isn't convenient to place those associations close to each other, a **copy of the class** may be portrayed with a diagonal slash across the corner and with no attributes included in the class. A reader who sees a class illustrated in such a manner should look elsewhere on the diagram to see the details of that class. Exhibit 7-18 illustrates the re-labeling of the associations so that each association has a unique name. The result is an integrated conceptual model containing the core events, resources, and agents for a revenue and acquisition cycle of a small enterprise.

Exhibit 7-14 Revenue Cycle View Model

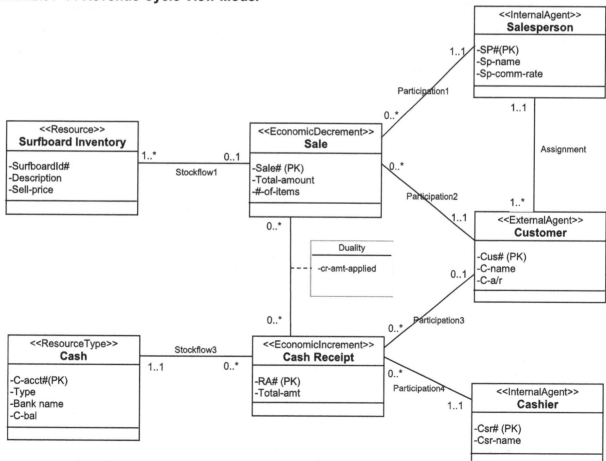

Exhibit 7-15 Acquisition Cycle View Model

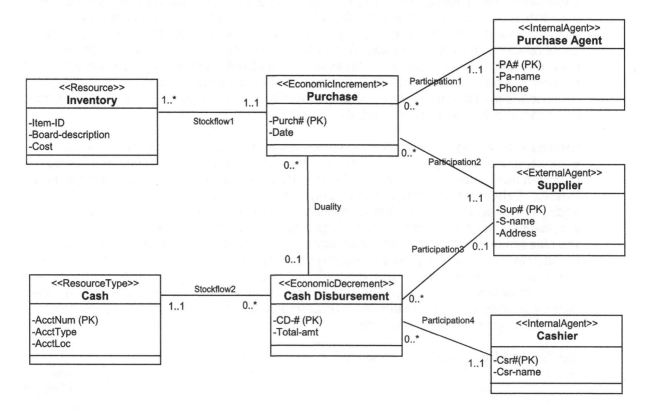

REA Accounting Systems: Resources-Events-Agents: An ontology for designing, controlling, and using integrated enterprise systems

233

Exhibit 7-16 Identify Common Classes

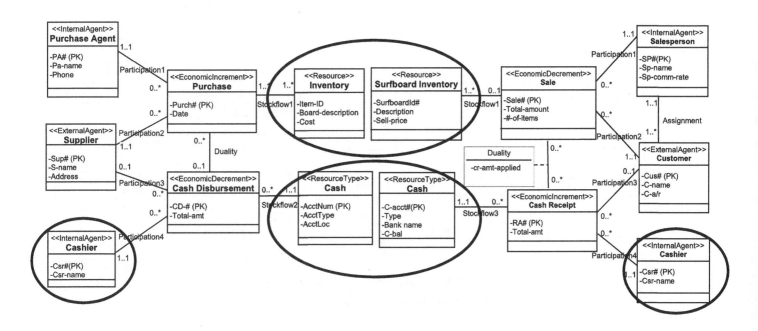

Exhibit 7-17 Merge on Common Classes

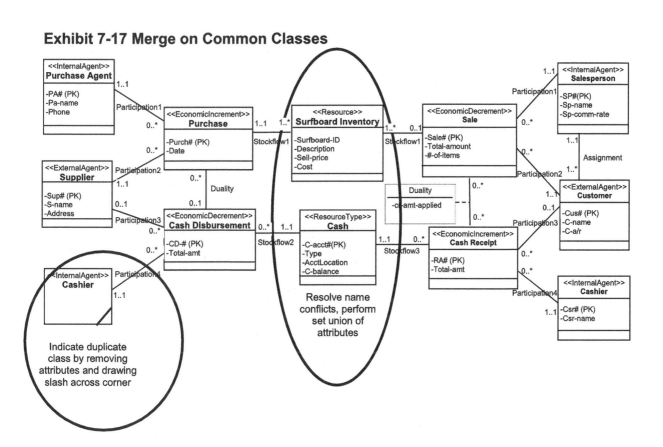

Exhibit 7-18 Resolve Association Name Conflicts

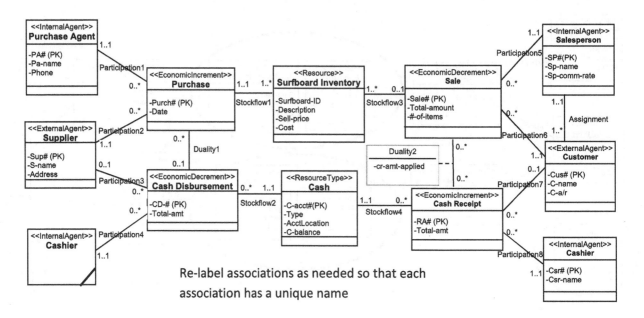

Re-label associations as needed so that each
association has a unique name

CONCLUDING COMMENTS

This chapter reviewed the activities in the acquisition and revenue cycles and demonstrated the extended REA ontology as it applies to those cycles. Whether an enterprise sells hot dogs at a small stand outside a university library or sells custom-made computers via orders placed on its website, whether it sells dental services, insurance, or some combination of products and services, the activities in these cycles fit the REA pattern. The event labels for an enterprise may be different from those used in this textbook; therefore the concepts learned here cannot be routinely applied with rote memorization. The key for discovering the pattern fit for a specific enterprise is to think about the nature of the events and the resources affected by them. Thinking at the value system level first may help – what resources does the enterprise exchange with its customers and suppliers? Thinking at the value chain level next may also help – what resources are provided to the acquisition cycle and what does the acquisition cycle trade those for and in turn make available to other cycles? What resources are provided to the revenue cycle and what does the revenue cycle trade those for and in turn make available to other cycles?

Once you are confident you are thinking effectively about resources and events that are part of the acquisition and revenue cycles and you have identified the economic increment and decrement events that comprise the duality associations in those cycles, then it should be relatively easy to determine the commitment events and instigation events that led to each economic event and to connect resources, internal agents, and external agents to each event as needed. Finally, consider what additional relationships apply, such as custody or assignment or others that are unique to the enterprise you are modeling. As long as the foundation of the system database is consistent with REA, extra constructs may be added without compromising the advantages the pattern provides for automated reasoning and inter-enterprise integration.

KEY TERMS AND CONCEPTS

Association name conflict
Association structure conflict
Attribute conflict
Class name conflict
Commitment event
Copy of class
Economic reversal event
Fulfillment
Homonym
Instigation event

Mutual commitment event
Proposition
Reciprocal
Reservation
Reversal
Synonym
Typification
View integration
View modeling

Review Questions

LO1   R1.   Which association in an enterprise revenue cycle contains information regarding open sale orders?

LO5,6   R2.   Identify typical resources, internal agents, and external agents associated with each of the following events:
     a.   Sales call
     b.   Sale order
     c.   Sale, shipment, or service engagement
     d.   Cash receipt
     e.   Sale return

LO5,6   R3.   Identify typical resources, internal agents, and external agents associated with each of the following events:
     a.   Purchase requisition
     b.   Purchase order
     c.   Purchase
     d.   Cash disbursement
     e.   Purchase return

LO10   R4.   What three basic steps are involved in view integration?

LO9   R5.   What are two types of class name conflicts that must be resolved when identifying common classes in multiple view models?

LO9   R6.   In view integration, what is attribute conflict and how is it resolved?

LO10   R7.   What notation is used in a conceptual model to represent a duplicate copy of a class that is already used elsewhere in the model?

Multiple Choice Questions

LO1, LO2

1.   Each of the following is an instigation event in the revenue cycle, EXCEPT:
     A) Sales call
     B) Advertising campaign
     C) Customer inquiry
     D) Shipment
     E) All of the above are instigation events in the revenue cycle

LO1, LO3

2.   What type of event is a customer order?
     A) Instigation Event
     B) Mutual Commitment Event
     C) Economic Decrement Event
     D) Economic Increment Event
     E) Economic Reversal Event

LO1, LO3, LO4, LO5

3.   In the revenue cycle, which of the following association(s) involve an economic decrement event?
           I. Duality   II. Fulfillment   III. Stockflow   IV. Reversal
     A) I and II only
     B) I, II, and III
     C) II and III only
     D) I, II, III, and IV
     E) II, III, and IV only

REA Accounting Systems: Resources-Events-Agents: An ontology for designing, controlling, and using integrated enterprise systems

237

LO1, LO4
4. What kind of event is a sale return?
    A) Economic increment reversal event
    B) Economic decrement reversal event
    C) Instigation event
    D) Economic increment event
    E) Economic commitment event

LO1, LO5
5. What relationship in the sales/collection process represents the association between a commitment event and the resource the event commits to increase or decrease?
    A) Proposition relationship
    B) Participation relationship
    C) Reservation relationship
    D) Fulfillment relationship
    E) Duality relationship

LO1, LO3
6. Each of the following is an example of a mutual commitment event in the acquisition/payment cycle EXCEPT:
    A) Cash disbursement
    B) Purchase order
    C) Rental agreement
    D) Service agreement
    E) All of the above are mutual commitment events in the acquisition/payment cycle

LO1, LO2
7. Which of the following represents an unfulfilled request by a department supervisor for the purchasing department to acquire a good or service?
    A) Open purchase order file
    B) Closed purchase order file
    C) Open purchase requisition
    D) Closed purchase requisition
    E) Acquisition voucher

LO1, LO5
8. Which relationship in the acquisition cycle represents an association between an instigation event and the resource the event proposes to increase or decrease?
    A) Reservation
    B) Participation
    C) Stockflow
    D) Proposition
    E) Fulfillment

LO1, LO4
9. What type of event is a purchase return in the acquisition/payment process?
    A) Economic increment reversal event
    B) Mutual commitment event
    C) Economic decrement reversal event
    D) Instigation event
    E) Economic increment event

LO8
10. The creation of separate models for different portions of a system is called:
    A) View integration
    B) Logical level implementation
    C) Decomposition
    D) View modeling
    E) Differentiation

LO9
11. What conflict exists if different attributes have been identified as important for describing the same entity in various views?
    A) Attribute conflict
    B) Name conflict
    C) View conflict
    D) Integration conflict
    E) Homonym conflict

LO9
12. The name conflict that results from the use of different names to describe the same entity or process involves the use of:
    A) Homonyms
    B) Synonyms
    C) Antonyms
    D) None of the above

LO11
13. Which of the following is typically an integration point between the revenue and acquisition cycles for a wholesale distributor?
    A) Salesperson
    B) Supplier
    C) Inventory
    D) Sale Order
    E) Purchase

Applied Learning

LO7   A1. Tom owns a small recreational trailer business in a suburban community located close to the mountains. The community is relatively small but growing at a fast rate. Tom's business is growing, not because of his effective sales style and personality, but by growth of the community. Currently, Tom's competition has been nearly nonexistent, but as the area grows he expects to encounter increasing competition.

Tom sells mostly trailers for vacationing and camping. When customers arrive on Tom's lot, they are greeted by a salesperson. The salesperson may show the customers the trailers on the lot, but the salesperson need not be present during the entire showing. Depending on customer preference, the salesperson will either take the customer on a tour or the customer may roam the lot freely, inspecting trailers at their leisure.

Since recreational trailers are fairly large-ticket items, customers will often leave the lot without making a purchase, only to return another day after making the decision to purchase a trailer. When a customer decides to make a purchase, the salesperson initiates a series of procedures to properly document the order and sale transaction. First, the salesperson determines the model of the selected trailer and offers the customer a list of options that correspond to the particular model. The customer may (1) purchase a trailer off the lot with no added features, (2) purchase a trailer off the lot with additional features, or (3) special order a trailer that is not currently on the lot.

In most cases, customers do not pay cash for their trailers. If, however, the customer pays cash, a simple sales contract is prepared and the customer drives off with his or her trailer. The majority of the customers use an installment method of purchase. Before an installment purchase is authorized, the customer's credit must be verified to determine credit worthiness.

With an installment purchase, an installment agreement is prepared in addition to the sales contract. Tom has arranged financing through a local bank for all installment sales. When an installment sale is made, the bank sends Tom a lump-sum payment equal to the price of the trailer. Instead of making payment to Tom, customers pay the bank plus interest. In either case, Tom receives a lump-sum payment for each trailer sold, whether that lump-sum comes from the customer or from the bank.

Once the credit is approved, the customer can take delivery of the trailer. This involves a delivery person who checks the trailer before delivering it to the customer. The customer may pick up the trailer or have it delivered by Tom.

Required

Tom's Trailer Sales has identified the following events of interest: Customer Looks at Trailers; Customer Orders Trailer; Deliver Trailer; and Receive Payment.
a. What business process is described in this narrative?
b. What resource flows (in and out) exist in this business process?
c. For each resource inflow, identify the economic event that uses it up, and for each resource outflow, identify the economic event that produces it.
d. Create an REA business process level model for this business process; make sure to include attributes and multiplicities. Use judgment to determine at least two attributes for each class. List any assumptions you make to determine multiplicities for which the narrative is inconclusive.
e. Convert your conceptual model from part (d) into relational database tables.

LO11 A2. Surfer Dudes Inc Acquisition and View Integration. You should have already completed the Surfer Dudes Inc (SDI) Revenue cycle problem before attempting this problem (see chapter 6, problem A1). The information in this narrative is in addition to that already stated in the revenue cycle narrative. Assume that SDI employs purchasing agents who buy the handcrafted surfboards from local boardmakers who are reluctant to sell to the public because they don't really like people very much. SDI does a great job of identifying which boardmakers will relate the best to which of its purchasing agents and assigns each purchasing agent specifically to the boardmakers accordingly. Purchasing agents may be entered into the system before being assigned to any boardmakers and may be assigned to more than one. Each boardmaker is immediately assigned to exactly one purchasing agent as he/she is entered into the system or the first time. Purchasing agents visit boardmakers to see their available boards. When making a purchase, the agent selects the boards to buy on behalf of SDI, immediately pays the boardmaker with a check for the entire purchase, and takes the boards back to SDI. SDI has identified the following attributes of interest for its acquisitions of surfboards:

Surfboard number	Boardmaker address
Buyer ID	Cash disbursement ID
Date of purchase	Cash account ID
Length of board	Cash balance for an account
Unit cost of board	Total purchase dollar amount
Buyer name	Purchase ID
Buyer phone number	Total cash disbursement dollar
Boardmaker name	amount
Boardmaker phone number	Boardmaker ID

Required

Create an REA class diagram for SDI's acquisition of surfboards cycle. Be sure to include all relevant classes, associations, attributes, and multiplicities. Don't add any attributes or represent anything that can't be identified. Integrate the two views into one class diagram.

LO11   A3. Quandrax Computers is a store that buys computer components for low prices, assembles the components into computers, and then sells the computers at high prices. Each computer is assigned a unique identification number, and computers that have common configurations are categorized into types (e.g., Longitude is a laptop that is easily networked and is recommended for businesses, Element is a desktop that is intended for home and small businesses). Categories can be entered into the database before any computers in the categories are actually assembled. The computer components are purchased from wholesalers. One of Quandrax's purchasing agents submits an order to the wholesaler that has listed a given component for sale. If the order is accepted, one of Quandrax's inventory clerks receives the items. Multiple orders accepted by the same supplier may be consolidated into one purchase. Orders are accepted in their entirety or not at all. Nearly all of Quandrax's orders are accepted. Sometimes the incorrect components are delivered to Quandrax and Quandrax has to return them to the appropriate supplier. Sometimes Quandrax returns components to suppliers for other reasons, such as the result of a change in planned production of a certain category of computers. Only about 10 percent of Quandrax's purchased components are returned to suppliers, and any return would result from only one purchase.

When payment is due for a purchase, one of Quandrax's cashiers issues one check for payment in full for the items on that purchase. Sometimes if multiple purchases have been made from the same supplier within a short time, Quandrax pays for those purchases with just one check. One of Quandrax's managers is required to not only authorize all purchase orders greater than $5,000 but also to sign all checks (including checks written for expenditures other than purchases of computer components). Quandrax needs to keep track of the managers' participation in these events as well as the participation of other employees in these events. In physically implementing the conceptual model into the database tables, Quandrax wants to combine all employee types into just one table. This means Quandrax would keep the separate employee entities on the E-R diagram, but make just one employee table to represent all of the employee entities, then post keys or make relationship tables as necessary to implement all relationships of employees to the relevant events.

All sales are handled via mail or e-mail, as Quandrax does not have any showrooms. Quandrax assigns salespeople to its large corporate customers and the salespeople take sample computers to the customer locations to demonstrate features as part of their sales calls. Only a small percentage of Quandrax's sales calls result in orders, and sometimes a salesperson might need to make several sales calls to the same customer to obtain one order from that customer. Orders also result from customers surfing the Internet and seeing descriptions of the computers on Quandrax's website. These customers are not assigned to specific salespeople; Quandrax only tracks the salesperson that actually took the order. Some of Quandrax's salespeople are hired to handle just such orders and as such are not assigned specifically to any customers.

If a customer orders multiple computers on one sale order and some of the computers are immediately available whereas the others are not yet assembled, Quandrax ships the available computers right away and then ships the remainder of the order when the rest of the computers are assembled. Sometimes Quandrax combines computers from multiple sale orders into a single shipment. For example, once a customer ordered 10 computers and the next day decided that wouldn't be enough so he ordered 4 more. Quandrax shipped all 14 computers in one shipment. Quandrax only accepts checks for its sales of computers; customers can pay for multiple sales with a single check, but no partial payments are accepted. Each sale transaction is tracked by a shipment ID; an invoice is sent to the customer that is due within 10 days, with no discounts allowed. Quandrax does not allow any sale returns; that is, all sales are final. Cash receipts are never split between two cash accounts; rather each receipt is assigned to one of Quandrax's cash accounts by one of Quandrax's cashiers. Quandrax also receives cash from other activities, such as loans, so the database must allow for that.   Suppliers, employees, and customers need to be entered into the database before any transactions involving them occur.

The following attributes are of interest to Quandrax. Do not add attributes to the list. Use the boldface abbreviations in parentheses next to the attributes in the list. List any assumptions you make, along with the reasons behind your assumptions (i.e., state what you think is vague in the problem, say what you are going to assume to clear up the ambiguity and make a case for that assumption).

- Purchase Order Number (**PO#**)
- Supplier ID (**SuppID**)
- Employee ID (**EmpID**)
- Purchase Order Date (**PODate**)
- Purchase Date (**PurchDate**)
- Location of cash account (**Ca-Loc**)
- Cash Account Number (**CashAcct#**)
- Name of supplier (**SupName**)
- Receiving Report Number (**RR#**)
- Computer Category ID code (**Cat-ID**)
- Component ID code (**CompoID**)
- Cash Disbursement Date (**CD-Date**)
- Name of employee (**EmpName**)
- Purchase return ID (**PR-ID**)

- Cash Disbursement Number (**CD#**)
- Sale Order ID (**SO-ID**)
- Shipment ID (**Ship-ID**)
- Date of sales call (**SC-Date**)
- Customer check number (**CR-Chk#**)
- Sales Call ID (**SC-ID**)
- Cash Receipt ID (**CR-ID**)
- Customer ID (**Cust-ID**)
- Date of cash receipt (**CR-Date**)
- Name of Customer (**Cust-Name**)
- Total sale dollar amount (**Sale-Amt**)
- Type of employee (**EmpType**)
- Date of sale order (**SO-Date**)
- Date of purchase return (**PR-Date**)
- Dollar amount of cash receipt (**CR-Amt**)
- Current balance of cash account (**AcctBal**)
- Shipping address for a customer (**Cust-Ship**)
- Date of sale/shipment of computers (**Ship-Date**)
- Description of a computer category (**Cat-Desc**)
- Computer component description (**Comp-desc**)
- Total dollar amount of a cash disbursement (**CD-Amt**)
- Standard cost for a computer component (**Std-Cost**)
- Quantity of a computer component returned (**Qty-Ret**)
- Type of supplier (i.e., wholesaler or individual) (**SupType**)
- Identification number for a finished computer (**CompuID**)
- Quantity of a computer component ordered on purchase order (**Qty-Ord**)
- Proposed selling price for a type of computer on a sales call (**Prop-SP**)
- Ordered cost for a computer component on a purchase order (**PO-Unit-Cost**)
- Suggested selling price for computers [hint: by category] (**List-price**)
- Date assembly was completed for a finished computer (**Assemb-Date**)
- Quoted selling price for each item on a sale order (**Ord-SP**)
- Actual selling price for a particular finished computer (**Act-SP**)
- Quantity of a computer component received on a purchase (**Qty-Rec**)
- Actual cost of a computer component on a particular purchase (**Item-Unit-Cost**)

Required

Create a UML Class diagram using the REA ontology for Quandrax Computers. You may want to first create the revenue cycle model, then create the acquisition cycle model, and then integrate the two to form a single UML class diagram. Note that because the narrative and attribute list are for the two cycles combined, you should not encounter class and attribute conflicts.

CHAPTER 8

Database Design Implementation with Microsoft Access

LEARNING OBJECTIVES

The primary objective of this chapter is to describe a procedure for converting a logical relational database model on paper into a physical Microsoft Access database implementation. This chapter also introduces querying and illustrates means by which information can be retrieved from relational databases to meet demands for enterprise decisions. After studying this chapter, you should be able to

1. Convert a logical relational model into a Microsoft Access physical implementation
2. Enter transaction data into a relational database in Microsoft Access
3. Interpret a physical database implementation in Microsoft Access to determine what the underlying conceptual model must have been
4. Recognize and implement application level controls to facilitate the integrity of data entered into a relational database

INTRODUCTION

As discussed in Chapter 6, conceptual models are created to represent the reality of enterprise classes and associations. Conceptual models are independent of any logical model or software package; they are converted into logical models once the type of database to be used has been determined. Logical models are independent of any specific software package, but may only be implemented using a software package based on the logical model choice. Logical models may be relational, object-oriented, hierarchical, network, and so forth. Logical models are converted into physical database implementations using the chosen software.

Because most enterprises use relational database software of some kind, and because most universities make relational database software available to students, we have chosen in this book to focus only on the relational database logical model. For the physical database model we illustrate the concepts discussed in this chapter using Microsoft Access 2010 because of its wide availability both in academia and in practice and because of its ease of use. Please understand that the constructs discussed may also be applied to other relational database packages.

PHYSICAL IMPLEMENTATION OF RELATIONAL MODEL IN MICROSOFT ACCESS

Once the relational tables are established on paper, forming a logical model, the model may be implemented into physical form using a particular database software package. Microsoft Access is used in this chapter to demonstrate the conversion of a logical model to a physical model. Keep in mind that the procedures will be similar but not exactly the same with other relational database software packages.

This chapter will not provide you with comprehensive assistance on every aspect of Access. Instead it will provide you with an introduction to creating tables in Access and communicating information to Access about the links between the tables (i.e., telling Access which primary keys are posted into other tables as foreign keys or as parts of concatenated primary keys). If you need additional Access instructions, you may use the electronic help facility provided in Access or use an Access reference manual.

To get to the appropriate area of the help facility, once Access is open, click on the white question mark inside the blue circle near the top right corner of your Access window. If you are connected to the Internet, the help function will default to Office.com and the Access Help window will appear as illustrated in Exhibit 8-1. The help available offline is not nearly as extensive as that available when you are connected.

Exhibit 8-1 Microsoft Access Help Window if Connected to Office.com

You may then choose to review the Getting Started with Access 2010 section or go directly to the section of interest under Browse Access 2010 support. As indicated on Exhibit 8-1, the area within help that you are most likely to need for this chapter is the Tables section.

Creating and Working With Databases

In order to enter tables in Microsoft Access, you must first create a database file in which to store the tables. For those of you who have used other Microsoft software products, notice that this is different from some of those products. In Microsoft Word or Excel, you may begin creating content in a blank document or spreadsheet and then save it to a file later. Microsoft Access requires you to create a file (and name it) before entering any tables or data. Additions and changes are then automatically saved as Microsoft Access accepts them.

When you start Microsoft Access, a window appears in which you specify whether you want to open an existing database or (a) create a blank database, (b) create a blank web database, or (c) use a template to create a blank database. See Exhibit 8-2. To open an existing database, click on the Open folder near the top of the left hand menu bar. To create a blank database, click on the icon indicated by (a). To create a blank web database, click on the icon indicated by (b). To create a blank database with a template, find the appropriate template under one of the choices indicated by (c).

Exhibit 8-2: Create a Database using Blank Access Database

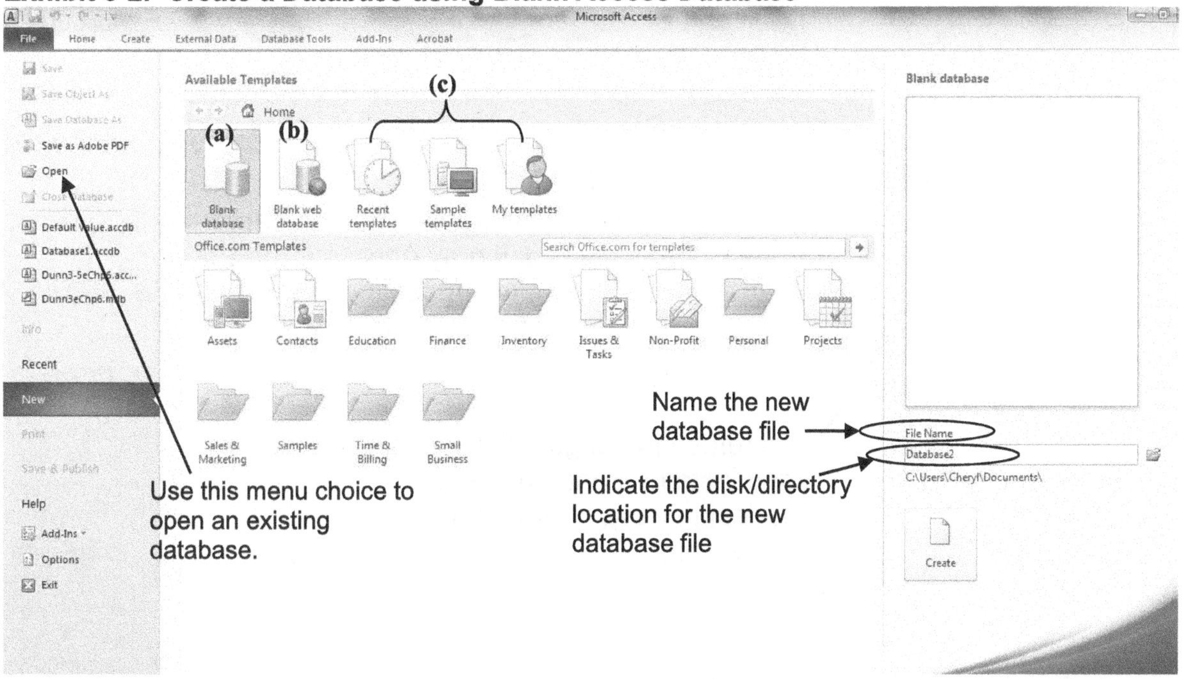

When you are using Microsoft Access in conjunction with materials in this textbook, do NOT use any wizards or templates. These wizards and templates use defaults that you must understand and know when and how to override when appropriate. We do not cover that knowledge in this book, so we caution you not to use wizards or templates at all, or to use them at your own risk.

Once you tell Access to create a blank database, you are required to name the database file before you can enter any tables or data into it. Specify the disk drive and folder in which you want your database to be stored directly below the database file name. See the right side of Exhibit 8-2. Be sure to note the disk drive and folder you specified so that you will know where to find the database file the next time you want to use it.

When you create or open an existing database, Microsoft Access by default displays its database window with the Table Tools section open and a Table1 open in datasheet view. The **database window** is a container for all objects stored in the database, including tables, queries, forms, and reports. For this chapter we will focus only on tables.

As shown in Exhibit 8-3, when you start a new database, Access automatically opens a new table for you; this table is opened in datasheet view. **Datasheet view** assumes you want to create a table simply by entering data. This is not the option we recommend using. Instead, change the view to design view by clicking on the View icon near the top left corner of the Table Tools window and then click on Design view. **Design view** gives you control over all choices that need to be made during table creation, such as specifying data types and field properties for each attribute in the table. A **data type** or **field property** determines what kind of data values may be entered into a database table's column. Examples include text, numbers, currency, date/time, and so forth.

Exhibit 8-3 Microsoft Access Database Window – Table Tools

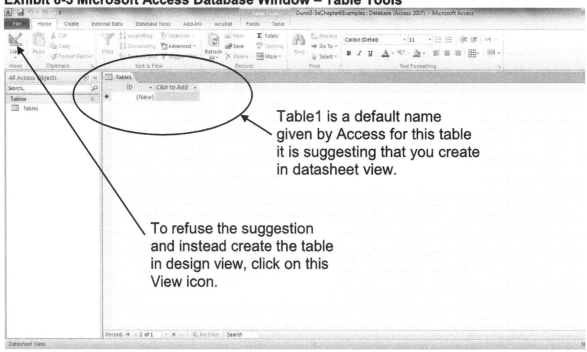

Table1 is a default name given by Access for this table it is suggesting that you create in datasheet view.

To refuse the suggestion and instead create the table in design view, click on this View icon.

In response to clicking on the View icon, Access prompts you with a popup window to save the table and offers you a chance to give it a different name. See Exhibit 8-4. For example purposes, we will change the table's name to Sale.

Exhibit 8-4 Popup Window to Save and Rename Table When Switching to Design View

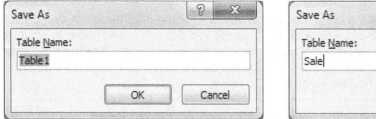
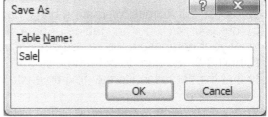

Once the table is saved as Sale in design view, the resulting window appears as illustrated in Exhibit 8-5.

Exhibit 8-5: Microsoft Access Table Design View

Section 1 of Exhibit 8-5 shows the overall layout of the table. The fields (attributes) of the table are listed on the left; in the middle column you can choose the appropriate data type for each field (e.g. text, currency, date, number, etc. The right-hand column provides space for the table designer to write a description of what that field represents. The description may be left blank, and we suspect in most databases, most of the descriptions are left blank because, unfortunately, people generally don't take the time or see the need for documenting their system design. A quick note about the default attribute that Access displays: ID with AutoNumber as its Data Type. Access knows that every table should have a primary key attribute and that if a naturally occurring primary key does not exist then the database designer should create and assign numbers to each record in the table. By suggesting the use of this field, Access reminds database designers to either use it or replace that field with a naturally occurring primary key (changing the data type to whatever is appropriate).

In Section 2 (the field properties panel) you may set additional properties for each field, such as the field size, customized format, default value (the value to be used if the user doesn't enter a value), validation rules, or a specification as to whether the field is required to contain data (or whether it's okay for it to have blank values). The panel in section 2 changes based on which field the cursor is pointed to in Section 1. That is because the field properties for one field can be different from the properties for a different field.

We next work through two examples to give you some experience creating physical implementations of relational logical models in Access 2010. You may want to work through these examples on a computer as you read the rest of this chapter. (If you have not been working along up to this point, you will want to catch yourself up by creating a new blank database, then creating a new table labeled Sale so that your screen resembles Exhibit 8-5).

The first logical model we will implement is that illustrated in Exhibit 8-6 and consists of two tables: Sale and Salesperson.

Exhibit 8-6: Sale – Salesperson Logical Model

Sale

SaleID	Date	Amount	Salesperson
061401A	6/14	$4,218	*123456*
061401B	6/14	$6,437	*654321*
061501A	6/15	$1,112	*654321*
061501B	6/15	$3,300	
061501C	6/15	$1,776	

Salesperson

SalespersonID	Name	Telephone
123456	Fred	555-0063
654321	Francis	555-0007

Example 1: Creating and Connecting Class Tables
To finish creating the Sale table, enter the four fields (SaleID, Date, Amount, and Salesperson) in the leftmost column and change each data type to its appropriate value. You may have noticed that Access set a default data type as "Text". Move to the middle column of Section 1 of Exhibit 8-5. Click on the arrowhead next to "Text" and a popup list of data type choices will appear. A good rule of thumb to use when determining appropriate data types is given in the next sentence.

> If the data type is not a date, and you do not need to be able to perform calculations with it, then set the data type as text; if you do need to perform calculations with it, then set the data type as number, unless it is a dollar value in which case you should set it as currency.

That rule is simplistic, but it works well for most situations. For our example, we will specify SaleID as Text, Date as Date, Amount as Currency, and Salesperson as Text. Notice the field properties panel change as you click from one field to the next in the top section, but don't change anything in the field properties section yet. You may wonder why we used "Text" for Salesperson, when all the data values we have are numeric. Go back to the rule of thumb. Are we likely to need to calculate anything based on the salesperson ID? No. And it is possible that someday we may start adding letters into our salesperson IDs, so we are better off specifying the type as text.

Now let's think about the field properties section, but without going into detail on most of these settings. One thing you need to be aware of with respect to field properties (and data type, which is also a field property) is that if the properties of two fields are different, then Access considers the values in those fields to be different even if the content is the same. Why is that important? Think about posted foreign keys. In our example, the identification number for salesperson is a field in both of our tables. In the Salesperson table (which we haven't yet made) it is the primary key. In the Sale table (which we are currently creating) it is a foreign key. Now, recall from earlier in this chapter the referential integrity principle that relational databases are supposed to meet. That principle said for a data value entered in the Salesperson field in the Sale table to be acceptable, it must either be blank or it must match exactly a data value in the SalespersonID field in the Salesperson table. Because the data type becomes part of the value of the data, we must be very careful with changing field properties, especially for fields that are primary and foreign keys.

For learning the basics in this textbook, our recommendation is that the only field properties you change for any fields are the data type and the "Required?" field property that specifies whether data entry in the field is mandatory. The data entry requirement property for a field determines whether null values are allowed or not. Therefore you must know something about the enterprise's business rules to make this decision.

This is especially important for foreign keys, as in many cases the multiplicities are manifestations of business rules and the degrees of multiplicities are reflected in foreign key postings. For the Exhibit 8-6 example, we did not start with a conceptual model so we don't immediately know multiplicity information. But we can figure out the multiplicities from the table data. We know that Sale's participation in the association with Salesperson is 0..1 That is, a sale may not involve a salesperson and each sale may relate to a maximum of one salesperson.

How do we know this? Null values are included in the Salesperson column of the Sale table, so that indicates a sale can exist without a related salesperson (minimum = 0). And because Salesperson is posted into Sale as a foreign key, it cannot have more than one value (maximum = 1).

Do we know Salesperson's multiplicities with respect to Sale? From the data in these tables we note that we currently have no salespeople in our database who do not yet have a related sale. But common sense would tell us that we need to enter new salespeople in our database when they are hired, at which point we would not have expected them to have already made a sale. So we will assume the minimum is 0. We know for sure that the maximum is *, because we have a salesperson (Francis) who has made multiple sales. In our example, then, neither class has mandatory participation in the association, so we need not change the requirement property to yes for any of the fields. [To test your understanding - What if we determined that a sale cannot exist without a salesperson and we therefore change the minimum multiplicity beside Salesperson to 1? Then in the Sale table we would need to set the *Required data entry* property of the Salesperson field to Yes.] The **Required data entry field property** in Microsoft Access is a choice specified in table design view that will result in a user not being allowed to enter a record into the table without including a value for that field. A user may leave any field except the primary key field(s) blank for which this property is not set to yes. Microsoft Access automatically enforces entity integrity (a principle that says primary keys must never have null values) so there is no need to set the required data entry field property to "yes" for primary key fields).

Getting back to our example from Exhibit 8-6 (with no mandatory participation), we have no need to change any field properties other than the data types, which we already changed. At this point, your table design should look like Exhibit 8-7 below.

Exhibit 8-7: Example Sale table design

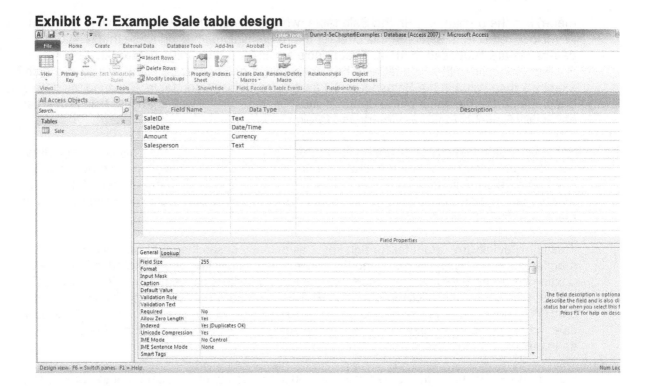

Look on your screen at the grey box immediately to the left of SaleID. If it has a small key symbol in it as is shown in Exhibit 8-7, that resulted from replacing the autonumbered id field suggested by Access with the text SaleID field. If instead of replacing that initial field you had deleted it and then added SaleID as a new field, you may not have a key icon next to the SaleID. If that is the case, you need to add it to communicate to Access that field is the primary key of the Sale table. To give this information to Access, click on the small gray box to the immediate left of the field and then click on the Primary key icon near the top left corner of the TableTools window. Once you do this, your window should look like Exhibit 8-7. For the moment, we are finished with the Sale table's design, so we need to save the table. You may either choose File, Save from the top menu bar, or click on the icon with the diskette symbol on it. Name the table Sale and then close the table. You will notice that your database window now contains a table object called Sale.

Next create the Salesperson table, following similar steps. From the database window, double-click on "create table in design view". Enter the three fields: SalespersonID, SalespersonName, and SalespersonTelephoneNumber. None of these are dates, and none are fields that would likely be part of a calculation, so don't change the data type or any field properties. Set SalespersonID as the primary key. Save the table, giving it the name Salesperson, and close the table. Your database window should now resemble Exhibit 8-8 below.

REA Accounting Systems: Resources-Events-Agents: An ontology for designing, controlling, and using integrated enterprise systems

251

Exhibit 8-8: Database Window after Designing Sale and Salesperson Tables

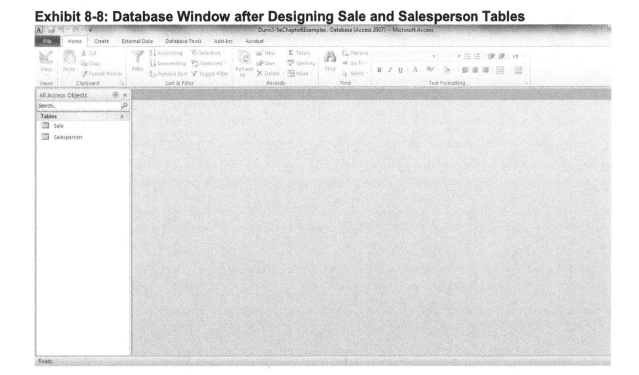

Did you notice that we left one very important piece of information out in what we communicated to Access in designing these tables?

No, we are not talking about the entry of data values into the tables, although that certainly also needs to be done. We are talking about the need to specify to Access how the tables are linked together. At this point, Access understands that we have a table representing a class called Sale and Access understands that we have a table representing a class called Salesperson, but Access doesn't have a clue that there is an association between sale and salesperson.

Recall that we established that association in our logical model by posting salesperson as a foreign key into the Sale table. To Access, salesperson looks like just another attribute, because we have done nothing to differentiate it from any other attribute in the Sale table. We could, of course, type "foreign key from Salesperson table" in the description area for that field (and for system documentation purposes that is a very good thing to do). However, Access doesn't understand natural language and Access doesn't do any processing based on information in description cells. The way to communicate foreign keys (and concatenated primary keys that are formed from posting two different class' primary keys into an association table) to Access is by establishing a relationship between the two tables. To do this, go to the **relationship layout**, which is a window in which relationships between tables are visually depicted. To go to the relationship layout, click on the menu choice for Database Tools and then click on the icon labeled Relationships (see circled items on Exhibit 8-9).

Exhibit 8-9: Database Tools, Relationships

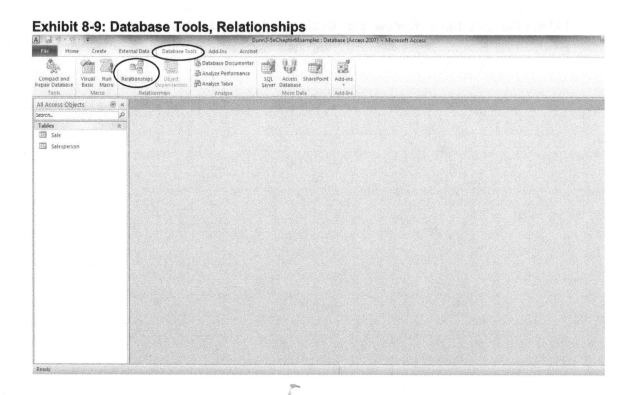

The screen that initially appears when you open the relationship layout is the **show table window** – that is a screen from which the user may choose which tables to include in the relationship layout or in a query design. See Exhibit 8-10. This screen automatically appears if there are no tables already in the relationship layout; if you want to add more or different tables later you must go to the relationship tools menu and click on the icon labeled Show Table.

Exhibit 8-10: "Show Table" Window

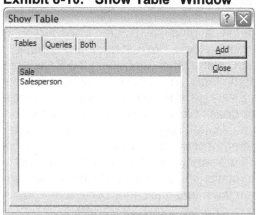

Highlight both tables and add them to the layout by clicking Add after they are both highlighted. Then close the "show table" window (but leave the relationship layout window open). Your relationship layout should look like Exhibit 8-11 (without the arrows and labels).

Exhibit 8-11: Relationship Layout with tables added

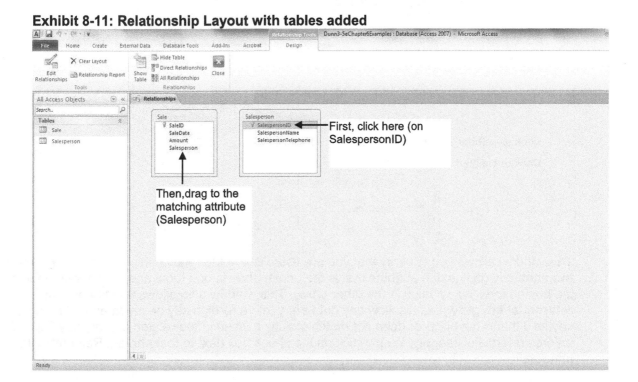

Note that you may move a table around on the layout by clicking on its titlebar and dragging it to the desired location. You may also resize the table windows within the layout if you want to (sometimes you will need to in order to see all the fields).

Next you need to explain to Access that you posted a foreign key. To do this, start with your cursor on SalespersonID in the Salesperson table. Click and drag the cursor to Salesperson in the Sale table. Make sure you drag the primary key to the posted foreign key because those are the fields that you expect to have matching data values.

When you "drop" the primary key onto the matching foreign key to which you dragged it, Access will display an "Edit Relationships" window, as shown in Exhibit 8-12.

Exhibit 8-12: Edit Relationships Window

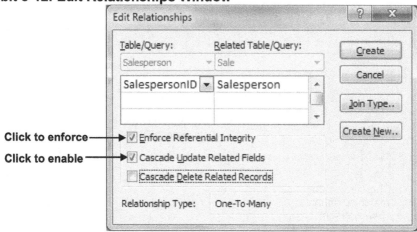

This window allows you to verify that you are establishing the relationship between the correct two attributes (that is, the attribute that is the primary key in one table and the attribute that is the posted foreign key value in the other table). This window also allows you to **enforce referential integrity** (i.e., disallow any data entry into a foreign key or concatenated primary key field that is not blank or does not match exactly a value in the related primary key field. To enforce referential integrity, simply click on the check box next to that phrase. Remember that principle?

Microsoft Access does not require that this principle be enforced. That tells you that Access allows you to create databases that are not fully relational. This can cause serious problems with querying if users are not well-trained and very careful. For purposes of this textbook, always enforce referential integrity unless it is impossible because of choices made in the conceptual model. You also have the option of setting updates in the primary key field to "cascade" to also update the related field, and of setting deletions of the record that is represented by the primary key to "cascade" to also delete records in which it was a participant. The first option is usually a good option, because if you change the value of a primary key such as SalespersonID then you want the corresponding posted foreign key values to also be changed, such as the Salesperson values in the Sale table. The second option is somewhat risky, because you don't want to unintentionally lose data that you may later need.

One important note regarding cascade updates: Many people get the false impression that enabling this option causes data entry of new primary key values to automatically become entered into the related foreign key fields. That cannot happen, because Access does not have any way of knowing which specific records in the table in which the foreign key is posted are related to the record in the table from which the foreign key is posted until the data itself is actually entered. In our sales-salesperson example, when we enter records into the Sale table, Access can't possibly know which salesperson made the sale unless we tell it which one made the sale by entering the value of the foreign key. Notice that simply adding a salesperson to the salesperson table does NOT inform Access as to which sales the salesperson has made and will make in the future. However, once you have created a link between the fields themselves by establishing the association, enabling cascade updates, and by entering common data into the primary and foreign key fields, if you were to decide to re-number salesperson 123456 to be 1234560, when you change that primary key data value in the Salesperson table, the change will flow through and change all the foreign key values in the Sale table that are 123456 to 1234560.

After enforcing referential integrity and enabling cascade updates, click on "Create" to establish the relationship. The relationship layout will appear, and will now display the relationship you just created, as shown in Exhibit 8-13.

Exhibit 8-13 Relationship Layout

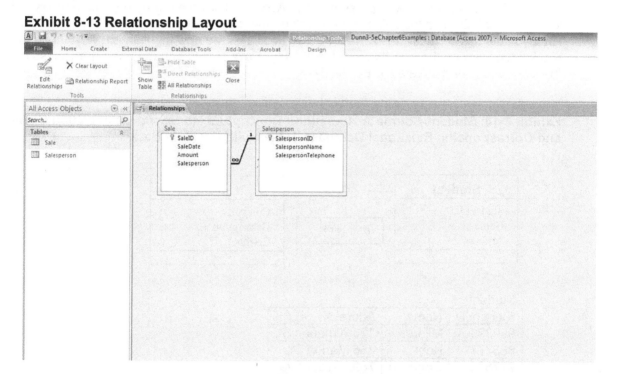

Although the relationship layout resembles a UML class diagram, it is not! Remember, the only purpose for the relationship layout is to communicate to Access information about posted key relationships – including the posting of foreign keys and the posting of concatenated primary keys.

The 1 and ∞ symbols on the Relationship Layout resemble multiplicities, however, they are not exactly the same concept. The 1 and ∞ reveal how many times the same data value can be stored in that field of the table to which the symbol is connected. For example, the 1 next to Salesperson says that the same data value for SalespersonID can exist in the Salesperson table only one time. That is, there can be no duplicate values, which makes sense because SalespersonID is the primary key and must be unique. The ∞ next to Salesperson in the Sale table indicates that the same data value for that attribute may exist multiple times in the Sale table. That also makes sense given that there is no restriction on foreign key fields to be unique. Salesperson 654321 can only exist in the Salesperson table (in which it is the primary key) once, but can exist in the Sale table (in which it is a foreign key) as many times as that salesperson makes sales.

Example 2: Creating and Connecting Association Class Tables to Class Tables
The second example demonstrates the physical implementation of the tables from Exhibit 8-14. To begin, create a new blank database following the steps in Exhibits 8-2. Following the same

basic procedure that was illustrated in Exhibits 8-3 through 8-5, add two new tables in design view. One should be named Student, and should include the following fields: StudentID (text, primary key), Name (text), Address (text). The other should be named Course, and should include the following fields: CourseID (text, primary key), Description (text), and Credits (number). Next, create another new table in design view and include the following fields: Student ID (text), CourseID (text) and Grade earned (text). For this third table a primary key needs to be specified, but in this example it is a concatenated primary key made up of both StudentID and CourseID. To represent this in Access, click on the grey box immediately to the left of Student ID. Hold the shift key and click on the grey box immediately to the left of Course ID. If you did this correctly, the rows for those two fields are now highlighted. With those rows highlighted, click on the icon that looks like a key. Keys should appear in the grey boxes next to the field names as illustrated in Exhibit 8-15.

Exhibit 8-14: Student-Course Association: Conceptual Model with Association Class and Corresponding Relational Database Tables with Example Data

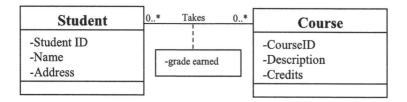

Student

StudentID	Name	Address
999888	Mildred	123 Almanac St.
888777	Kent	456 Market Dr.
777666	Candace	789 Harriet Ave.

Course

CourseID	Description	Credits
ACG611	Advanced AIS	3
FIN642	Financial Markets	3
MIS650	IT Management	3

Takes

StudentID	CourseID	Grade earned
999888	ACG611	B
999888	MIS650	A-
888777	MIS650	B+

Name the table "StudentTakesCourse". Next add the Student, Course, and StudentTakesCourse tables to the relationship layout following the same basic procedure used in Exhibit 8-9 and 8-10. Recall that the relationship layout is used to inform Access as to the existence of primary keys that are posted into other tables either as foreign keys or as parts of concatenated primary keys. Therefore you need to "tell" Access you posted the primary keys from Student and Course into the StudentTakesCourse table to form its concatenated primary key. To do this you simply click on StudentID in the Student table and drag the cursor to StudentID in the StudentTakesCourse table, similar to what was done in Exhibit 8-11. When you release the mouse, the "Edit Relationships" window will appear, as it did in Exhibit 8-12. Check the appropriate boxes to enforce referential integrity and enable cascade updates, similar to what you did for Exhibit 8-13. Click on OK. A join line should appear connecting StudentID in the Student table to StudentID in the StudentTakesCourse table. Next click on CourseID in the Course table and drag the cursor to CourseID in the StudentTakesCourse table and check the boxes in the "Edit Relationships" window to enforce referential integrity and enable cascade updates. Your relationship layout should resemble Exhibit 8-16.

Exhibit 8-15: Specifying a concatenated primary key in Microsoft Access

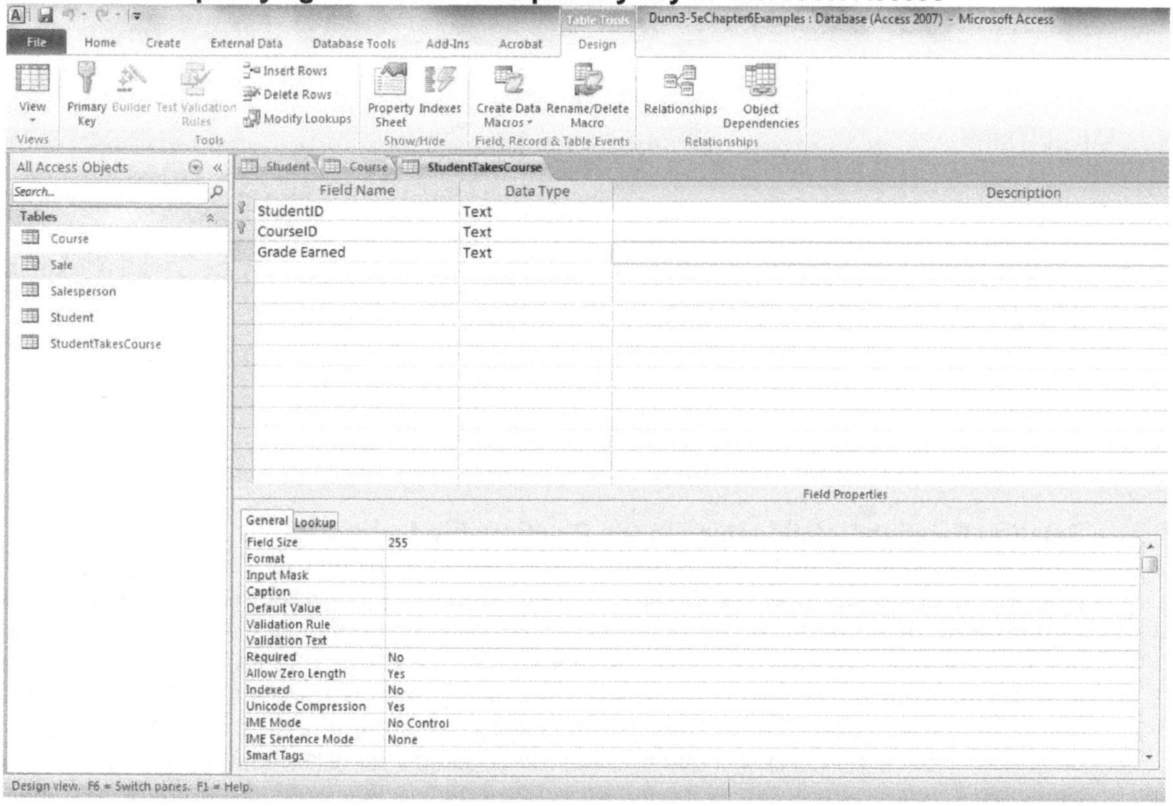

Notice that any given value for StudentID can exist in the Student table only once because it is the sole primary key of that table and must be unique; however, that same value for StudentID can exist multiple times in the StudentTakesCourse table because it is only a part of the concatenated primary key and it is the combination of StudentID and CourseID that must be unique. Likewise any given value for CourseID can exist only once in the Course table in which it is the sole primary key, but can exist multiple times in the StudentTakesCourse table as long as each time it appears in that table it is paired with a different StudentID. In our example from Exhibit 8-14, Mildred's student ID of 999888 can appear in the Student table only once, because there can't be another student with that same ID. However, Mildred's student ID 999888 can appear multiple times in the StudentTakesCourse table as long as it is paired with different values of CourseID, such as ACG611 and MIS650. The course number MIS650 can appear only once in the Course table because there can't be another course with the same

ID. However, Course MIS650 may be taken by multiple students and therefore can appear in the StudentTakesCourse table multiple times as long as it is paired with different values of Student ID such as 999888 and 888777.

Exhibit 8-16: Association Class Table Linked to Two Class Tables

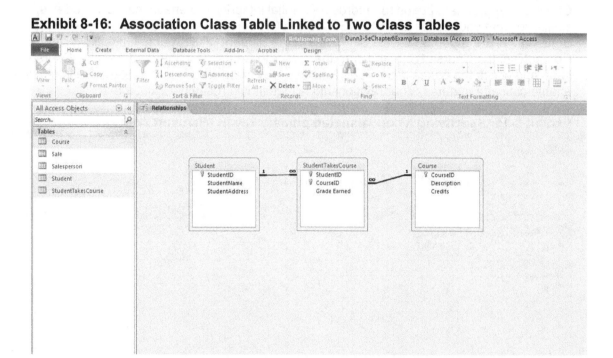

Deleting Existing Relationships in the Relationship Layout

What if you make a mistake and create a relationship you didn't really want? Open the relationship layout. Single-click the line for the relationship you want to delete (**make sure it's highlighted**), and then press the Delete key. Notice that you must delete the relationship itself, not just one table that was part of the relationship. If you delete a table from the relationship layout (by selecting the table and pressing the Delete key) the relationship will appear to be gone. However, if you click on "Design" on the top menu bar and then click "Show All" as circled on Exhibit 8-17, you will see that the relationship was retained in Access's memory. Similarly, if you are frustrated with your layout and decide you want to start over, you may notice the "Clear Layout" icon that is also circled on Exhibit 8-17. Beware! The layout will be cleared, but all the relationships are still in Access's memory so you have not deleted them. As soon as you click on "Relationships, Show All" they will be back. If you want to delete relationships from your layout you MUST highlight each relationship line and press the Delete key. Access will ask you if you really want to permanently delete the relationship, to which you would reply yes. If Access didn't ask you that question, then you didn't delete the relationship!

REA Accounting Systems: Resources-Events-Agents: An ontology for designing, controlling, and using integrated enterprise systems

259

Exhibit 8-17: Relationship Layout Design Tools

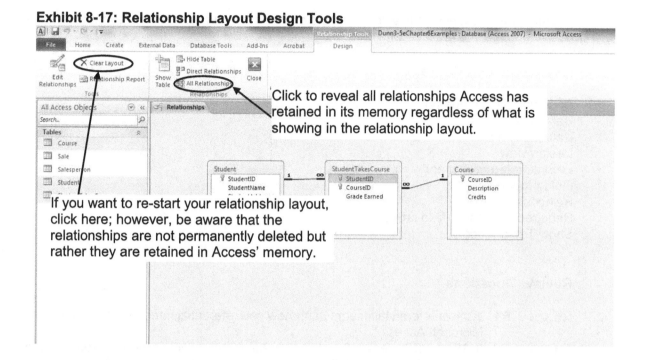

Entering Data into Microsoft Access Tables

Once all of your tables are created and you have verified that the relationship layout correctly communicates the posted key information, you are ready to begin entering data into the tables. Two views exist for entering data into a table: datasheet view and form view. We will only discuss datasheet view in this chapter; that is the standard row-column format that most people are used to, and which is available in most relational database packages.

Enter the appropriate data records, using the TAB key to move between fields. You can also use the mouse to move the cursor to a desired field or record. As you tab out of one record to another record, the software automatically saves the record, displaying an error message if it was unable to save the record because of a data entry problem (such as violations of referential integrity). Often, you may see a pencil icon in the left hand, gray column. The pencil indicates the current record (the one being "pointed to" in memory). After you finish adding records, choose File, Close from the main menu. Experiment with the arrow keys at the bottom of the table window. They allow you to view different fields and records. Don't worry about entering data in alpha or numeric order. The computer will sort the data via the primary key attribute field.

Keep in mind that if you have enforced referential integrity (as you should have) and established mandatory data entry for appropriate fields (e.g., foreign keys posted from a 1..1 class table), you must be careful about the order in which you enter the data. Consider the multiplicities in your underlying conceptual model and picture the company's reality in your mind. Think about the order in which data would be entered in real life. Generally information about resources and agents is input to corporate databases before any transactions involving them occur. Most of the time, you should enter your resource and agent data before you enter your event data and association data. If you encounter error messages while you are entering data, pay attention to them and try to figure out whether you are entering the data incorrectly or whether you in fact have a flaw in your table design or in your relationship layout that needs to be fixed before you proceed with data entry.

Key Terms and Concepts

Data type (field property)
Database window
Datasheet view
Design view
Enforce referential integrity
Field property
Relationship layout
Required data entry (field property
Show Table window

Review Questions

LO1, LO4   R1. What is referential integrity and how can referential integrity be enforced in Microsoft Access?

LO1, LO4   R2. In Microsoft Access, what does it mean to set a field property to require data entry? Is that the same thing as enforcing referential integrity? If not, what is the purpose for setting a field property to require data entry?

LO2   R3. In a Microsoft Access database, suppose you have a sale table, a customer table, an inventory table, and a stockflow-sale-inventory table. Customer ID is posted into the sale table as a foreign key. Referential integrity is enforced on all relationships between tables. Describe the data entry into these tables. When will data be entered into each table? Will data be entered into every table when a sale is made? Or is some of it entered at other times? Will the order in which data is entered into the tables matter? Explain.

LO1   R4. How do you establish a concatenated primary key in Microsoft Access?

LO3   R5. When you create a relationship layout in Microsoft Access that includes relationships between tables for which referential integrity is enforced, Access marks the relationships with notations of 1 and ∞. What do those notations indicate?

Applied Learning

LO2   A1.   Examine the data in the partial database tables illustrated below. Determine what connections must exist between tables.

Required

a.   Draw the most likely underlying conceptual model in UML class diagram format.

b.   Enter each of the tables into a database in Microsoft Access; create the relationship layout and enforce referential integrity where it seems appropriate.

Sale Event Table

SaleNbr	Date	Terms	Salesperson ID	Customer ID
1	11/5	2 10, net 30	2	2543
2	11/5	2 10, net 30	4	635
3	11/5	COD	6	1845

Sale-Inventory Table

SaleNbr	Inventory Item #	Quantity Sold	Price each
1	876	10	1.25
1	674	8	0.875
1	451	30	0.995
2	887	54	1.475
2	513	188	0.525
3	736	36	24.995
3	001	58	7.875
3	302	16	8.00
3	224	114	8.75

Salesperson Table

Salesperson ID	Last Name	First Name
2	Cleaves	Mateen
4	Warrick	Peter
6	Peterson	Morris
8	Janakowski	Sebastian

Cashier Table

Cashier ID	Last Name	First Name
1	Weinke	Chris
2	Outzen	Marcus

Cash Receipt Event Table

Cash Rec Nbr	Date	Check Nbr	Cashier ID	Sale Nbr	Cust ID	Cash Account	Amount Received
1001	11/6	11097	12	2	635	110146758	$ 178.35

Customer Table

Customer ID	Last Name	First Name	Address	City	State	Zip
101	Conrad	Chris	5629 Longfellow Dr.	Paragould	AK	65323
183	Anderson	Paul	674 Sunderland Lane	Sioux City	IA	63126
635	Padgham	Donna	1264 Algonquin Road	Mason	MI	48854
1845	Oliver	Andrew	8512 Bonita Dr.	Clearwater	FL	33051
2543	Cook	Carol	536 Secondary Ave.	Fremont	CA	75518

Cash Table

Cash #	Type of account	Bank Name
110146758	Regular checking	North First
1203948102	Payroll checking account	Credit Grantors

Inventory Table

Inventory Item #	Description
001	XL T-shirt
224	XL Sweatshirt
302	XXL T-shirt
451	Felt pennant
513	Ping pong ball
674	Golf ball
736	XL Polo shirt
876	Bumper sticker
887	Foam football

LO1, LO2   **A2.** Laker Sport Shop has the following conceptual model and additional information.

Laker Sports Shop Conceptual Model

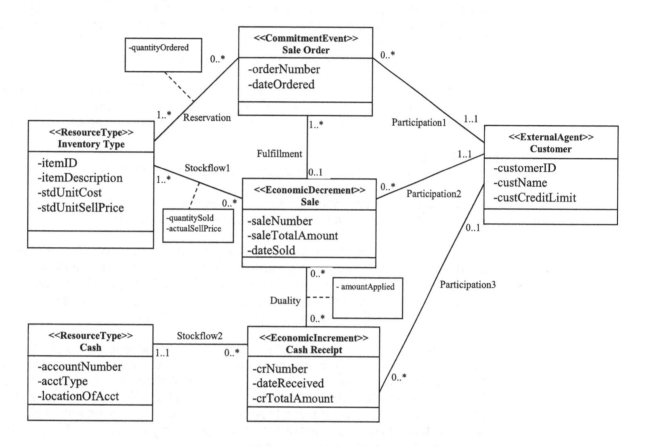

Other information you may need to know:

LSS is able to fill more than 80% of the orders placed by customers.

While LSS occasionally receives cash from loans or from purchase returns, more than 90% of its cash receipts come from customers as a result of sales.

The main purpose of this exercise is to provide hands-on experience with the physical level of the database design process. You will also need to draw upon your knowledge of the conceptual and logical levels of this process. This exercise requires you to convert a conceptual level model into a logical level relational model, create the resulting tables on paper, then implement them in Microsoft Access and enter some representative data into the database. Successful completion of this exercise will provide you with an enhanced understanding of Microsoft Access as well as the entire database design process. You should also solidify your understanding of multiplicities.

As you have learned, the first steps in designing a relational database are actually performed prior to even turning on the computer. These steps include requirements analysis and conceptual modeling of the business processes, and then converting the conceptual model into a set of minimal relational database table structures. A benefit of conceptual modeling we discussed is that it is independent of any particular database system (such as Microsoft Access). At the logical level, a choice has been made as to the type of database system (relational for this text) but it is still independent of specific software (i.e., Oracle, Paradox, or some other relational database software could be used instead of Access). The physical level involves specific database software (in this case Microsoft Access) that is used to create a new database, add tables to the database, specify relationships between those tables, and enter transaction data into those tables.

The material covered in chapters 6-8, and the help facility in Microsoft Access should provide sufficient guidance for you to perform the following six required tasks to complete this exercise. You are strongly advised to finish one task before going on to the next.

Required Tasks
Please do NOT add any additional classes, associations, or attributes to the model.

1. Convert the conceptual model for Laker Sports Shop into a logical level relational database model (i.e., derive a set of relational tables on paper).

2. Create a new database file in Microsoft Access that has your last name followed by 8a2 as the name of the database (e.g., adler8a2 for a project submitted by Amy Adler) Access will add an .accdb file extension that indicates the file is a Microsoft database file. It is always a good idea to make backups of your work to avoid losing more than necessary in case of a hardware or operating system failure.

3. Add each table from your relational solution for task 1 above to the database, defining the data types for each field and identifying the primary key(s) for each table. For foreign keys, enter "foreign key from _____table" (filling in the name of the table from which it was posted) into the field's description field. This is not required by Access and in fact communicates nothing to Access; however, it is a good habit for documentation purposes to provide communication to yourself in the future or for other members of your database design team.

   For each foreign key field, if the related minimum multiplicity requires mandatory participation, set the field's required property to "yes". For example, say you have a Purchase Agent 1..1 – 0..* Purchase relationship implemented with PAgentID posted into the Purchase table. PAgentID is a foreign key in the Purchase table, and the participation of Purchase in its relationship with Purchase Agent is mandatory. That is, we cannot enter data about a purchase without specifying which purchase agent was responsible for that purchase. In that case, PAgentID must be set for required data entry = "yes" in the Purchase table.

4. Create and save the relationship layout for the database, including ALL tables and relationships in the database (this should be done after you have entered all of the tables from task 3 above). Set referential integrity on all relationships.

5. Make up data to enter into the database tables. Each table must have at least 3 records and you must enter data that is internally consistent and that conforms to the minimum and maximum cardinalities. For <u>internal consistency</u>, you need to make sure the data makes sense when viewed as a whole. For example, if you indicate that cash disbursement #478 was applied to purchase #1764, and purchase #1764 was made

from vendor #2, then cash disbursement #478 should also be indicated as paid to vendor #2. For the <u>minimum multiplicities</u>, if there is optional participation (for example, a purchase agent can be entered into the database before any transactions occur) you need to have data reflect this (e.g., a row for a purchase agent in the "Purchase Agent" table that is not included in any of the rows in the Purchase table – in other words, create a purchase agent that hasn't yet made a purchase). If participation is mandatory (such as: a purchase has to have a vendor) you need to have data reflect this (every purchase record has a vendor associated with it). If you followed the instructions in task 3 above and specified such fields as required, Access will force you to enter a data value for those mandatory cases that involved foreign keys. However, for mandatory participation in relationships that are implemented with separate tables, you will need to enter the data appropriately and will get no warning from Access. For the <u>maximum multiplicities</u>, your data should illustrate either "at most one" or "at most many" participation. For example, say there is a relationship between purchase and inventory such that one purchase receipt can include multiple inventory stock numbers and one inventory stock number may be included on multiple purchase receipts. Your data should reflect at least one purchase that includes multiple inventory items, and at least one inventory item number that is purchased more than once. Note that in some cases conforming to the maximum cardinalities may require you to enter more than 3 records in a table. Do not enter more than 6 records in any one table.

CHAPTER 9

Introduction to Querying

LEARNING OBJECTIVES

Sound database design is a necessary but not sufficient requirement for valid **information retrieval**, that is, repossession or capture of data that was previously entered into a database or other data storage structure. Querying logic and skills are also necessary for valid information retrieval. If a database is not designed correctly, information retrieved from it may be meaningless; however, an enterprise database may be perfectly designed and still produce meaningless information if it is retrieved incorrectly. By considering the relational algebra operators introduced in this chapter, and by working through the examples in this chapter with SQL and with QBE in Microsoft Access, you should develop querying logic and skills. After studying this chapter you should be able to

1. Identify and understand the purpose of the three primary relational algebra operators
2. Identify and understand the primary components of a Structured Query Language (SQL) query statement
3. Identify the relational algebra operations achieved by a given SQL statement
4. Create a SQL statement to retrieve requested information from a relational database
5. Examine a SQL statement and the tables to which it will be applied and identify the query result
6. Find errors in a SQL statement
7. Create a Microsoft Access Query By Example (QBE) query to retrieve information from relational tables
8. Examine a Microsoft Access QBE query and the tables to which it applies and identify the query result
9. Find errors in a Microsoft Access QBE query

QUERYING RELATIONAL DATABASES

Two philosophies for providing information to decision makers are prevalent in practice. One approach has information systems professionals pre-determine what information users need from the database. Then the IS professionals create queries and build interfaces that allow the users to run the queries without knowing any specifics of how they are constructed. The other approach does not pre-suppose what information a user may need but instead allows users to query the database in an ad hoc fashion. A **query** is a request for information submitted to a database engine. **Ad hoc querying** is direct retrieval of information by end-users from a database whereby the retrieval was not planned (i.e. no pre-formulated queries or interfaces were developed in anticipation of needing the information). The ad hoc querying approach requires users to be trained in whatever querying language is used for the database software in which the enterprise database is implemented. Of course, these approaches may be combined by some enterprises such that an interface is created to allow retrieval of some pre-determined types of information and ad hoc querying is allowed for other information needs.

The need for learning how to retrieve information from relational databases for those who desire to become information systems professionals is obvious. However, the need is equally great for anyone who may perform ad hoc querying of a database to support their decision-making, or for anyone who may evaluate the integrity of information retrieved from an enterprise database. In short, all business professionals should be versed in the techniques of relational database querying. This chapter includes a three-pronged approach to database querying. First some elements of relational algebra are discussed to lay the foundation of the underlying logical procedures in querying. **Relational algebra** is the original data manipulation language that was constructed as part of the relational database model and therefore is based on set theory and predicate logic. The second prong discussed is **Structured Query Language (SQL)**, which is a querying language shared by many relational database software packages. The third prong discussed is **Query By Example (QBE)**, which is a type of query interface intended to be more "point and click" in nature and to require less user expertise. This chapter illustrates the QBE version used in Microsoft Access. Different relational database software packages have slightly different QBE interfaces; however, familiarity with the Microsoft Access QBE interface should help you to also understand QBE interfaces in other relational database software.

Enterprises need information in many different formats to support different types of decisions. Much of the information is derived from the same underlying data, but that data must be aggregated in different ways. For example, the marketing manager for the southeast region of an enterprise may need to know last month's sales dollar value for the southeast region. That same marketing manager may also need to know what last month's sales quantity was for a particular product or product line in the southeast region. The accountant for the enterprise needs to know last month's total sales for the entire enterprise to report on the income statement. These three pieces of information are based on the same underlying data – that is, the disaggregated sales data which includes sale dates, locations, products sold, cash receipts received in exchange, and internal and external participating agents.

Because the data is stored in a format that is different from that format in which it needs to be retrieved, it takes a certain skill set to be able to effectively query a database. Several ingredients are necessary for good information retrieval. First, the database itself must have been well-designed. If the tables are not fully relational, if the tables are incompletely specified, or if the conceptual model has not been correctly converted into relational format, querying will be difficult or even impossible. Second, the query designer must have a thorough knowledge of the database table structures and of the nature of the data in the tables. To understand the database table structures, the query designer must have some basic knowledge of database design. Third, the query designer must completely understand the desired output – that is, what information is actually needed to support the decision of interest? Fourth, the query designer must have good logic and reasoning skills. Finally, the query designer must know the querying language used to retrieve information from the enterprise's database. Several querying language choices exist, but not all of them are available for every database package. We will discuss three of the prevalent choices.

Relational Algebra
When the relational database model was initially created, Codd[12] specified relational algebra as a language for retrieving data from the tables. Because the tables were created in conformance with set theory and predicate logic, it makes sense that the means for retrieving data from the tables is also based on set theory and predicate logic.

---

[1] Codd, E.F. "Derivability, Redundancy, and Consistency of Relations Stored in Large Data Banks." *IBM Research Report* RJ599, August 19, 1969.

[2] Codd, E.F. "A Relational Model of Data for Large Shared Data Banks." CACM 13, No. 6, June 1970. Republished in *Milestones of Research: Selected Papers 1958-1982.* CACM 25th Anniversary Issue, CACM 26, No. 1, January 1983.

There are many relational algebra operators used to allow complete manipulation of relational database tables; however, most basic queries are covered by three of these operators: PROJECT, SELECT, and JOIN. In applying these operators, we will discuss horizontal and vertical subsets of tables. Rows form the horizontal part of a relational table; columns form the vertical part of a table. Therefore a **horizontal subset** is a part of the table that includes only some of the table's rows (but includes all the columns). A **vertical subset** is a part of the table that includes only some of the table's columns (but includes all the rows). **PROJECT** (pronounced prō-JĔCT') is an operator that retrieves a vertical subset of a table. The **SELECT** operator retrieves a horizontal subset of a table. The **JOIN** operator is the most powerful of the relational algebra operators, allowing us to combine separate but related tables by linking them on their common attributes.

We will use the following tables to give examples of each of the relational algebra operators.

Employee

EmpID	SocialSec#	LastName	FirstName	Street Address	Pay rate	Telephone	DeptID
E1	123345678	Adams	Anita	144 Apple St.	$10	555-1234	D4
E2	234456789	Boston	Benjamin	255 Banana Rd.	$12	555-2345	D2
E3	345567890	Crabb	Charlie	366 Cherry Ave.	$14	555-3456	D2
E4	456678901	Davis	Deborah	477 Dip Dr.	$32	555-4567	D1
E5	567789101	Engler	Edward	588 Eggplant St.	$11	555-5678	D4
E6	678891012	Folkert	Fawn	699 Fruity Ave.	$23	555-6789	D3

Department

DeptID	Name
D1	Exec Mgmt
D2	Accounting
D3	InfoSystems
D4	Operations

Training Courses

CourseID	Description	Length
AC1	Accounting Fundamentals	2 days
AC2	Chart of Accounts	5 days
IS1	Basic Information Systems	5 days
IS2	Database Design	5 days
MD100	ERP Systems	10 days

Employee Takes Course

EmpID	CourseID	DateTaken
E3	AC1	May 1-2
E3	AC2	June 24-28
E6	IS1	June 24-28
E6	IS2	July 8-12
E4	AC1	Oct 14-15

PROJECT Example

Imagine the enterprise wants to create an emergency phone tree – a list of employee names and their telephone numbers. The first step is to determine which table or tables contain the attributes that need to be accessed by the user. Only one table is needed – the Employee table. However, the enterprise does not want to simply print out the employee table because they do not want sensitive information such as social security numbers and pay rates to be included on the phone tree; they only want the names and phone numbers to appear. Therefore they need a vertical subset of the Employee table. A relational algebra query that makes use of a PROJECT will provide the requested information:

PROJECT Employee Over (LastName, FirstName, Telephone) Giving Answer

REA Accounting Systems: Resources-Events-Agents: An ontology for designing, controlling, and using integrated enterprise systems

269

This command tells the database software package to list a vertical subset of the Employee table, with that subset consisting of the three columns that contain the last name, first name, and telephone, and to present that subset in a new "table" called "answer".

The result of this relational algebra operation is:

Answer

LastName	FirstName	Telephone
Adams	Anita	555-1234
Boston	Benjamin	555-2345
Crabb	Charlie	555-3456
Davis	Deborah	555-4567
Engler	Edward	555-5678
Folkert	Fawn	555-6789

SELECT Example

Imagine this has been a difficult economic year for the enterprise, especially in terms of cash flow, and as a result the enterprise has decided to give cost-of-living raises to only those employees whose current pay rate is less than $15 per hour. Since only the payroll department personnel are going to see the information, there is no need to leave out any attributes from the query result. Therefore they need a horizontal subset of the Employee table, filtering out those employees who make $15 or more per hour. A relational algebra query that makes use of a SELECT will provide the requested information:

SELECT Employee Where PayRate <15 Giving Answer

This command tells the database software package to list a horizontal subset of the Employee table, with that subset consisting of the employees for which the PayRate data value is less than 15, and to present that subset in a new "table" called "answer".

The result of this relational algebra operation is:

Answer

EmplD	SocialSec#	LastName	FirstName	Street Address	Pay rate	Telephone	DeptID
E1	123345678	Adams	Anita	144 Apple St.	$10	555-1234	D4
E2	234456789	Boston	Benjamin	255 Banana Rd.	$12	555-2345	D2
E3	345567890	Crabb	Charlie	366 Cherry Ave.	$14	555-3456	D2
E5	567789101	Engler	Edward	588 Eggplant St.	$11	555-5678	D4

JOIN Examples

A JOIN combines two (or more) tables on the basis of a common attribute. Recall from chapter 6 that relationships between entities are represented in relational database tables by posting attributes from some tables into other tables (e.g. by posting a foreign key into another table, or by creating a concatenated primary key by posting keys from two different tables to form a new table). Joins are used to establish these links between tables for querying purposes when information from two (or more) related tables is needed to answer a question or create a report.

Two types of joins are of interest for most enterprise queries. One is called an **inner join** or an **equi-join**. This type of join combines the tables together, keeping only those rows for which the data values of the common attribute match exactly. Note that the JOIN operator in relational algebra will retain all attributes of both tables. Performing a PROJECT operation on the answer will then eliminate unwanted columns.

Imagine the enterprise wants to prepare a list of employees and the names of the departments to which they are assigned. Most of the information needed for this query is available in the Employee table; however, to obtain the names of the departments, the Department table isalso needed. Begin with a JOIN relational algebra command as follows:

JOIN Employee Department Where Employee.DeptID=Department.DeptID Giving Answer

The result of this command is:

Answer

EmpID	SocialSec#	LastName	FirstName	Street Address	Pay rate	Telephone	DeptID	DeptID	Name
E1	123345678	Adams	Anita	144 Apple St.	$10	555-1234	D4	D4	Operations
E2	234456789	Boston	Benjamin	255 Banana Rd.	$12	555-2345	D2	D2	Accounting
E3	345567890	Crabb	Charlie	366 Cherry Ave.	$14	555-3456	D2	D2	Accounting
E4	456678901	Davis	Deborah	477 Dip Dr.	$32	555-4567	D1	D1	Exec Mgmt
E5	567789101	Engler	Edward	588 Eggplant St.	$11	555-5678	D4	D4	Operations
E6	678891012	Folkert	Fawn	699 Fruity Ave.	$23	555-6789	D3	D3	InfoSystems

To filter out all columns other than the employee names and department names (if those were the only attributes needed) a PROJECT command can be issued as follows:
PROJECT Answer Over (LastName, FirstName, Name) Giving Answer2

The result of this command is:

Answer2

LastName	FirstName	Name
Adams	Anita	Operations
Boston	Benjamin	Accounting
Crabb	Charlie	Accounting
Davis	Deborah	Exec Mgmt
Engler	Edward	Operations
Folkert	Fawn	InfoSystems

For this example, an inner join yielded complete information because all employees are assigned to departments, and all departments have at least one employee assigned to them.

Sometimes an inner join will leave out some information that is important for a given decision. Using the example tables given, imagine the enterprise wants a list of the employee names and the ids and descriptions of each training course each employee has completed. The data needed to satisfy this information need is located in the Employee and Training Courses tables. However, the table that establishes the relationship between these entities is also needed in completing the query because that is where the common attributes between Employee and Training Course are located. In other words, there are no common attributes in the Employee and Training Course tables. However, the Employee and Employee Takes Course tables contain a common attribute (EmplID), and the Training Course and Employee Takes Course tables contain a common attribute (CourseID). Thus we need to perform two join operations as follows:

JOIN Employee Employee_Takes_Course Where Employee.EmplID=Employee_Takes_Course.EmplID Giving Answer

JOIN Answer Training_Course Where Answer.CourseID=Training_Course.CourseID Giving Answer2

The result of the first JOIN is too wide to fit on the page, so it is shown in two sections. These sections would connect with PayRate as the next column after Street Address.

Answer

EmplD	SocialSec#	LastName	FirstName	Street Address
E3	345567890	Crabb	Charlie	366 Cherry Ave.
E3	345567890	Crabb	Charlie	366 Cherry Ave.
E4	456678901	Davis	Deborah	477 Dip Dr.
E6	678891012	Folkert	Fawn	699 Fruity Ave.
E6	678891012	Folkert	Fawn	699 Fruity Ave.

PayRate	Telephone	DeptID	EmplID	CourseID	DateTaken
$14	555-3456	D2	E3	AC1	May 1-2
$14	555-3456	D2	E3	AC2	June 24-28
$32	555-4567	D1	E4	AC1	Oct 14-15
$23	555-6789	D3	E6	IS1	June 24-28
$23	555-6789	D3	E6	IS2	July 8-12

The result of the second JOIN is likewise too wide to fit on this page, so it is also divided into two sections. These sections would connect with DeptID as the next column after Telephone.

Answer2

EmplD	SocialSec#	LastName	FirstName	Street Address	Pay rate	Telephone
E3	345567890	Crabb	Charlie	366 Cherry Ave.	$14	555-3456
E3	345567890	Crabb	Charlie	366 Cherry Ave.	$14	555-3456
E4	456678901	Davis	Deborah	477 Dip Dr.	$32	555-4567
E6	678891012	Folkert	Fawn	699 Fruity Ave.	$23	555-6789
E6	678891012	Folkert	Fawn	699 Fruity Ave.	$23	555-6789

DeptID	EmplID	CourseID	DateTaken	CourseID	Description	Length
D2	E3	AC1	May 1-2	AC1	Accounting Fundamentals	2 days
D2	E3	AC2	June 24-28	AC2	Chart of Accounts	5 days
D1	E4	AC1	Oct 14-15	AC1	Accounting Fundamentals	2 days
D3	E6	IS1	June 24-28	IS1	Basic Information Systems	5 days
D3	E6	IS2	July 8-12	IS2	Database Design	5 days

Next we need to perform a PROJECT operation to eliminate the duplicate columns and to filter out any columns that are not needed based on the information request, as follows:

PROJECT Answer2 Over (LastName, FirstName, CourseID, Description) Giving Answer3

The result of this command is:

Answer3

LastName	FirstName	CourseID	Description
Crabb	Charlie	AC1	Accounting Fundamentals
Crabb	Charlie	AC2	Chart of Accounts
Davis	Deborah	AC1	Accounting Fundamentals
Folkert	Fawn	IS1	Basic Information Systems
Folkert	Fawn	IS2	Database Design

Examine closely the Answer3 result to determine whether it meets our information need: a list of employee names and the course id and description of courses they have taken. If we only want a list of employees that have taken firm-offered training courses, then our need is met. However, what if we want all our employees included on this list, with blanks left next to those who have not yet taken a firm-offered training course? Then our need was not met, because three of our employees (Anita Adams, Benjamin Boston, and Edward Engler) do not appear in Answer3. Let's backtrack to figure out when and why they were deleted. Notice that they did not appear in Answer2 either. Indeed, they were eliminated when the first JOIN of Employee and Employee Takes Course was performed, because their employee ids did not appear in the Employee Takes Course table and the JOIN was an inner join. To include all the employees in our answer, we must perform a different type of join. An **outer join** is a combination of tables based on a common attribute that keeps unmatched records from both tables and pairs them with null values. A full outer join keeps unmatched records from both sides, and the final answer (with the projection done) would look as follows:

Answer3 (result of full outer join and projection)

LastName	FirstName	CourseID	Description
Adams	Anita		
Boston	Benjamin		
Crabb	Charlie	AC1	Accounting Fundamentals
Crabb	Charlie	AC2	Chart of Accounts
Davis	Deborah	AC1	Accounting Fundamentals
Engler	Edward		
Folkert	Fawn	IS1	Basic Information Systems
Folkert	Fawn	IS2	Database Design
		MD100	ERP Systems

A right outer join, also called a **right join**, is a combination of tables based on a common attribute that keeps unmatched records from the second table listed in the join and eliminates unmatched records from the first table in the join. The answer for our example with a right outer join is:

Answer3 (result of right outer join and projection)

LastName	FirstName	CourseID	Description
Crabb	Charlie	AC1	Accounting Fundamentals
Crabb	Charlie	AC2	Chart of Accounts
Davis	Deborah	AC1	Accounting Fundamentals
Folkert	Fawn	IS1	Basic Information Systems
Folkert	Fawn	IS2	Database Design
		MD100	ERP Systems

A left outer join, also called a **left join**, is a combination of tables based on a common attribute that keeps unmatched records from the first table listed in the join and eliminates unmatched records from the second table in the join. The answer for our example with a left outer join is:

Answer3 (result of left outer join and projection)

LastName	FirstName	CourseID	Description
Adams	Anita		
Boston	Benjamin		
Crabb	Charlie	AC1	Accounting Fundamentals
Crabb	Charlie	AC2	Chart of Accounts
Davis	Deborah	AC1	Accounting Fundamentals
Engler	Edward		
Folkert	Fawn	IS1	Basic Information Systems
Folkert	Fawn	IS2	Database Design

Which of these answers best satisfies the information need we were trying to meet? The left outer join provides a list of all employees (whether or not they have taken a training course) and for those who have taken training courses, it lists the training courses taken. Therefore for this information need, the left outer join provided the best solution. For other information needs, an inner join, or a right outer join, or a full outer join may provide the best data. The best answer depends on the question being asked!

Structured Query Language
Although relational algebra was developed as part of the relational model, it is not the most commonly used data manipulation language today. **Data manipulation** is the specification of operations to be performed on one or more data fields to obtain additional information, and is a major component of querying. One weakness of relational algebra is that each operator must be accomplished in a separate query. That is, a projection and a selection are not accomplished in the same query; two queries need to be executed to accomplish the two operations. Structured Query Language (SQL) was developed to enable the performance of multiple operations in a single query. It was also believed that use of a standard format for every query would simplify the task of query development, which had proven to be very difficult for many users. For relational algebra, users must learn different syntax for each of the various relational algebra operators (including the three we have discussed as well as several others). In SQL, every information retrieval query follows a structured, pre-defined **Select-From-Where** syntax as follows:

SELECT <u>attribute name(s)</u>
FROM <u>table name(s)</u>
WHERE <u>condition criteria is met</u>;

Note that the semi-colon at the end of the SQL statement is very important if the system you are using allows more than one SQL statement to be executed in the same call to a database server, because it communicates to the database software that the end of the query statement has been reached. If that is left off, the query will not be executed. Most current relational database software packages automatically put the semi-colon at the end of the statement to help avoid the syntax error that may occur when it is missing. For some queries not every component in this syntax is necessary, and for other queries additional components must be included, but in general every SQL statement must conform to this format. Although most companies and most database software packages do not make direct use of relational algebra syntax, it is helpful when you are deriving queries to consider the three major relational algebra operators and determine how you will accomplish those in either SQL or QBE. First we examine how the selection, projection, and join operators are achieved in SQL.

The first component of each SQL statement (that is, the SELECT component) specifies which attribute(s) are to be included in the answer to the query. Recall that attributes are the columns of the table(s). Thus this component of the SQL statement accomplishes the projection relational algebra operator. The second component of each SQL statement (that is, the FROM component) specifies the tables that contain the data to include in the answer. If there is just one table, this component of the SQL statement simply identifies which table it is. If multiple tables are needed to meet the information request, this component helps to achieve the relational algebra JOIN operation (but does not achieve the join without the next component). The third component of the SQL statement can serve two purposes. In combination with the FROM component, it helps to achieve the relational algebra JOIN by specifying the fields for which the two joined tables should have equal values. Alternatively (or additionally) the WHERE component specifies criteria to be met by records in order to be included in the answer. Thus the WHERE component of an SQL statement accomplishes the relational algebra selection operator. Table 9-1 summarizes the SQL statement components that correspond to each of the relational algebra operators.

Table 9-1 Comparison of Relational Algebra Operators and SQL Statement Components

Relational Algebra Operator	SQL Statement Component(s)
PROJECT	SELECT attribute name(s)
SELECT	WHERE criteria is met
JOIN	FROM table names WHERE posted key field data values match

Next we use SQL to demonstrate the same queries that we formulated earlier.

PROJECT Example
The first query generated a list of employees' names and phone numbers to be used for an emergency phone tree. The query required a projection operator only. In SQL the query is stated as follows:

```
SELECT LastName, FirstName, Telephone
FROM Employee;
```

REA Accounting Systems: Resources-Events-Agents: An ontology for designing, controlling, and using integrated enterprise systems

275

Notice that when we are not trying to accomplish a relational algebra JOIN nor a relational algebra SELECT operator, there are no criteria to be met and thus there is no WHERE component to the statement.

SELECT Example

The second query we formulated with relational algebra was the list of employees (including all attributes) whose pay rate is less than $15 per hour. This query required the relational algebra selection operator but no projection or join operators. The SQL statement for this query is as follows:

```
SELECT *
FROM Employee
WHERE PayRate <15.00;
```

Note that the * (asterisk) is a wildcard symbol and simply tells the database software package to include all attributes in the query result.

Combining SELECT and PROJECT in SQL

Notice that it is very easy to combine a relational algebra selection operator with a projection operator in a single SQL statement. Say you wanted to retrieve the names and telephone numbers of the employees whose pay rate is less than 15 so you could call those employees to tell them they are getting a cost-of-living raise. The following SQL statement accomplishes everything the previous two statements did.

```
SELECT LastName, FirstName, Telephone
FROM Employee
WHERE PayRate <15.00;
```

JOIN Examples

Next let's examine how to accomplish the information request for a list of all employees and the name of the department to which they are assigned. We begin with a SQL statement that accomplishes only the JOIN operation (that is equivalent to the first relational algebra JOIN statement).

The SQL statement is as follows:

```
SELECT *
FROM Employee, Department
WHERE Employee.DeptID=Department.DeptID;
```

In our relational algebra example of this query, we had to execute a second query to accomplish the PROJECT operation. Our SQL statement may be revised slightly to accomplish both the JOIN and the PROJECT in just one query as follows:

```
SELECT LastName, FirstName, Name
FROM Employee, Department
WHERE Employee.DeptID=Department.DeptID;
```

Keep in mind that the latter query replaces the former query. Whereas in relational algebra we must use two separate queries to accomplish the two separate operations, in SQL we combined them into just one query.

To specify that a JOIN needs to be an outer join (to retrieve all records from a table for which no match is available in the joined table), the syntax needs to be varied slightly. The outer join must be specified as a Left Join or a Right Join in the From clause of your SQL statement. Whether you use a left or right outer join depends on the order in which you list the tables in your SQL statement. Pretend for our employees and departments example we want the list to include the DeptName in our answer, and we want the names of all departments even if they do not have any employees assigned to them. Our statement should be formulated as follows:

```
SELECT DeptName, LastName, FirstName, Name
FROM Department LeftJoin Employee
On Department.DeptID=Employee.DeptID;
```

The following Right Join statement would accomplish exactly the same thing:

```
SELECT DeptName, LastName, FirstName, Name
FROM Employee RightJoin Department
On Department.DeptID=Employee.DeptID;
```

Some other clauses are needed to accomplish many queries for decision-making purposes. For example, we need to be able to calculate amounts based on fields in our database. You may recall from chapter 5 that it is undesirable to store any derivable attributes for which the value will change upon the entry of new data. For example, "Quantity On Hand" as an attribute in an Inventory table has a value that needs to be increased every time a purchase is made of an inventory item and decreased every time a sale is made of an inventory item. Unless the database is capable of using a concept called triggers, which in essence stores a formula instead of a value in the table's cell, it is preferable not to store this as an attribute in the inventory table, but instead to create a query we can run whenever we need an updated value for this field. Therefore we need to be able to create formulas within our queries to calculate such values.

Using Mathematical, Special Comparison, and Logical Operators in SQL Queries

Mathematical comparison operators are criteria that compare data values to determine whether or not they should be included in a query result. Examples of mathematical comparison operators include:

=	equal to
<	less than
>	greater than
<=	less than or equal to
<=	greater than or equal to
<>	not equal to (in some software this is denoted as !=)

These comparison operators may be applied to any type of field. For date fields, dates that are earlier in time are considered to be "less than" dates that are later in time. For example, April 1, 1980 is less than June 1, 1980. Most database software packages are able to compare and to perform calculations with date fields because they store the "Julian date" rather than the text format of the date. The "Julian date" is the value assigned to a date based on a continuous count assignment to days on the Julian calendar starting January 1, 4713 BCE (before common era). That date is assigned a Julian value of 1. Today's Julian date value (depending on when you are reading this) is likely somewhere in the 2.5-3 million range. For text fields, earlier letters in the alphabet are considered to be "less than" later letters in the alphabet. For example, *apple* is less than *banana*. Because comparison operators assist in isolating certain rows (i.e. relational algebra's selection operation) they are included in the WHERE clause of an SQL statement. The query used earlier as an example accomplishing a SELECT in SQL (SELECT * FROM Employee WHERE PayRate < 15.00;) used a mathematical comparison operator.

BETWEEN is a special comparison operator that is used to identify instances within a certain range of values. The endpoints of the range are included. Use of a BETWEEN operator is equivalent to using a combination of less than or equal to with greater than or equal to. For example, a query to include all sales for the month of June 2015 in its answer could be constructed using WHERE SaleDate >=6/1/2015 AND SaleDate <=6/30/2015, or it could be constructed using WHERE SaleDate BETWEEN 6/1/2015 and 6/30/2015.

IS NULL is a special comparison operator that is used to identify instances for which an attribute value does not exist. EXISTS is a special comparison operator that is used to identify instances for which an attribute value does exist.

Queries may also include **logical operators**, which are Boolean search terms used in queries to define which records are included in the query result. Example of logical operators include AND, OR, and NOT. The AND operator accomplishes a set intersection; an answer to a query connecting two criteria by an "AND" will contain only the instances that meet both criteria. The OR operator accomplishes a set union; an answer to a query connecting two criteria by an "OR" will contain all instances that meet at least one of the criteria. The NOT operator identifies instances that do not meet one or more conditions.

Using Calculations and Aggregation Functions in SQL Queries

There are two types of calculations we may need in queries. One type of calculation performs mathematical operations within a particular column of data values, such as a computation of the average or sum of a set of values. Calculations within a column are called **aggregation functions**, and several are standard in SQL. To compute the average of a column in a query, you would simply add (AVG) in front of the field name in the SELECT clause of the SQL statement. For example, if we wanted to compute the average payrate for all of our employees, we could specify:

        SELECT AVG(PayRate)
        FROM Employee;

Other aggregation functions (that are applied the same way) include SUM (to add a column), MAX (to find the largest value in a column), MIN (to find the smallest value in a column), and COUNT (to tell how many data values are in a column).

When we use aggregation functions in querying, we may not always want aggregate results for the table in its entirety. Sometimes we want aggregate results for certain combinations of rows in the table. For example, we may want to calculate total sales for each date, or we may want to know total purchase amount for each vendor. **GROUP BY** is a component that may be added after the WHERE component of a SQL statement to achieve this sub-totaling. Whatever field(s) the query is asked to group by will be grouped together and any aggregation function that is used will be applied to the subgroups rather than to the entire table. Examine the following Sale table.

Sale

SaleID	Date	Amount	Customer
S108	April 26	$432.00	C76
S109	April 26	$118.00	C83
S110	April 27	$625.00	C19
S111	April 28	$375.00	C38
S112	April 28	$864.00	C76

If you wanted to calculate total sales separately for each date, you will need to GROUP BY date. The query is formulated as follows:

    SELECT Date, SUM(Amount)
    FROM Sale
    GROUP BY Date;

The answer that results from this query is:

SalesByDate

Date	SumofAmount
April 26	$550.00
April 27	$625.00
April 28	$1,239.00

If instead, you wanted to calculate total sales separately for each customer, you will need to GROUP BY customer. The query is formulated as follows:

    SELECT Customer, SUM(Amount)
    FROM Sale
    GROUP BY Customer;

The answer that results from this query is:

SalesByCustomer

Customer	SumofAmount
C19	$625.00
C38	$375.00
C76	$1,296.00
C83	$118.00

The other type of calculation needed in some queries is a calculation that computes a mathematical function using data values from two different fields in a record. Examine the following table that represents a stockflow relationship between Sale and Inventory.

Stockflow

ItemID	SaleID	QtySold	UnitSellPrice
I1	S108	10	$25.00
I1	S109	4	$25.00
I1	S111	15	$25.00
I2	S108	10	$15.00
I2	S112	41	$14.00
I3	S108	4	$8.00
I3	S109	2	$9.00
I3	S112	29	$10.00
I5	S110	25	$25.00

To calculate the sale line extension for a stockflow record, a new field must be created and defined as the product of QtySold and UnitSellPrice. The query is formulated as follows:

```
SELECT QtySold*UnitSellPrice As SaleLineExtension
FROM Stockflow;
```

Query By Example (QBE) in Microsoft Access

Much of the ad hoc querying that is done to support enterprise decision-making is done by users who are not trained in SQL. Although most relational database software can run queries that are created in SQL form, most packages also offer an interface intended to make querying have more of a point and click feel. Such an interface is called Query By Example (QBE) because it has the user provide an example of what they want the answer to their query to look like. The user doesn't need to learn SQL code in order to generate many useful queries. However, it is very important to understand exactly what the different elements of the QBE interface accomplish when developing a query. If you do not ask the correct question, you will not get the correct answer! Query By Example can seem easier than it really is. Think about this: the less you understand the language of a person (or computer software) to whom you are asking a question, the more likely you are to make a mistake in asking that question. *You* may understand what you are trying to ask, but if you cannot adequately communicate the question to the database software, you will not get the answer you need. The dangerous thing is that you may not even realize the answer is incorrect! Of course that warning is also true for users querying with SQL, but our own anecdotal experience leads us to believe QBE is more likely than SQL to cause a false sense of security for untrained users. Most users who are trained in SQL are instructed to test their query construction before relying on the result; whereas many QBE users do not receive such instruction.

Because we are using Microsoft Access as our physical implementation software, we will next examine some elements of querying with the QBE interface in Access. Note that Access also offers a **SQL view**, a mode for viewing the underlying SQL statement for a query. Users may directly enter queries in SQL format using the SQL view, so if you are comfortable with SQL you may choose to bypass the QBE interface.

To create a new query in Microsoft Access, you first need to open a database. It is important for you to have a solid understanding of both the design and content of the tables from which you are trying to retrieve information before you create any queries. The overall approach to Querying By Example in Access is as follows

(1) Select the table(s) and/or query(ies) that contain the fields that eventually need to appear in the query result, and establish any joins that are needed (make sure to use the appropriate join type).

(2) Drag the fields that need to be manipulated or that need to appear in the query result into the **query grid** (the lower half of the QBE view into which fields are dragged and in which aggregations or horizontal calculations may be created to establish the desired logic for a query)

(3) Complete whatever steps are needed to develop the answer

    a.   Set criteria to filter out irrelevant records

    b.   Use aggregation functions within fields for which such calculations are appropriate OR create calculated fields using standard mathematical operators

    c.   Apply any other needed functions such as Group By or Sort

Keep in mind that you may need to accomplish your end result with a series of queries that build on each other. You will generally end up with a wrong answer if you mix **horizontal calculations**, which are row computations that combine data from multiple columns of one or more tables, and **vertical calculations**, which aggregate data values within a column according to specified functions. Access doesn't know which to do first, the vertical calculations or the horizontal calculations and if the query runs at all, it may create an answer that includes every possible combination of everything. It is best to create one query that applies the aggregation functions and then create a new query (using the first query as the starting object) that accomplishes the horizontal calculations, or vice versa, depending on the query demands.

Familiarization With Database
To allow a comparison and contrast with relational algebra and SQL, we use the same queries introduced earlier for discussing QBE. The database we use therefore consists of the same tables we used earlier in the chapter. We display them here in Microsoft Access as Exhibit 9-1 so you can see that we are using the same data. You are also provided with the Access data file in case you want to follow along on a computer as you read.

Exhibit 9-1 Example Tables in Microsoft Access

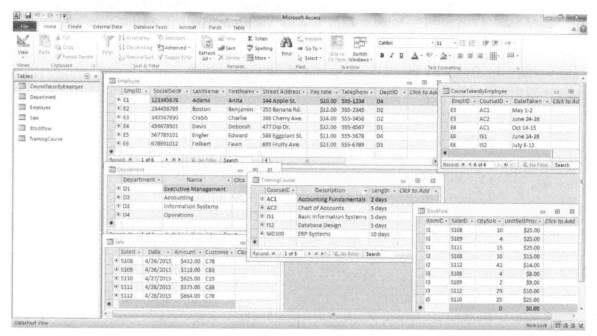

To display each of these tables on the screen simultaneously we simply opened each one in data sheet view and resized the table windows so they would fit on the screen. We next display the relationship layout as Exhibit 9-2 so you can familiarize yourself with the relationships between tables that are formed by the use of posted keys.

Exhibit 9-2 Relationship Layout for Employee Example Tables

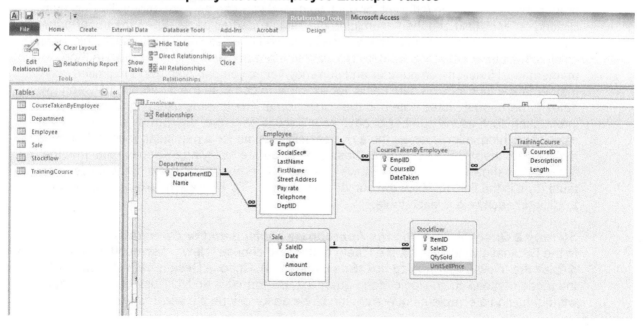

Please note that this is not intended to be a complete database. Only the tables necessary to illustrate the query examples are included. It is important for you to familiarize yourself with each table's design. The table design view for the Employee and related tables that are used for most of the queries are displayed as Exhibit 9-3.

Exhibit 9-3 Design View of Employee and Related Tables

It is more informative to look at the design view within Microsoft Access itself, because the field properties panel may be different for each field, and you can only see those differences by clicking on each field and then examining the field properties panel. From the upper panel you can see the data type, which in many cases is all you need to know about each field when using it in a query. Knowing the data type is important because you can only use most mathematical functions on number and currency fields; you can also perform limited mathematical functions on date fields, for example to compute the difference between two dates or between a stored date and the current date. The latter is useful for calculating information such as the number of days an invoice is past due; the former is useful for calculating information such as the average delivery time for a particular vendor. You must be familiar with the structure of the database tables you are querying. Keep in mind that the screen shot shown in Exhibit 9-3 shows only the field properties for one of the fields in each table (that is the field in which the cursor was placed). To view each field's property you need to click on each field in each table.

Starting a Query and Adding the Appropriate Table(s) and/or Query(ies)
In the Database window, click the Query button and choose "New". Microsoft Access will then display the "New Query" dialog box (See Exhibit 9-4). Choose Design View (the **design view** is the mode that depicts the logic of the query in QBE format -- do NOT use query wizards without having a complete understanding of the assumptions the wizards make).

REA Accounting Systems: Resources-Events-Agents: An ontology for designing, controlling, and using integrated enterprise systems

283

Exhibit 9-4 Starting a New Query

(a)

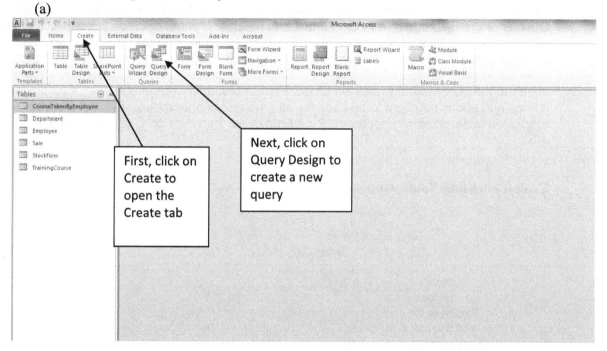

The result of clicking on Query Design will be the following windows – notice Show Table is a separate window that is on top of the query window. The **query window** is the screen in which the query is created – in that window the user may toggle between QBE design, SQL design, and datasheet views.

(b)

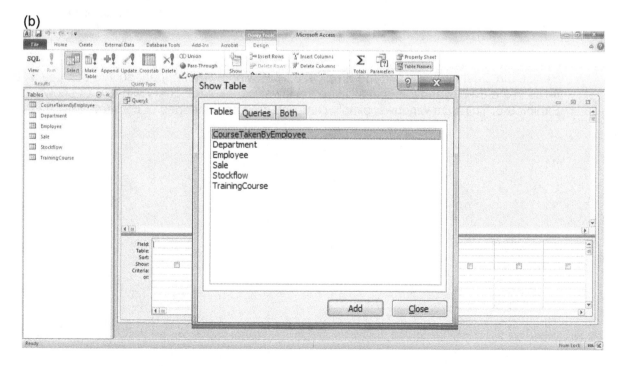

The **show table window** displays a list of tables and queries in your database (the default is to show the tables; if you want to base a query on an existing query, you can click on either the Queries or the Both tab). To include table(s) in the query, either double-click on each table name or click each name and click the Add button. To select multiple tables and add them simultaneously, press the Ctrl key while you click on the table names and when all the chosen table names are highlighted, click on Add. When all appropriate tables and/or queries are added to the query window, click on Close. For our first query (generate a list of employees' names and phone numbers to be used for an emergency phone tree) we only need the Employee table, so simply double-click on Employee, then click on Close as shown in Exhibit 9-5.

Exhibit 9-5 Show Table window

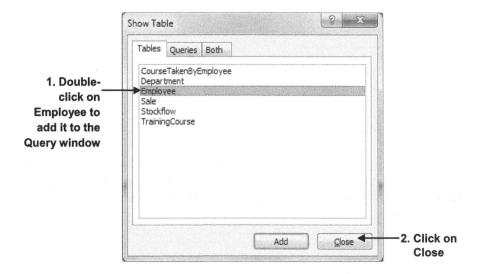

Resize the Query window and the Employee table window that appear so you can see all the fields in the Employee table and still see the lower panel of the query window as shown in Exhibit 9-6. To resize windows, simply click and drag on the edges or corners.

Exhibit 9-6 Query Window

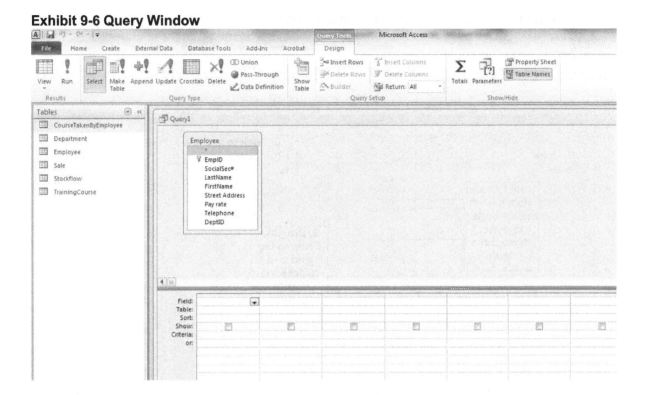

The next step is to add field names from the table to the query grid (the lower panel of the query window). This can be accomplished either by clicking the field name(s) and dragging them down to the grid or by double-clicking each field name to add it to the grid. For our query we need only the names and phone numbers for the emergency phone tree. Therefore we add Last Name, First Name, and Telephone to the query grid as illustrated in Exhibit 9-7.

Exhibit 9-7 Employee Phone Tree Query Design

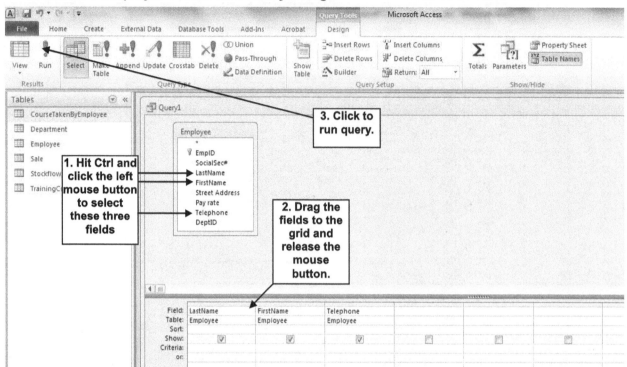

Because our query only needed to accomplish a PROJECT relational algebra operation, our query is complete. To see the results of the query, either click on the icon that looks like an exclamation mark (!), or switch to **Datasheet view** (the view that is row/column format and looks like a table) by clicking datasheet toolbar button or by selecting View, Datasheet View.

A query's answer in Microsoft Access is not actually a table, but is called a dynaset. A **dynaset** looks and behaves like a table but is not actually stored as a table -- it is generated as a view each time the query is run. New data added to the database that affects the query result is reflected in the dynaset the next time the query is run. The answer to our first query is shown in Exhibit 9-8.

Exhibit 9-8 Employee Phone Tree Query Result

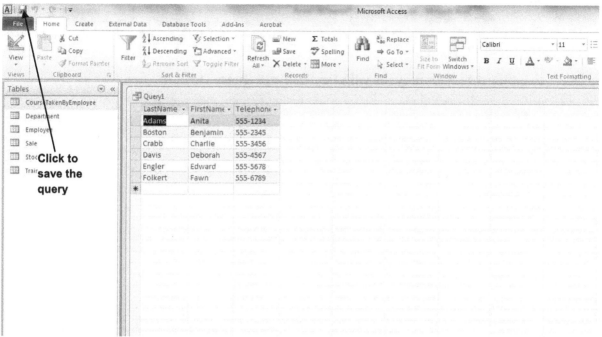

Once we are certain our query is executing properly, we need to save the query so it can be run again in the future. To save the query, either click on the Save icon (it looks like a diskette) as indicated on Exhibit 9-8, or click on File, Save on the menu. That will bring up a "Save As" window into which you can type a meaningful name for your query and click on OK. See Exhibit 9-9.

Exhibit 9-9 "Save As" window.

Our second query (a list of all attributes of employees whose pay rate is less than $15) accomplishes the relational algebra SELECT operator. To begin, create a new query and add the Employee table to the query window following the same steps illustrated in Exhibits 9-4 through 9-6. The next step is to add all the fields from the Employee table into the query grid. Then specify the criteria by which the horizontal subset is to be defined. In this example, the field for which the criteria needs to be specified is PayRate, and the criteria is <15. The query grid includes a line labeled "Criteria" on which to enter the logical operator expression. Criteria should be entered on the same line in the appropriate fields for any query that includes the logical operator AND. Criteria should be entered in the Criteria line for one of the appropriate fields and on the "Or" line for the other appropriate field for a query that includes the logical operator OR.

Exhibit 9-10 (a) illustrates the appropriate design for this query, and Exhibit 9-10 (b) shows the resulting dynaset.

Exhibit 9-10 (a) Employees with PayRate <15 Query Design

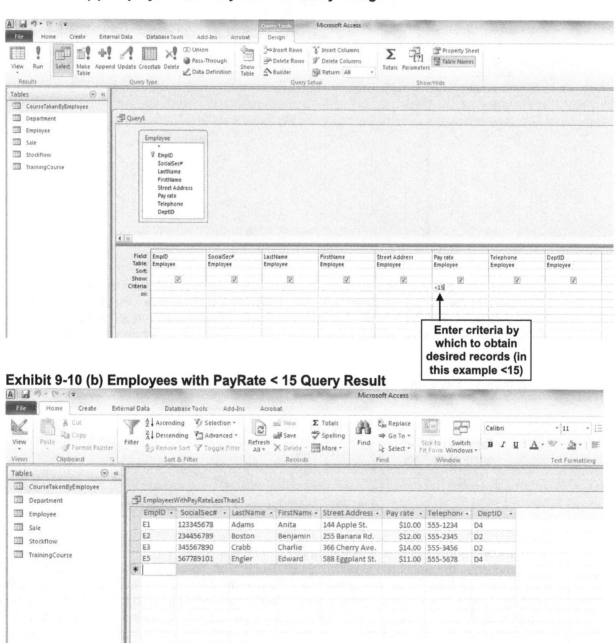

Enter criteria by which to obtain desired records (in this example <15)

Exhibit 9-10 (b) Employees with PayRate < 15 Query Result

EmpID	SocialSec#	LastName	FirstName	Street Address	Pay rate	Telephone	DeptID
E1	123345678	Adams	Anita	144 Apple St.	$10.00	555-1234	D4
E2	234456789	Boston	Benjamin	255 Banana Rd.	$12.00	555-2345	D2
E3	345567890	Crabb	Charlie	366 Cherry Ave.	$14.00	555-3456	D2
E5	567789101	Engler	Edward	588 Eggplant St.	$11.00	555-5678	D4

REA Accounting Systems: Resources-Events-Agents: An ontology for designing, controlling, and using integrated enterprise systems

289

The third query we generated earlier in this chapter in relational algebra and SQL was one that created a list of employees and the names of the departments to which they are assigned. This query required a JOIN relational algebra operator as well as a PROJECT to narrow down the answer to only include the employee name and department name columns. In SQL we were able to combine those two operators into one query. In QBE we are also able to accomplish both operators with a single query. To formulate this query in QBE, follow the steps in Exhibits 9-4 through 9-6 adding both the Employee and the Department tables to the query window. Then add the LastName and FirstName fields from the Employee table and add the Name field from the Department table to the query window. Exhibit 9-11 shows the result of these steps. Notice that a join line automatically appeared between Employee and Department, linking the Department ID field in the Department table with the DeptID field in the Employee table. This line represents the join that was established in the relationship layout as Access's means for knowing that DeptID in the Employee table is a posted foreign key from the Department table.

Exhibit 9-11 Employee and Department Names JOIN Query Design

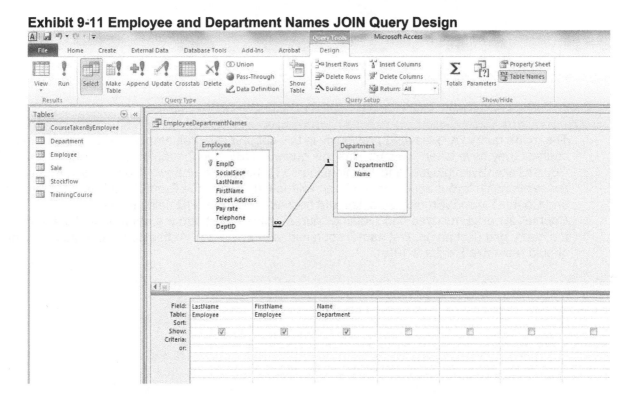

Exhibit 9-12 shows the result of this query.

Exhibit 9-12 Employee and Department JOIN Query Result

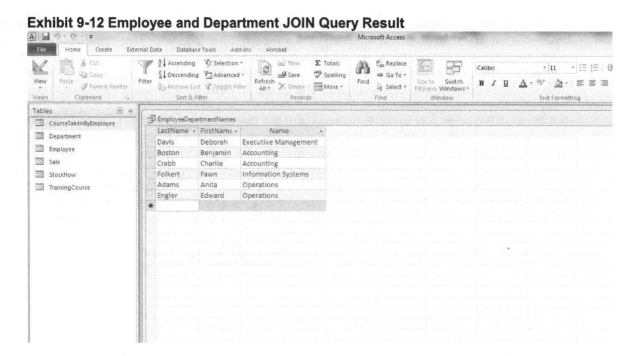

The fourth query we examined previously in this chapter listed all employees and the training courses they have taken. To formulate this query in QBE add the tables Employee, CourseTakenByEmployee, and TrainingCourse to the query window. The joins established in the relationship layout appear in the query window (between the EmpIID fields in the Employee and CourseTakenByEmployee tables and between the CourseID fields in the CourseTakenByEmployee and TrainingCourse tables). Next add the appropriate field names to the query grid (last name, first name, course id, course name). At this point your query design should resemble Exhibit 9-13(a).

REA Accounting Systems: Resources-Events-Agents: An ontology for designing, controlling, and using integrated enterprise systems

291

Exhibit 9-13 (a) Initial Query Design Employees and Courses Taken

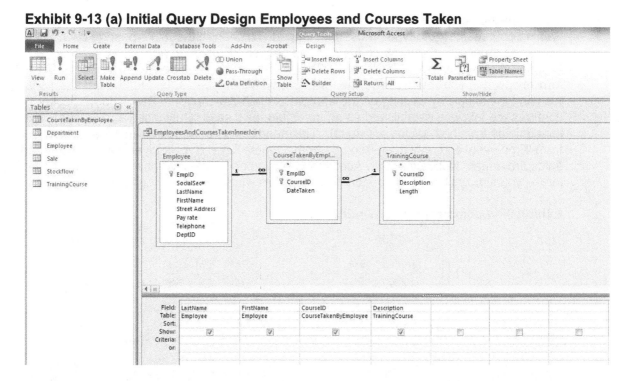

Running this query results in the dynaset shown in Exhibit 9-13(b). What does this answer tell you about the type of join Access uses by default? It must be an inner join, because only those employees who have actually taken courses show up in our answer.

Exhibit 9-13 (b) Result of Initial Query Design Employees and Courses Taken

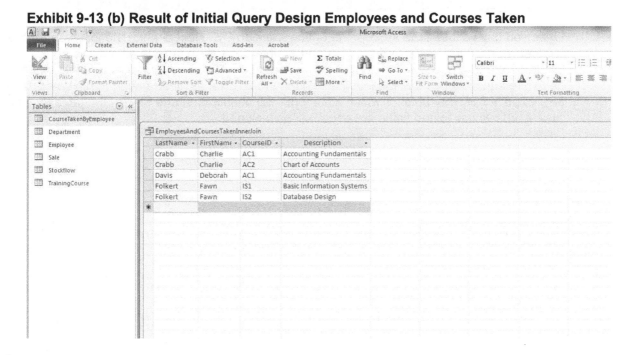

To include ALL employees in the list, showing a blank for those who have not taken any training courses, the join types must be changed. To change the join types, go back to the query design and double-click on the join line between Employee and CourseTakenByEmployee. A window will appear similar to the one shown in Exhibit 9-14. The **join properties window** displays the three possible join types such that the user can change the join type simply by clicking on the appropriate join description. This window display confirms the join was established as an inner join, as it says "Only include rows where the joined fields from both tables are equal." This needs to be changed to "Include ALL records from 'Employee' and only those records from 'CourseTakenByEmployee' where the joined fields are equal." Notice that with Access's QBE you don't specify "inner join", "left join" or "right join" – you simply choose the option that describes what you are trying to accomplish.

Exhibit 9-14 Join Properties Window

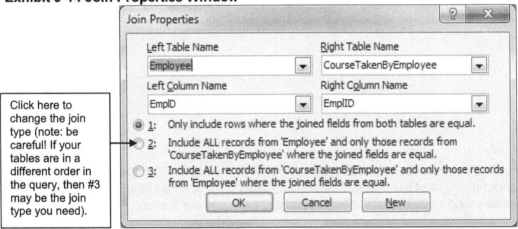

Once you have chosen the appropriate option, click on OK. Next change the join type for the join between CourseTakenByEmployee and TrainingCourse to include all records from 'CourseTakenByEmployee' and only those records from 'TrainingCourse' where the joined fields are equal. Notice that the join lines change to arrows, as illustrated in Exhibit 9-15. The arrows point from the table for which all records will be included and toward the table for which the records whose joined fields are equal will be included.

Exhibit 9-15 Revised Join Lines

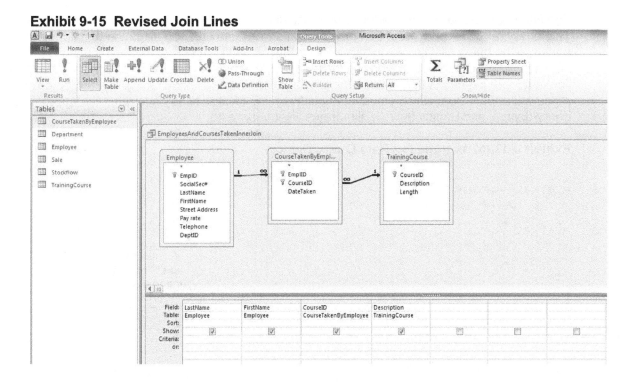

When you run the query again, your answer should resemble Exhibit 9-16.

Exhibit 9-16 Result of Revised Query Design Employees and Courses Taken

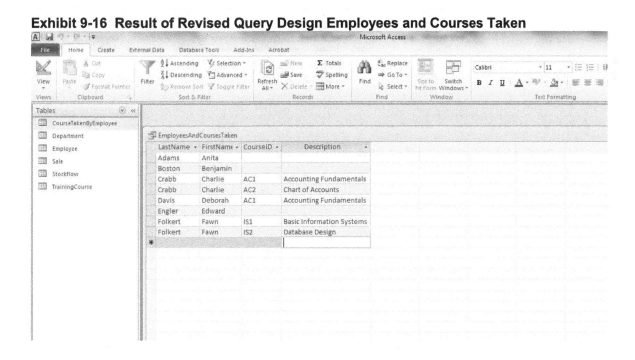

The fifth query we examined earlier was to calculate the average pay rate for our employees. This query requires an aggregation function called AVG. In QBE aggregation functions may be added to the query grid by clicking on an icon that looks like a summation symbol and is labeled as Totals. When that icon is clicked, a "Total" line is added to the query grid. When this line is added, it defaults to a "Group By" aggregation. If you click on Group By, a drop down menu will appear from which you can select "Avg". Exhibit 9-17 (a) illustrates the appropriate query design, and Exhibit 9-17 (b) illustrates the query result

Exhibit 9-17 (a) Average PayRate Query Design

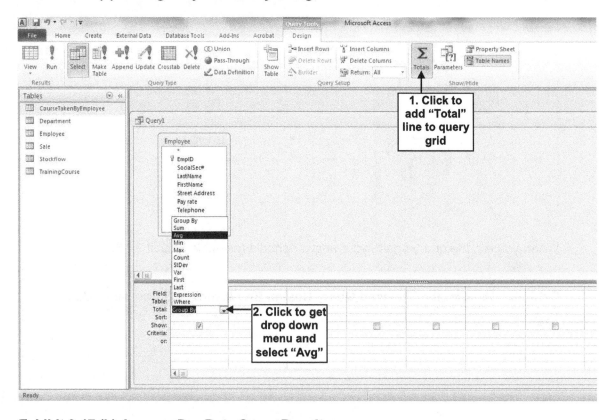

Exhibit 9-17 (b) Average Pay Rate Query Result

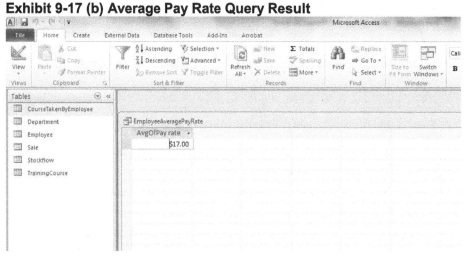

REA Accounting Systems: Resources-Events-Agents: An ontology for designing, controlling, and using integrated enterprise systems

295

The sixth query we examined earlier in this chapter calculated total sales separately for each date. In QBE this query is accomplished by adding the Sale table to the query window, dragging the date and amount fields to the query grid, adding the Total line to the query grid, and setting the Total line to Group By for the Date field and to Sum for the Amount field. This query design is illustrated in Exhibit 9-18 (a) and the result is displayed in Exhibit 9-18 (b).

Exhibit 9-18 (a) Total Sales By Date Query Design

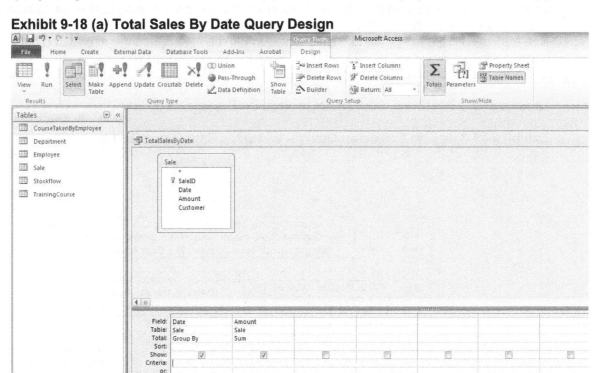

Exhibit 9-18 (b) Total Sales by Date Query Result

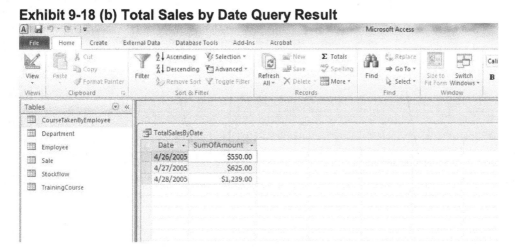

If instead, you wanted to calculate total sales separately for each customer, you would need to drag the Customer and Amount fields to the query grid, GROUP BY Customer and SUM Amount. It is important when you are using aggregation functions that you only drag the fields to the query grid that actually participate in an aggregation. If you drag the Date, Customer, and Amount fields, it is going to first group by Date and then group by Customer (or vice versa depending on which field is listed first). This will not give you the sum you want!

The final query we examined earlier required a calculation of quantity sold multiplied by the unit sales price to compute a sale line extension for a stockflow record. To accomplish this query in QBE, add the Stockflow table to the query window. Drag all the fields to the query grid. Save the query as SaleLineExtension. Saving the query with fields in the query grid makes those fields available for manipulation in a tool called the expression builder. The **expression builder** is an application within Microsoft Access that assists in creating horizontal calculations within queries. With the cursor in the next available blank field in the query grid, click on the icon that looks like a magic wand, as illustrated in Exhibit 9-19. Once the expression builder is open, double-click on the QtySold field to place it in the expression window. Then click on the asterisk symbol for multiplication. Double-click on the UnitSellPrice field to place it into the expression window. The expression tells Access this field should store the multiplication of QtySold and UnitSellPrice. Click on OK to close the Expression Builder.

Exhibit 9-19 Sale Line Extension Query – Using the Expression Builder

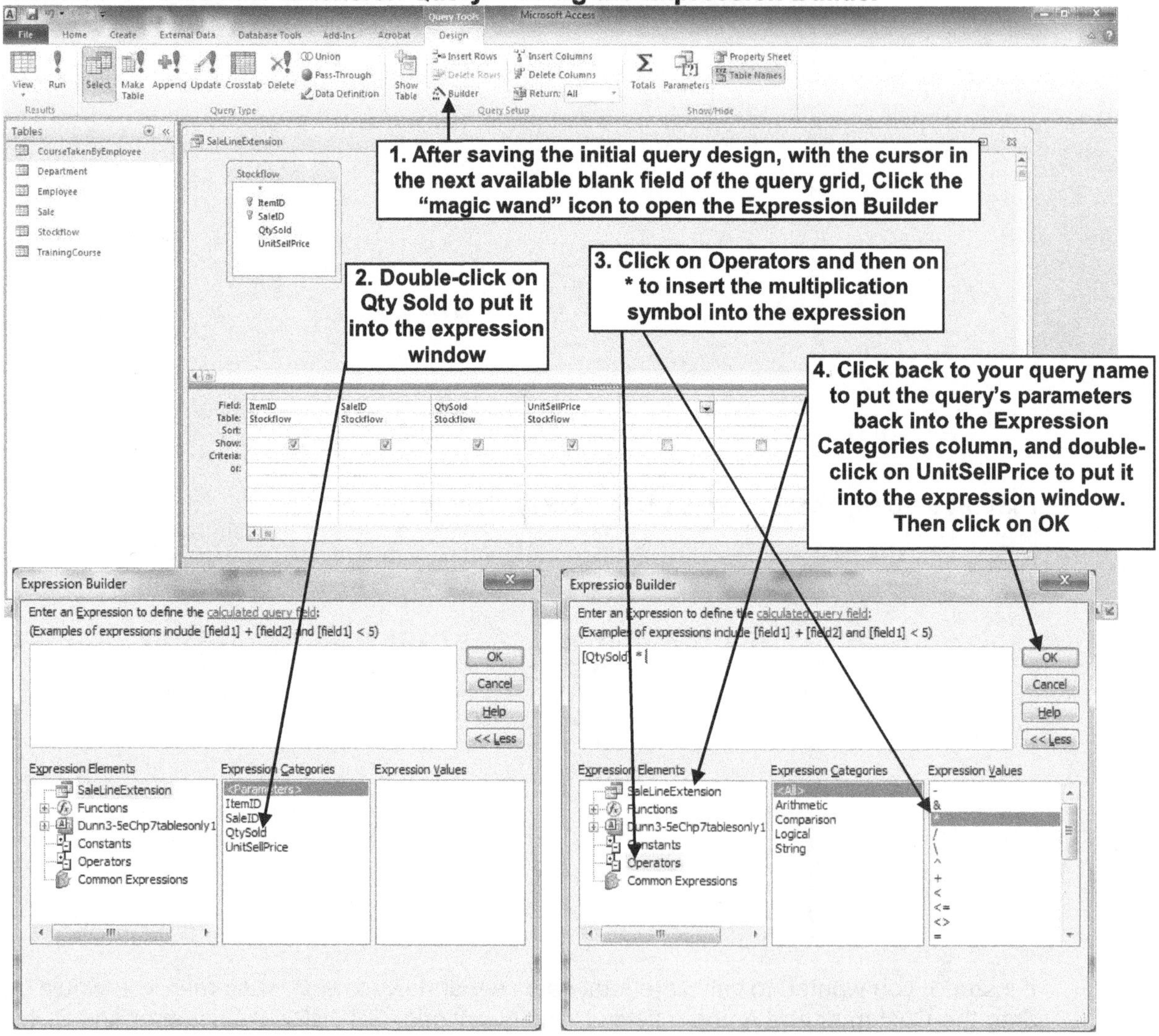

REA Accounting Systems: Resources-Events-Agents: An ontology for designing, controlling, and using integrated enterprise systems

297

Exhibit 9-20 Sale Line Item Extension Query Result

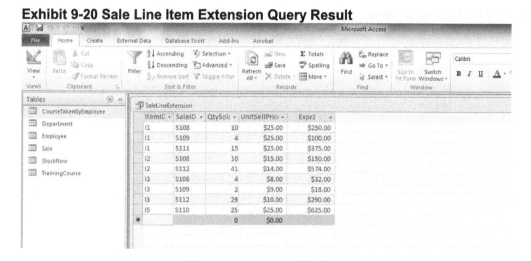

Exhibit 9-20 shows the result of running the SaleLineExtension query.

In the dynaset, the expression is labeled with a generic term "Expr1". To change this to a more meaningful name, switch back to the query's design view and in the expression's field, highlight the Expr1 and type the more meaningful name, as shown in Exhibit 9-21.

Exhibit 9-21 Renaming a Field

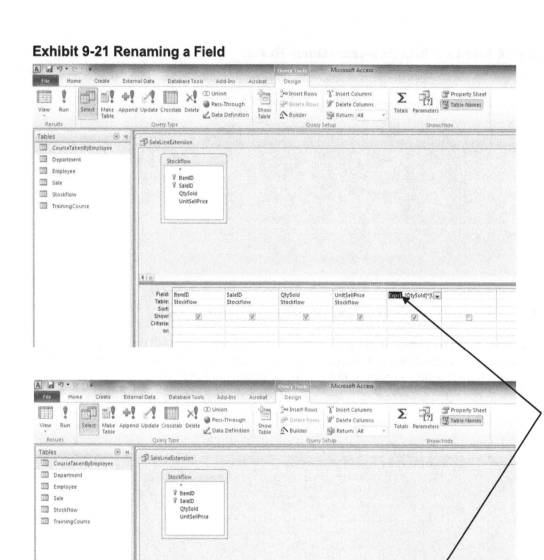

To change a field name, highlight the field name and type the desired field name. The field name is whatever text appears before the colon.

We noted earlier that Access allows query entry via a SQL view as an alternative to the QBE view. Let's enter the SQL statement for the final query directly into Access instead of using the QBE interface as an illustration. Start a new query, and when the Show Table window appears, hit close without adding any tables or queries to your query window. In the upper left corner, the SQL with the small down arrow next to it indicates the path to switch to SQL view. Click on the arrow next to SQL to display the SQL view, as shown in Exhibit 9-22.

Exhibit 9-22 Creating a Query in Microsoft Access SQL View

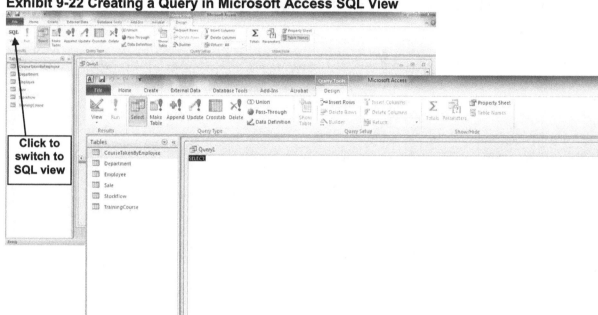

The SQL view appears with the word SELECT followed by a semicolon. Access knows that every SQL statement begins with the word SELECT and ends with a semicolon. All that is needed is the detail that goes in between. Type the SQL statement in as shown in Exhibit 9-23, then run the query to see the same dynaset that resulted earlier using QBE. Compare Exhibit 9-23 with Exhibit 9-20; the only difference is the other ItemID, SaleID, QtySold, and UnitSellPrice attributes do not appear in Exhibit 9-23. That is because the SQL statement did not specifically ask for those to be included. A slight revision to the SQL statement will cause those fields to appear in the dynaset, as follows:

SELECT ItemID, SaleID, QtySold, UnitSellPrice, QtySold*UnitSellPrice As SaleLineExtension FROM Stockflow;

Exhibit 9-23 SQL Statement and Resulting Dynaset

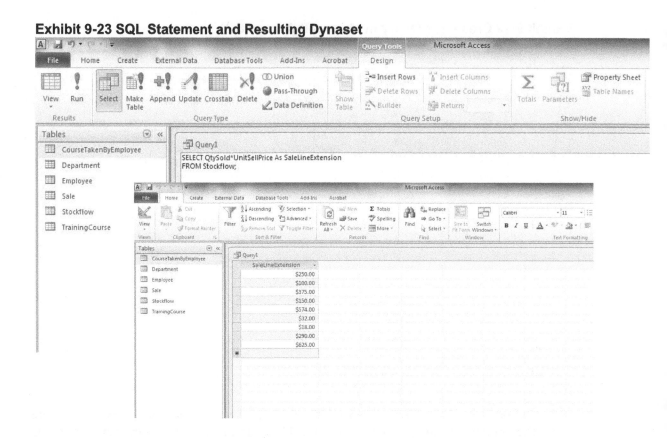

Parameter Queries

Often users need to re-use ad hoc queries they construct on a regular basis, changing only the date criteria. For example, a marketing manager who wants to know the total sales for a specific inventory item for a week or for a month could use the same query with different date constraints. A **date constraint** is a restriction placed on a date field in a query to limit the query results to include only records for which the date values meet the restriction. To increase the re-usability of queries, Access offers the option of creating parameter queries. A **parameter query** specifies variables in lieu of data values as part of the query's selection criteria, allowing the user to specify the data values to be used each time the query is run. Consider a query that specifies a date range as the criteria: BETWEEN 1/1/15 and 1/31/15. If the user wants to re-use this query in the future for a different date range (e.g. BETWEEN 2/1/15 and 2/28/15), he or she must change the design of the query to change the date constraint. A parameter query for this situation would not specify the exact dates, instead it would include parameter names for each date, for example BETWEEN [BeginDate] and [EndDate]. When the query is run, Access realizes that it doesn't know what BeginDate and EndDate are, so Access prompts the user to specify the values of these parameters. This enables the user to change the dates each time the query is run without changing the design of the query.

Exhibit 9-24 (a) illustrates the design of a parameter query. Access's syntax for parameters requires that they be enclosed in square brackets. Parts (b), (c), and (d) of Exhibit 9-24 show the prompts for the parameter values and the final query result.

Exhibit 9-24 (a) Parameter Query Design

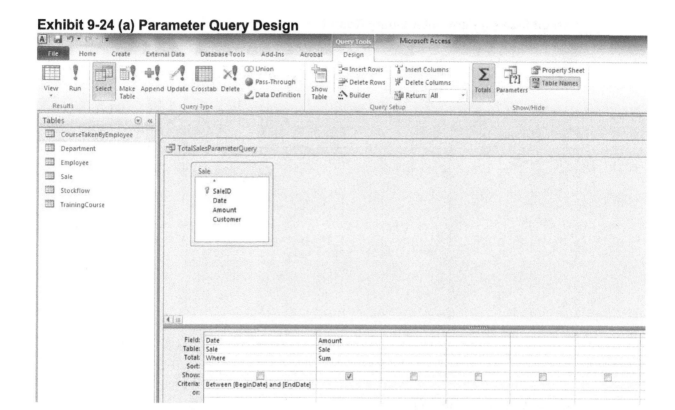

Exhibit 9-24(b) Prompt for value for the [BeginDate] parameter

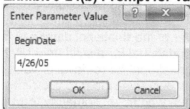

Exhibit 9-24 (c) Prompt for value for the [EndDate] parameter

Exhibit 9-24 (d) Parameter Query Result

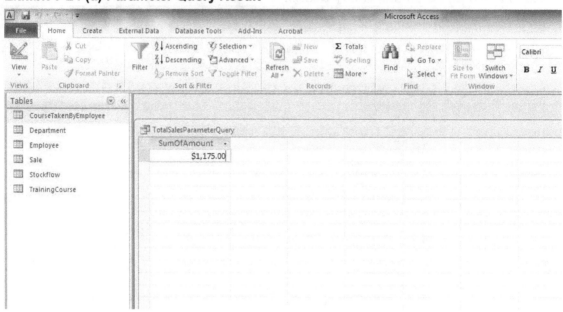

CONCLUDING COMMENTS

In chapters 5 through 8, you have learned how to create a conceptual representation (on paper) of an enterprise's reality and convert it, first into a logical set of relational tables (also on paper) and then into a physical implementation of relational tables using Microsoft Access 2010 software. You also learned how to retrieve information from the tables using a structured approach. It is in the querying capabilities that the real power of the relational database is found; however, a solid understanding of table design is foundational for a solid understanding of querying. In turn, a solid understanding of querying is foundational for retrieval of valid data, which is crucial for sound decision making. Perhaps it is now becoming clear to you (if it wasn't already clear) why all enterprise system users (that is, anyone who might someday form an ad hoc query of a relational database) must understand the basics of relational database design. Hopefully seeing the translation of the conceptual models into an actual working database has helped clarify some of the concepts that we covered in chapters 2 and 5 by making them more concrete. You may find it worthwhile to go back and re-read those chapters now that you have a better understanding of the end result.

Once you unlock the mystery of query construction, whether you prefer SQL or QBE, you can tap into the wealth of information that is at your fingertips in a well-designed relational database. Enterprises today typically store vast amounts of data in relational databases that can be retrieved in a variety of different formats for different decision-making purposes. To ensure the information retrieved is valid, users should be well versed in relational database design, semantic query logic, and the syntax of the particular query language used. This chapter is intended only to provide you with a cursory introduction to querying in SQL and Microsoft Access's QBE. To become proficient at querying, you MUST practice and learn through trial and error. The automated help facility in Microsoft Access contains more examples of queries and will help you to solidify your understanding of the query window, QBE grid, Expression Builder, and other syntactic features of Microsoft Access QBE.

REA Accounting Systems: Resources-Events-Agents: An ontology for designing, controlling, and using integrated enterprise systems

303

If you do an Internet search using a search engine such as www.google.com and keywords SQL tutorial you will find several tutorial sites that provide help with understanding SQL syntax. Note, however, that you won't find solutions for the semantic nature of queries you need to formulate. Rather, you must first figure out where the desired information is in your database and determine how to get that information (thinking about this in terms of the relational algebra operators can be very helpful). We strongly recommend using a pencil and a calculator (or exporting data to a spreadsheet) to figure solutions out manually before attempting to create a query in Microsoft Access. That ensures that you understand the logic of the query before enveloping the logic into the syntax of either QBE or SQL, and it also gives you some "check figures" to use in determining whether the query is functioning as planned. Comprehensive testing of queries that are intended to be re-used is crucial to ensure they will work for different dates (if date constraints are included), and after new data is entered into the database.

Key Terms and Concepts

General Terms and Concepts
Ad hoc querying
Aggregation functions
Data manipulation
Date constraint
Equi-join
Group By
Horizontal calculation
Horizontal subset of a table
Information retrieval
Inner join
JOIN
Left join
Logical operator
Mathematical comparison operator
Outer join
PROJECT
Query
QBE (Query By Example)
Relational Algebra

Right join
SELECT (in relational algebra)
SELECT-FROM-WHERE (in SQL)
Structured Query Language (SQL)
Vertical calculation
Vertical subset of a table

Microsoft Access Terms and Concepts
Datasheet view
Design view
Dynaset
Expression builder
Join properties window
Parameter query
Query grid
Query window
Show Table window
SQL view

Review Questions

LO1 R1. Which of the relational algebra operators is needed to retrieve a vertical subset (i.e., a subset of columns) from a relational database table?

LO1 R2. Which of the relational algebra operators is needed to retrieve a horizontal subset (i.e., a subset of rows) from a relational database table?

LO1 R3. Which of the relational algebra operators is needed to combine two tables together in a query?

LO2 R4. What is the standard format of a SQL query statement?

LO3 R5. Which component of a SQL statement accomplishes a relational algebra SELECT operation?

LO3 R6. Which component of a SQL statement accomplishes a relational algebra PROJECT operation?

LO3 R7. Which components of a SQL statement accomplish a relational algebra JOIN operation?

LO7 R8. What is the advantage to creating a query that includes a date constraint as a parameter query?

LO4,LO7 R9. What is the difference between an aggregation (vertical calculation) and a horizontal calculation?

LO4,LO7 R10. Give an example of a query for which you would need to use a left join instead of an inner join.

Multiple Choice Questions

1. Which of the following query interfaces is intended to be more point-and-click in nature and to require less user expertise?
    A) Relational Algebra
    B) Structured Query Language (SQL)
    C) Query By Example
    D) Standard Query
    E) Relational Calculus

2. Which of the following is necessary for effective information retrieval?
    A) The database is well designed
    B) The query designer has a thorough knowledge of the database table structures and the nature of the data in the tables.
    C) The query designer adequately understands the desired output.
    D) The query designer knows the querying language used to retrieve information from the enterprise's database.
    E) All of the above are necessary for effective information retrieval.

3. Which of the following is **NOT** a relational algebra operator used in basic queries?
    A) Locate
    B) Project
    C) Join
    D) Select
    E) All of the above are relational algebra operators used in basic queries.

REA Accounting Systems: Resources-Events-Agents: An ontology for designing, controlling, and using integrated enterprise systems

305

4. Which relational algebra operator can be used to eliminate duplicate columns or filter out columns that are not needed based on the information request?
    A) Locate
    B) Project
    C) Join
    D) Select
    E) Request

5. If a table contained 50 rows and you want to use only 20 of the rows that meet a specific criteria, you would create a query to get
    A) A vertical subset
    B) A horizontal subset
    C) A diagonal subset
    D) A JOIN
    E) An OPEN

6. What is currently the most commonly used data manipulation language?
    A) Relational Algebra
    B) Structured Query Language (SQL)
    C) Query By Example
    D) Fortran
    E) Pascal

7. In SQL, every information retrieval query follows what structured, predefined syntax?
    A) SELECT *attribute name(s)*, FROM *table name(s)*, WHERE *condition criteria is met*;
    B) SELECT *attribute name(s)*, JOIN *table name(s)*, WHERE *condition criteria is met*;
    C) SELECT *attribute name(s)*, QUERY *table name(s)*, WHEN *condition criteria is met*;
    D) SELECT *attribute name(s)*, FROM *table name(s)*, WHEN *condition criteria is met*;
    E) SELECT *attribute name(s)*, from QUERY *table name(s)*, LOCATED *in database name*;

8. Which of the following is true regarding the use of an outer join in SQL?
    A) The outer join must be specified in the SELECT clause of an SQL statement.
    B) The outer join need not be specified as an outer join, because most database software automatically recognizes whether a join should be inner or outer.
    C) The outer join must be specified as a Left Join or a Right Join.
    D) An outer join is also commonly called an Equi-Join.
    E) The outer join must be specified in the PROJECT clause of an SQL statement.

9. What does the asterisk (*) in SQL mean?
    A) The asterisk (*) is a standard symbol used to start most or all queries
    B) The asterisk (*) is a standard symbol used to end most or all queries
    C) The asterisk (*) is a wildcard symbol that requests inclusion of all attributes
    D) The asterisk (*) is a wildcard attribute that means to disregard any attributes that follow its use
    E) The asterisk (*) is an interruption symbol used to abort a query if it takes longer to process than a prescribed time length.

10. Which SQL statement will multiple Table A's Field P by Table A's Field Q?
    A) Project Field P times Field Q From Table A;
    B) Select Field P From Table A Where Field Q = Field P * 2;
    C) Select Sum (Field P, Field Q) From Table A;
    D) Select (Field P * Field Q) From Table A;
    E) Select Table A Field P and Table A Field Q, Multiply P*Q;

11. If Table A is on the left and Table B is on the right, a right outer join will include in its answer
    A) Only the rows for which the values of the two tables' common attribute match exactly.
    B) All the rows from Table A, with the corresponding detail of Table B for those rows for which the values of the two tables' common attribute match exactly.
    C) All the rows from Table B, with the corresponding detail of Table A for those rows for which the value of the two tables' common attribute match exactly.
    D) All rows from both Table A and Table B.
    E) None of the rows from either table

12. A query's answer in Microsoft Access is referred to as a
    A) Project
    B) Dynaset
    C) Dataset
    D) Interface
    E) None of the above

Discussion Questions

LO1,2,3   D1.   What are the advantages (and/or disadvantages) of SQL compared to Relational Algebra?

LO2,7   D2.   What are the advantages (and/or disadvantages) of QBE compared to SQL?

LO5,6,8,9 D3.   Explain why a poor database design will result in information retrieval problems.

LO5,6,8,9 D4.   Explain how incorrect information retrieval results may be obtained even from a perfectly designed database.

LO4   D5.   Create a query in SQL that will list the last name, first name, and telephone number for all the customers who live in Florida. States are entered in the database using their two digit postal abbreviation (Florida is FL). The customer table structure (field types are noted) follows:

Customer

CustomerID	LastName	FirstName	Telephone	City	State	CreditLimit	AcctsReceivableBalance
Text	Text	Text	Text	Text	Text	Currency	Currency

CHAPTER 10

Acquisition and Revenue Cycle Information Retrieval

LEARNING OBJECTIVES

This chapter illustrates use of the REA ontology to determine and meet information needs within the acquisition and revenue cycles. This chapter focuses on relatively uncomplicated queries that involve single classes or associations within each cycle. After studying this chapter you should be able to

1. Identify common information needs within the acquisition cycle
2. Identify common information needs within the revenue cycle
3. Create queries to meet common information needs within the acquisition cycle
4. Create queries to meet common information needs within the revenue cycle

INFORMATION NEEDS AND MEASURES IN THE ACQUISITION AND REVENUE CYCLES

Information customers, i.e., people who need information in order to make decisions, often need information found within the acquisition and revenue cycles.

Within any business process, information needs fit into the following categories:
Internal users need information about internal phenomena.
- Internal users need information about external phenomena.
- External users need information about internal phenomena.
- External users need information about external phenomena.

For example, salespeople (internal users) need information about the products they sell (internal phenomena). Salespeople also need information about the customers to whom they make sales (external phenomena). Suppliers (external users) need information about the products the company wants to purchase (internal phenomena). Purchase agents need information about new products its suppliers offer (external phenomena). Other examples within each of these categories may include information at different levels of detail. We next analyze each of the classes and associations in the business process level REA pattern to give some ideas about the queries that may be needed to satisfy information needs regarding these objects for internal and external users. The queries presented are not a comprehensive set of queries (there are simply too many potentially useful queries to list them all). However, the set provided should provide you guidance for creating similar queries to satisfy similar information needs. To describe example queries needed in the acquisition and revenue cycles we use the database tables in Exhibit 10-1.

Exhibit 10-1 Database Tables for Example Queries

Cash (Resource Type)

CashAccountID	AccountType	Location	DateAccountEstablished
Ca123501	Checking	1st Local Bank	April 1, 2015
Ca789125	Savings	1st Local Bank	April 1, 2015
Ca351235	Petty	Onsite - Cashier Desk drawer	April 15, 2015
Ca351327	Petty	Onsite - CEO Assistant's File Cabinet	April 22, 2015

Inventory Type (Resource Type)

Item ID	Description	UnitOfMeasure	Standard Cost	List Price
BIS1	Big Stuff	Each	$20.00	$50.00
HUS1	Huge Stuff	Each	$30.00	$70.00
LIS1	Little Stuff	Box of 6	$36.00	$72.00
MIN1	Miniature Stuff	Box of 24	$56.00	$110.00
TIS1	Tiny Stuff	Box of 12	$48.00	$96.00
TTP12	Tiara	Each	$10.00	$25.00

Operating Assets (Resource)

Asset TagID	Description	AcqDate	AcqCost	Asset Category	Estimated LifeYrs	Estimated Salvage	IRSListed Property
OA1	Building	4/01/2015	$200,000.00	Buildings	40	$20,000.00	No
OA2	Property	4/01/2015	$300,000.00	Land	0	$0.00	No
OA3	Executive desk	4/10/2015	$2,000.00	Furniture	10	$200.00	No
OA4	Manager desk	4/10/2015	$1,500.00	Furniture	10	$100.00	No
OA5	Manager desk	4/10/2015	$1,500.00	Furniture	10	$100.00	No
OA6	Administrator desk	4/10/2015	$1,000.00	Furniture	10	$100.00	No
OA7	Administrator desk	4/10/2015	$1,000.00	Furniture	10	$100.00	No
OA8	Executive desk chair	4/10/2015	$500.00	Furniture	7	$50.00	No
OA9	Manager task chair	4/10/2015	$350.00	Furniture	7	$50.00	No
OA10	Manager task chair	4/10/2015	$350.00	Furniture	7	$50.00	No
OA11	Task chair	4/10/2015	$175.00	Furniture	7	$25.00	No
OA12	Task chair	4/10/2015	$175.00	Furniture	7	$25.00	No
OA13	Task chair	4/10/2015	$175.00	Furniture	7	$25.00	No
OA14	Task chair	4/10/2015	$175.00	Furniture	7	$25.00	No
OA15	Toshiba tecra	4/15/2015	$3,000.00	Computers	5	$300.00	Yes
OA16	Dell optima desktop	4/15/2015	$2,000.00	Computers	5	$200.00	Yes
OA17	Dell optima desktop	4/15/2015	$2,000.00	Computers	5	$200.00	Yes
OA18	Dell optima desktop	4/15/2015	$2,000.00	Computers	5	$200.00	Yes
OA19	Warehouse shelving	4/16/2015	$10,000.00	Fixtures	40	$0.00	No
OA20	Fax machine	4/17/2015	$400.00	Comm Equip	3	$0.00	Yes

Sales Call (Instigation) Event

Sales Call ID	Date	StartTime	EndTime	Location	SalesRepID[FK]	CustomerID[FK]
42	5/04/2015	9:12 a.m.	10:00 a.m.	Customer	E23	C2323
43	5/04/2015	9:27 a.m.	10:35 a.m.	Ours	E26	C4731
44	5/05/2015	10:30 a.m.	11:15 a.m.	Customer	E23	C6125

Exhibit 10-1 (cont.) Database Tables for Example Queries

Purchase Requisition (Instigation) Event

Purch ReqID	Date	Maximum Budget for this purchase	Date Needed	SuperID^{FK}	Purch AgentID^{FK}	Recommended SupplierID^{FK}
R17	4/22/2010	$30,000	5/02/2010	E5	E12	V7
R18	5/05/2010		5/23/2010	E5	E12	V14
R19	5/06/2010		5/20/2010	E5	E12	V7
R20	5/15/2010		5/25/2010	E5	E12	
R21	5/18/2010		5/26/2010	E5	E12	V7

Sale Order (Mutual Commitment) Event

Sale Order ID	Order Date	Date Needed	Dollar Total	Sales Tax	Shipping Charge	Sales CallID^{FK}	Sales RepID^{FK}	Customer ID^{FK}
14	5/04/2015	5/07/2015	$1,100.00	$0	$0	42	E23	C2323
15	5/04/2015	5/12/2015	$3,050.00	$0	$0	43	E26	C4731
16	5/06/2015	5/09/2015	$4,305.00	$0	$0	42	E23	C2323
17	5/08/2015	5/17/2015	$8,280.00	$0	$0	43	E26	C4731

Purchase Order (Mutual Commitment) Event

Purchase OrderID	OrderDate	DateNeeded	DollarTotal	Purchase ReqID^{FK}	Purchase AgentID^{FK}	Supplier ID^{FK}
PO16	4/24/2010	5/2/2010	$28,450.00	R17	E12	V7
PO17	5/05/2010	5/8/2010		R18	E12	V14
PO18	5/05/2010	5/12/2010		R18	E12	V90
PO19	5/06/2010	5/10/2010		R19	E12	V14
PO20	5/06/2010	5/24/2010		R19	E12	V7
PO21	5/16/2010	5/24/2010		R20	E12	V14

Sale (Economic Decrement) Event

Sale ID	Date	Dollar Total	PickListID	PackListID	BOL#	SalesRepID^{FK}	CustomerID^{FK}	CashReceiptID^{FK}
12	5/05/2015	$1,100.00	15	15	15	E23	C2323	RA20
13	5/07/2015	$3,050.00	16	16	16	E26	C4731	RA21
14	5/08/2015	$2,100.00	17	17	17	E23	C2323	RA20
15	5/10/2015	$2,205.00	18	18	18	E23	C2323	

Cash Receipt (Economic Increment) Event

CashReceiptID	Date	Dollar Total	CashAccountID^{FK}	CustomerID^{FK}	CashierID^{FK}
RA20	5/19/2015	$3,060.00	Ca123501	C2323	E111
RA21	5/24/2015	$3,050.00	Ca123501	C4731	E111
RA22	5/31/2015	$25,000.00	Ca123501		E111

Purchase (Economic Increment) Event

Receiving ReportID	Date	Dollar Amount	Receiving ClerkID^{FK}	SupplierID^{FK}	Vendor Invoice#	Invoice Amount	Cash DisbID^{FK}
RR18	4/30/2015	$28,450.00	E111	V7	VI4167	$28,450.00	40
RR19	5/08/2015	$1,100.00	E111	V14	821536	$1,100.00	
RR21	5/10/2015	$3,240.00	E111	V14	821983	$3,240.00	
RR22	5/12/2015	$2,000.00	E111	V7	VI5213	$2,000.00	
RR25	5/12/2015	$480.00	E111	V90	312353	$480.00	

Exhibit 10-1 (cont.) Database Tables for Example Queries

Cash Disbursement (Economic Decrement) Event

DisbVoucherID	VoucherDate	DollarAmount	CheckNbr	CashAcctID^FK	APClerkID^FK	PayeeID^FK
39	5/15/2015	$746.57	41234	Ca123501	E36	E23
40	5/25/2015	$28,450.00	41235	Ca123501	E36	V7
41	5/29/2015	$398.12	41236	Ca123501	E36	E41

Sales Return (Economic Decrement Reversal) Event

Sale ReturnID	Date	Dollar Amount	Receiving ReportNo.	Credit Memo#	Credit MgrID	SaleID^FK	CustomerID^FK	Receiving ClerkID^FK
SR1	5/12/2015	$140.00	RR25	1	E16	12	C2323	E247

Purchase Return (Economic Increment Reversal) Event

Purchase ReturnID	Date	Dollar Amount	Packing Slip#	Debit Memo#	Receiving ReportID^FK	SupplierID^FK	Dept SuperID^FK	Shipping ClerkID^FK
PR3	5/17/2015	$480.00	22	3	RR25	V90	E5	E41

Customer (External Agent)

Customer ID	Name	Address	Telephone	Credit Rating
C2323	Needmore Stuff	86906 Enterprise Court	555-8989	A+
C2831	Targeted One	41352 Price Ln.	555-1771	B+
C4731	Gottahave Moore	1207 Emperor Dr.	555-5688	B
C6125	Don't Wantmuch	3421 Carradine St.	555-9098	A+

Supplier (External Agent)

SupplierID	Name	Address	Telephone	PerformanceRating
V7	Joe's Favorite Vendor	89056 Ransom Hwy.	555-7655	Excellent
V14	Reliable Rudy's	34125 Michigan Ave.	555-1199	Very Good
V90	Trina's Trinkets	1612 Myway Rd.	555-2424	Very Good

Cashier (Internal Agent)

CashierID	Name	Address	Telephone	DateOfBirth
E111	Missy Witherspoon	1710 Crestwood Dr.	555-9392	May 11, 1960
E222	Eponine Eldridge	1003 Zenker Dr.	555-9099	July 29, 1972

Receiving Clerk (Internal Agent)

ClerkID	Name	Address	Telephone	DateOfBirth
E247	Kenneth Barki	4312 Monticello Dr.	556-4891	April 14, 1945
E251	Rita Barki	4312 Monticello Dr.	556-4891	May 22, 1948

Sales Representative (Internal Agent)

Sales Rep ID	Name	Address	Telephone	DateOfBirth
E23	Jimmy Vitale	425 ConAir Drive	555-5678	Aug 18, 1962
E26	Cyndie North	122 Front St.	555-6353	Apr 4, 1961
E30	Wayland Stindt	3506 Carthan St.	555-0621	Dec 29, 1973

Shipping Clerk (Internal Agent)

ShippingClerkID	Name	Address	Telephone	DateOfBirth
E41	Amy Milano	8892 Eddy Ave.	555-9557	January 3, 1964

Exhibit 10-1 (cont.) Database Tables for Example Queries

Department Supervisor (Internal Agent)

DeptSupervisorID	Name	Address	Telephone	DateOfBirth
E5	Patrick Wellesley	53125 Fenton Dr.	555-1112	March 4, 1958

Accounts Payable Clerk (Internal Agent)

APClerkID	Name	Address	Telephone	DateOfBirth
E36	Diane Bowersox	9115 Wolfgang Ct.	555-7244	September 15, 1963

Receiving Clerk (Internal Agent)

ClerkID	Name	Address	Telephone	DateOfBirth
E247	Kenneth Barki	4312 Monticello Dr.	556-4891	April 14, 1945
E251	Rita Barki	4312 Monticello Dr.	556-4891	May 22, 1948

Proposition Relationship (Sales Call – Inventory)

Sales Call ID	Item ID	Customer Reaction to Product
42	BIS1	Negative
42	LIS1	Positive
42	HUS1	Negative
42	TIS1	Positive
42	MIN1	Undecided
43	BIS1	Positive
43	LIS1	Undecided
43	HUS1	Positive
43	TIS1	Negative
43	MIN1	Negative
44	BIS1	Negative
44	LIS1	Negative
44	HUS1	Negative
44	TIS	Negative
44	MIN1	Negative

Proposition2 Relationship (Purchase Requisition – Inventory Type)

PurchReqID	Item ID	QuantityNeeded	EstimatedUnitCost
R17	BIS1	100	$20.00
R17	LIS1	200	$36.00
R17	HUS1	150	$30.00
R17	TIS1	300	$48.00
R18	MIN1	20	$56.00
R18	TTP12	20	$10.00
R19	MIN1	60	$56.00
R19	BIS1	100	$20.00
R20	TTP12	20	$10.00
R21	LIS1	200	$36.00

Exhibit 10-1 (cont.) Database Tables for Example Queries

Reservation Relationship (Sale Order – Inventory Type)

Sales Order ID	Item ID	Quantity Ordered	Quoted Unit Price
14	LIS1	2	70.00
14	TIS1	10	96.00
15	BIS1	40	60.00
15	HUS1	13	50.00
16	MIN1	41	105.00
17	LIS1	120	69.00

Reservation3 Relationship (Purchase Order – Inventory Type)

PurchOrderID	ItemID	QuantityOrdered	QuotedUnitPrice
PO16	BIS1	100	$20.00
PO16	LIS1	200	$35.50
PO16	HUS1	150	$29.00
PO16	TIS1	300	$50.00
PO17	MIN1	20	$55.00
PO18	TTP12	20	$10.00
PO19	MIN1	60	$54.00
PO20	BIS1	100	$20.00
PO21	TTP12	20	$11.00

Fulfillment2 Relationship (Sale Order – Sale)

Sale Order ID	Sale ID
14	12
15	13
16	14
16	15

Fulfillment4 Relationship (Purchase Order – Purchase)

PurchaseOrderID	PurchaseID
PO16	RR18
PO17	RR19
PO18	RR25
PO19	RR21
PO20	RR22

Stockflow Relationship (Sale – Inventory)

Sale ID	Item ID	Quantity Sold	Actual Unit Price
12	LIS1	2	70.00
12	TIS1	10	96.00
13	BIS1	40	60.00
13	HUS1	13	50.00
14	MIN1	20	105.00
15	MIN1	21	105.00

Stockflow3 Relationship (Sale Return – Inventory)

Sale Return ID	Item ID	Quantity Returned	Actual Unit Price	Condition of Goods	Reason Returned
12	LIS1	2	70.00	Perfect	Too big

Exhibit 10-1 (cont.) Database Tables for Example Queries

Stockflow4 Relationship (Purchase – Inventory Type)

PurchaseID	ItemID	PurchaseQuantity	ActualUnitCost
RR18	BIS1	100	$20.00
RR18	LIS1	200	$35.50
RR18	HUS1	150	$29.00
RR18	TIS1	300	$50.00
RR19	MIN1	20	$55.00
RR21	MIN1	60	$54.00
RR22	BIS1	100	$20.00
RR25	TTP12	48	$10.00

Stockflow6 Relationship (Purchase Return – Inventory Type)

PurchReturnID	Item ID	QuantityReturned	ActualUnitCost
PR3	TTP12	48	$10.00

Resource Queries in the Sales/Collection and Acquisition/Payment Processes

Internal and external users may need information regarding an enterprise resource or resource type. A **resource query** is one that asks questions about a single table containing data that describe enterprise resources or resource types. The resources and resource types most commonly present in the Sales/Collection and Acquisition/Payment processes are inventory or services (specifically identified inventory, inventory types, or service types), operating assets, and cash. Users may need either detailed or summarized information about each resource instance or about only those resource instances meeting specific criteria. That information may include all characteristics of the resource instances, or it may include only a subset of the characteristics.

Information regarding inventory, service types, operating assets, and cash that may be needed by internal users (such as salespeople) and by external users (such as customers) includes:

- A list of each inventory item, item type, or service type offered for sale by an enterprise.
- A list of all inventory items, item types, or service types that possess certain characteristics (e.g., all books, real estate listings with lake frontage, toys with selling prices within a certain range, video games in GameBoy Advance format, and preventive dental care services.)
- Quantity on hand of an inventory item type as of a specified date.
- Total cost value of inventory on hand as of a specified date.
- A list of all cash accounts owned by an enterprise as of a specified date.
- Balance in a specific cash account as of a specified date.
- Total balance in all cash accounts as of a specified date.
- A list of general and administrative supply and service types the enterprise purchases and for which the enterprise maintains descriptive data.
- A list of fixed assets owned by an enterprise.
- Book value of a depreciable fixed asset owned by an enterprise on a specified date.
- Average age of an enterprise's machinery on a specified date.

Notice that some of the information needs listed above fall completely within either the sales/collection process or the acquisition/payment process, whereas others require data from both processes and therefore cannot be provided by single-table queries unless the database allows the storage of volatile derivable attributes (triggers). For example, calculation of quantity on hand of inventory requires the use of quantities purchased of inventory along with the quantities sold of inventory. Purchased quantities are part of the acquisition/payment process and quantities sold are part of the sales/collection process. Therefore, unless quantity on hand is stored as a triggered update field attribute in the inventory table, the query will be complex and will involve tables from multiple business processes. Similarly, calculation of the total cash balance requires the use of cash receipts from multiple business processes (primarily financing and sales/collection) and the use of cash disbursements from multiple business processes (primarily from acquisition/payment, payroll, and financing). Therefore unless the balance of each cash account is stored as a triggered update field in the cash resource type table, the query will involve multiple tables from multiple business processes. We will review some of these queries later in this chapter.

A list of each inventory item or item type offered for sale by an enterprise is a query that can be answered using a single-table query of the inventory or inventory type table. The structured query language code for this query based on the tables in Exhibit 10-1 is

SELECT * FROM InventoryType;

The asterisk (*) is a wild card that indicates all characteristics of the inventory type are to be included in the answer. There is no WHERE clause, because all instances of inventory type are to be included. Notice that because there is no selection of specific instances nor any projection of characteristics, the answer is simply a listing of the inventory type table. In Microsoft Access, therefore, the information can be obtained by simply opening the inventory type table in datasheet view. Or a query could be constructed with SQL as noted above; the same query in Query-By-Example (QBE) format is displayed along with the query result in Exhibit 10-2.

Exhibit 10-2 Microsoft Access QBE View of Query to List Each Inventory Item Type

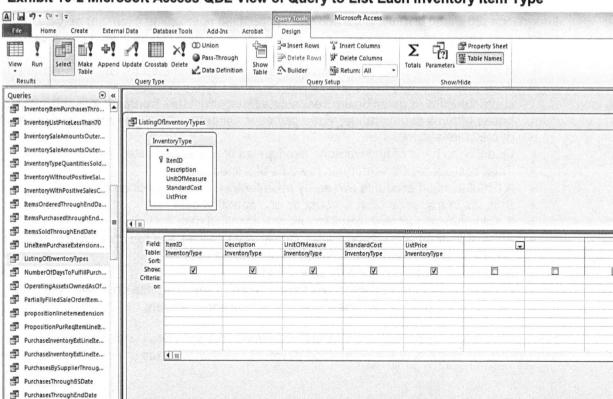

Exhibit 10-2 Continued: Answer for Query to Generate Listing of Inventory Types

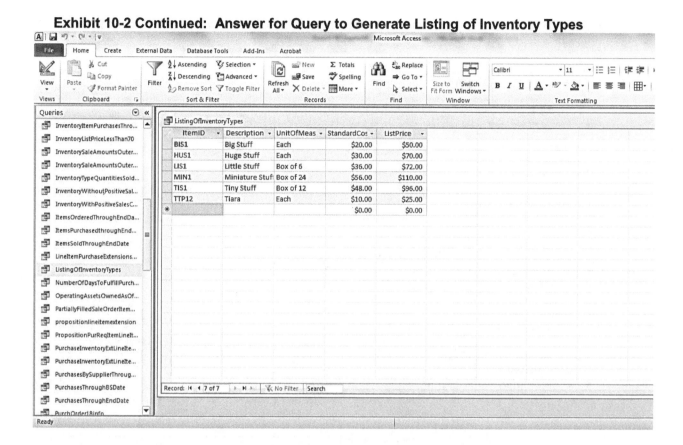

This single-table query could easily be revised to list only the inventory item types that possess specific characteristics, such as those with list selling prices less than $70.00 or those with "each" as a unit of measure. The query also could provide only selected characteristics, for example, when providing inventory information to customers, perhaps the enterprise doesn't want to include the standard cost information. To meet such an information need, a query could be constructed similar to the following query that lists only the description, unit of measure, and list price of those items that have list prices less than $70.00. The SQL code for this query using the tables from Exhibit 10-1 is

SELECT Description, UnitOfMeasure, ListPrice
FROM InventoryType
WHERE ListPrice < 70;

The Microsoft Access QBE and query results are illustrated in Exhibit 10-3.

Exhibit 10-3 Query to List Selected Characteristics of Items with List Price < $70.00

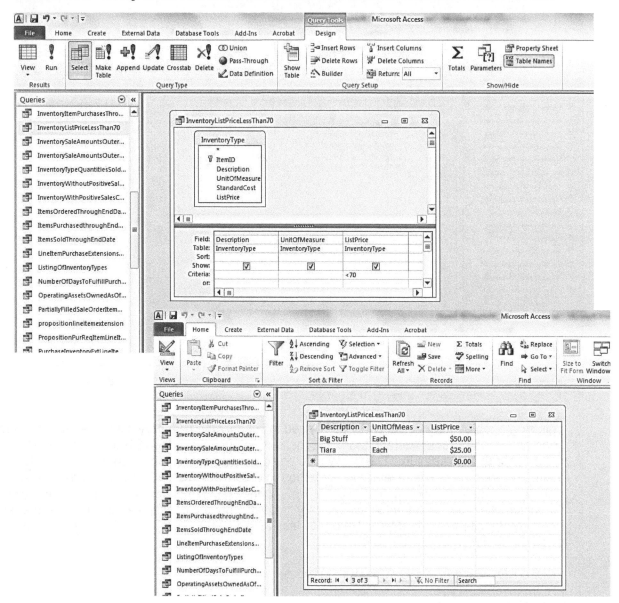

A list of each fixed asset owned by an enterprise on May 31, 2015 is a query that can be answered using a single-table query of the operating assets table, assuming no assets have been disposed of, as the example database does not include adequate information to determine disposals. The structured query language code for this query based on the tables in Exhibit 10-1 is

SELECT *
FROM OperatingAssets
WHERE AcquisitionDate <= 5/31/2015;

The same query in Query-By-Example (QBE) format in Microsoft Access is displayed in Exhibit 10-4, along with the query result.

Exhibit 10-4 QBE to List Each Fixed Asset Owned on 5/31/2015

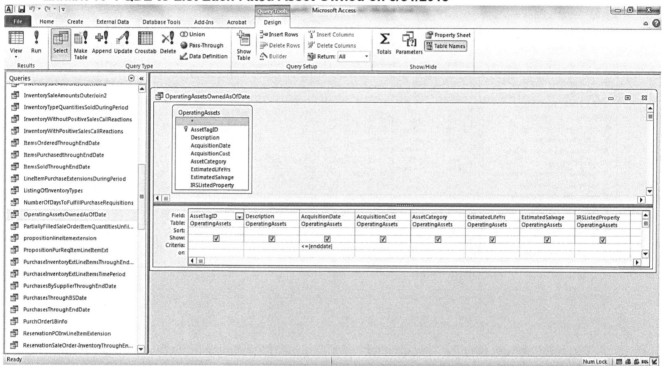

Notice the query is a parameter query (see chapter 9 for a discussion of parameter queries) so the user will see the following window when running the query

Entering the date 5/31/2015 into the parameter window yields the following result

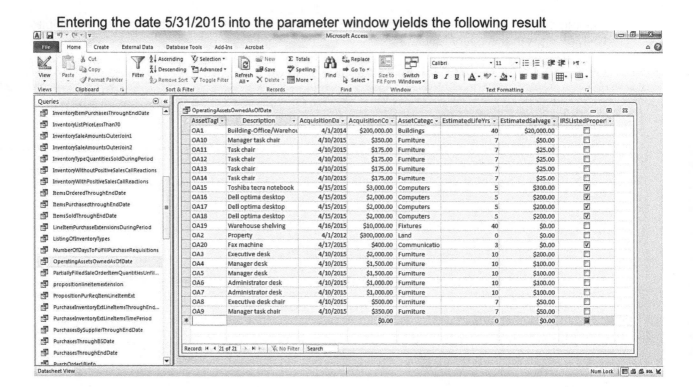

You may wonder why the resource table for operating assets includes the acquisition date as that characteristic may be more appropriately assigned to the relationship between purchase and operating asset. Because the operating assets are each specifically identified, they are not included in the operating asset table until they have been acquired (thus won't have a null value) and the same asset is not purchased multiple times (no redundancy). Hence, there is no design disadvantage to including the characteristic in the asset table. There are query advantages (as in the previous example) to including acquisition date in the asset table; therefore the acquisition date was placed in the asset table.

Of course the query from Exhibit 10-4 could be easily revised to list only the operating assets that possess certain characteristic values; for example, those with estimated salvage values greater than $200 or those classified as listed property by the Internal Revenue Service. To meet information needs such as these, queries could be constructed that are similar to the following query that lists the asset tag Id, description, acquisition date, acquisition cost, estimated useful life in years, and estimated salvage value of all computers owned by the enterprise on May 1, 2015, based on the tables in Exhibit 10-1. The SQL code for this query is

SELECT AssetTagID, Description, AcquisitionDate, AcquisitionCost, EstimatedLifeYrs, EstimatedSalvage
FROM OperatingAssets
WHERE AssetCategory=Computers AND AcquisitionDate<=5/1/2015;

The Microsoft Access QBE and query results are illustrated in Exhibit 10-5.

REA Accounting Systems: Resources-Events-Agents: An ontology for designing, controlling, and using integrated enterprise systems

319

Exhibit 10-5 Query to List Selected Characteristics of Computers Owned as of 5/1/2015

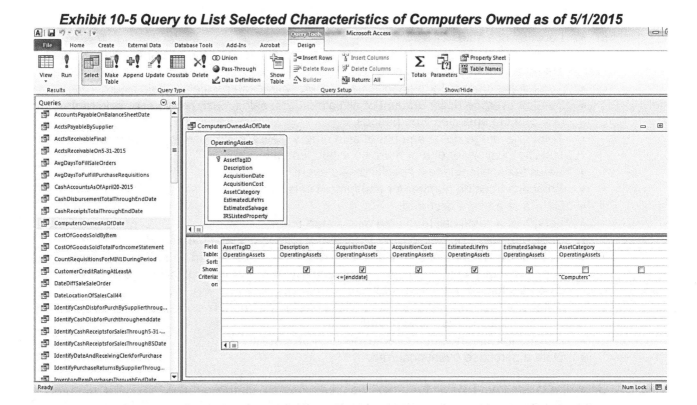

The query in Exhibit 10-5 is a parameter query so to run it we entered the date 5/1/2015 when the parameter window popped up. Notice in the query design that the asset category field is included in the query grid to set the criteria but it does not appear in the answer because the "Show" box is not checked. Finally, notice that to establish the **AND** logic operator for the criteria (thereby including only those records in the answer that meet both criteria), both criteria (acquisitiondate<=[enddate] and assetcategory="computers") are listed on the same line of the query grid. If they were listed on separate lines, the logic operator to combine the criteria would become **OR** and any records that meet either criteria would be included in the answer.

Event Queries

Internal and external users may need information regarding events. An **event query** asks a question that can be answered by using a single table that contains data detailing a set of events. The most common events in the sales/collection process are sales calls, sale orders, sales, cash receipts, and sale returns. The most common events in the acquisition/payment process are purchase requisitions, purchase orders, purchases, cash disbursements, and purchase returns. Users may need either detailed or summarized information about each event or about only those event instances meeting specific criteria.

Examples of information needs in the sales/collection and acquisition/payment process are

- Location of a sales call
- Total number of sales calls, sale orders, or sales that occurred at a specified location or during a specified time period
- Total dollar amount for a specific sale order, sale, cash receipt, or sale return
- Total or average dollar amount of all sale orders, sales, cash receipts, or sale returns for one or more specified time periods
- Total or average dollar amount of sale orders, sales, cash receipts, or sale returns in a specific location for one or more specified time periods
- Sales tax applicable to a specified sale event
- Shipper's tracking number for a shipment sale event
- Date a sale event occurred
- Length of a sales call (end time minus start time)
- Total number of purchase orders made during a specified time period.
- Total dollar amount for a specific purchase order, general and administrative service and supplies acquisition, operating asset acquisition, inventory acquisition, cash disbursement, or purchase return.
- Total or average dollar amount of all acquisition/payment events of a specified type for one or more specified time periods.
- Seller's tracking number for an expected purchase event.
- Date a purchase event occurred.

Using the tables from Exhibit 10-1, next we create some example queries for similar information needs. For one query a user wants to know the date and location of sales call 44. The SQL code for such a query is

SELECT SalesCallID, Date, Location
FROM SalesCall
WHERE SalesCallID=44;

For Microsoft Access, the QBE and resulting solution are illustrated in Exhibit 10-6.

REA Accounting Systems: Resources-Events-Agents: An ontology for designing, controlling, and using integrated enterprise systems

321

Exhibit 10-6 Query and Result for Date and Location of Sales Call 44

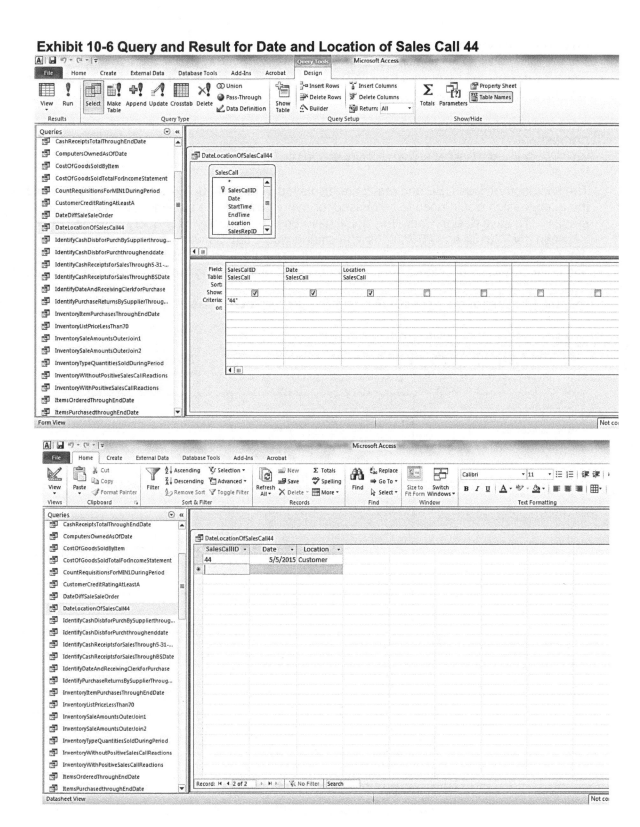

An event query with a vertical aggregation that can be constructed from the tables in Exhibit 10-1 is the total sales dollar amount for a specified time period. Say the accountants need that figure for the income statement they are preparing for the week May 1-7, 2015. The SQL code for this query is

SELECT Sum(DollarTotal)
FROM Sale
WHERE Date BETWEEN 5/1/2015 AND 5/7/2015;

The Microsoft Access QBE and result are displayed in Exhibit 10-7. As written, the dates within the query design would need to be revised for every new income statement the accountants prepare. To save design work, they could have designed a parameter query – instead of Between #5/1/2015# and #5/7/2015#, the criteria would say Between [begin date] and [end date]. When the query is run, first a window will pop up asking the user to enter the begin date and once that value is entered another window will pop up asking the user to enter the end date.

Exhibit 10-7 Microsoft Access QBE and Result for Total Sales May 1-7, 2015

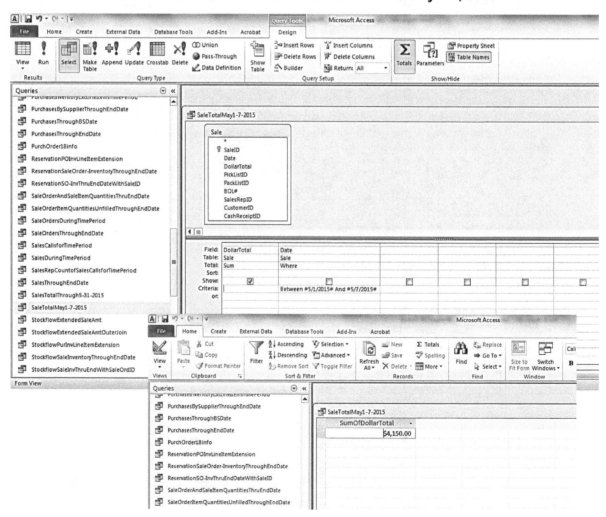

Agent Queries

An **agent query** is a question that can be answered by querying a single table that contains data which describe an internal or an external agent. The internal agents most often present in the sales/collection process are salespersons, credit managers, inventory/shipping clerks, cashiers, and service-providing employees (such as consultants, medical care providers, and waitresses). The internal agents who typically participate in the acquisition/payment process are purchase agents, accounts payable clerks, inventory/receiving clerks, and supervisors. The external agents usually associated with the sales/collection process are customers, clients, patrons, or patients. The external agents most likely to participate in the acquisition/payment process are suppliers or vendors. These lists are not intended to be comprehensive but simply to provide a representative set of potential internal and external agents found in those processes. Users may need either detailed or summarized information about each agent or about only those agent instances that meet specific criteria.

Examples of information needs with respect to various types of agents in the sales/collection and acquisition/payment processes include (but are not limited to):

- A list of all salespeople, cashiers, inventory clerks, credit managers, purchase agents, accounts payable clerks, inventory clerks, or supervisors for an enterprise
- A list of all employees that possess certain characteristics (e.g., all waiters and waitresses who are at least 21 years old, all staff auditors who have passed the CPA exam, or all salespeople whose pay is commission-based)
- A list of all employee names and telephone numbers for an emergency phone tree
- A list of all customers who live in a specific zip code
- A list of all suppliers who are ISO compliant

An example agent query that can be constructed using the tables in Exhibit 10-1 is one that identifies and lists all attributes of customers with at least an "A" credit rating. The SQL code is

```
SELECT *
FROM Customer
WHERE CreditRating ="A" or CreditRating="A+";
```

The Microsoft Access QBE and query result are displayed in Exhibit 10-8.

Exhibit 10-8a Microsoft Access Query for Customers with Credit Rating A or A+

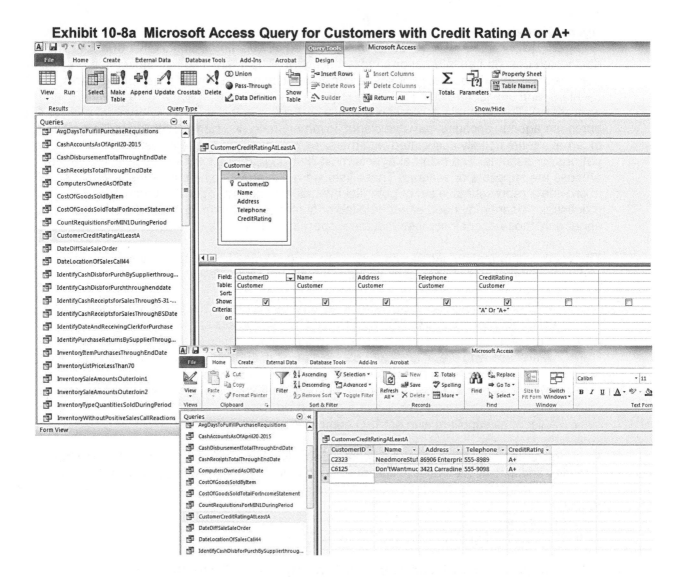

Association Queries

Although resource, event, and agent queries satisfy some information needs, many information needs can be satisfied only by combining information about resources, events, and/or agents. For example, for an event it is not always sufficient to know only what happened (and when and where) but also what resources were affected by or involved in the event, who was affected by or involved in the event, why did the event occur (e.g., what other events led to the event) or what was the result of the event (what subsequent events occurred)? Therefore let's examine each association in the REA business process pattern to study what types of queries help to satisfy information needs arising from these relationships.

REA Accounting Systems: Resources-Events-Agents: An ontology for designing, controlling, and using integrated enterprise systems

325

Duality Association and/or Reversal Association Queries

Duality associations represent exchanges comprised of two or more events, and reversal associations represent the negation of part or all of an exchange. **Duality association queries** ask questions about economic exchanges, and **reversal association queries** ask questions about the negations of exchanges. Some types of information needs with respect to duality associations in general are
- Identification as to whether a specified exchange is completed.
- Identification of completed exchanges for a specified time period.
- Identification of incomplete exchanges for a specified time period.
- Calculation of the amount of claims, such as prepaid expenses, payables, unearned revenues, or receivables, either in total or for a specific exchange event.
- Calculation of the total or average length of the timing differences between the events involved in one or more exchanges.

Queries involving economic events often include adjustments for any reversals of the economic events. Therefore our focus is not only on duality but also on reversal associations.

In the acquisition cycle the most common economic increment and economic decrement events that participate in duality and reversal associations are purchases or service acquisitions, cash disbursements, and purchase returns. If a purchase or service acquisition (increment) occurs without corresponding cash disbursements (decrements) or purchase returns (increment reversals) that total the purchase amount, there exists a claim typically called accounts payable. If a cash disbursement (decrement) occurs without corresponding purchases (increments) that total the cash disbursement amount, there exists a claim typically called prepaid expense. If a purchase return (increment reversal) occurs without corresponding purchases (increments) that total the purchase return amount, then there is an error because something that never happened cannot be reversed.

Some information needs for which queries can be created using the duality relationship in the acquisition/payment process are
- Calculation of the outstanding payable balance for a purchase or service acquisition
- Calculation of total accounts payable at a point in time
- Calculation of prepaid expenses at a point in time
- Aging of accounts payable
- Calculation of the average number of days it takes to pay vendor invoices

Similarly, in the revenue cycle the most common economic decrement and economic increment events that participate in duality and/or reversal associations are sales, rentals, or service engagements, cash receipts, and sale returns. Although the relationship between a sale and a sale return is reversal rather than duality, the reversal of a sale indicates it will not be requited by a cash receipt. If a sale (decrement) occurs without corresponding cash receipts (increments) or sale returns (decrement reversals) that total the sale amount, then there exists a claim that is typically called accounts receivable. The sales invoices that represent the sales for which cash receipts have not yet occurred in full are called open sales invoices. If a cash receipt (increment) occurs without corresponding sales (decrements) that total the cash receipt amount, then there exists a claim that is typically called deferred revenue. If a sale return (decrement reversal) occurs without corresponding sales (decrements) that total the sale return amount, then there is an error because something that never happened cannot be reversed.

Some information needs for which queries can be created using the duality association in the sales/collection process are:

- Calculation of the outstanding receivable balance for a sale, rental, or service engagement invoice
- Creation of an open sales invoice file (a list of open sale invoices)
- Calculation of total accounts receivable at a point in time
- Calculation of prepaid revenue at a point in time
- Aging of accounts receivable
- Calculation of the average number of days it takes to collect receivables

Using the tables in Exhibit 10-1 we can construct a query to calculate the total dollar amount of accounts receivable on a particular date (we call it the balance sheet date because accounts receivable is a line item on an enterprise's balance sheet). Consider the information needed for such a query. Accounts receivable is calculated as the total dollar amount of all sales minus any cash receipts applicable to those sales and minus any sales returns. The calculation should only include those events that occurred during the time period up to and including the balance sheet date. For example, if a sale for $1,000 occurred on June 29, then $200 of the merchandise was returned on July 6 and the customer paid the remaining $800 on July 15, then as of June 30 accounts receivable for the sale was $1,000; as of July 7, accounts receivable for the sale was $800; and as of July 31 accounts receivable for the sale was $0. If the dates are not properly constrained or if the information is not linked together correctly in constructing the query, the result may be incorrect. Notice that there is no beginning date constraint; even if the sale took place last year, if it was not returned nor was cash received to settle the receivable, then it is still a receivable. When bad debts exist, an enterprise may need to add an event entity to the conceptual model for bad debt writeoffs that would also be subtracted from sales in calculating accounts receivable.

Procedures for computing accounts receivable in aggregate are generally as follows:

1) Calculate total sales dollar value through the balance sheet date by using the sale table.

2) Calculate total cash receipts that applied to sales, for which the cash receipts occurred before or on the balance sheet date, using the duality relationship to isolate only those cash receipts that applied to sales (because the cash receipt table may include other cash receipts from financing or purchase returns).

   a. If the duality relationship is represented with a separate table, join the cash receipt table to the duality table, establish the constraint on the cash receipt date, and sum the cash receipt amounts.

   b. If duality is represented with the cash receipt identifier posted as a foreign key in the sale table, then join the cash receipt table to the sale table and establish the constraint on the cash receipt date. Then, in another query, sum the cash receipt amounts (Note: Do not combine these steps into one query, because any cash receipt that paid for multiple sales will be counted multiple times in the sum and your query result will be incorrect.)

REA Accounting Systems: Resources-Events-Agents: An ontology for designing, controlling, and using integrated enterprise systems

327

3) Calculate total sale returns that occurred through the balance sheet date, using the sale return table.

4) Subtract the amounts calculated in steps 2 and 3 from the amount calculated in step 1.

These procedures cannot be accomplished in a single query because steps 1 through 3 each involve vertical aggregations based on different tables and step 4 involves a horizontal calculation using those results. Multiple strategies exist to formulate the queries needed to generate this accounts receivable figure; the queries shown in Exhibit 10-9 are one possibility.

Exhibit 10-9 Queries to Calculate Accounts Receivable as of May 31, 2015

Query Step 1: Total Sales Through May 31, 2015

Exhibit 10-9 cont. Queries to Calculate Accounts Receivable as of May 31, 2015
Query Step 2a: Identify Cash Receipts Applicable to Sales Received Through May 31, 2015

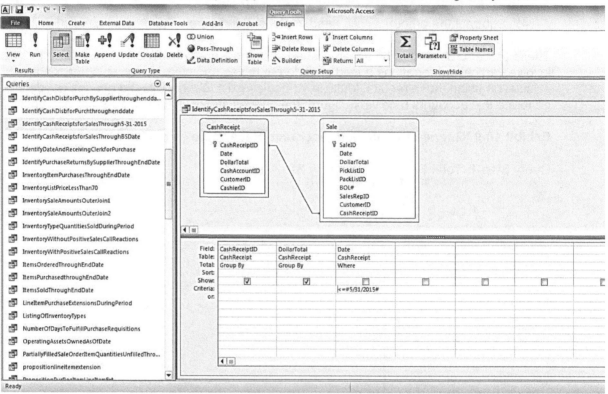

Result of Step 2a: Identify Cash Receipts applicable to Sales Received through May 31, 2015

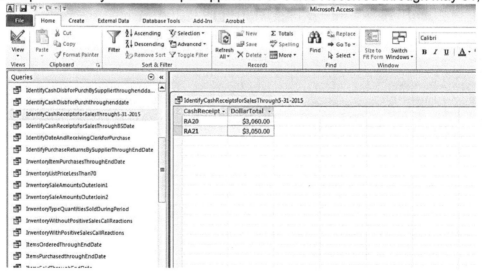

Exhibit 10-9 cont. Queries to Calculate Accounts Receivable as of May 31, 2015

Query Step 2b: Sum Cash Receipts Applicable to Sales Received Through May 31, 2015

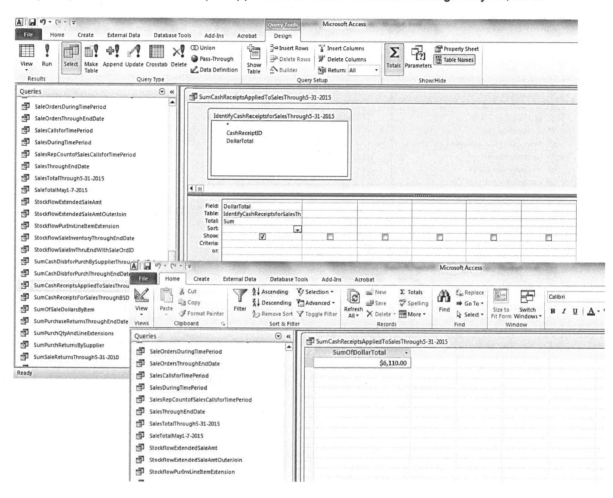

Exhibit 10-9 cont. Queries to Calculate Accounts Receivable as of May 31, 2015

Query Step 3: Total Sale Returns Through May 31, 2015

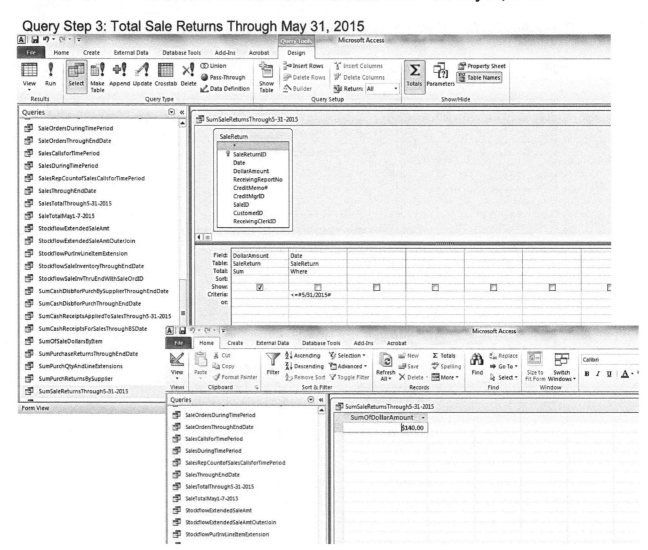

REA Accounting Systems: Resources-Events-Agents: An ontology for designing, controlling, and using integrated enterprise systems

331

Exhibit 10-9 cont. Queries to Calculate Accounts Receivable as of May 31, 2015

Query Step 4: Calculate Query 1 Result – Query 2 Result – Query 3 Result

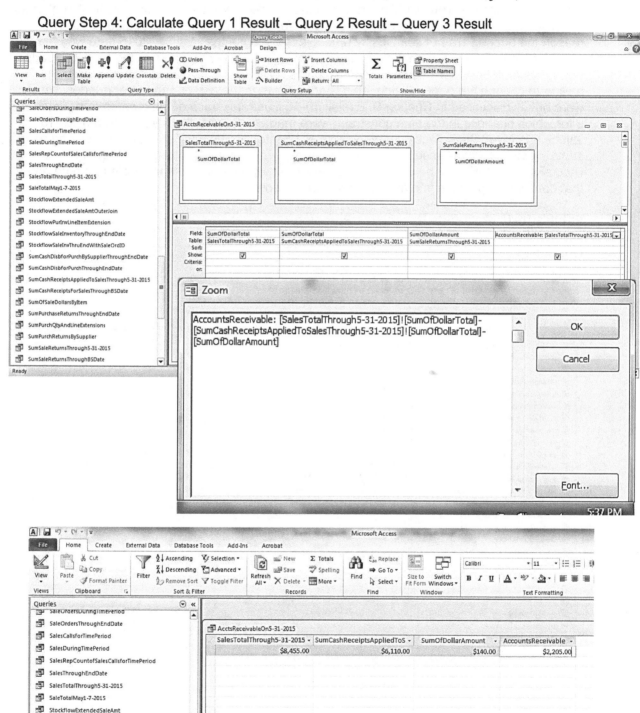

The number of queries it took to generate accounts receivable may dismay you. Especially when you realize that you would need to change the design of the accounts receivable queries when you need to generate accounts receivable for a different date, such as June 30. The reason the queries are not seamlessly reusable is because the May 31, 2015 date was hard-wired into the queries. Fear not! A relatively simple tweak may be made to the May 31 queries that will enable any user to generate an accounts receivable figure as of any date without having to change the query design. This is done through the use of parameter queries, which were briefly discussed in Chapter 9. Exhibit 10-10 illustrates each of the queries from Exhibit 10-9 for which changes in the date constraint were made to remove the hard-wired 5/31/2015 values and insert their places a variable name "bsdate" (for balance sheet date). As long as the same variable name is used in all related queries, when the user runs the final query (AcctsReceivableFinal), the user will only have to enter the balance sheet date one time and that date will be plugged into all the related sub-queries.

Exhibit 10-10 Accounts Receivable Parameter Queries

Query step 1

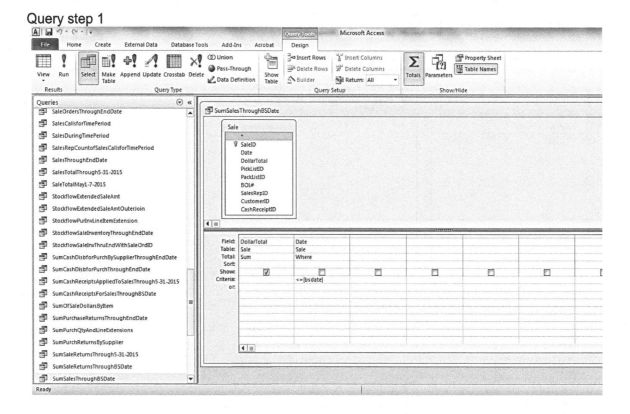

REA Accounting Systems: Resources-Events-Agents: An ontology for designing, controlling, and using integrated enterprise systems

333

Exhibit 10-10 cont. Accounts Receivable Parameter Queries

Query step 2a

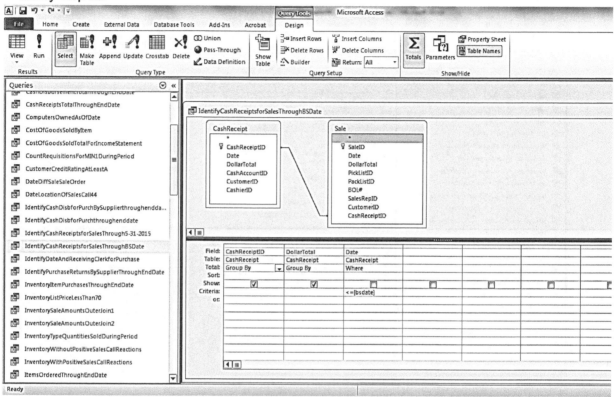

Query step 2b

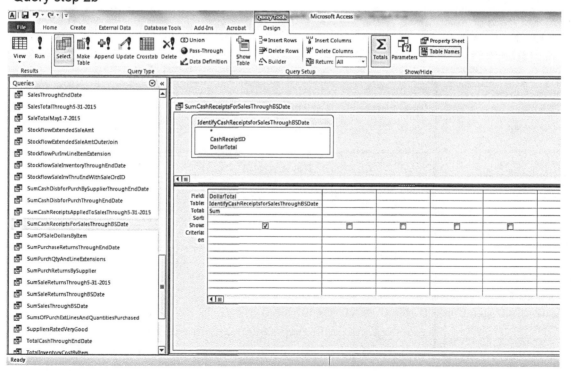

Exhibit 10-10 cont. Accounts Receivable Parameter Queries

Query step 3

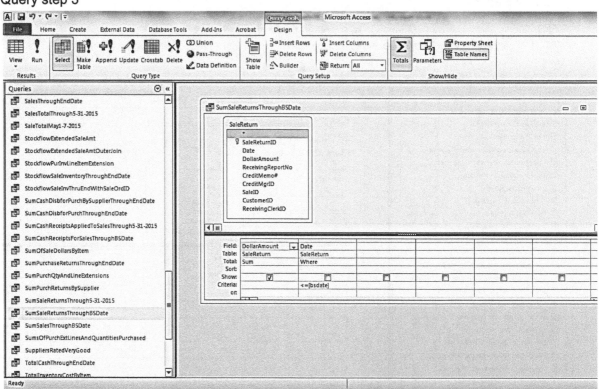

Query step 4

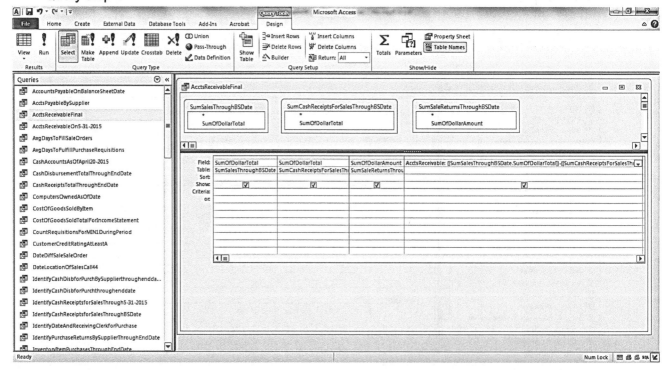

REA Accounting Systems: Resources-Events-Agents: An ontology for designing, controlling, and using integrated enterprise systems

335

Exhibit 10-10 cont. Accounts Receivable Parameter Queries

A user who runs the query "AcctsReceivableFinal" will see:

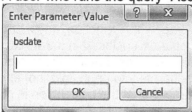

A user who enters 5/31/2015 in the box as bsdate will see:

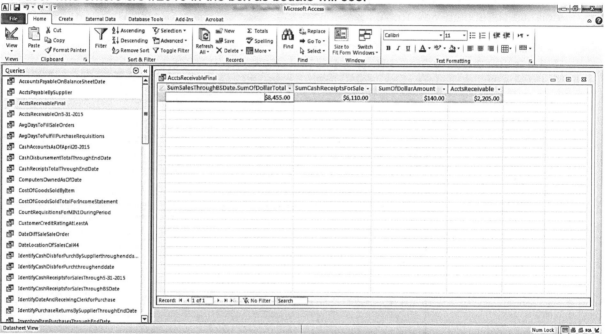

When developing queries, you must test them adequately by entering different dates to ensure a query works for various time periods. The query run with the date 5/31/2015 works fine. However, try running the query with 5/15/2015. It does not work. See Exhibit 10-11.

Exhibit 10-11 Result of Previous Query with May 15, 2015 Balance Sheet Date

The problem is that no cash receipts were applied to sales prior to 5/15/2015, and as a result the field SumCashReceiptsForSales has a null value. In mathematics, a null value cannot be used in a calculation – the result of any expression that includes a null value is also a null value. Therefore, the AcctsReceivable field is also a null value. Microsoft Access has available a **null to zero function** that treats null values as if they are zero. To apply this function, any factor in a query's calculation that could potentially have a null value should be enclosed in parentheses and preceded by Nz. The null to zero function does not actually change a null value to a zero; it simply treats the field as if it were zero. Nz must be applied separately to each field, not applied to the overall calculation, otherwise Access will evaluate whether the entire calculation is null and if so, treat it as zero. That would result in Accounts Receivable of zero, when in fact it should have a balance of $8,315. Exhibit 10-12 illustrates the use of Nz in the calculation for the final query step of Exhibit 10-10 and the resulting answer when the query is run for the balance sheet date May 15, 2015.

Exhibit 10-12 Query Step 4 Revised to Include Nz (Null-to-Zero) Function

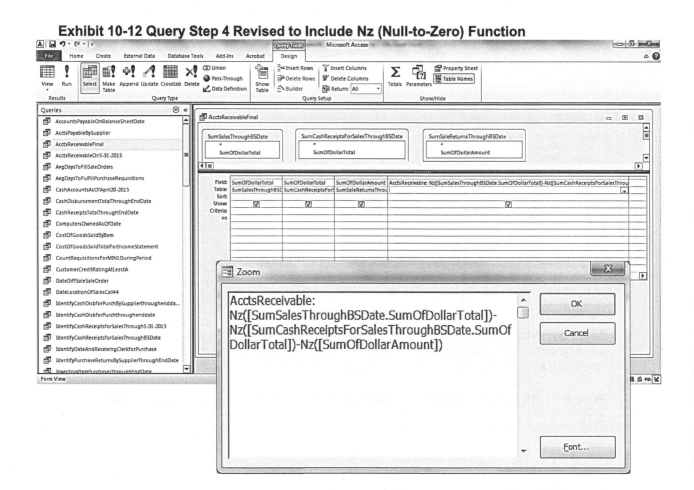

REA Accounting Systems: Resources-Events-Agents: An ontology for designing, controlling, and using integrated enterprise systems

337

Exhibit 10-12 cont. Query Step 4 Revised to Include Nz (Null-to-Zero) Function

Result for May15, 2015 balance sheet date

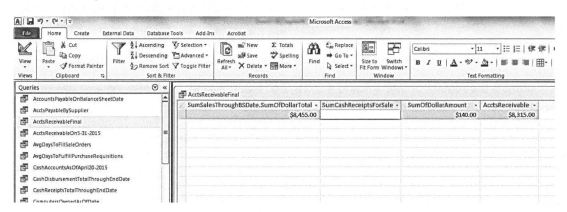

Using the tables in Exhibit 10-1 we can construct a similar set of queries to calculate the total dollar amount of accounts payable for a balance sheet date. Accounts payable is calculated as the total dollar amount of all acquisitions minus any cash disbursements applicable to those purchases and minus any purchase returns. The calculation should include only those events that occurred during the time period up to and including the balance sheet date. For example, if a purchase for $3,000 occurred on June 29, and then $600 of the merchandise was returned on July 6 and the company paid the remaining $2,400 on July 15, then as of June 30 accounts payable for the purchase was $3,000; as of July 7, accounts payable for the purchase was $2,400; and as of July 31 accounts payable for the purchase was $0. If the dates are not properly constrained in the query or if the query does not link the fields together properly, the result will be inaccurate. Notice that there is no beginning date constraint; even if the purchase took place last year, if it was not returned nor paid for, then it is still payable.

Procedures for computing accounts payable in aggregate are generally as follows: Determine what kinds of acquisitions are represented in your database (do NOT include labor acquisitions, because unpaid labor acquisitions are called wages payable rather than accounts payable) and for each kind of acquisition follow these steps:

1. Determine which table contains the acquisition date and dollar amount (usually these are found in the acquisition event table).

2. Sum the acquisition amount through the balance sheet date (with no beginning date constraint).

3. Determine which tables contain the cash disbursements that applied to those acquisitions and calculate the applicable cash disbursements total. To determine this, examine the duality relationship.

   a. When the duality relationship is represented with a separate table, join the duality table to the cash disbursement table, establish the ending date constraint on the cash disbursement date field (with no beginning date constraint), and sum the cash disbursement amount applied to the acquisition.

b. When the duality relationship is represented with the cash disbursement identifier posted as a foreign key into the acquisition table, join the cash disbursement table to the acquisition table, establish the ending date constraint on the cash disbursement date field (with no beginning date constraint), and sum the cash disbursement amounts.

4. Calculate total purchase returns that occurred through the balance sheet date, using the purchase returns table.

5. Subtract the results of steps 3 and 4 from the result of step 2 to get accounts payable as of the balance sheet date.

These procedures cannot be accomplished in a single query because steps 1 through 4 each involve vertical aggregations based on different tables and step 5 involves a horizontal calculation using those results. Exhibit 10-13 outlines a set of queries to calculate accounts payable for inventory acquisitions for the tables in Exhibit 10-1. Additional queries would be needed to calculate accounts payable for operating asset purchases and general and administrative supply and service acquisitions (notice that the partial set of tables in Exhibit 10-1 does not include sufficient detail of those acquisitions to be able to calculate the payables for those). The set of queries in Exhibit 10-13 is constructed in parameter format to increase re-usability, and the final query uses the Nz function for the same reasons discussed with respect to the accounts receivable queries.

Exhibit 10-13 Queries to Calculate Accounts Payable for Inventory Purchases

Query Steps 1and 2: Determine Acquisition Types and Sum Acquisition Dollar Amounts Through the Balance Sheet Date.

Note: For the partial database table set given, purchases of inventory are the only acquisitions for which enough detail is given to compute accounts payable.

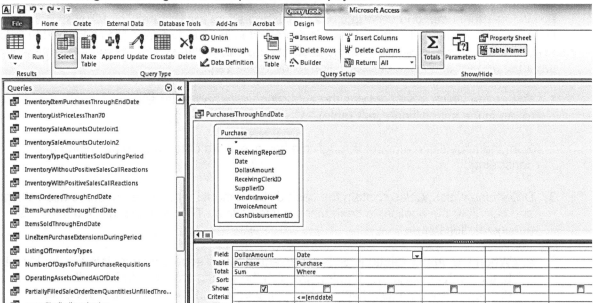

Exhibit 10-13 cont. Queries to Calculate Accounts Payable for Inventory Purchases

Result for May 31, 2015

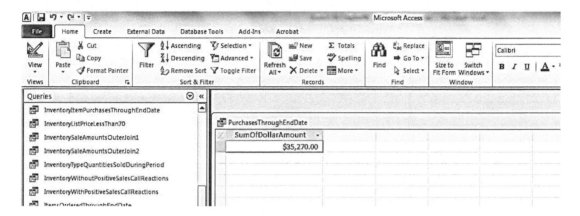

Query Step 3a: Identify Cash Disbursements Applicable to Purchases for which Payment was Made Prior to or on Balance Sheet Date

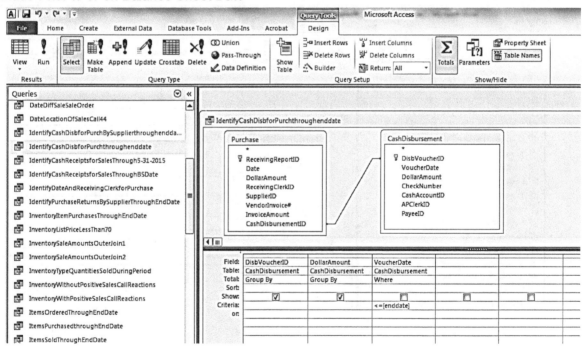

Exhibit 10-13 cont. Queries to Calculate Accounts Payable for Inventory Purchases

Result for May 31, 2015

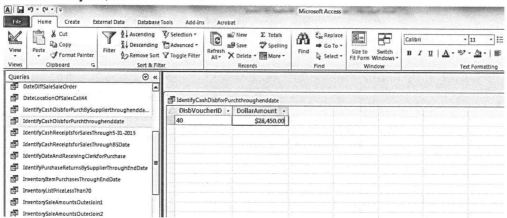

Query Step 3b: Sum Cash Disbursements Applicable to Purchases Paid Through Balance Sheet Date

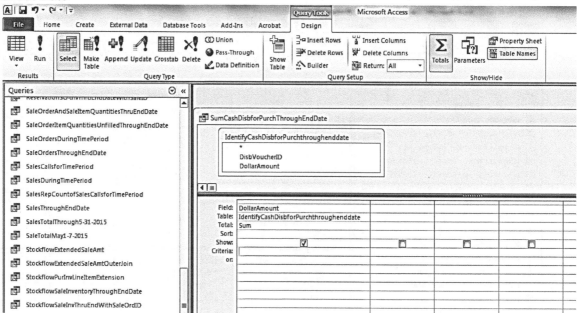

Exhibit 10-13 cont. Queries to Calculate Accounts Payable for Inventory Purchases

Result for May 31, 2015

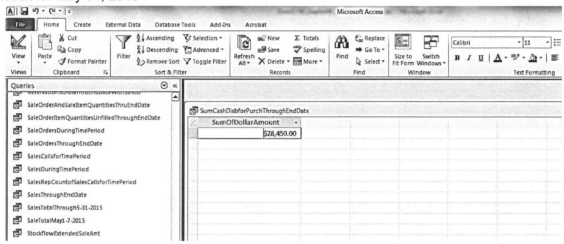

Query Step 4: Calculate Total Purchase Returns Through Balance Sheet Date

Exhibit 10-13 cont. Queries to Calculate Accounts Payable for Inventory Purchases

Result for May 31, 2015

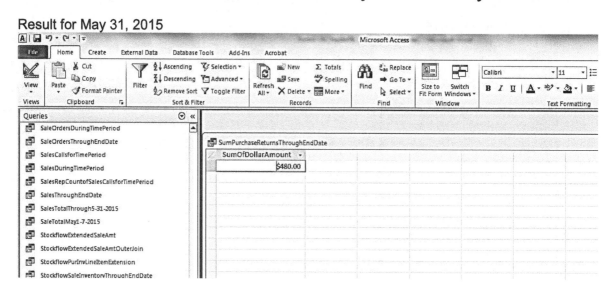

Query Step 5: Calculate Query 2 Result – Query 3 Result – Query 4 Result

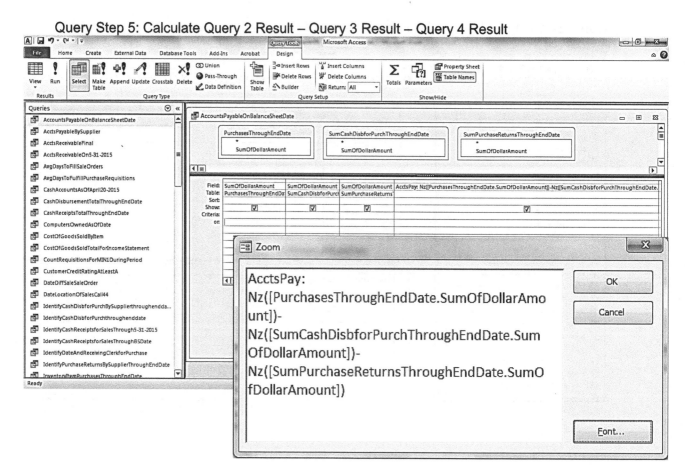

Exhibit 10-13 cont. Queries to Calculate Accounts Payable for Inventory Purchases

Result for May 31, 2015

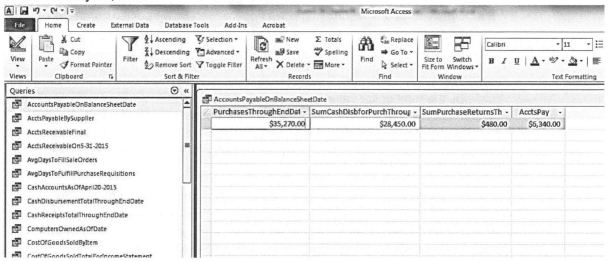

PurchasesThroughEndDat	SumCashDisbforPurchThroug	SumPurchaseReturnsTh	AcctsPay
$35,270.00	$28,450.00	$480.00	$6,340.00

Stockflow Association Queries

Stockflow associations represent relationships between economic increment or decrement events and the resources that are increased or decreased by those events. A **stockflow association query** is one that attempts to satisfy information needs about the effect of economic events on resources or about the resources involved in events. Some common information needs are:

- What resources or resource types were increased or decreased by an economic event?
- What quantity of a resource or resource type was increased or decreased by an economic event?
- What dollar value of a resource or resource type was increased or decreased by an economic event?
- When did an event increase or decrease a specific resource or resource type?
- Where did an event increase or decrease a specific resource or resource type?

Such information needs can require detailed descriptions of specific transactions or they may require aggregations such as sums or averages. The preceding types of information may be used as part of a trend analysis to project future events and their expected effects on resources or resource types, and/or they may be compared to similar information for competitors to gauge the level of competitive advantage (or disadvantage) the enterprise may have.

Within the acquisition/payment process, some common information needs of these types are
- Which inventory types were increased by a specific purchase event?
- What quantity of each inventory type was increased by a specific purchase event?
- Which inventory types were decreased by a purchase return event?
- What quantity of each inventory type was decreased by a specific purchase return event?
- What unit cost was charged for an inventory type on a specific purchase event?
- What unit cost was granted as credit for an inventory type on a specific purchase return event?
- What was the total dollar value of purchases for a specified time period? (Note: If the total purchase dollar amount is stored in the purchase event table, then it is not necessary to use the stockflow relationship to meet this information need.)
- What is the average dollar value of purchases of a specified inventory type for a specified time period?

Within the sales/collection process, some common information needs of these types are
- Which inventory types were decreased by a specific sale event?
- What quantity of each inventory type was decreased by a specific sale event?
- Which inventory types were increased by a sale return event?
- What quantity of each inventory type was increased by a specific sale return event?
- What selling price was charged for an inventory type on a specific sale event?
- What selling price was granted as credit for an inventory type on a specific sale return event?
- What was the total dollar value of sales for a specified time period? (Note: If the total sale amount is stored in the sale event table, then it is not necessary to use the stockflow relationship to meet this information need.)
- What is the average dollar value of sales of a specified inventory type for a specified time period?

Assume a marketing manager has requested two reports of sales dollars by inventory item to see which inventory item has generated the most sales and the least. The first report covers the week of May 1-7, 2015 and the second report covers the week of May 8-14, 2015. In each report, the manager wants the ItemID, the item description, and the total sales dollar amount for each item. How would you construct a query from the tables in Exhibit 10-1 to meet the manager's need?

Begin by examining the tables to see which tables you need. Because this query combines information about sales and inventory, you need to look at the stockflow association and related classes and determine which of the database tables represent those constructs. Then examine those tables to see which contain the relevant information. In this case the Sale, InventoryType, and StockflowSaleInventory tables contain the desired information. Exhibit 10-14 displays the Microsoft Access QBE and result. The query is constructed as a parameter query so that the same query may be run for each week.

Exhibit 10-14: Queries to Determine Dollar Value Sold of Each Inventory Item

Query Step 1 Join tables, Constrain dates, and Extend Sale Amounts

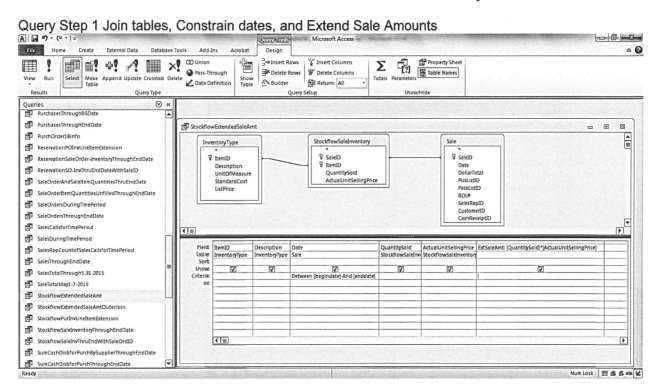

Query Step 2 Sum Extended Sale Amounts for Each Item

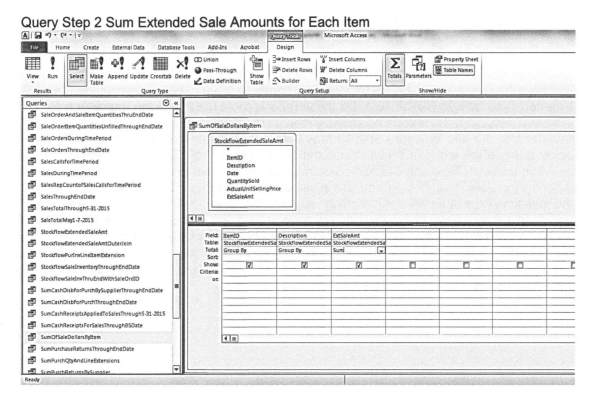

Exhibit 10-14 cont.: Queries to Determine Dollar Value Sold of Each Inventory Item

Result for May 1-7, 2011

Result for May 8-14, 2010

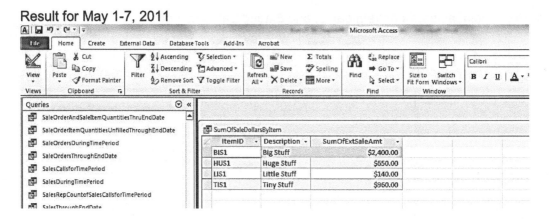

Examine the results in Exhibit 10-14. Carefully compare them to each other and to the InventoryType table in Exhibit 10-1. Do these reports meet the marketing manager's need? No. Why not? Although the reports adequately identify the item with the highest dollar sales (Big Stuff for May 1-7 and Miniature Stuff for May 8-14), they do not display the items with lowest dollar sales, which are in fact those items that haven't sold at all. That is because the join type between InventoryType and StockflowSaleInventory is an inner join, which results in a solution that only includes instances with matching values in both tables. To keep instances that exist in the InventoryType table without matching values in the StockflowSaleInventory table, the join type between those two tables must be changed to an outer join. Because the Query Step 1 as shown in Exhibit 10-14 contains three tables, the join between InventoryType and StockflowSaleInventory cannot simply be changed to an outer join. Three table outer joins are too ambiguous for Access to understand. Exhibit 10-15 illustrates the revised query steps that better satisfy the marketing manager's information need.

REA Accounting Systems: Resources-Events-Agents: An ontology for designing, controlling, and using integrated enterprise systems

347

Exhibit 10-15 Queries to Identify Highest and Lowest Selling Inventory

Query Step 1 Constrain Dates and Calculate Extended Sale Amounts for Inventory Sales

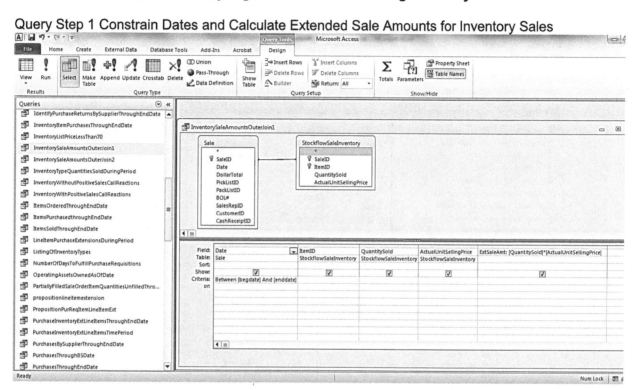

Query Step 2 Join Extended Sale Amounts for Sold Inventory to Inventory Type Table

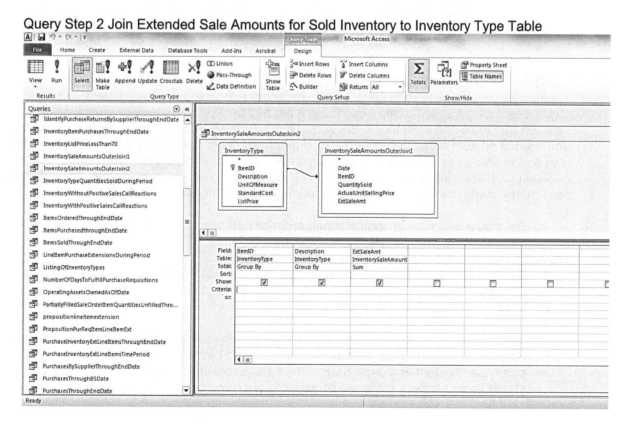

Exhibit 10-15 cont.: Queries to Identify Highest and Lowest Selling Inventory

Results for May 1-7, 2015 and for May 8-14, 2015

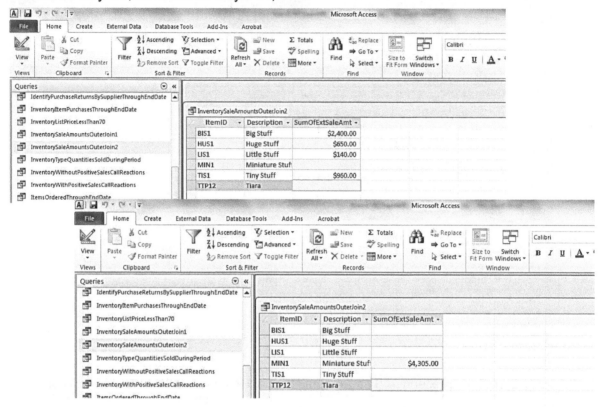

Weighted Average Unit Costing

Enterprises commonly need to calculate the weighted average unit cost of inventory items purchased during a specific time period. Such a query involves the stockflow relationship between purchase and inventory in the acquisition/payment process. The **weighted average unit cost** of an item is calculated as the total purchase dollar amount for that item during the time period divided by the total quantity purchased of that item during the time period. The general procedures for determining weighted average unit cost (i.e., the **weighted average unit cost query steps**) for each inventory item during a time period are as follows.

1. Determine which table contains the purchase date attribute (usually this is in the table that represents the purchase economic event).

2. Determine which table contains the purchase quantities and actual unit cost information (usually these attributes are in the table that represents the stockflow relationship between purchase and inventory).

3. Join the tables together, set the date constraints (beginning and ending dates for desired time period) and multiply the quantities purchased by the actual unit costs to get the total purchase line-item amounts. Note: If the total purchase line-item amount is already stored as an attribute in the stockflow table, then you don't need to calculate it.

REA Accounting Systems: Resources-Events-Agents: An ontology for designing, controlling, and using integrated enterprise systems

349

4. Group the result from step 3 by inventory item and sum the purchase quantity and the total purchase line-item dollar amount.

5. Start with the result from step 4 and, still grouping by inventory item, divide the sum of the total purchase line item by the sum of the total purchased quantity.

Exhibit 10-16 displays the Microsoft Access QBE and result for the queries to provide the requested information for the weighted average unit cost for inventory types purchased in a specified time period. The query is constructed as a parameter query so that the query may be run for alternative time periods.

Note on Weighted Average Unit Costing for Financial Statements
The procedures described are only for use in the time period in which the items are purchased. When using weighted average unit cost for valuing Cost of Goods Sold on the Income Statement or Inventory on the Balance Sheet, Step 3 will need to be modified to use only an ending date constraint. The modification is needed because the time period for which the Income Statement is calculated may not be the same as the time period in which the inventory items are purchased. For example, items that are purchased in March may be sold in April. If the query is intended to value cost of goods sold for the month of April, the seemingly logical beginning date constraint to use is April 1. However, if April 1 is set as a beginning date constraint, those items will not be assigned a cost value because they weren't purchased during April. Because the weighted average unit cost flow assumption indicates no physical matching of items sold to items purchased, no beginning date constraint can be used. To avoid having unreasonably old inventory costs assigned to Cost of Goods Sold and Inventory, a company may instead want to use a moving weighted average which would require programming and is beyond the scope of this textbook.

Exhibit 10-16 Queries to Determine Weighted Average Unit Cost of Inventory Types

Join Purchase & Stockflow Tables, Constrain Purchase Date, Calculate Line Item Extensions

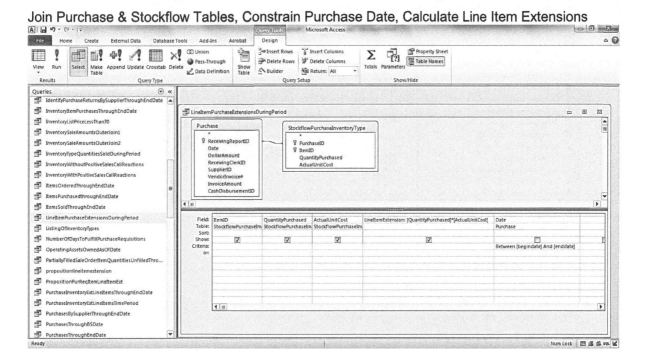

Exhibit 10-16 cont.: Queries to Determine Weighted Average Unit Cost of Inventory Types

Sum Purchase Quantities and Line Item Extensions for Each Item Id

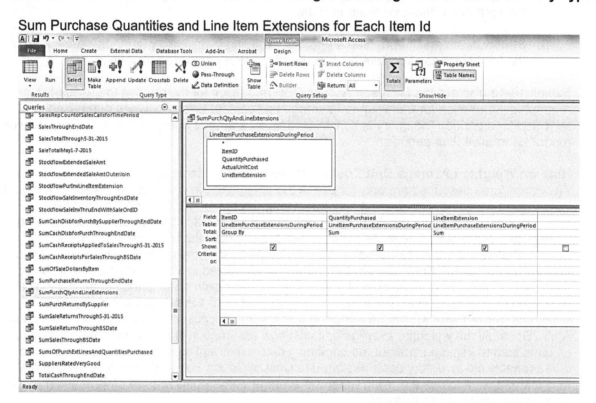

Divide Total Line Item Extensions by Total Purchase Quantities for Each Item Id

Exhibit 10-16 cont.: Queries to Determine Weighted Average Unit Cost of Inventory Types

Result for May 1-31, 2015

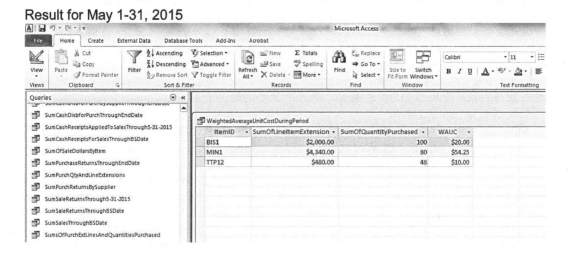

WeightedAverageUnitCostDuringPeriod

ItemID	SumOfLineItemExtension	SumOfQuantityPurchased	WAUC
BIS1	$2,000.00	100	$20.00
MIN1	$4,340.00	80	$54.25
TTP12	$480.00	48	$10.00

Fulfillment Association Queries

Fulfillment associations are similar to duality associations in that both associations represent relationships between events. Whereas duality associations focus on economic exchanges, fulfillment associations focus on events that led up to the economic exchanges. A **fulfillment association query** is one that answers one or more questions about the relationship between an instigation event and the commitment event to which it led or about the relationship between a commitment event and the resulting economic event. Therefore some of the information needs to be satisfied with fulfillment relationships include:

- Identification of unfulfilled commitments or instigation events
- Identification of fulfilled commitments or instigation events
- Identification of commitment events that were not preceded by instigation events, or identification of economic events that were not preceded by commitment events
- Calculation of length of time between instigation and commitment events or between commitment and economic events
- Identification of causes of commitments and/or of economic events
- Identification of results of instigations and/or of commitment events

In the acquisition/payment process the most common instigation events are purchase requisitions; the most common commitment events that fulfill the purchase requisitions are purchase orders; and the most common economic increment events that fulfill the purchase orders are purchases (i.e., receipt of goods or services). If a purchase requisition occurs without a corresponding purchase order, the purchase requisition is unfulfilled. If a purchase order occurs without a corresponding purchase, the purchase order is unfulfilled. Some information needs for which queries can be created using the fulfillment relationships in the acquisition/payment process are:

- List of unfilled purchase orders
- Identification of filled purchase requisitions (i.e., those purchase requisitions that resulted in purchase orders)
- Calculation of average number of days the enterprise takes to fill purchase requisitions for a given time period
- Identify the purchase order that corresponds to a purchase

In the sales/collection process the most common instigation events are sales calls; the most common commitment events that fulfill the sales calls are sale orders, rental contracts, or service engagement contracts; and the most common economic decrement events that fulfill the sale orders are sales, rentals, or service engagements. If a sales call occurs without a corresponding sale order, the sales call is unfulfilled. If a sale order occurs without a corresponding sale, the sale order is unfulfilled. A list of unfilled sales orders is often called an open sales order file. Some example information needs for which queries can be created using the fulfillment relationships in the sales/collection process are

- List of open sale orders
- Identification of successful sales calls (i.e., those sales calls that resulted in orders)
- Calculation of number of average days the enterprise takes to fill sale orders

Using the tables in Exhibit 10-1, a query can be constructed to calculate the number of days the enterprise took to fill each sale order, and a further query can be constructed to calculate the average number of days the enterprise takes to fill sale orders for that time period. Exhibit 10-17 illustrates the queries needed to satisfy these information needs. Note that if the date fields must be designed as Date/Time fields in order to be subtracted to calculate the number of days to fill the order.

Exhibit 10-17 Calculation of Days to Fill Sale Orders

Query Step 1 Calculate Number of Days to Fill Each Sale Order (result for May 2015 orders)

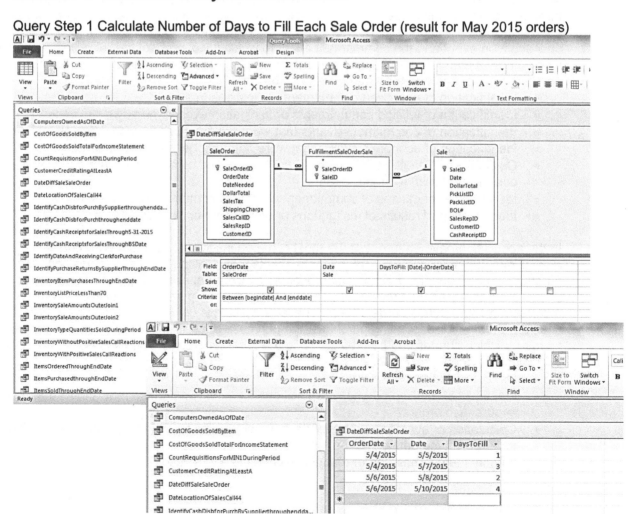

REA Accounting Systems: Resources-Events-Agents: An ontology for designing, controlling, and using integrated enterprise systems

353

Exhibit 10-17 cont.: Calculation of Days to Fill Sale Orders

Query Step 2 Calculate Average of Days to Fill Orders

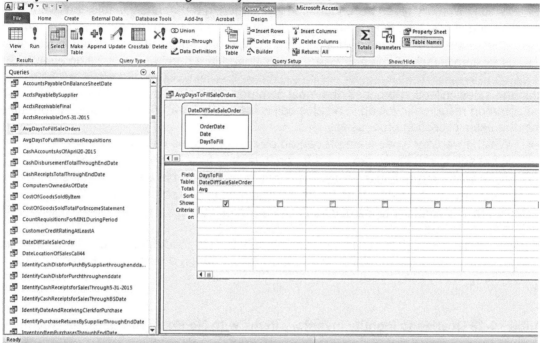

Result of Query Step 2 for May 2015

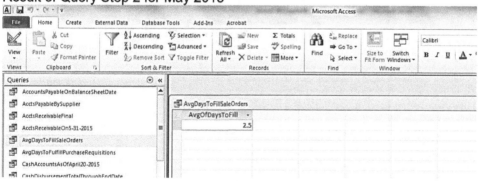

Proposition Association Queries

Proposition associations represent relationships between instigation events and the resources the events propose to increase or decrease. A **proposition association query** is one created to satisfy information needs about the proposed effect of instigation events on resources or about the resources involved in instigation events. Some common information needs are

- What resources or resource types does the instigation event propose to increase or decrease?
- What quantity of a resource or resource type is the proposed increase or decrease for an instigation event?
- When did an instigation event propose to increase or decrease a specific resource or resource type?

Within the acquisition/payment process, the most common instigation events are purchase requisitions, and the most common resource involved in a purchase requisition is inventory type. Some common information needs within the acquisition/payment process are

- Which inventory types were identified as needed in a purchase requisition event?
- What unit cost was estimated for an inventory type in a purchase requisition event?
- How many times has a specified inventory type been requisitioned during a time period?
- How many types of inventory were requisitioned in a purchase requisition event?

Within the sales/collection process, the most common instigation events are sales calls, and the most common resource involved in a sales call is inventory type. Some common information within the sales/collection process are

- Which inventory types were presented as part of a sales call event?
- What selling price was proposed for an inventory type in a specific sales call event?
- What was the reaction to each inventory type presented in a specific sales call event?
- Have any inventory types never been presented in any sales call event?
- How many different types of inventory were presented in a specific sales call event?

Using the tables in Exhibit 10-1, a query can be constructed to identify which (if any) inventory items have never received a positive customer reaction during a sales call. Exhibit 10-18 displays the query needed to satisfy this information need.

Exhibit 10-18 Queries to Identify Inventory Items with No Positive Customer Reactions

Query Step 1 Identify Items in Sales Calls with Positive Reactions

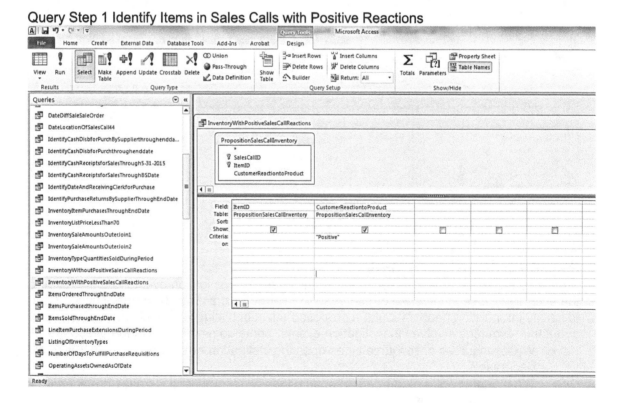

Exhibit 10-18 cont. Queries to Identify Inventory Items with No Positive Customer Reactions

Query Step 2 Outer Join InventoryType to Positive Reactions, Identify Those Without Positives

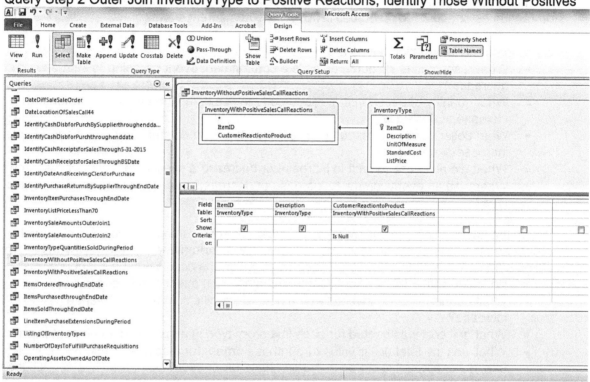

Result

Reservation Association Queries

Reservation associations represent relationships between commitment events and the resources the events are committing to increase or decrease. A **reservation association query** is one that attempts to satisfy information needs about the eventual effect of commitment events on resources or about the resources involved in commitment events.

Some common information needs are
- What resources or resource types is a commitment event agreeing to increase or decrease?
- What quantity of a resource or resource type is a commitment event agreeing to increase or decrease?
- What dollar value of a resource or resource type is a commitment event agreeing to increase or decrease?
- When did an event commit to increase or decrease a specific resource or resource type?
- Where did an event commit to increase or decrease a specific resource or resource type?

Within the acquisition/payment process, the most common commitment events are purchase orders and the most common resource associated with commitment events is inventory type. Some common information needs of these types within the acquisition/payment process are
- Which inventory types does a specific commitment event agree to increase?
- What quantity of each inventory type does a specific commitment event agree to increase?
- What unit cost was quoted for each inventory type in a specific commitment event?
- What was the total dollar value of purchase orders for a specified time period? (Note: If total dollar amount is stored in the purchase order event table, then it is not necessary to use the reservation relationship to meet this information need.)
- What is the average dollar value of purchase orders of a specified inventory type for a specified time period?

Within the sales/collection process, the most common commitment events are sale orders and the most common resource associated with commitment events is inventory type. Some common information needs of these types within the sales/collection process are
- Which inventory types does a specific commitment event agree to decrease?
- What quantity of each inventory type does a specific commitment event agree to decrease?
- What selling price was quoted for each inventory type in a specific commitment event?
- What was the total dollar value of sale orders for a specified time period? (Note: If the total dollar amount is stored in the sale order event table, then it is not necessary to use the reservation relationship to meet this information need.)
- What is the average dollar value of sale orders of a specified inventory type for a specified time period?

Because these queries are very similar to the examples already illustrated for the proposition and stockflow association queries, no additional examples are displayed in detail.

REA Accounting Systems: Resources-Events-Agents: An ontology for designing, controlling, and using integrated enterprise systems

357

Participation Association Queries

Participation associations represent relationships between various events and the agents who participate in the events. A **participation association query** is one that attempts to satisfy information needs for identification of which agents participated in events or the events in which agents have participated. Any common information needs on this list could be required for either internal or external agents.

- Which agents participated in a specified event?
- In how many events of a specified type has a specified agent participated?
- What is the total dollar value of events of a specific type in which a specified agent has participated for a specified time period?
- When did a specified event in which a specified agent participated occur?
- Where did a specified event in which a specified agent participated occur?

Within the acquisition/payment process, some common information needs of these types are:

- From which supplier was a purchase made?
- By which purchase agent was a purchase order placed?
- How many purchase orders did a purchase agent make during a time period?
- What is the total or average dollar amount of purchases made by each purchasing agent during a specified time period?
- When was a purchase received, and by which receiving clerk (include clerk's Id, name, and telephone number)?
- To which supplier have the most purchase returns been made?

Within the sales/collection process, some common information needs of these types are

- To which customer was a sale made?
- By which salesperson was a sale order accepted?
- How many sales calls did a specified salesperson make during a specified time period?
- What is the total (or average) dollar amount of sales made by each salesperson during a specified time period?
- When was a shipment sent to a customer?
- Where did a sales call to a customer take place?

Using the database tables in Exhibit 10-1, a query can be constructed to calculate the number of sales calls made by each salesperson for a time period. The tables needed are SalesCall and Salesperson, since the relevant participation relationship is implemented with SalespersonID posted as a foreign key in the SalesCall table. Exhibit 10-19 displays the query.

Exhibit 10-19 Query for Number of Sales Calls Made by Each Salesperson in a Time Period

Query Step 1 Constrain Dates on Sales Calls

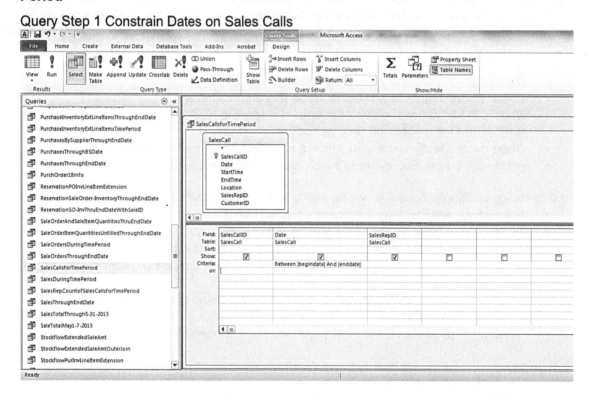

Query Step 2 Join Sales Calls to Sales Representatives and Count Sales Calls Made by Each, with results for May 1-15, 2015

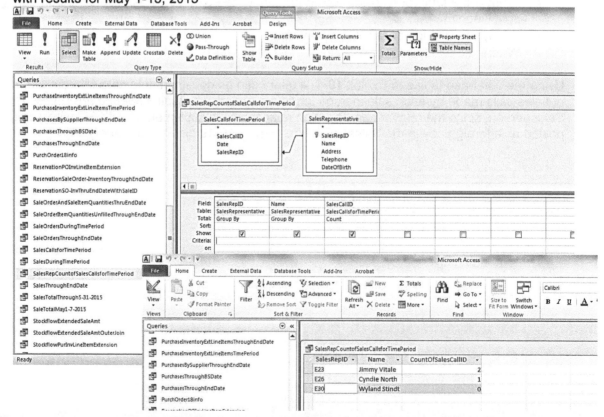

You may be wondering why the query in Exhibit 10-19 was constructed in two steps rather than combining both steps into one. If both steps are combined, any sales representative who has not made any sales calls during the time period identified by the date constraints will not appear in the solution at all; thus E30 Wyland Stindt does not appear on the list. Try it!

CONCLUDING COMMENTS

This chapter applied the information retrieval concepts discussed in chapter 9 to the revenue and acquisition cycles discussed in chapters 3, 6 and 7 to illustrate how to satisfy representative example information needs with queries. This chapter focused on the relatively simple queries – those that require information from within one cycle and within one class or association. The queries presented represent only a small fraction of the many different information needs that enterprises have on a daily basis. One goal of this chapter is to enable students who one day may be faced with meeting an enterprise's information needs to be able to think creatively and generate queries to meet those information needs. The database tables presented in this chapter are not comprehensive. Database tables in real-world enterprise system applications have dozens (sometimes even hundreds) of attributes. Examination of the attributes available in an enterprise system database is a critical step in developing queries that report values of those attributes in the format needed by a user. Practicing the queries illustrated in this chapter is a good starting point, but you will need to exercise your creativity and critical thinking to apply similar thinking to build queries for the same information needs using alternative databases and to build queries for different information needs.

KEY TERMS AND CONCEPTS
Agent queries
Duality association queries
Event queries
Fulfillment association queries
Null to zero function in Microsoft Access
Participation association queries
Proposition association queries
Reservation association queries
Resource queries
Reversal association queries
Stockflow association queries
Weighted average unit cost

Multiple Choice Questions

1. Which of the following information needs can be met using only one relationship in the revenue cycle?
    A) Which sale orders have been partially filled?
    B) Which salesperson presented a specific inventory type to a specific customer?
    C) Which inventory types were delivered in a specific sale event?
    D) What is the total dollar value of accounts receivable for a specific customer at a point in time?
    E) None of the above

2. Which of the following is an example of an information need that could be satisfied by an event query in the revenue cycle?
    A) What is the name and address of the salesperson with the highest dollar sales for a specific time period?
    B) A list of open sale orders
    C) What is the total dollar amount of a specific sale?
    D) A list of inventory items that have a list selling price higher than $100
    E) What quantity of a specific inventory type was sold on a specific sale?

3. Which of the following information needs in the acquisition/payment process requires multiple relationships?
    A) To which supplier have the most purchase returns been made?
    B) Which inventory types were identified as needed in a purchase requisition event?
    C) On which requisitions was a specific inventory type requested from a specific recommended supplier?
    D) When was a specific purchase received, and by which receiving clerk?
    E) Which purchase orders are unfilled as of a specific date?

4. When should a beginning date constraint **not** be used for a query set to generate weighted average unit costs of inventory items?
    A) When the weighted average unit cost is to be assigned to cost of goods sold on the income statement
    B) When the weighted average unit cost is to be assigned to inventory on the balance sheet
    C) When the weighted average unit cost is to be assigned to all goods purchased within a time period
    D) Both A and B above (the beginning date constraint should not be used for either A or B)
    E) None of the above (the beginning date constraint should always be used)

5. A list of all science fiction titles owned by a bookstore is an information need that could be answered by what type of query?
    A) Event query
    B) Agent query
    C) Resource query
    D) Fulfillment query
    E) Duality query

Applied Learning

A1. Your instructor should have available an Access database file that contains the tables with data illustrated in this chapter, but with no queries created. Using that file, work through the examples in this chapter to create, save, and run the queries.

A2. Using the file mentioned in A1 above, create queries for six of the other suggested information needs. For example, create a query to generate a list of all products sold by the enterprise whose database this is. The six queries you create should be from different categories – for example, don't create six resource queries; instead you could create one resource query, one event query, one agent query, one stockflow query, one duality query, and one fulfillment query.

CHAPTER 11

Advanced Acquisition and Revenue Cycle Information Retrieval

LEARNING OBJECTIVES

This chapter builds on the concepts introduced in chapter 10, presenting more complicated information needs and demonstrating sets of queries to meet those information needs. Rather than focusing on single classes or associations, the examples in this chapter require use of multiple associations, either within the acquisition or revenue cycle, or combining information from both cycles. After studying this chapter, you should be able to

1. Identify information needs that require information across multiple associations and across multiple business processes
2. Create queries to satisfy information needs that require information from multiple business processes

QUERIES REQUIRING MULTIPLE ASSOCIATIONS

Sometimes information that crosses multiple associations must be retrieved to satisfy an information need. For example, a query that requires information about both a resource and an agent that were involved in an economic event needs to use both a stockflow association and a participation association. These types of queries are the most complicated to construct, and yet are typically the most powerful tools for meeting information needs.

Within the sales/collection process, some common information needs that require use of multiple associations are

- Which sale orders have been partially filled? (Requires stockflow, reservation, and fulfillment-sale-order-sale associations.)
- What is the total dollar value of accounts receivable for a specific customer at a point in time? (Requires duality, participation-customer-sale, and participation-customer-cash receipt associations.)
- What inventory types have been presented to a specific customer in sales calls during a specified time period? (Requires proposition and participation-customer-sales-call associations.)
- Which salesperson presented a specific inventory type to a specific customer? (Requires proposition, participation-customer-sales call, and participation-salesperson-sales-call associations.)
- What is the total dollar amount of sales of an inventory type that have been made to customers in a specific region? (Requires stockflow and participation-customer-sale associations.)
- In what region have sales calls involving a specific inventory type been the most successful? (Requires proposition, fulfillment-sales-call-sale-order, and reservation associations.)

Within the acquisition/payment process, some common information needs that require use of multiple associations are:

- Which purchase orders have been partially filled? (requires stockflow, reservation, and fulfillment-purchaseorder-purchase associations)
- What is the total dollar value of accounts payable to a given supplier at a point in time? (requires duality, participation-supplier-purchase, and participation-supplier-cash disbursement associations)
- On which requisitions has a specific vendor been the recommended supplier for a given inventory type? (requires proposition and participation-purchaserequisition-supplier associations)
- Which purchase agent ordered a specific inventory type from a given supplier? (requires reservation, participation-supplier-purchaseorder, and participation-purchaseagent-purchaseorder associations)
- What is the total dollar amount of purchases of an inventory type made from suppliers in a given region? (requires stockflow-purchase-inventory and participation-supplier-purchase associations)

In the discussion of fulfillment association queries in Chapter 10, we designed a query set to calculate the average number of days an enterprise had taken to fill sale orders (revisit Exhibit 10-17). That query set has one weakness; it does not distinguish a filled sale order from a partially filled sale order. As long as the enterprise has sent something from a customer's order to the customer, it counts the order as having been filled for purposes of calculating the days it took to fill the order. When the remainder of the order is filled, that sale date is also factored into the calculation of days to fill the order; in the average calculation it is as if the two parts of the order that are shipped separately are two different orders with the same order date. Over a reasonably long time frame, this distinction is not usually crucial so the query shown in Exhibit 10-17 may be useful. If, however, the firm does not want to count an order as filled until it is *completely* filled, or if the firm wants to determine which sale orders have been only partially filled, additional association information is needed.

Using the database tables in Chapter 10, Exhibit10-1, a query can be constructed to determine which sale orders have been only partially filled. This query requires information from the sale order event, reservation association, fulfillment association, sale event, and stockflow association. The data needed regarding the sale order event are the order ID (to link to the reservation and fulfillment associations) and the date on which the order was placed. The data needed regarding the sale event are the sale ID (to link to the fulfillment and stockflow associations) and the date on which the sale occurred. In a previous query we saw that it is useful to complete date constraints as a preliminary step in queries that join multiple items together, as it helps to prevent filtering out records that should be included in an answer. The first two steps of the query demonstrated in Exhibit 11-1 therefore isolate the sale orders through a user-specified date and isolate the sales through a user-specified date.

The third step joins the date-constrained sale orders to the reservation association, thereby date-constraining the reservation association. The fourth step joins the date-constrained sales to the stockflow association table, thereby date-constraining the stockflow association. The fifth step joins the date-constrained reservation result to the fulfillment association table to add the related sale ID to each reservation record; similarly, the sixth step joins the date-constrained stockflow result to the fulfillment association table to add the related sale order ID to each stockflow record. The seventh step joins the results from steps 5 and 6 together based on sale

ID, sale order ID, and inventory item ID. The quantity sold field is summed so that if multiple sales applied to the same sale order the total sold can be compared to the quantity ordered. The final step subtracts that total sold from the quantity ordered to calculate the unfilled quantity of each item on sale orders that have been at least partially filled. This series of query steps does not include sale orders that have not been filled at all; additional steps would be needed to include those in the answer. As you can see, queries of multiple associations can become quite complex. It is important to organize your thinking and not combine too many steps.

Exhibit 11-1: Query to Identify Partially Filled Sale Orders

Query Step 1 Constrain Sale Order Date to Have Occurred up to User-Specified Ending Date

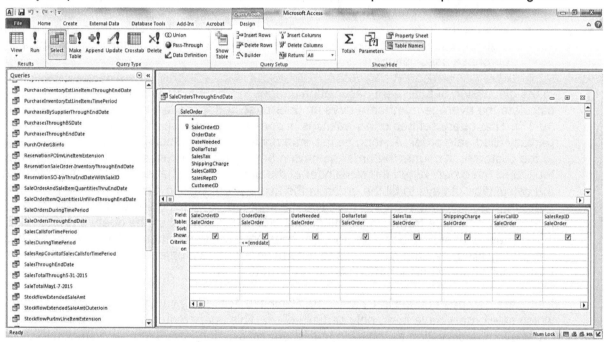

REA Accounting Systems: Resources-Events-Agents: An ontology for designing, controlling, and using integrated enterprise systems

365

Exhibit 11-1 cont.: Query to Identify Partially Filled Sale Orders

Query Step 2 Constrain Sale Date to Have Occurred up to User-Specified Ending Date

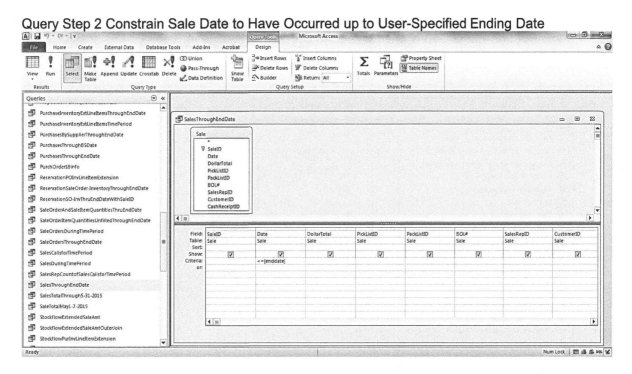

Query Step 3 Join Date-Constrained Sale Orders With Reservation Association to Identify Quantities of Items Ordered (in Effect Date-Constraining the Reservation Association)

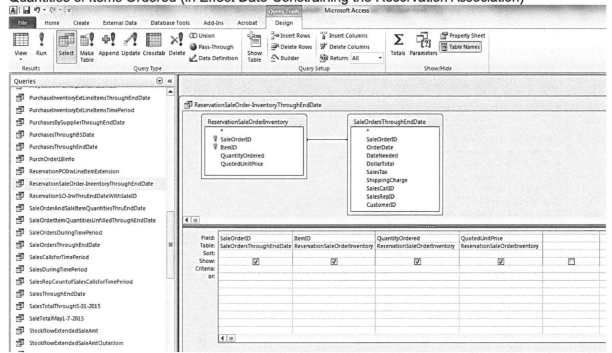

Exhibit 11-1 cont.: Query to Identify Partially Filled Sale Orders

Query Step 4 Join Date-Constrained Sales with Stockflow Association to Identify Quantities of Items Sold (in Effect Date-Constraining the Stockflow Association)

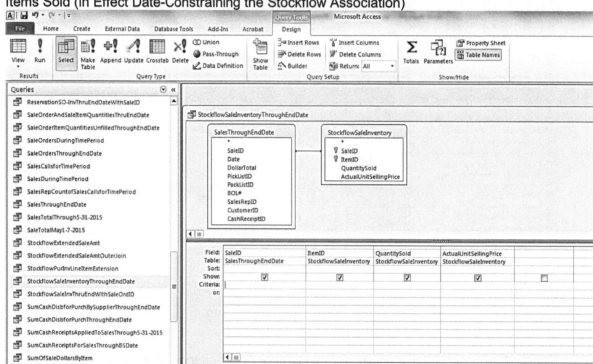

Query Step 5 Join Date-Constrained Reservation with Fulfillment to Link Sale Orders to Sale Ids

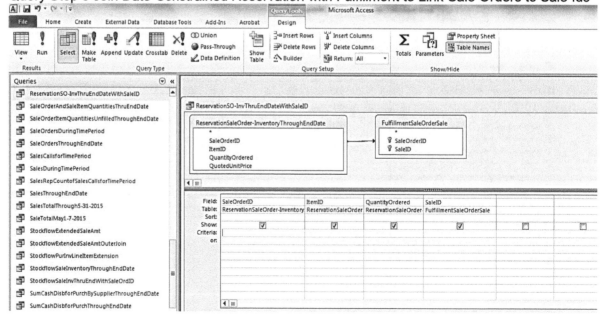

Exhibit 11-1 cont.: Query to Identify Partially Filled Sale Orders

Query 6 Join Date Constrained Stockflow with Fulfillment to Link Sales with Sale Order Ids

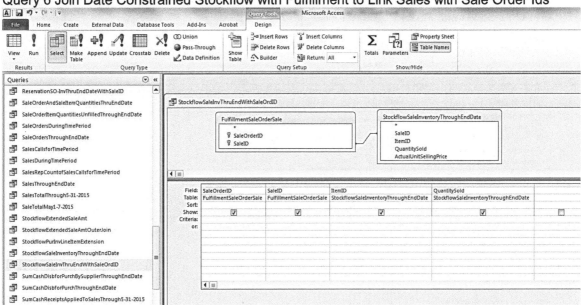

Query 7 Join the results of Queries 5 and 6, linking them via Sale ID, Sale Order ID, and Item ID; Group by Sale Order ID; Sum Quantities Sold

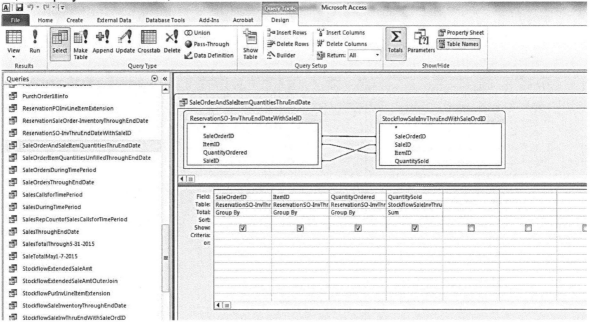

Exhibit 11-1 cont.: Query to Identify Partially Filled Sale Orders

Query 8 Using the result of Query 7, subtract Sum of Quantity Sold from Quantity Ordered to Get Unfilled Quantities of Partially Filled Sale Orders

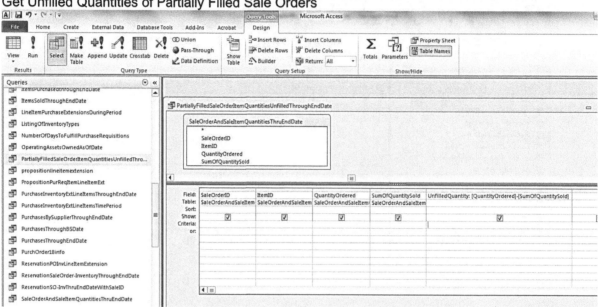

Result for Query Run with 5/8/2015 as End Date

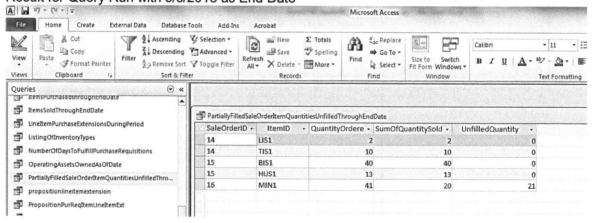

SaleOrderID	ItemID	QuantityOrdere	SumOfQuantitySold	UnfilledQuantity
14	LIS1	2	2	0
14	TIS1	10	10	0
15	BIS1	40	40	0
15	HUS1	13	13	0
16	MIN1	41	20	21

Accounts Payable By Supplier

In the acquisition/payment process, the procedures for calculating individual supplier payable balances are similar to those for calculating total accounts payable in aggregate; however, they are slightly more complicated by the addition of the participation associations. The general procedures are as follows:

Determine what kinds of acquisitions are represented in your database (except for labor acquisitions) and for each kind of acquisition follow these steps:

1. Determine which tables contain the acquisition date, dollar amount, and related supplier (usually these are found in the acquisition event table). Group by supplier, and sum the acquisition amount through the balance sheet date (with no beginning date constraint).

2. Determine which tables contain the cash disbursements that applied to those acquisitions. To determine this, examine the duality-purchase-cashdisbursement association.

    a. If the duality association is represented with a separate table, join the duality table to the cash disbursement table, establish the ending date constraint on the cash disbursement date field (with no beginning date constraint), group by supplier, and sum the cash disbursement amount applied to the acquisition.

    b. If the duality association is represented with the cash disbursement identifier posted as a foreign key into the acquisition table, join the cash disbursement table to the acquisition table, establish the ending date constraint on the cash disbursement date field (with no beginning date constraint), group by supplier and sum the cash disbursement amounts.

3. Determine which tables contain purchase returns that applied to those acquisitions. To determine this, examine the duality-purchase-purchasereturn association

    a. If the purchase-purchase return association is represented with a separate table, join the purchase return table to the acquisition table, establish the ending date constraint on the purchase return table date field (with no beginning date constraint), group by supplier and sum the purchase return amount applied to the acquisition.

    b. If the purchase-purchase return association is represented with purchase Id posted as a foreign key in the purchase return table, establish the ending date constraint on the purchase return table date field (with no beginning date constraint), group by supplier and sum the purchase return amount applied to the acquisition.

4. Subtract the results of steps 2 and 3 from the result of step 1 to get accounts payable for each supplier as of the balance sheet date.

Exhibit 11-2 illustrates a query set to calculate accounts payable balances on a given date for each supplier based on the database tables in Chapter 10, Exhibit 10-1.

Exhibit 11-2 Query - Accounts Payable Balances for Each Supplier

Query 1: Constrain Purchase Date and Sum Purchase Dollar Amount for Each Vendor

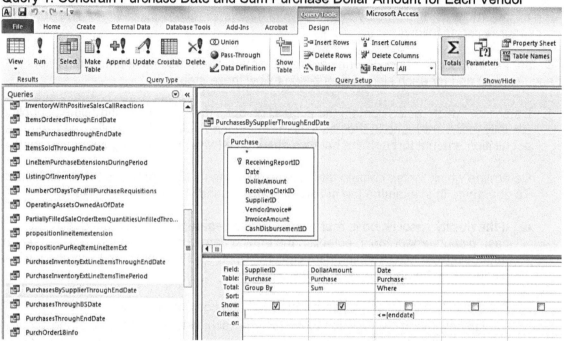

Query 2: Join Purchase, Cash Disbursement Tables, Group by Supplier, Constrain Cash Disbursement Date

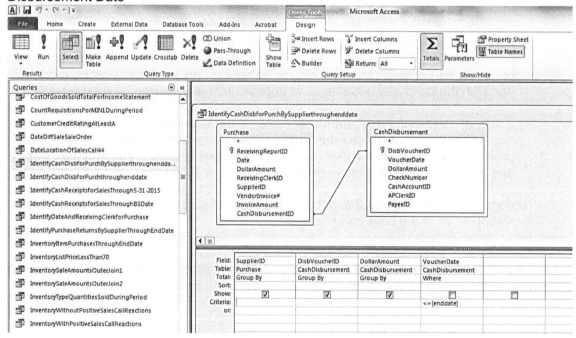

REA Accounting Systems: Resources-Events-Agents: An ontology for designing, controlling, and using integrated enterprise systems

371

Exhibit 11-2 cont.: Query - Accounts Payable Balances for Each Supplier

Query 3: Sum the Cash Disbursements by Supplier

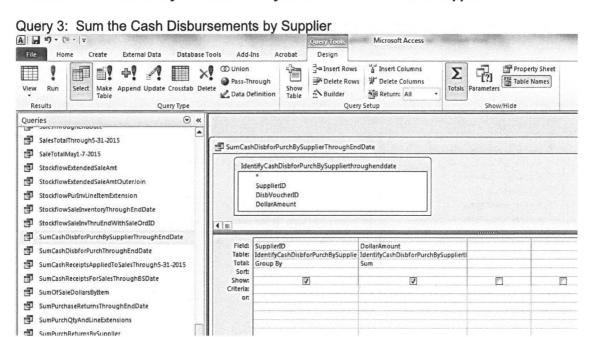

Query 4: Join Purchase and Purchase Return Tables; Constrain Purchase Return Date

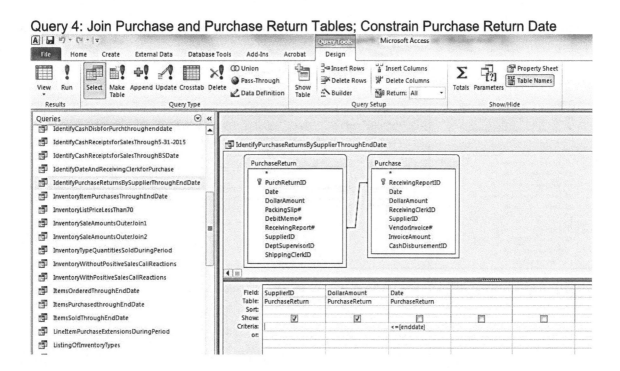

Exhibit 11-2 cont.: Query - Accounts Payable Balances for Each Supplier

Query 5: Sum Purchase Returns by Supplier

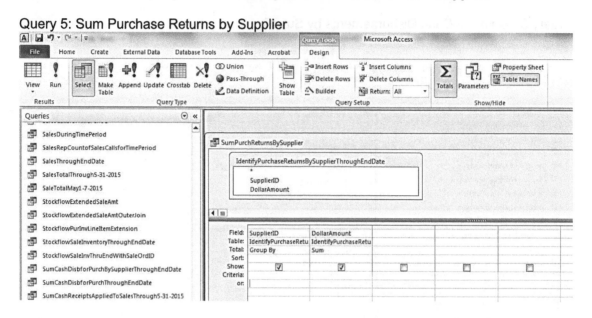

Query 6: Combine Purchases and Purchase Returns by Supplier to Get Unreturned Purchases

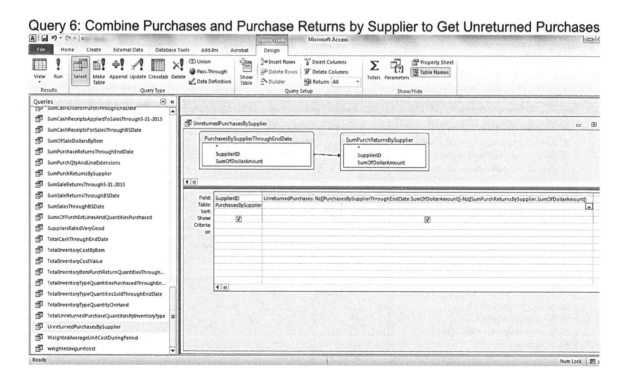

Exhibit 11-2 cont.: Query - Accounts Payable Balances for Each Supplier

Query 7: Combine Unreturned Purchases and Cash Disbursements by Supplier to Get Unpaid Purchases

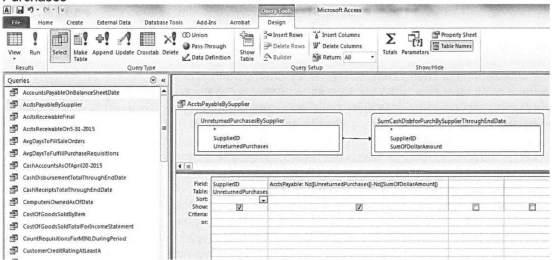

(Note: Queries 6 and 7 cannot be combined into a single query step because outer joins are needed to include purchases from suppliers to whom neither payments nor returns have been made. Inclusion of two outer joins in the same query is too ambiguous for Microsoft Access to evaluate.)

Result for May 31, 2015

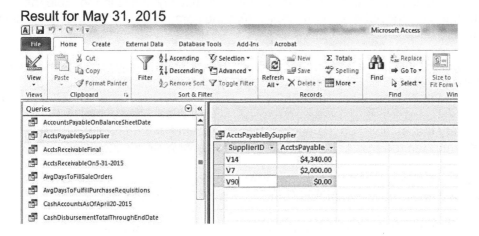

INFORMATION NEEDS THAT REQUIRE DATA FROM MULTIPLE BUSINESS PROCESSES

Consideration of the value system and value chain levels of the REA ontology reveals that resources typically are the objects on which business process model views are integrated. Information needs that involve multiple business processes are therefore likely to be focused on resources. Many of the information needs that involve both the revenue cycle and the acquisition cycle involve cash and inventory, resources shared by those business processes.

Cash Balance

The calculations of cash balances (either for one or more specific accounts or for the total balance of all cash accounts) are typically affected by all the transaction cycles except the conversion process. In a database these accounts are usually represented in a cash class table; however, the account balance is a volatile derivable attribute that is not stored unless the software is capable of triggers. Therefore a set of queries is needed to calculate the total cash receipts through the date for which the balance is needed; then to calculate the total cash disbursements through the date for which the balance is needed; and finally to subtract the total cash disbursements from the total cash receipts. If the cash receipt amounts and the cash disbursement amounts are stored as attributes in the cash receipt and cash disbursement tables, respectively, the querying is quite simple. If the company only stores amounts in duality association tables, then all the appropriate duality tables need to be joined to the cash receipt and disbursement event tables to apply the date constraints and get the totals. Most companies recognize the value of storing the amount field in the cash receipt and disbursement event tables, so we consider that case and ignore the more complicated possibility.

The process for querying to provide the cash balance on a given date is typically as follows.

1. Determine which table contains the cash receipt date (usually this is in the table that represents the cash receipt event) and make sure the same table also contains the cash receipt amount field.

2. Determine which table contains the cash disbursement date (usually this is in the table that represents the cash disbursement event) and make sure the same table also contains the cash disbursement amount field.

3. Create a query that establishes the ending date constraint (with no beginning date constraint) and **sum** the dollar amount field in the table identified in step 1.

4. Create a query that establishes the ending date constraint (with no beginning date constraint) and sum the dollar amount field in the table identified in step 2.

5. Create a query that subtracts the total in step 4 from the total in step 3.

Exhibit 11-3 depicts a query set to generate the cash balance for the enterprise represented in the tables in Chapter 10, Exhibit 10-1.

Exhibit 11-3: Query - Calculate Cash Balance on a Given Date

Query 1: Sum Dollar Amounts of Cash Receipts Through Ending Date (No Beginning Date)

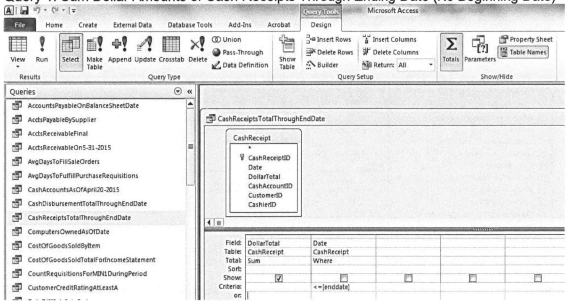

Query 2: Sum Cash Disbursement Dollar Amounts Through Ending Date (No Beginning Date)

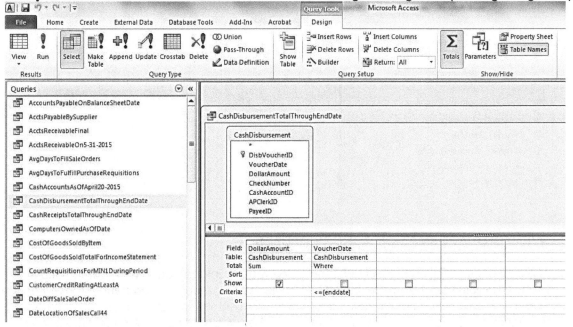

Exhibit 11-3 cont.: Query - Calculate Cash Balance on a Given Date

Query 3: Subtract Sum of Cash Disbursements from the Sum of Cash Receipts

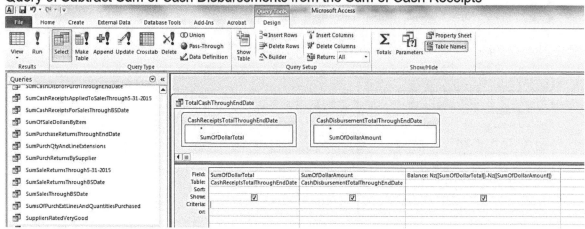

Result as of May 31, 2015

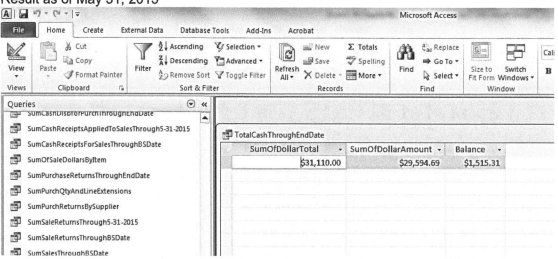

INVENTORY INFORMATION ACROSS CYCLES

Several needs for inventory-related information require integration of data from multiple business processes. Examples include calculations of the quantity on hand for inventory on a given date, calculations of the dollar cost value of inventory on hand on a specific date, and calculations of the dollar cost value of inventory that was sold during a given time period. Exhibit 11-4 demonstrates an example query set to calculate quantity on hand of each inventory item based on the enterprise database tables in Chapter 10, Exhibit 10-1. Queries to calculate dollar values of inventory on hand and cost of inventory sold are described in Exhibits 11-5 through 11-7.

Inventory Quantities On Hand

Quantity on hand consists of quantities purchased minus quantities returned minus quantities sold through a given ending date (with no beginning date constraint). Notice the similarity to the calculation of cash balance, which was the amount of cash receipts minus the amount of cash disbursements through a specific date. The pattern for both calculations is balance equals inflows minus outflows. An important difference between the queries in Exhibit 11-3 for the total cash balance and the queries to be developed for the quantity on hand of each inventory item is the fact that the latter requires a separate balance for each item whereas for the cash query we did not compute a separate balance for each cash account (although that certainly is another information need of most enterprises for which we could employ similar procedures as those we are about to describe).

The procedures for calculating inventory item quantities on hand typically are as follows.

1. Determine which table contains the purchase date attribute (usually this is in the table that represents the purchase economic event).

2. Determine which table contains the purchase quantity attribute and the item ID (usually this is in the table that represents the stockflow association between the purchase economic event and the inventory resource).

3. Determine which table contains the purchase return date attribute (usually this is in the table that represents the purchase return economic event).

4. Determine which table contains the quantity returned attribute and the item ID (usually this is in the table that represents the stockflow association between the purchase return economic event and the inventory resource).

5. Determine which table contains the sale date attribute (usually this is in the table that represents the sale economic event).

6. Determine which table contains the quantity sold attribute and the item id (usually this is in the table that represents the stockflow association between the sale economic event and the inventory resource).

7. Determine which table contains the sale return date attribute (usually this is in the table that represents the sale return economic event).

8. Determine which table contains the quantity returned attribute and the item ID (usually this is in the table that represents the stockflow association between the sale return economic event and the inventory resource).

9. Join the tables identified in steps 1 and 2, group by inventory item, set the ending date constraint (with no beginning date constraint) and sum the quantity purchased to get the total quantity purchased per inventory item. Make sure to include the inventory item identifier attribute in the query result to provide a means for linking to the results of other steps.

10. Join the tables identified in steps 3 and 4, group by inventory item, set the ending date constraint (with no beginning date constraint) and sum the quantity returned to get the total quantity returned per inventory item. Make sure to include the inventory item identifier attribute in the query result to provide a means for linking to the results of other steps.

11. Join the tables identified in steps 5 and 6, group by inventory item, set the ending date constraint (with no beginning date constraint) and sum the quantity sold to get the total quantity sold per inventory item. Make sure to include the inventory item identifier attribute in the query result to provide a means for linking to the results of other steps.

12. Join the tables identified in steps 7 and 8, group by inventory item, set the ending date constraint (with no beginning date constraint) and sum the quantity returned to get the total quantity of sale returns per inventory item. Be sure to include the inventory item identifier attribute in the query result to provide a means for linking to the results of other steps.

13. Join the results from steps 9 and 10. Change the join type to include all records from the total quantity purchased query and the matches from the total quantity returned query. The null to zero (Nz) function is necessary in the calculation to subtract the total quantity returned from the total quantity purchased. For example, this calculation expression would look something like this (depending on the query's variable names):

    Nz(SumPurchaseQty) – Nz(SumQtyReturned).

    This formula results in the unreturned purchase quantities for each item.

14. Join the results from steps 11 and 12. Change the join type to include all records from the total quantity sold query and the matches from the total sale return quantity. The null to zero (Nz) function is necessary in the calculation to subtract the total quantity returned from the total quantity sold. For example, this calculation expression would look something like this (depending on the query's variable names):

    Nz(SumQtySold)-Nz(SumSaleReturnQty).

15. Join the results from step 13 with the results from step 14. Change the join type to include all records from the total unreturned quantities purchased query and the matches from the total unreturned quantities sold query. The null to zero (Nz) function is needed in the calculation to subtract the total unreturned quantity sold from the total unreturned purchase quantity. For example, this calculation expression would look something like this (depending on the query's variable names):

    Nz(SumUnreturnedPurchaseQty) – Nz(SumUnreturnedSaleQty)

    This query result yields the total quantity on hand separately for each inventory item.

REA Accounting Systems: Resources-Events-Agents: An ontology for designing, controlling, and using integrated enterprise systems

379

Exhibit 11-4: Query - Calculate Quantities on Hand for Inventory Types

Query 1: Accomplish steps 1, 2, and 9 – Constrain purchase date, sum quantities by type

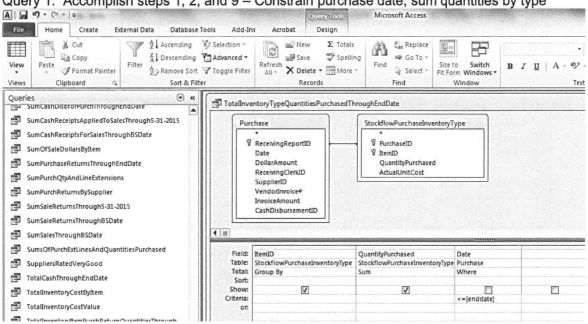

Query 2: Accomplish steps 3, 4, and 10 – Constrain return date, sum quantities by type

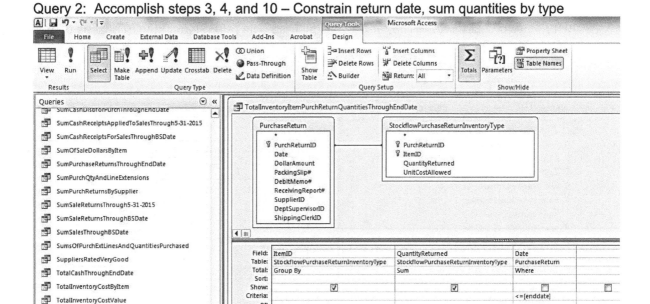

Exhibit 11-4 cont.: Query - Calculate Quantities on Hand for Inventory Types

Query 3: Accomplish steps 5, 6, and 11 – Constrain sale date; Sum quantities sold by type

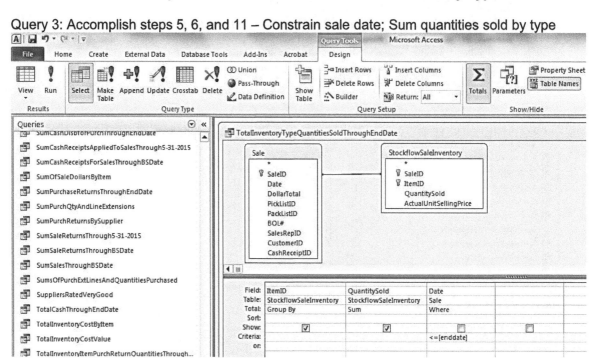

Query 4: Accomplish steps 7, 8, and 12 - Constrain sale return date, sum quantities by type

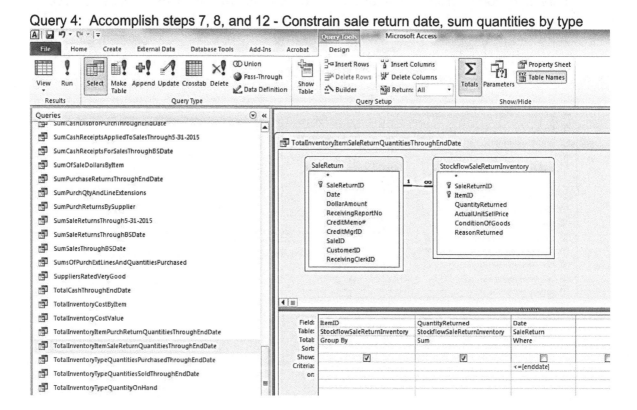

REA Accounting Systems: Resources-Events-Agents: An ontology for designing, controlling, and using integrated enterprise systems

381

Exhibit 11-4 cont.: Query - Calculate Quantities on Hand for Inventory Types

Query 5: Accomplish step 13 – Compute unreturned purchase quantities by item

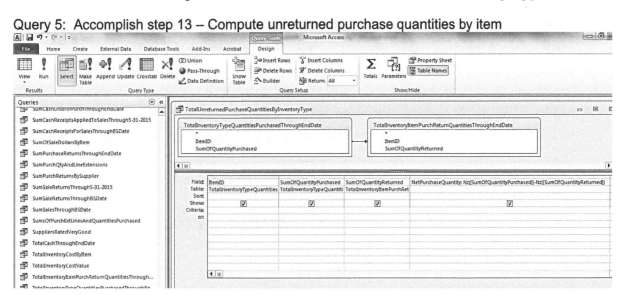

Query 6: Accomplish step 14 – Calculate unreturned sale quantities by item

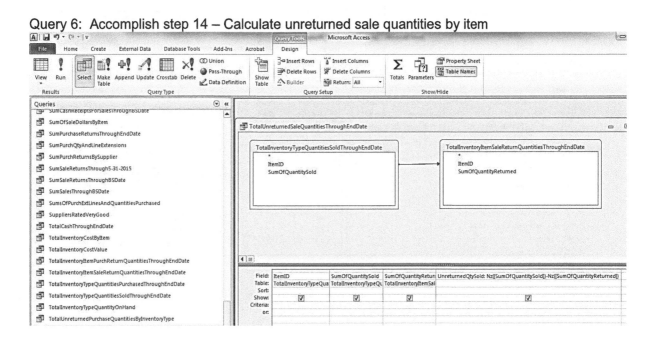

Exhibit 11-4 cont.: Query - Calculate Quantities on Hand for Inventory Types

Query 7: Accomplish step 15 - Calculate quantity on hand by item

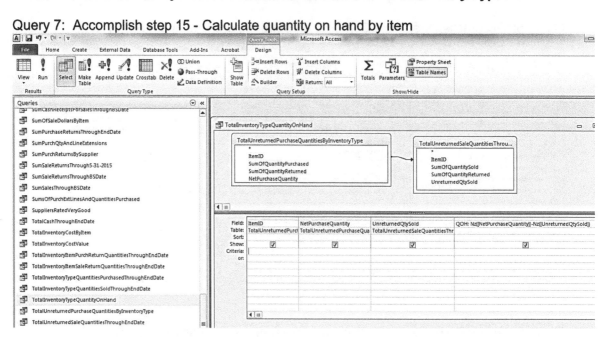

Result for May 31, 2015

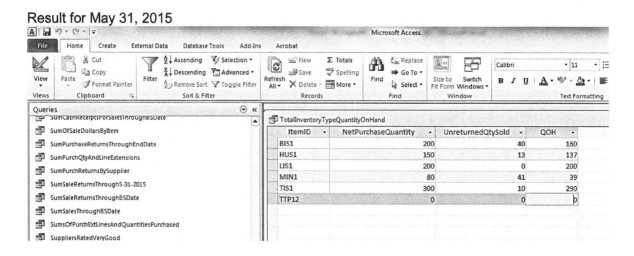

Inventory Cost (Dollar Value for Balance Sheet)

Once the quantities on hand of inventory types are calculated for a given date, an enterprise also may want to assign cost values to those inventory types. Various cost assumptions may be used to assign costs to inventory types, including weighted average unit cost, first-in-first-out (FIFO), and last-in-first-out (LIFO). The assignment of costs based on FIFO or LIFO entails the writing of program code that is too complex for this textbook. The assignment of weighted average unit costs to inventory types on hand is less complex and can be accomplished without extensive program code, as demonstrated in Chapter 10, Exhibit 10-16. As Exhibit 11-5 demonstrates, the result from a set of queries similar to the query set in Chapter 10, Exhibit 10-16 (but with no beginning date constraint on the purchase date) may be joined together with the result from the query set in Exhibit 11-4 to get the total cost value of each inventory type on hand.

Exhibit 11-5: Query set to assign weighted average costs to inventory types on hand

Multiply weighted average unit costs by quantities on hand

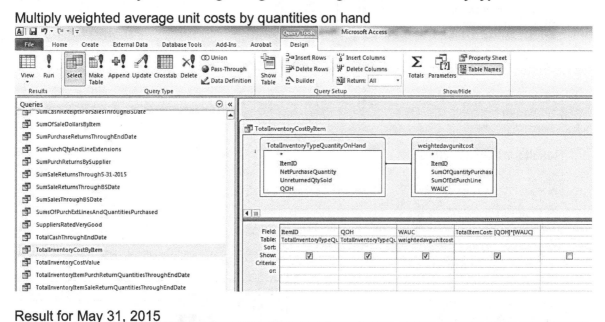

Result for May 31, 2015

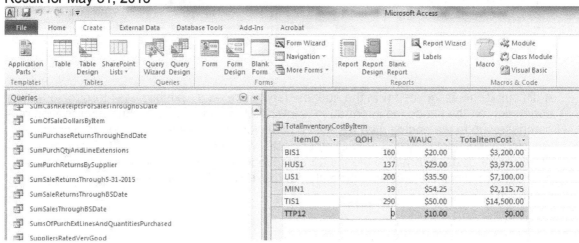

The result from Exhibit 11-5 may be summed as illustrated in Exhibit 11-6 to get a single dollar value such as is needed for the enterprise balance sheet.

Exhibit 11-6: Query - Calculate Total Inventory Cost Value on a Specific Date

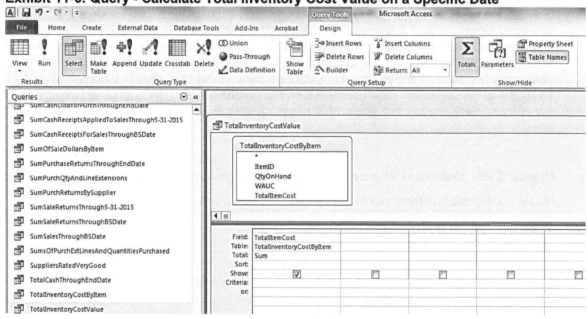

Result for May 31, 2015

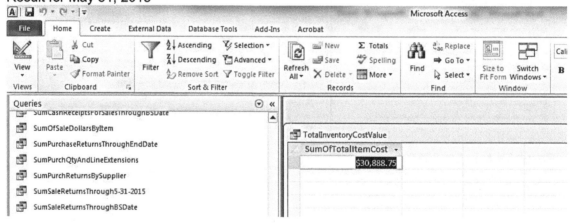

A difficult issue associated with the queries demonstrated in Exhibits 11-4 through 11-6, depending on the needs the information is intended to address, is that the aggregation of all purchases up to the ending date results in the inclusion of relatively old costs. For some decision needs that may be fine; but other decision needs may require consideration of only the more recent costs. Alternative means for computing weighted average unit costs may be employed to allocate the costs differently; for this textbook we only illustrate the simplest approach.

Cost of Goods Sold

Cost of goods sold is a line item on enterprise income statements that is similar to the calculation of the dollar value of inventory on hand. Whereas the calculation of inventory on hand applies an assumed cost value to the quantities of inventory types on hand; the calculation of cost of goods sold applies an assumed cost value to the quantities of inventory types sold during a specified time period. The total cost value of inventory on hand appears as a line item on enterprise balance sheets. The same cost value assumption must be used in calculating inventory on the balance sheet and cost of goods sold on the income statement. Therefore, if weighted average unit cost is used as the costing assumption for inventory, it must also be used for cost of goods sold.

The overall procedures to calculate cost of goods sold for a given time period are as follows:

1. Determine which table contains the sale date attribute; usually this is in the table that represents the sale economic event.

2. Determine which table contains the sale quantities; usually this is in the table that represents the stockflow association between sale and inventory.

3. Join the tables together; set date constraints for the beginning and ending of the income statement period; group by inventory ID, and sum the quantity sold.

4. Join the result of step 3 with the the result of a query set similar to that in Chapter 10, Exhibit 10-16 (except without the beginning date constraint on the purchase date). Join them on Item ID – recall that Chapter 10, Exhibit 10-16 calculated the weighted average unit cost per item type. Multiplying the quantity sold of each item type by the weighted average unit cost of each item type yields the total weighted average cost of goods sold for each inventory type.

5. Create a final query that sums the weighted average cost per inventory item type sold to get the total COGS for the income statement.

Exhibit 11-7: Query - Cost of Goods Sold

Query 1: Accomplish steps 1, 2, 3: Constrain sale date; sum quantity sold by item

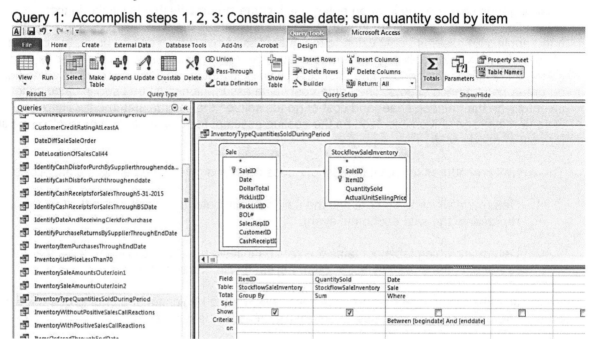

Query 2: Accomplish step 4 – Calculate COGS by item as quantity sold x weighted average unit cost

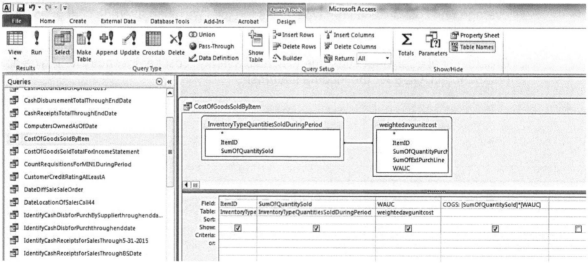

REA Accounting Systems: Resources-Events-Agents: An ontology for designing, controlling, and using integrated enterprise systems

387

Exhibit 11-7 cont.: Query - Cost of Goods Sold

Query 3: Accomplish step 5 - Sum COGS by item to get total cost of goods sold

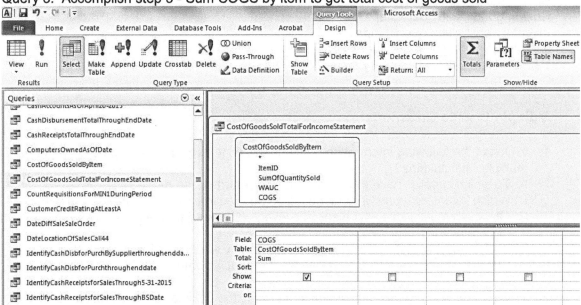

Result for May 1 – May 31, 2015

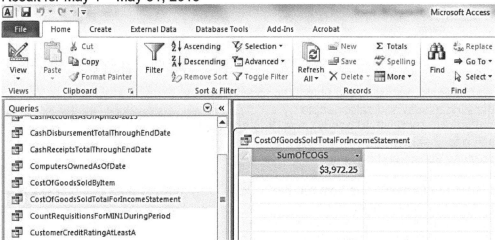

CONCLUDING COMMENTS

This chapter applied the information retrieval concepts discussed in chapter 7 to the revenue and acquisition cycles discussed in chapter 6 to illustrate how to satisfy representative example information needs with queries. This chapter focused on relatively complicated examples – those that require data across multiple associations and/or across multiple transaction cycles. As with Chapter 10, the examples presented represent only a small fraction of the many different information needs that enterprises have on a daily basis. Students will need to think creatively and critically to be able to apply the knowledge gained from practicing these examples to alternative databases and alternative information needs.

Key Terms and Concepts

Accounts payable by supplier query steps
Cash balance query steps
Cost of goods sold query steps
Inventory cost value query steps
Inventory quantity on hand query steps
Partially filled sale orders query steps

Multiple Choice Questions

1. Which of the following information needs in the acquisition/payment process requires multiple relationships?
   A) To which supplier have the most purchase returns been made?
   B) Which inventory types were identified as needed in a purchase requisition event?
   C) On which requisitions was a specific inventory type requested from a specific recommended supplier?
   D) When was a specific purchase received, and by which receiving clerk?
   E) Which purchase orders are unfilled as of a specific date?

2. Which transaction cycle typically does not affect the calculation of cash balances?
   A) Acquisition process
   B) Sales process
   C) Financing process
   D) Conversion process
   E) Payroll process

3. What resources are involved in most information needs that encompass both the revenue and acquisition cycles?
   A) Raw materials inventory and finished goods inventory
   B) Operating assets and salespeople
   C) Merchandise (or finished goods) inventory and cash
   D) Cash and cashiers
   E) Operating assets and raw materials inventory

4. Which financial statement line item requires details from multiple business processes?
   A) Sales on the income statement
   B) Cost of goods sold on the income statement
   C) Accounts receivable on the balance sheet
   D) Accounts payable on the balance sheet
   E) Rent expense on the income statement

5. Which financial statement line item should use a beginning date constraint?
   A) Cash
   B) Accounts Payable
   C) Accounts Receivable
   D) Inventory
   E) Cost of Goods Sold

CHAPTER 12

Advanced REA Modeling Concepts

LEARNING OBJECTIVES

The objective of this chapter is to introduce the policy infrastructure of the REA ontology, which includes advanced conceptual modeling concepts such as typification and generalization. After studying this chapter, you should be able to

1. Explain the difference between typification and generalization
2. Explain the difference between the accountability and policy infrastructures in REA modeling
3. Create business process level REA models that include typification and generalization
4. Identify and create common conceptual level, logical level, and physical level implementation compromises
5. Explain common reasons for compromising implementations

ADVANCED BUSINESS PROCESS LEVEL REA MODELING

Business process conceptual models in the REA ontology have two components: the accountability or operational infrastructure, and the policy infrastructure. The **accountability infrastructure** represents the economic and commitment activities that actually have happened. The **policy infrastructure** represents the economic and commitment activities that should, could, or must happen in a company. The policy infrastructure reflects the results of planning and control efforts by the enterprise management.

Most of the concepts introduced in chapter 6 for core business process level REA modeling are part of the accountability infrastructure. The policy infrastructure extends those concepts through the use of abstraction mechanisms such as generalization and typification. **Abstraction** is the ignoring or hiding of details to highlight or capture some kind of commonality between different instances.

Generalization

Generalization is the abstraction from a class of objects to a superclass (less detailed, higher level) via the creation of an "is-a" relationship between the subclass and superclass. Subclasses contain more specific instances of superclasses. For example, the classes oboe, bassoon, and english horn all participate in an "is-a" relationship with the double-reed instrument class.

Generalization relationships may even be chained together to form a hierarchy; for example, oboe is a double-reed instrument, a double-reed instrument is a woodwind instrument, a woodwind instrument is a musical instrument. Generalization relationships are used in conceptual modeling when some of the characteristics that we want to include in the model are common to all subtype entities but other characteristics are unique to specific subtypes.

Subclasses inherit the characteristics of the superclass as well as possessing their own attributes.

Consider the Employee class for an enterprise. Employees hold many kinds of positions in a typical enterprise, and the enterprise may need to store different attributes for employees in different positions. For example, the enterprise may want to store the CPA license number for its accountants, the driver's license numbers for its truck drivers, and the fidelity bond rating for its cashiers. The values of those attributes would be null for all employees who do not hold those respective positions, therefore, the enterprise should not store those attributes for all employees. Other attributes should be stored for all employees, such as employee id, last name, first name, address, telephone number, date of birth, and so forth.

Generalization allows us to store the attributes that are common to all employees as attributes of the Employee superclass and to store the others as attributes of the appropriate subclass. Exhibit 12-1 illustrates these concepts in conceptual model form and Exhibit 12-2 provides representative example data in the corresponding relational tables. Notice that the conceptual model uses arrows to point from the subclasses to the superclass. No multiplicities are needed – by definition each member of the subclass is also a member of the superclass, and a member of the superclass can only be a member of one subclass and may not be a member of any of the subclasses. So if multiplicities were listed, they would be 1..1 next to the superclass and 0..1 next to each subclass. In the relational tables, you would never use a foreign key to implement the generalization association because the superclass and subclasses already share the same primary key.

Exhibit 12-1 Generalization Conceptual Model and Corresponding Relational Tables

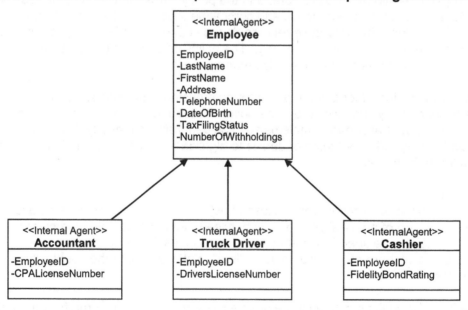

Exhibit 12-2 Relational Tables Corresponding to Exhibit 12-1

Employee

EmployeeID	Last Name	First Name	Address	Telephone Number	Date of Birth	Tax Status	Number of Withholdings
E1	Frank	Ryan	123 Neat St.	616-342-1235	8/27/1990	S	1
E2	Daniels	Jackie	83156 Elm St.	616-531-1381	4/5/1980	MFJ	3
E3	Burger	Chase	921 Oak St.	517-326-5213	10/3/1966	MWS	2
E4	Newman	Marcus	444 Ash St.	616-883-9980	6/10/1964	MFJ	6
E5	Q	Susie	765 Beech St.	616-892-2638	11/5/1989	HH	2
E6	Tuttle	Franklin	329 Maple St.	517-319-5130	7/7/1989	S	1
E7	Grace	Sal	901 Oak St.	517-513-3123	1/3/1970	HH	4
E8	Place	Sharon	2991 Birch St.	616-883-1269	5/5/1964	MFJ	5
E9	Maxx	Angel	3552 Rider Dr.	616-831-9056	3/14/1990	S	1
E10	Curie	George	6312 Peach Ct.	616-315-1235	2/12/1956	MWS	2

Accountant

EmployeeID	CPA License Number
E7	M12351
E8	M90123

Truck Driver

EmployeeID	Drivers License Number
E2	D500315120531289
E9	M800312315012986

Cashier

EmployeeID	Fidelity Bond Rating
E3	AA
E5	A

Notice that the instances of the subclasses are also instances of the superclass. That is, the E7 who is an accountant is also the same E7 who is an employee and the E3 who is a cashier is the same E3 who is an employee. To get all details of any specific employee, the Employee table could be joined to the relevant subclass table. For example, joining Employee to Truck Driver would allow us to get all details for Jackie Daniels and also for Angel Maxx. You may notice that some of the employees in the Employee superclass table are not included in any of the subclass tables. That simply indicates that no separate attributes are stored for whatever type of position those employees hold in the enterprise. They are members of the superclass but are not members of any of the subclasses.

Typification

Typification allows us to store characteristics about categories, or types of objects. For example, an enterprise may want to track certain characteristics of the categories of employees it has such as the pay range and benefit plan for which each employee position type is eligible. We saw typification in chapter 5 for inventory. Recall that inventory may be specifically identified with unique tags or serial numbers for each separate physical unit, as is often the case with vehicles or electronics. In the language of chapter 2, this is token-level representation. Alternatively, inventory may be identified with model numbers, catalog product numbers, or skus, in which case each model number represents many different physical units. That is often the case with groceries, office supplies (other than electronics), clothing, and many other products. In the language of chapter 2, this is type-level representation and may be used when each instance of the type would have identical values for the characteristics of interest. We said back in Chapter 6 that the uniquely identified inventory is a resource and the catalog inventory is a resource type. The association between the inventory and inventory type classes is called typification. Even enterprises that track inventory at the token level may also find it useful to track it at the type level. For example, a computer manufacturer advertises information about the types of computers it has available to sell by assigning model numbers to identify the specific features a finished computer will have. Customers will order by model number to indicate the bundle of features they want – not by serial number to indicate the exact physical computer. As long as the company sends the customer a computer that has all the ordered features, the customer won't care whether the computer has serial number xyz1235123-1235y or whether it has serial number xyz3e212351231sah-235. Once the enterprise actually sells the computer, then the enterprise will track the specifically identified computer.

Exhibit 12-3 shows a conceptual model for a typification association between Employee and Employee Type and the corresponding relational database tables.

Exhibit 12-3 Typification Conceptual Model and Corresponding Relational Tables

Employee

EmployeeID	Last Name	First Name	Address	Telephone Number	Date of Birth	Tax Status	Number of Withholdings	PositionType (FK)
E01	Frank	Ryan	123 Neat St.	616-342-1235	8/27/1990	S	1	Line Worker
E10	Curie	George	6312 Peach Ct.	616-315-1235	2/12/1956	MWS	2	Executive
E02	Daniels	Jackie	83156 Elm St.	616-531-1381	4/5/1980	MFJ	3	Truck Driver
E03	Burger	Chase	921 Oak St.	517-326-5213	10/3/1966	MWS	2	Cashier
E04	Newman	Marcus	444 Ash St.	616-883-9980	6/10/1964	MFJ	6	Executive
E05	Q	Susie	765 Beech St.	616-892-2638	11/5/1989	HH	2	Cashier
E06	Tuttle	Franklin	329 Maple St.	517-319-5130	7/7/1989	S	1	Line Worker
E07	Grace	Sal	901 Oak St.	517-513-3123	1/3/1970	HH	4	Accountant
E08	Place	Sharon	2991 Birch St.	616-883-1269	5/5/1964	MFJ	5	Accountant
E09	Maxx	Angel	3552 Rider Dr.	616-831-9056	3/14/1990	S	1	Truck Driver

Employee Type

Employee Position Type	Benefit Plan	Minimun of Pay Range	Maximum of Pay Range
Accountant	Full	$40,000.00	$112,000.00
Truck Driver	Full	$25,000.00	$56,000.00
Cashier	Health only	$22,000.00	$36,000.00
Line Worker	Health only	$22,000.00	$42,000.00
Admin Assistant	Health only	$25,000.00	$56,000.00
Executive	Full	$60,000.00	$999,000.00

Notice that the Employee Position Type that is the primary key of the Employee Type table is posted as a foreign key in the Employee table to implement the typification association. If the multiplicities indicated that one employee could hold multiple position types, then the association should be implemented with a separate table.

Also notice that the instances of the Employee Type table are the position types, not the employees. That is the key to understanding the difference between generalization and typification. With generalization, the instances of the subclasses are also instances of the super class. With typification, the instances of the object class and the typified object class are different things – the instances of the object class are the objects and the instances of the typified object class are categories to which the objects belong.

As noted earlier, generalization and typification are usually used in the policy infrastructure part of the REA conceptual models – that is, the part of the model that identifies what could, should, or must occur. Any object class may be typified if doing so is useful for planning, controlling, or evaluating the company's activities. That is, you may have Event Types and Agent Types as well as the Resource Types we saw in Chapter 6.

Policy specification often involves associations between types. For example, a company may classify its salespeople according to experience such that it has master salespeople, senior salespeople, associate salespeople, and staff salespeople. The company may also classify its customers such that the company has relationship customers, choice customers, and transaction customers. Extending the REA conceptual model to include types will allow the company to specify a policy as to which types of salespeople may be assigned to which types of customers. For example, the company may specify that only master salespeople and senior salespeople may be assigned to relationship customers and that staff salespeople may only be assigned to transaction customers.

Not only can we typify objects once, but we can then further typify the object types. Recall the example of the specific computers categorized into model numbers, resulting in a typification relationship between finished computers and computer types. We could then further classify the computer types into categories such as premium gaming computers, premium business computers, moderate gaming computers, moderate business computers, and economy computers.

OPERATIONAL (ACCOUNTABILITY) AND POLICY INFRASTRUCTURES

Enterprises have two levels of infrastructure: operational and policy. In 2006, Geerts & McCarthy published a paper that discussed the application of REA constructs at two levels of enterprise infrastructure: operational (which they also call accountability) and policy. The **operational infrastructure** is composed of the daily activities of the enterprise carrying out its mission – in other words, what is actually happening. The policy infrastructure is composed of the rules, procedures, policies, and goals set by enterprise management – in other words, what should be, could be and must be. Exhibit 12-1 from Geerts & McCarthy's paper summarizes the interaction of these infrastructure levels.

Exhibit 12-1 from Geerts & McCarthy, 2006, Policy Level Specifications in REA Enterprise Information Systems, *Journal of Information Systems*, Vol. 20, Iss. 2, pp. 37-64.

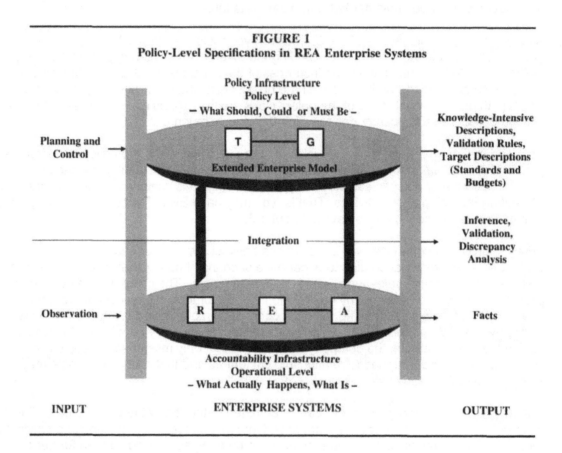

FIGURE 1
Policy-Level Specifications in REA Enterprise Systems

Since 2006, Geerts and McCarthy have continued to develop these ideas and added a third layer of what is planned or scheduled to complete the time expansion of REA. Their 3 layers of time expansion are shown in Exhibit 12-2. As the figure illustrates, the original REA constructs - Resources, Events, Agents, and the associations between them – comprise the operational/accountability infrastructure. They represent the past and near present activities of the enterprise, i.e., what has actually occurred or is currently occurring.

The typified REA constructs – Resource Types, Event Types, and Agent Types – are combined to form policies, as further illustrated in Exhibit 12-3. For example, the company may create a policy that an event type may only be done by certain agent types. As such, any association between two typified REA constructs is called a policy, and represents what could be or what should be. The time focus is therefore on the future. However, we can analyze operational data post hoc to determine its compliance with policies. Adding this policy infrastructure dimension to REA is an important advancement to facilitate the COSO framework objectives. Recall from chapter 4 that the COSO objectives include designing control activities (policies and procedures enterprises use to ensure necessary actions are taken to minimize risks associated with achieving enterprise objectives) and monitoring the quality of internal control performance over time. Declaring such policies in the database structure allows queries to be run to identify instances of non-compliance which can be addressed by management.

Exhibit 12-2: Three layers of time expansion with REA
Source: William McCarthy, Michigan State University

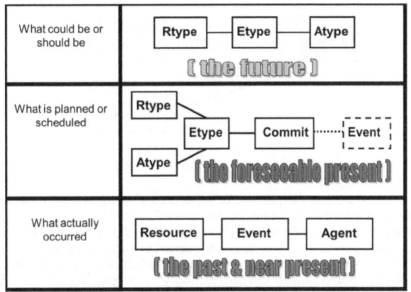

the elevator pitch for time expansion

Exhibit 12-3: Policy formation between typified REA constructs
Source: William McCarthy, Michigan State University

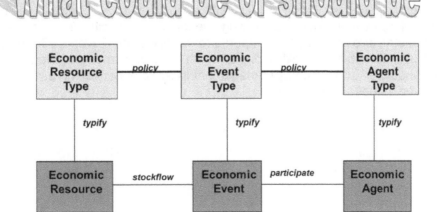

Exhibit 12-4: Abstract specification of commitments

Source: William McCarthy, Michigan State University

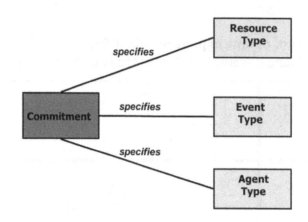

What is planned or scheduled

Exhibit 12-4 further illustrates the planned or scheduled element of the time expansion of REA modeling. While we introduced commitment events in earlier chapters, the commitments had more in common with the operational level than they did with the policy level. We tracked the resources that we expected to give or take, we tracked the economic events that fulfilled the commitment events, and we tracked the agents who participated in the agreements. However, we didn't track other details of what the commitment events specified. To more fully describe the enterprise activities and to help bridge the policy and operational infrastructures, Geerts & McCarthy advocate tracking the resource types, event types, and agent types that are specified by a commitment event. The specification between the commitment and the resource type is what we have previously discussed as reservation. The commitment reserves a resource or resource type so that it is not used for some other purpose when the economic event occurs to which the commitment agreed. None of our previously introduced associations are equivalent to the specifications between commitment and event type and between commitment and agent type. While we related commitment events to the economic events that fulfilled them, that fulfillment association is different from specification of the types of events to which the commitment agrees. Similarly while we tracked the agents who agreed to the commitment events, that participation is different from specification of the types of agents the commitment agrees will participate in the eventual fulfilling events. Such specifications are essentially part of the policy infrastructure and may be compared to the operational events after they occur to monitor compliance with the specifications to which the commitments agreed. Findings of non-compliance should be addressed by management to avoid negative impressions of the external agents involved in those commitments.

REA Accounting Systems: Resources-Events-Agents: An ontology for designing, controlling, and using integrated enterprise systems

397

IMPLEMENTATION COMPROMISE

An ideal information system is a model of perfection – it is what the information system would be if we could make it everything we desire. Unfortunately such an information system is not usually achievable. **Implementation compromises** are deviations from the identified ideal information system design due to practical considerations, insufficient measurement techniques, and other constraints. In this section we discuss some common implementation compromises in the design of enterprise-wide databases. Some of the implementation compromises we discuss are made at the conceptual level, some are made at the logical level, and some are made at the physical implementation level.

Conceptual Level Modeling Compromises

A **conceptual level compromise** is the use of less than ideal representation in a conceptual model because of an inability or lack of need to completely and accurately represent an object. Such compromises occur anytime we determine we cannot adequately represent or measure an object in reality. Common compromises made at the conceptual level include

- Exclusion of a class or association because of inadequate measurement mechanisms or because no decision need exists for that data.
- Consolidation of conceptually congruent classes.
- Materialization of tasks as event classes.

It is only practical to include measurable and definable phenomena in a conceptual model from which a database will be designed. Often we can identify the existence of phenomena that we cannot measure; it is an implementation compromise to exclude those objects from the conceptual model. For example, we may be aware that in an enterprise's revenue cycle, many different resources are being used up in the process of generating revenue. Fixed assets such as the storefront display room, the warehouse, the shelving within those facilities, equipment such as cash registers, supplies such as cash register tape, pens, and staplers, and the labor of sales personnel and support staff are consumed to varying degrees within the revenue cycle. However, trying to measure the extent to which each of those resources (and possibly others) are consumed within that cycle is a challenge. Until cost-effective means for directly measuring and tracing the resources consumed to the resources acquired as a result, the conceptual model for the revenue cycle must be compromised to exclude those immeasurable items. The cost of those resources may still be tracked via the acquisition cycle conceptual model; however, those costs must be represented only as period expenses rather than directly matched to the revenues they helped to produce.

In other cases measurement mechanisms may exist, but no decision need exists and therefore an enterprise may decide to exclude an entity or relationship. For example, if an enterprise has only one purchasing agent, and intends to always have only one purchasing agent, then there is no need to track which internal agent is responsible for purchases. Or if an enterprise sells merchandise only to cash customers and has no need to track information about individual customers, the enterprise could choose not to materialize a class for customer data. Sometimes an enterprise chooses not to implement all the associations called for by the REA pattern. For example, an enterprise may make a declarative/procedural trade-off, whereby it decides to exclude the declarative duality association between purchase and cash disbursement because the enterprise determines no need to apply payments directly to individual purchases and by procedurally tracing purchases and cash disbursements each to the related vendor, the enterprise may be able to determine accounts payable by vendor (though not by purchase).

In some enterprises, certain pairs or groups of events always occur simultaneously. Such events are called **conceptually congruent events**. The practical compromise is to collapse, or consolidate, the classes for conceptually congruent events. For example, consider Only Gas, a gas station/convenience store that sells only gasoline. Only Gas sells gasoline for cash – no credit cards, checks, or sales on account are permitted. Only Gas's procedures are as follows:

- Customers are required to bring their car keys and driver's licenses to the cashier's window, which is conveniently located adjacent to the gas pumps.
- Cashiers unlock the appropriate pumps, enabling the customers to pump gas.
- Customers pump gas into vehicles or containers, then return to the cashier's window; pay for the gas, retrieve their car keys and driver's licenses, and drive away.

These activities encompass multiple events within the sales/collection process, including the sale order, sale, and cash receipt. There is no identifiable need to separate these events for Only Gas, because they are conceptually congruent. That is, each occurrence of a sale order is automatically accompanied by an occurrence of sale and an occurrence of cash receipt. Another way of looking at this is that the multiplicity pattern is

Sale Order 1..1 – 1..1 Sale 1..1 – 1..1 Cash Receipt.

A sale order would not be entered into Only Gas's system without also entering exactly one sale and exactly one cash receipt. This allows the classes to be collapsed (consolidated) into a single class in the conceptual model. Therefore instead of the normal conceptual model reflecting

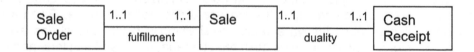

The compromised conceptual model could be portrayed as follows:

```
┌──────────┐
│ Cash     │
│ Sale     │
└──────────┘
```

The consolidation of conceptually congruent events simplifies the conceptual model as compared to the full REA ontology pattern. Another type of implementation compromise – **materialization of tasks as classes**, i.e., the representation of an activity that could be re-engineered away as a base object class – increases the complexity of the conceptual model. Recall from earlier chapters that workflow tasks that comprise an event may involve preparation of multiple documents. For example, the sale event as described in Chapters 3 and 5 may sometimes involve picking, packing, and shipping of inventory and may involve preparation of as many as four documents: picking slip, packing list, bill of lading, and sale invoice. Or the purchase requisition event as described in Chapters 3 and 5 may involve requesting quotes or bids from potential vendors to help determine the one with whom to place a purchase order. Some companies may determine they have a need to keep the attributes from each of these tasks separate from each other rather than combining them into the event they comprise. Therefore a company may choose to model the requests for quotes and the receipt of quotes from vendors as events between the purchase requisition and purchase order as follows:

Because the enterprise also would need to track each resource and agent involved with each of these activities, the complexity added to the conceptual model may be burdensome. Also, if workflow changes in the future, the database design will need to change. Enterprises should exercise caution in determining whether or not to materialize tasks as classes; in general it is not recommended. To make the determination, enterprises should consider what is needed to plan, control, execute, and evaluate its activities and employees. If the attributes can be stored and retrieved effectively for the needed decisions using the standard REA template, then the standard template should be used. If the attributes cannot be stored and retrieved effectively in the standard template for an enterprise, then separate classes should be created in which to store the task attributes.

Logical Level Modeling Compromises

Compromises are also made at the logical level. **Logical level compromises** are the deviations from pure theory made when converting a conceptual model into database objects such as relational tables. In fact, the procedures recommended in Chapter 5 for posting a foreign key for appropriate cardinality patterns that would result in high **load** (the percentage of non-null values for a posted foreign key) are a logical level implementation compromise. A theoretically pure relational database would never allow a null value in a table. To be completely consistent with the relational model theory, Chapter 5's step 5 should require relationships that have cardinality patterns of 0..1-0..1; 0..1-0..*; 0..1-1..*; 0..*-0..1; and 1..*-0..1 to be implemented with separate tables.

Such an implementation would avoid the possibility of null values. The trade-off is the extra storage space needed and the increased complexity of queries that involve multiple tables. Because queries often focus on relationships, relationships that are implemented with separate tables often require the use of three tables. By compromising the logical level for relationships for which a posted foreign key results in a relatively low number of null values, an enterprise usually can reduce query complexity.

A similar type of compromise is sometimes made when a class is related to two or more other classes and the associations are mutually exclusive; that is, an instance of Class A will be related to either an instance of Class B or to an instance of Class C. For example, Cash Disbursement is an event in multiple transaction cycles. In the payroll cycle, cash disbursements are made to employees. In the acquisition/payment cycle, cash disbursements are made to vendors. In the financing cycle, cash disbursements are made to creditors or investors. However, each cash disbursement is made to an instance of only one of those related classes.

Panel A of Exhibit 12-4 illustrates the integrated conceptual model with the cash disbursement class participating in three separate associations with external agents. Theoretically these three associations would either require three separate tables or (if more than half of all cash disbursements are made to one of these sets of external agents) a posted foreign key for the association with high load and two separate tables for the other two associations.

An implementation compromise could be made to post a single foreign key; for example, Payee, to implement all three associations. Such posting of a single foreign key to implement multiple associations is called **combined class key posting**. Panel B of Exhibit 12-4 illustrates this compromise. The value for the Payee would be an employee foreign key for a record that disburses cash to an employee, the value would be a supplier foreign key for a record representing cash disbursed to a supplier, and the value would be a creditor or investor foreign key for a record representing cash disbursed to a creditor or investor.

Exhibit 12-4: Combined Class Key Posting

Panel A: Conceptual Model

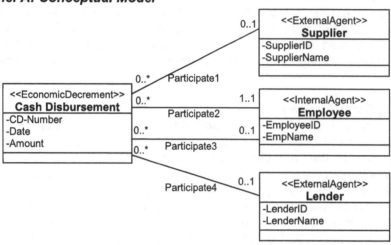

Note: Participate2 represents the association with the employee who processes payments (e.g., cashier, a/p clerk, or payroll clerk). Participate3 represents the association with the employee to whom the cash disbursement is made (e.g., a worker being paid in the payroll cycle).

Panel B: Logical Relational Model

Cash Disbursement (Economic Decrement Event)

CashDisbursement#	Date	Amount	EmplID^{FK}	Payee^{FK}

Employee (Internal and External Agent)

EmplID	Name

Supplier (External Agent)

Supplier ID	Name

Lender (External Agent)

Lender ID	Name

Participate1 is implemented via Supplier Payee ID posted from Supplier into Cash Disbursement.
Participate2 is implemented via EmplID posted from Employee into Cash Disbursement.
Participate3 is implemented via Employee Payee ID posted from Employee into Cash Disbursement.
Participate4 is implemented via Lender Payee ID posted from Lender into Cash Disbursement.

A disadvantage that results from combined class key posting is the inability to enforce referential integrity. In the example shown, the value for Payee could be posted from any of three different tables and referential integrity only verifies the value against one reference table. Therefore referential integrity for Participate1, Participate3, and Participate4 cannot be enforced. An alternative implementation compromise that could be used is to combine agents of different types about which similar attributes need to be stored into a single class. For example, employees, suppliers, and lenders could be combined into one class without the use of a generalization hierarchy as long as no specific attributes need to be stored about each subtype. The conceptual model for the previous example could be compromised as shown in Exhibit 12-5.

Exhibit 12.5: Combination of Classes Without Generalization

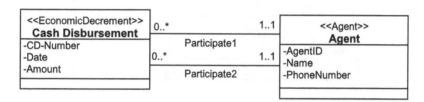

In this case, Participate1 portrays the relationship of the cash disbursement to the internal agent who processes it and Participate2 represents the relationship of the cash disbursement to the external agent to whom it is sent. Referential integrity may now be enforced. Because lenders, employees, and suppliers all had the same attributes stored for them, all that is necessary is the consolidation of any data values already entered into the tables when they were separate.

Physical Implementation Compromises

Compromises may also be made at the physical implementation level. A **physical level compromise** is a deviation from the theoretical ideal when converting the logical database model into specific database software to implement the working database. Physical implementation compromises include storage of **derivable attributes** (attributes whose value can be calculated from the values of other stored attributes) and event activity roll-ups. As described in Chapter 5, we recommend the storage of static derivable attributes because the cost of the extra storage space taken up by those attributes is likely outweighed by the benefit of less complexity, and therefore less processing power needed for queries that use those attributes. For example, if the enterprise sells mass-produced merchandise inventory, attributes such as quantity sold and actual unit selling price may be used to derive the total dollar amount of a sale. That is a static derivable attribute; that is, once the total dollar amount for Sale 1 is computed, it does not change as additional sales are added to the enterprise system. If the total sale dollar amount is stored as an attribute in the Sale event table, it simplifies all additional queries the enterprise needs that include total sales dollar amounts as components (e.g., accounts receivable, or total sales by salesperson)

Another physical implementation compromise is that of **event activity roll-up** – the aggregation of a group of event records into a single summary record once historical detail is no longer needed. This compromise recognizes that enterprise databases exist in a finite storage space and also recognizes that the larger the size of the database, the less efficient querying becomes. A benefit of enterprise information systems founded on enterprise-wide databases is the ability to produce financial statements without actually closing the books. This is sometimes called a virtual close. The disadvantage of never closing the books is the uncontrolled growth of the database – the database may quickly grow too large for optimized, proficient querying. One means of controlling that growth is to wait until such a time as event activity detail is not needed and then roll that data up into a single event occurrence. In Exhibit 12-6 we illustrate event activity roll-up.

Exhibit 12-6: Event Activity Roll-up

Sale – Original table

SaleID	Date	Amount	Customer	Salesperson
S1	1/1	$400.00	C23	SP4
S2	1/1	$450.00	C17	SP2
S3	1/5	$875.00	C46	SP3
S4	1/5	$125.00	C72	SP4
S5	1/6	$350.00	C14	SP3
S6	1/7	$500.00	C17	SP2
S7	1/8	$700.00	C46	SP3

Sale table with event activity rolled up

SaleID	Date	Amount	Customer	Salesperson
SR1	1/1	$3,400.00	C0	SP0

SR1 represents the set of sales 1 through 7.
C0 is set up as a placeholder customer (a customer number that indicates we can't track the customer).
SP0 is set up as a placeholder salesperson (indicates we can't track the salesperson).

CONCLUDING COMMENTS

This chapter discussed advanced concepts used in the policy infrastructure level of the REA ontology to support enterprise planning and control activities. The abstraction mechanisms generalization and typification allow for rich policy specification to be embedded into the enterprise database. This chapter also discussed the need for systems that aren't theoretically pure as a result of practical constraints such as hardware limitations and available measurement tools. Such implementation compromises must be applied with full understanding of what benefits the compromises may provide but also what opportunities they prevent.

Key Terms and Concepts

Abstraction	Implementation compromise
Accountability infrastructure	Load
Combined class key posting	Logical level compromise
Conceptual level compromise	Materialization of tasks as classes
Conceptually congruent events	Operational infrastructure
Derivable attribute	Physical level compromise
Event activity roll-up	Policy infrastructure
Generalization	Typification

Review Questions

R1. List and describe three conceptual level implementation compromises.

R2. List and describe three logical level implementation compromises.

R3. List and describe two physical level implementation compromises.

R4. The word compromise may seem like a negative concept – something we don't really want to do. In a database environment, are implementation compromises bad? Explain.

R5. Why might a company decide to roll up its cash disbursement event activity?

R6. Glorious Bea Enterprises (GBE) receives cash from various external business partners – investors, creditors, customers, and suppliers. GBE wants to store information about all external business partners in a single database table. Describe at least three of the implementation compromises GBE will need to make and discuss the pros and cons of its approach.

R7. Exhibit 12-1 illustrates generalization of employees. Think of another example of something an enterprise may need to keep track of a different levels of abstraction and draw a corresponding generalization in UML class diagram format.

R8. Explain the difference between typification and generalization.

R9. Explain the difference between the operational infrastructure and the policy infrastructure of an enterprise. Under which infrastructure are most accounting applications most appropriately classified? Explain.

R10. In the REA ontology, what name is given to associations between a commitment and the kinds of resources, events, and agents to which the commitment agrees?

Multiple Choice Questions

1. What abstraction mechanism creates an "is-a" relationship between a super-class and one or more sub-classes?
    A) Generalization
    B) Typification
    C) Conversion
    D) Fulfillment
    E) Specification

2. In the REA ontology, a relationship between two types (e.g. resource type and event type or event type and agent type) likely represents
    A) Typification
    B) Generalization
    C) Specification
    D) Policy
    E) Internal Control

3. In the REA ontology, a relationship between a commitment event and a resource type or an agent type likely represents
    A) Typification
    B) Generalization
    C) Specification
    D) Policy
    E) Internal Control

4. In the REA ontology, representation of what could be, should be, or must be is part of the
   A) Operational infrastructure
   B) Accountability infrastructure
   C) Policy infrastructure
   D) Both A and B above
   E) None of the above

5. Which compromise is commonly made at the conceptual level?
   A) Materialization of tasks as event entities.
   B) Consolidation of conceptually congruent entities.
   C) Exclusion of an entity or relationship because of inadequate measurement mechanisms or because no decision need exists for those data.
   D) Two of the above.
   E) All of the above.

6. In some enterprises, certain pairs or groups of events always occur simultaneously. These events are called:
   A) Logically congruent events
   B) Physically congruent events
   C) Conceptually congruent events
   D) Economically congruent
   E) None of the above

7. Which of the following is a disadvantage that results from combined class key posting?
   A) Inability to run queries
   B) Inability to enforce referential integrity
   C) Uncontrolled growth of the database
   D) The need for outer join queries
   E) All of the above

8. Which of the following is a physical level compromise?
   A) Event activity (or event history) roll-up
   B) Combined entity key posting
   C) Consolidation of conceptually congruent event entities
   D) Materialization of tasks as event entities
   E) Exclusion of an entity or relationship in a model because of inadequate measurement mechanisms or because no decision need exists for those data

9. Posting a foreign key to implement a relationship when it results in a high load is an example of a:
   A) Physical level implementation compromise
   B) Logical level implementation compromise
   C) Conceptual level implementation compromise
   D) None of the above.

REA Accounting Systems: Resources-Events-Agents: An ontology for designing, controlling, and using integrated enterprise systems

405

10. Which compromise recognizes that enterprise databases exist in a finite storage space and also recognizes that the larger the size of the database, the less efficient querying becomes?
A) Event activity (or event history) roll-up
B) Storage of derivable attributes
C) Combined entity key posting
D) Consolidation of conceptually congruent event entities
E) None of the above

CHAPTER 13

The Conversion Business Process

LEARNING OBJECTIVES

The objectives of this chapter are to introduce the conversion business process; to discuss the REA ontology representation of conversion processes, and to describe some of the typical information needs in the conversion business process. After studying this chapter you should be able to

1. Identify the activities common to most conversion business processes
2. Recognize similarities and differences between different types of conversion processes
3. Identify the various components of the REA ontology in the Conversion business process
4. Create a REA business process level model for an enterprise's Conversion process
5. Identify common information needs that exist within the Conversion process
6. Create database queries to retrieve Conversion process information from a relational database

INTRODUCTION TO THE CONVERSION BUSINESS PROCESS

The **conversion process** includes the business events associated with converting raw inputs such as materials, labor, machinery, and other fixed assets into finished outputs. Most of the time the conversion process involves the manufacture or production of finished goods, so it is sometimes called the manufacturing process or the production process. As you analyze and model a business process, you must clearly understand its purpose and objectives. You will better understand this process if you can base your understanding on some personal experience. Have you ever been involved in a conversion cycle? Perhaps you do not have experience in the manufacturing process of a corporation or other business entity; however, most people have participated in the production of some type of finished product. Have you ever cooked, made crafts, created something on a computer, written a story, or made lemonade? If so, then you have some real life experience with conversion cycle activities. In this chapter we use the example of baking cookies to demonstrate many of the concepts[1]. If you have never baked cookies before, we recommend you find a recipe and bake a batch of your favorite cookies before reading the rest of this chapter!

It may seem to you that the conversion processes for most firms will be different because the products they produce are so different. Indeed, the specific workflow tasks vary greatly among enterprises. However, the REA business process level pattern underlies all conversion processes. In analyzing the conversion process for an enterprise, you must first realize how the conversion process fits into the value system of the enterprise as a whole. As discussed in chapter 2, at the value system level the conversion process is completely inside the enterprise bubble (see Exhibit 13-1). It is an internal business process that typically does not provide a point of contact with any external agents. Although an enterprise may need information from external agents or may need to provide information to external agents regarding the conversion

---

[1] Thank you to Julie Smith David of the American Accounting Association for the idea of using cookie baking to illustrate conversion cycle concepts.

REA Accounting Systems: Resources-Events-Agents: An ontology for designing, controlling, and using integrated enterprise systems

407

process, keep in mind that the value system level depicts *resource* flows, *not* information flows. Typically any resource flows between the enterprise and the external agents are part of either the acquisition/payment or the revenue processes that interface with the conversion process.

Exhibit 9-1 Conversion Process in the Enterprise Value System

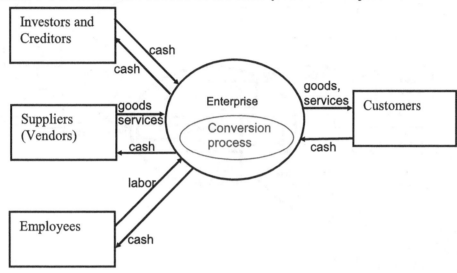

Consider also the value chains we discussed in chapter 2. Value chain reveal resource interfaces between business processes. Exhibit 13-2 illustrates the typical value chain for manufacturers. Materials and machinery are made available to the conversion process as a result of the acquisition/payment process. Labor is made available to the conversion process as a result of the human resource/payroll process. The conversion process turns those inputs (materials, machinery, and labor) into finished products, which are made available to the revenue process. In order to convert the labor, materials, equipment, and overhead items such as utilities and supplies into finished goods, the conversion process must include economic events that use up those inputs (**labor operation** uses up labor, **raw material issuance** uses materials, and **machine operation** consumes equipment) and an economic event that produces the finished products.

Exhibit 13-2: Typical Value Chain for a Manufacturer

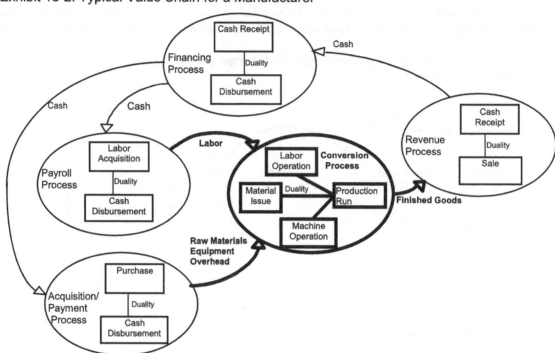

CONVERSION BUSINESS PROCESS LEVEL REA MODELS

Conversion processes can be broadly categorized into two types: batch processes and continuous processes. Batch processes involve the production of an established number of units of a product, or they may involve the completion of a job such as a car repair, the printing of a customized wedding invitation, or a consulting engagement. Continuous processes produce a homogeneous product somewhat continuously. Examples include the production of cement, petroleum products, flour, beer, and steel. The main difference between batch processes and continuous processes is that for batch processes, natural starting and ending points exist for assigning costs to the production run, whereas for continuous processes, artificial starting and ending points must be created for cost assignment purposes. Usually these start and end points are arbitrarily chosen boundaries of a time period. The time period may span minutes, hours, days, weeks, or even months, depending on the nature of the enterprise's conversion process. Presumably the time periods should be chosen such that they are long enough to include the production of at least one identifiable resource. For example, the time period used for the economic increment event for an agricultural crop may be designated as the growing season, whereas an hour may be deemed an appropriate time period for a production run of breakfast cereal. Once the production run event is determined as either a batch, job, time period, etc., cost assignment is relatively straightforward. The assignment of manufacturing costs to units produced is an averaging process; you simply divide the manufacturing costs (accumulated either by job, batch, or time period) by the number of units produced in that job, batch, or time period.

We begin our detailed discussion of the conversion process by reviewing some of its more common events in the context of cookie baking. While it is true that a wide variety of workflow activities may be included in a conversion process, and as a result the task level modeling will vary accordingly, a pattern exists into which the activities can be categorized for data storage and for data exchange purposes for most, if not all, enterprises.

Recall that the REA pattern captures data to answer the *who, what, where, when, why* questions regarding a transaction cycle. Answers to the *when* and *where* questions are typically stored as attributes, unless the location is also a resource, e.g. a specific warehouse or machine. Answers to the *who, what*, and *why* questions are provided by the associations captured in the core REA pattern as illustrated for the conversion cycle in Exhibit 13-3. The participation associations identify the *who* for each event, and the stockflow associations indicate the *what* for each event. The duality association reveals *why* the enterprise engages in the economic events of the cycle.

Exhibit 13-3 Conversion Cycle Core REA Pattern

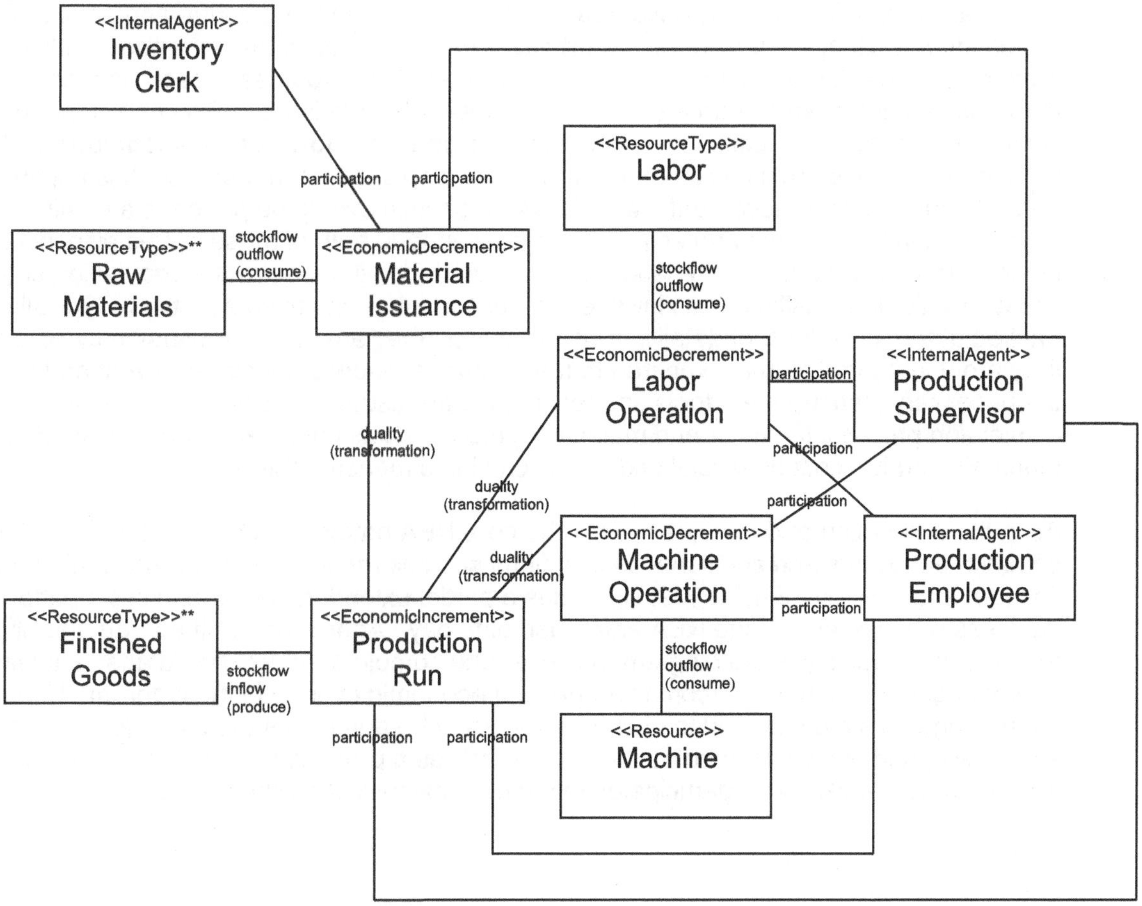

** If each physical instance of raw material or of finished goods is uniquely identified, then that class would be stereotyped as Resource rather than Resource Type

The core REA pattern for the conversion cycle consists of the same components as the core pattern for the sales/collection and acquisition/payment processes. Recall that the core REA pattern for those cycles contains economic increment events paired by duality with economic decrement events. Each economic event is linked to the resource or resource type that the event increases or decreases, and each economic event is linked to at least one initiator agent (who may be internal or external) and at least one responsible agent (who is typically internal). In the conversion cycle instead of only two paired economic exchange events, typically four economic events are tracked in detail. Three of these events are economic decrement events that represent the using up of the machinery, labor, and raw materials. The fourth event is the economic increment event – the **production run** that produces the finished goods. Although the duality association is in essence a 4-way relationship between four events, for ease of implementation we represent it as three binary relationships, each of which has the inherent causality of duality. The company gives up the labor in the labor operation because it expects to end up with the finished good from the production run. Likewise the company gives up the materials in the material issuance and gives up use of the machinery in the machine operation because it expects to end up with the finished good from the production run.

The duality association in the conversion cycle is slightly different from the duality associations in the sales/collection and acquisition/payment processes. In the revenue and acquisition cycles, duality usually is a **transfer duality association**. That is, the enterprise trades one or more resource(s) for another resource. Usually one of the resources is cash and the other resource is a non-cash resource such as **raw materials** or finished goods inventory. In the conversion process, the duality association is a **transformation duality association**. That is, the enterprise transforms raw input resources into a finished good resource. It is important to note that there is no requirement that only two economic events be paired in a duality association in the revenue and acquisition cycles; in fact, both of those cycles also include labor operations that use up the labor resource. Activities in those cycles may also use up fixed assets, equipment, utilities, etc. However, the use of labor and fixed assets are typically not tracked at the same level of detail in those cycles as they are in the conversion cycle, because they are usually immaterial compared to the primary economic decrement event and because the necessary measurement tools and techniques are usually cost-prohibitive. In the conversion process, the labor and machine operation costs often exceed the costs of the raw materials and it is cost beneficial and in fact crucial to measure them.

As in the acquisition and revenue cycles, the core REA pattern has been extended to include commitment events and additional associations such as reservation, reciprocal, fulfillment, linkage, and custody. Exhibit 13-4 illustrates a partial extended conversion cycle pattern for the business process level of the REA enterprise ontology. Agents are omitted from this illustration to improve readability of the diagram; however, the complete model should attach at least one internal agent to each event (commitments and economic events) in the diagram. Usually two internal agents are connected to each event – one who authorizes the event (such as a supervisor) and one who executes the event (such as a production employee). A **production employee** is a worker who participates in the manufacture of finished goods.

Exhibit 13-4 Extended REA Conversion Cycle Business Process Level Pattern

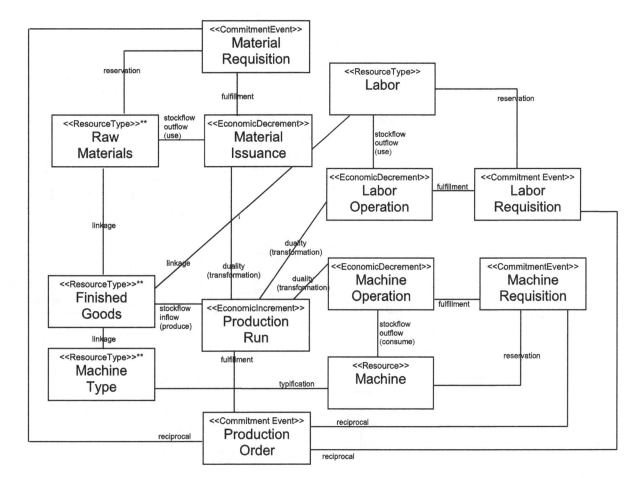

As in the acquisition and revenue cycles, the specific labels on the resources, events, and agents will differ depending on the nature of the enterprise's conversion cycle. Exhibit 13-5 illustrates labels that could be used for an enterprise whose conversion cycle involves cookie baking.

Exhibit 13-5 Cookie Baking Example Conversion Business Process Level Model

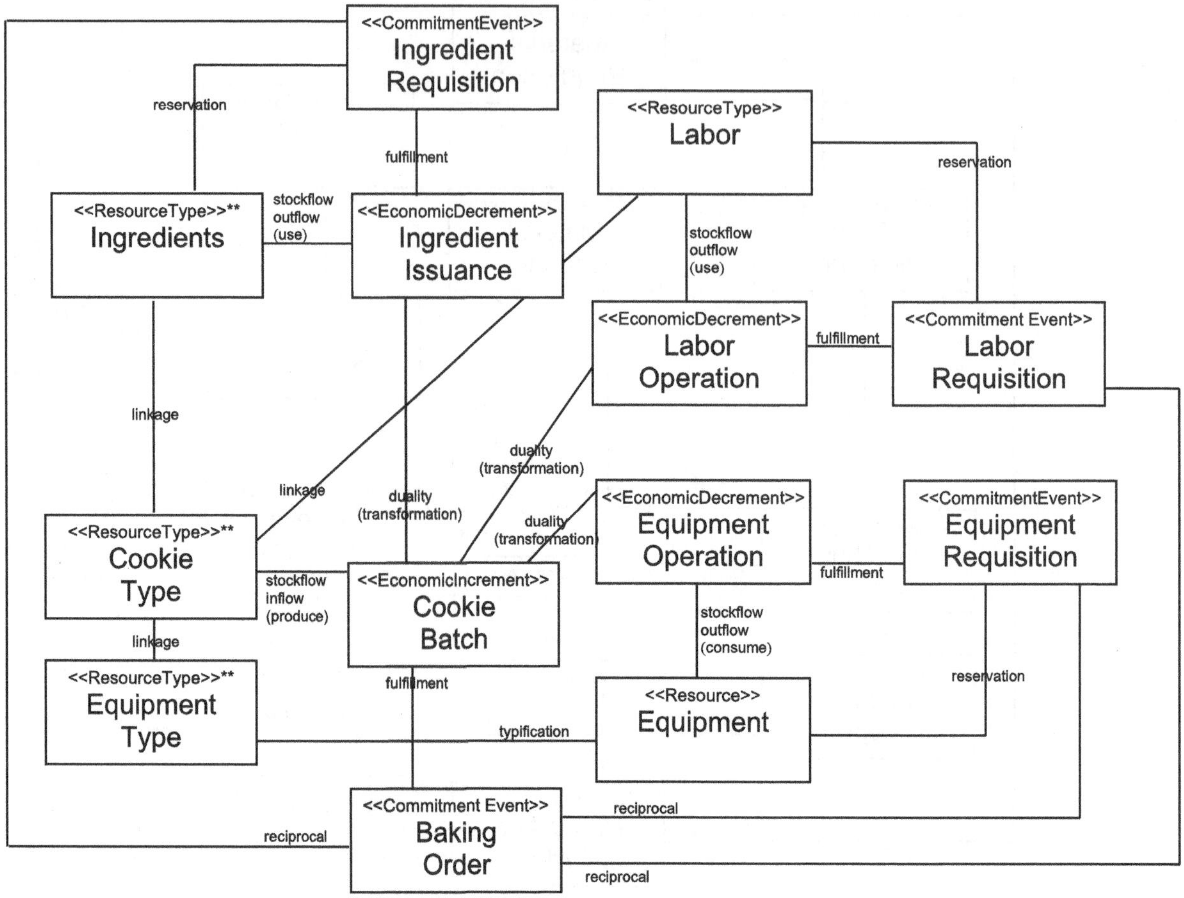

Economic Increment Event: Production Run

The center of the pattern is made up of the duality association and the events that participate in that relationship. The event that usually comes to mind when contemplating the conversion process is the production run, because that is the event that actually increases the quantity of a finished good. In other words, the production run is the event that is intended to achieve the overall objective of the conversion process – the production of a finished product resource. In the example of Exhibit 13-5, the cookie batch is the economic increment event – that is, the production run event that produces finished cookies. Data typically captured regarding production run events are an assigned identifier for the event, the date/time the event started, and the date/time the event ended. Data are also recorded as to what resources and agents are involved.

The relational tables in Exhibit 13-6 illustrate some of the data attributes that may be captured with respect to the cookie batch event and its related resources and agents. The cookie batch table stores the event data that pertains to each batch as a whole – when it started, when it ended, how many cookies the batch was supposed to produce as well as how many cookies the batch actually did produce, and the supervisor in charge of the batch. The cookie type table stores the resource data that describes the finished cookies. In this case the resources are not individually identified (e.g. with a separate identification number for each physical cookie) but instead are identified at the type or category level (i.e., each separate kind of cookie is assigned a different identification code). For some enterprises, each physical product may need to be specifically identified with a serial number. In that case, both a finished resource class and a resource-type class need to be included in the conceptual model. We will discuss such a situation later in the chapter.

The stockflow table stores the data needed to identify which type of cookie was produced in each cookie batch. The baking supervisor table stores data that describes supervisors, such as their names and phone numbers. The participation association between baking supervisor and cookie batch is not represented with a separate table, but is traceable via a posted foreign key of supervisor id in the cookie batch table. The baking employee table stores data that describes production employees, such as their names, phone numbers, and which supervisor is assigned responsibility for them. The participation-cookiebatch-bakingemployee table represents the relationship between baking employees and cookie batches, enabling users to identify which employees worked on each separate cookie batch.

In this example, we can see that Larry, Moe, and Curly baked 40 frosted sugar cookies with candy sprinkles under the supervison of Ricky. They started on July 15, 2015 at 6:30 a.m. and finished that same day at 7:15 a.m. Fred and Ethel baked 48 snickerdoodles under the supervision of Lucy. They also started on July 15, 2015 at 6:30 a.m.; however, they took longer to finish their batch, ending at 7:37 a.m.

Exhibit 13-6 Relational Database Tables Encompassing Cookie Batch Event

CookieBatch

BatchID	StartTime	CompletionTime	Scheduled Quantity	Actual Quantity	SupervisorID
WJ1	7/15/2015 6:30:00 AM	7/15/2015 7:15:00 AM	40	40	S2
WJ2	7/15/2015 6:30:00 AM	7/15/2015 7:37:00 AM	48	48	S1

StockflowCookieBatch-CookieType

BatchID	FinishedCookieTypeID
WJ1	FSCS
WJ2	SN

CookieType

CookieID	Description	UnitsPerPackage	ListPrice
CC	Chocolate chip plain	12	$2.99
CCP	Chocolate chip with pecans	12	$2.99
FSCS	Frosted sugar cookies with candy sprinkles	10	$3.59
M	Molasses	12	$3.29
OR	Oatmeal raisin	12	$2.99
PB	Peanut butter	12	$2.99
SC	Sugar cookies plain	12	$2.99
SN	Snickerdoodles	12	$3.59

Exhibit 13-6 cont.: Relational Database Tables Encompassing Cookie Batch Event

BakingSupervisor

SupervisorID	SupervisorName	SupervisorPhone
S1	Lucy	1-1234
S2	Ricky	1-4321

Baking Employee

EmployeeID	EmployeeName	EmployeePhone	SupervisorID
PE1	Fred	1-6789	S2
PE2	Ethel	1-9876	S2
PE3	Larry	1-7698	S1
PE4	Moe	1-6798	S1
PE5	Curly	1-8796	S1

ParticipationCookieBatchBakingEmployee

BatchID	EmployeeID
WJ1	PE3
WJ1	PE4
WJ1	PE5
WJ2	PE1
WJ2	PE2

Economic Decrement Event: Material Issuance

The cookie batch event is also involved in the duality association, which as noted earlier, was separated from a four-way relationship into three binary duality relationships that identify what economic decrement events the enterprise must engage in such that the economic increment event can occur. In other words, it identifies what the enterprise needed to use up in order to produce the finished cookies. One economic decrement event that typically exists is the using up of raw materials in the production process. Those raw materials are usually transformed into finished goods and lose their own identity and nature in the process. Such an event is given a label such as material issuance and the stockflow association between the issuance event and the raw materials is specified as a **use stockflow association** to reflect the fact that the materials are completely used up. In the cookie-baking example, the label ingredient issuance has been used for the materials issuance event. Data typically captured regarding material issuance events are an assigned identifier for the issuance, the date/time of the issuance, and the location of the issuance. Data are also recorded as to what resources and agents are involved and the underlying **production order**, which is a document that captures information about a production order event.

A **move ticket** is typically used to document the issuance of raw materials into production; therefore, sometimes the move ticket number becomes the assigned identifier used to identify the event. See Exhibit 13-7 for an example move ticket document.

REA Accounting Systems: Resources-Events-Agents: An ontology for designing, controlling, and using integrated enterprise systems

415

Exhibit 13-7 Example Move Ticket document

Move Ticket
No. _____

Batch Number _____

Move Date: _____

Moved From: _____   Taken by: _____

Moved To: _____   Received by: _____

Production Order Number: _____

The relational tables in Exhibit 13-8 illustrate some of the data attributes that may be captured with respect to the ingredient issuance event and its associations with ingredients, inventory clerks, supervisors, and with the cookie batch event. The duality table identifies which ingredient issuances apply to which cookie batches. The ingredient issuance table stores the event data that pertains to each issuance, such as when and where it occurred, who authorized it (supervisor) and who executed it (inventory clerk). In the example shown, the participation associations between baking supervisor and ingredient issuance and between inventory clerk and ingredient issuance are not represented by separate tables, but are traceable via posted foreign keys of supervisor id and employee id in the ingredient issuance table.

The ingredients table stores the resource data that describes the types of ingredients available for use in the production process. As with the finished cookies, the ingredients are not individually identified but instead are identified at the type or category level (i.e., each separate kind of ingredient is assigned a different identification code). The stockflow table stores the data needed to identify which type of ingredient (and how much of each) was actually issued in each ingredient issuance event.

In this example, we can see that Ted and Alice issued several different ingredients to Ricky and to Lucy for the frosted sugar cookie and snickerdoodle cookie batches on July 15, 2015 between 6:20 and 6:30 a.m. Each of the ingredients was issued to the workcenter where the initial work involving the ingredients was to take place.

Exhibit 13-8 Relational Database Tables Encompassing Ingredient Issuance Event

DualityCookieBatch-IngredientIssuance

BatchID	IngredientIssuanceID
WJ1	RMI4238
WJ1	RMI4239
WJ1	RMI4240
WJ2	RMI4241
WJ2	RMI4242
WJ1	RMI4243
WJ2	RMI4244
WJ1	RMI4245
WJ2	RMI4246

IngredientIssuance

IngredientIssuanceID	IssuanceTime	Location	InventoryClerkID	SupervisorID
RMI4238	7/15/2015 6:20:00 AM	WorkcenterA	IC1	S2
RMI4239	7/15/2015 6:22:00 AM	WorkcenterB	IC2	S2
RMI4240	7/15/2015 6:24:00 AM	WorkcenterC	IC2	S2
RMI4241	7/15/2015 6:28:00 AM	WorkcenterD	IC1	S1
RMI4242	7/15/2015 6:26:00 AM	WorkcenterE	IC2	S1
RMI4243	7/15/2015 6:29:00 AM	WorkcenterC	IC1	S2
RMI4244	7/15/2015 6:29:30 AM	WorkcenterE	IC1	S1
RMI4245	7/15/2015 6:29:00 AM	WorkcenterC	IC2	S2
RMI4246	7/15/2015 6:29:30 AM	WorkcenterE	IC2	S1

StockflowIssuanceofIngredients

IngredientID	IssuanceID	QuantityIssued	UnitOfMeasure
WS	RMI4238	5	cups
FL	RMI4238	7	cups
EG	RMI4239	4	each
SH	RMI4239	2	cups
VN	RMI4239	3	teaspoons
SL	RMI4238	2	teaspoons
CS	RMI4240	1	cup
WS	RMI4241	6	cups
FL	RMI4241	8	cups
EG	RMI4242	4	each
SH	RMI4242	3	cups
VN	RMI4242	4	teaspoons
SL	RMI4241	2	teaspoons
CN	RMI4241	1	cup
PK	RMI4243	4	each
PK	RMI4244	4	each
ILFS	RMI4245	4	each
ILSN	RMI4246	4	each

Exhibit 13-8 Continued

Ingredients

IngredientID	Description	UnitOfMeasure	StandardCostPerUnitOfMeasure
WS	White sugar	50 lb bag	$10.00
EG	Eggs, large AA grade	2 dozen carton	$1.29
FL	Flour, white sifted	100 lb bag	$20.00
VN	Vanilla, pure	1 liter bottle	$20.00
SL	Salt, iodized	5 lb bag	$1.00
PB	Peanut butter	10 lb jar	$8.37
CN	Cinnamon	16 oz tin	$3.29
CM	Chocolate morsels	10 lb bag	$19.49
PE	Pecans	2 lb bag	$5.32
SH	Shortening	10 lb can	$12.10
CS	Candy sprinkles	1 lb tin	$3.18
BU	Butter	10 lb box	$3.98
BS	Brown sugar	50 lb bag	$9.47
PK	Plastic container	each	$0.12
ILFS	Ingredient label - frosted sugar	each	$0.01
ILSN	Ingredient label - snickerdoodle	each	$0.01

InventoryClerk

InventoryClerkID	ClerkName	ClerkPhone
IC1	Ted	1-5678
IC2	Alice	1-8765

Baking Supervisor

SupervisorID	SupervisorName	SupervisorPhone
S1	Lucy	1-1234
S2	Ricky	1-4321

Economic Decrement Event: Labor Operation

The labor operation event is an economic decrement event that represents the performance of a specific activity in the conversion process by a production employee, thereby using up the resource of that person's labor. Many people often are confused as to the difference between labor (also called **labor type**) and labor operation. Labor is a resource-type class that represents a list of the types of labor that can be performed in labor operations. Labor operations are the actual using up of the available labor. Data typically captured to describe labor types are the description and standard or budget information such as the standard hourly cost of each type of labor. Data typically captured to describe labor operations are the starting and ending date/time of the labor operation events and the total elapsed time of each labor operation. Keep in mind that data regarding labor types and labor operations will only be captured and stored if measurement techniques exist and are cost-effective. In the acquisition and revenue cycle, labor operations and labor types are typically not measured and recorded. In the conversion process, labor operations are often (but not always) measured and recorded.

When they are measured and recorded, labor operations are usually documented on **job time tickets**, documents that detail start and stop times and descriptions of labor operations on a specific date by a specific employee. Some enterprises call these documents time tracks instead of job time tickets. Either way, the document number typically serves as an identifier for the labor operation event. See Exhibit 13-9 for an example job time ticket.

Exhibit 13-9 Example Job Time Ticket form

Job Time Ticket No._____					
Employee ID _____		Name _____		Date _____	
Start time	Stop time	Total time	Rate	Total Amount	Job Number
Approved by _____ Department Supervisor					

The relational tables in Exhibit 13-10 illustrate some of the data attributes that may be captured with respect to the labor operations event and its associations with labor, baking employees, baking supervisors, and with the cookie batch event. The duality table identifies which labor operations apply to which cookie batches. The labor operations table stores the event data that pertains to each labor operation, such as when it began and ended, who authorized it (supervisor) and who executed it (employee). The labor table stores the resource data that describes the types of labor available for use in the production process. The stockflow table stores the data needed to identify which type of labor (and how much of each) was actually used in each labor operation event.

The participation association between baking supervisor and labor operation is not represented with a separate table, but is traceable via a posted foreign key of supervisor id in the labor operations table. Similarly, the participation association between baking employee and labor operations is represented with the employee id posted as a foreign key in the labor operations table.

In this example, we can see that to make the frosted sugar cookies, Larry took 10 minutes to mix the dry ingredients while Moe took 12 minutes to mix the moist ingredients. Curly took 5 minutes to combine the dry and moist ingredients. Larry took 5 minutes to form the cookies into dough and put them onto a cookie sheet. Curly took 1 minute to put the cookie sheet into the oven and set the timer. Twelve minutes later, Curly took the cookies out of the oven. Four and a half minutes later Larry took 4 minutes to frost the cookies, then Moe took 1 minute to add candy sprinkles and Curly took 2 minutes to package the final cookies.

Meanwhile, to bake the snickerdoodles, Fred took 10 minutes to mix the dry ingredients while Ethel took 10 minutes to mix the moist ingredients. Ethel then took 5 minutes to combine the dry and moist ingredients and then she took 2 minutes to form the dough and put the cookies onto the cookie sheet. Fred took 1 minute to put the cookies into the oven and set the timer. Twelve minutes later Fred took 30 seconds to take the cookies out of the oven. Nearly 35 minutes later, Ethel took 2 minutes to package the finished cookies. Notice that one of the things the tables don't show us is the reason for significant gaps in time – for example, why did they wait 35 minutes to package the cookies? It turns out that Fred thought Ethel had packaged them already, whereas Ethel thought that was Fred's responsibility. Lucy was in a comic mood and had been keeping them so well entertained they didn't realize they weren't finished until Ricky came in to gloat to Lucy that his crew had already finished their cookies even though they had the harder cookies to make (harder in that they involved more labor operations).

Exhibit 13-10 Relational Database Tables Encompassing Labor Operation Event

LaborOperation

LaborOperationID	StartTime	EndTime	EmployeeID	SupervisorID	LaborReqID
LO21	7/15/2015 6:30:00 AM	7/15/2015 6:40:00 AM	PE3	S2	LR2
LO22	7/15/2015 6:30:00 AM	7/15/2015 6:40:00 AM	PE4	S2	LR2
LO23	7/15/2015 6:40:00 AM	7/15/2015 6:45:00 AM	PE5	S2	LR2
LO24	7/15/2015 6:45:00 AM	7/15/2015 6:50:00 AM	PE3	S2	LR2
LO25	7/15/2015 6:50:00 AM	7/15/2015 6:51:00 AM	PE5	S2	LR2
LO26	7/15/2015 7:03:00 AM	7/15/2015 7:03:30 AM	PE5	S2	LR2
LO27	7/15/2015 7:08:00 AM	7/15/2015 7:12:00 AM	PE3	S2	LR2
LO28	7/15/2015 7:12:00 AM	7/15/2015 7:13:00 AM	PE4	S2	LR2
LO29	7/15/2015 7:13:00 AM	7/15/2015 7:15:00 AM	PE5	S2	LR2
LO30	7/15/2015 6:30:00 AM	7/15/2015 6:40:00 AM	PE1	S1	LR1
LO31	7/15/2015 6:30:00 AM	7/15/2015 6:40:00 AM	PE2	S1	LR1
LO32	7/15/2015 6:40:00 AM	7/15/2015 6:45:00 AM	PE2	S1	LR1
LO33	7/15/2015 6:45:00 AM	7/15/2015 6:47:00 AM	PE2	S1	LR1
LO34	7/15/2015 6:47:00 AM	7/15/2015 6:48:00 AM	PE1	S1	LR1
LO35	7/15/2015 7:00:00 AM	7/15/2015 7:00:30 AM	PE1	S1	LR1
LO36	7/15/2015 7:35:00 AM	7/15/2015 7:37:00 AM	PE2	S1	LR1

Baking Employee

EmployeeID	EmployeeName	EmployeePhone	SupervisorID
PE1	Fred	1-6789	S2
PE2	Ethel	1-9876	S2
PE3	Larry	1-7698	S1
PE4	Moe	1-6798	S1
PE5	Curly	1-8796	S1

Exhibit 13-10 Continued

DualityCookieBatch-LaborOperation

BatchID	LaborOperationID
WJ1	LO21
WJ1	LO22
WJ1	LO23
WJ1	LO24
WJ1	LO25
WJ1	LO26
WJ1	LO28
WJ1	LO29
WJ2	LO30
WJ2	LO33
WJ2	LO34
WJ2	LO35
WJ2	LO36

Labor Type

LaborTypeID	Description
L1	Mix dry ingredients
L2	Mix moist ingredients
L3	Combine dry and moist ingredients
L4	Add morsels to mixed dough
L5	Add nuts to mixed dough
L6	Form dough into cookies
L7	Put cookies onto cookie sheet
L8	Put cookie sheet into oven
L9	Set cookie timer
L10	Take cookie sheet out of oven
L11	Frost cookies
L12	Sprinkle cookies
L13	Package cookies

REA Accounting Systems: Resources-Events-Agents: An ontology for designing, controlling, and using integrated enterprise systems

421

Exhibit 13-10 Continued

StockflowLaborTypeinLaborOperation

LaborTypeID	LaborOperationID
L1	LO21
L2	LO22
L3	LO23
L6	LO24
L7	LO24
L8	LO25
L9	LO25
L10	LO26
L11	LO27
L12	LO28
L13	LO29
L1	LO30
L2	LO31
L3	LO32
L7	LO33
L8	LO34
L9	LO34
L10	LO35
L13	LO36

Economic Decrement Event: Machine Operation

Along with using up materials and labor, conversion processes also often use up machinery and equipment. An economic decrement event called machine operation is included in the REA enterprise ontology to capture the consumption of a portion of the machine's useful life. The machine operation event is slightly different in nature from the material issuance and labor operation economic decrement events, in that the machinery typically still exists in its original form (although with some added wear and tear) after the machine operation occurs. In contrast, the material issuance and labor operation events result in the materials and available labor being completely used up – they no longer exist in their original form but have been transformed into finished goods. Nevertheless, part of the machine's useful life has been consumed and represents a resource decrease that in some cases is cost-beneficial to measure and record. Although machine operations could be tracked using a separate document similar to a job time ticket, usually machine operations are only tracked on the production run cost sheet.

In our cookie baking example it makes sense to label this event as equipment operation as that more closely describes the types of machines used in baking cookies: ovens, mixers, utensils, pans, and measuring devices. Notice that we are using the term machine loosely – to represent any fixed asset used in production; some enterprises may prefer to only track consumption of fixed assets that exceed a certain cost value. The relational tables in Exhibit 13-11 illustrate some of the data attributes that may be captured with respect to the equipment operation event and its associations with equipment, baking employees, baking supervisors, and with the cookie batch event. The duality table identifies which equipment operations apply to which cookie batches. The equipment operation table stores the event data that pertains to each equipment operation, such as when it began and ended, who authorized it (supervisor) and who executed it (employee). The equipment table stores the resource data that describes the equipment available for use in the production process. Each piece of equipment or machine is specifically identified with a unique id; that is, this is a token-level class rather than a type-level class. Specific identification of fixed assets allows the tracking of cost allocation in accordance with generally accepted accounting principles.   The stockflow table stores the data needed to identify which equipment was actually used in each equipment operation event. The equipment does not get completely used up in the equipment operation; rather, it is partially consumed. Thus the stockflow association between equipment and an equipment operation event is called a **consume stockflow** association. The same piece of equipment can thus be used in multiple equipment operations.

The participation associations between baking supervisor and equipment operation and between baking employee and equipment operation are not represented with separate tables, but are traceable via posted foreign keys of supervisor id and employee id in the equipment operations table.

In this example, we can see that the sugar cookie production run (batch) required three equipment operations. The first was a measure and mix operation that partially consumed a heavy duty mixer and measuring device set. The second was a baking operation that partially consumed a cookie sheet and an oven. The third was a finishing operation that partially consumed frosting utensils. The snickerdoodle batch required only two machine operations. The first was a measure and mix operation that partially consumed a heavy duty mixer and a measuring device set. The second was a baking operation that partially consumed a cookie sheet and an oven.

Exhibit 13-11 Relational Database Tables Encompassing Equipment Operation Event

DualityCookieBatchEquipmentOperation

BatchID	EquipOperationID
WJ1	MO12
WJ1	MO13
WJ1	MO14
WJ2	MO15
WJ2	MO16

MachineOperation

MachineOperationID	StartTime	EndTime	EmployeeID	SupervisorID	EquipReqID
MO12	7/15/2015 6:30:00 AM	7/15/2015 6:45:00 AM	PE5	S2	ER2
MO13	7/15/2015 6:51:00 AM	7/15/2015 7:03:00 AM	PE5	S2	ER2
MO14	7/15/2015 7:08:00 AM	7/15/2015 7:12:00 AM	PE3	S2	ER2
MO15	7/15/2015 6:30:00 AM	7/15/2015 6:45:00 AM	PE2	S1	ER1
MO16	7/15/2015 6:40:00 AM	7/15/2015 7:00:00 AM	PE2	S1	ER1

Exhibit 13-11 Continued

Equipment

FixedAssetID	Description	Acquisition Date	Cost	Estimated LifeYears	Estimated SalvageValue
FA1	Oven	1/3/2015	$400.00	10	$50.00
FA2	Oven	4/2/2014	$500.00	3	$100.00
FA3	Heavy duty mixer	3/17/2014	$150.00	3	$0.00
FA4	Measuring device set	2/16/2014	$80.00	5	$10.00
FA5	Cookie sheet	2/18/2014	$10.00	3	$0.00
FA6	Cookie sheet	1/3/2015	$15.00	3	$0.00
FA7	Frosting utensils	1/3/2015	$10.00	5	$0.00
FA8	Heavy duty mixer	2/15/2015	$170.00	3	$0.00
FA9	Measuring device set	2/15/2015	$75.00	5	$10.00

StockflowEquipmentinEquipmentOperation

FixedAssetID	EquipOperationID
FA1	MO13
FA2	MO16
FA3	MO12
FA4	MO12
FA5	MO13
FA6	MO16
FA7	MO14
FA8	MO15
FA9	MO15

Commitment to Economic Increment Event: Production Order
The discussion thus far has centered on the core economic exchange pattern in the REA ontology at the business process level. We next discuss the extension of the pattern to include commitment events and related resource and agent associations. In the conversion cycle the commitments that make up a mutual commitment event are typically not bundled together into a single event as they are in the revenue and acquisition processes. Therefore in the conversion process, one event commits to an economic decrement event and another event commits to an economic increment event. In theory each economic event is preceded by a commitment to that event. The **production order event** is the event that represents the enterprise's commitment to engage in a production run. That is, the production order is the commitment to an economic increment event that will increase the finished goods resource. Production order information is typically captured on a document (or data entry screen) that is called a production order. An example production order document is illustrated in Exhibit 13-12.

Exhibit 13-12 Example Production Order

Production Order No. _____						
Date _____		Product Number_____		Description_____		
Approved by: _____		Deliver to: _____		Begin Date: _____	Complete by: _____	
WorkCenter	Operation	Quantity Completed	Labor Type Description	Start Date / Time	End Date / Time	

The relational tables in Exhibit 13-13 illustrate some of the data attributes that may be captured with respect to the production order event (in this example it is called a baking order) and its asoociations with finished cookies, baking employees, baking supervisors, and with the cookie batch event. The duality table identifies which machine operations apply to which cookie batches. The production order table stores the event data that pertains to each production order, such as the order date, the requested completion date, and who authorized it (supervisor). The finished cookies table stores the resource data that describes the finished goods the production order is committing to increase. Notice that this is the same finished cookie table that was described in relation to the production run economic increment event. The reservation table stores the data needed to identify how many of each finished cookie type is going to be produced when the production order is fulfilled.

We can see in this example that baking order PO1 committed the company to produce 40 frosted sugar cookies and called for Larry, Moe, and Curly to be the baking employees and for Ricky to be the supervisor for the job. Cookie batch WJ1 fulfilled baking order PO1; tracing back to the tables in Exhibit 13-6 reveals that WJ1 produced all 40 frosted sugar cookies. We can also see that baking order PO2 committed the company to produce 44 snickerdoodles and called for Fred and Ethel to be the baking employees and for Lucy to be the supervisor for the job. Cookie batch WJ2 fulfilled baking order PO2; tracing back to the tables in Exhibit 13-6 reveals that WJ2 produced 48 snickerdoodles, more than needed. Whether that is good or bad depends on the company policy. We might suspect that 48 were produced because the recipe for the company (which we will discuss later in the linkage associations section) is designed to make multiples of 12, and the snickerdoodles are typically packaged by the dozen.

Exhibit 13-13 Relational Database Tables Encompassing Baking Order Event

BakingOrder

BakingOrderID	BakingOrderDateTime	RequestedCompletion	SupervisorID
PO1	7/14/2015 4:30:00 PM	7/15/2015 8:00:00 AM	S2
PO2	7/14/2015 4:31:30 PM	7/15/2015 8:00:00 AM	S1
PO3	7/15/2015 4:45:00 PM	7/16/2015 8:00:00 AM	S1
PO4	7/15/2015 4:46:00 PM	7/16/2015 8:00:00 AM	S1
PO5	7/15/2015 4:50:00 PM	7/16/2015 8:00:00 AM	S2

ReservationBakingOrderFinishedCookieType

CookieID	BakingOrderID	QuantityReserved
FSCS	PO1	40
SN	PO2	44

FinishedCookieType

CookieID	Description	UnitsPerPackage	ListPrice
CC	Chocolate chip plain	12	$2.99
CCP	Chocolate chip with pecans	12	$2.99
FSCS	Frosted sugar cookies with candy sprinkles	10	$3.59
M	Molasses	12	$3.29
OR	Oatmeal raisin	12	$2.99
PB	Peanut butter	12	$2.99
SC	Sugar cookies plain	12	$2.99
SN	Snickerdoodles	12	$3.59

BakingSupervisor

SupervisorID	SupervisorName	SupervisorPhone
S1	Lucy	1-1234
S2	Ricky	1-4321

ParticipationBakingEmployeeScheduledForBakingOrder

EmployeeID	ProductionOrderID
PE1	PO2
PE2	PO2
PE3	PO1
PE4	PO1
PE5	PO1

Exhibit 13-13 continued

BakingEmployee

EmployeeID	EmployeeName	EmployeePhone	SupervisorID
PE1	Fred	1-6789	S2
PE2	Ethel	1-9876	S2
PE3	Larry	1-7698	S1
PE4	Moe	1-6798	S1
PE5	Curly	1-8796	S1

CookieBatchFulfillsBakingOrder

BatchID	BakingOrderID
WJ1	PO1
WJ2	PO2

Commitment to Economic Decrement Event: Materials Requisition
Theoretically every economic decrement event is preceded by a corresponding commitment for that decrement. The commitment for the material issuance economic decrement in the example given is the raw material requisition event. Because the word requisition may bring to your mind a purchase requisition (an instigation event in the acquisition/payment process as described in chapter 5), we must point out that a material requisition is not the same thing as a purchase requisition. A materials requisition (sometimes called a **raw material requisition**) is a commitment event whereby the inventory clerk or warehouse supervisor commits to the production supervisor to transfer materials from the materials warehouse to the production floor. A materials requisition assumes the raw materials are available within the enterprise, and is reserving them for use. In contrast, warehouse personnel initiate purchase requisitions to indicate the need to acquire the items from an external source. Thus, if a materials requisition is initiated for which insufficient materials are on-hand in the warehouse, this will likely trigger a purchase requisition and thereby instigate events in the acquisition/payment process. However, the raw materials requisition event occurs within the conversion cycle and the purchase requisition event occurs within the acquisition/payment cycle. Data captured regarding raw materials requisitions typically includes the date/time of requisition and information about the resources and agents involved in the event. Each requisition is assigned a unique identifier. Requisition data is typically captured on a document or data entry screen that is called a materials requisition. Exhibit 13-14 illustrates an example material requisition form.

Exhibit 13-14 Example Material Requisition

Materials Requisition No. _____	
Date _____	Production Order Number _____
Approved by _____	Deliver to _____

Material ID	Description	Quantity	Unit Cost	Total Cost

The relational tables in Exhibit 13-15 illustrate some of the data attributes that may be captured with respect to the materials requisition event (in this example it is called an ingredient requisition) and its associations with ingredients, inventory clerks, baking supervisors, and with the production order event. The fulfillment association identifies which ingredient issuances fulfill which ingredient requisitions. The ingredient requisition table stores the event data that pertains to each ingredient requisition, such as the requisition date, the requested completion date, and who authorized it (supervisor). The ingredients table in Exhibit 13-15 is the same one shown in Exhibit 13-8; it stores the resource data that describes the ingredients that are available for reservation by the ingredient requisition. The Reservation association table depicts which ingredients the ingredient requisition is committing to decrease.

We can see in this example that ingredient requisition 1002 reserves the ingredients that are needed for the 40 frosted sugar cookies per baking order P01, and requisition 1003 reserves the ingredients that are needed for the 44 snickerdoodles per baking order PO2. We can see that the ingredient issuances fulfilled the ingredient requisitions; a close examination reveals that more ingredients were issued for the snickerdoodles than were requisitioned. The issuance amounts were sufficient to make 48 cookies rather than 44 cookies.

Exhibit 13-15 Relational Database Tables Encompassing Ingredient Requisition Event

IngredientRequisition

RequisitionID	RequisitionDate	SupervisorID	BakingOrderID
1002	7/14/2015 4:35:00 PM	S2	PO1
1003	7/14/2015 4:35:30 PM	S1	PO2

Exhibit 13-15 Continued

Baking Supervisor

SupervisorID	SupervisorName	SupervisorPhone
S1	Lucy	1-1234
S2	Ricky	1-4321

ParticipationInventoryClerkIngredientRequisition

InventoryClerkID	IngredientRequisitionID
IC1	1002
IC1	1003
IC2	1002
IC2	1003

Inventory Clerk

InventoryClerkID	ClerkName	ClerkPhone
IC1	Ted	1-5678
IC2	Alice	1-8765

ReservationIngredientRequisitionIngredients

IngredientID	IngredientRequisitionID	QuantityReserved	Unit of Measure
CN	1003	0.5	cup
CS	1002	1	cup
EG	1002	4	each
EG	1003	4	each
FL	1002	8	cups
FL	1003	6	cups
ILFS	1002	4	each
ILSN	1003	4	each
PK	1002	4	each
PK	1003	4	each
SH	1002	2.67	cups
SH	1003	1.75	cups
SL	1002	2	teaspoons
SL	1003	1.75	teaspoons
VN	1002	4	teaspoons
VN	1003	2.75	teaspoons
WS	1002	6	cups
WS	1003	4.66	cups

REA Accounting Systems: Resources-Events-Agents: An ontology for designing, controlling, and using integrated enterprise systems

429

Exhibit 13-15 Continued

IngredientIssuanceFulfillsIngredientRequisition

IngredientIssuanceID	IngredientRequisitionID
RMI4238	1003
RMI4239	1003
RMI4240	1002
RMI4241	1002
RMI4242	1002
RMI4243	1002
RMI4244	1003
RMI4245	1002
RMI4246	1003

Commitment to Economic Decrement Event: Labor Requisition

A labor requisition is a commitment event whereby the production supervisor schedules employees to perform the labor operations for a production run. A document to represent such a commitment event can take many forms and may not even exist on paper. Many companies simply use the labor schedule that is made as part of the payroll cycle or the production order itself as documentation of this event. The information captured for a labor requisition event should include the production order to which the labor requisition applies, the requesting supervisor, what types of employees are needed to perform the labor operations and/or what types of labor need to be performed, and what quantity of hours of each type of labor are needed. The requisition may also specify the location at which the labor will be performed and the supervisor to which the scheduled employees should report to begin the scheduled labor operations. The relational tables in Exhibit 13-16 illustrate some of the data attributes that may be captured for the labor requisition event.

Exhibit 13-16 Relational Tables Encompassing Labor Requisition Event & related classes

LaborRequisition

LaborReqID	DateOfRequisition	Number Employees Needed	Hours Needed	SchedulingSupervisor	Baking Order ID
LR1	7/14/2015	2	1.00	S3	PO2
LR2	7/14/2015	3	1.00	S3	PO1
LR3	7/15/2015	4	2.00	S3	PO3

BakingOrderCommitmentEvent

BakingOrderID	BakingOrderDateTime	RequestedCompletion	SupervisorID
PO1	7/14/2015 4:30:00 PM	7/15/2015 8:00:00 AM	S2
PO2	7/14/2015 4:31:30 PM	7/15/2015 8:00:00 AM	S1
PO3	7/15/2015 4:45:00 PM	7/16/2015 8:00:00 AM	S1
PO4	7/15/2015 4:46:00 PM	7/16/2015 8:00:00 AM	S1
PO5	7/15/2015 4:50:00 PM	7/16/2015 8:00:00 AM	S2

Exhibit 13-16 continued

ReservationLaborRequisitionLaborType

LaborReqID	LaborTypeID
LR1	L1
LR1	L2
LR1	L3
LR1	L10
LR1	L13
LR1	L7
LR1	L8
LR1	L9
LR2	L1
LR2	L10
LR2	L11
LR2	L12
LR2	L13
LR2	L2
LR2	L3
LR2	L6
LR2	L7
LR2	L8
LR2	L9

LaborOperation

LaborOperationID	StartTime	EndTime	EmployeeID	SupervisorID	LaborReqID
LO21	7/15/2015 6:30:00 AM	7/15/2015 6:40:00 AM	PE3	S2	LR2
LO22	7/15/2015 6:30:00 AM	7/15/2015 6:40:00 AM	PE4	S2	LR2
LO23	7/15/2015 6:40:00 AM	7/15/2015 6:45:00 AM	PE5	S2	LR2
LO24	7/15/2015 6:45:00 AM	7/15/2015 6:50:00 AM	PE3	S2	LR2
LO25	7/15/2015 6:50:00 AM	7/15/2015 6:51:00 AM	PE5	S2	LR2
LO26	7/15/2015 7:03:00 AM	7/15/2015 7:03:30 AM	PE5	S2	LR2
LO27	7/15/2015 7:08:00 AM	7/15/2015 7:12:00 AM	PE3	S2	LR2
LO28	7/15/2015 7:12:00 AM	7/15/2015 7:13:00 AM	PE4	S2	LR2
LO29	7/15/2015 7:13:00 AM	7/15/2015 7:15:00 AM	PE5	S2	LR2
LO30	7/15/2015 6:30:00 AM	7/15/2015 6:40:00 AM	PE1	S1	LR1
LO31	7/15/2015 6:30:00 AM	7/15/2015 6:40:00 AM	PE2	S1	LR1
LO32	7/15/2015 6:40:00 AM	7/15/2015 6:45:00 AM	PE2	S1	LR1
LO33	7/15/2015 6:45:00 AM	7/15/2015 6:47:00 AM	PE2	S1	LR1
LO34	7/15/2015 6:47:00 AM	7/15/2015 6:48:00 AM	PE1	S1	LR1
LO35	7/15/2015 7:00:00 AM	7/15/2015 7:00:30 AM	PE1	S1	LR1
LO36	7/15/2015 7:35:00 AM	7/15/2015 7:37:00 AM	PE2	S1	LR1

Exhibit 13-16 continued

BakingSupervisor

SupervisorID	SupervisorName	SupervisorPhone
S1	Lucy	1-1234
S2	Ricky	1-4321
S3	Louie	1-5678

Commitment to Economic Decrement Event: Machine/Equipment Requisition
A machine or equipment requisition is a commitment event whereby the production supervisor schedules the fixed assets of the company to be used in operations for a production run. A document to represent such a commitment event can take many forms and may not even exist on paper. Many companies simply create an equipment schedule that serves as summarized documentation of all equipment requisitions for a time period. The information captured for a machine/equipment requisition event should include the production order to which the requisition applies, the requesting supervisor, what types of machines/equipment are needed, and for what quantity of hours. The requisition may also specify the supervisor who will be in charge of the machine operations that fulfill the machine/equipment requisition. The relational tables in Exhibit 13-17 illustrate some of the data attributes that may be captured for the machine/equipment requisition event and related events, resources, and agents.

Exhibit 13-17 Relational Tables Encompassing Machine/Equipment Requisition Event

EquipmentRequisition

EquipReqID	EReqDate	DateEquipmentNeeded	BakingOrderID	SchedulingSupervisor
ER1	7/13/2015	7/15/2015	PO2	S3
ER2	7/13/2015	7/15/2015	PO1	S3
ER3	7/15/2015	7/16/2015	PO3	S3
ER4	7/15/2015	7/16/2015	PO4	S3

BakingOrderCommitmentEvent

BakingOrderID	BakingOrderDateTime	RequestedCompletion	SupervisorID
PO1	7/14/2015 4:30:00 PM	7/15/2015 8:00:00 AM	S2
PO2	7/14/2015 4:31:30 PM	7/15/2015 8:00:00 AM	S1
PO3	7/15/2015 4:45:00 PM	7/16/2015 8:00:00 AM	S1
PO4	7/15/2015 4:46:00 PM	7/16/2015 8:00:00 AM	S1
PO5	7/15/2015 4:50:00 PM	7/16/2015 8:00:00 AM	S2

MachineOperation

MachineOperationID	StartTime	EndTime	EmployeeID	SupervisorID	EquipReqID
MO12	7/15/2015 6:30:00 AM	7/15/2015 6:45:00 AM	PE5	S2	ER2
MO13	7/15/2015 6:51:00 AM	7/15/2015 7:03:00 AM	PE5	S2	ER2
MO14	7/15/2015 7:08:00 AM	7/15/2015 7:12:00 AM	PE3	S2	ER2
MO15	7/15/2015 6:30:00 AM	7/15/2015 6:45:00 AM	PE2	S1	ER1
MO16	7/15/2015 6:40:00 AM	7/15/2015 7:00:00 AM	PE2	S1	ER1

Exhibit 13-17 continued

ReservationEquipReqEquipment

EquipReqID	EquipmentID
ER1	FA2
ER1	FA6
ER1	FA8
ER1	FA9
ER2	FA1
ER2	FA3
ER2	FA4
ER2	FA5
ER2	FA7

BakingEmployee

EmployeeID	EmployeeName	EmployeePhone	SupervisorID
PE1	Fred	1-6789	S2
PE2	Ethel	1-9876	S2
PE3	Larry	1-7698	S1
PE4	Moe	1-6798	S1
PE5	Curly	1-8796	S1

BakingSupervisor

SupervisorID	SupervisorName	SupervisorPhone
S1	Lucy	1-1234
S2	Ricky	1-4321
S3	Louie	1-5678

Exhibit 13-18: Partial Business Process Conversion Cycle Model with Custody and Responsibility

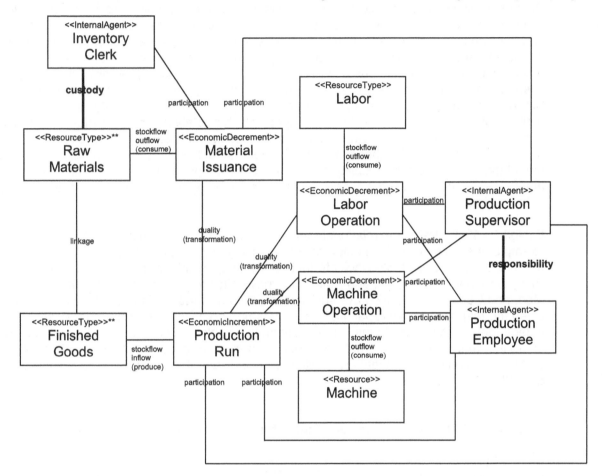

Custody Association

Companies often give custody of materials (and possibly finished goods) to a set of inventory clerks to protect the goods from theft or other misappropriation. Because agents were omitted from Exhibits 13-4 and 13-5, no custody association is illustrated in those exhibits. Exhibit 13-18 shows a partial business process model that includes a custody association between inventory clerk and raw materials. To help you find it, that association is on the left portion of the model and appears in bolder font. Custody associations should only be included in a business process level REA model if there is a direct relationship between a resource or resource type such as raw materials or finished goods and an internal agent. That relationship must exist independently of their mutual participation in an event such that it would need to be tracked separately from the associations that connect the common event to the resource and to the agent. In other words, if you simply need to know which inventory clerk issued which raw materials in an issuance event, there is no need for a custody association – that information is already captured and communicated by the stockflow association and participation associations.

Responsibility Association

Responsibility associations exist when there is a need to track a direct relationship between two types of agents. As with custody, such a relationship must be independent of their mutual participation in a common event. Responsibility associations vary depending on the types of agents that are being connected. Relationships between an internal and an external agent (such as the salesperson to customer relationship in the revenue cycle) are called assignment associations. In the conversion cycle the most common agent-to-agent association is between two internal agents and represents the fact that one type of internal agent is in charge of, or is responsible for, the other type of internal agent. Such a relationship is called a responsibility association. Because agents were omitted from Exhibits 13-4 and 13-5, no responsibility association is illustrated in those exhibits. Exhibit 13-18 illustrates a partial business process model that includes a responsibility association between production supervisor and production employee. To help you find it, that association is on the right portion of the model and appears in bolder font.

Exhibit 13-19 illustrates the relational tables that include the responsibility association. In this example, the supervisor id is posted as a foreign key in the baking employee table to represent the association. These tables indicate that Lucy is responsible for Larry, Moe, and Curly and Ricky is responsible for Fred and Ethel. You may notice that for WJ1, Ricky supervised Larry, Moe, and Curly and for WJ2, Lucy supervised Fred and Ethel. This may seem disturbing to you given the responsibility association; however, remember that the responsibility association is independent of the agents' mutual participation in a cookie batch event. Ricky and Lucy can share information about the employees' performance; the responsibility association indicates that Lucy will officially evaluate Larry, Moe, and Curly and that Ricky will officially evaluate Fred and Ethel.

Exhibit 13-19 Relational Database Tables for Responsibility Association

Baking Supervisor

SupervisorID	SupervisorName	SupervisorPhone
S1	Lucy	1-1234
S2	Ricky	1-4321

Baking Employee

EmployeeID	EmployeeName	EmployeePhone	SupervisorID
PE1	Fred	1-6789	S2
PE2	Ethel	1-9876	S2
PE3	Larry	1-7698	S1
PE4	Moe	1-6798	S1
PE5	Curly	1-8796	S1

Reciprocal Association

The **reciprocal association** in Exhibit 13-4 is the equivalent of duality only for the commitment events rather than for the economic events. The commitment for an economic increment event must be accompanied by a commitment for an economic decrement event to reflect the inherent nature of give and take in business processes. Production orders (the commitment to the economic increment event) trigger the commitments to the various economic decrement

REA Accounting Systems: Resources-Events-Agents: An ontology for designing, controlling, and using integrated enterprise systems

435

events: the requisitioning of materials, the requisitioning of labor, and the requisitioning of machinery/equipment. The reciprocal association represents a schedule of what is to be produced and what will need to be used and consumed in the production run event. In Exhibit 13-5 three reciprocal associations are depicted, between the ingredient requisition and the baking order event, between the labor requisition and the baking order event, and between the equipment requisition and baking order event. Exhibit 13-20 illustrates the relational tables that include the reciprocal associations. Baking order id is posted as a foreign key in the ingredient requisition table to represent the first reciprocal association. These tables indicate that requisition 1002 is related to baking order PO1 and requisition 1003 is related to baking order PO2. The reciprocal association between labor requisition and baking order is represented with the baking order id posted as a foreign key in the labor requisition table.

Exhibit 13-20 Relational database tables for Reciprocal associations

IngredientRequisition

RequisitionID	RequisitionDate	SupervisorID	BakingOrderID
1002	7/14/2015 4:35:00 PM	S2	PO1
1003	7/14/2015 4:35:30 PM	S1	PO2
1004	7/15/2015 4:50:00 PM	S1	PO3
1005	7/15/2015 4:51:00 PM	S1	PO4
1006	7/15/2015 4:55:00 PM	S2	PO5

LaborRequisition

LaborReqID	DateOfRequisition	Number Employees Needed	Hours Needed	SchedulingSupervisor	Baking Order ID
LR1	7/14/2015	2	1.00	S3	PO2
LR2	7/14/2015	3	1.00	S3	PO1
LR3	7/15/2015	4	2.00	S3	PO3

EquipmentRequisition

EquipReqID	EReqDate	DateEquipmentNeeded	BakingOrderID	SchedulingSupervisor
ER1	7/13/2015	7/15/2015	PO2	S3
ER2	7/13/2015	7/15/2015	PO1	S3
ER3	7/15/2015	7/16/2015	PO3	S3
ER4	7/15/2015	7/16/2015	PO4	S3

BakingOrder

BakingOrderID	BakingOrderDateTime	RequestedCompletion	SupervisorID
PO1	7/14/2015 4:30:00 PM	7/15/2015 8:00:00 AM	S2
PO2	7/14/2015 4:31:30 PM	7/15/2015 8:00:00 AM	S1
PO3	7/15/2015 4:45:00 PM	7/16/2015 8:00:00 AM	S1
PO4	7/15/2015 4:46:00 PM	7/16/2015 8:00:00 AM	S1
PO5	7/15/2015 4:50:00 PM	7/16/2015 8:00:00 AM	S2

Linkage Associations

The **linkage associations** in Exhibit 13-4 and in Exhibit 13-5 provide a means for identifying the materials of which a finished good is composed and the types of labor that are needed to produce a finished good. Information about the linkage association between materials and finished good is often captured on a bill of materials. A **bill of materials** is a document that lists the names and quantities of all the materials needed to produce a specified size batch of finished product. It is similar to the ingredient list portion of a recipe. An example bill of materials is illustrated in Exhibit 13-21.

Exhibit 13-21 Bill of Materials

Bill of Materials _____		
Product ID _____ Standard Batch Quantity_____		
Product Description_____		
Material ID	Material Description	Quantity Needed

Information about the linkage association between labor types and finished goods is usually captured on an operations list. An **operations list** is a document that identifies the labor types and standard processing and setup times for each of those labor types needed to produce a specified size batch of finished product. It is similar to the instruction portion of a recipe, but with more detail. Exhibit 13-22 illustrates an example operations list document.

Exhibit 13-22 Example Operations List

Operations List _____

Product ID _____   Standard Batch Quantity _____

Description _____

WorkCenter	Labor Type	Description	Standard Time/Unit	
			Setup	Processing

The relational tables shown in Exhibit 13-23 illustrate some of the attributes often stored with respect to the linkage associations between raw materials and finished goods, between labor and finished goods, and between equipment and finished goods. Such information provides standards against which actual commitments and production may be compared for variance analyses and performance evaluations. The bills of materials and operations lists are typically used in the planning stages of the conversion process for made-to-stock finished goods. These documents are used to help in preparing the production order document that represents the commitment to the economic increment event.

Exhibit 13-23 Relational database tables encompassing the linkage associations

LinkageIngredientsNeededForFinishedCookies

CookieTypeID	IngredientID	QuantityNeeded	UnitOfMeasure	CookieBatchSize
FSCS	CS	0.25	cup	10
FSCS	EG	1	each	10
FSCS	FL	1.75	cups	10
FSCS	ILFS	1	each	10
FSCS	PK	1	each	10
FSCS	SH	0.5	cup	10
FSCS	SL	0.5	teaspoon	10
FSCS	VN	0.75	teaspoon	10
FSCS	WS	1	cup	10
SN	CN	3	teaspoons	12
SN	EG	1	each	12
SN	FL	1.5	cups	12
SN	ILSN	1	each	12
SN	PK	1	each	12
SN	SH	0.67	cup	12
SN	SL	0.5	teaspoon	12
SN	VN	1	teaspoon	12
SN	WS	1.5	cups	12

Ingredient

IngredientID	Description	UnitOfMeasure	StandardCostPerUnitOfMeasure
BS	Brown sugar	50 lb bag	$9.47
BU	Butter	10 lb box	$3.98
CM	Chocolate morsels	10 lb bag	$19.49
CN	Cinnamon	16 oz tin	$3.29
CS	Candy sprinkles	1 lb tin	$3.18
EG	Eggs, large AA grade	2 dozen carton	$1.29
FL	Flour, white sifted	100 lb bag	$20.00
ILFS	Ingredient label - frosted sugar	each	$0.01
ILSN	Ingredient label - snickerdoodle	each	$0.01
PB	Peanut butter	10 lb jar	$8.37
PE	Pecans	2 lb bag	$5.32
PK	Plastic container	each	$0.12
SH	Shortening	10 lb can	$12.10
SL	Salt, iodized	5 lb bag	$1.00
VN	Vanilla, pure	1 liter bottle	$20.00
WS	White sugar	50 lb bag	$10.00

Exhibit 13-23 Continued

Finished Cookie Type

CookieID	Description	UnitsPerPackage	ListPrice
CC	Chocolate chip plain	12	$2.99
CCP	Chocolate chip with pecans	12	$2.99
FSCS	Frosted sugar cookies with candy sprinkles	10	$3.59
M	Molasses	12	$3.29
OR	Oatmeal raisin	12	$2.99
PB	Peanut butter	12	$2.99
SC	Sugar cookies plain	12	$2.99
SN	Snickerdoodles	12	$3.59

LaborType

LaborTypeID	Description
L1	Mix dry ingredients
L10	Take cookie sheet out of oven
L11	Frost cookies
L12	Sprinkle cookies
L13	Package cookies
L2	Mix moist ingredients
L3	Combine dry and moist ingredients
L4	Add morsels to mixed dough
L5	Add nuts to mixed dough
L6	Form dough into cookies
L7	Put cookies onto cookie sheet
L8	Put cookie sheet into oven
L9	Set cookie timer

LinkageLaborNeededForFinishedCookieType

CookieTypeID	LaborTypeID
FSCS	L1
FSCS	L10
FSCS	L11
FSCS	L12
FSCS	L13
FSCS	L2
FSCS	L3
FSCS	L6
FSCS	L7
FSCS	L8
FSCS	L9
SN	L1
SN	L10
SN	L13
SN	L2
SN	L3
SN	L7
SN	L8
SN	L9

Exhibit 13-20 Continued

LinkageEquipTypeCookieType

EquipmentType	CookieType	Quantity Needed	Unit of Measure
Cookie sheet	FSCS	1	each
Cookie sheet	SN	1	each
Frosting utensils	FSCS	1	set
Heavy duty mixer	FSCS	1	each
Heavy duty mixer	SN	1	each
Measuring device set	FSCS	1	set
Measuring device set	SN	1	set
Oven	FSCS	1	each
Oven	SN	1	each

EquipmentType

EquipTypeName	Standard Cost	Average Expected Life
Cookie sheet	$12.00	3
Frosting utensils	$10.00	4
Heavy duty mixer	$160.00	3
Measuring device set	$78.00	5
Oven	$450.00	7

In the Linkage1 association table in our example we can see the quantity of each ingredient needed to make a batch of 20 frosted sugar cookies and the quantity of each ingredient needed to make a batch of 24 snickerdoodles. The batch size used for the materials linkage association is an arbitrary choice depending on the needs of the enterprise. Some enterprises will attempt to list the quantity needed to produce a single unit of the finished product. Such an approach would require us to divide each of the quantities in the Linkage1 table by 20 for the frosted sugar cookies and by 24 for the snickerdoodles. Keeping the measurement at such a fine level of detail may not always be practical or useful. How do you divide an egg by 20 or 24? The linkage2 labor type association in our model does not indicate a particular quantity of labor for each finished cookie type. However, such an attribute could be added as a standard to which actual labor use could be compared. If a quantity (e.g. number of minutes) of each labor type is indicated, a batch size would also need to be included similar to that shown for the linkage1 association table. In this example it was determined that although you could double the quantity of materials needed for a batch size that was twice as big and get a valid measure, you couldn't double the number of minutes for each labor type for a double-sized batch and get a meaningful number, therefore the attributes were not captured. In other words, if it takes 4 minutes to mix the dry ingredients (1 cup of white sugar, 1 3/4 cups of flour, and a ½ teaspoon of salt) to make a batch of 10 cookies, it will likely not take 16 minutes to mix the dry ingredients (4 cups of white flour, 7 cups of flour, and 2 teaspoons of salt) to make a batch of 40 cookies. The third linkage association table includes the quantity and unit of measure for equipment needed; some of these may need to be multiplied to produce multiple batches; others may not. To help you make sense of the linkage associations you can think of them as the two parts of a recipe. Recipes in a cookbook typically contain a list of ingredients along with the quantities needed to make an identified quantity of a food dish. Recipes also include a list of instructions with steps and equipment needed to prepare the food dish.

INFORMATION NEEDS AND MEASURES IN THE CONVERSION PROCESS

The most common information customers for the conversion process include top management, production personnel, accountants, and auditors. There are typically no external information customers directly associated with the conversion process. Results of the conversion process are typically summarized indirectly in various line items on financial statements prepared by accountants and made available to the public.

We next analyze each of the classes and associations in the conversion process pattern to provide some ideas as to the types of queries that may be needed to satisfy information needs in the conversion process. The queries presented are not a comprehensive set of queries (there are simply too many potential queries to list them all); however, the set provided should provide you guidance for creating similar types of queries. To describe example queries needed in the conversion process we will use the database tables shown in Exhibits 13-6, 13-8, 13-10, 13-11, 13-13, 13-15, 13-16, 13-17, and 13-20.

Resource Queries in the Conversion Process

The resources and resource types that most commonly exist in the conversion process are raw materials inventory, labor type, machinery, and finished goods inventory. For each resource, users may need any of the following:
- Detailed status information at one or more points in time for each resource instance
- Detailed status information at one or more points in time for only those resource instances meeting specified criteria
- Summarized status information at one or more points in time for all resource instances
- Summarized status information at one or more points in time for only those resource instances meeting specified criteria

With regard to each of the above, users may need to know all characteristics of the instances in the answer set, or they may need only a subset of the characteristics.

Raw materials and finished goods inventory may be tracked at the type level and/or may be specifically identified. Therefore queries may be needed at either of those levels of detail. Labor is typically tracked only at the type level. Machinery and other operating assets are usually specifically identified, but may also be tracked at the category level. For example, most enterprises assign an identification tag to each operating asset that has a cost value exceeding a certain threshold; however, they also keep track of the category to which the asset belongs (i.e. furniture, computer equipment, office equipment, etc.). Since the raw materials and machinery resources in the conversion process are the same as those acquired in the acquisition/payment process and the finished goods resources in the conversion process is the same as the inventory resources in the revenue process, any query that focuses solely on a resource table will be very similar to the resource queries displayed in Exhibits 10-2 through 10-5 in Chapter 10.

Event Queries in the Conversion Process

Users may need information regarding events. The most common events in the conversion process are materials requisitions, materials issuances, labor operations, machine operations, production orders, and production runs. For each of these types of events, users may need any of the following:

- Detailed information about each event instance (i.e., what happened, when did it begin and end, at which workstation did it occur, etc.)
- Detailed information about each event instance that meets specified criteria (e.g. events of a specified type that occurred during a specified time period or that occurred at a specified workstation)
- Summarized information for all instances of an event type for a specified time period (e.g. total of the event instances during a specified time period)
- Summarized information for only those instances of an event type for a specified time period that meet specified criteria (e.g. average dollar value of the event instances for a specified location during a specified time period)

Examples of information needs in the conversion process regarding events are (among many other possibilities):

- Length of a specific production run (end time minus start time)
- Average length of the production runs within a specified time period
- Total number of production runs that occurred at a specified plant or workstation or during a specified time period
- Date and/or time an issuance of materials occurred

From the event tables in the cookie manufacturing example (IngredientRequisition, BakingOrder, CookieBatch, IngredientIssuance, LaborOperation, and MachineOperation) some specific queries (among many possibilities) that may be developed are:

- How long did it take to produce a specific batch of cookies?
  - Using the CookieBatch table, calculate the difference between the start time and the completion time for a specified batch
- Count the number of ingredient issuances that were made to Workcenter E
  - Using the IngredientIssuance table, use the Count function to count the issuances for which the Location field is WorkcenterE
- When did the most recent ingredient requisition take place?
  - Using the IngredientRequisition table, use the Max function to identify the largest (most recent) date in the RequisitionDate field
- Which baking orders are requested for completion on a particular day?
  - Using the BakingOrder table, specify the desired day as criteria by which to select the corresponding orders
- How many machine operations took longer than 14 minutes to complete?
  - Using the MachineOperation table, create an expression to calculate the difference in start and end times and then use the expression as criteria by which to select the corresponding machine operations.

A caution before you try to do each of these example queries in Microsoft Access. The queries that involve calculations with date/time fields may not provide meaningful results because of the complexities of formatting the results; to make them meaningful involves use of Visual Basic code that is beyond the scope of most courses for which this textbook is appropriate. Therefore you may not want to try the queries that involve date/time calculations.

Agent Queries in the Conversion Process

Because the conversion process does not typically involve external agents, the agent queries center on various types of employees. The employees commonly involved in conversion processes are production supervisors, production workers, and inventory clerks. **Production supervisors** are the internal agents who authorize conversion cycle events. Production workers are the internal agents who do the conversion work. Inventory clerks are internal agents who issue materials and equipment into production. Queries may be needed to obtain any of the following:

- Detailed status information at one or more points in time for each employee
- Detailed status information at one or more points in time for each employee who meets specified criteria
- Summarized status information at one or more points in time for all employees
- Summarized status information at one or more points in time for all employees who meet specified criteria

Because the agent tables in the cookie manufacturing example (BakingSupervisor, BakingEmployee, and InventoryClerk) only include employee ids, names, and telephone numbers, not many queries can be constructed other than a list of employees and their telephone numbers. A complete database would typically include many other attributes of employees that could provide useful information for decision-makers.

Association Queries in the Conversion Process

Combining information from various resource, event, and agent tables in accordance with the associations in which they participate can provide much richer data than single table queries. We next discuss queries based on the various types of associations in the conversion process.

Duality Association Queries

As explained earlier, duality associations in conversion processes represent transformations rather than exchanges. Raw inputs are not exchanged for finished goods; rather they are converted into finished goods. The duality association connects raw material issuances, machine operations, and labor operations that use up the inputs to the production runs that produce the finished goods. Information needs with respect to duality associations in conversion processes include (among other possibilities):

- Identification of labor operations related to one or more specified production runs
- Identification of machine operations related to one or more specified production runs
- Identification of raw material issuances related to one or more specified production runs
- Calculation of the time taken for a labor (or machine) operation as a percentage of a complete production run
- Count the number of raw material issuances (or labor operations or machine operations) related to a specified production run

For the cookie manufacturing example, duality queries could investigate

- Which labor operations (or machine operations or ingredient issuances) related to batch WJ1 and which related to batch WJ2?
- How many ingredient issuances were associated with each cookie batch?
- How many machine operations were necessary to make cookie batch WJ1?
  - Join the MachineOperations table to the DualityCookieBatchMachineOperations table; set the criteria for the Batch ID = WJ1 and count the Machine Operations ID field
- How much of the total production time for batch WJ1 consisted of machine operations and how much of the time consisted of labor operations?

As noted earlier, queries that calculate differences in date/time fields are very difficult to successfully create in Microsoft Access so we do not recommend you try the last one above.

Stockflow Association Queries

Stockflow associations in the conversion process represent the use or consumption of input resources by economic decrement events and the production of finished good resources by economic increment events. Therefore stockflow associations are commonly used in queries to identify the effect of economic events on resources or to identify the resources used up or produced by the economic events. Some common information needs that can be addressed by stockflow associations in general are:

- What resources or resource types were increased or decreased by an economic event?
- What quantity of a resource or resource type was increased or decreased by an economic event?
- What dollar value of a resource or resource type was increased or decreased by an economic event?
- When did an event increase or decrease a specific resource or resource type?
- Where did an event increase or decrease a specific resource or resource type?

These information needs may be addressed at a detailed level or they may be aggregated for groups of events and/or resources/resource types. The information may be used in isolation or used as part of a trend analysis to project future events and their expected effects on resources or resource types. Within the conversion process, some common stockflow information needs (among many other possibilities) are:

- Which raw material types were decreased by a material issuance?
- What quantity of each raw material inventory type was decreased by a material issuance?
- What types of labor were used in a labor operation?
- What equipment was used (and/or for how long) in a machine operation?
- What finished goods were produced by a production run?
- What quantity of each finished good was produced by a production run?
- What is the standard unit cost of the raw materials used by a materials issuance?

In the cookie manufacturing example, questions such as the following could be answered via stockflow association queries:

- How long did it take to sprinkle the cookies in labor operation 28?
  - Because this involves a date/time calculation, you should not attempt this in Microsoft Access
- How many frosted sugar cookies with candy sprinkles were produced on July 15, 2015 and in which batch(es)?
  - Join the FinishedCookieType table to the StockflowCookieBatch-FinishedCookieType table using Cookie Type ID to determine which batches were for frosted sugar cookies with candy sprinkles. Join StockflowCookieBatch-FinishedCookieType table to CookieBatch table using the Batch ID, constrain the Date = 7/15/2015 and sum the Actual Quantity Produced.
- What kind of cookies were produced in batch WJ1?
  - Join the FinishedCookieType table to the StockflowCookieBatchFinishedCookie table using Cookie Type ID. Enter criteria =WJ1 in the Batch ID field and display the Batch ID, Cookie Type ID, and the Cookie Type Description

Fulfillment Queries in the Conversion Process

Fulfillment associations in the conversion process represent associations between the production order and production run (the production run fulfills the production order) and between the materials (or labor or equipment) requisition and the materials issuance (or labor or machine operation). Fulfillment association queries in the conversion process in general include:

- Identification of unfilled commitment events (e.g. production orders for which production runs have not yet occurred, materials requisitions for which materials issuances have not yet occurred, etc.)
- Identification of filled commitment events (e.g. production orders for which production runs have occurred, materials requisitions for which materials issuances have occurred, etc.)
- Identification of economic events for which commitments were not made (e.g. production runs that were not ordered or material issuances that were not requisitioned)
- Calculation of length of time between commitment events and economic events (e.g. length of time between production order and production run or between material requisition and material issuance)
- Identification of causes for economic events (e.g. which production order led to a production run or which material requisition led to a material issuance)
- Identification of results of commitment events (e.g. which production run fulfilled a production order or which material issuance fulfilled a material requisition)

In the cookie manufacturing example, questions such as the following could be answered via fulfillment association queries:

- Has baking order PO4 been fulfilled?
  - Join the BakingOrderCommitmentEvent table to the CookieBatch table with an outer join keeping all baking orders; include the BakingOrder ID from the BakingOrderCommitmentEvent table and the Batch ID from the CookieBatch table; set criteria to select the Baking Order =PO4
- Have any ingredient issuances occurred that were not related to ingredient requisitions?
  - Join the IngredientIssuance table to the IngredientIssuanceFulfillsIngredientRequisition table with an outer join keeping all ingredient issuances; include the Issuance ID from the IngredientIssuance table and the Ingredient Requisition Number from the IngredientIssuanceFulfillsIngredientRequisition table; set criteria to select null ingredient requisitions
- What is the average length of time between baking orders and cookie batches for this company?
  - Because this involves a date/time calculation, you should not attempt this in Microsoft Access
- What baking order triggered cookie batch WJ2?
  - Join the CookieBatch table to the CookieBatchFulfillsBakingOrder table using the Cookie Batch ID; include the Baking Order ID; set the criteria to select Batch ID = WJ2

Reservation Queries in the Conversion Process

Reservation associations in the conversion process represent associations between commitment events such as production orders and materials requisitions and the resources those events are committing to increase or decrease. Therefore reservation associations are commonly used in queries to satisfy information needs as to the eventual effect of commitment events on resources or as to the resources involved in commitment events. Some common information needs in the conversion process are:

- What finished good or finished good type is a production order agreeing to produce?
- What quantity of a finished good or finished good type is a production order agreeing to produce?
- What is the dollar value of the finished good or finished good type a production order is agreeing to produce?
- When did a production order commit to produce a specific finished good or finished good type?
- What material or material type is a materials requisition agreeing to use up?
- What quantity of each material type is a materials requisition agreeing to use up?
- What is the standard or actual unit cost for each material a materials requisition is agreeing to use up?
- When did a materials requisition commit to using up a material or material type?

In the cookie manufacturing example, questions such as the following could be answered via reservation association queries:

- What kind of cookies is baking order PO5 agreeing to produce and when are they scheduled to be produced?
    - o Join the ReservationBakingOrderFinishedCookie table to the FinishedCookieType and to the BakingOrder tables to see that PO5 is agreeing to produce molasses cookies by July 16, 2015 at 8:00 a.m.
- How many peanut butter cookies are scheduled to be produced on July 16, 2015 and which production order represents the agreement to produce them?
    - o Join ReservationBakingOrderFinishedCookie table to the FinishedCookieType and to the BakingOrder tables to determine that PO4 has scheduled 36 peanut butter cookies for production
- What are the descriptions of the ingredients that were scheduled to be used up by ingredient requisition 1002?
    - o Join Ingredients table to ReservationIngredientRequisitionIngredient. Enter criteria =1002 in IngredientRequisitionID field and display the ingredient description

Participation Queries in the Conversion Process

Participation associations in the conversion cycle typically represent the associations between production orders, materials requisitions, material issuances, machine operations, labor operations, and production runs and the employees who authorize those events (typically supervisors) and the employees who accomplish the events (typically production workers or inventory clerks). Therefore participation associations are commonly used in queries to satisfy information needs as to the identification of employees who participated in events or as to the events in which specified employees participated. Some common information needs are:

- Which production supervisor authorized a machine operation?
- By how many production orders has a production employee been scheduled to work?
- How long did a production employee take to perform a labor operation?
- How many production orders have been authorized by a specific production supervisor?
- Which inventory clerk accomplished a materials issuance?

In the cookie manufacturing example, questions such as the following could be answered via participation association queries:
- What is the name of the supervisor who authorized machine operation MO13?
  - Join the MachineOperation table to the BakingSupervisor table; enter criteria =MO13 in the MachineOperationID field and display the supervisor name field
- What are the names of the employees who were scheduled on baking order PO2?
  - Join the ParticipationBakingOrderBakingEmployee table to the BakingEmployee table; enter criteria =PO2 in the baking order id field and display the employee name field
- What are the names and phone numbers of the inventory clerks who processed ingredient issuances #RMI4240-RMI4245?
  - Join the IngredientIssuance table to the InventoryClerk table; enter criteria BETWEEN RMI4240 and RMI4245 in the ingredient issuance ID field and display the ClerkName and ClerkPhone fields
- How many production runs has Lucy supervised?
  - Join the CookieBatch table to the BakingSupervisor table; enter criteria =Lucy in the supervisor name field; enter aggregate function COUNT in the BatchID field

Linkage Queries in the Conversion Process
Linkage associations in the conversion cycle typically represent the associations between finished goods and raw materials and also between finished goods and labor type. As described earlier, the information content within the linkage between finished goods and raw materials is often captured by enterprises on bill of materials documents, and the information content within the linkage between finished goods and labor types is often captured on operations list documents. Therefore queries encompassing the linkage associations ask the same kinds of questions that could be answered from one of those documents. Some examples are:
- What raw materials are needed to produce a finished good or finished good type?
- What quantity of each raw material is needed to produce a finished good or finished good type?
- Which finished goods contain a specified raw material or a specified labor type?
- What labor types are needed to produce a finished good or finished good type?

In the cookie manufacturing example, questions such as the following could be answered via linkage association queries:
- How much white sugar is needed to make a batch of snickerdoodles?
  - Join the FinishedCookieType, Ingredients, and Linkage tables; enter criteria =Snickerdoodles in the finished cookie type description field; enter criteria =white sugar in the ingredient description field; display the quantity needed and unit of measure fields
- Which finished cookie types contain brown sugar?
  - Join the FinishedCookieType, Ingredients, and LinkageIngredientsInCookieType tables; enter criteria =brown sugar in the ingredient description field; display the finished cookie type description field
- Which finished cookie types require the labor type frost cookies?
  - Join the FinishedCookieType, LaborType, and LinkageLaborTypeNeededForFinishedCookieType tables; enter criteria =Frost cookies in labor type description field; display the finished cookie type description field

CONCLUDING COMMENTS

This chapter presented an overview of the activities in the conversion process and discussed the extended REA pattern as it applies to this process. Whether enterprises produce cereal, video games, furniture, or some other type of resource, the REA pattern for the necessary components of their conversion processes will be similar to each other. Designing an information system that supports the complexities and intricacies of a conversion process requires a careful analysis and a detailed understanding of the objectives of the process. Traditionally, organizations have generated multiple systems to support the conversion process. In fact, organizations often develop financial accounting systems and a variety of separate cost/managerial accounting systems. By using the REA ontology to design an integrated enterprise information system, organizations can derive financial statement information and other information needed to support a variety of programs (including activity-based costing, quality management, just-in-time inventories, and material requirements planning).

Key Terms and Concepts

Bill of materials	Production order (document)
Consume stockflow association	Production order (event)
Conversion process	Production run
Job time ticket	Production supervisor
Labor operation	Raw material issuance
Labor type	Raw material requisition
Linkage association	Raw materials
Machine operation	Reciprocal association
Move ticket	*Transfer* duality association
Operations list	*Transformation* duality association
Production employee	*Use* stockflow association

Multiple Choice Questions

1. Most of the time the conversion process involves the manufacture or production of:
   A) Work in Process
   B) Finished Goods
   C) Raw Materials
   D) Labor
   E) Overhead

2. Which type of manufacturing process involves the production of an established number of product units, or particular jobs such as car repair, the printing of a customized wedding invitation, or a consulting engagement?
   A) Continuous processes
   B) Established run processes
   C) Batch processes
   D) Production employee processes
   E) Ongoing run processes

3. Which kind of association identifies the *who* for each event in a conversion process?
A) Duality
B) Stockflow
C) Fulfillment
D) Participation
E) Reservation

4. Which kind of association in a conversion cycle reveals *why* the enterprise engages in the economic events of the cycle?
A) Duality
B) Stockflow
C) Fulfillment
D) Participation
E) Reservation

5. An association in which an enterprise trades one or more resources for one or more different resources is called a(n) _____ duality association.
A) Transformation
B) Trade
C) Exchange
D) Swap
E) Transfer

6. Which is NOT an economic decrement event in the conversion cycle?
A) Production run
B) Material issuance
C) Labor operation
D) Machine operation
E) All of the above are economic decrement events in the conversion cycle

7. What form is often used in a conversion cycle to document the actual use of raw materials?
A) Bill of lading
B) Job time ticket
C) Bill of materials
D) Move ticket or initialing of line items on material requisition by inventory clerk
E) Packing slip

8. Which of the following is FALSE regarding labor operations in a conversion process?
A) Labor Operations are the actual using up of the available labor.
B) Labor or Labor Type is a resource-type class that represents a list of the types of labor that can be performed in the labor operations.
C) When they are measured and recorded, labor operations are usually documented on move tickets, which serve as an identifier for the labor operations event.
D) The labor operation event is an economic decrement event.
E) All of the above are true statements.

9. The REA ontology label for an association in an enterprise conversion cycle that connects the classes machine and machine operation, whereby a machine does not get completely used up by a machine operation is:
A) Use stockflow
B) Consume stockflow
C) Machine outflow
D) Production inflow
E) Operating outflow

10. A move ticket
A) Captures information related to the movement of raw materials into production
B) Captures information related to the movement of goods from our supplier to receiving dock
C) Captures information related to the movement of customers from one address to another
D) Captures information related to the movement of employees from one job to another
E) Captures information related to the movement of employees from one address to another

11. Which association is the equivalent of the duality association, but for commitment events instead of economic events?
A) Linkage
B) Reciprocal
C) Custody
D) Association
E) Reservation

12. What documents in the conversion cycle capture the same information as the Linkage associations?
A) Operations list and Bill of materials
B) Materials requisition and Production order
C) Job time ticket and Production order
D) Bill of materials and Materials requisition
E) Move ticket and Materials requisition

13. What is the association between two conversion cycle commitment events?
A) Custody
B) Duality
C) Reciprocal
D) Fulfillment
E) Reservation

14. The resource typically made available to the conversion process by the payroll process is
A) Cash
B) Labor
C) Machinery
D) Raw materials
E) Finished goods

15. Which transaction cycle typically includes an event called Material Issuance?
    A) Financing
    B) Acquisition/payment
    C) Human resources
    D) Conversion
    E) Revenue

16. On which class or association should one focus to answer the question of when the most recent material requisition occurred?
    A) Material Requisition event
    B) Material Issuance event
    C) Fulfillment association between Material Requisition and Material Issuance
    D) Reservation association between Material Requisition and Raw Materials
    E) Stockflow association between Material Issuance and Raw Materials

17. What pair of classes are likely to participate in a conversion cycle Custody association?
    A) Cash and Cashier
    B) Materials Inventory and Inventory Clerk
    C) Materials Inventory and Production Run
    D) Inventory Clerk and Materials Issuance
    E) Materials Inventory and Finished Goods Inventory

18. Which of the following attributes is LEAST likely to be assigned to the Raw Materials Inventory class in a conversion cycle business process level REA model?
    A) ID-number
    B) Description
    C) Unit of measure
    D) Standard Unit Cost
    E) Unit List Selling Price

Bentley Balloons Narrative

Bentley Balloons is an enterprise that specializes in providing helium filled balloons for customers' special occasions. They only sell balloons in large quantities; for example they provide balloons to large corporations who are having celebrations, or to department stores that want to advertise a special sale with the help of some balloons (they even have some balloons that say "Clearance Sale" on them); or to circuses or carnivals that intend to re-sell the balloons. Bentley acquires the balloons, helium tanks, ribbons, and weights in bulk from various suppliers. Bentley's inventory clerks identify the need for those items and request the purchasing department to get them, and often the inventory clerks identify a particular vendor from whom they want purchasing to place the order (this does not obligate the purchasing department to do so, but they will need to track the information). Some requisitions are rejected by purchasing agents and are never filled. Others are approved and purchase orders are prepared and sent to vendors for the requested goods. Some purchase orders are rejected by vendors and are never filled. Others are accepted and the goods are sent by the vendors and received by Bentley's receiving clerks. Once goods are received, one of Bentley's accounting clerks issues an electronic payment to the corresponding vendor from one of its checking accounts. To meet demand, Bentley's production supervisors perform the scheduling of production jobs, the scheduling consists of ordering production (documented by production orders) and requisitioning materials (documented by materials requisitions). No equipment is needed, when new helium tanks are delivered by vendors, they take back the empty helium tanks. Production supervisors receive materials into production and oversee the production employees who perform the work in the production jobs. Bentley sees no need to track specific labor operations with respect to the production of the helium-filled balloons, as it is a very simple process.

Following is a cycle-level REA diagram that is intended to represent the materials acquisition and conversion (manufacturing) cycles.

REA Conceptual Model for Bentley's Balloons

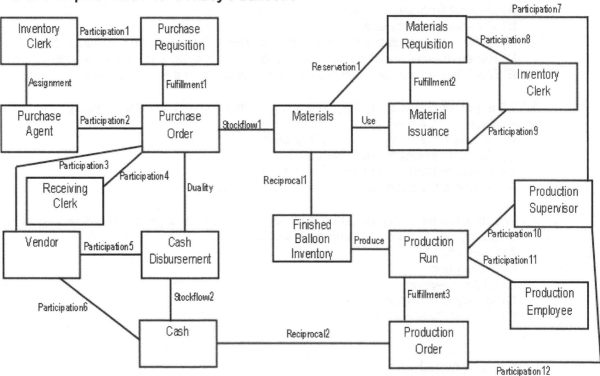

Use the narrative and conceptual model for Bentley's Balloons to answer questions 19 through 28.

19. What event is missing from the Acquisition/Payment part of the conceptual model for Bentley's Balloons?
    A) No event is missing
    B) Cash Receipt
    C) Purchase/Receipt of Goods
    D) Bill of Materials
    E) Linkage

20. Examine the association between Purchase Order and Cash Disbursement that is labeled Duality. Is that the correct label for that association, and if not, what should it be called instead?
    A) Yes it is correct
    B) No, it should be called Reciprocal
    C) No, it should be called Stockflow
    D) No, it should be called Fulfillment
    E) No, it should be called Linkage

21. Examine the association between Cash and Production Order that is labeled as Reciprocal2. Is that the correct label for that association, and if not, what should it be called instead?
    A) Yes it is correct
    B) No, it should be called Stockflow
    C) No, it should be called Fulfillment
    D) No, it should be called Linkage
    E) No, it should not even exist so it shouldn't have a label

22. What are the associations labeled Use and Produce more specific examples of?
    A) Duality
    B) Fulfillment
    C) Linkage
    D) Participation
    E) Stockflow

23. What stereotype would be most appropriate for the Purchase Requisition class?
    A) Instigation Event
    B) Commitment Event
    C) Economic Increment Event
    D) Economic Decrement Event
    E) Economic Increment Reversal Event

24. What stereotype would be most appropriate for the Materials Requisition class?
    A) Instigation Event
    B) Commitment Event
    C) Economic Increment Event
    D) Economic Decrement Event
    E) Economic Increment Reversal Event

25. What is the current label of the association that should be called Linkage?
    A) Produce
    B) Stockflow1
    C) Reciprocal1
    D) Reciprocal2
    E) Reservation1

26. What is the current label of the association(s) in the model that should not exist – that is, for which association that is currently created should the two connected classes not have a connection between them in most business contexts and certainly not for Bentleys Balloons.
    A) Assignment
    B) Participation4
    C) Participation6
    D) Reciprocal2
    E) All of the above – i.e., none of the associations in A through D above should exist

27. What internal agent is missing from Bentley's model that should be included?
    A) Accounting clerk
    B) Warehouse supervisor
    C) Bank
    D) Supplier
    E) Customer

28. Currently the model does not show an association connecting the Materials and Production Run classes. Should there be, and if so, what should it be called?
    A) No
    B) Yes, Linkage
    C) Yes, Stockflow
    D) Yes, Reservation
    E) Yes, Reciprocal

CHAPTER 14

The Human Resource Business Process
aka The Payroll Cycle

LEARNING OBJECTIVES

The objectives of this chapter are to introduce the human resource business process, also called the payroll cycle; to discuss the REA ontology representation of human resource processes, and to describe some of the typical information needs in the payroll cycle. After studying this chapter you should be able to

1. Identify the activities and documents common to most payroll cycles
2. Identify the various components of the REA ontology in the human resource process
3. Create a REA business process level model for an enterprise's human resource process
4. Identify common information needs that exist within the human resource process
5. Create database queries to retrieve human resource process information from a relational database

HUMAN RESOURCE BUSINESS PROCESS IN AN ENTERPRISE VALUE SYSTEM

The human resource business process encompasses all of the activities needed to acquire and pay for employee labor. Although the specific workflow activities differ in various enterprises' human resource processes, we discuss the pattern for the information system's base objects that has been identified as common to most payroll cycles. Activities in the human resource process include hiring, training, evaluating, terminating, and paying employees for their labor, knowledge, and skills. Often these activities are separated into two subprocesses: personnel and payroll. The **personnel function** hires, trains, evaluates, and terminates employees. The **payroll function** disburses payments to employees. In this chapter, we use the terms *human resource process* and *payroll cycle* as synonyms, so please don't confuse payroll cycle with the payroll function that is a subset of the cycle as a whole.

The **human resource process** is in essence a special case of the acquisition/payment cycle. The personnel function acquires and maintains employee labor and the payroll function pays for employee labor. Because the acquisition of and payment for goods and outside services often result in different information needs than the acquisition of and payment for labor, both with respect to the types of resources acquired and the types of agents from whom they are acquired, the payroll cycle is usually kept separate from the acquisition/payment cycle.

As you analyze and model a business process, you must clearly understand its purpose and objectives. You must realize how the business process fits into the value system and enterprise value chain. At the value system level, the human resource process is the point of contact between the enterprise and its employees. At this point of contact, the **employees** are external business partners to the enterprise; in other words they are engaging in arms' length exchanges. Whereas in other business processes we have considered employees as internal agents; in the human resource process the only employees we consider as internal agents are those whose job functions involve processing payroll. Those payroll processing employees are also members of the external agent employee entity set with respect to their own provision of labor to the enterprise.

At arm's length, the enterprise gives cash to the employees in exchange for the employees' labor as highlighted in Exhibit 14-1. Along with their labor (described as time worked at a particular wage rate), the employees also provide knowledge and skills to the enterprise. However, the enterprise usually does not end up owning the employees' knowledge and skills so we assume measurements of the knowledge and skills are encompassed in the wage rate and time worked. Today many enterprises are attempting to develop techniques for owning employees' skills and knowledge such that those can be separated to some extent from the simple time-worked construct. To accomplish this, enterprises are creating knowledge bases and artificial intelligence based decision support systems in which to store the knowledge and procedural decision-making processes of its most valuable knowledge-intensive employees. Although significant progress has been made in the area of knowledge bases and decision support systems, most information systems can still only measure labor acquisition as time-worked.

Exhibit 14-1   Human Resource Process in the Enterprise Value System

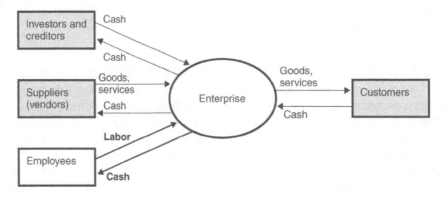

The value chain reveals interfaces between the payroll process and other business processes. Exhibit 14-2 illustrates the typical value chain interfaces.

Exhibit 14-2 Human Resource Process in the Value Chain

Partial Value Chain

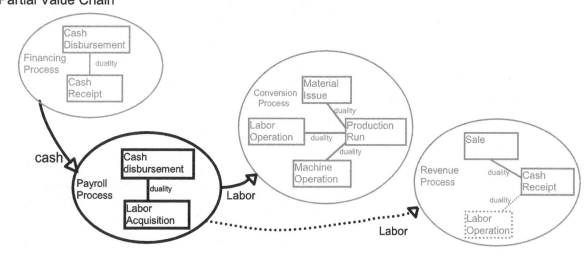

Notice that the solid arrows of Exhibit 14-2 only depict the human resource process making labor available to the conversion process. In many companies the conversion cycle is the only process wherein the use of labor is tracked at a specific enough level to justify including it at the value chain level. If we specifically track labor use in another business process we similarly show labor as an output of payroll and as an input to the other process. The dashed arrow in Exhibit 14-2 illustrates the value chain depiction of labor made available to the revenue process; as a result the specific use of that labor is included in the revenue process as an economic decrement event called labor operation. A similar depiction would be used for labor that is specifically tracked in the acquisition/payment and/or financing processes.

The primary objective of the human resource process is to provide the human labor and expertise the enterprise needs to function efficiently and effectively. Because employees' labor is a valuable asset for many enterprises, we must model its acquisition and payment for it as correctly and completely as possible in a cost effective manner.

We begin our business process level discussion of the payroll cycle by reviewing some of its more common events. Two important reminders before we begin the discussion. Because we discuss the activities in a sequential fashion, it may seem that the human resource process is linear. That is not necessarily true. Increasingly, business processes and the activities that comprise those processes are dynamic, rather than linear and static. Also, remember that the activities in this process are linked to and sometimes overlap activities in other processes. We are concentrating on one process at a time to simplify our analysis.

HUMAN RESOURCE BUSINESS PROCESS LEVEL REA MODELS
Recall that the extended REA ontology described in several chapters in this book and that is illustrated in Exhibit 14-3 identifies the pattern underlying each transaction cycle. Included are instigation events, mutual commitment events, economic exchange events, resources, agents, types, and various associations such as stockflow, duality, fulfillment, reservation, proposition, and participation. In this section we describe the extended REA ontology components specific to the human resource business process.

Exhibit 14-3 Payroll Cycle Extended REA Ontology Database Design Pattern

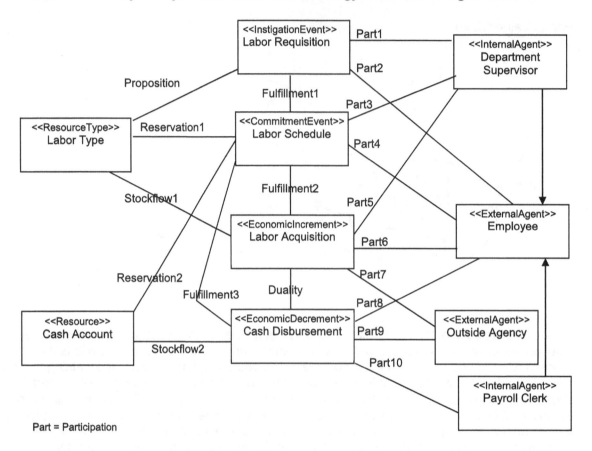

Part = Participation

We remind you that instigation events and the associations in which they participate (such as proposition) are not part of the published REA ontology. We added them to the business process level models in this text as a convenient means of fleshing out the complete story of each business process. A proposal is made in the instigation event. The proposal is acted upon and a mutual agreement is reached in the commitment event. The mutual commitment is fulfilled by the economic events that comprise the exchange of resources. These base objects exist in every cycle for every enterprise; however, measurement and storage of all the details of them is not always cost-effective.

The *REA* pattern aids in analyzing business processes and events by highlighting the *what* (the resources involved in the event) and the *who* (the internal and external agents) involved in each event. The *where* and the *when* are often stored as attributes of each event. The events, agents, and resources involved in the human resource process vary somewhat from enterprise to enterprise. The general pattern discussed in this chapter can be adapted and applied to meet the exact requirements of any enterprise.

Resources
Human capital is the resource acquired in the human resource process. Human capital is made up of the work employees perform and the knowledge and skills employees use in performing that work. Because human capital is mostly intangible, it is very difficult to measure. Ownership is also difficult to establish, as discussed earlier in this chapter. If we could resolve the

ownership and measurement issues, then we would directly represent the human capital resource as a class in the enterprise's business process level model. Instead, we typically substitute a class called labor type. The **labor type resource** class serves as an inventory of the kinds of labor an enterprise may need to acquire and use in its operations. The attributes typically captured to represent labor types include an identifier, a description, and a standard (budgeted) hourly wage rate for that type of labor.

Cash is the resource given in exchange for labor. Cash in the payroll cycle is typically represented by the cash accounts from which paychecks are written. Paychecks are usually written from either a regular checking account or from an imprest checking account. An **imprest checking account** is an account that normally maintains a zero balance. For example, when the amount of cash disbursements needed for a payroll period is determined, a company that uses an imprest checking account transfers the total amount of the paychecks from one of its regular checking accounts to its imprest account. Paychecks to each specific employee are drawn on the imprest checking account. As time passes, if the imprest account balance is positive, that indicates employees are not all cashing their paychecks. If the imprest account balance becomes negative, a mistake likely occurred. Either situation warrants investigation. Attributes typically captured to represent the set of cash accounts include an identifier, type, description, and location of each account. If financial institutions (such as banks or credit unions) maintain most of the cash accounts, then the account numbers assigned by the financial institutions also need to be captured. Cash account balance is an example of a volatile derivable attribute for which a stored query may be created and reused for quick retrieval.

Instigation Events - Need Identification and Request for Labor
Supervisors determine the need for labor by monitoring enterprise growth (or lack thereof), production plans, sales forecasts, employee turnover, and other trends and projections. Identification of a need for labor often is labeled as a **labor requisition event** as shown in Exhibit 14-3. Labor requests occur on an ongoing basis as part of normal operations and involve identification of the number of hours (or some similar basis) existing employees are needed to provide specific types of labor. The labor requisition event is fulfilled by the scheduling of one or more employees to provide that labor.

Agents involved in instigation events in the payroll cycle usually are department supervisors (internal agents who authorize the requisition) and employees (external agents whose skills and knowledge are the subject of the request). As noted earlier, because labor is intangible it is usually measured via categories and is specified as labor type. Attributes of labor requisitions that typically should be captured include the date and time of the requisition. The requisition event data should be linked to data regarding the related supervisor, requested employees (if any are specified), and the type of labor requested. Documentation of need identification for labor may vary widely. Although theoretically we could expect to see a labor requisition form that looks much like a purchase requisition form as shown in the acquisition/payment cycle chapter, not many enterprises use such forms for routine labor need identification. Indeed, most need for labor is identified by department supervisors who themselves also approve the request based on their own department's budget. A **staffing plan** is the most commonly used form of documentation on which a department supervisor communicates a department's need for labor for a given time period. Such a plan indicates the types and quantities of labor needed without assigning specific employees to provide the labor. Exhibit 14-4 illustrates a staffing plan.

Exhibit 14-4 Sample Document for Labor Requisition Event: Staffing Plan

Your Source Company
Staffing Plan ___7___
For Period April 1, 2015 – April 7, 2015

Date Plan Approved __2/24/2015_____   Approved by _E5_____

Labor type	4/1	4/2	4/3	4/4	4/5	4/6	4/7	Total	Std Wage Rate	Ext. Amount
	Quantity of Labor Needed (in hours)									
CT2 Cashier duties	16	16	16	16	16	0	0	80	$12.00	$960.00
US3 Cleaning/janitorial	8	8	8	8	8	12	0	52	$9.00	$468.00
AP1 Sales tax preparation	12	12	12	12	12	0	0	60	$18.00	$1,080.00
CT1 Data entry	12	12	12	12	12	12	12	84	$11.00	$924.00
Totals	48	48	48	48	48	24	12	276		$3,432.00

List IDs and names of any requested employees here, as well as for what type of labor

___E23 James Worthwhile for tax preparation_____

The set of relational tables illustrated in Exhibit 14-5 correspond to Exhibit 14-3's UML class diagram representation of the labor requisition event, the associations in which it participates (proposition, fulfillment1, participation1, and participation2), and the related classes (labor type, labor schedule, department supervisor, and employee. Alternative tables could be derived depending on the association multiplicities. Data from the form in Exhibit 14-4 have been entered into the database tables; however, some of these data (e.g. labor type and employee information) would have existed already in the database tables before the requisition data was added to the tables so only the association information that links them to the event is recorded for those objects. New data that would be entered as a result of the labor requisition event is shown in bold italic font.

Exhibit 14-5 Relational Tables Encompassing Labor Requisition Event (partial data)

LaborRequisition (Instigation) Event

LaborReqID	Date	Maximum Budget for request	Total Estimated Budget request	Labor Request Period	SuperID^FK
LR7	2/24/2015	$3,600.00	$3,432.00	4/1/2015-4/7/2015	E5

Proposition Association

LaborReqID	LaborTypeID	Hours Needed	Estimated Hourly Wage
LR7	CT2	80	$12.00
LR7	US3	52	$9.00
LR7	AP1	60	$18.00
LR7	CT1	84	$11.00

ParticipationLaborRequisitionEmployee (Participation2) Association

LaborReqID	Requested EmployeeID
LR7	E23

DepartmentSupervisor (Internal Agent)

SuperID	Authorized Spending Limit
E5	$425,000

Employee (External Agent)

EmpID	Name	Address	Telephone	DateOfBirth	Rating	Position	Type	Wage
E5	Patrick Wellesley	53125 Fenton Dr.	555-1112	March 4, 1958	Excellent	Supervisor	Salary	$35.50
E15	Donna Davis	149 Rovetta Dr.	555-9932	Feb. 3, 1954	Superior	Cashier	Hourly	$13.50
E16	Nancy Hardaway	271 Rovetta Dr.	555-2117	June 11, 1956	Excellent	Cashier	Hourly	$12.75
E17	Joe Thompson	535 Olson St.	555-2277	Apr. 24, 1947	Excellent	Custodian	Hourly	$9.20
E18	Freda Matthews	3214 Deerlake St.	555-1222	Aug. 6, 1940	Good	Custodian	Hourly	$8.90
E19	John Matthews	3214 Deerlake St.	555-1222	Oct. 14, 1940	Good	Custodian	Hourly	$8.90
E20	Paula Cosgrove	5006 Jazz Ct.	555-5200	Apr. 18, 1958	Excellent	Data Entry	Hourly	$11.50
E21	Rob Fordham	4444 Zephyr Ln.	555-4545	June 4, 1975	Excellent	Data Entry	Hourly	$11.00
E22	Francis Johnson	1261 Mason Dr.	555-0129	May 5, 1980	Good	Data Entry	Hourly	$10.75
E23	James Worthwhile	5432 Wadsworth Ln	555-7777	Apr. 14, 1964	Superior	Accountant	Salary	$18.00
E36	Diane Bowersox	9115 Wolfgang Ct	555-7244	Sept 15, 1963	Superior	Payroll	Hourly	$11.75

LaborType (Resource Type)

Item ID	Description	Standard Hourly Wage
CT2	Cashier duties	$12.00
US3	Clean sales showroom and stockroom	$9.00
AP1	Prepare quarterly sales tax return	$18.00
CT1	Enter data for sales transactions	$11.00

LaborSchedule (Mutual Commitment) Event

Labor ScheduleID	Date Schedule Approved	Begin Date	End Date	Total Dollar Amt	LaborReqID^FK	SuperID^FK

Note: Fulfillment1 association is implemented with LaborReqID posted into Labor Schedule table; Participation1 association is implemented with SuperID posted into Requisition table; Fulfillment1 data is not yet entered, assuming a time lag between requisition and schedule.

Mutual Commitment Event (Labor Schedule)

A mutual commitment event exists when an enterprise and an external business partner have each agreed to exchange specific quantities of resources at a defined future time. In the payroll process a labor schedule serves as a mutual commitment event. A **labor schedule**, also called an **employee schedule**, is typically prepared by a supervisor with inputs from the employee as to when the employee is and is not available to work. This is similar to a purchase agent's preparation of a purchase order with input from a supplier as to the availability of goods or services. The employee schedule represents a commitment by the employee to provide the labor as specified and a commitment by the enterprise to pay the employee the contracted wage rate for the labor provided. If the employee does not work his or her scheduled hours, (as when a supplier doesn't fill a purchase order for goods) the enterprise is not obligated to pay for those hours not worked.

Attributes of labor schedule events that typically should be captured include the date the schedule was approved, the total dollar amount to which the schedule commits, and the time period covered by the schedule (often in the form of a beginning date and an ending date). The labor schedule should also be linked to data regarding the related labor types, employees, supervisor, labor acquisition event, and labor requisition event. Data regarding labor schedule events are often captured on a form such as that shown in Exhibit 14-6. This form may either be a paper document, an electronic spreadsheet, or part of a software application interface that is used to update the enterprise database.

Exhibit 14-6 Labor Schedule

Your Source Company
Employee Schedule ___7___
For Period April 1, 2015 – April 7, 2015

Date Schedule Approved ___3/4/2015___   Approved by ___E5___

Empl ID	Name	4/1/15	4/2/15	4/3/15	4/4/15	4/5/15	4/6/15	4/7/15	Total Hours
E15	Donna Davis	7-4	7-4	7-4	7-4	7-4			40
E16	Nancy Hardaway	9-6	9-6	9-6	9-6	9-6			40
E17	Joe Thompson	7-4	7-4	7-4	7-4	7-4			40
E18	Freda Matthews						7-2		6
E19	John Matthews						7-2		6
E20	Paula Cosgrove	9-1	9-1	9-1	9-1	9-1	9-1	9-1	28
E21	Rob Fordham	8-5	8-5	8-5	8-5	8-5			40
E22	Francis Johnson						8-5	8-5	16
E23	James Worthwhile	8-8	8-8	8-8	8-8	8-8			60

The set of relational tables in Exhibit 14-7 correspond to Exhibit 14-3's UML class diagram representation of the labor schedule event and the associations in which it participates (reservation1, fulfillment1, fulfillment2, participation3, and participation4). Other possible tables could be derived, depending on the association multiplicities. Data from the form in Exhibit 14-6 have been entered into the database tables; however, some of these data (e.g. labor type, supervisor, and employee information) would have existed already in the database tables before the labor schedule data was added to the tables so only the association information that links them to the labor schedule should be added for those objects. The new data entered to record the labor schedule event are shown in bold italic font.

Exhibit 14-7 Relational Tables Encompassing Labor Schedule Event (partial data)

LaborSchedule (Mutual Commitment) Event

Labor ScheduleID	Date Schedule Approved	Begin Date	End Date	Total Dollar Amt	LaborReqID^{FK}	SuperID^{FK}
LS7	3/4/2015	4/1/2015	4/7/2015	$3,538.80	LR7	E5

LaborRequisition (Instigation) Event

LaborReqID	Date	Maximum Budget for request	Estimated Budget for request	Labor Request Period	SuperID^{FK}
LR7	2/24/2015	$3,600.00	$3,432.00	4/1/2015-4/7/2015	E5

ReservationLaborScheduleLaborType (Reservation1) Relationship

LaborScheduleID	LaborTypeID	HoursScheduled
LS7	CT2	80
LS7	US3	52
LS7	AP1	60
LS7	CT1	84

ParticipationLaborScheduleEmployee (Participation4) Relationship

LaborScheduleID	Scheduled EmployeeID	Hours Scheduled	Wage Rate
LS7	E15	40	$13.50
LS7	E16	40	$12.75
LS7	E17	40	$9.20
LS7	E18	6	$8.90
LS7	E19	6	$8.90
LS7	E20	28	$11.50
LS7	E21	40	$11.00
LS7	E22	16	$10.75
LS7	E23	60	$18.00

DepartmentSupervisor (Internal Agent)

SuperID	Authorized Spending Limit
E5	$425,000

Employee (External Agent)

EmpID	Name	Address	Telephone	DateOfBirth	Rating	Position	Type	Wage
E5	Patrick Wellesley	53125 Fenton Dr.	555-1112	March 4, 1958	Excellent	Supervisor	Salary	$35.50
E15	Donna Davis	149 Rovetta Dr.	555-9932	Feb. 3, 1954	Superior	Cashier	Hourly	$13.50
E16	Nancy Hardaway	271 Rovetta Dr.	555-2117	June 11, 1956	Excellent	Cashier	Hourly	$12.75
E17	Joe Thompson	535 Olson St.	555-2277	Apr. 24, 1947	Excellent	Custodian	Hourly	$9.20
E18	Freda Matthews	3214 Deerlake St.	555-1222	Aug. 6, 1940	Good	Custodian	Hourly	$8.90
E19	John Matthews	3214 Deerlake St.	555-1222	Oct. 14, 1940	Good	Custodian	Hourly	$8.90
E20	Paula Cosgrove	5006 Jazz Ct.	555-5200	Apr. 18, 1958	Excellent	Data Entry	Hourly	$11.50
E21	Rob Fordham	4444 Zephyr Ln.	555-4545	June 4, 1975	Excellent	Data Entry	Hourly	$11.00
E22	Francis Johnson	1261 Mason Dr.	555-0129	May 5, 1980	Good	Data Entry	Hourly	$10.75
E23	James Worthwhile	5432 Wadsworth Ln	555-7777	Apr. 14, 1964	Superior	Accountant	Salary	$18.00
E36	Diane Bowersox	9115 Wolfgang Ct	555-7244	Sept 15, 1963	Superior	Payroll	Hourly	$11.75

Exhibit 14-7 continued

LaborType (Resource Type)

Item ID	Description	Standard Hourly Wage
CT2	Cashier duties	$12.00
US3	Clean sales showroom and stockroom	$9.00
AP1	Prepare quarterly sales tax return	$18.00
CT1	Enter data for sales transactions	$11.00

FulfillmentLaborAcquisitionLaborSchedule (Fulfillment2) Relationship

LaborScheduleID	LaborAcquisitionID

Note: Participation3 association is implemented with SuperID posted into the Labor Schedule table; Fulfillment1 association is implemented with Requisition ID posted into Labor Schedule table; Fulfillment2 data is not yet entered, assuming a time lag between schedule and labor acquisition.

Economic Increment Event (Labor Acquisition)

Labor acquisition is the primary economic increment event in the human resource process. This event represents the provision of labor to an enterprise by an employee. Because labor is intangible, the acquisition of labor is also somewhat intangible. While in theory labor is acquired continuously, most enterprises aggregate labor acquisitions according to a defined time period. Each instance of the labor acquisition set therefore represents the purchase of labor for a defined time period. The time period may be the same as the enterprise pay period, or each days' time worked by each employee may serve as an instance of the labor acquisition event. Daily (or even more frequent) recording of labor acquisitions allows for a more complete picture of the enterprise on a continual basis because the time lag between the company receiving the benefit of the economic increment event and the recording of that benefit (and the related liability) is minimized.

The primary document prepared by the enterprise in conjunction with the economic increment event is a time card. Time cards may be completed on a daily, weekly, or other basis. Time cards are typically completed by employees and approved by supervisors. Time cards list the times employees started working (punched in) and stopped working (punched out) for each day in the covered time period.

Most large enterprises have not used hand-written paper time cards for many years, but instead use electronic time clocks with punch cards that enable automated data processing. Some have further upgraded to scanning of employee id cards or badges upon arrival and departure, with direct transmission of that data to the computerized payroll application. In such automated systems, the data captured are similar to the paper time cards; the difference is in the speed with which the system is updated. Such systems enable the daily or more frequent recording of labor acquisitions recommended earlier.

What about labor acquired from salaried employees, for which no time clock data is collected? For purposes of determining accruals for compensated sick time and vacation time, most enterprises assume such employees work forty hours per week at a wage rate equivalent to their annual salary divided by 2,080 (the number of hours in the year calculated as 52 weeks x 40 hours per week). While they don't require employees to punch a clock, they do typically require employees to report sick time or vacation time taken.

Exhibit 14-8 illustrates a time card representing the type of data collected regardless of whether the data is captured on paper or electronically, and whether the data are based on actual time worked or assumed time worked.

Exhibit 14-8: Time Card

Time Card # ___49___   Pay Period ___4/1/2015 – 4/7/2015___

Employee ID __E23__   Employee Name __James Worthwhile__

Monday 4/1				Tuesday 4/2				Wednesday 4/3				Thursday 4/4				Friday 4/5				Saturday 4/6				Sunday 4/7			
In	Out	In	Out	In	Out	In	Out	In	Out	In	Out	In	Out	In	Out	In	Out	In	Out	In	Out	In	Out	In	Out	In	Out
7	-	-	7	7	-	-	7	7	-	-	7	7	-	-	7	7	-	-	7								

I hereby ascertain that I worked the hours recorded above.

James S. Worthwhile   ___4/5/2015___
Employee Signature   Date

Approved by _E5_   Date: _4/8/2015_
Initials   _PW_

In addition to the time card data, to record the labor acquisition event, the enterprise must also use data stored in its system as to any applicable withholdings. That information is not needed to determine the cost of the labor acquisition. However, it is needed to allocate the amounts of that cost that are payable to the employee and to other outside agencies such as the IRS, state government, or insurance providers. When enterprises record payroll-related expenses, wages or salaries expense is recorded as the gross pay dollar amount. Wages or salaries payable is recorded as the net pay dollar amount – that represents the amount that is payable to the employees. The difference is made up of the **withholdings**, also called **payroll deductions**. These represent amounts that are not to be paid directly to the employee but instead are to be paid on behalf of the employee (sometimes by statute, sometimes voluntarily) to government agencies, benefit providers, or other outside agencies. In the United States, amounts withheld for federal income taxes, social security tax, and medicare tax typically are payable to the Internal Revenue Service. Amounts withheld for state income taxes are payable to the appropriate state government agencies. Amounts withheld for employees' premiums for insurance benefits (health, dental, life, and so forth) are payable to the appropriate insurance providers. Other deductions may be payable to other types of agencies such as charitable organizations.

In theory enterprises could simply record the gross pay as the labor acquisition cost and then wait to record the various withholdings as part of the duality association once the checks are written to the employees and outside agencies. However, because the amounts are available (either by predefined calculations or reference files) and because the enterprise's economic story is more complete sooner by including them when recording the acquisition event, there is no reason to postpone their recognition.

Associations in which the labor acquisition event in the human resource process participates typically include stockflow (allowing the enterprise to trace the labor type resource that was acquired), fulfillment (enabling the enterprise to trace which labor schedule event the acquisition fulfilled), duality (allowing the enterprise to trace the related cash disbursements), and participation associations with the supervisor who authorized the acquisition, the employee who provided the labor, and the outside agencies that are entitled to compensation based on the employee providing the labor.

The set of relational tables in Exhibit 14-9 correspond to Exhibit 14-3's UML class diagram representation of the labor acquisition event and the associations in which it participates (stockflow1, fulfillment2, participation5, participation6, participation7 and duality). Other possible tables could be derived, depending on the association multiplicities. Data from the form in Exhibit 14-8 have been entered into the database tables; however, some of this data (e.g. labor type and employee information) would already have existed in the database tables before the labor acquisition data were added to the tables so only the association information that links them to the labor acquisition event is added for those objects. The new data to be added upon provision of labor by employees are shown in bold italic font.

Exhibit 14-9 Relational Tables Encompassing Labor Acquisition (partial data)

LaborAcquisition (Economic Increment) Event

AcqID	BeginDate	EndDate	Hours	GrossPay	FICA	Medica	FIT	SIT	Net Pay	EmpID^{FK}	SupID^{FK}
TC49	*4/1/2015*	*4/7/2015*	*60*	*$1,080.00*	*$66.96*	*$15.66*	*$216*	*$43.20*	*$738.18*	*E23*	*E5*

ParticipationLaborAcquisitionOutsideAgency Association

LaborAcquisitionID	AgencyID	Amount
TC49	*IRS*	*$298.62*
TC49	*Mich*	*$43.20*

LaborSchedule (Mutual Commitment) Event

Labor ScheduleID	Date Schedule Approved	Begin Date	End Date	Total Dollar Amt	LaborReqID^{FK}	SuperID^{FK}
LS7	3/4/2015	4/1/2015	4/7/2015	$3,538.80	LR7	E5

StockflowLaborAcquisitionLaborType (Stockflow1) Relationship

AcquisitionID	LT-ID	Hours worked	wage
TC49	*AP1*	*60*	*$18.00*

DualityLaborAcquisitionCashDisb Relationship

LaborAcquisitionID	Voucher#	AmountApplied

DepartmentSupervisor (Internal Agent)

SuperID	Authorized Spending Limit
E5	$425,000

LaborType (Resource Type)

Item ID	Description	Standard Hourly Wage
CT2	Cashier duties	$12.00
US3	Clean sales showroom and stockroom	$9.00
AP1	Prepare quarterly sales tax return	$18.00
CT1	Enter data for sales transactions	$11.00

FulfillmentLaborAcquisitionLaborSchedule (Fulfillment2) Relationship

LaborScheduleID	LaborAcquisitionID
LS7	TC49

Employee (External Agent)

EmpID	Name	Address	Telephone	DateOfBirth	Rating	Position	Type	Wage
E5	Patrick Wellesley	53125 Fenton Dr.	555-1112	March 4, 1958	Excellent	Supervisor	Salary	$35.50
E15	Donna Davis	149 Rovetta Dr.	555-9932	Feb. 3, 1954	Superior	Cashier	Hourly	$13.50
E16	Nancy Hardaway	271 Rovetta Dr.	555-2117	June 11, 1956	Excellent	Cashier	Hourly	$12.75
E17	Joe Thompson	535 Olson St.	555-2277	Apr. 24, 1947	Excellent	Custodian	Hourly	$9.20
E18	Freda Matthews	3214 Deerlake St.	555-1222	Aug. 6, 1940	Good	Custodian	Hourly	$8.90
E19	John Matthews	3214 Deerlake St.	555-1222	Oct. 14, 1940	Good	Custodian	Hourly	$8.90
E20	Paula Cosgrove	5006 Jazz Ct.	555-5200	Apr. 18, 1958	Excellent	Data Entry	Hourly	$11.50
E21	Rob Fordham	4444 Zephyr Ln.	555-4545	June 4, 1975	Excellent	Data Entry	Hourly	$11.00
E22	Francis Johnson	1261 Mason Dr.	555-0129	May 5, 1980	Good	Data Entry	Hourly	$10.75
E23	James Worthwhile	5432 Wadsworth Ln	555-7777	Apr. 14, 1964	Superior	Accountant	Salary	$18.00
E36	Diane Bowersox	9115 Wolfgang Ct	555-7244	Sept 15, 1963	Superior	Payroll	Hourly	$11.75

OutsideAgencies (External Agent)

AgencyID	AgencyName	MailingAddress
S315	Internal Revenue Service	PO Box 123512
S320	State Government	PO Box 321533
S325	Blue Health	31253 Elm St.
S330	Best Dental	1472 Beech St.

Note: Participation5 is implemented with SuperID posted into Labor Acquisition table;
Participation6 is implemented with EmplID posted into Labor Acquisition table;
Participation7 is implemented as a separate table with LaborAcquisitionID and AgencyID as combined primary key
Duality data is not yet entered, assuming a time lag between Labor Acquisition and Cash Disbursement

Economic Decrement Event (Cash Disbursement)

Cash disbursements are economic decrement events that decrease the enterprise's cash balance. Cash disbursements in the payroll cycle may be made via paper check, electronic funds transfer (direct deposit), or cash payment. Most enterprises use either paper checks or direct deposit to pay employees. Paycheck or direct deposit stubs typically contain information such as gross pay, net pay, and the various withholdings that make up the difference between gross and net pay (such as income tax, social security tax, medicare tax, health insurance premiums, and retirement plan contributions). Exhibit 14-10 illustrates a direct deposit stub.

Exhibit 14-10: Sample Direct Deposit Notification

Your Source Company Direct Deposit Notification Employee ID _23_ Name James Worthwhile	Time card 49	Gross Pay $1,080	Federal Income Tax W/H $216.00	FICA W/H $66.96	Medicare W/H $15.66	State Income Tax W/H $43.20	No. __49__ Net Pay $738.18

Your Source Company	No. __49__
	Voucher No. _89_
	Date 4/14/2015
James S. Worthwhile	

Your net pay has been transmitted electronically (EFT)
to your financial institution according to your instructions

Cash disbursements may occur at various times during the human resource process. Most enterprises pay employees only after acquiring labor from the employees. Some enterprises do offer advances to employees; those are advance payments for which the employee is obliged either to provide the corresponding labor or to repay the cash with interest. Attributes captured regarding cash disbursements usually include a cash disbursement identifier (such as a disbursement voucher number), date, amount paid, payee identification (for paychecks, that is the employee who supplied labor or the outside agency who benefitted from the employee supplying labor), clerk identification (i.e., the employee who wrote the check), the cash account number from which the cash is disbursed, and the voucher or check number of the payment.

Exhibit 14-11 shows a set of relational tables that correspond to Exhibit 14-3's UML class diagram representation of the cash disbursement event and the payroll cycle associations in which it participates (duality, stockflow2, participation8, participation9, and participation10). Other possible tables could be derived, depending on the association multiplicities. Additional tables are necessary to correspond to associations in which the cash disbursement event participates in other transaction cycles such as acquisition/payment and financing. The tables shown in Exhibit 14-11 are applicable to the human resource process. Data from the form in Exhibit 14-10 have been entered into the database tables; however, some of this data (e.g. labor acquisition, cash, and employee information) would already have existed in the database tables before the cash disbursement data were added to the tables. Only the association information that links those objects to the cash disbursements is added to the database upon the cash disbursement. The new data to be added for the cash disbursement event are shown in bold italic font.

Exhibit 14-11 Relational Tables Encompassing Cash Disbursement Event (partial data)

CashDisbursement (Economic Decrement) Event

Disb Voucher ID	Voucher Date	Dollar Amount	Check Number	Cash AccountID^{FK}	Payroll ClerkID^{FK}	PayeeID^{FK}
88	4/14/2015	$2,637.82	40404	Ca123501	E36	Ca987654
89	4/14/2015	$738.18	49	Ca987654	E36	E23
90	4/14/2015	$298.62	50	Ca987654	E36	S315
91	4/14/2015	$43.20	51	Ca987654	E36	S320

Cash (Resource Type)

CashAccountID	AccountType	Location
Ca123501	Checking	1st Local Bank
Ca987654	Imprest checking	1st Local Bank

DualityLaborAcquisitionCashDisb Relationship

LaborAcquisitionID	Voucher#	Amount Applied
TC49	89	$738.18
TC49	90	$298.62
TC49	91	$43.20

LaborAcquisition (Economic Increment) Event

AcqID	BeginDate	EndDate	Hours	GrossPay	FICA	Medica	FIT	SIT	Net Pay	EmpID^{FK}	SupID^{FK}
TC49	4/1/2015	4/7/2015	60	$1,080.00	$66.96	$15.66	$216	$43.20	$738.18	E23	E5

PayrollClerk (Internal Agent)

PayrollClerkID	Fidelity Bond Rating
E36	AA

Employee (External Agent)

EmpID	Name	Address	Telephone	DateOfBirth	Rating	Position	Type	Wage
E5	Patrick Wellesley	53125 Fenton Dr.	555-1112	March 4, 1958	Excellent	Supervisor	Salary	$35.50
E15	Donna Davis	149 Rovetta Dr.	555-9932	Feb. 3, 1954	Superior	Cashier	Hourly	$13.50
E16	Nancy Hardaway	271 Rovetta Dr.	555-2117	June 11, 1956	Excellent	Cashier	Hourly	$12.75
E17	Joe Thompson	535 Olson St.	555-2277	Apr. 24, 1947	Excellent	Custodian	Hourly	$9.20
E18	Freda Matthews	3214 Deerlake St.	555-1222	Aug. 6, 1940	Good	Custodian	Hourly	$8.90
E19	John Matthews	3214 Deerlake St.	555-1222	Oct. 14, 1940	Good	Custodian	Hourly	$8.90
E20	Paula Cosgrove	5006 Jazz Ct.	555-5200	Apr. 18, 1958	Excellent	Data Entry	Hourly	$11.50
E21	Rob Fordham	4444 Zephyr Ln.	555-4545	June 4, 1975	Excellent	Data Entry	Hourly	$11.00
E22	Francis Johnson	1261 Mason Dr.	555-0129	May 5, 1980	Good	Data Entry	Hourly	$10.75
E23	James Worthwhile	5432 Wadsworth Ln	555-7777	Apr. 14, 1964	Superior	Accountant	Salary	$18.00
E36	Diane Bowersox	9115 Wolfgang Ct	555-7244	Sept 15, 1963	Superior	Payroll	Hourly	$11.75

OutsideAgencies (External Agent)

AgencyID	AgencyName	MailingAddress
S315	Internal Revenue Service	PO Box 123512
S320	State Government	PO Box 321533
S325	Blue Health	31253 Elm St.
S330	Best Dental	1472 Beech St.

Note: Stockflow2 is implemented with Cash AccountID posted into Cash Disbursement table; Participation8 and Participation9 are both implemented with PayeeID posted into Cash Disbursement table – this is an example of Combined class key posting as discussed in Chapter 12; Participation10 is implemented with PayrollClerkID posted into Cash Disbursement table

INFORMATION NEEDS IN THE HUMAN RESOURCE PROCESS

The most common information customers for the human resource business process include management, employees, accountants, and auditors. We next analyze each of the REA ontology classes and associations in the human resource process to provide ideas as to the types of queries that may be needed to satisfy information needs in the payroll cycle. The queries presented are not a comprehensive set of queries because there are simply too many potential queries exist to list them all. However, the following set should provide you guidance for creating similar types of queries. To describe example queries needed in the payroll cycle use the database tables shown in Exhibits 14-5, 14-7, 14-9, and 14-11.

Class Queries

Among the simplest of queries to create are those that involve single classes. Because each class is implemented as a table, each class query will require consideration of only one table.

Resource Queries in the Human Resource Process

Labor type and cash are the resources that most commonly exist in the human resource process. For each resource, users may need any of the following:

- Detailed status information at one or more points in time for each resource instance
- Detailed status information at one or more points in time for only those resource instances meeting specified criteria
- Summarized status information at one or more points in time for all resource instances
- Summarized status information at one or more points in time for only those resource instances meeting specified criteria

With regard to each list item, users may need to know all characteristics of the instances in the answer set, or they may need only a subset of the characteristics.

Labor is typically tracked only at the type level. Cash is tracked by the accounts in which the cash is stored. Some example queries and procedures for creating the queries based on the tables in this chapter are as follows:

- *What are the descriptions for all labor types for the enterprise?* Use the labor type table; display all fields
- *Which labor types have standard hourly wage rates less than $10?* Use the LaborType table; enter criteria <10 in the StdHourlyWageRate field; display labor type description
- *Does the enterprise own any imprest cash accounts?* Use the Cash table; enter criteria LIKE *imprest* in the AccountType field; display the cash account id. (The LIKE command coupled with the wild card * symbols will identify any account type that includes the word imprest in the type name).
- *What is the average standard hourly wage rate for all labor types?* Use the LaborType table; apply the AVG aggregation function to the standard hourly wage field

Event Queries in the Human Resource Process

Users may need information regarding events. The most common events in the human resource process are labor requisitions, labor schedules, labor acquisitions, and cash disbursements. For each of these types of events, users may need any of the following:
- Detailed information about each event instance
- Detailed information about each event instance that meets specified criteria
- Summarized information for all instances of an event type for a specified time period
- Summarized information for only those instances of an event type for a specified time period that meet specified criteria

Some example queries to satisfy information needs regarding events in the human resource process are (among many other possibilities) as follows:
- *What is the maximum budget amount for labor requisition LR7?* Use the LaborRequisition table; enter criteria =LR7 in the labor requisition id field; apply the MAX aggregation function to the budget for request field
- *When was labor schedule LS7 approved?* Use the LaborSchedule table; enter criteria =LS7 in the labor schedule id field; display the date schedule approved field
- *How many days of labor are included on labor acquisition TC49?* Use the LaborAcquisition table; enter criteria =TC49 in the acquisition id field; create an expression to subtract the begin date field from the end date field
- *How many cash disbursements were made on 4/14/2015?* Use the CashDisbursement table; enter criteria =4/14/2015 in the voucher date field; apply the COUNT aggregation function to the disbursement voucher id field
- *What is the dollar value of wages expense for April, 2015?* Use the LaborAcquisition table; enter criteria >=4/1/2015 in begin date field and enter criteria <= 4/30/2015 in the end date field; apply the SUM aggregation function to the gross pay field. *Note:* this query reveals the need for companies to track labor acquisitions at a finer level of detail than in this example. If the desired wages expense period only includes part of the time card period, it will be impossible to isolate what portion of the gross pay applied to the desired wages expense period.
- *What total dollar amount of withholdings should have been added to the payable account for state government as a result of labor acquisitions during April 2015?* Use the LaborAcquisition table; enter criteria >=4/1/2015 in begin date field and enter criteria <=4/30/2015 in the end date field; apply the SUM aggregation operator to the SIT field.

Agent Queries in the Human Resource Process

The agents commonly involved in human resource processes are the employees from whom labor is acquired, the department supervisors who authorize labor acquisitions, and the payroll clerks who generate the paychecks (cash disbursements). Queries may be needed to obtain any of the following:
- Detailed status information at one or more points in time for each employee
- Detailed status information at one or more points in time for each employee who meets specified criteria
- Summarized status information at one or more points in time for all employees
- Summarized status information at one or more points in time for all employees who meet specified criteria

Some example queries based on the tables in this chapter are as follows:

- *What are the names and positions of the employees who have been rated as excellent?* Use the Employee table; enter criteria =Excellent in the rating field; display the name and position fields
- *What is the average wage of the data entry employees?* Use the Employee table, enter criteria = "Data Entry" in the position field; apply the AVG aggregation function to the Wage field
- *What are the names and birth dates of employees who were born in 1960 or earlier?* Use the Employee table; enter criteria <=12/31/1960 in the date of birth field; display the name and date of birth fields

Association Queries

Combining information from various resource, event, and agent tables according to the associations in which they participate can provide much richer data than single class queries. We next discuss queries based on the various types of associations in the human resource process.

Duality Association Queries in the Human Resource Process

The duality association in the human resource process connects labor acquisitions to cash disbursements, as it represents exchanges of cash for labor. Information needs with respect to duality associations in the human resource process include (among other possibilities):

- Calculation of the outstanding wages payable balance at a point in time
- Identification of the labor acquisition for which a cash disbursement was made
- Identification of cash advances made to employees
- Identification and calculation of amounts withheld from gross pay amounts for employee and employer payroll-related taxes

Based on the tables in this chapter, duality queries could investigate

- *Had labor acquisition TC49 been paid for as of 4/10/2015?* Join the LaborAcquisition table to the DualityLaborAcquisitionCashDisb and CashDisbursement tables; enter criteria =TC49 in the acquisition id field; enter <=4/10/2015 in the voucher date field
- *What is the balance of wages payable as of April 30, 2015?* **Query 1:** Wages payable are increased by net pay amounts that represent the cost of labor acquired net of taxes and other withholdings amounts (those amounts are classified into other liability accounts). To find the net pay amounts for labor acquisitions that occurred through April 30, 2015, use the LaborAcquisition table; enter criteria <=4/30/2015 in the end date field; apply the SUM aggregation operator to the net pay field. **Query 2:** Wages payable is decreased by paychecks, those are the cash disbursements that applied to the labor acquisitions' net pay amounts (not the cash disbursements that applied to the withheld portions of the labor acquisitions). To find the paycheck amounts that occurred through April 30, 2015, join the LaborAcquisition, DualityLaborAcquisitionCashDisb, and CashDisbursement tables using the acquisition id to join labor acquisition to duality and the disbursement voucher id to join duality to cash disbursement; and also join EmpID in the LaborAcquisition table to PayeeID in the Cash Disbursement table. Enter criteria <=4/30/2015 in the cash disbursement voucher date field; apply the SUM aggregation operator to the AmountApplied field in the DualityLaborAcquisitionCashDisb table. **Query 3**: Subtract the sum of amounts applied calculated in query 2 from the sum of net pay amounts calculated in query 1 to get wages payable.

Stockflow Association Queries in the Human Resource Process

Stockflow relationships in the human resource process represent the connections between resources labor type and cash and the economic events that increase labor and decrease cash. Some common stockflow information needs in the human resource process (among other possibilities) are:

- Which cash account was decreased by a cash disbursement?
- What is the total dollar amount of cash disbursements made from a specified cash account during a time period?
- What quantity of each labor type was acquired by a labor acquisition event?
- How many different labor types were acquired by a labor acquisition event?
- Which labor acquisitions have involved a specified labor type?

Based on the tables in this chapter, stockflow queries could investigate:

- *What total dollar amount of cash disbursements were made from imprest checking accounts during the month of April, 2015?* Join the CashDisbursement table to the Cash table; enter criteria LIKE *imprest* in the cash account type field; enter criteria BETWEEN 4/1/2015 and 4/30/2015 in the cash disbursement voucher date field; apply the SUM aggregation operator to the cash disbursement dollar amount field
- *How many different types of labor were acquired on labor acquisition TC49?* Join the LaborAcquisition table to the StockflowLaborAcquisitionLaborType table using the acquisition id; enter criteria =TC49 in the stockflow acquisition id field; apply the COUNT aggregation operator to the stockflow labor type field

Fulfillment Queries in the Human Resource Process

The fulfillment associations typically materialized in the human resource process represent relationships between the labor requisitions and labor schedules (the schedules fulfill the requisitions)and between the labor schedules and labor acquisitions (the acquisitions fulfill the schedules). Fulfillment association queries in the human resource process in general include:

- Identification of unfilled commitment events (e.g. schedules for which work has not yet been performed, requisitions for which schedules have not yet been developed)
- Identification of filled commitment events (e.g. schedules for which labor was acquired, labor requisitions for which schedules were developed)
- Identification of economic events for which commitments were not made (e.g. labor acquisitions that were not scheduled)
- Identification of results of commitment events (e.g. which labor acquisitions resulted from a labor schedule, and were there any discrepancies between the scheduled and actual acquisitions)

Based on the example tables in this chapter, questions such as the following could be answered via fulfillment association queries in the human resource process:

- *Has staffing plan 7 been fulfilled?* Join LaborRequisition table to LaborSchedule table on LaborReqID with an outer join keeping all labor requisitions from the LaborRequisition table; include LaborReqID from LaborRequisition table and LaborScheduleID from LaborSchedule table; set criteria to select LaborReqID = LR7
- *Have any labor acquisitions occurred that were not scheduled?* Join LaborAcquisition table FulfillmentLaborAcquisitionLaborSchedule table with an outer join on AcquisitionID, keeping all acquisitions; include AcquisitionID from LaborAcquisition table and LaborScheduleID from the fulfillment table; set criteria on LaborScheduleID to IS NULL

- *What is the average length of time between labor schedules and labor acquisitions for this company?* Because this involves a date/time calculation, you should not attempt this in Microsoft Access
- *What staffing plan triggered labor schedule LS7?* Join LaborSchedule table to LaborRequisition table on LaborReqID; include LaborReqID; set criteria on LaborScheduleID = LS7

Reservation Queries in the Human Resource Process

The reservation association that is typically materialized in the human resource process represent the relationships between labor schedules and the types of labor the schedules commit to acquire. Some enterprises also materialize the reservation associations between the labor schedules and the cash resource the schedules commit to decrease. Therefore reservation associations in the human resource process are commonly used in queries to satisfy information needs as to the eventual effect of labor schedules on cash or as to the labor types involved in labor schedules. Some information needs (among many others) in the payroll cycle are:

- What labor type or types is a labor schedule agreeing to acquire?
- How many hours of a specified labor type is a labor schedule committing to acquire?
- What is the dollar value of cash reserved by a labor schedule?
- On what dates is a labor schedule committing to acquire a specified labor type?

Based on the tables in this chapter, questions such as the following could be answered via reservation relationship queries in the payroll cycle:

- *What are the descriptions of the labor types that labor schedule LS7 commits to acquire?* Join the ReservationLaborScheduleLaborType table to the LaborType table on labor type id; enter criteria =LS7 in the labor schedule id field; display the labor type description field
- *How many hours of cashier duties does labor schedule LS7 commit to acquire?* Join ReservationLaborScheduleLaborType table to the LaborType table on labor type id; enter criteria LIKE *cashier* in the labor type description field; enter criteria =LS7 in the labor schedule id field; display the hours scheduled field

Participation Queries in the Human Resource Process

Participation associations in the payroll cycle typically represent the associations between labor requisitions, labor schedules, labor acquisitions, and cash disbursements and the employees who authorize those events (typically supervisors for labor acquisition and payroll clerks for cash disbursements) and the employees who accomplish those events (typically a generalized employee entity set). The labor acquisition and cash disbursement events are also typically associated with outside agencies that benefit from employees labor, because a portion of the employees' compensation becomes compensation to the agencies. Therefore participation associations are commonly used in queries to satisfy information needs as to the identification of employees who participated in events or as to the events in which specified employees participated. Some common payroll cycle information needs are:

- Which department supervisor authorized a labor requisition?
- By how many labor schedules has an employee been scheduled to work?
- How many hours did an employee work on a labor acquisition?
- How many labor schedules has a specific department supervisor authorized?
- Which payroll clerk issued a specific cash disbursement?

Based on the tables in this chapter, questions such as the following could be answered via participation association payroll cycle queries:

- *What is the name of the supervisor who authorized labor requisition LR7?* Join the LaborRequisition table to the DepartmentSupervisor and Employee tables; enter criteria =LR7 in the labor requisition id field and display the supervisor name field
- *What are the names of the employees who were scheduled on labor schedule LS7?* Join the ParticipationLaborScheduleEmployee table to the Employee table on employee id; enter criteria =LS7 in the labor schedule id field and display the employee name field
- *Who worked on labor acquisition TC49 and how many hours did the employee work?* Join the LaborAcquisition table to the Employee table on employee id; enter criteria =TC49 in the labor acquisition id field; display the employee name field and the total hours field

CONCLUDING COMMENTS

This chapter presented an overview of the activities in the human resource process and discussed the extended REA ontology as it applies to this process. Information needs associated with the human resource business process were also described in this chapter, although those identified needs are not a comprehensive list. Enterprises with database systems patterned according to the REA ontology should be able to satisfy most or even all of their human resource process information needs by constructing queries based on their database tables.

Key Terms and Concepts

Employee
Employee schedule
Human capital
Human resource process
Imprest checking account
Labor acquisition event
Labor requisition event
Labor schedule
Labor type resource
Payroll cycle
Payroll deduction
Payroll function
Personnel function
Staffing plan
Withholdings

Review Questions

R1. What is the primary objective of the human resource process?

R2. How is the human resource process related to the conversion process, the sales/collection process, the acquisition/payment process, and the financing process?

R3. Which functions in the human resource process are typically thought of as personnel functions, and which functions are typically thought of as payroll functions?

R4. Identify the resources, internal agents, external agents, and possible locations associated with each of the following business events in the human resource process:

   a. Schedule (Commitment to Increment) event

   b. Labor Acquisition (Economic Increment) event

   c. Budget (Commitment to Decrement) event

   d. Cash Disbursement (Economic Decrement) event

R5. Describe the information required by each of the following in performing their role in the human resource process:

   a. Management

   b. Payroll

   c. Accounting

   d. Personnel

Multiple Choice Questions

MC1. Which document typically represents the same phenomena as the labor acquisition (economic increment) event?
   A. Payroll register
   B. Operations list
   C. Timecard
   D. Schedule

MC2. The labor acquisition process represents the point of contact between the enterprise and which set of external business partners?
   A. Investors and Creditors
   B. Suppliers
   C. Customers
   D. Employees

MC3. The resource made available by the Human Resource process to the Conversion process in a typical enterprise value chain is:
   A. Inventory
   B. Property, plant, and equipment
   C. Labor
   D. Cash

REA Accounting Systems: Resources-Events-Agents: An ontology for designing, controlling, and using integrated enterprise systems

477

MC4. Which of the following entities are usually paired in a stockflow relationship in the Human Resource process?
   A. Labor acquisition and Employee
   B. Labor type and Schedule
   C. Cash and Cash Disbursement
   D. Employee and Supervisor

MC5. Which of the following events reflects the commitment of the enterprise to receive an employee's labor for a future time period?
   A. Schedule
   B. Labor acquisition
   C. Cash budget
   D. Cash disbursement

Discussion Questions

D1. How do you compute the dollar amount of wages payable for financial statement purposes using a database designed with the REA ontology?

D2. How does training provided to employees affect the resources in the human resource process?

D3. Consider the tables in Exhibit 14-7. Describe the necessary procedures to construct a query to determine the number of hours for which Freda Matthews is scheduled to work during the first week of April, 2010.

D4. Consider the tables in Exhibit 14-5. Describe the necessary procedures to construct a query to determine the total number of labor hours needed for unfulfilled labor requisitions.

Applied Learning

A1. Customers engage Kravenhall Katering to provide food and beverages at upscale parties. When one of Kravenhall's supervisors is notified about an upcoming party that has been assigned to him or her, he or she must determine his or her staffing needs. The supervisor records the number of hours they need of each different type of labor (cooking, baking, serving, bartending, etc.) for the party on a staffing plan. The supervisor then creates a schedule by calling employees who have the skills needed for each type of labor needed and verifying their availability and willingness to participate in the catering job. The schedule lists each employee and the dates and times the employee will need to work on this job. When the party job occurs, details of the hours worked by each employee are recorded on time cards (one time card per employee). The department supervisor verifies the accuracy of each time card and then sends the timecards to the Payroll department. A payroll clerk calculates the gross pay, net pay, and withholdings dollar amounts and enters the information into the database. The net pay amounts are transferred to the employees' bank accounts via direct deposit and pay stubs are given to the employees (one stub per employee) for their own recordkeeping purposes.

Cash disbursements are tracked via a voucher number, since the check numbers and direct deposit numbers for its different checking accounts may overlap. Kravenhall's cash accounts are all located in banks; Kravenhall has multiple accounts in some banks and single accounts in other banks. For example, Kravenhall has checking, savings, and money market accounts at First National Bank and only a certificate of deposit account at Uniontown Bank. Less than half of the checks Kravenhall issues are for payroll; other checks are written to vendors, stockholders, lenders, etc.

Kravenhall also wants to track the various skills needed for each type of labor, and the degree of skill level needed. For example, to bake a soufflé, a high degree of baking skill may be needed; whereas to bake a cake, a low degree of baking skill may be needed. To aid in scheduling, Kravenhall wants to be able to track which employees possess each skill, and to document how the employee acquired the skill (e.g. by taking a class, through experience, or by some other means).

Required: Prepare an REA model for Kravenhall in ER diagram format including all relevant entities, relationships, and participation cardinalities. Also convert your model into a set of minimal relational table structures. The following attributes are of interest to Kravenhall and should be included in your solution. Do not add or subtract any attributes.

-Payroll clerk ID	-Labor type description
-Employee ID	-Bank name
-Voucher number	-Direct deposit amount (net pay)
-Employee Schedule ID	-Employee name
-Cash account number	-Std wage rate for labor type
-Check or direct deposit number	-Time card date
-Bank ID	-Date staff plan approved
-Check or direct deposit date	-Bank address
-Cash account type	-Payroll clerk fidelity bond rating
-Employee phone number	-Employee address
-Time card number	-Date employee schedule approved
-Labor TypeID	-Skill type ID
-Supervisor ID	-Skill type description
-Staffing plan number	-Gross pay amount

-Maximum number of subordinates allowed for a supervisor
-Requested hours on a staffing plan for each type of labor
-Total scheduled hours for each employee on an employee schedule
-Total hours worked by each employee on a time card
-Std wage rate for a labor type used on a staffing plan
-Estimated wage rate for each employee on an employee schedule
-Means by which an employee acquired a skill
-Actual regular wage rate for an employee on a timecard
-Actual overtime wage rate for an employee on a timecard
-Degree of skill type required by a labor type
-Degree of skill type possessed by an employee

CHAPTER 15

The Financing Business Process

CHAPTER OBJECTIVES

The objectives of this chapter are to introduce the financing business process; to discuss the REA ontology representation of financing processes, and to describe some of the typical information needs in the financing business process. After studying this chapter you should be able to:

1. Identify the activities common to most financing business processes
2. Identify the various components of the REA ontology in the financing process
3. Create a REA business process level model for an enterprise's financing process
4. Identify common information needs that exist within the financing process
5. Create database queries to retrieve financing process information from a relational database

FINANCING BUSINESS PROCESS IN AN ENTERPRISE VALUE SYSTEM

The financing business process provides the capital resources an enterprise needs to fund all aspects of its operations. A substantial portion of cash is used to fund two of the business processes we have discussed already: the acquisition/payment process and the human resource process. Much of the cash available to the financing process comes from the sales/collection process. However, when insufficient cash is available via the sales/collection process, other financing alternatives are used.

The financing process includes the activities associated with acquiring and paying for the use of cash through various debt and equity financing mechanisms. Activities in the financing process are triggered by an enterprise's need to obtain cash from an external source. The most obvious time of need for external cash is when an enterprise is new, before it has engaged in any operations. However, at other times enterprises may have insufficient internal cash available either because of timing differences between cash outflows and expected cash inflows or because of the need to expand operations, add capacity, etc. One mechanism for acquiring cash is **debt financing**, whereby the enterprise borrows cash from one or more external business partners for a specified period of time and with the agreement that the enterprise will pay a specified interest rate as well as repayment of the principal balance. Another mechanism for acquiring cash is **equity financing**, whereby the enterprise issues **shares of stock** (that represent the right to share in various ownership interests) in exchange for cash.

The financing process is in essence a special case of the acquisition/payment cycle; in it the enterprise acquires and pays for various types of financing. Because different information needs often exist with respect to the acquisition and payments for cash as compared to the exchange of cash for goods and services, the financing cycle is usually maintained as a separate transaction cycle. In this chapter we discuss the strategy, objectives, and nature of the financing process.

As you analyze and model a business process, you must clearly understand its purpose and objectives. You must realize how the business process fits into the value system and enterprise value chain. At the value system level, the financing process is the point of contact between the enterprise and its investors and creditors. The enterprise gives cash to its investors and creditors in exchange for cash they previously provided to the enterprise, as highlighted in Exhibit 15-1.

Exhibit 15-1 Financing Process in the Enterprise Value System

The value chain reveals interfaces between the financing process and other business processes. Exhibit 15-2 illustrates the typical value chain interfaces.

Exhibit 15-2 Financing Process in the Value Chain

Partial Value Chain

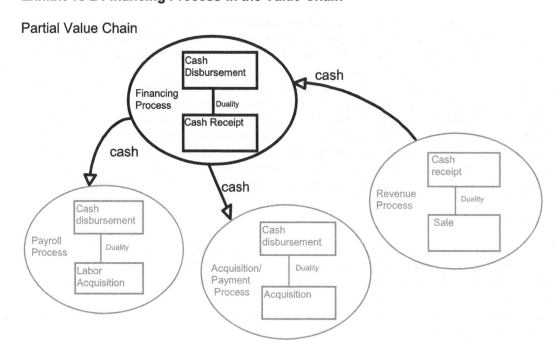

The arrows in Exhibit 15-2 depict the financing process accepting responsibility for cash made available by the revenue process and for making cash available to the payroll and acquisition/payment processes. The payroll process disburses that cash in exchange for acquisition of labor from employees. The acquisition/payment process disburses that cash in exchange for acquisitions of goods and services from suppliers. Cash received in the revenue process is made available to the financing process wherein it is disbursed to investors and creditors in exchange for the earlier described cash receipts or it is re-invested in the enterprise by being made available to the various acquisition processes. Although only one instance of the acquisition/payment process is illustrated in Exhibit 15-2, many enterprises have multiple instances of the acquisition/payment process, separating their purchases of inventory, operating assets, and general & administrative services. Such enterprises' value chains would simply be expanded to reflect every instance of acquisition/payment, with cash arrows going from the financing process to each of the acquisition/payment process instances.

The primary objective of the financing process is to provide the financial capital the enterprise needs to function efficiently and effectively. The objectives of this process are to have the liquid funds needed to run the enterprise while not letting cash sit idle. Sufficient cash availability enables enterprises to purchase in quantity to obtain more favorable prices and to take advantage of cash discounts. Having cash available to pay obligations on time and the ability to pay in cash give an organization a great deal of power.

We begin our business process level discussion of the financing cycle by reviewing some of its more common events. Two important reminders before we begin the discussion. Because we discuss the activities in a sequential fashion, it may seem that the financing process is linear. That is not necessarily true. Increasingly, business processes and the activities that comprise those processes are dynamic, rather than linear and static. Although the specific workflow activities differ in various enterprises' financing processes, we discuss the pattern for the information system's base objects that has been identified as common to most financing processes. Also, remember the activities in this process are linked to and sometimes overlap activities in other processes. We are concentrating on one process at a time to simplify our analysis.

FINANCING BUSINESS PROCESS LEVEL REA MODELS
Recall that the extended REA ontology described in chapter 6 and illustrated in Exhibit 15-3 identifies the pattern underlying each transaction cycle, which consists of instigation events, mutual commitment events, economic exchange events, resources, agents, types, and various relationships such as stockflow, duality, fulfillment, reservation, proposition, and participation. In this section we describe the extended REA ontology components specific to the financing business process.

We remind you that instigation events and the relationships in which they participate (such as proposition) are not part of the published REA ontology. We have added them to the business process level models in this text as a convenient means of fleshing out the complete "story" of each business process. A proposal is made in the instigation event. The proposal is acted upon and a mutual agreement is reached in the commitment event. The mutual commitment is fulfilled by the economic events that comprise the exchange of resources. These base objects exist in every cycle for every enterprise; however, it may not be cost-effective to measure and store the details of all these phases.

Exhibit 15-3 Financing Cycle Extended REA Ontology Database Design Pattern

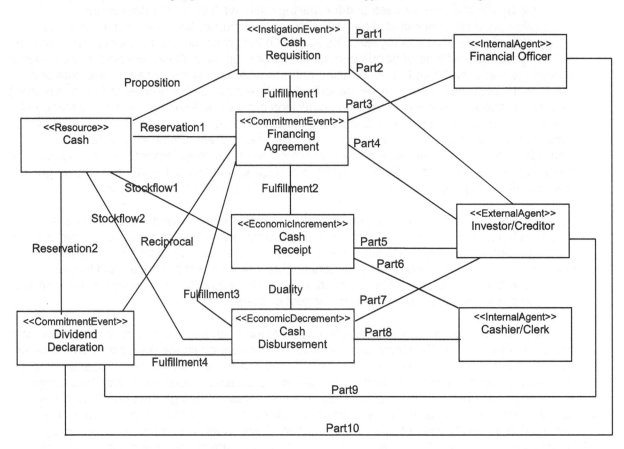

Part = Participation

Note 1: Internal agents illustrated on this diagram are not representative of all enterprises; however, they are common to many.

Note 2: Fulfillment3 association applies only to debt financing agreements; The Dividend Declaration event and all associations connected to it apply only to equity financing agreements.

The REA pattern aids in analyzing business processes and events by highlighting the *what* (the resources involved in the event) and the *who* (the internal and external agents) of each event. Notice that the *where* and the *when* are often stored as attributes of each event. The events, agents, and resources involved in the financing process vary somewhat from enterprise to enterprise. The general pattern discussed in this chapter can be easily adapted and applied to meet the exact financing requirements of any enterprise (e.g., nonprofit or governmental agencies, wholesalers, retailers, service providers, manufacturers, etc.).

Resources

Cash is both the resource acquired and the resource given in the financing process. Cash is represented in an enterprise system as the various stores of cash owned by the enterprise. Bank accounts, petty cash accounts, on-hand cash accounts, and other types of cash accounts are all potential instances of the cash resource for an enterprise. Cash is a resource type class,

REA Accounting Systems: Resources-Events-Agents: An ontology for designing, controlling, and using integrated enterprise systems

483

because it is normally not practical and cost-effective to identify and represent the serial number of each piece of currency owned by an enterprise. Instead, the amounts of currency and coin and negotiable cash instruments (such as checks, money orders, etc.) are combined together into cash accounts of various types such as checking, savings, petty, etc.

The attributes typically captured to represent cash accounts include an identification number or name, the type of cash account it is (e.g. savings, checking, etc.), the location, an account number assigned by the financial institution in which the account is located (if applicable), and the balance of the account. Because cash account balance is a volatile derivable attribute, it should only be included in a relational database table for cash if the database software allows the use of triggered update fields. Otherwise, a stored query may be created and reused for quick retrieval of the cash account balance attribute.

Instigation Events - Need Identification and Request for Cash

Financial officers typically determine the need for cash by monitoring enterprise growth (or lack thereof), production plans, sales forecasts, employee turnover, and other trends and projections, and creating a **cash budget** that incorporates expected cash receipts from the revenue and financing transaction cycles and expected cash disbursements from the various acquisition/payment processes and financing cycle. Forecasted cash shortfalls result in decisions to acquire cash from external sources via either debt or equity financing. This identification of need for cash is often labeled as a **cash requisition** event as shown in Exhibit 15-3. The cash requisition event is fulfilled by the financing agreement.

Agents involved in instigation events in the financing cycle usually are financial officers (internal agents who authorize the requisitions) and **investors/creditors** (external agents identified as potential sources of cash via equity/debt financing). Attributes of cash requisitions that typically should be captured include the date, time, and dollar amount of the requisition. The requisition event data should also be linked to data regarding the related financial officer, investor and/or creditor, and the type of financing agreement requested. Documentation of need identification for cash may vary widely. Some enterprises use a cash requisition form that looks much like a purchase requisition form as shown in the acquisition/payment cycle chapter. Others simply issue a memorandum summarizing the need for additional cash and the mechanism by which the enterprise proposes to obtain the cash. In Exhibit 15-4 we illustrate a cash requisition form.

Exhibit 15-4 Cash Requisition Document

YOUR SOURCE COMPANY CASH REQUISITION			No. ___3___	
Date Prepared: 4/05/2015	Prepared by: E64	Date Needed: 5/2/2015	Suggested Source: V41	
Cash Account	Amount Needed	Reason Needed		
Ca123501	$1,450,000	Cash Flow Budget created 4/05/2015 for the fiscal year reveals $1,429,413 cash shortfall due to expansion plans		
Approved by: E62		Approval Signature:	Date Approved: 4/15/2015	

The set of relational tables illustrated in Exhibit 15-5 correspond to Exhibit 15-3's UML class diagram representation of the cash requisition event, the associations in which it participates (proposition, fulfillment1, participation1, and participation2), and the related classes (cash, financing agreement, financial officer, and proposed investor/creditor). Alternative tables could be derived depending on the association multiplicities. Data from the form in Exhibit 15-4 have been entered into the database tables; however, some of this data (e.g. cash account, employee information, and investor/creditor information) would already have existed in the database tables before the requisition data were added to the tables. Therefore only the association information that links them to the event is recorded for those objects. New data that would be entered as a result of the cash requisition event is shown in bold italic font.

Exhibit 15-5 Sample Relational Tables Encompassing Cash Requisition Event

CashRequisition (Instigation) Event

CashReqID	Date	Dollar Amount Requested	OfficerID^{FK}	Suggested Investor/Creditor^{FK}
3	*4/15/2015*	*$1,450,000*	*E64*	*V41*

PropositionCashReqCashAcct (Proposition) Relationship

CashReqID	CashAccountID	Amount Needed
3	*Ca123501*	*$1,450,000*

FinancialOfficer (Internal Agent)

OfficerID	Authorized Debt Limit
E64	$2,500,000

Investor/Creditor (External Agent)

CreditorID	Name	Address	Telephone	Performance Rating
V41	First Chance Bank	43221 Financial Institute Way	555-5576	Excellent

Cash (Resource Type)

CashAccountID	AccountType	Location
Ca123501	Checking	1st Local Bank

DebtFinancingAgreement (Mutual Commitment) Event

LoanID	LoanDate	MaturityDate	InterestRate	Amount	CashReqID^{FK}	CreditorID^{FK}	OfficerID^{FK}

EquityFinancingAgreement (Mutual Commitment) Event

StockID	IssueDate	Type	#shares	Par Value	Amount	CashReqID^{FK}	InvestorID^{FK}	OfficerID^{FK}

Note: Fulfillment1 association is implemented with CashReqID posted into Debt Financing Agreement table and with CashReqID posted into Equity Financing Agreement table; Participation1 association is implemented with Suggested Investor/CreditorID posted into Cash Requisition table; Participation2 association is implemented with OfficerID posted into Cash Requisition table; Fulfillment1 data is not yet entered, assuming a time lag between cash requisition and financing agreements.

Mutual Commitment Event (Financing Agreement)

A mutual commitment event exists when an enterprise and an external business partner have each agreed to exchange specified quantities of resources at a defined future time. Because debt financing and equity financing are different types of financing mechanisms, with different information needs resulting from the commitment agreements for each, most enterprises need to separately represent financing agreements involving debt and equity. For debt financing, the mutual commitment is called a **loan**, a promissory note, a mortgage, or a **bond certificate**. For equity financing, the mutual commitment is typically called a **stock issuance**, the sale of the shares of stock to a sharesholder. The primary difference between debt financing and equity financing is the specification and timing of the resulting cash inflows and outflows.

Debt financing agreements usually specify a determinable dollar amount and timing of the cash inflow (loan proceeds) and of the cash outflows (loan repayments). That is not to say that the exact dollar amounts are certain; in fact, the exact dollar amounts may vary depending on the timing of the cash flows. However, a formula for determining the dollar amounts is certain.

Equity financing agreements specify a determinable dollar amount and timing of the cash inflow (stock proceeds); however, the cash outflows (dividend payments or stock re-purchases) are less certain as to both the timing and the dollar amounts. A **dividend** is a portion of the enterprise's earnings that is paid to its owners (shareholders). Investors buy enterprise stock (and thus provide cash to the enterprise) with the expectation of getting cash back in the form of dividend payments and capital appreciation such that the investor can sell the stock in the stock market for more than the amount for which the investor purchased the stock. However, the enterprise has no legal obligation to repurchase stock itself, nor to pay dividends unless the enterprise has declared a dividend.

Attributes of debt financing agreement events that typically should be captured include the agreement date, the total dollar amount of principal to which the agreement commits, the interest rate that applies to the agreement, and the maturity date of the agreement. The debt financing agreement should also be linked to data regarding the cash account into which the proceeds will be deposited, the financial officer responsible for the loan, the creditor from which the financing is to be acquired, the resulting cash receipt and cash disbursement events, and the cash requisition event the agreement fulfills. Debt financing agreements are typically represented on paper as promissory notes or as bond certificates. In Exhibit 15-6 we illustrate a promissory note, and in Exhibit 15-7, a bond certificate.

Attributes of equity financing agreements that typically should be captured include the date the stock was issued, the par value and type of the stock, the number of shares issued, and the dollar amount for which the stock was issued. Exhibit 15-8 illustrates a **share of stock**, also called a **stock certificate** that indicates the equity financing agreement terms. As mentioned earlier, the shares of stock do not guarantee future cash flows. Preferred stock may indicate a percentage or dollar amount for which preferred shareholders have dividend preference over common shareholders, however that does not guarantee dividends will ever be paid to anyone. Therefore some may not consider the equity financing agreement to be a mutual commitment event although the stock carries an implicit commitment on the part of the enterprise. Explicit commitments related to equity financing agreements are called dividend declarations. A **dividend declaration** is an announcement by an enterprise that it will pay dividends of a specific amount on a specific date; this declaration creates a legal obligation for the enterprise. That is, once a dividend is declared the enterprise is required by law to actually pay the dividend. Dividend declarations are typically represented as commitment events that are related via reciprocal associations to the equity financing agreement commitment events.

Dividend declarations should also be linked to data regarding the cash that they reserve for future payment, to the internal and external agents, and to the cash disbursement events that fulfill the commitments.

Exhibit 15-6 Promissory Note

PROMISSORY NOTE
SAMPLE for illustration purposes only

$450,000.00   Date: May 1, 2015

For value received, the undersigned Your Source Company (the "Borrower"), at123 Main St., Anytown, USA 12345, promises to pay to the order of First Chance Bank, (the "Lender"), at 43221 Financial Institute Way, (or at such other place as the Lender may designate in writing) the sum of $450,000.00 with 10% interest payments due on April 30 of each year beginning with April 30, 2016.

The unpaid principal shall be payable in full on April 30, 2022 (the "Due Date").

All payments on this Note shall be applied first in payment of accrued interest and any remainder in payment of principal.

If any payment obligation under this Note is not paid when due, the remaining unpaid principal balance and any accrued interest shall become due immediately at the option of the Lender.

The Borrower reserves the right to prepay this Note (in whole or in part) prior to the Due Date with no prepayment penalty.

If any payment obligation under this Note is not paid when due, the Borrower promises to pay all costs of collection, including reasonable attorney fees, whether or not a lawsuit is commenced as part of the collection process.

If any of the following events of default occur, this Note and any other obligations of the Borrower to the Lender, shall become due immediately, without demand or notice:
1) the failure of the Borrower to pay the principal and any accrued interest in full on or before the Due Date;
2) the death of the Borrower or Lender;
3) the filing of bankruptcy proceedings involving the Borrower as a debtor;
4) the application for the appointment of a receiver for the Borrower;
5) the making of a general assignment for the benefit of the Borrower's creditors;
6) the insolvency of the Borrower;
7) a misrepresentation by the Borrower to the Lender for the purpose of obtaining or extending credit.

If any one or more of the provisions of this Note are determined to be unenforceable, in whole or in part, for any reason, the remaining provisions shall remain fully operative.

All payments of principal and interest on this Note shall be paid in the legal currency of the United States. The Borrower waives presentment for payment, protest, and notice of protest and nonpayment of this Note.

No renewal or extension of this Note, delay in enforcing any right of the Lender under this Note, or assignment by Lender of this Note shall affect the liability or the obligations of the Borrower. All rights of the Lender under this Note are cumulative and may be exercised concurrently or consecutively at the Lender's option.

Signed this __1st__ day of __May, 2015__, at

Borrower: Your Source Company
By:___*Woodrow D. James*_____
      Mr. Woodrow D. James, on behalf of Your Source Company

EXHIBIT 15-7   Bond Certificate

EXHIBIT 15-8   Stock Certificate

The set of relational tables in Exhibit 15-9 correspond to Exhibit 15-3's UML class diagram representation of the financing agreement events (with debt financing agreements and equity financing agreements in separate tables), the dividend declaration commitment event and the associations in which the various commitment events participate (reservation1, reservation2, fulfillment1, fulfillment2, participation3, participation4, participation9, and participation10). Alternative table configurations could be derived from this example, depending on the association multiplicities.

You may have noticed that the cash requisition in this example had only suggested a creditor as the source of cash. However, apparently the financial officer decided to obtain most of the needed financing via issuance of common stock.

Data from the forms in Exhibits 15-6 and 15-8 have been entered into the database tables; however, some of these data (e.g. cash account, financial officer, and investor/creditor information) would already have existed in the database tables before the financing agreement data was added to the tables so only the association information that links them to the financing agreement should be added for those objects. The new data entered to record the financing agreement event are shown in bold italic font. The new data entered to record the dividend declaration that is reciprocally related to the equity finance agreement is shown in non-bold italic print.

Exhibit 15-9 Relational Tables Encompassing Commitment Event(s)

Debt FinancingAgreement (Mutual Commitment) Event

LoanID	LoanDate	MaturityDate	InterestRate	Amount	CashReqID^{FK}	CreditorID^{FK}	OfficerID^{FK}
L1	*5/1/2015*	*4/30/2022*	*10%*	*$450,000*	*3*	*V41*	*E64*

EquityFinancingAgreement (Commitment) Event

StockID	IssueDate	Type	#shares	Par Value	Amount	CashReqID^{FK}	InvestorID^{FK}	OfficerID^{FK}
E1	*5/1/2015*	*Common*	*50,000*	*$4*	*$500,000*	*3*	*I234*	*E64*
E2	*5/1/2015*	*Common*	*50,000*	*$4*	*$500,000*	*3*	*I235*	*E64*

ReservationFinanceAgreementCashAcct (Reservation1) Relationship

FinanceAgreementID	CashAccountID	Amount Reserved
L1	*Ca123501*	*$450,000*
E1	*Ca123501*	*$500,000*
E2	*Ca123501*	*$500,000*

ReciprocalDivDecEquityFinancing (Reciprocal) Relationship

StockID	DividendDeclarationID
E1	*DD1*
E2	*DD1*

DividendDeclaration (Commitment) Event

DividendDeclarationID	DeclarationDate	DollarAmountperShare	PaymentDate	OfficerID^{FK}
DD1	*4/30/2015*	*$.50*	*5/17/2015*	*E64*

ParticipationDivDecInvestor (Participation10) Relationship

DividendDeclarationID	InvestorID
DD1	*I234*
DD1	*I235*

REA Accounting Systems: Resources-Events-Agents: An ontology for designing, controlling, and using integrated enterprise systems

489

Exhibit 15-9 Continued

CashRequisition (Instigation) Event

CashReqID	Date	Dollar Amount Requested	OfficerID^{FK}	Suggested Investor/Creditor^{FK}
3	4/15/2015	$1,450,000	E64	V41

FinancialOfficer (Internal Agent)

OfficerID	Name	Authorized Debt Limit
E64	Donald James	$2,500,000

Investor/Creditor (External Agent)

Investor/CreditorID	Name	Address	Telephone	Performance Rating
V41	First Chance Bank	43221 Financial Institute Way	555-5576	Excellent
I234	CREF	1 Retirement Dr.	555-9988	Excellent
I235	Schwarb	852 Mutual Manor Ct.	555-7312	Excellent

Cash (Resource Type)

CashAccountID	AccountType	Location
Ca123501	Checking	1st Local Bank

FulfillmentCashReceiptFinancing (Fulfillment2) Relationship

FinancingAgreementID	CashReceiptID

FulfillmentCashDisbDebtFinancing (Fulfillment3) Relationship

LoanID	CashDisbursementID	Principal Pmt Amt	Interest Pmt Amt

Note: Participation3 relationship is implemented with OfficerID posted into Financing Agreement tables. Participation4 relationship is implemented with InvestorID posted into Equity Financing Agreement table and with CreditorID posted into Debt Financing Agreement table. Participation9 relationship is implemented with OfficerID posted into Dividend Declaration table. Fulfillment1 relationship is implemented with CashReqID posted into Financing Agreement tables. Fulfillment2, Fulfillment3, and Fulfillment4 data is not yet entered, assuming a possible time lag between commitment events and the resulting cash receipts and cash disbursements. There is also a time lag between the financing agreements and the dividend declaration commitment event; this is indicated via the dates entered.

Economic Increment Event (Cash Receipt)

Cash Receipt is the primary economic increment event in the finance process. For debt financing agreements, the cash receipt event represents the receipt of the cash proceeds of the loan or bond. For equity financing agreements, the cash receipt event represents the receipt of the cash proceeds of the stock issuance. In both cases, the cash receipt event fulfills the commitment of the investors and creditors to provide cash to the enterprise; at the point of cash receipt, the enterprise has not yet fulfilled its commitment to provide loan repayments or dividend payments to the investors and creditors. As in the Sales/Collection process, the receipt of cash is a custodial function. The document typically involved in task activities that comprise the cash receipt event in the financing cycle is a deposit slip. When cash from financing is received (usually in the form of checks), internal agents (usually cashiers) verify the payment information is correctly recorded on a deposit slip. A copy of the deposit slip is retained by the enterprise and the original is sent with the proceeds to the bank for deposit. In some cases investors and creditors may electronically transfer funds to the enterprise rather than sending checks through the mail. In such cases the investors and creditors may send a direct deposit notification, otherwise the monthly bank statement will serve as notification of the cash receipt.

Associations in which the cash receipt event in the financing process participates typically include fulfillment (enabling the enterprise to trace which debt or equity financing agreement event the cash receipt fulfilled), duality (allowing the enterprise to trace the related cash disbursements), stockflow (to trace the cash account into which the cash receipt was deposited), and participation associations with internal agents (typically cashiers) and external agents (investors or creditors).

The set of relational tables in Exhibit 15-10 correspond to Exhibit 15-3's UML class diagram representation of the cash receipt event and the associations in which it participates (stockflow1, fulfillment2, participation5, participation6, and duality). Other possible tables could be derived, depending on the association multiplicities. Example data regarding cash receipt events have been entered into the database tables; however, some of this data (e.g. cash account, financing agreement, investor and creditor information, and employee information) would already have existed in the database tables before the cash receipt data were added to the tables so only association information that links them to the cash receipt event is added for those objects. The new data to be added upon receipts of cash from financing agreements are printed in bold italic font.

Exhibit 15-10 Relational Tables Encompassing Cash Receipts

CashReceipt (Economic Increment) Event

CashReceiptID	Date	DollarAmount	CashAccountID^{FK}	ExtAgentID^{FK}	CashierID^{FK}
RA14	*5/1/2015*	*$450,000*	*Ca123501*	*V41*	*E111*
RA15	*5/1/2015*	*$500,000*	*Ca123501*	*I234*	*E111*
RA16	*5/1/2015*	*$500,000*	*Ca123501*	*I235*	*E111*

FulfillmentCashReceiptFinancingAgreement (Fulfillment2) Relationship

FinancingAgreementID	CashReceiptID
L1	RA14
E1	RA15
E2	RA16

DebtFinancingAgreement (Mutual Commitment) Event

LoanID	LoanDate	MaturityDate	InterestRate	Amount	CashReqID^{FK}	CreditorID^{FK}	OfficerID^{FK}
L1	5/1/2015	4/30/2022	10%	$450,000	3	V41	E64

EquityFinancingAgreement (Mutual Commitment) Event

StockID	IssueDate	Type	#shares	Par Value	Amount	CashReqID^{FK}	InvestorID^{FK}	OfficerID^{FK}
E1	5/1/2015	Common	50,000	$4	$500,000	3	I234	E64
E2	5/1/2015	Common	50,000	$4	$500,000	3	I235	E64

Cashier (Internal Agent)

CashierID	Name	Address	Telephone	DateOfBirth
E111	Missy Witherspoon	1710 Crestwood Dr.	555-9392	May 11, 1960

REA Accounting Systems: Resources-Events-Agents: An ontology for designing, controlling, and using integrated enterprise systems

491

Exhibit 15-10 continued

Investor/Creditor (External Agent)

Investor/CreditorID	Name	Address	Telephone	Performance Rating
V41	First Chance Bank	43221 Financial Institute Way	555-5576	Excellent
I234	CREF	1 Retirement Dr.	555-9988	Excellent
I235	Schwarb	852 Mutual Manor Ct.	555-7312	Excellent

Cash (Resource Type)

CashAccountID	AccountType	Location
Ca123501	Checking	1st Local Bank

DualityCashDisbursementCashReceipt Relationship

CashReceipt	CashDisbursementID

Note: Participation5 relationship is implemented with CashierID posted into Cash Receipt table;
Participation6 relationship is implemented with ExtAgentID posted into Cash Receipt table;
Duality data is not yet entered, assuming a time lag between Cash Receipt and Cash Disbursement

Economic Decrement Event (Cash Disbursement)

Cash disbursements are economic decrement events that decrease the enterprise's cash balance. Cash disbursements in the financing cycle are typically made by paper check or electronic funds transfer and are made to fulfill the terms of the financing agreement, in exchange for the cash receipts that occurred at a previous point in time. Attributes captured regarding cash disbursements usually include a cash disbursement identifier (such as a disbursement voucher number), date, amount paid, the check number of the payment, payee identification (investor or creditor), employee identification (i.e., employee who wrote the check), the cash account from which the cash is disbursed, and links to the reason for the cash disbursement (i.e. what commitment it is fulfilling and the economic increment event that began the exchange). Exhibit 15-11 shows a set of relational tables that correspond to Exhibit 15-3's UML class diagram representation of the cash disbursement event and the financing cycle associations in which it participates (duality, fulfillment3, fulfillment4, stockflow2, participation7, and participation8). Alternative table configurations could be derived, depending on the association multiplicities. As noted in the acquisition/payment cycle chapter, additional tables are necessary to correspond to relationships in which the cash disbursement event participates in other transaction cycles such as acquisition/payment and payroll.

The tables shown in Exhibit 15-10 are applicable to the financing process. Data for cash disbursements applicable to the financing process have been entered into the database tables; however, some of this data (e.g. financing agreements, dividend declaration, cash accounts, investor/creditor information, and employee information) would already have existed in the database tables before the cash disbursement data was added to the tables. Only association information that links those objects to the cash disbursements is added to the database upon entry of the cash disbursement. The new data to be added for the cash disbursement event are shown in bold italic font.

Exhibit 15-11 Relational Tables Encompassing Cash Disbursement Event

CashDisbursement (Economic Decrement) Event

Disb Voucher ID	Voucher Date	Dollar Amount	Check Number	Cash AccountID^{FK}	Financing ClerkID^{FK}	PayeeID^{FK}
124	4/30/2016	$45,000	921	Ca123501	E36	V41
138	5/17/2016	$25,000	935	Ca123501	E36	I234
139	5/17/2016	$25,000	936	Ca123501	E36	I235

DualityCashDisbursementCashReceipt Relationship

CashReceipt	CashDisbursementID
RA14	124
RA15	138
RA16	139

FulfillmentCashDisbDebtFinancing (Fulfillment3) Relationship

LoanID	CashDisbursementID	PrincipalPaid	InterestPaid
L1	124	$0	$45,000

FulfillmentCashDisbEquityFinancing (Fulfillment4) Relationship

DividendDeclarationID	CashDisbursementID
DD1	138
DD1	139

Cash (Resource Type)

CashAccountID	AccountType	Location
Ca123501	Checking	1st Local Bank

CashReceipt (Economic Increment) Event

CashReceiptID	Date	DollarAmount	CashAccountID^{FK}	ExtAgentID^{FK}	CashierID^{FK}
RA14	5/1/2015	$450,000	Ca123501	V41	E111
RA15	5/1/2015	$500,000	Ca123501	I234	E111
RA16	5/1/2015	$500,000	Ca123501	I235	E111

DebtFinancingAgreement (Mutual Commitment) Event

LoanID	LoanDate	MaturityDate	InterestRate	Amount	CashReqID^{FK}	CreditorID^{FK}	OfficerID^{FK}
L1	5/1/2015	4/30/2022	10%	$450,000	3	V41	E64

Investor/Creditor (External Agent)

Investor/CreditorID	Name	Address	Telephone	Performance Rating
V41	First Chance Bank	43221 Financial Institute Way	555-5576	Excellent
I234	CREF	1 Retirement Dr.	555-9988	Excellent
I235	Schwarb	852 Mutual Manor Ct.	555-7312	Excellent

FinancingClerk (Internal Agent)

FinancingClerkID	Name	Fidelity Bond Rating
E36	Diane Bowersox	AA

Note: Stockflow2 is implemented with Cash AccountID posted into Cash Disbursement table; Participation7 is implemented with FinancingClerkID posted into Cash Disbursement table; Participation8 is implemented with PayeeID posted into Cash Disbursement table.

REA Accounting Systems: Resources-Events-Agents: An ontology for designing, controlling, and using integrated enterprise systems

493

INFORMATION NEEDS AND MEASURES IN THE FINANCING PROCESS

The most common information customers for the financing business process include top management, investors, creditors, accountants, and auditors. We next analyze each of the classes and associations in the financing cycle pattern to provide some ideas as to the types of queries that may be needed to satisfy information needs in the financing cycle. The queries presented are not a comprehensive set of queries (there are simply too many potential queries to list them all); however, the set described should guide you in creating similar types of queries. To describe queries needed in the financing cycle we use the database tables shown in Exhibits 15-5, 15-9, 15-10, and 15-11.

Resource Queries in the Financing Process

Cash is the resource that most commonly exists in the financing process. Cash is usually tracked by the accounts in which the cash is stored. Cash queries are described in chapters 10 to 14 so we do not repeat those details here.

Event Queries in the Financing Process

Users may need information regarding events. The most common events in the financing process are cash requisitions, debt and equity financing agreements, cash receipts, dividend declarations, and cash disbursements. For each of these types of events, users may need any of the following:

- Detailed information about each event instance
- Detailed information about each event instance that meets specified criteria
- Summarized information for all instances of an event type for a specified time period
- Summarized information for only those instances of an event type for a specified time period that meet specified criteria

Queries based on the tables in this chapter to satisfy information needs regarding events in the financing process include (among many other possibilities):

- *What dollar amount was requested on cash requisition 3?* Using the CashRequisition table, enter criteria =3 in the cash requisition id field; display the dollar amount requested field

- *Which loans bear interest rates > 9%, and what are the dollar amounts of those loans?* Using the DebtFinancingAgreement table, enter criteria >.09 in the interest rate field; display the loan id and amount fields

- *How many shares of common stock have been issued as of 5/31/2015?* Using the EquityFinancingAgreement table, enter criteria <=5/31/2015 in the issue date field; enter criteria =common in the type field; apply the SUM aggregation operator to the #shares field

- *How many cash receipts occurred in May, 2015?* Using the CashReceipt table, enter criteria BETWEEN 5/1/2015 and 5/31/2015 in the date field; apply COUNT aggregation function to the cash receipt id field

Agent Queries in the Financing Process

The agents commonly involved in financing processes are the financial officers who authorize the financing transactions, the investors and creditors from whom financing is acquired, and the cashiers or other clerks who process the cash receipts and cash disbursements. Queries may be needed to obtain any of the following:

- Detailed status information at one or more points in time for each financial officer, investor, creditor, cashier, or clerk
- Detailed status information at one or more points in time for each financial officer, investor, creditor, cashier, or clerk who meets specified criteria
- Summarized status information at one or more points in time for all financial officers, investors, creditors, cashiers, or clerks
- Summarized status information at one or more points in time for all financial officers, investors, creditors, cashiers, or clerks who meet specified criteria

Queries based on the tables in this chapter include, but are not limited to:

- *What are the names and addresses of the investors who have been rated as excellent?* Using the Investor/Creditor table, enter criteria =Excellent in the performance rating field; display the name and address fields

- *Which financial officer has the highest limit for which to authorize debt?* Using the FinancialOfficer table, apply the MAX aggregation function to the authorized debt limit field; display the officer id field

Association Queries

Combining information from various resource, event, and agent tables in accordance with the relationships in which they participate can provide much richer data than single table queries. We next discuss queries based on the various types of relationships in the financing process.

Duality and Fulfillment Association Queries in the Financing Process

The duality association in the financing process connects cash receipts (financing acquisitions) to cash disbursements (financing payments), as it represents exchanges of cash for cash. Because the financing cash receipts may result from either debt or equity financing, the direct duality relationship between cash receipts and cash disbursements is often somewhat ambiguous. Other than identifying which cash disbursements applied to a cash receipt, and vice versa, there is not much information content to be gained from examining the duality association in the financing process. Much more informative are the fulfillment associations between the financing agreement and the cash receipts and between the financing agreement and the cash disbursements.

In the financing process, each financing agreement (whether equity or debt) is associated with at least one cash receipt and at least one cash disbursement. Debt obligations are cash receipts that relate to debt financing agreements. Cash disbursements related to debt financing agreements indicate repayments of debts. Comparisons of the debt obligations to repayments of those debts reveal loans or notes payable balances.

REA Accounting Systems: Resources-Events-Agents: An ontology for designing, controlling, and using integrated enterprise systems

495

Fulfillment association queries in the financing process include:

- Identification of unfilled commitment events (e.g. financing agreements for which cash has not yet been received and/or for which cash disbursements have not been made in full)
- Identification of filled commitment events (e.g. financing agreements for which cash was received and cash was repaid according to payment terms)

Based on the example tables in this chapter, questions such as the following could be answered via fulfillment association queries in the financing process:

- *What is the outstanding principal balance of debt financing agreement L1 as of May 1, 2015?* **Query 1:** the outstanding principal balance for a loan is increased by cash receipt amounts that represent the principal acquired. To find the principal amounts acquired through May 1, 2015, Join the CashReceipt and FulfillmentCashReceiptDebtFinancing tables; enter criteria =L1 in the financing agreement id field; enter criteria <=5/1/2015 in the cash receipt date field; apply the SUM aggregation operator to the cash receipt dollar amount field. **Query 2:** the outstanding principal balance for a loan is decreased by cash disbursement amounts that represent repayments of principal. To find the principal repayment amounts that occurred through May 1, 2015, join the FulfillmentCashDisbDebtFinancing table to the CashDisbursement table; enter criteria =L1 in the loan id field; enter criteria <=5/1/2015 in the cash disbursement voucher date field; apply the SUM aggregation operator to the prinicipalpaid field. **Query 3:** Subtract the sum calculated in query 2 from the sum calculated in query 1.

- *Have any cash receipts occurred that were not related to financing agreements?* Join CashReceipts table to FulfillmentCashReceiptFinancing table with an outer join keeping all cash receipts; include cash receipt id from CashReceipt table and financing agreement id from FulfillmentCashReceiptFinancing table; set criteria to IS NULL in the financing agreement id field

Stockflow Queries in the Financing Process

Stockflow associations in the financing process represent the connections between cash and the economic events that increase and decrease cash. Some common stockflow information needs in the financing process (among other possibilities) are:

- Which cash account was decreased by a cash disbursement?
- What is the total dollar amount of cash disbursements made from a specified cash account during a time period?
- Which cash account was increased by a cash receipt?
- What is the total dollar amount of cash receipts for a specified cash account during a time period?

Examples of these types of stockflow queries have been illustrated in chapters 10-13 therefore we do not repeat these details here.

Reservation Queries in the Financing Process

The reservation association typically materialized in the financing process represents the set of relationships between financing agreements and the cash the agreements commit to acquire and repay. Therefore reservation associations in the financing process are commonly used in queries to satisfy information needs as to the eventual effect of financing agreements on cash. Some common information needs (among many others) in the financing cycle are:

- What dollar amount is a financing agreement committing to acquire for a specific cash account?
- From which cash accounts will any dividend declarations that occurred during a specific time period be paid?
- What is the dollar value of cash reserved by a dividend declaration?
- On what dates is a financing agreement committing to acquire cash?

Based on the tables in this chapter, questions such as the following could be answered via reservation association queries in the financing cycle:

- *What dollar amount is financing agreement E1 committing to acquire for cash account Ca123501?* Use the ReservationFinanceAgreementCashAcct table; enter criteria =E1 in the finance agreement id field; enter criteria =Ca123501 in the cash account id field; display the amount reserved field

- *What is the total dollar amount reserved for cash account CA123501 by financing agreements during the month of May, 2015?* **Query 1:** To determine the dollar amount reserved for cash account Ca123501 by equity financing agreements during May 2010, join the ReservationFinanceAgreementCashAcct table to the EquityFinancingAgreement table; enter criteria =Ca123501 in the cash account id field; enter criteria BETWEEN 5/1/2015 and 5/31/2015 in the issue date field; apply the SUM aggregation operator to the amount reserved field. **Query 2:** To determine the dollar amount reserved for cash account Ca123501 by debt financing agreements during May 2010, join the ReservationFinanceAgreementCashAcct table to the DebtFinancingAgreemnet table; enter criteria =Ca123501 in the cash account id field; enter criteria BETWEEN 5/1/2015 and 5/31/2015 in the loan date field; apply the SUM aggregation operator to the amount reserved field. **Query 3:** Add the sum from query 1 to the sum from query 2 to get the total reserved amount for cash account Ca123501 during May 2015.

Participation Queries in the Financing Process

Participation associations in the financing cycle typically represent the relationships between cash requisitions, debt financing agreements, equity financing agreements, cash receipts, dividend declarations, and cash disbursements and the employees who authorize those events (typically financial officers), the employees who accomplish those events (typically cashiers), and the investors and creditors with whom cash is exchanged. Therefore participation associations are commonly used in queries to satisfy information needs as to the identification of employees, investors, or creditors who participated in financing events or as to the financing events in which specific employees, investors, or creditors participated.

Some common financing cycle information needs are:
- Which financial officer authorized a cash requisition?
- How many debt financing agreements has a financial officer approved?
- What is the total dollar amount of cash disbursements paid to a specific creditor?
- How many shares of common stock has a specific investor purchased?
- Which cashier processed a specific cash receipt?

Based on the tables in this chapter, questions such as the following could be answered via participation association financing cycle queries:

- *What is the name of the financial officer who authorized cash requisition 3?* Join the CashRequisition table to the FinancialOfficer table; enter criteria =3 in the cash requisition id field and display the officer name field

- *How many debt financing agreements has Donald James approved?* Join the DebtFinancingAgreement table to the FinancialOfficer table; enter criteria =Donald James in the officer name; apply the COUNT aggregation operator to the LoanID field

- *What is the name of the cashier who processed cash receipt RA15?* Join the CashReceipt table to the Cashier table; enter criteria =RA15 in the cash receipt id field; display the cashier name field

- *What are the name and address of the investor(s) to which the most shares of common stock have been issued?* **Query 1:** to sum the number of shares issued to each investor, use the EquityFinancingAgreement table; apply the GROUP BY aggregation operator to the investor id field; apply the SUM aggregation operator to the #shares field **Query 2:** to identify the names and addresses of the investors to which the most shares have been issued, Join the result of Query 1 to the Investor/Creditor table; apply the MAX aggregation operator to the sum of #shares field; display the investor name and investor address fields

CONCLUDING COMMENTS

This chapter presented an overview of the activities in the finance process and discussed the extended REA pattern as it is applied to this process. Information needs associated with the finance business process were also described in this chapter, although those identified are not a comprehensive list. An enterprise with an enterprise system based on the REA pattern is able to satisfy most (if not all) of the information needs by constructing queries based on its database tables.

Key Terms and Concepts

Bond certificate

Cash budget

Cash requisition

Creditor

Debt financing

Dividend declaration

Dividend

Equity financing

Financial officer

Investor

Loan

Shares of stock

Stock certificate

Stock issuance

Review Questions

R1. What is the primary objective of the financing business process?

R2. How is the financing process related to the conversion process, the sales/collection process, the acquisition/payment process, and the payroll process?

R3. What is the difference between a bond certificate and a stock certificate?

R4. What document(s) is(are) typically used to represent a debt financing agreement event?

R5. Identify the resources, internal agents, and external agents associated with each of the following events in the finance process:

   a. Cash Requisition (Instigation) event

   b. Loan (Mutual commitment) event

   c. Stock Issuance (Commitment to Increment) event

   d. Dividend Declaration (Commitment to Decrement) event

   e. Cash Receipt (Economic Increment) event

   f. Cash Disbursement (Economic Decrement) event

Multiple Choice Questions

MC1. Which document typically represents the same phenomena as the cash receipt (economic increment) event?

   A. Disbursement voucher

   B. Deposit slip

   C. Stock certificate

   D. Promissory note

MC2. The financing process represents the point of contact between the enterprise and which set of external business partners?

   A. Investors and Creditors

   B. Suppliers

   C. Customers

   D. Employees

REA Accounting Systems: Resources-Events-Agents: An ontology for designing, controlling, and using integrated enterprise systems

499

MC3. The resource made available by the Finance process to the Payroll process in a typical enterprise value chain is:
   A. Finished goods inventory
   B. Machinery and equipment
   C. Labor
   D. Cash

MC4. Which of the following entities are usually paired in a stockflow relationship in the Finance process?
   A. Cash Receipt and Employee
   B. Cash and Debt Financing Agreement
   C. Cash and Cash Receipt
   D. Stock Issuance and Cash Receipt

MC5. Which of the following events reflects the commitment of the enterprise to receive and to repay cash provided by a creditor?
   A. Debt Financing Agreement
   B. Dividend Declaration
   C. Cash requisition
   D. Cash disbursement

Discussion Questions

D1. Describe at least two financing process information needs for each of the following:
   a. Management

   b. Finance and Accounting

   c. Investors and Creditors

D2. What classes and/or associations should most likely be included in a query to calculate the loan payable balance for each creditor (assume the balance is not stored as a volatile derivable attribute in the creditor table)?

D3. When determining how much cash to keep on hand, what are some of the factors financial officers need to consider, and how can the database tables based on the REA business process level model help them determine a cash budget?

CHAPTER 16

Current Accounting and Enterprise Systems

LEARNING OBJECTIVES

One objective of this chapter is to describe the historical development of accounting and enterprise systems and illustrate how the REA enterprise ontology fits into those systems. Another objective of this chapter is to speculate as to the future development of accounting and enterprise systems and to discuss the potential for REA to help shape that development. After studying this chapter, you should be able to

1. Compare the goals of current accounting and enterprise systems with those of the REA enterprise ontology
2. Describe the characteristics of accounting and enterprise systems in the various categories presented in the chapter
3. Identify information integration tools commonly used in practice (e.g. electronic data interchange, extensible markup language, enterprise application integration software, and electronic business extensible markup language) to integrate accounting systems with other parts of enterprise systems
4. Discuss strengths and weaknesses of integration tools commonly used in practice
5. Discuss strengths and weaknesses of the REA enterprise ontology as a foundation for accounting-based integrated enterprise systems

ORGANIZING PRINCIPLES OF CURRENT ACCOUNTING AND ENTERPRISE SYSTEMS[1]

Accounting systems in practice range in complexity. Some are very simple, with no connection to other information systems in the enterprise. Others are very complex, with connections to other information systems within the enterprise and some even with connections to external information systems. Categories of accounting and enterprise systems discussed in this chapter include those that support a singular focus, those that are enterprise-centric, and those that are community focused.

Singularly Focused Systems
Singularly focused systems are typically designed to keep track of transactions that affect just one resource of an enterprise. Usually that resource is cash. **Single-entry systems** are the simplest of accounting systems. Consider a manual checkbook register that categorizes expenditures such as that shown in Exhibit 16-1. Its purpose is to track the inflow and outflow of cash, classifying those inflows and outflows as needed for reporting purposes. Computerized software that has the same purpose and thus fits into this category includes Quicken, Microsoft Money, Ace Money, and YNAB. Such systems are ideal for very simple enterprises with few reporting requirements and a very small number of decision makers. A sole proprietor may effectively use such software to track its cash inflows and outflows.

---

[1] Acknowledgement: Points made in this chapter come in part from David, J.S., McCarthy, W.E. and Sommer, B.E. 2003. Agility: The Key to Survival of the Fittest in the Software Market. *Communications of the ACM.* May. 46:5. 65-69.

REA Accounting Systems: Resources-Events-Agents: An ontology for designing, controlling, and using integrated enterprise systems

501

Because of the low cost and ease of use, individuals also use these types of systems to keep track of their finances; in fact, some label these types of systems as personal finance software. Benefits of using the software include the automated accurate calculations, easily generated summaries of expenditures within expense codes, and the ease of backing up the data file.

Exhibit 16-1 Example checkbook register

DATE	CHECK NUMBER	RECORD ALL CHARGES OR CREDITS THAT AFFECT YOUR ACCOUNT					
		DESCRIPTION	PAYMENT	C ✓	DEPOSIT	BALANCE $	
MEMO LINE:			EXPENSE CODE:				
MEMO LINE:			EXPENSE CODE:				
MEMO LINE:			EXPENSE CODE:				
MEMO LINE:			EXPENSE CODE:				
MEMO LINE:			EXPENSE CODE:				

Enterprise-Centric Systems

Enterprise-centric systems capture, store, and report data about various types of transactions or other activities within an enterprise. They are broader in scope than the single-entry systems discussed in the previous system; however their scope is primarily within the enterprise. While such systems may produce information that is transmitted to external business partners, and may receive information electronically from external business partners, these systems typically are not truly integrated with the systems of the enterprise's external business partners. Systems within this category range from the simplest double-entry accounting systems to the most complex ERP systems, with hybrid systems that are in the midst of that range.

Double-entry Bookkeeping Systems

In 1494 the first accounting textbook was authored by Luca Pacioli, who instructed readers on the mechanics of double-entry bookkeeping. While archaeological evidence suggests that double-entry bookkeeping had been used for hundreds of years prior to 1494, its use was not widespread until many years after Pacioli's book was published. The organizing structure of the **double-entry bookkeeping system** is the accounting equation Assets = Liabilities + Owners Equity.

The primary components of double-entry accounting systems include a chart of accounts, journals, and ledgers. In computerized double-entry bookkeeping systems, the journals may be called transaction files and the ledgers may be called master files. The **chart of accounts** is a list of all the asset, liability, owners' equity, revenue, and expense accounts that are used by the enterprise to store transaction details. Double-entry systems record accounting transactions in chronological order in a journal, specifying the applicable accounts affected by each transaction. Early systems used only a **general journal**, a chronological record of enterprise transactions that includes the date of each transaction and which accounts should be debited and credited to reflect the effect of the transactions on the **general ledger**, a collection of the asset, liability, and equity accounts an enterprise uses to summarize the financial results of its activities. Later systems recognized benefits of recording like entries together and adopted the use of special journals including sales, cash receipts, cash disbursements, purchases, and payroll.

Journal entries are posted to the general ledger to update the account balances. Early bookkeeping systems included only the general ledger. Later systems added **subsidiary ledgers** in which to store the details of accounts that are made up of sub-account-balances that may need to be reported individually. Accounts Receivable, Accounts Payable, Fixed Assets, and Employee Earnings are the most common subsidiary ledgers.

Exhibits 16-2 through 16-6 illustrate typical journals and ledgers in a double-entry bookkeeping system.

Exhibit 16-2: Example General Ledger

GENERAL LEDGER

1000 Cash

DATE	DESCRIPTION	POST REF	DEBIT	CREDIT	BALANCE $	

1010 Accounts Receivable

DATE	DESCRIPTION	POST REF	DEBIT	CREDIT	BALANCE $	

1020 Inventory

DATE	DESCRIPTION	POST REF	DEBIT	CREDIT	BALANCE $	

(Note: while only three accounts are shown in this exhibit, the general ledger would actually include all the accounts on the company's chart of accounts.)

Exhibit 16-3 Example General Journal

GENERAL JOURNAL				PAGE _____
DATE	TRANSACTION DESCRIPTION	POST REF	DEBIT	CREDIT

Exhibit 16-4 Example Accounts Receivable Subsidiary Ledger

ACCOUNTS RECEIVABLE SUBSIDIARY LEDGER

Customer Account Number:　　　　　Customer Address:
Customer Name:

DATE	TRANSACTION DESCRIPTION	POST REF	DEBIT	CREDIT	BALANCE	
					DEBIT	CREDIT

Customer Account Number:　　　　　Customer Address:
Customer Name:

DATE	TRANSACTION DESCRIPTION	POST REF	DEBIT	CREDIT	BALANCE	
					DEBIT	CREDIT

Customer Account Number:　　　　　Customer Address:
Customer Name:

DATE	TRANSACTION DESCRIPTION	POST REF	DEBIT	CREDIT	BALANCE	
					DEBIT	CREDIT

Exhibit 16-5 Example Sales Journal

SALES JOURNAL   PAGE _____

DATE	INVOICE#	CUSTOMER	POST REF	ACCOUNT RECEIVABLE DEBIT SALES CREDIT

Exhibit 16-6 Example Cash Receipts Journal

CASH RECEIPTS JOURNAL   PAGE _____

DATE	PAYER	POST REF	ACCOUNTS RECEIVABLE CREDIT	SALES CREDIT	SALES TAX PAYABLE CREDIT	OTHER ACCOUNT CREDIT	CREDIT CARD EXPENSE DEBIT	CASH DEBIT

Accounting transactions are activities that have an economic effect on an enterprise; in other words, they affect the company's assets, liabilities, and/or equity accounts. Accounting transactions are the only activities for which information is captured in double-entry bookkeeping systems. Activities such as sale orders (the customer has ordered goods or services but the enterprise has not yet delivered the goods or performed the services) that have no immediate effect on an asset, a liability, or an owners' equity account cannot be entered into these types of systems. Accounting transactions are entered into the applicable journal and then posted to the applicable ledger(s).

Cash sales are entered into the cash receipts journal with the amount placed in the sales credit column and in the cash debit column. At a predefined point in time (e.g., when the end of the page is reached, at the end of each day, or at the end of each week), the cash receipts journal column totals will be posted to the corresponding general ledger accounts. Using the **special journals** and posting the column totals rather than having to post each individual line item saves much effort.

Credit sales are entered into the sales journal with the amount placed in the accounts receivable debit, sales credit column. At a predefined point in time, the total of that column will be posted to the general ledger as a debit to the accounts receivable account and as a credit to the sales account. Each individual sale amount is posted to the corresponding customer's account in the accounts receivable subsidiary ledger.

Transactions for which no special journals apply are entered into the general journal and posted to the appropriate general ledger accounts. In practice manual double-entry bookkeeping systems are rarely used because of the availability of inexpensive double-entry bookkeeping software such as QuickBooks, Peachtree, or Simply Accounting. The overall structure of such software is very similar to that of manual double-entry bookkeeping. Some capability is added to allow tracking of activities such as sales orders that lead to accounting transactions, and of course the benefit of automated posting with the corresponding decrease in effort and mathematical errors is well worth the cost of the software.

Hybrid Systems or Mid-range ERP Systems
The accounting equation Assets = Liabilities + Owners Equity is still a part of the primary organizing structure of **hybrid systems**. However, such systems expand the structure to also include material requirements planning (MRP) and activity-based costing (ABC) phenomena. These additions yield better support of manufacturing processes and attempt to identify activities that actually result in expenditures rather than simply allocating costs based on direct labor or material usage. While hybrid systems represent an important step forward from pure double-entry bookkeeping systems, the integration between the financial accounting, MRP, and ABC parts of the system is typically somewhat loose. Examples of hybrid systems include Microsoft Dynamics and SysPro.

ERP Systems
While larger-scale ERP systems still process financial accounting transactions, the accounting system does not provide the overall organizing structure. Rather, their foundation is Michael Porter's enterprise-wide value chain concept. **ERP systems** are groups of software applications that are integrated to form enterprise-wide information systems. At the time of this writing the dominant ERP software vendors are SAP and Oracle, however there are dozens of companies in this market. ERP systems have their strongest roots in MRP (materials resource planning) system software; however, they also encompass general ledger software, human resource planning software, and other types of software that were previously considered separate systems. ERP systems originally focused on back-office applications such as accounting and human resources. **Back-office** is a term that is often used in business to describe activities or systems that are only seen and used by people within enterprises; external partners such as vendors and customers do not usually see back-office activities. The systems and activities external partners normally do see are referred to as **front-office** systems and activities. For example, activities and systems used in the sales showroom are front-office dealings because customers see and interact with them. Many applications that were originally created as **bolt-on applications** (software programs that can be added to existing ERP software) have since been incorporated into the main ERP products. Therefore most ERP systems now incorporate front-office applications such as supply chain optimization, customer relationship management, and sales force automation. Non-ERP vendors developed most of these bolt-on applications; however, in some cases the ERP vendors acquired the companies that developed the applications in order to more fully integrate the products' functionality into their own software.

Community Focused Enterprise Systems
Enterprise information needs often extend beyond the boundaries of the enterprise. Although some ERP systems have added front-office applications, the extent to which they are able to become truly outwardly organized depends on the building blocks with which their systems are built. On the outside, many ERP systems look alike. Examine the sales literature of ten different ERP vendors and you are likely to see many of the same features and benefits described. Yet, the foundational structure of different ERP systems may be very different from each other. Some ERP software packages have tens of thousands of tables in the underlying databases and are somewhat inflexible, requiring enterprises to adapt their business to the

software rather than making the software fit the business. Other ERP software packages, especially those developed recently, have less tables and more flexibility.

An ideal **community focused enterprise system** would be an inter-enterprise system connecting multiple enterprises and tracking all of their data, both within each separate firm and across firms. Any transaction that involves two enterprises, for example, a shipment of goods from one firm to another, would be captured as an independent view, with identification of the originating and destination companies, from which their respective enterprise-centric views of the transaction as a sale and a purchase may be recognized. As globalization of enterprises and industries increases, the need for outwardly organized enterprise systems increases. Systems that capture detailed semantics about business resources and events such as those built with semantic technology and ontological foundations such as REA are the best equipped to enable outward focus. Two examples of agile systems that provide ERP functionality but show promise for extending their reach to the trading partner and/or independent view include Plex Online and Workday.

GOALS AND METHODS OF ERP SOFTWARE AND THE REA ONTOLOGY

The REA enterprise ontology discussed throughout this textbook has been described as a theoretical foundation for ERP systems. In fact, Workday used REA as a foundation during the development of its software. Therefore it is important to consider the similarities and differences between the goals of ERP and REA. The objective in this chapter is not to compare REA to any specific software package. Rather, the objective is to provide a high level overview of similarities and differences between ERP systems and REA systems. To provide such a high-level overview the goals of each are examined along with the methods by which the goals are achieved. Keep in mind that ERP software packages are not all created equal, so some packages will achieve the goals using methods similar to REA; others will achieve them in other ways or will not achieve them.

Three features may be used to compare some of the goals of ERP software-based systems and REA-based systems: a database orientation, a semantic orientation, and a structuring orientation[2]. We discuss each of these in turn.

Database Orientation

One goal of both ERP software-based systems and REA-based systems is the achievement of integrated enterprise-wide storage, maintenance, and reporting of data needed for decision-making. This goal may be referred to as a **database orientation**; and it requires the following three conditions to be met

- Data must be stored at their most primitive levels, at least for a defined time period
- Data must be stored only once, and such that all authorized decision makers can access the data
- Data must be stored so as to allow retrieval in various formats as needed for different purposes

The most **primitive level for data** is the level at which the data cannot be further decomposed. Total sales for the day is not primitive level data because it may be further decomposed into finer levels of detail such as the dollar amounts applicable to each of sales #42 through #89. Similarly the total dollar amounts of each of sales #42 through #89 may be further decomposed

---

[2] Dunn, C.L. and McCarthy, W.E. 1997. REA Accounting Systems: Intellectual Heritage and Prospects for Progress. *Journal of Information Systems.* 11:1. 31-51.

REA Accounting Systems: Resources-Events-Agents: An ontology for designing, controlling, and using integrated enterprise systems

507

into the quantities sold and the dollar unit selling prices for each good or service on each of the sales.

The three database orientation conditions ensure data is stored at the finest level of detail for which decisions may need to be made, so that data may be retrieved and aggregated as needed to make those decisions. The conditions also attempt to eliminate uncontrolled redundancy in the data. Non-integrated systems (often called legacy or traditional systems) typically record duplicate data about the same object many times (once for each functional area that needs access to the data), thus the data is stored multiple times. For example, in many legacy systems the marketing department records information about customers that have been identified as potential buyers. Once a customer order is received, the sales order entry function (which in a legacy system environment is not usually linked with marketing) records information about the customer from whom the order was received. The sales order entry function may request information about the customer from the credit management function; credit management will retrieve whatever information is in the customer master file and if inadequate information is available to establish a credit rating, credit management may in turn seek and enter additional data from outside sources. That data is stored and maintained by credit management and is made available to the order entry function only upon request. The sales order entry function typically passes along information about customers to the shipping function and to the customer service function; in those areas the information is entered into their customer master files (either via re-keying or by electronic transmittal). The result is customer data stored in several different customer master files by several different functional areas, which is a maintenance nightmare. Many customers have been frustrated by the fact that when they call their sellers to change their addresses, some mailings from the sellers reflect the changed addresses but other mailings continue to be sent to the old addresses. Such frustration occurs because the customers' calls trigger changes in only one application (that of whichever functional area the customers called) whereas the customers' address is stored in several applications.

In fully-implemented ERP software systems and REA systems, data items are stored only once and may be accessed from any authorized functional area in various formats, thus meeting the three database orientation conditions. The extent to which the three database orientation conditions are achieved using ERP software varies for different enterprises depending on whether they use single source ERP software packages, whether they implement "best of breed" ERP solutions, whether they install bolt-on applications in addition to their ERP software, and whether they implement the ERP software enterprise-wide or only in some parts of the enterprises. A single-source ERP solution implemented for an entire enterprise typically maintains a single database and meets the three conditions for the database orientation. The implementation of selected modules of an ERP software package, or the installation of a "best of breed" ERP system is less likely to completely satisfy the database orientation. Such an implementation is more likely to store the same data in multiple places, since different modules will have to overlap to some extent. Bridges may be built (similar to the Lego/K'nex connectors described in chapter 1 of this textbook) to minimize data redundancy and to facilitate data synchronization. However, the retrieval of data from the different modules in combination may be difficult or even impossible. View integration for views created with different building blocks may not be seamless.

Semantic Orientation
A second goal of REA-based systems is a **semantic orientation**. This goal requires objects in the system's conceptual model to correspond as closely as possible to objects in the underlying reality. At first glance both ERP-based systems and REA-based systems share the

semantic orientation goal. Horror stories abound of ERP software implementations for which the business processes did not match the software[3]. In fact, ERP system implementations are often regarded as business process re-engineering efforts because the business process tasks must be changed to match those supported by the software. Therein lies a subtle difference between REA-based systems and many ERP software-based systems. Whereas ERP software requires the business to be changed to match the software, REA tailors the system to match the business's reality. This difference may be critical for the long-term success of the system and the enterprise.

A semantic orientation also precludes the use of artificial constructs such as debits, credits, and accounts as base objects in the enterprise system. Chapters 9,10, and 11 demonstrated the derivation of many accounting numbers using queries, with no debits, credits, or accounts in the REA-based system. Most ERP software preserves the use of debits, credits, and accounts to satisfy accounting information needs rather than generating the accounting numbers from the underlying economic events and relationships. One probable reason for the preservation of accounting artifacts as base objects in ERP software is market demand; another related reason is lack of education as to how to generate accounting numbers procedurally on-demand rather than storing them in accounts.

Some vendors offer an optional "virtual" general ledger (i.e., a view that is generated on demand), but the market largely rejects that approach and opts for the vendors' "hardwired" general ledgers (i.e., general ledgers that are permanently stored and updated). Whether the market prefers the hardwired general ledger approach for efficiency reasons, because of lack of education, because of simple resistance to change, or some other reason, is a question for future research. We know only that REA and most ERP systems differ to some extent in their semantic orientations. A notable exception is Workday, a software system that is billed as "beyond ERP" and was developed with REA as its foundational organizing structure. Its semantic orientation is consistent with REA; while debits, credits, and accounts may be shown as part of the user interface and reports, they represent views of the underlying data rather than storage structures to house that data.

Structuring Orientation
A **structuring orientation** demands the use of a pattern as a foundation for the enterprise system. A pattern-based system design is important to facilitate automated reasoning by intelligent software interfaces to the enterprise system. Academic research is ongoing to develop software applications that can reason with the objects in the REA pattern to aid in decision-making. Pattern-based system design is also important to facilitate integration of systems between enterprises. If two enterprises merge their business operations and both used the same pattern-based approach to designing their systems, their systems will be much easier to combine than if they each followed a task-based or haphazard approach. REA-based systems obviously incorporate the REA pattern discussed throughout this textbook. ERP software-based systems do not seem to be intentionally built using any particular pattern; instead they are built to support best practices at the task level. That is, it appears that ERP developers identify the tasks performed by the enterprises that are believed to be most efficient or effective in an industry and build the software such that it supports those tasks. Different versions of the software are created for different industries because the best practices for one industry are not always the best practices for another industry. This reveals a significant

---

[3] Davenport, T.H. 2000. *Mission Critical: Realizing the Promise of Enterprise Systems.* Harvard Business School Press.

difference in the structuring orientations of ERP-based systems and REA-based systems, as most tasks are not used as base objects in REA-based systems.

INTRA-ENTERPRISE INTEGRATION

ERP systems attempt to integrate applications and data within enterprises. In theory, an ERP system is a single software program that serves the information needs of all users throughout an enterprise. Installed correctly, ERP systems can have a tremendous payback.

In practice many enterprises that have implemented ERP systems have not realized complete system integration. One reason is that many companies have implemented "best of breed" enterprise systems or have only implemented ERP software for part of their enterprises. "Best of breed" enterprise system implementations install different ERP software applications that best meet the needs of different areas of the enterprise. For example, an enterprise may determine that Peoplesoft best meets its human resource information needs, and that Oracle Applications is best suited for its financial information needs, while SAP is ideal for tracking information in its manufacturing processes. Another enterprise may determine that its main integration needs are for financial reporting purposes and therefore decide only to implement the financial module of an ERP software package.

Within enterprises that have best of breed, partial ERP implementations, or any other types of non-integrated information systems, two common integration solutions are often employed. One is the in-house creation of integration programs tailored to the parts of the separate systems that need to be connected. Another is the adoption of packaged **enterprise application integration (EAI) software**. Consider the Lego/K'nex example from chapter 1. The in-house creation of integration programs is similar to the example of developing a building block with a Lego connector on one end and a K'nex connector on the other end and using it to connect the disparate systems. The use of EAI software is more similar to designing a building block with a Lego (or K'nex) connector on one end and a generic connector on the other end. A typical EAI solution builds bridges from existing applications to a generic central hub that integrates the pieces.

The level of integration used for intra-enterprise systems depends on the goal of the system integration. If the goal is consolidation of information for corporate reporting purposes, integration may be achieved at a high level by creating some sort of shell reporting model and requiring each system to report its results in compliance with that shell. Once each piece is submitted in the shell format, the pieces may be easily combined. Such integration is not as complex as the EAI hub solutions.

ERP systems were originally developed with an intra-enterprise focus. The overall objective was to make information more available and more consistent within enterprises for internal decision-making purposes. Similarly, REA in its earliest phases was also inwardly focused. The pattern discovered and applied to each transaction cycle was examined from only one enterprise's perspective. In recent years, the trend for ERP systems and for REA research has shifted to an outwardly organized, supply-chain perspective. The increasing growth of electronic commerce and the increasing benefits of supply chain management have been catalysts for the changing nature of enterprise systems. We next explore the advancements in REA related to e-commerce and inter-enterprise system design.

ELECTRONIC COMMERCE, INTER-ENTERPRISE SYSTEM DESIGN, and REA

E-commerce is increasingly important in today's global networked economy. E-commerce occurs in various forms; the two most general forms are B2B (business-to-business) and B2C (business-to-consumer). Most people envision B2C transactions when they think about e-commerce; however, most e-commerce activity is actually B2B. If you have ever purchased an item via the Internet using a credit card, then you have engaged in B2C e-commerce (as the consumer). Consideration of ERP systems and REA patterns for a B2C environment isn't significantly different from consideration of ERP systems and REA patterns for a catalog mail order or telephone order environment. In those scenarios a customer inquires (or is informed through a marketing event) about goods or services, the customer places an order for goods or services to be delivered, the enterprise delivers the goods or services to the customer, and the customer renders payment to the enterprise for the goods or services. The simple change in communication technology by which the order is placed and/or by which the payment is rendered doesn't change the nature of the business process or the structure of the system needed to capture relevant information.

The primary differences in B2C commerce enabled by electronic technology are the breaking down of time, place, and form barriers. The time barrier is broken in that no longer is consumer access to certain business information restricted to normal business hours; information may be posted to web sites and made accessible 24 hours per day, 7 days per week, 52 weeks per year. The place barrier is broken in that consumers do not need to physically transport themselves to business locations in order to engage in transactions with the businesses. They can shop from the comfort of their easy chair with a few clicks of a mouse, and they can obtain product information and products from suppliers around the world from whom they may not have been able to obtain information before the advent of B2C e-commerce. B2C e-commerce also breaks the form barrier in that businesses no longer need to be a particular form or size in order to attract and satisfy customers. A small enterprise that can't afford a fancy physical storefront may be able to attract customers with a well-designed web-based storefront. Consumers typically do not have automated information systems that need to be seamlessly integrated with the businesses' information systems. Thus e-commerce technology advances create little apparent need to change the focus of enterprise systems from an intra-enterprise view to an inter-enterprise view.

In the B2B arena; however, a shift has occurred that requires an inter-enterprise view of enterprise systems. This shift is away from a traditional linear supply chain/value system to the current "value webs" in which enterprises need information not just about their most direct external partners but also about indirect partners. For example, enterprises today increasingly need information about product demand by their customers' customers. It is difficult to say whether this shift occurred because of advances in technology or whether the increasing information needs driving enterprises toward e-commerce in fact necessitated the technological developments.

Some researchers and practitioners say what we know today as e-commerce began over a century ago with the inventions of the telegraph and the telephone. Indeed a telecommunications infrastructure is necessary to support e-commerce. Other more recent foundations for e-commerce are EDI (**electronic data interchange**) and the Internet. EDI began in the 1960's but wasn't widely used until the 1980's. EDI involves the exchange of data between enterprises in a prescribed electronic format, usually through a VAN (value added network). The VAN connections between enterprises and the software used to accomplish EDI were proprietary and expensive. Enterprises that recognized the need for better and faster information to manage their supply chains justified the expense. Such enterprises realized how much money they had tied up in inventory sitting idle in warehouses and targeted inventory management costs for reduction. Inventory management practices at that time focused on anticipating demand for products and having products available when needed to meet that demand. Enterprises believed that reducing the time it took for upstream supply chain partners (i.e. their suppliers) to process their purchase orders would allow the enterprises to stock lower inventory levels and to better predict downturns in customer demand, thus reducing inventory obsolescence while still meeting customer demand. Large enterprises did benefit from more efficient and effective supply chain management enabled by EDI. In fact, some large enterprises required their suppliers to become EDI-capable if they wanted to remain approved vendors. Some smaller suppliers were unable to afford the investment in the proprietary hardware and software necessary for EDI so they either dissolved their businesses or shifted their business strategies to target different customers.

Many enterprises today still use EDI; however, many efforts in the past two decades have focused on developing standards to make EDI more consistent across industries. In the early years of EDI different industries had different standards, so it was extremely difficult for enterprises whose supply chains crossed industries to use EDI. A decade later the small suppliers that were forced out of business because of EDI would have an easier time engaging in B2B e-commerce with their customers. The Internet eliminated the need for proprietary hardware connections to accomplish EDI, significantly reducing the cost of EDI. Proprietary software was still required in order to partner with some companies; however, efforts such as Open-EDI attempted to eliminate the need for proprietary bilateral EDI arrangements by creating standards available to all enterprises involved in business transactions.

Cost reduction and process efficiency efforts continue to focus on supply chain issues today, and attempts are still being made to develop standards for inter-enterprise exchange of business transaction data. Customer relationship management bolt-on ERP software applications provide interfaces to allow automated interactions with customers in order to better satisfy customer information needs. Supplier relationship management bolt-on ERP software applications similarly provide suppliers with self-service capabilities via the purchaser's Internet website. Advanced planning systems and logistics applications are other examples of bolt-on ERP software applications that attempt to make enterprise systems more outwardly focused.[4] Supply chain management for some enterprises has transformed to the extent that a new term has emerged to describe their efforts: collaborative planning, forecasting, and replenishment (CPFR). CPFR is a business technique whereby trading partners agree upon a joint plan and sales forecast; they monitor the extent to which the plan and forecast are met, replenishing inventory as needed, and they recognize and respond to any exceptions.[5]

The REA enterprise ontology as introduced in this textbook is primarily inwardly focused. How might it be adjusted to shift its focus outward? As described in the previous section, e-commerce requires connections between enterprise systems of upstream and downstream supply chain partners. To achieve CPFR, these connections must be as seamless as possible. Creation of these connections is somewhat similar to view integration. In the view integration chapter in this textbook, we only discussed intra-enterprise connections. These connections between transaction cycles typically occurred via the resource flows of the value chain. For inter-enterprise view integration, then, it seems logical that connections between enterprises

[4] David, J.S., McCarthy, W.E. and Sommer, B.E. 2003. Agility: The Key to Survival of the Fittest in the Software Market. *Communications of the ACM*. May. 46:5. 65-69.

[5] Andraski, J.C. and Haedicke, J. 2003. CPFR: Time for the Breakthrough? *Supply Chain Management Review*. May/June. 7:3. 55-60.

would occur via the resource exchanges in the value system level model. Let's consider the possibility of connecting two enterprise systems at the value system level. Recall the Legos/K'nex toy trains example in chapter 1. To be able to seamlessly connect two enterprise systems at the value system level would require both systems to be created from the same building blocks. Theoretically REA constructs serve as a great set of building blocks. However, in the short term we will unlikely convince either or both enterprises to tear apart their systems and start building from scratch. Instead, the REA constructs have been enveloped into the information exchange standards that comprise the bridges between many enterprise systems. ISO 15944-4[6] is an international standard that incorporates most of the REA ontology as foundational elements. This standard was jointly published by the ISO (International Organization for Standardization) and the IEC (International Electrotechnical Commission).

Consider some of the difficulties of inter-enterprise view integration to support CPFR. The process of entity/class and attribute conflict resolution discussed in chapter 7 is complicated by the fact that entities labeled as sales/collection cycle phenomena by one enterprise are labeled as acquisition/payment phenomena by the other enterprise. When Enterprise Q sells merchandise inventory to Enterprise R in exchange for cash, Enterprise Q records a sale and a cash receipt. Enterprise R records a purchase and a cash disbursement. To merge these two views, therefore, is a non-trivial exercise. Once merged, the integrated view would include two events, a transfer of goods and a transfer of cash. Each event would need to be related to both Enterprise Q and Enterprise R, with an indication of which enterprise gave up goods to get cash and which one gave up cash to get goods. This merging at first glance may appear relatively simple; indeed the problems are more political than technical. For example, where would the data reside, who would enter the data, who would own the data, and who would maintain the data? The complexities multiply once Enterprises S, T, U, and V are added to the supply web. This textbook does not attempt to solve the problems associated with inter-enterprise view integration. Research on REA as an ontology to support collaborative planning, forecasting, and replenishment is ongoing, and as the research progresses, future editions of this textbook will incorporate the results of that research.

CONCLUDING COMMENTS

Most of you probably want to know what this discussion of current systems and different levels of integration means to you. In other words, what are you most likely to see once you graduate and start working? You could encounter systems with any of the organizing principles discussed in the first section; however, in the first few years of your career you are most likely to work with the hybrid and ERP systems. You may not be able to see a direct tie between REA and the software (unless you end up using Workday); however, the parallels will most likely be there if you look for them.

If you end up using a hybrid or ERP system that maintains the double-entry bookkeeping artifacts as storage structures then the connections to REA will be found primarily in the non-financial-accounting modules of the system. The benefit of recording transaction details of instigation and commitment events, the ability to track the related resources and agents, and the ability to track those events to the resulting economic events and reversal events will accrue primarily to the managers and managerial accountants when planning and budgeting. If you end up using an ERP system (or beyond ERP system) that generates accounting

---

[6] ISO/IEC 2007, ISO 15944-4 Information technology -- Business Operational View -- Part 4: Business transaction scenarios -- Accounting and economic ontology.
http://standards.iso.org/ittf/PubliclyAvailableStandards/index.html

numbers from the underlying transaction data, the connections to REA will be more evident and the queries included in chapter 10 that generated financial statement numbers will be especially useful. Whether you end up working with a system in which REA is clearly evident or not, do not lose sight of the advantages of pattern-based thinking and the insights the REA pattern should provide for you in understanding the operations of enterprises. Whether you are working for a large manufacturer, a mega-retailer, or a medium-sized service provider, they all have the same basic transaction cycles made up of economic exchanges of resources by agents. The labels may differ, but the concepts are the same.

Key Terms and Concepts

Accounting transactions	General journal
Back-office systems	General ledger
Bolt-on application	Hybrid systems
Chart of accounts	ISO 15944-4
Community focused enterprise systems	Mid-range ERP systems
Database orientation	Primitive level data
Double-entry bookkeeping systems	Semantic orientation
Electronic data interchange (EDI)	Single-entry systems
Enterprise application integration software	Singularly focused systems
Enterprise-centric systems	Special journals
ERP systems	Structuring orientation
Front-office systems	Subsidiary ledger

Review Questions

R1. Explain the three conditions that must be met to satisfy a database orientation.

R2. "Bolt-on applications" and "Best of breed software" are both concepts associated with ERP software. What is the difference between these concepts?

R3. What is the difference between intra-enterprise integration and inter-enterprise integration?

R4. What does it mean to have data stored at its most primitive level?

R5. What is the difference between back-office and front-office activities?

R6. To what extent is B2C e-commerce different from B2C commerce?

R7. How has B2B commerce changed with advances in electronic technology?

R8. Which technology makes information exchange between a small supplier and a large customer more feasible: electronic data interchange or the Internet?

Multiple Choice Questions

1. Which of the following is an example of a back-office activity?
   A) An in-store sale of merchandise
   B) Ordering of merchandise from a vendor
   C) Processing of a sale order for a mail-order catalog sales company
   D) Rental of an office building from a landlord
   E) None of the above

2. Which is characteristic of a semantic orientation of a system?

A) Data must be stored at their most primitive levels at least for a defined time period
B) Data must be stored only once, and such that all authorized decision makers can access the data
C) A pattern based system design is evident
D) Objects in the system's conceptual model correspond as closely as possible to objects in the underlying reality
E) Both A and B above

3. Which systems are primarily outward focused?
   A) Single-entry systems
   B) Double-entry bookkeeping systems
   C) Hybrid or mid-range ERP systems
   D) ERP systems
   E) REA systems as introduced in most of this textbook
   F) None of the above

4. A system that stores data only once in such a way that all authorized decision makers can access the data has at least one characteristic of a
   A) Database orientation
   B) Semantic orientation
   C) Structuring orientation
   D) Community orientation
   E) None of the above

REA Accounting Systems: Resources-Events-Agents: An ontology for designing, controlling, and using integrated enterprise systems

515

Glossary of Terms and Concepts

Abstraction – the ignoring or hiding of details to capture some kind of commonality between different instances. Examples of abstraction mechanisms in conceptual modeling include generalization and typification., p.389

Access control matrix – identifies the functions each user is allowed to perform and what data and programs the user can access once he or she gains access to the system, p.130

Accountability infrastructure – in the REA ontology, the economic and commitment activities that actually have happened, p.389

Accounting transactions – activities that affect an enterprise's assets, liabilities, and/or equity accounts, p.504

Accounts payable by supplier query steps, p.369-373
Determine what kinds of acquisitions are represented in your database (except for labor acquisitions which would be part of salaries and wages payable) and for each kind of acquisition follow these steps:
1. Determine which tables contain the acquisition date, dollar amount, and related supplier (usually these are found in the acquisition event table). Group by supplier, and sum the acquisition amount through the balance sheet date (with no beginning date constraint).
2. Determine which tables contain the cash disbursements that applied to those acquisitions. To determine this, examine the duality-purchase-cashdisbursement association.
    a. If the duality association is represented with a separate table, join the duality table to the cash disbursement table, establish the ending date constraint on the cash disbursement date field (with no beginning date constraint), group by supplier, and sum the cash disbursement amount applied to the acquisition.
    b. If the duality association is represented with the cash disbursement identifier posted as a foreign key into the acquisition table, join the cash disbursement table to the acquisition table, establish the ending date constraint on the cash disbursement date field (with no beginning date constraint), group by supplier and sum the cash disbursement amounts.
3. Determine which tables contain purchase returns that applied to those acquisitions. To determine this, examine the duality-purchase-purchasereturn association
    a. If the purchase-purchase return association is represented with a separate table, join the purchase return table to the acquisition table, establish the ending date constraint on the purchase return table date field (with no beginning date constraint), group by supplier and sum the purchase return amount applied to the acquisition.
    b. If the purchase-purchase return association is represented with purchase Id posted as a foreign key in the purchase return table, establish the ending date constraint on the purchase return table date field (with no beginning date constraint), group by supplier and sum the purchase return amount applied to the acquisition.
4. Subtract the results of steps 2 and 3 from the result of step 1 to get accounts payable for each supplier as of the balance sheet date.

Acquisition cycle or **Acquisition/Payment process** – transaction cycle in which cash or some other form of compensation is disbursed in exchange for goods and services; encompasses all activities associated with the purchase of and payment for those goods and services; also called the "procure-to-pay" mega-process or the expenditures cycle, p.36, p.74

Ad hoc querying – direct retrieval of information by end-users from a database whereby the retrieval was not planned (i.e. no pre-formulated queries or interfaces were developed in anticipation of needing the information), p.266

Agent – an individual, department, division, or organization that participates in the control and/or execution of one or more events, p.35, p.176

Agent queries – queries that involve single tables containing data that describes internal or external agents; typically such queries are used to list one or more internal or external agents who possess one or more specific characteristics, p.323

Aggregation function – a mathematical operation used in querying to summarize information within a single column; also called a vertical calculation, p.277

Application control – a feature created in a software program to help ensure transactions are valid, properly authorized, and completely and accurately processed, p.132

Area of responsibility – a department, a section within a department, or an individual employee who is held accountable for flow of information or physical objects through a system; used in system flowcharting to clearly identify changes in accountability for a document as the document moves through the system, p.70

Artificial construct – a thing that is artificially created or developed as opposed to something naturally occurring; also called an artifact, p. 23

Assignment – a relationship between an internal and external agent that represents responsibility given to the internal agent to communicate with and service the external agent on a regular basis; this relationship is independent of their mutual participation in an event, p.178

Association – a relationship between two or more classes, p.147

Association class – an association that possesses characteristics of its own and for which there can be only one link between the related classes, p.148

Association name conflict – a discrepancy in the labels used to name associations in different view models – either the same name used for different associations or different names used for the same association, p.231

Association structure conflict – a discrepancy in the assignment of multiplicities for the same association in different view models, p.231

Attribute – a characteristic possessed by a class or association class, p.148

Attribute conflict – differences in the list of characteristics identified as important for describing the same class or association class in various view models; resolve in view integration by including a set union of the attributes for the class or association class in the integrated view, p.230

Back-office systems – activities or systems that are only seen and used by people within enterprises; external partners such as vendors and customers do not usually see back-office activities or systems, p.505

REA Accounting Systems: Resources-Events-Agents: An ontology for designing, controlling, and using integrated enterprise systems

517

Barter transaction – exchange of a non-cash resource for a different non-cash resource, p.43

Base object – a foundational building block of an enterprise information system; because they are foundational, removal of base objects causes serious problems and requires rebuilding of the system, p.22

Batch control total – an internal control used to verify that all transactions within a batch were processed correctly, p.135

Batch processing – accumulates data for a period of time to collect a group of transaction data, after which all transactions are posted to the master file in one processing run, p.74

Best-of-breed – an approach to ERP software implementation in which an enterprise chooses different software packages for different areas of its business such that each package best suits the business area for which it is chosen. For example, an enterprise may choose one package for manufacturing process, another for human resources, and another for financials, p.19

Bill of lading – a document that indicates transfer of custody of goods from the enterprise to a common carrier; includes details about how many boxes made up the shipment and the dimensions and/or weight of those boxes, p.82

Bill of materials – a document that identifies the types and quantities of raw materials needed to create a finished good item; similar to the ingredient list portion of a recipe, p.436

Bolt-on application – software programs that can be added to existing ERP software applications, p.505

Bond certificate – a debt financing agreement that indicates the amount and timing of the expected cash receipts and resulting repayments per the loan terms, p.485

Bonding – the process of purchasing insurance on the employees who handle cash for an enterprise; the insurer performs background checks on the employees, determines the likelihood the employees will steal from the enterprise, and agrees to compensate the enterprise in the case of employee theft; is primarily a corrective control, p.119

Budget – a plan for future inflows and/or outflows of resources

Business-entrepreneur script – The stereotypical sequence of enterprise events that says (from the enterprise's point of view) the enterprise gets some money, engages in value-added exchanges, pays back the money, and lives off the profit, p.36

Business interruption – a temporary halt in normal operations due to an incident such as a threat or catastrophe

Business process – a term widely used in business to indicate anything from a single activity such as printing a report to a set of activities such as an entire transaction cycle; in this text business process is used as a synonym of transaction cycle, p.21

Business process level REA model – a representation of an enterprise's resources, events, agents, and appropriate associations between them within one or more transaction cycles; this conceptual representation is often used to design the logical enterprise database design, p.36

Business process risks – possibilities of loss associated with actual business process objects, including resources, events, agents, and relationships among resources, events, and agents, p.117

Candidate key – an attribute value that could be used as a primary key for some class (not necessarily for the class in whose table it exists), p.156

Cash balance query steps, p.374-376
1. Determine which table contains the cash receipt date (usually this is in the table that represents the cash receipt event) and make sure the same table also contains the cash receipt amount field.
2. Determine which table contains the cash disbursement date (usually this is in the table that represents the cash disbursement event) and make sure the same table also contains the cash disbursement amount field.
3. Create a query that establishes the ending date constraint (with no beginning date constraint) and sum the dollar amount field in the table identified in step 1.
4. Create a query that establishes the ending date constraint (with no beginning date constraint) and sum the dollar amount field in the table identified in step 2.
5. Create a query that subtracts the total in step 4 from the total in step 3.

Cash-related economic event – an event that has the effect of increasing or decreasing cash

Cash disbursement/Cash disbursement economic event – an event that has the effect of decreasing cash; also called a payment, p.80

Cash budget – a plan that delineates expected cash receipts from the revenue and financing transaction cycles and expected cash disbursements from the various acquisition/payment processes and financing cycle. Results in identification of the need to obtain additional cash; forecasted shortfalls result in decisions to acquire cash from external sources via debt or equity financing, p.483

Cash receipt – an economic event that has the effect of increasing cash, p.91

Cash requisition – a document indicating the identification of need for cash, p.483

Cash resource – usually a list of cash accounts (whether in banks or in petty or on-hand accounts) owned by an enterprise; in essence is a resource type, p.482

Chart of accounts – a list of an enterprise's general ledger account names arranged in the order in which they customarily appear in financial statements, p.503

Check – a document used to authorize the transfer of cash from one person or enterprise to another, p.80

Check digit – a number that is appended to and maintained as a part of an account number, part number, or other identifier as determined by a predefined formula, p.134

Check register – a listing of the checks written to disburse cash from a bank account

Claim – a timing difference between an economic increment event and the related economic decrement event; receivables and payables are examples of claims, p.176

Class – a set of entities, i.e., real world objects that have separate physical or conceptual existence, p.147

Class name conflict – discrepancies in the labeling of classes in different views; may result from synonyms (same class given two different labels) or homonyms (different classes given the same label), p.230

Closed loop verification – an internal control that helps the user verify the correct record is being processed and updated by displaying details of the record the user should recognize as belonging to the record; e.g., display of a customer's name upon the user entering the customer number, p.133

Collusion – two or more employees acting together to perpetrate a fraud, p.119

Column – the data values of an attribute (field) for various records (rows) in a database table

Combined class key posting – a logical level implementation compromise whereby a single foreign key is placed into a table to represent two or more different relationships, p.399

Committee of Sponsoring Organizations (COSO) – a committee of the Treadway Commission that issues reports with guidance/requirements as to components of internal control systems and methods of evaluating internal controls, p.109

Commitment event – an event whereby an enterprise becomes obligated to engage in a future economic event, p.209

Community-focused enterprise systems – information systems that connect multiple enterprises and track data from an independent viewpoint, from which the enterprise-centric views may be derived, p.506

Completeness check – an edit check internal control that verifies that all critical field data are entered; only verifies that some value has been entered for each field; does not verify accuracy, p.134

Composite attribute – a characteristic that is a combination of other characteristics, p.149

Concatenated primary key – a unique and universal identifier for a class or association class that is made up of multiple attributes, p.149

Conceptual level compromise – the use of less than ideal representation in a conceptual model because of an inability (e.g. inadequate measurement technique) or lack of need to completely and accurately represent an object, p.397

Conceptual (database) model – a representation that depicts the important objects and relationships between the objects that must be captured in a database; is independent of any hardware, software, or even any type of software, p.146

Conceptually congruent events – two or more events that are inseparable, that always occur simultaneously, p.397

Consume **stockflow association**– a relationship between a resource and an economic decrement event whereby the resource is partially used up by the decrement but still exists when the decrement is complete, p.422

Context – the circumstances or setting in which an event occurs; determines which script is invoked in attempting to understand and make predictions about the event, p.34

Contingency plan – an approach to be followed in case of a future business interruption or other emergency, p.118

Contract – an agreement that commits two or more enterprises to engage in one or more future exchanges of resources, p.76

Control activity – one of COSO's five interrelated components of an internal control system; a policy or procedure used to ensure necessary actions are taken to minimize risks associated with achieving enterprise objectives; may be preventive, detective, or corrective in nature, p.111

Control environment – one of COSO's five interrelated components of an internal control system; "the tone at the top;" the foundation that provides discipline and structure upon which all other components of internal control are built, p.110

Control Objectives for Business and Information Technology (COBIT) – a framework for internal controls that has gradually added emphases on enterprise governance and risk, p.110

Conversion cycle or conversion process – transaction cycle in which materials, labor, machinery, and other resources are transformed into finished goods or services; also called the manufacturing cycle, p.36, p.406

Copy of class – a duplicate representation of a class placed in a separate position on a conceptual model; must be marked as a copy and have no attributes assigned to it in order to avoid the creation of duplicate database tables, p.231

Corrective control – a control activity that focuses on recovering from, repairing the damage from, or minimizing the cost of errors or irregularities, p.111

Cost of goods sold query steps, p.385-387
1. Determine which table contains the sale date attribute; usually this is in the table that represents the sale economic event.
2. Determine which table contains the sale quantities; usually this is in the table that represents the stockflow association between sale and inventory.
3. Join the tables from steps 1 and 2 together; set date constraints for the beginning and ending of the income statement period; group by the inventory item identifier, and sum the quantity sold.
4. Join the result of step 3 with a query result that contains the calculated weighted average unit cost per inventory item. Multiplying the quantity sold by the weighted average unit cost yields the total weighted average cost of goods sold for each inventory type.
5. Create a final query that sums the weighted average cost per inventory item sold to get the total COGS for the income statement.

Credit memorandum or credit slip – an internal document used to communicate to the accounting department that a journal entry needs to be made with a credit to the customer's account receivable; a copy may be given to the customer to confirm their account balance was decreased, p.94

Creditor – an external agent (business partner) from whom the enterprise borrows cash and to whom the enterprise repays cash, p.483

Custody – a relationship between an agent and a resource that represents the agent having responsibility for the physical security of the resource; this relationship is independent of any mutual participation of the agent and the resource in an event, p.177

Customer – a person or organization to which an enterprise sells its goods and services, p.39

Customer order – information in the customer's own format regarding what goods and services the customer is committing to purchase from an enterprise, p.85

Customer statement – a document that summarizes the economic transactions for a customer and reflects the customer's account balance status, p.92

Data manipulation – the specification of operations to be performed on one or more data fields to obtain additional information; may create aggregations, horizontal calculations, subset selections, and so forth, p.273

Data type (field property) (in Microsoft Access) – specification as to what kind of data values may be entered into a database table's column, p.246

Database orientation – a goal for integrated enterprise-wide data storage which requires data to (a) be stored at their most primitive levels, at least for a defined time period (b) be stored only once, and such that all authorized decision makers can access the data, and (c) be stored so as to allow retrieval in various formats as needed for different purposes, p.506

Database window (in Microsoft Access) – a screen that depicts the components of the selected database (e.g., tables, queries, forms), p.245

Datasheet view (in Microsoft Access) – a mode that presents a relational table or a query result in row/column format, p.245, p.286

Date constraint – a restriction placed on a date field in a query to limit the query results to include only records for which the date values meet the restriction, p.300

Debit memorandum – an internal document used to communicate the need for a journal entry to debit (decrease) the enterprise's accounts payable balance for a supplier to whom goods were returned, p.82

Debt financing – a mechanism for obtaining cash whereby the firm borrows cash from one or more external business partners called creditors for a specified period of town p. 479

Default value – a software option that sets a data field's contents to a pre-specified (default) value; in some cases the default values may be overridden, while in other cases they may not, p.134

Deposit slip – a document used to summarize the cash receipts that are added to an enterprise's bank account at a specified point in time, p.92

Derivable attribute – a characteristic of a class or an association class that can be calculated based on the values of other stored characteristics, p.149, p.401

Design view (in Microsoft Access) – for relational tables, a mode that displays details about the fields of a table and allows the user to specify various design parameters such as which field(s) comprise the primary key, whether a field is set to required data entry, and the data type for a field; for queries, a mode that depicts the logic of a query in QBE format, p.245, p.282

Detective control – a control activity that focuses on identifying that errors or irregularities have occurred, p.111

Direct access – allows each record to be retrieved without reading all the records that precede it in the file, p.73

Disbursement/payment voucher – a document that indicates underlying documents have been examined to confirm goods or services were received and thus payment should be made, p.80

Dividend – a portion of enterprise earnings that is paid to shareholders, p.485

Dividend declaration commitment event – a commitment to a future economic decrement event in the equity financing cycle; is a legal obligation of the enterprise – once a dividend is declared the enterprise is required by law to actually pay the dividend, p.485

Document/procedure flowchart – a graphical representation that depicts the movement of and processing procedures for documents through a system, p.63

Double-entry bookkeeping systems – enterprise information systems that have the components of the accounting equation (Assets = Liabilities + Equity) as foundational elements of the systems' organizing structure, p.501

Duality – the causal link between a give (economic decrement) event and a take (economic increment) event, p.47, p.16

Duality association queries – queries that involve the tables that comprise a relationship between an economic decrement and an economic increment event such as that between sale and cash receipt or between cash disbursement and purchase; typically such queries are used to identify incomplete exchanges or to calculate dollar values of claims such as accounts receivable and accounts payable, p.325

Dynaset (in Microsoft Access) – a query's result; looks and behaves like a table but is not actually stored as a table; it is generated as a view each time the query is run, p.286

Economic decrement event – an activity that decreases one or more resources, p.176
Economic event – an activity that either increases or decreases one or more resources, p.35

Economic increment event – an activity that increases one or more resources, p.176

Economic reversal event – an activity that undoes a previous event that had increased (decreased) a resource; therefore the reversal event decreases (increases) the resource, p.210

Economy risks – threats of loss associated with factors that affect the entire economy, p.114

Edit check – a control incorporated into computer program instructions to verify and validate the completeness, reasonableness, and/or accuracy of data, p.134

Electronic data interchange (EDI) – the exchange of transaction level data between enterprises in a prescribed electronic format, usually through a proprietary value added network, p.510

Employee schedule – a mutual commitment event in the human resource business process wherein the employee agrees to provide labor as specified in the schedule and the enterprise commits to pay the employee the contracted wage rate for the labor provided, also called labor schedule, p.462

Encryption – a process of encoding data entered into a system, storing or transmitting the data in coded form, and then decoding the data upon its use or arrival at its destination to prevent unauthorized access to the data while it is stored or as it is transmitted, p.131

Enforce referential integrity (in Microsoft Access) – a choice selected in the relationship layout to determine whether the referential integrity principle will be enforced in a relationship between two tables as the user enters data into the database, p.254

Enterprise – an organization established to achieve a particular undertaking involving industrious, systematic activity; may be profit driven or charitably motivated, p.12

Enterprise application integration software – a software solution that builds bridges from existing applications to a generic central hub that integrates the pieces, p.509

Enterprise-centric systems – systems that capture, store, and report data about various types of transactions or other activities within an enterprise; while information from the system may be transmitted to external users, and the system may receive electronically transmitted information from external business partners, enterprise-centric systems are not truly integrated with the external business partners' systems, p. 501

Enterprise resource planning (ERP) system software – a group of software applications integrated to form an enterprise-wide information system solution, p.19, p.505

Enterprise risks– threats of loss to the enterprise as a result of internal and external factors that result from the actions or circumstances of the enterprise itself or of one of its external business partners, p.115

Entity – an object that has either a physical or conceptual existence, p.147

Entity integrity – a principle in the relational database model that requires the primary key of each tuple (row) to contain a non-null value; guarantees the uniqueness of entity instances and enables proper referencing of primary key values by foreign key values, p.155

Equi-join – a join that combines the tables together based on a common attribute, keeping only those rows for which the data values of the common attribute match exactly; also called an inner join; accomplishes a set intersection of the tables, p.269

Equity financing – a mechanism for acquiring cash whereby the enterprise issues shares of stock (that represent the right to share in various ownership interests) in exchange for cash, p.479

Error – an unintended mistake on the part of an employee or external business partner, p.111

ERP software – Internally developed or packaged software (such as SAP or Oracle Applications) that aims to provide one integrated enterprise-wide system with a common database, p.19

Event – an activity within an enterprise that needs to be planned, controlled, executed, and evaluated, p.35, p.176

Event-driven systems – systems whose foundational building blocks are representations of the actual underlying activities, p.23

Event activity rollup – the aggregation of a group of event records into a single summary entry; is an implementation compromise made at the physical level after transaction data is entered into the database once the historical detail is no longer needed, p.401

Event queries –queries that involve single tables containing data that describes events; typically such queries are used to list one or more events that meet specific criteria (such as those that occurred during a defined time period or those that exceeded a certain amount), p.319

Exchange – a trade or swap of one resource for a different resource between business partners, p.36

REA Accounting Systems: Resources-Events-Agents: An ontology for designing, controlling, and using integrated enterprise systems

525

Exposure – the potential impact of a threat of loss on an enterprise, i.e. uncontrolled risk, p.105

Expression builder (in Microsoft Access) – an application within Microsoft Access that assists the user in creating horizontal calculations within queries, p.296

Extension – the rows in a relational database table; they represent the specific instances that are members of the entity or relationship set, p.154

External agent – a person or organization with which an enterprise trades resources; also called external business partner, p.176

External business partner – a person or organization with which an enterprise trades resources; also called external agent, p.35

Fact – the pairing of a candidate key data value with another attribute data value; facts are found in a table's extension (rows), p.156

Field – a column in a relational database table, p.154

Field (mode) check – an instruction in a computer program that verifies the entered data type is the appropriate mode (e.g. text, numeric, date) for the field into which the data is entered, p.134

Field property (in Microsoft Access) – defines the type of data that is allowed to be entered into a column of a database table, p.246

Financial/numeric control total – the sum of a financial field, such as an invoice amount, of all records in a batch, p.136

Financial officer – internal agent who authorizes events in the financing business process, p.483

Financing process – transaction cycle in which cash is exchanged for cash at a later point in time; may include debt and/or equity financing, p.36

Flow line – a symbol on a flowchart used to indicate the movement of a document, a physical object, or data to the next point in a system, p.63

Flowchart symbols – specific notations used to communicate constructs on a system flowchart; numerous different symbols are used to represent different constructs, p.63

Foreign key – an attribute from one relational database table that is added as a column in another relational database table in order to establish a link between the two tables, p.154

Fraud – an intentional effort to cause harm to an enterprise; an irregularity, p.108

Front-office systems – systems and activities that are typically visible to external partners such as customers and vendors, p.505

Fulfillment – an association between instigation and commitment events whereby the commitment event fulfills the instigation event OR an association between commitment events and economic events whereby the economic event fulfills the commitment event, p.210

Fulfillment association queries – queries that involve the tables that comprise a relationship either between an instigation event and a commitment event or between a commitment event and an economic event; typically such queries are used to identify or to calculate total values of unfulfilled (open) items such as open purchase requisitions, open purchase orders, open sale orders, open production orders, and so forth, p.351

General controls – all controls over data center operations, access security, systems software acquisition and maintenance, and application system development and maintenance, p.131

General journal – a chronological record of enterprise transactions that includes the date of each transaction and which accounts should be debited and credited to reflect the effect of the transactions on the general ledger, p.501

General ledger – a collection of the asset, liability, and equity accounts an enterprise uses to summarize the financial results of its activities, p.501

Generalization – the abstraction from a class of objects to a superclass (less detailed, higher level) via the creation of an "is-a" relationship between the subclass and superclass. Subclasses contain more specific instances of superclasses., p.389

Group by – a querying function used to create subgroups to which aggregations may be applied; a means for creating subtotals, p.277

Hash control total – the sum of an attribute in a file that has no real meaning or use; for example, the sum of the customer number field of all the records in a batch, p.136

Homonym – one word used to designate multiple different things, p.230

Horizontal calculation – a row computation in a query that combines data from two or more separate columns of one or more tables, p.280

Horizontal subset of a table – a part of a table that includes only some of the table's rows, but includes all the columns, p.268

Human capital – the resource acquired in the human resource process, made up of the work employees perform and the knowledge and skills employees use in performing that work, p.458

Human resources process – transaction cycle in which cash is exchanged with employees for labor; also called the payroll cycle, p.36, p.455

Hybrid systems – enterprise information systems that are primarily organized using the accounting equation (Assets = Liabilities + Equity) structure; however, the structure is expanded to also include material requirements planning (MRP) and activity-based costing (ABC) phenomena, p.505

REA Accounting Systems: Resources-Events-Agents: An ontology for designing, controlling, and using integrated enterprise systems

527

Implementation compromise – deviation from the identified ideal information system design due to practical considerations, insufficient measurement techniques, and other constraints, p.397

Imprest checking account – an account that normally maintains a zero balance and works as follows: A company determines and deposits the total amount of cash disbursements needed for a payroll period from its regular checking account into its imprest checking account; paychecks are written from the imprest checking account. If all is as expected, the total paychecks written and cashed will equal the deposits made to the account and the balance will be zero, p.463

Independent checks on performance – verification of accuracy of an employee's performance by a different employee (or by an automated procedure), p.126

Industry risks – threats of loss associated with factors that affect an enterprise's industry, p.114

Inflow – the flowing in (receipt) of a resource to an enterprise, p.177

Information and communication – one of COSO's five interrelated components of an internal control system; prescribes features of the information system to ensure information quality and also prescribes open channels of communication to ensure employees understand what is expected of them in achieving internal control objectives, p.112

Information process risks– Risks associated with recording, maintaining, and reporting information about resources, events, and agents, p.117

Information retrieval – repossession or capture of data that was previously entered into a database or other data storage structure, p.266

Information system – the network of all communication channels used within an organization, including all paths by which enterprise employees and business partners impart and receive information (e.g. telephone conversations, written documents, fax transmittals, computer technology etc.), p.13

Inner join – a join that combines the tables together based on a common attribute, keeping only those rows for which the data values of the common attribute match exactly; also called an equi-join; accomplishes a set intersection of the tables, p.269

Instigation event – an activity in which need for a resource is identified; is typically the event that starts a transaction cycle, p.209

Intension – The columns in a relational database table; they represent the attributes of the entity or relationship set; also called the schema of the table, p.154

Internal agent – an individual, department, or division within an enterprise that participates in the control and/or execution of one or more events, p.176

Internal control – an activity performed to minimize or eliminate risk, p.106

Inventory cost value query steps, p.383-384

1. Join the result of a set of queries to calculate inventory quantity on hand for each item type the result of a set of queries that contains the calculated weighted average unit cost per inventory item. This join should be done using the inventory item identifier. Multiply the quantity on hand by the weighted average unit cost to get the cost value of each separate item type.

2. Create a final query that sums the cost value of each inventory item on hand to get the total Inventory dollar cost value for the balance sheet.

Inventory quantity on hand query steps, p.377-382

1. Determine which table contains the purchase date attribute (usually this is in the table that represents the purchase economic event).

2. Determine which table contains the purchase quantity attribute and the item ID (usually this is in the table that represents the stockflow association between the purchase economic event and the inventory resource).

3. Determine which table contains the purchase return date attribute (usually this is in the table that represents the purchase return economic event).

4. Determine which table contains the quantity returned attribute and the item ID (usually this is in the table that represents the stockflow association between the purchase return economic event and the inventory resource).

5. Determine which table contains the sale date attribute (usually this is in the table that represents the sale economic event).

6. Determine which table contains the quantity sold attribute and the item id (usually this is in the table that represents the stockflow association between the sale economic event and the inventory resource).

7. Determine which table contains the sale return date attribute (usually this is in the table that represents the sale return economic event).

8. Determine which table contains the quantity returned attribute and the item ID (usually this is in the table that represents the stockflow association between the sale return economic event and the inventory resource).

9. Join the tables identified in steps 1 and 2, group by inventory item, set the ending date constraint (with no beginning date constraint) and sum the quantity purchased to get the total quantity purchased per inventory item. Be sure to include the inventory item identifier in the query result to provide a means for linking to the results of other steps.

10. Join the tables identified in steps 3 and 4, group by inventory item, set the ending date constraint (with no beginning date constraint) and sum the quantity returned to get the total quantity returned per inventory item. Be sure to include the inventory item identifier in the query result to provide a means for linking to the results of other steps.

11. Join the tables identified in steps 5 and 6, group by inventory item, set the ending date constraint (with no beginning date constraint) and sum the quantity sold to get the total quantity sold per inventory item. Be sure to include the inventory item identifier in the query result to provide a means for linking to the results of other steps.

12. Join the tables identified in steps 7 and 8, group by inventory item, set the ending date constraint (with no beginning date constraint) and sum the quantity returned to get the total quantity of sale returns per inventory item. Be sure to include the inventory item identifier in the query result to provide a means for linking to the results of other steps.

REA Accounting Systems: Resources-Events-Agents: An ontology for designing, controlling, and using integrated enterprise systems

529

13. Join the results from steps 9 and 10. Change the join type to include all records from the total quantity purchased query and the matches from the total quantity returned query. The null to zero (Nz) function is necessary in the calculation to subtract the total quantity returned from the total quantity purchased. For example, this calculation expression would look something like this (depending on the query's variable names):
    Nz(SumPurchaseQty) – Nz(SumQtyReturned).
    This formula results in the unreturned purchase quantities for each item.

14. Join the results from steps 11 and 12. Change the join type to include all records from the total quantity sold query and the matches from the total sale return quantity. The null to zero (Nz) function is necessary in the calculation to subtract the total quantity returned from the total quantity sold. For example, this calculation expression would look something like this (depending on the query's variable names):
    Nz(SumQtySold)-Nz(SumSaleReturnQty).

15. Join the results from step 13 with the results from step 14. Change the join type to include all records from the total unreturned quantities purchased query and the matches from the total unreturned quantities sold query. The null to zero (Nz) function is needed in the calculation to subtract the total unreturned quantity sold from the total unreturned purchase quantity. For example, this calculation expression would look something like this (depending on the query's variable names):
    Nz(SumUnreturnedPurchaseQty) – Nz(SumUnreturnedSaleQty)
    This query result yields the total quantity on hand separately for each inventory item.

Investor – an external agent with whom the enterprise exchanges partial ownership of the enterprise for cash, p.483

Irregularity – an intentional effort to cause harm to an enterprise; a fraud, p.111

ISO 15944-4 – an international standard for commerce that incorporates most of the REA ontology as foundational elements. This standard was jointly published by the ISO (International Organization for Standardization) and the IEC (International Electrotechnical Commission)., p.512

Job time ticket – a document that indicates starting and stopping times and descriptions for labor operations performed on a specific date by a specific employee; the document's number often serves as an identifier for the labor operation event; also called a time track document, p.418

Join – to combine separate but related tables by linking them on their common attributes; one of the three primary relational algebra operators discussed in this text, p.268

Join properties window (in Microsoft Access) – a screen that appears when a user double-clicks on a join line to reveal whether the join is an inner join, a left join, or a right join; a user can change the join type in this window; used in the relationship layout and in query designs, p.292

Key verification (rekeying) – the keying of input data twice, with the computer comparing the two entries and highlighting any discrepancies for correction, p.134

Labor acquisition event – an economic increment event in which employee labor is purchased; each instance covers some time period; often represented by a timecard document, p.464

Labor operation – an economic decrement event that uses up the employee labor resource, p.407

Labor requisition event – identification of the need for labor; most commonly documented by a staffing plan, p.459

Labor schedule – a mutual commitment event in the human resource business process wherein the employee agrees to provide labor as specified in the schedule and the enterprise commits to pay the employee the contracted wage rate for the labor provided, also called employee schedule, p.462

Labor type resource – a resource type class that represents a list of the kinds of labor activities that can be performed in labor operations, p.417, p.459

Lapping – a method of stealing cash whereby an employee steals cash from a customer payment and delays posting a payment to the customer's account, and then uses funds from a subsequent customer payment to post to the first customer's account; the process continues with the employee continually stealing from subsequent customer payments to post as prior customer payments, p.120

Left Join – a combination of tables based on a common attribute that includes unmatched records from the first table in the join and does not include unmatched records from the second table in the join; is a partial outer join, is also called left outer join, p.273

Linkage association – a relationship between two resource types to represent the fact that one of the resources is composed of the other; in the conversion cycle this provides a means for identifying the materials of which a finished good is composed and the types of labor that are needed to produce a finished good. A bill of materials manifests the linkage between materials and finished goods. An operations list manifests the linkage between labor type and finished goods. An equipment list manifests the linkage between equipment type and finished goods., p.436

Load (high and low) – the percentage of data values for an attribute that are non-null; if most cells in a column have actual values, the load is high; if most cells in a column have null values, the load is low, p.158, p.399

Loan mutual commitment event – a debt financing agreement between an enterprise and a creditor external business partner that specifies determinable dollar amounts and timing of the cash inflow (loan proceeds) and of the cash outflows (loan repayments), p.485

Logical access control – restrict unauthorized access to the programs and data in systems, p.130

Logical level compromise – an implementation compromise made when converting a conceptual model into database objects, p.399

Logical model – in database design, a model into which the conceptual model is converted once the type of database software to be used has been chosen (e.g. relational or object-oriented); is hardware independent and is somewhat software independent (if relational is chosen as the database type, then any relational software may be chosen but object-oriented software may not), p.147

Logical operator – Boolean search terms used in queries to define which records are included in the query result; Examples include AND, OR, and NOT, p.277

Machine operation – an economic decrement event that partially consumes a machine in the conversion cycle, p.407

Magnetic tape – stores data from source documents and reports in a format that is computer readable; examples include audiocassette tapes and vcr tapes, p.72

Mandatory participation – represents a requirement that an instance of a class must be associated with at least one instance of an associated class in order to be included in the database; a minimum multiplicity equal to one, p.150

Marketing event – an activity such as a sales call, advertising campaign, or promotion intended to inform customers about products and/or services and persuade them to trigger the sales/collection process; an internally instigated instigation event

Master file – contain balance data or the status of an entity at a point in time, p.72

Master reference check – verifies that an event/transaction record has a corresponding master record to be updated, p.135

Material – see raw material

Material issuance – see raw material issuance

Material requisition – see raw material requisition

Materiality of risk – a function of the size of the potential loss, its impact on achieving the enterprise's objectives, and the likelihood of the loss, p.107

Materialization of tasks as classes – a conceptual model level implementation compromise in which an activity that could be re-engineered is established as a class (base object), p.398

Mathematical comparison operator – criterion by which data values are compared to determine whether or not they should be included in a query result, p.276

Maximum multiplicity – represents the maximum number of times an instance of a class may participate in an association with instances of a related class; legal values are 1 and * (many), p.150

Mid-range ERP systems – see **hybrid systems**

Minimum multiplicity – represents the minimum number of times an instance of a class must participate in an association with instances of a related class; legal values are 0 and 1, p.150

Model – a representation intended to serve as a plan or blueprint for something to be created; an object that represents in detail another (usually larger and more complex) object; used in systems design to help control complexity, p.30

Monitoring – one of COSO's five interrelated components of an internal control system; the process of assessing the quality of internal control performance over time and taking corrective actions as needed, p.112

Move ticket – a document typically used in the conversion cycle to indicate the actual use of raw materials (i.e., the materials issuance event), p.414

Mutual commitment event – an event that obligates an enterprise to participate in at least two future economic events, one that increments a resource and another that decrements a resource, p.76, p.210

Null value – a blank cell in a database table; a cell into which no data has been entered, p.155

Null to zero function (in Microsoft Access) – a Microsoft Access procedure used in querying that treats null values as if they are zeros; each factor in an expression that could potentially have a null value should be enclosed in parentheses and preceded by Nz; for example Cash: Nz(CashReceipts)-Nz(CashDisbursements), p.336

Object – a thing that has a physical or conceptual existence, p.31

Object pattern – a commonly observed constellation of things and associations between those things, p.32

One fact, one place rule – a principle in database design that prohibits a pairing of a candidate key value with another attribute value from appearing multiple places in a database table and also prohibits multiple pairings of candidate key values with other attribute values in the same place; helps to ensure well-behaved relational tables, p.156

Online processing – the computer input device is connected to the CPU so that master files are updated as transaction data are entered, p.74

Ontology – the study of what things exist, p.23

Open purchase order file – a repository that contains information about purchase order events that have not yet been fulfilled by purchase events; a collection of unfilled purchase orders, p.77

Operational infrastructure – the daily activities of an enterprise carrying out its mission, also called the accountability infrastructure, p.393

Operations list – a document that identifies the labor types needed to create a finished good; captures the same information as the linkage relationship between labor types and finished goods, p.436

Opportunity – a potential for reward, p.106

Optional participation – represents a minimum multiplicity of zero; an instance of a class may be included in the database without being related to an instance of the associated class, p.150

Outer join – a combination of tables based on a common attribute that includes unmatched records from both sides; accomplishes a set union of the tables, p.272

Outflow – the flowing out (disbursement or distribution) of a resource from an enterprise, p.177

Packing slip – a document that detail the contents of a package shipped to an external business partner such as a customer or a vendor (in the case of a purchase return), p.88

Parameter query (in Microsoft Access) – a query in which variables are used in lieu of data values as part of the query's selection criteria; allows the user to specify the data value to be used each time the query is run, thereby allowing re-use of the same query many times for different decisions, p.300

Partially filled sale orders query steps (note: results of this query series would not include orders that have not been at least partially filled), p.363-368
1. Step 1 Isolate sale orders that occurred through a user-specified date
2. Step 2 Isolate sales that occurred through a user-specified date
3. Step 3 Join date-constrained sale orders with Reservation association to identify quantities of items ordered (in effect date-constraining the reservation association)
4. Step 4 Join date-constrained sales with Stockflow association to identify quantities of items sold (in effect date-constraining the stockflow association)
5. Step 5 Join date-constrained reservation result to the fulfillment association to link the sale orders to the sales (in essence adding the sale identifier to the sale orders/reservation detail)
6. Step 6 Join date-constrained stockflow result to the fulfillment association to link the sales to the sale orders (in essence adding the sale order identifier to the sales/stockflow detail)
7. Step 7 Join the results of steps 5 and 6, linking them via the sale identifier, the sale order identifier, inventory item identifier, and then grouping by the sale order identifier, sum the quantity sold
8. Step 8 Using the result of step 7, subtract the sum of quantity sold from the quantity ordered to get the unfilled quantity of each sale order; any orders for which the unfilled quantity is greater than zero are partially filled.

Participation – a relationship between an event and an internal or external agent, p.177

Participation association queries – queries that involve the tables that comprise a relationship between an event and an agent (either internal or external); typically such queries are used to identify information about the agents who participated in an event or to aggregate event data by agent (for example, total sales by salesperson), p.357

Password –a unique identifier that only an authorized user of a system or application should know and that the user is required to enter each time he/she logs onto the system; a weak form of protection; a logical access control, p.130

Pattern – an arrangement of repeated or recognizably consistent objects or actions, p.32

Paving the cowpaths – automating existing processes as is, without considering whether they are the most efficient and effective means of achieving the goal, p.20

Payroll cycle – transaction cycle in which cash is exchanged with employees for labor; also called the human resource process, p.36, p.455

Payroll deduction – amounts withheld from paychecks to be paid on behalf of the employee (sometimes by statute, sometimes voluntarily) to government agencies, benefit providers, or other outside agencies, also called withholdings p.465

Payroll function – the function within the payroll cycle that pays employees for the labor the enterprise acquired from the employees, p.455

PCAOB Auditing Standard 5 (AS5) – regulation that provides a comprehensive and rigorous expectation of the responsibilities of auditors involved in an engagement that includes both audits of a company's financial statements and of the company's management's assessment of internal control over financial reporting, p.109

Performance – the fulfillment of an obligation in a manner that releases the performer from all liabilities; an activity or action that fulfills an obligation, p.78

Performance review – a review of some element of an enterprise's performance that provides a means for monitoring; examples include comparison of actual data to budgeted or prior period data, comparison of operating data to financial data, and comparison of data within and across various units, subdivisions, or functional areas of the enterprise, p.112

Personnel function – function within the payroll cycle that acquires and maintains employee labor, i.e., the function that hires, trains, evaluates, and terminates employees, p.455

Physical access control – method of prevention of unauthorized access to physical resources, p.119

Physical database model – a working database system; is dependent on the hardware, software, and type of software chosen during the design stages, p.147

Physical level compromise – a deviation from the theoretical ideal when converting the logical database model into specific database software to implement the working database, p.401

Picking slip – a document that identifies the goods that have been taken out of the warehouse and made available to be shipped, p.88

Policy infrastructure – in the REA ontology, the economic and commitment activities that should, could, or must happen in a company. The policy infrastructure reflects the results of planning and control efforts by the enterprise management., p.389

Preventive control – a control activity that focuses on preventing errors or irregularities either from occurring or from being entered into the enterprise information system, p.111

Primary key attribute – a characteristic that uniquely and universally identifies each instance in an entity or relationship set, p.148

Primitive level data – data that cannot be decomposed into any component parts, p.506

Production employee – an internal agent involved in labor operations and production runs in the conversion process; a worker who participates in the manufacture of finished goods, p.410

Production order (document) – a document that captures information about a production order event, p.414

Production order (event) – an event that represents the enterprise's commitment to engage in a future economic increment event (a production run) that will increase the finished goods resource, p.423

Production run – an economic increment event that increases the quantity of a finished good resource; sometimes referred to as a job, a batch, or a work-in-process job, p.410

Production supervisor – an internal agent who authorizes events in the conversion cycle, p.443

Project – a relational algebra operator (pronounced pro-JECT' rather than PRO'-ject) that specifies a vertical subset to be included in the query result, p.268

Proposition – a relationship between an instigation event and a resource or resource type; often specifies quantity and proposed cost or selling price for the item(s) identified as needed, p.210

Proposition association queries – queries that involve the tables that comprise a relationship between an instigation event and a resource or resource type; typically such queries are used to list the quantities or dollar values of the items included in the event or to aggregate them for a time period, p.353

Public Company Accounting Oversight Board (PCAOB) – a non-profit organization intended to monitor public accounting firms to be sure they are conducting high quality audits, p. 108
Purchase – an economic increment event in which services or the title to goods transfers from a supplier to the enterprise; also called an acquisition, p.78

Purchase order – a mutual commitment event in which a supplier agrees to transfer title of goods to the enterprise at an agreed upon future time and price and the enterprise agrees to pay for those goods; a document reflecting the terms of the mutual commitment event, p.76

Purchase requisition – an instigation event in which the need for goods or services is identified; an internal document that communicates this need to the enterprise purchasing function, p.75

Purchase return – an economic increment reversal event in which the title to goods previously transferred from a supplier to the enterprise is transferred back to the supplier, p.81

Query – a request for information submitted to a database engine, p.266

Query By Example (QBE) – a type of query interface intended to be more "point and click" in nature than is SQL; in this interface the user creates a visual example of what tables and fields should be included in a query result and specifies any calculations to be included, p.267

Query grid (in Microsoft Access) – the lower half of the QBE view into which fields are dragged and in which aggregations or horizontal calculations may be created to establish the desired logic for a query, p.280

Query window (in Microsoft Access) – the screen in which queries are created; user may toggle back and forth between QBE design, SQL design, and Datasheet (result) views within the query window, p.284

Quote – an offer by a vendor to sell an item at a stated price, p.76

Random storage – information may be stored in any order on the disk device, p.73

Range check – an instruction in a computer program that compares entered data to a predetermined acceptable upper and/or lower limit and rejects data that falls outside the specified limits unless special authorization is obtained, p.134

Raw material – an input resource in the conversion process that is completely used up in the transformation to finished goods; also called **material**, p.410

Raw material issuance – an economic decrement event involving the using up of raw materials in the production process; the raw materials are usually transformed into finished goods and lose their own identity and nature in the process; also called **material issuance**, p.407

Raw material requisition – a commitment event whereby the inventory clerk or warehouse supervisor commits to the production supervisor to transfer materials from the materials warehouse to the production floor; also called **material requisition**; assumes the raw materials are available within the enterprise and reserves them for use – if they are not, the raw material requisition (commitment event) in the conversion cycle may trigger a purchase requisition (instigation) in the acquisition cycle, p.426

REA Ontology – a domain ontology founded by Bill McCarthy at Michigan State University that attempts to defined constructs that are common to all enterprises and demonstrate how those constructs may be represented in an integrated enterprise information system. The REA ontology is made up of four layers: the value system, value chain, business process, and task levels, p.23, p.38

Real-time processing – updates master files as a business activity occurs, p.74

Reality – that which exists objectively and in fact, p.30

Reasonableness check – an instruction in a computer program to verify whether the amount of an event/transaction record appears reasonable when compared to other elements associated with each item being processed, p.135

Receiving Report document – a document that lists the items and the quantities and condition of each item received in an acquisition event; the receiving report identifier is often used as the identifier for the acquisition event, p.79

Reciprocal – a relationship between a commitment to an economic increment and a commitment to an economic decrement; the commitment level equivalent of the duality relationship; in the conversion cycle, represents a schedule of what is to be produced and what will need to be used and consumed in the production process, p.210, p.434

Reconciliation of physical to recorded quantities – a comparison of a quantity of a resource on hand per a count to the quantity listed as on hand in the information system, p.120

Record – a row in a relational database table, p.154

Record count control total – the total number of records in a batch, p.136

REA Accounting Systems: Resources-Events-Agents: An ontology for designing, controlling, and using integrated enterprise systems

537

Redundancy – in database design, duplicate storage of the same information, p.156

Reengineering – the redesign of business processes or systems to achieve a dramatic improvement in enterprise performance, p.20

Referential integrity – a principle in relational databases that requires a value for a foreign key attribute to either be null (blank) or to match exactly a data value in the table in which the attribute is a primary key, p.135, p.155

Reified association – an association that possesses characteristics of its own and for which there may be multiple links between the related classes, p.148

Relation – a two dimensional storage structure with rows and columns, more commonly referred to as a table, p.154

Relational algebra – the original data manipulation (querying) language that was constructed based on set theory and predicate logic as part of the relational database model; primary operators include Select, Project, and Join; however, other operators are also part of the relational algebra, p.267

Relational model – a logical level database design model based developed by E.F. Codd based on set theory and predicate logic; primary constructs are relations (tables) that represent classes and associations between classes, p.154

Relationship layout (in Microsoft Access) – a window in which relationships between tables are visually depicted, p.251

Remittance advice – a document (usually the portion of a customer invoice or statement that says "return this stub with payment") that advises the enterprise the customer is remitting payment; often used as the identifier for a cash receipt event, p.92

Rental – an economic decrement event that does not involve the transfer of title of goods, but instead involves a transfer of the right to use goods for an agreed upon length of time; begins when the right to temporary possession of the goods transfers from the lessor to the lessee and ends when possession of the goods transfers back from the lessee to the lessor, p.88

Rental agreement – a mutual commitment event in which a vendor agrees to make an asset available for an enterprise to use for a specific future time period at a specific price and the enterprise agrees to pay for that usage, p.76

Repeating group – multiple facts stored in one place; the same value of a key attribute field associated with multiple values of another attribute, p.156

Report-time processing – data used to generate a requested report is processed as the report is created, p.74

Representation – a surrogate for something; a symbol that closely resembles the actual construct; the closer the resemblance to the real object, the better the representation, p.30

Request for quote (RFQ) – notification to a potential supplier asking for price and availability of one or more products, p.75

Request to return – notification to a supplier of the enterprise's dissatisfaction with goods that seeks permission to return those goods in lieu of making payment (or in exchange for a refund), p.81

Required data entry (field property) (in Microsoft Access) – a choice specified in table design view; a user will not be allowed to enter a record into the table without including a value for any field(s) for which this property is set to "yes"; a user may leave any field except the primary key field(s) blank for which this property is not set to "yes" (Microsoft Access automatically enforces entity integrity so there is no need to set the required data entry field property to "yes" for primary key fields), p.249

Reservation – a relationship between a commitment event and a resource or resource type; often specifies quantity and budgeted cost or selling price for the resources involved in the agreement, p.210

Reservation association queries – queries that involve the tables that comprise a relationship between a commitment event and a resource or resource type; typically such queries are used to list the quantities or dollar values of the items included in the event or to aggregate them for a time period, p.356

Resource – a thing of economic value (with or without physical substance) that is provided or consumed by an enterprise's activities and operations, p.35, p.175

Resource queries – queries that involve single tables containing data that describes resources or resource types; typically such queries are used to identify one or more resources that possess specific characteristics (e.g. all inventory types that weigh more than 50 lbs), p.313

Resource type – a resource that is tracked only by the category into which it is classified such that one identifier is assigned to represent the category and the individual instances are interchangeable and indistinguishable; also may be referred to as a bulk resource

Responsibility – an association between two types of internal agents that is separate from any event in which they might both participate, and that indicates one agent is responsible in some way for the other agent, p.178

Return authorization – document or verbally granted information giving permission to a customer to return goods through the mail or via a common carrier in exchange for which the enterprise will refund payment or credit the customer's account receivable, p.94

Revenue cycle (also called Sales/Collection process) – transaction cycle in which goods or services are exchanged to customers or clients for cash or some other form of compensation, p.84

Reversal – a relationship between an economic reversal event and the economic event it reverses, e.g. between sale and sale return or between purchase and purchase return, p.210

Reversal association queries – queries that involve the tables that comprise a relationship between an economic event and a reversal event that negates part or all of the economic event; typically such queries are used to identify or aggregate the net event activity (e.g. to calculate net purchases as purchases minus purchase returns for a specific time period), p.325

REA Accounting Systems: Resources-Events-Agents: An ontology for designing, controlling, and using integrated enterprise systems

539

RFID (Radio frequency identification) tags – tags that communicate electronically with a reader via radio waves that enable tracking of resources, p.123

Right join – a combination of tables based on a common attribute that includes unmatched records from the second table in the join and does not include unmatched records from the first table in the join; is a partial outer join, is also called right outer join, p.272

Risk – a chance of injury or loss, p.105

Risk assessment – one of COSO's five interrelated components of an internal control system; the identification and analysis of relevant risks associated with the enterprise achieving its objectives; forms the basis for determining what risks need to be controlled and the controls required to manage them, p.111

Sale – an economic decrement event in which title to goods is transferred from the enterprise to a customer; may also be called a shipment or a delivery; if sale involves services instead of goods, the event is usually called service engagement or something similar p.87

Sale order – a mutual commitment event in which the enterprise agrees to transfer title of goods to a customer at an agreed upon future time and price and the customer agrees to pay for those goods; a document reflecting the terms of the mutual commitment event, p.86

Sales call – An internally initiated instigation event; typically is a meeting between an enterprise sales representative and a customer in which the sales rep describes features of products or services in an attempt to generate sales; usually is pre-arranged and face-to-face, p.84

Sale invoice – a document used to communicate to a customer the fact that the enterprise has fulfilled a commitment to transfer title of goods to the customer; sometimes also serves as a request or reminder for the customer to fulfill its commitment and remit payment to the enterprise, p.90

Sale order – a mutual commitment event in which the enterprise agrees to deliver goods to a customer and the customer agrees to pay for those goods by a future date; a sale order document is typically prepared after receipt of a customer purchase order indicating the enterprise's acceptance of the order and authorizing the sale, p.86

Sale return – an economic decrement reversal event in which the title to goods previously transferred to a customer transfers back to the enterprise, p.94

Sales/Collection business process – transaction cycle in which goods or services are exchanged to customers or clients for cash or some other form of compensation, p.36, p.84

Sarbanes Oxley Act (SOX) – section 404 – legislation that requires management to assess internal controls, p.108

Schema – the column headings, or intension, of a relational database table, p.154

Script pattern – a sequence of events that typically occur in combination with each other, p.34

Select – a relational algebra operator that specifies a horizontal subset to be included in the query result, p.268

Select-From-Where – the format of SQL queries; the Select clause specifies a vertical subset to be included in the query result; the From clause specifies which table(s) are to be queried and any sub-grouping to be done; the Where clause specifies a horizontal subset to be included in the query result, and if multiple tables are included, helps to define the join, p.273

Semantic orientation – a goal of REA-based systems that requires objects in the system's conceptual model to correspond as closely as possible to objects in the underlying reality, p.507

Separation of duties (segregation of duties) – the structuring of employees' job functions such that one employee is prohibited from performing two or more of the following functions: authorization of transactions involving assets, custody of assets, record keeping, and reconciliation; reduces the opportunity for one employee to steal enterprise assets and to conceal the theft in the normal course of his or her work, p.119

Sequence check – a control used to verify the records in a batch are sorted in the proper sequence and/or to highlight missing batch items, p.135

Sequential access – requires all data to be read in sequential order; to find a particular record requires all previous records to be read first, p.72

Sequential storage – records are stored one after another in some order (chronologically, or in numeric order, p.72

Service agreement – a mutual commitment event in which a vendor agrees to provide services to an enterprise at an agreed upon future time and price and the enterprise agrees to pay for those services, p.76

Service engagement – an economic decrement event in which the enterprise transfers services to a customer, p.88

Share of stock – an document that represents partial ownership of the enterprise as a result of providing equity financing, also called a stock certificate, p.485

Show Table window (in Microsoft Access) – a screen from which the user may choose which table(s) to include in the relationship layout or in a query, p.252

Silo operations – division of enterprises into functional areas such that different activities occur in different parts of the enterprise, p.15

Silo systems – separate information systems for each of the different functional areas of an enterprise, p.15

Simple attribute – a characteristic of an entity or relationship that cannot be further decomposed into component characteristics, p.149

Single-entry systems, also called **Singularly focused systems** – the simplest of accounting systems, designed to record the inflow and outflow transactions that affect just one resource of an enterprise (such as cash), p.500

Smart card or token – a logical access control that authenticates a user through a hardware device combined with a log-in password process; the smart card generates a random code that changes at predetermined intervals and must be matched against the host system; the user must also enter a password to gain access to the system, p.130

Special journal – chronological record of transactions affecting pre-defined accounts such that an entire column can be summed and posted to one account; examples include sales, cash receipts, cash disbursements, purchases, and payroll journals, p.504

SQL view (in Microsoft Access) – a mode for viewing the underlying SQL statement for a query; even if a query was created in QBE mode, Microsoft Access generates a corresponding SQL statement that the user may view to evaluate the query's logic, p.279

Statement on Auditing Standards (SAS) 94 – an auditing statement that largely established current standards as to the effect of information technology on auditor consideration of internal control, p.109

Statement on Auditing Standards (SAS) 115 – an auditing statement that largely established current standards as to the communication of internal control matters identified in an audit, p.109

Static derivable attribute – a derivable attribute for which the derived value will not change if additional transaction data is entered into the database, p.149

Staffing plan – a document on which a supervisor communicates a department's need for labor for a given time period, that indicates the types and quantities of labor needed but does not assign specific employees to provide the labor, p.459

Stock certificate – an document that represents partial ownership of the enterprise as a result of providing equity financing, also called a stock certificate, p.485

Stock issuance commitment event – an equity financing agreement that commits an investor to provide a determinable cash dollar amount (stock proceeds) on a specified date, p.485

Stockflow – an association between an economic event and a resource or an association between an economic reversal event and a resource; often specifies quantity and actual cost or selling price for the item(s) involved in the event, p.47, p.177

Stockflow association queries – queries that involve the tables that comprise a relationship between an economic event or a reversal event and a resource or resource type; typically such queries are used to list the quantities or dollar values of the items included in the event or to aggregate them for a time period, p.343

Strategy – an enterprise's planned course of action for achieving an objective, p.39

Structured Query Language (SQL) – a query language developed to enable the performance of multiple operations in a single query and to use a standard format for every query statement (Select-From-Where) to simplify the task of query development, p.267, p.273

Structuring orientation – a goal of REA-based systems that demands the use of a pattern as a foundation for the enterprise system to facilitate automated reasoning by intelligent software interfaces to the enterprise system, p.508

Subsidiary ledger – stores the details of general ledger accounts that are made up of sub-account-balances that may need to be reported individually, such as accounts receivable, accounts payable, fixed assets, inventory, and employee earnings, p.502

Supplier – a person or organization from which an enterprise purchases goods or services, p.39

Supply chain – the entire network of enterprises (e.g., retailers, wholesalers, transportation firms) involved in providing a particular product or service to an end customer, p.39

Symbol – something that stands for or represents something else, p.30

Synonym – a word that has the same meaning as one or more other words, p.230

System flowchart – a graphical representation of the inputs, processes, and outputs of an enterprise information system; includes details about the physical as well as the logical aspects of the system components, p.63

Task level REA model – a task is a workflow step or activity that may be changed or eliminated without fundamentally changing the nature of the enterprise and therefore should not serve as a foundational element in an enterprise information system; task level models in the REA ontology are graphical representations of workflow processes for which there is no identified pattern, p.36

Threat – a situation or event that causes possible or probable loss to a person or enterprise, p.105

Timecard – the primary document prepared by the enterprise in conjunction with the economic increment event is a time card; may be completed on a daily, weekly, or other basis; are typically completed by employees and approved by supervisors, list the times employees started working (punched in) and stopped working (punched out) for each day in the covered time period, p.465

Token – an individual object; token-level representation uses a separate token for each individual instance in the piece of reality that is being modeled, p.31

Token system – use of a hardware device combined with a log-in password to protect against unauthorized access to a network; the hardware device is a smart card that works in sync with the host network to authenticate access, p.130

Transaction file – a file that contains activity data that is used to update the blanaces on master files, p.72

Transaction type check – a batch level internal control that verifies that all transactions within the batch are of the same category or type, p.135

REA Accounting Systems: Resources-Events-Agents: An ontology for designing, controlling, and using integrated enterprise systems

543

***Transfer* duality association** – a relationship between economic increment and economic decrement events in which the decremented resources are traded for the incremented resources, p.410

***Transformation* duality relationship** – an association between economic increment and economic decrement events whereby the decremented resources are converted into the incremented resources, p.410

Tuple – a row in a relational database table, p.154

Type – a category into which individual objects may be classified; type level representation uses one type to represent as many individual instances as fit the category, p.31

Typification – representation as a category or type rather than as an individual instance, p.210, p.391

Universal Modeling Language (UML) – a widely accepted diagrammatic notation for system analysis and design, UML includes several types of diagrams for different levels of analysis; its class diagrams are appropriate for conceptual modeling of REA concepts, p.146

***Use* stockflow association** – a relationship between a resource and an economic decrement event whereby the resource is completely subsumed by the decrement, i.e., the resource is completely used up, p.414

Valid sign check – an internal control used to assess whether a field's sign (positive or negative) makes sense; is used to highlight illogical values, particularly balances in master file records, p.135

Validity check – an internal control in which a comparison is made between entered data and pre-specified stored data to determine whether the entered data is valid, p.134

Value chain – the interconnection of business processes via resources that flow between them, with value being added to the resources as they flow from one process to the next, p.39

Value chain level REA model – a representation that depicts the interconnected business processes for an enterprise, the resource flows between the processes, and the duality relationships within each process, p.35

Value system – an enterprise placed into the context of its various external business partners such as suppliers, customers, creditors/investors, and employees, p.39

Value system level REA model - a representation that depicts the resource exchanges in which an enterprise engages with external business partners, p.35

Vendor invoice – document sent by a supplier to the enterprise to communicate the fact that the supplier has fulfilled its commitment to transfer title of goods to the enterprise; sometimes also serves as a request or reminder for the enterprise to fulfill its commitment and remit payment, p.79

Vertical calculation – a computation that is a summarization of data values within a single column; also called an aggregation function, p.280

Vertical subset of a table – a part of a table that includes only some of the table's columns (but includes all the rows), p.268

View-driven system – a system in which foundational building blocks are artificial constructs that represent a perspective needed for a particular decision-making need (e.g. debits, credits, journals, and ledgers), p.23

View integration – the process of combining separate conceptual models into one comprehensive model, p.229

View modeling – the creation of conceptual models to represent separate parts (usually transaction cycles) of an enterprise, p.229

Volatile derivable attribute – a derivable attribute for which the derived value will change if additional transaction data is entered into the database, p.149

Weighted average unit cost – an inventory costing method that divides the total cost of each type of item available for sale by the total quantity available; that unit cost is multiplied by the quantity sold during a time period to derive cost of goods sold and that unit cost is multiplied by the quantity on hand to get the cost balance of ending inventory, p.348

Weighted average unit cost query steps, p.348
1. Determine which table contains the purchase date attribute (usually this is in the table that represents the purchase economic event).
2. Determine which table contains the purchase quantities and actual unit cost information (usually these attributes are in the table that represents the stockflow relationship between purchase and inventory).
3. Join the tables together, set a <= balance sheet date constraint as a user-definable parameter and multiply the quantities purchased by the actual unit costs to get the total purchase line-item amounts. Note: If the total purchase line-item amount is already stored as an attribute in the stockflow table, then you don't need to calculate it.
4. Group the result from step 3 by the inventory item identifier and sum the purchase quantity and the total purchase line-item dollar amount.
5. Start with the result from step 4 and, still grouping by inventory item, divide the sum of the total purchase line item by the sum of the total purchased quantity.

Withholdings – amounts not paid on paychecks but retained by the company to be paid on behalf of the employee (sometimes by statute, sometimes voluntarily) to government agencies, benefit providers, or other outside agencies, also called payroll deductions, p.465